D1386912

Contents

Editorial Staff

Editors

Ian Brookes

Mary O'Neill

Supplement

Martin and Simon Toseland

For the publisher

Gerry Breslin

Hannah Dove

Kerry Ferguson

Using this Thesaurus

Main entry words are printed in bold blue type:

> **altogether**

Senses: If a word has several senses, each separate sense is introduced by a number:

> **accident 1 = crash**,
> smash, wreck, collision
> **2 = misfortune**, disaster

Parts of speech are provided at entry words that have multiple parts of speech, and are shown in small caps. Each change in part of speech is shown by an arrow:

> **act** VERB 1 = **do something**…
> ▷ NOUN 3 = **deed**

Alternatives (synonyms) are separated by commas, with the key synonym for each sense given in bold, preceded by an equals sign:

> **alternative** NOUN
> 1 = **substitute**, choice, other

Opposites (antonyms) are provided at the end of the lists of synonyms, and are preceded by the word 'opposite' in small capital letters:

> **anarchy** = **lawlessness**…
> **OPPOSITE:** order

Phrases involving a main entry word are marked with an arrow:

> **apply**…
> ▷ PHRASES: apply yourself

Usage and regional labels give information about the country, region, or particular context a word or sense is associated with. These are shown in italics, within round brackets:

> **drink**...hooch *or* hootch
> (*informal, chiefly US & Canad*)

Usage notes give information about how the word is used. These appear underneath the entry they belong to with a blue bar down the left side:

> **beside**...
> | **USAGE NOTE**
> | People occasionally confuse
> | *beside* and *besides*...

Related words appear underneath the entry they belong to with a blue bar down the left side:

> **air**...
> | **RELATED WORD**
> | *adjective:* aerial

Word list panels provide a brief encyclopaedic list of words associated with a particular subject:

SHADES OF BLUE	
aqua	Nile blue
aquamarine	Oxford blue
azure...	peacock blue...

Cross references to word list panels appear at related entries, introduced by 'See panel' in italics:

> **blue**...
> • *See panel* SHADES OF BLUE

Lists in the Thesaurus

Abbreviations

Austral	Australia/Australian
Brit	British
Canad	Canada/Canadian
N	North
NZ	New Zealand
®	trademark
S	South
Scot	Scottish
US	United States

Aa

abandon VERB 1 = **leave**, strand, ditch, forsake, run out on, desert, dump 2 = **stop**, give up, halt, pack in (*Brit informal*), discontinue, leave off **OPPOSITE:** continue 3 = **give up**, yield, surrender, relinquish **OPPOSITE:** keep
▷ NOUN 4 = **recklessness**, wildness **OPPOSITE:** restraint

abandonment = **desertion**, leaving, forsaking

abbey = **monastery**, convent, priory, nunnery, friary

abduct = **kidnap**, seize, carry off, snatch (*slang*)

abide = **tolerate**, suffer, accept, bear, endure, put up with, take, stand
▷ PHRASES: abide by something = **obey**, follow, agree to, carry out, observe, fulfil, act on, comply with

abiding = **enduring**, lasting, continuing, permanent, persistent, everlasting **OPPOSITE:** brief

ability 1 = **capability**, potential, competence, proficiency

OPPOSITE: inability 2 = **skill**, talent, expertise, competence, aptitude, proficiency, cleverness

able = **capable**, qualified, efficient, accomplished, competent, skilful, proficient **OPPOSITE:** incapable

abnormal = **unusual**, different, odd, strange, extraordinary, remarkable, exceptional, peculiar, daggy (*Austral & NZ informal*) **OPPOSITE:** normal

abnormality 1 = **strangeness**, peculiarity, irregularity, singularity 2 = **anomaly**, oddity, exception, peculiarity, deformity, irregularity

abolish = **do away with**, end, destroy, eliminate, cancel, get rid of, ditch (*slang*), throw out **OPPOSITE:** establish

abolition = **eradication**, ending, end, destruction, wiping out, elimination, cancellation, termination

abort 1 = **terminate** (*~a pregnancy*) 2 = **stop**, end, finish, check, arrest, halt, cease, axe (*informal*)

abortion = **termination**, deliberate miscarriage

abound = **be plentiful**, thrive, flourish, be numerous, proliferate, be abundant, be thick on the ground

about PREPOSITION
1 = **regarding**, on, concerning, dealing with, referring to,

relating to, as regards 2 = **near**, around, close to, nearby, beside, adjacent to, in the neighbourhood of
▷ ADVERB 3 = **approximately**, around, almost, nearly, approaching, close to, roughly, just about

above 1 = **over**, upon, beyond, on top of, exceeding, higher than **OPPOSITE:** under 2 = **senior to**, over, ahead of, in charge of, higher than, superior to, more powerful than **OPPOSITE:** subordinate to

abroad = **overseas**, out of the country, in foreign lands

abrupt 1 = **sudden**, unexpected, rapid, surprising, quick, rash, precipitate **OPPOSITE:** slow 2 = **curt**, brief, short, rude, impatient, terse, gruff, succinct **OPPOSITE:** polite

absence 1 = **time off**, leave, break, vacation, recess, truancy, absenteeism, nonattendance 2 = **lack**, deficiency, omission, scarcity, want, need, shortage, dearth

absent 1 = **away**, missing, gone, elsewhere, unavailable, nonexistent **OPPOSITE:** present 2 = **absent-minded**, blank, vague, distracted, vacant, preoccupied, oblivious, inattentive **OPPOSITE:** alert
▷ PHRASES: absent yourself = **stay away**, withdraw, keep away, play truant

absolute 1 = **complete**, total, perfect, pure, sheer, utter, outright, thorough 2 = **supreme**, sovereign, unlimited, ultimate, full, unconditional, unrestricted, pre-eminent 3 = **autocratic**, supreme, all-powerful, imperious, domineering, tyrannical

absolutely = **completely**, totally, perfectly, fully, entirely, altogether, wholly, utterly **OPPOSITE:** somewhat

absorb 1 = **soak up**, suck up, receive, digest, imbibe 2 = **engross**, involve, engage, fascinate, rivet, captivate

absorbed = **engrossed**, lost, involved, gripped, fascinated, caught up, wrapped up, preoccupied

absorbing = **fascinating**, interesting, engaging, gripping, compelling, intriguing, enticing, riveting **OPPOSITE:** boring

absorption 1 = **soaking up**, consumption, digestion, sucking up 2 = **immersion**, involvement, concentration, fascination, preoccupation, intentness

abstract ADJECTIVE 1 = **theoretical**, general, academic, speculative, indefinite, hypothetical, notional, abstruse **OPPOSITE:** actual
▷ NOUN 2 = **summary**, résumé,

outline, digest, epitome, rundown, synopsis, précis **OPPOSITE:** expansion

▷ **VERB 3** = **extract**, draw, pull, remove, separate, withdraw, isolate, pull out **OPPOSITE:** add

absurd = **ridiculous**, crazy (*informal*), silly, foolish, ludicrous, unreasonable, irrational, senseless **OPPOSITE:** sensible

abundance = **plenty**, bounty, exuberance, profusion, plethora, affluence, fullness, fruitfulness **OPPOSITE:** shortage

abundant = **plentiful**, full, rich, liberal, generous, ample, exuberant, teeming **OPPOSITE:** scarce

abuse NOUN **1** = **maltreatment**, damage, injury, hurt, harm, manhandling, ill-treatment **2** = **insults**, blame, slights, put-downs, censure, reproach, scolding, defamation **3** = **misuse**, misapplication, exploitation

▷ **VERB 4** = **ill-treat**, damage, hurt, injure, harm, molest, maltreat, knock about *or* around **OPPOSITE:** care for **5** = **insult**, offend, curse, put down, malign, scold, disparage, castigate **OPPOSITE:** praise

abusive 1 = **violent**, rough, cruel, savage, brutal, vicious, destructive, harmful **OPPOSITE:** kind **2** = **insulting**, offensive, rude, degrading, scathing,

contemptuous, disparaging, scurrilous **OPPOSITE:** complimentary

academic ADJECTIVE **1** = **scholastic**, educational **2** = **scholarly**, learned, intellectual, literary, erudite, highbrow, studious **3** = **theoretical**, abstract, speculative, hypothetical, impractical, notional, conjectural

▷ **NOUN 4** = **scholar**, intellectual, don, master, professor, fellow, lecturer, tutor, acca (*Austral slang*)

accelerate 1 = **increase**, grow, advance, extend, expand, raise, swell, enlarge **OPPOSITE:** fall **2** = **expedite**, further, speed up, hasten **OPPOSITE:** delay **3** = **speed up**, advance, quicken, gather momentum **OPPOSITE:** slow down

acceleration = **hastening**, hurrying, stepping up (*informal*), speeding up, quickening

accent NOUN **1** = **pronunciation**, tone, articulation, inflection, brogue, intonation, diction, modulation

▷ **VERB 2** = **emphasize**, stress, highlight, underline, underscore, accentuate

accept 1 = **receive**, take, gain, pick up, secure, collect, get, obtain **2** = **acknowledge**, believe, allow, admit, approve, recognize, yield, concede

acceptable = satisfactory, fair, all right, suitable, sufficient, good enough, adequate, tolerable **OPPOSITE:** unsatisfactory

acceptance 1 = accepting, taking, receiving, obtaining, acquiring, reception, receipt 2 = acknowledgement, agreement, approval, recognition, admission, consent, adoption, assent

accepted = agreed, common, established, traditional, approved, acknowledged, recognized, customary **OPPOSITE:** unconventional

access 1 = admission, entry, passage 2 = entrance, road, approach, entry, path, gate, opening, passage

accessible = handy, near, nearby, at hand, within reach, reachable, achievable **OPPOSITE:** inaccessible

accessory 1 = extra, addition, supplement, attachment, adjunct, appendage 2 = accomplice, partner, ally, associate, assistant, helper, colleague, collaborator

accident 1 = crash, smash, wreck, collision 2 = misfortune, disaster, tragedy, setback, calamity, mishap, misadventure 3 = chance, fortune, luck, fate, hazard, coincidence, fluke, fortuity

accidental 1 = unintentional, unexpected, incidental, unforeseen, unplanned **OPPOSITE:** deliberate 2 = chance, random, casual, unplanned, fortuitous, inadvertent

accidentally = unintentionally, incidentally, by accident, by chance, inadvertently, unwittingly, randomly, haphazardly **OPPOSITE:** deliberately

acclaim VERB 1 = praise, celebrate, honour, cheer, admire, hail, applaud, compliment ▷ NOUN 2 = praise, honour, celebration, approval, tribute, applause, kudos, commendation **OPPOSITE:** criticism

accommodate 1 = house, put up, take in, lodge, shelter, entertain, cater for 2 = help, support, aid, assist, cooperate with, abet, lend a hand to 3 = adapt, fit, settle, alter, adjust, modify, comply, reconcile

accommodating = obliging, willing, kind, friendly, helpful, polite, cooperative, agreeable **OPPOSITE:** unhelpful

accommodation = housing, homes, houses, board, quarters, digs (*Brit informal*), shelter, lodging(s)

accompaniment 1 = backing music, backing, support,

obbligato **2 = supplement**, extra, addition, companion, accessory, complement, decoration, adjunct

accompany 1 = go with, lead, partner, guide, attend, conduct, escort, shepherd **2 = occur with**, belong to, come with, supplement, go together with, follow

accompanying = additional, extra, related, associated, attached, attendant, complementary, supplementary

accomplish = realize, produce, effect, finish, complete, manage, achieve, perform **OPPOSITE:** fail

accomplished = skilled, able, professional, expert, masterly, talented, gifted, polished **OPPOSITE:** unskilled

accomplishment 1 = achievement, feat, act, stroke, triumph, coup, exploit, deed **2 = accomplishing**, finishing, carrying out, conclusion, bringing about, execution, completion, fulfilment

accord 1 = treaty, contract, agreement, arrangement, settlement, pact, deal (*informal*) **2 = sympathy**, agreement, harmony, unison, rapport, conformity **OPPOSITE:** conflict ▷ **PHRASES: accord with something = agree with**, match, coincide with, fit with, correspond with, conform with, tally with, harmonize with

accordingly 1 = consequently, so, thus, therefore, hence, subsequently, in consequence, ergo **2 = appropriately**, correspondingly, properly, suitably, fitly

account NOUN **1 = description**, report, story, statement, version, tale, explanation, narrative **2 = importance**, standing, concern, value, note, worth, weight, honour **3** (*Commerce*) **= ledger**, charge, bill, statement, balance, tally, invoice ▷ VERB **4 = consider**, rate, value, judge, estimate, think, count, reckon

accountability = responsibility, liability, culpability, answerability, chargeability

accountable = answerable, subject, responsible, obliged, liable, amenable, obligated, chargeable

accountant = auditor, book-keeper, bean counter (*informal*)

accumulate = build up, increase, be stored, collect, gather, pile up, amass, hoard **OPPOSITE:** disperse

accumulation 1 = collection, increase, stock, store, mass, build-up, pile, stack **2 = growth**, collection, gathering, build-up

a

accuracy = **exactness**, precision, fidelity, authenticity, correctness, closeness, veracity, truthfulness **OPPOSITE:** inaccuracy

accurate 1 = **precise**, close, correct, careful, strict, exact, faithful, explicit **OPPOSITE:** inaccurate 2 = **correct**, true, exact, spot-on (*Brit informal*)

accurately 1 = **precisely**, correctly, closely, truly, strictly, exactly, faithfully, to the letter 2 = **exactly**, closely, correctly, precisely, strictly, faithfully, explicitly, scrupulously

accusation = **charge**, complaint, allegation, indictment, recrimination, denunciation, incrimination

accuse 1 = **point a** *or* **the finger at**, blame for, denounce, hold responsible for, impute blame to **OPPOSITE:** exonerate 2 = **charge with**, indict for, impeach for, censure with, incriminate for **OPPOSITE:** absolve

accustom = **familiarize**, train, discipline, adapt, instruct, school, acquaint, acclimatize

accustomed 1 = **used**, trained, familiar, given to, adapted, acquainted, in the habit of, familiarized **OPPOSITE:** unaccustomed 2 = **usual**, established, expected, common, standard, traditional, normal, regular **OPPOSITE:** unusual

ace NOUN 1 (*Cards, dice*) = **one**, single point 2 (*informal*) = **expert**, star, champion, authority, professional, master, specialist, guru
▷ **ADJECTIVE** 3 (*informal*) = **great**, brilliant, fine, wonderful, excellent, outstanding, superb, fantastic (*informal*), booshit (*Austral slang*), exo (*Austral slang*), sik (*Austral slang*), ka pai (*NZ*), rad (*informal*), phat (*slang*), schmick (*Austral informal*)

ache VERB 1 = **hurt**, suffer, burn, pain, smart, sting, pound, throb
▷ **NOUN** 2 = **pain**, discomfort, suffering, hurt, throbbing, irritation, tenderness, pounding

achieve = **accomplish**, fulfil, complete, gain, perform, do, get, carry out

achievement = **accomplishment**, effort, feat, deed, stroke, triumph, coup, exploit

acid 1 = **sour**, tart, pungent, acerbic, acrid, vinegary **OPPOSITE:** sweet 2 = **sharp**, cutting, biting, bitter, harsh, barbed, caustic, vitriolic **OPPOSITE:** kindly

acknowledge 1 = **admit**, own up to, allow, accept, reveal, grant, declare, recognize **OPPOSITE:** deny 2 = **greet**, address, notice, recognize, salute, accost **OPPOSITE:** snub 3 = **reply to**, answer, notice, recognize, respond to, react to, retort to **OPPOSITE:** ignore

acquaintance 1 = **associate**, contact, ally, colleague, comrade **OPPOSITE:** intimate 2 = **relationship**, connection, fellowship, familiarity **OPPOSITE:** unfamiliarity

acquire = **get**, win, buy, receive, gain, earn, secure, collect **OPPOSITE:** lose

acquisition 1 = **acquiring**, gaining, procurement, attainment 2 = **purchase**, buy, investment, property, gain, prize, asset, possession

acquit = **clear**, free, release, excuse, discharge, liberate, vindicate **OPPOSITE:** find guilty ▷ **PHRASES:** acquit yourself = **behave**, bear yourself, conduct yourself, comport yourself

act VERB 1 = **do something**, perform, function 2 = **perform**, mimic ▷ **NOUN** 3 = **deed**, action, performance, achievement, undertaking, exploit, feat, accomplishment 4 = **pretence**, show, front, performance, display, attitude, pose, posture 5 = **law**, bill, measure, resolution, decree, statute, ordinance, enactment 6 = **performance**, show, turn, production, routine, presentation, gig (*informal*), sketch

acting NOUN 1 = **performance**, playing, performing, theatre, portrayal, impersonation, characterization, stagecraft ▷ **ADJECTIVE** 2 = **temporary**, substitute, interim, provisional, surrogate, stopgap, pro tem

action 1 = **deed**, act, performance, achievement, exploit, feat, accomplishment 2 = **measure**, act, manoeuvre 3 = **lawsuit**, case, trial, suit, proceeding, dispute, prosecution, litigation 4 = **energy**, activity, spirit, force, vitality, vigour, liveliness, vim 5 = **effect**, working, process, operation, activity, movement, functioning, motion 6 = **battle**, fight, conflict, clash, contest, encounter, combat, engagement

activate = **start**, move, initiate, rouse, mobilize, set in motion, galvanize **OPPOSITE:** stop

active 1 = **busy**, involved, occupied, lively, energetic, bustling, on the move, strenuous **OPPOSITE:** sluggish 2 = **energetic**, quick, alert, dynamic, lively, vigorous, animated, forceful **OPPOSITE:** inactive 3 = **in operation**, working, acting, at work, in action, operative, in force, effectual

activist = **militant**, partisan

activity 1 = **action**, labour, movement, energy, exercise,

a

spirit, motion, bustle **OPPOSITE:** inaction 2 = **pursuit**, project, scheme, pleasure, interest, hobby, pastime

actor or **actress** = **performer**, player, Thespian, luvvie (*informal*)

> **USAGE NOTE**
> The use of *actress* is now very much on the decline, and women who work in the profession invariably prefer to be referred to as *actors*.

actual = **real**, substantial, concrete, definite, tangible **OPPOSITE:** theoretical

> **USAGE NOTE**
> The words *actual* and *actually* are often used when speaking, but should only be used in writing where they add something to the meaning of a sentence. For example, in the sentence *he actually rather enjoyed the film*, the word *actually* is only needed if there was originally some doubt as to whether he would enjoy it.

actually = **really**, in fact, indeed, truly, literally, genuinely, in reality, in truth

acute 1 = **serious**, important, dangerous, critical, crucial, severe, grave, urgent 2 = **sharp**, shooting, powerful, violent, severe, intense, fierce, piercing 3 = **perceptive**, sharp, keen, smart, sensitive, clever, astute, insightful **OPPOSITE:** slow

adamant = **determined**, firm, fixed, stubborn, uncompromising, resolute, unbending, obdurate **OPPOSITE:** flexible

adapt 1 = **adjust**, change, alter, modify, accommodate, conform, acclimatize 2 = **convert**, change, transform, alter, modify, tailor, remodel

adaptation 1 = **acclimatization**, naturalization, familiarization 2 = **conversion**, change, variation, adjustment, transformation, modification, alteration

add 1 = **count up**, total, reckon, compute, add up, tot up **OPPOSITE:** take away 2 = **include**, attach, supplement, adjoin, augment, affix, append

addict 1 = **junkie** (*informal*), freak (*informal*), fiend (*informal*) 2 = **fan**, lover, nut (*slang*), follower, enthusiast, admirer, buff (*informal*), junkie (*informal*)

addicted = **hooked**, dependent

addiction 1 = **dependence**, habit, obsession, craving, enslavement 2 *with* **to** = **love of**, passion for, attachment to

addition 1 = **extra**, supplement, increase, gain, bonus, extension, accessory, additive 2 = **inclusion**, adding, increasing, extension, attachment, insertion,

incorporation, augmentation
OPPOSITE: removal
3 = **counting up**, totalling,
adding up, computation,
totting up **OPPOSITE:**
subtraction
▷ **PHRASES:** in addition to = **as
well as**, along with, on top of,
besides, to boot, additionally,
over and above, to say
nothing of
additional = **extra**, new, other,
added, further, fresh, spare,
supplementary
address NOUN 1 = **location**,
home, place, house, point,
position, situation, site
2 (*Computing*) = **URL**, website,
addy (*informal*), IP address,
web address 3 = **speech**, talk,
lecture, discourse, sermon,
dissertation, homily, oration
▷ **VERB** 4 = **speak to**, talk to,
greet, hail, approach, converse
with, korero (*NZ*)
adept ADJECTIVE 1 = **skilful**,
able, skilled, expert, practised,
accomplished, versed, proficient
OPPOSITE: unskilled
▷ **NOUN** 2 = **expert**, master,
genius, hotshot (*informal*), dab
hand (*Brit informal*)
adequate 1 = **passable**,
acceptable, average, fair,
satisfactory, competent,
mediocre, so-so (*informal*)
OPPOSITE: inadequate
2 = **sufficient**, enough
OPPOSITE: insufficient

adhere to = **stick to**, attach to,
cling to, glue to, fix to, fasten to,
hold fast to, paste to
adjacent = **adjoining**,
neighbouring, nearby
OPPOSITE: far away
adjoin = **connect with** *or*
to, join, link with, touch on,
border on
adjoining = **connecting**,
touching, bordering,
neighbouring, next door,
adjacent, abutting
adjourn = **postpone**, delay,
suspend, interrupt, put off,
defer, discontinue **OPPOSITE:**
continue
adjust 1 = **adapt**, change, alter,
accustom, conform 2 = **change**,
reform, alter, adapt, revise,
modify, amend, make conform
3 = **modify**, alter, adapt
adjustable = **alterable**, flexible,
adaptable, malleable, movable,
modifiable
adjustment 1 = **alteration**,
change, tuning, repair,
conversion, modifying,
adaptation, modification
2 = **acclimatization**,
orientation, change, regulation,
amendment, adaptation,
revision, modification
administer 1 = **manage**,
run, control, direct, handle,
conduct, command, govern
2 = **dispense**, give, share,
provide, apply, assign, allocate,
allot 3 = **execute**, give, provide,

apply, perform, carry out,
impose, implement

administration
1 = **management**, government,
running, control, handling,
direction, conduct, application
2 = **directors**, board,
executive(s), employers
3 = **government**, leadership,
regime

administrative = **managerial**,
executive, directing, regulatory,
governmental, organizational,
supervisory, directorial

administrator = **manager**,
head, official, director,
executive, boss (*informal*),
governor, supervisor, baas
(*S African*)

admirable = **praiseworthy**,
good, great, fine, wonderful,
excellent, brilliant, outstanding,
booshit (*Austral slang*), exo
(*Austral slang*), sik (*Austral slang*),
ka pai (*NZ*), rad (*informal*), phat
(*slang*), schmick (*Austral informal*)
OPPOSITE: deplorable

admiration = **regard**,
wonder, respect, praise,
approval, recognition, esteem,
appreciation

admire 1 = **respect**, value,
prize, honour, praise,
appreciate, esteem, approve of
OPPOSITE: despise 2 = **adore**,
like, love, take to, fancy (*Brit
informal*), treasure, cherish,
glorify 3 = **marvel at**, look at,
appreciate, delight in, wonder

at, be amazed by, take pleasure
in, gape at

admirer 1 = **fan**, supporter,
follower, enthusiast, partisan,
disciple, devotee 2 = **suitor**,
lover, boyfriend, sweetheart,
beau, wooer

admission 1 = **admittance**,
access, entry, introduction,
entrance, acceptance, initiation,
entrée 2 = **confession**,
declaration, revelation,
allowance, disclosure,
acknowledgement,
unburdening, divulgence

admit 1 = **confess**, confide,
own up, come clean (*informal*)
2 = **allow**, agree, accept, reveal,
grant, declare, acknowledge,
recognize **OPPOSITE:** deny
3 = **let in**, allow, receive,
accept, introduce, take
in, initiate, give access to
OPPOSITE: keep out

adolescence = **teens**, youth,
minority, boyhood, girlhood

adolescent ADJECTIVE
1 = **young**, junior, teenage,
juvenile, youthful,
childish, immature, boyish
2 = **immature**, young, teen
(*informal*)
▷ NOUN 3 = **teenager**, girl, boy,
kid (*informal*), youth, lad, minor,
young man

adopt 1 = **take on**, follow,
choose, maintain, assume, take
up, engage in, become involved
in 2 = **take in**, raise, nurse,

mother, rear, foster, bring up, take care of **OPPOSITE:** abandon

adoption 1 = **fostering**, adopting, taking in 2 = **embracing**, choice, taking up, selection, assumption, endorsement, appropriation, espousal

adore = **love**, honour, admire, worship, esteem, cherish, revere, dote on **OPPOSITE:** hate

adoring = **admiring**, loving, devoted, fond, affectionate, doting **OPPOSITE:** hating

adorn = **decorate**, array, embellish, festoon

adrift ADJECTIVE 1 = **drifting**, afloat, unmoored, unanchored 2 = **aimless**, goalless, directionless, purposeless
▷ ADVERB 3 = **wrong**, astray, off course, amiss, off target, wide of the mark

adult NOUN 1 = **grown-up**, mature person, person of mature age, grown or grown-up person, man or woman
▷ ADJECTIVE 2 = **fully grown**, mature, grown-up, of age, ripe, fully fledged, fully developed, full grown 3 = **pornographic**, blue, dirty, obscene, filthy, indecent, lewd, salacious

advance VERB 1 = **progress**, proceed, come forward, make inroads, make headway **OPPOSITE:** retreat 2 = **accelerate**, speed, promote, hasten, bring forward, crack on (informal) 3 = **improve**, rise, develop, pick up, progress, upgrade, prosper, make strides 4 = **suggest**, offer, present, propose, advocate, submit, prescribe, put forward **OPPOSITE:** withhold 5 = **lend**, loan, supply on credit **OPPOSITE:** withhold payment
▷ NOUN 6 = **down payment**, credit, fee, deposit, retainer, prepayment, loan 7 = **attack**, charge, strike, assault, raid, invasion, offensive, onslaught 8 = **improvement**, development, gain, growth, breakthrough, step, headway, inroads
▷ ADJECTIVE 9 = **prior**, early, beforehand
▷ PHRASES: in advance = **beforehand**, earlier, ahead, previously

advanced = **sophisticated**, foremost, modern, revolutionary, up-to-date, higher, leading, recent **OPPOSITE:** backward

advancement = **promotion**, rise, gain, progress, improvement, betterment, preferment

advantage 1 = **benefit**, help, profit, favour **OPPOSITE:** disadvantage 2 = **lead**, sway, dominance, precedence 3 = **superiority**, good

adventure = **venture**, experience, incident, enterprise,

a

undertaking, exploit,
occurrence, caper
adventurous = **daring**,
enterprising, bold, reckless,
intrepid, daredevil **OPPOSITE:**
cautious
adversary = **opponent**,
rival, enemy, competitor,
foe, contestant, antagonist
OPPOSITE: ally
adverse 1 = **harmful**,
damaging, negative,
destructive, detrimental,
hurtful, injurious, inopportune
OPPOSITE: beneficial
2 = **unfavourable**, hostile,
unlucky 3 = **negative**,
opposing, hostile, contrary,
dissenting, unsympathetic,
ill-disposed
advert (*Brit informal*)
= **advertisement**, notice,
commercial, ad (*informal*),
announcement, poster, plug
(*informal*), blurb, banner ad
advertise = **publicize**, promote,
plug (*informal*), announce,
inform, hype, notify, tout
advertisement = **advert** (*Brit
informal*), notice, commercial,
ad (*informal*), announcement,
poster, plug (*informal*), blurb
advice = **guidance**, help,
opinion, direction, suggestion,
instruction, counsel, counselling
advise 1 = **recommend**,
suggest, urge, counsel,
advocate, caution, prescribe,
commend 2 = **notify**, tell,

report, announce, warn,
declare, inform, acquaint
adviser = **counsellor**, guide,
consultant, aide, guru, mentor,
helper, confidant
advisory = **advising**, helping,
recommending, counselling,
consultative
advocate VERB
1 = **recommend**, support,
champion, encourage, propose,
promote, advise, endorse
OPPOSITE: oppose
▷ NOUN 2 = **supporter**,
spokesman, champion,
defender, campaigner,
promoter, counsellor,
proponent 3 (*Law*) = **lawyer**,
attorney, solicitor, counsel,
barrister
affair 1 = **matter**, business,
happening, event, activity,
incident, episode, topic
2 = **relationship**, romance,
intrigue, fling, liaison, flirtation,
amour, dalliance
affect[1] 1 = **influence**, concern,
alter, change, manipulate, act
on, bear upon, impinge upon
2 = **emotionally move**, touch,
upset, overcome, stir, disturb,
perturb
affect[2] = **put on**, assume, adopt,
pretend, imitate, simulate,
contrive, aspire to
affected = **pretended**, artificial,
contrived, put-on, mannered,
unnatural, feigned, insincere
OPPOSITE: genuine

affection = **fondness**, liking, feeling, love, care, warmth, attachment, goodwill, aroha (NZ)

affectionate = **fond**, loving, kind, caring, friendly, attached, devoted, tender **OPPOSITE**: cool

affiliate = **associate**, unite, join, link, ally, combine, incorporate, amalgamate

affinity 1 = **attraction**, liking, leaning, sympathy, inclination, rapport, fondness, partiality, aroha (NZ) **OPPOSITE**: hostility 2 = **similarity**, relationship, connection, correspondence, analogy, resemblance, closeness, likeness **OPPOSITE**: difference

affirm 1 = **declare**, state, maintain, swear, assert, testify, pronounce, certify **OPPOSITE**: deny 2 = **confirm**, prove, endorse, ratify, verify, validate, bear out, substantiate **OPPOSITE**: refute

affirmative = **agreeing**, confirming, positive, approving, consenting, favourable, concurring, assenting **OPPOSITE**: negative

afflict = **torment**, trouble, pain, hurt, distress, plague, grieve, harass

affluent = **wealthy**, rich, prosperous, loaded (slang), well-off, opulent, well-heeled (informal), well-to-do, minted (Brit slang) **OPPOSITE**: poor

afford 1 = **have the money for**, manage, bear, pay for, spare, stand, stretch to 2 = **bear**, stand, sustain, allow yourself 3 = **give**, offer, provide, produce, supply, yield, render

affordable = **inexpensive**, cheap, reasonable, moderate, modest, low-cost, economical **OPPOSITE**: expensive

afraid 1 = **scared**, frightened, nervous, terrified, shaken, startled, fearful, cowardly **OPPOSITE**: unafraid 2 = **reluctant**, frightened, scared, unwilling, hesitant, loath, disinclined, unenthusiastic 3 = **sorry**, apologetic, regretful, sad, distressed, unhappy **OPPOSITE**: pleased

after PREPOSITION 1 = **at the end of**, following, subsequent to **OPPOSITE**: before ▷ ADVERB 2 = **following**, later, next, succeeding, afterwards, subsequently, thereafter

▌ **RELATED WORD**
▌ prefix: post-

aftermath = **effects**, results, wake, consequences, outcome, sequel, end result, upshot

again 1 = **once more**, another time, anew, afresh 2 = **also**, in addition, moreover, besides, furthermore

against 1 = **beside**, on, up against, in contact with, abutting 2 = **opposed to**, anti (*informal*), hostile to, in opposition to, averse to, opposite to **3 = in opposition to**, resisting, versus, counter to, in the opposite direction of **4 = in preparation for**, in case of, in anticipation of, in expectation of, in provision for

> **RELATED WORDS**
> *prefixes:* anti-, contra-, counter-

age NOUN **1 = years**, days, generation, lifetime, length of existence **2 = old age**, experience, maturity, seniority, majority, senility, decline, advancing years **OPPOSITE:** youth **3 = time**, day(s), period, generation, era, epoch
▷ VERB **4 = grow old**, decline, weather, fade, deteriorate, wither **5 = mature**, season, condition, soften, mellow, ripen

aged = old, getting on, grey, ancient, antique, elderly, antiquated **OPPOSITE:** young

agency 1 = business, company, office, firm, department, organization, enterprise, establishment **2** (*Old-fashioned*) = **medium**, means, activity, vehicle, instrument, mechanism

agenda = programme, list, plan, schedule, diary, calendar, timetable

agent 1 = representative, rep (*informal*), negotiator, envoy, surrogate, go-between **2 = author**, worker, vehicle, instrument, operator, performer, catalyst, doer **3 = force**, means, power, cause, instrument

aggravate 1 = make worse, exaggerate, intensify, worsen, exacerbate, magnify, inflame, increase **OPPOSITE:** improve **2** (*informal*) = **annoy**, bother, provoke, irritate, nettle, get on your nerves (*informal*) **OPPOSITE:** please

aggregate NOUN **1 = total**, body, whole, amount, collection, mass, sum, combination
▷ ADJECTIVE **2 = collective**, mixed, combined, collected, accumulated, composite, cumulative
▷ VERB **3 = combine**, mix, collect, assemble, heap, accumulate, pile, amass

aggression 1 = hostility, malice, antagonism, antipathy, ill will, belligerence, destructiveness, pugnacity **2 = attack**, campaign, injury, assault, raid, invasion, offensive, onslaught

aggressive 1 = hostile, offensive, destructive, belligerent, unfriendly, contrary, antagonistic, pugnacious, aggers (*Austral slang*), biffo (*Austral slang*) **OPPOSITE:** friendly **2 = forceful**, powerful, convincing, effective, enterprising, dynamic, bold, militant **OPPOSITE:** submissive

agitate 1 = **stir**, beat, shake, disturb, toss, rouse 2 = **upset**, worry, trouble, excite, distract, unnerve, disconcert, fluster **OPPOSITE:** calm

agony = **suffering**, pain, distress, misery, torture, discomfort, torment, hardship

agree 1 = **concur**, be as one, sympathize, assent, see eye to eye, be of the same opinion **OPPOSITE:** disagree 2 = **correspond**, match, coincide, tally, conform ▷ **PHRASES: agree with someone** = **suit**, get on with, befit

agreement 1 = **treaty**, contract, arrangement, alliance, deal (*informal*), understanding, settlement, bargain 2 = **concurrence**, harmony, compliance, union, agreeing, consent, unison, assent **OPPOSITE:** disagreement 3 = **correspondence**, similarity, consistency, correlation, conformity, compatibility, congruity **OPPOSITE:** difference

agricultural = **farming**, country, rural, rustic, agrarian

agriculture = **farming**, culture, cultivation, husbandry, tillage

ahead 1 = **in front**, in advance, towards the front, frontwards 2 = **at an advantage**, in advance, in the lead 3 = **in the lead**, winning, leading, at the head, to the fore, at an advantage 4 = **in advance**, in front, before, in the lead

aid NOUN 1 = **help**, backing, support, benefit, favour, relief, promotion, assistance **OPPOSITE:** hindrance ▷ **VERB** 2 = **help**, support, serve, sustain, assist, avail, subsidize, be of service to **OPPOSITE:** hinder 3 = **promote**, help, further, forward, encourage, favour, facilitate, pave the way for

aide = **assistant**, supporter, attendant, helper, right-hand man, second

ailing 1 = **weak**, failing, poor, flawed, unstable, unsatisfactory, deficient 2 = **ill**, poorly, sick, weak, crook (*Austral & NZ informal*), unwell, infirm, under the weather (*informal*), indisposed

ailment = **illness**, disease, complaint, disorder, sickness, affliction, malady, infirmity

aim VERB 1 = **try for**, seek, work for, plan for, strive, set your sights on 2 = **point** ▷ **NOUN** 3 = **intention**, point, plan, goal, design, target, purpose, desire

air NOUN 1 = **wind**, breeze, draught, gust, zephyr 2 = **atmosphere**, sky, heavens, aerosphere 3 = **tune**, song, theme, melody, strain, lay, ai'

a

4 = **manner**, appearance, look, aspect, atmosphere, mood, impression, aura
▷ VERB 5 = **publicize**, reveal, exhibit, voice, express, display, circulate, make public
6 = **ventilate**, expose, freshen, aerate

RELATED WORD
adjective: aerial

airborne = **flying**, floating, in the air, hovering, gliding, in flight, on the wing

airing 1 = **ventilation**, drying, freshening, aeration
2 = **exposure**, display, expression, publicity, vent, utterance, dissemination

airplane (*US & Canad*) = **plane**, aircraft, jet, aeroplane, airliner

airs = **affectation**, arrogance, pretensions, pomposity, swank (*informal*), hauteur, haughtiness, superciliousness

aisle = **passageway**, path, lane, passage, corridor, alley, gangway

alarm NOUN 1 = **fear**, panic, anxiety, fright, apprehension, nervousness, consternation, trepidation OPPOSITE: calmness
2 = **danger signal**, warning, bell, alert, siren, alarm bell, hooter, distress signal
▷ VERB 3 = **frighten**, scare, panic, distress, startle, dismay, daunt, unnerve OPPOSITE: calm

alarming = **frightening**, shocking, scaring, disturbing, distressing, startling, horrifying, menacing

alcoholic NOUN 1 = **drunkard**, drinker, drunk, toper, lush (*slang*), tippler, wino (*informal*), inebriate, alko *or* alco (*Austral slang*)
▷ ADJECTIVE 2 = **intoxicating**, hard, strong, stiff, brewed, fermented, distilled

alert ADJECTIVE 1 = **attentive**, awake, vigilant, watchful, on the lookout, circumspect, observant, on guard OPPOSITE: careless 2 = **quick-witted**, bright, sharp
▷ NOUN 3 = **warning**, signal, alarm, siren OPPOSITE: all clear
▷ VERB 4 = **warn**, signal, inform, alarm, notify, tip off, forewarn OPPOSITE: lull

alien NOUN 1 = **foreigner**, incomer, immigrant, stranger, outsider, newcomer, asylum seeker OPPOSITE: citizen
▷ ADJECTIVE 2 = **foreign**, strange, imported, unknown, exotic, unfamiliar 3 = **strange**, new, foreign, novel, unknown, exotic, unfamiliar, untried OPPOSITE: similar

alienate = **antagonize**, anger, annoy, offend, irritate, hassle (*informal*), estrange, hack off (*informal*)

alienation = **estrangement**, setting against, separation, turning away, disaffection, remoteness

alight¹ 1 = **get off**, descend, get down, disembark, dismount 2 = **land**, light, settle, come down, descend, perch, touch down, come to rest **OPPOSITE:** take off

alight² = **lit up**, bright, brilliant, shining, illuminated, fiery

align 1 = **ally**, side, join, associate, affiliate, cooperate, sympathize 2 = **line up**, order, range, regulate, straighten, even up

alike ADJECTIVE 1 = **similar**, close, the same, parallel, resembling, identical, corresponding, akin **OPPOSITE:** different
▷ ADVERB 2 = **similarly**, identically, equally, uniformly, correspondingly, analogously **OPPOSITE:** differently

alive 1 = **living**, breathing, animate, subsisting, existing, functioning, in the land of the living (*informal*) **OPPOSITE:** dead 2 = **in existence**, existing, functioning, active, operative, in force, on-going, prevalent **OPPOSITE:** inoperative 3 = **lively**, active, vital, alert, energetic, animated, agile, perky **OPPOSITE:** dull

all DETERMINER 1 = **the whole amount**, everything, the total, the aggregate, the totality, the sum total, the entirety, the entire amount 2 = **every**, each, every single, every one of, each

and every
▷ ADJECTIVE 3 = **complete**, greatest, full, total, perfect, entire, utter
▷ ADVERB 4 = **completely**, totally, fully, entirely, absolutely, altogether, wholly, utterly

allegation = **claim**, charge, statement, declaration, accusation, assertion, affirmation

allege = **claim**, charge, challenge, state, maintain, declare, assert, uphold **OPPOSITE:** deny

alleged = **claimed**, supposed, declared, assumed, so-called, apparent, stated, described

allegiance = **loyalty**, devotion, fidelity, obedience, constancy, faithfulness **OPPOSITE:** disloyalty

allergic = **sensitive**, affected, susceptible, hypersensitive

allergy = **sensitivity**, reaction, susceptibility, antipathy, hypersensitivity, sensitiveness

alleviate = **ease**, reduce, relieve, moderate, soothe, lessen, lighten, allay

alley = **passage**, walk, lane, pathway, alleyway, passageway, backstreet

alliance = **union**, league, association, agreement, marriage, connection, combination, coalition **OPPOSITE:** division

allied 1 = **united**, linked, related, combined, integrated, affiliated, cooperating, in league 2 = **connected**, linked, associated

allocate = **assign**, grant, distribute, designate, set aside, earmark, give out, consign

allocation 1 = **allowance**, share, portion, quota, lot, ration 2 = **assignment**, allowance, allotment

allow 1 = **permit**, approve, enable, sanction, endure, license, tolerate, authorize **OPPOSITE:** prohibit 2 = **let**, permit, sanction, authorize, license, tolerate, consent to, assent to **OPPOSITE:** forbid 3 = **give**, provide, grant, spare, devote, assign, allocate, set aside 4 = **acknowledge**, accept, admit, grant, recognize, yield, concede, confess
▷ **PHRASES: allow for something** = **take into account**, consider, plan for, accommodate, provide for, make provision for, make allowances for, make concessions for

allowance 1 = **portion**, lot, share, amount, grant, quota, allocation, stint 2 = **pocket money**, grant, fee, payment, ration, handout, remittance 3 = **concession**, discount, reduction, repayment, deduction, rebate

all right 1 = **satisfactory**, O.K. or okay (informal), average, fair, sufficient, standard, acceptable, good enough **OPPOSITE:** unsatisfactory 2 = **well**, O.K. or okay (informal), whole, sound, fit, safe, healthy, unharmed **OPPOSITE:** ill

ally NOUN = **partner**, friend, colleague, associate, mate, comrade, helper, collaborator, cobber (Austral & NZ old-fashioned informal), E hoa (NZ) **OPPOSITE:** opponent
▷ **PHRASES: ally yourself with something** or **someone** = **unite with**, associate with, unify, collaborate with, join forces with, band together with

almost = **nearly**, about, close to, virtually, practically, roughly, just about, not quite

alone ADJECTIVE 1 = **solitary**, isolated, separate, apart, by yourself, unaccompanied, on your tod (slang) **OPPOSITE:** accompanied 2 = **lonely**, abandoned, isolated, solitary, desolate, forsaken, forlorn, destitute
▷ ADVERB 3 = **solely**, only, individually, singly, exclusively, uniquely 4 = **by yourself**, independently, unaccompanied, without help, on your own, without assistance **OPPOSITE:** with help

aloud = **out loud**, clearly, plainly, distinctly, audibly, intelligibly

already = **before now**, before, previously, at present, by now, by then, even now, just now

also = **and**, too, further, in addition, as well, moreover, besides, furthermore

alter 1 = **modify**, change, reform, vary, transform, adjust, adapt, revise 2 = **change**, turn, vary, transform, adjust, adapt

alternate VERB
1 = **interchange**, change, fluctuate, take turns, oscillate, chop and change
2 = **intersperse**, interchange, exchange, swap, stagger, rotate
▷ ADJECTIVE 3 = **alternating**, interchanging, every other, rotating, every second, sequential

alternative NOUN
1 = **substitute**, choice, other, option, preference, recourse
▷ ADJECTIVE 2 = **different**, other, substitute, alternate

alternatively = **or**, instead, otherwise, on the other hand, if not, then again, as an alternative, as another option

although = **though**, while, even if, even though, whilst, albeit, despite the fact that, notwithstanding

altogether 1 = **absolutely**, quite, completely, totally, perfectly, fully, thoroughly, wholly 2 = **completely**, fully, entirely, thoroughly, wholly, in every respect **OPPOSITE:**

partially 3 = **on the whole**, generally, mostly, in general, collectively, all things considered, on average, for the most part 4 = **in total**, in all, all told, taken together, in sum, everything included

USAGE NOTE

The single-word form *altogether* should not be used as an alternative to *all together* because the meanings are very distinct. *Altogether* is an adverb meaning 'absolutely' or, in a different sense, 'in total'. *All together*, however, means 'all at the same time' or 'all in the same place'. The distinction can be seen in the following example: *altogether there were six or seven families sharing the flat's facilities* means 'in total', while *there were six or seven families all together in one flat*, means 'all crowded in together'.

always 1 = **habitually**, regularly, every time, consistently, invariably, perpetually, without exception, customarily **OPPOSITE:** seldom 2 = **forever**, for keeps, eternally, for all time, evermore, till the cows come home (*informal*), till Doomsday 3 = **continually**, constantly, all the time, forever, repeatedly, persistently, perpetually, incessantly

amass = **collect**, gather, assemble, compile, accumulate, pile up, hoard

amateur = **nonprofessional**, outsider, layman, dilettante, layperson, non-specialist, dabbler

amaze = **astonish**, surprise, shock, stun, alarm, stagger, startle, bewilder

amazement = **astonishment**, surprise, wonder, shock, confusion, admiration, awe, bewilderment

amazing = **astonishing**, surprising, brilliant, stunning, overwhelming, staggering, sensational (*informal*), bewildering

ambassador = **representative**, minister, agent, deputy, diplomat, envoy, consul, attaché

ambiguity = **vagueness**, doubt, uncertainty, obscurity, equivocation, dubiousness

ambiguous = **unclear**, obscure, vague, dubious, enigmatic, indefinite, inconclusive, indeterminate **OPPOSITE:** clear

ambition 1 = **goal**, hope, dream, target, aim, wish, purpose, desire 2 = **enterprise**, longing, drive, spirit, desire, passion, enthusiasm, striving

ambitious = **enterprising**, spirited, daring, eager, intent, enthusiastic, hopeful, striving **OPPOSITE:** unambitious

ambush VERB 1 = **trap**, attack, surprise, deceive, dupe, ensnare, waylay, bushwhack (*US*)
▷ NOUN 2 = **trap**, snare, lure, waylaying

amend = **change**, improve, reform, fix, correct, repair, edit, alter

amendment 1 = **addition**, change, adjustment, attachment, adaptation, revision, modification, alteration 2 = **change**, improvement, repair, edit, remedy, correction, revision, modification

amends = **compensation**, redress, reparation, restitution, atonement, recompense

amenity = **facility**, service, advantage, comfort, convenience

amid *or* **amidst** 1 = **during**, among, at a time of, in an atmosphere of 2 = **in the middle of**, among, surrounded by, amongst, in the midst of, in the thick of

ammunition = **munitions**, rounds, shot, shells, powder, explosives, armaments

amnesty = **general pardon**, mercy, pardoning, immunity, forgiveness, reprieve, remission, clemency

among *or* **amongst** 1 = **in the midst of**, with, together with, in the middle of, amid, surrounded by, amidst, in the thick of 2 = **in the group of**, one of, part of,

included in, in the company of, in the class of, in the number of
3 = **between**, to

amount = **quantity**, measure, size, supply, mass, volume, capacity, extent

▷ **PHRASES:** amount to something 1 = **add up to**, mean, total, equal, constitute, comprise, be equivalent to
2 = **come to**, become, develop into, advance to, progress to, mature into

> **USAGE NOTE**
> Although it is common to use a plural noun after *amount of*, for example in *the amount of people* and *the amount of goods*, this should be avoided. Preferred alternatives would be to use *quantity*, as in *the quantity of people*, or *number*, as in *the number of goods*.

amphibian
• *See panel* **AMPHIBIANS**

ample 1 = **plenty of**, generous, lavish, abundant, plentiful, expansive, copious, profuse **OPPOSITE:** insufficient 2 = **large**, full, extensive, generous, abundant, bountiful

amply = **fully**, completely, richly, generously, abundantly, profusely, copiously **OPPOSITE:** insufficiently

amuse 1 = **entertain**, please, delight, charm, cheer, tickle **OPPOSITE:** bore 2 = **occupy**, interest, involve, engage, entertain, absorb, engross

amusement 1 = **enjoyment**, entertainment, cheer, mirth, merriment **OPPOSITE:** boredom 2 = **diversion**, fun, pleasure, entertainment
3 = **pastime**, game, sport,

AMPHIBIANS

axolotl	midwife toad
brown-striped frog (*Austral*)	mud puppy
bullfrog	natterjack
caecilian	newt *or* (*dialect or archaic*) eft
cane toad (*Austral*)	olm
congo eel *or* snake	pipa *or* Surinam toad
eft	Queensland cane toad
frog *or* (*Caribbean*) crapaud	salamander
Goliath frog	siren
hairy frog	toad *or* (*Caribbean*) crapaud
hellbender	tree frog
hyla	

a

joke, entertainment, hobby, recreation, diversion

amusing = funny, humorous, comical, droll, interesting, entertaining, comic, enjoyable **OPPOSITE:** boring

anaesthetic NOUN
1 = **painkiller**, narcotic, sedative, opiate, anodyne, analgesic, soporific
▷ **ADJECTIVE** 2 = **pain-killing**, dulling, numbing, sedative, deadening, anodyne, analgesic, soporific

analogy = similarity, relation, comparison, parallel, correspondence, resemblance, correlation, likeness

analyse 1 = **examine**, test, study, research, survey, investigate, evaluate, inspect
2 = **break down**, separate, divide, resolve, dissect, think through

analysis = examination, test, inquiry, investigation, interpretation, breakdown, scanning, evaluation

analytic or **analytical** = **rational**, organized, exact, precise, logical, systematic, inquiring, investigative

anarchy = lawlessness, revolution, riot, disorder, confusion, chaos, disorganization **OPPOSITE:** order

anatomy 1 = **structure**, build, make-up, frame, framework, composition 2 = **examination**, study, division, inquiry, investigation, analysis, dissection

ancestor = forefather, predecessor, precursor, forerunner, forebear, antecedent, tupuna or tipuna (NZ) **OPPOSITE:** descendant

ancient 1 = **classical**, old, former, past, bygone, primordial, primeval, olden
2 = **very old**, aged, antique, archaic, timeworn 3 = **old-fashioned**, dated, outdated, obsolete, out of date, unfashionable, outmoded, passé **OPPOSITE:** up-to-date

and 1 = **also**, including, along with, together with, in addition to, as well as 2 = **moreover**, plus, furthermore

> **USAGE NOTE**
> The forms try and do something and wait and do something should only be used in informal or spoken English. In more formal writing, use try to and wait to, for example: we must try to prevent this happening (not try and prevent).

anecdote = story, tale, sketch, short story, yarn, reminiscence, urban myth, urban legend

angel 1 = **divine messenger**, cherub, archangel, seraph
2 (informal) = **dear**, beauty, saint, treasure, darling, jewel, gem, paragon

anger NOUN 1 = **rage**, outrage, temper, fury, resentment, wrath, annoyance, ire **OPPOSITE:** calmness
▷ VERB 2 = **enrage**, outrage, annoy, infuriate, incense, gall, madden, exasperate **OPPOSITE:** soothe

angle 1 = **gradient**, bank, slope, incline, inclination 2 = **intersection**, point, edge, corner, bend, elbow, crook, nook 3 = **point of view**, position, approach, direction, aspect, perspective, outlook, viewpoint

angry = **furious**, cross, mad (informal), outraged, annoyed, infuriated, incensed, enraged, tooshie (Austral slang), off the air (Austral slang), aerated **OPPOSITE:** calm

> **USAGE NOTE**
> Some people feel it is more correct to talk about being angry with someone than being angry at them. In British English, angry with is still more common than angry at, but angry at is used more commonly in American English.

angst = **anxiety**, worry, unease, apprehension **OPPOSITE:** peace of mind

anguish = **suffering**, pain, distress, grief, misery, agony, torment, sorrow

animal NOUN 1 = **creature**, beast, brute 2 = **brute**, devil, monster, savage, beast, bastard (informal offensive), villain, barbarian
▷ ADJECTIVE 3 = **physical**, gross, bodily, sensual, carnal, brutish, bestial, animalistic
• See panels AMPHIBIANS, ANIMALS, BATS, BIRDS, CARNIVORES, DINOSAURS, FISH, INSECTS, INVERTEBRATES, MARSUPIALS, MONKEYS, APES AND OTHER PRIMATES, REPTILES, RODENTS, SEA MAMMALS

animate ADJECTIVE 1 = **living**, live, moving, alive, breathing, alive and kicking
▷ VERB 2 = **enliven**, excite, inspire, move, fire, stimulate, energize, kindle **OPPOSITE:** inhibit

animated = **lively**, spirited, excited, enthusiastic, passionate, energetic, ebullient, vivacious **OPPOSITE:** listless

animation = **liveliness**, energy, spirit, passion, enthusiasm, excitement, verve, zest

announce = **make known**, tell, report, reveal, declare, advertise, broadcast, disclose, post, tweet **OPPOSITE:** keep secret

announcement 1 = **statement**, communication, broadcast, declaration, advertisement, bulletin, communiqué, proclamation 2 = **declaration**, report, reporting, revelation, proclamation

a

ANIMALS
Collective Animals

antelopes	herd
apes	shrewdness
asses	pace *or* herd
badgers	cete
bears	sloth
bees	swarm *or* grist
birds	flock, congregation, flight, *or* volery
bitterns	sedge *or* siege
boars	sounder
bucks	brace *or* lease
buffaloes	herd
capercailzies	tok
cats	clowder
cattle	drove *or* herd
choughs	chattering
colts	rag
coots	covert
cranes	herd, sedge, *or* siege
crows	murder
cubs	litter
curlews	herd
curs	cowardice
deer	herd
dolphins	school
doves	flight *or* dule
ducks	paddling *or* team
dunlins	flight
elk	gang
fish	shoal, draught, haul, run, *or* catch
flies	swarm *or* grist
foxes	skulk
geese	gaggle *or* skein
giraffes	herd
gnats	swarm *or* cloud
goats	herd *or* tribe
goldfinches	charm

grouse	brood, covey, or pack
gulls	colony
hares	down or husk
hawks	cast
hens	brood
herons	sedge or siege
herrings	shoal or glean
hounds	pack, mute, or cry
insects	swarm
kangaroos	troop
kittens	kindle
lapwings	desert
larks	exaltation
leopards	leap
lions	pride or troop
mallards	sord or sute
mares	stud
martens	richesse
moles	labour
monkeys	troop
mules	barren
nightingales	watch
owls	parliament
oxen	yoke, drove, team, or herd
partridges	covey
peacocks	muster
pheasants	nye or nide
pigeons	flock or flight
pigs	litter
plovers	stand or wing
pochards	flight, rush, bunch, or knob
ponies	herd
porpoises	school or gam
poultry	run
pups	litter
quails	bevy
rabbits	nest
racehorses	field or string

Collective Animals *continued*

ravens	unkindness
roes	bevy
rooks	building *or* clamour
ruffs	hill
seals	herd *or* pod
sheep	flock
sheldrakes	dopping
snipe	walk *or* wisp
sparrows	host
starlings	murmuration
swallows	flight
swans	herd *or* bevy
swifts	flock
swine	herd, sounder, *or* dryft
teal	bunch, knob, *or* spring
whales	school, gam, *or* run
whelps	litter
whiting	pod
wigeon	bunch, company, knob, *or* flight
wildfowl	plump, sord, *or* sute
wolves	pack, rout, *or* herd
woodcocks	fall

annoy = **irritate**, trouble, anger, bother, disturb, plague, hassle (*informal*), madden, hack you off (*informal*) **OPPOSITE:** soothe

annoying = **irritating**, disturbing, troublesome, maddening, exasperating **OPPOSITE:** delightful

annual 1 = **once a year**, yearly 2 = **yearlong**, yearly

annually 1 = **once a year**, yearly, every year, per year, by the year, every twelve months, per annum 2 = **per year**, yearly, every year, by the year, per annum

anomaly = **irregularity**, exception, abnormality, inconsistency, eccentricity, oddity, peculiarity, incongruity

anonymous 1 = **unnamed**, unknown, unidentified, nameless, unacknowledged, incognito **OPPOSITE:** identified 2 = **unsigned**, uncredited, unattributed **OPPOSITE:** signed

answer VERB 1 = **reply**, explain, respond, resolve, react, return, retort OPPOSITE: ask
▷ NOUN 2 = **reply**, response, reaction, explanation, comeback, retort, return, defence OPPOSITE: question
3 = **solution**, resolution, explanation 4 = **remedy**, solution

ant
• See panel ANTS, BEES, AND WASPS

anthem = **song of praise**, carol, chant, hymn, psalm, paean, chorale, canticle

anthology = **collection**, selection, treasury, compilation, compendium, miscellany

anticipate 1 = **expect**, predict, prepare for, hope for, envisage, foresee, bank on, foretell
2 = **await**, look forward to, count the hours until

anticipation = **expectancy**, expectation, foresight,

ANTS, BEES, AND WASPS

Amazon ant
ant or (archaic or dialect) emmet
army ant or legionary ant
bee
blue ant (Austral)
bulldog ant, bull ant, or (Austral) bull Joe
bumblebee or humblebee
carpenter bee
cicada hunter (Austral)
cuckoo bee
digger wasp
driver ant
flower wasp (Austral)
gall wasp
honeybee or hive bee
honeypot ant or honey ant (Austral)
horntail or wood wasp
ichneumon fly or ichneumon wasp
killer bee

kootchar (Austral)
leafcutter ant
leafcutter bee
mason bee
mason wasp
minga (Austral)
mining bee
mud dauber
native bee or sugarbag fly (Austral)
Pharaoh ant
policeman fly (Austral)
ruby-tail wasp
sand wasp
Sirex wasp (Austral)
slave ant
spider-hunting wasp
termite or white ant
velvet ant
wasp
wood ant
yellow jacket (US & Canad)

a

premonition, prescience, forethought

antics = **clowning**, tricks, mischief, pranks, escapades, playfulness, horseplay, tomfoolery

antique NOUN 1 = **period piece**, relic, bygone, heirloom, collector's item, museum piece
▷ ADJECTIVE 2 = **vintage**, classic, antiquarian, olden

anxiety = **uneasiness**, concern, worry, doubt, tension, angst, apprehension, misgiving **OPPOSITE:** confidence

anxious 1 = **eager**, keen, intent, yearning, impatient, itching, desirous **OPPOSITE:** reluctant
2 = **uneasy**, concerned, worried, troubled, nervous, uncomfortable, tense, fearful **OPPOSITE:** confident

apart 1 = **to pieces**, to bits, asunder 2 = **away from each other**, distant from each other
3 = **aside**, away, alone, isolated, to one side, by yourself
▷ PHRASES: apart from = **except for**, excepting, other than, excluding, besides, not including, aside from, but

apartment 1 (US) = **flat**, room, suite, penthouse, duplex (US & Canad), crib, bachelor apartment (Canad) 2 = **rooms**, quarters, accommodation, living quarters

apathy = **lack of interest**, indifference, inertia, coolness,

passivity, nonchalance, torpor, unconcern **OPPOSITE:** interest

apiece = **each**, individually, separately, for each, to each, respectively, from each **OPPOSITE:** all together

apologize = **say sorry**, express regret, ask forgiveness, make an apology, beg pardon

apology = **regret**, explanation, excuse, confession
▷ PHRASES: apology for something or someone = **mockery of**, excuse for, imitation of, caricature of, travesty of, poor substitute for

appal = **horrify**, shock, alarm, frighten, outrage, disgust, dishearten, revolt

appalling 1 = **horrifying**, shocking, alarming, awful, terrifying, horrible, dreadful, fearful **OPPOSITE:** reassuring
2 = **awful**, dreadful, horrendous

apparatus 1 = **organization**, system, network, structure, bureaucracy, hierarchy, setup (informal), chain of command
2 = **equipment**, tackle, gear, device, tools, mechanism, machinery, appliance

apparent 1 = **seeming**, outward, superficial, ostensible **OPPOSITE:** actual 2 = **obvious**, marked, visible, evident, distinct, manifest, noticeable, unmistakable **OPPOSITE:** unclear

apparently = seemingly, outwardly, ostensibly

appeal VERB 1 = **plead**, ask, request, pray, beg, entreat **OPPOSITE:** refuse
▷ NOUN 2 = **plea**, call, application, request, prayer, petition, overture, entreaty **OPPOSITE:** refusal
3 = **attraction**, charm, fascination, beauty, allure **OPPOSITE:** repulsiveness
▷ PHRASES: appeal to someone = **attract**, interest, draw, please, charm, fascinate, tempt, lure

appealing = **attractive**, engaging, charming, desirable, alluring, winsome **OPPOSITE:** repellent

appear 1 = **look (like** or **as if)**, seem, occur, look to be, come across as, strike you as 2 = **come into view**, emerge, occur, surface, come out, turn up, be present, show up (informal) **OPPOSITE:** disappear

appearance 1 = **look**, form, figure, looks, manner, expression, demeanour, mien (literary) 2 = **arrival**, presence, introduction, emergence
3 = **impression**, air, front, image, illusion, guise, façade, pretence

appease 1 = **pacify**, satisfy, calm, soothe, quiet, placate, mollify, conciliate **OPPOSITE:** anger 2 = **ease**, calm, relieve, soothe, alleviate, allay

appendix = **supplement**, postscript, adjunct, appendage, addendum, addition

appetite 1 = **hunger** 2 = **desire**, liking, longing, demand, taste, passion, stomach, hunger **OPPOSITE:** distaste

applaud 1 = **clap**, encourage, praise, cheer, acclaim **OPPOSITE:** boo 2 = **praise**, celebrate, approve, acclaim, compliment, salute, commend, extol **OPPOSITE:** criticize

applause = **ovation**, praise, cheers, approval, clapping, accolade, big hand

appliance = **device**, machine, tool, instrument, implement, mechanism, apparatus, gadget

applicable = **appropriate**, fitting, useful, suitable, relevant, apt, pertinent **OPPOSITE:** inappropriate

applicant = **candidate**, claimant, inquirer

application 1 = **request**, claim, appeal, inquiry, petition, requisition 2 = **effort**, work, industry, trouble, struggle, pains, commitment, hard work 3 = **program**, package, software, app (informal), killer application or killer app

apply 1 = **request**, appeal, put in, petition, inquire, claim, requisition 2 = **be relevant**, relate, refer, be fitting, be appropriate, fit, pertain, be applicable 3 = **use**, exercise,

carry out, employ, implement, practise, exert, enact **4 = put on**, work in, cover with, lay on, paint on, spread on, rub in, smear on
▷ **PHRASES: apply yourself = work hard**, concentrate, try, commit yourself, buckle down (*informal*), devote yourself, be diligent, dedicate yourself

appoint 1 = assign, name, choose, commission, select, elect, delegate, nominate **OPPOSITE:** fire **2 = decide**, set, choose, establish, fix, arrange, assign, designate **OPPOSITE:** cancel

appointed 1 = decided, set, chosen, established, fixed, arranged, assigned, designated **2 = assigned**, named, chosen, selected, elected, delegated, nominated **3 = equipped**, provided, supplied, furnished, fitted out

appointment 1 = selection, naming, election, choice, nomination, assignment **2 = job**, office, position, post, situation, place, employment, assignment **3 = meeting**, interview, date, arrangement, engagement, fixture, rendezvous, assignation

appraisal = assessment, opinion, estimate, judgment, evaluation, estimation

appreciate 1 = enjoy, like, value, respect, prize, admire,

treasure, rate highly **OPPOSITE:** scorn **2 = be aware of**, understand, realize, recognize, perceive, take account of, be sensitive to, sympathize with **OPPOSITE:** be unaware of **3 = be grateful for**, be obliged for, be thankful for, give thanks for, be indebted for, be in debt for, be appreciative of **OPPOSITE:** be ungrateful for **4 = increase**, rise, grow, gain, improve, enhance, soar **OPPOSITE:** fall

appreciation 1 = admiration, enjoyment **2 = gratitude**, thanks, recognition, obligation, acknowledgment, indebtedness, thankfulness, gratefulness **OPPOSITE:** ingratitude **3 = awareness**, understanding, recognition, perception, sympathy, consciousness, sensitivity, realization **OPPOSITE:** ignorance **4 = increase**, rise, gain, growth, improvement, escalation, enhancement **OPPOSITE:** fall

apprehension 1 = anxiety, concern, fear, worry, alarm, suspicion, dread, trepidation **OPPOSITE:** confidence **2 = arrest**, catching, capture, taking, seizure **OPPOSITE:** release **3 = awareness**, understanding, perception, grasp, comprehension **OPPOSITE:** incomprehension

apprentice = **trainee**, student, pupil, novice, beginner, learner, probationer **OPPOSITE:** master

approach VERB 1 = **move towards**, reach, near, come close, come near, draw near 2 = **make a proposal to**, speak to, apply to, appeal to, proposition, solicit, sound out, make overtures to 3 = **set about**, tackle, undertake, embark on, get down to, launch into, begin work on, commence on
▷ NOUN 4 = **advance**, coming, nearing, appearance, arrival, drawing near 5 = **access**, way, drive, road, passage, entrance, avenue, passageway 6 *often plural* = **proposal**, offer, appeal, advance, application, invitation, proposition, overture 7 = **way**, means, style, method, technique, manner

appropriate ADJECTIVE 1 = **suitable**, fitting, relevant, to the point, apt, pertinent, befitting, well-suited **OPPOSITE:** unsuitable
▷ VERB 2 = **seize**, claim, acquire, confiscate, usurp, impound, commandeer, take possession of **OPPOSITE:** relinquish 3 = **allocate**, allow, budget, devote, assign, designate, set aside, earmark **OPPOSITE:** withhold 4 = **steal**, take, nick (*slang, chiefly Brit*), pocket, pinch (*informal*), lift (*informal*), embezzle, pilfer

approval 1 = **consent**, agreement, sanction, blessing, permission, recommendation, endorsement, assent 2 = **favour**, respect, praise, esteem, acclaim, appreciation, admiration, applause **OPPOSITE:** disapproval

approve = **agree to**, allow, pass, recommend, permit, sanction, endorse, authorize **OPPOSITE:** veto
▷ PHRASES: **approve of something** *or* **someone** = **favour**, like, respect, praise, admire, commend, have a good opinion of, regard highly

apt 1 = **appropriate**, fitting, suitable, relevant, to the point, pertinent **OPPOSITE:** inappropriate 2 = **inclined**, likely, ready, disposed, prone, liable, given, predisposed 3 = **gifted**, skilled, quick, talented, sharp, capable, smart, clever **OPPOSITE:** slow

arbitrary = **random**, chance, subjective, inconsistent, erratic, personal, whimsical, capricious **OPPOSITE:** logical

arbitration = **decision**, settlement, judgment, determination, adjudication

arc = **curve**, bend, bow, arch, crescent, half-moon

arcade = **gallery**, cloister, portico, colonnade

a

arch¹ NOUN 1 = **archway**, curve, dome, span, vault 2 = **curve**, bend, bow, crook, arc, hunch, sweep, hump
▷ VERB 3 = **curve**, bridge, bend, bow, span, arc

arch² = **playful**, sly, mischievous, saucy, pert, roguish, frolicsome, waggish

archetypal = **typical**, standard, model, original, classic, ideal, prototypic or prototypical

architect = **designer**, planner, draughtsman, master builder

architecture 1 = **design**, planning, building, construction 2 = **construction**, design, style 3 = **structure**, design, shape, make-up, construction, framework, layout, anatomy

archive NOUN 1 = **record office**, museum, registry, repository
▷ PLURAL NOUN 2 = **records**, papers, accounts, rolls, documents, files, deeds, chronicles

Arctic = **polar**, far-northern, hyperborean

arctic (informal) = **freezing**, cold, frozen, icy, chilly, glacial, frigid

ardent 1 = **enthusiastic**, keen, eager, avid, zealous OPPOSITE: indifferent 2 = **passionate**, intense, impassioned, lusty, amorous, hot-blooded OPPOSITE: cold

area 1 = **region**, quarter, district, zone, neighbourhood, locality 2 = **part**, section, sector, portion

3 = **realm**, part, department, field, province, sphere, domain

arena 1 = **ring**, ground, field, theatre, bowl, pitch, stadium, enclosure 2 = **scene**, world, area, stage, field, sector, territory, province

argue 1 = **quarrel**, fight, row, clash, dispute, disagree, squabble, bicker 2 = **discuss**, debate, dispute 3 = **claim**, reason, challenge, insist, maintain, allege, assert, uphold

argument 1 = **reason**, case, reasoning, ground(s), defence, logic, polemic, dialectic 2 = **debate**, questioning, claim, discussion, dispute, controversy, plea, assertion 3 = **quarrel**, fight, row, clash, dispute, controversy, disagreement, feud OPPOSITE: agreement

arise 1 = **happen**, start, begin, follow, result, develop, emerge, occur 2 (Old-fashioned) = **get to your feet**, get up, rise, stand up, spring up, leap up 3 = **get up**, wake up, awaken, get out of bed

aristocrat = **noble**, lord, lady, peer, patrician, grandee, aristo (informal), peeress

aristocratic = **upper-class**, lordly, titled, elite, gentlemanly, noble, patrician, blue-blooded OPPOSITE: common

arm¹ = **upper limb**, limb, appendage

arm² VERB 1 = **equip**, provide, supply, array, furnish, issue with,

deck out, accoutre
▷ **PLURAL NOUN 2 = weapons**,
guns, firearms, weaponry,
armaments, ordnance,
munitions, instruments of war
armed = carrying weapons,
protected, equipped, primed,
fitted out
armour = protection, covering,
shield, sheathing, armour
plate, chain mail, protective
covering
armoured = protected,
mailed, reinforced, toughened,
bulletproof, armour-plated,
steel-plated, ironclad
army 1 = soldiers, military,
troops, armed force, legions,
infantry, military force, land
force **2 = vast number**, host,
gang, mob, flock, array, legion,
swarm
aroma = scent, smell, perfume,
fragrance, bouquet, savour,
odour, redolence
around PREPOSITION
1 = approximately, about,
nearly, close to, roughly, just
about, in the region of, circa (~*of*
a date) **2 = surrounding**, about,
enclosing, encompassing,
framing, encircling, on all sides
of, on every side of
▷ **ADVERB 3 = everywhere**,
about, throughout, all over,
here and there, on all sides, in all
directions, to and fro **4 = near**,
close, nearby, at hand, close
at hand

USAGE NOTE
In American English, *around* is
used more often than *round*
as an adverb and preposition,
except in a few fixed phrases
such as *all year round*. In
British English, *round* is more
commonly used as an adverb
than *around*.

arouse 1 = stimulate,
encourage, inspire, prompt,
spur, provoke, rouse, stir up
OPPOSITE: quell **2 = inflame**,
move, excite, spur, provoke, stir
up, agitate **3 = awaken**, wake
up, rouse, waken
arrange 1 = plan, agree,
prepare, determine, organize,
construct, devise, contrive,
jack up (*NZ informal*) **2 = put**
in order, group, order, sort,
position, line up, organize,
classify, jack up (*NZ informal*)
OPPOSITE: disorganize
3 = adapt, score, orchestrate,
harmonize, instrument
arrangement 1 *often plural*
= plan, planning, provision,
preparation **2 = agreement**,
contract, settlement,
appointment, compromise,
deal (*informal*), pact, compact
3 = display, system, structure,
organization, exhibition,
presentation, classification,
alignment **4 = adaptation**,
score, version, interpretation,
instrumentation, orchestration,
harmonization

array NOUN 1 = **arrangement**, show, supply, display, collection, exhibition, line-up, mixture 2 (*poetic*) = **clothing**, dress, clothes, garments, apparel, attire, finery, regalia
▷ VERB 3 = **arrange**, show, group, present, range, display, parade, exhibit 4 = **dress**, clothe, deck, decorate, adorn, festoon, attire

arrest VERB 1 = **capture**, catch, nick (*slang, chiefly Brit*), seize, detain, apprehend, take prisoner **OPPOSITE:** release 2 = **stop**, end, limit, block, slow, delay, interrupt, suppress **OPPOSITE:** speed up 3 = **fascinate**, hold, occupy, engage, grip, absorb, entrance, intrigue
▷ NOUN 4 = **capture**, bust (*informal*), detention, seizure **OPPOSITE:** release 5 = **stoppage**, suppression, obstruction, blockage, hindrance **OPPOSITE:** acceleration

arresting = **striking**, surprising, engaging, stunning, impressive, outstanding, remarkable, noticeable **OPPOSITE:** unremarkable

arrival 1 = **appearance**, coming, arriving, entrance, advent, materialization 2 = **coming**, happening, taking place, emergence, occurrence, materialization 3 = **newcomer**, incomer, visitor, caller, entrant

arrive 1 = **come**, appear, turn up, show up (*informal*), draw near **OPPOSITE:** depart 2 = **occur**, happen, take place 3 (*informal*) = **succeed**, make it (*informal*), triumph, do well, thrive, flourish, be successful, make good

arrogance = **conceit**, pride, swagger, insolence, high-handedness, haughtiness, superciliousness, disdainfulness **OPPOSITE:** modesty

arrogant = **conceited**, proud, cocky, overbearing, haughty, scornful, egotistical, disdainful **OPPOSITE:** modest

arrow 1 = **dart**, flight, bolt, shaft (*archaic*), quarrel 2 = **pointer**, indicator, marker

arsenal 1 = **store**, supply, stockpile 2 = **armoury**, storehouse, ammunition dump, arms depot, ordnance depot

art 1 = **artwork**, style of art, fine art, creativity 2 = **skill**, craft, expertise, competence, mastery, ingenuity, virtuosity, cleverness

article 1 = **feature**, story, paper, piece, item, creation, essay, composition 2 = **thing**, piece, unit, item, object, device, tool, implement 3 = **clause**, point, part, section, item, passage, portion, paragraph

articulate ADJECTIVE 1 = **expressive**, clear, coherent, fluent, eloquent, lucid

OPPOSITE: incoherent
▷ **VERB** 2 = **express**, say, state, word, declare, phrase, communicate, utter 3 = **pronounce**, say, talk, speak, voice, utter, enunciate

artificial 1 = **synthetic**, manufactured, plastic, man-made, non-natural 2 = **insincere**, forced, affected, phoney *or* phony (*informal*), false, contrived, unnatural, feigned **OPPOSITE:** genuine 3 = **fake**, mock, imitation, bogus, simulated, sham, counterfeit **OPPOSITE:** authentic

artillery = **big guns**, battery, cannon, ordnance, gunnery

artistic 1 = **creative**, cultured, original, sophisticated, refined, aesthetic, discerning, eloquent **OPPOSITE:** untalented 2 = **beautiful**, creative, elegant, stylish, aesthetic, tasteful **OPPOSITE:** unattractive

as CONJUNCTION 1 = **when**, while, just as, at the time that 2 = **in the way that**, like, in the manner that 3 = **since**, because, seeing that, considering that, on account of the fact that ▷ **PREPOSITION** 4 = **in the role of**, being, under the name of, in the character of

ashamed 1 = **embarrassed**, sorry, guilty, distressed, humiliated, self-conscious, red-faced, mortified **OPPOSITE:**

proud 2 = **reluctant**, embarrassed

ashore = **on land**, on the beach, on the shore, aground, to the shore, on dry land, shorewards, landwards

aside ADVERB 1 = **to one side**, separately, apart, beside, out of the way, on one side, to the side ▷ **NOUN** 2 = **interpolation**, parenthesis

ask 1 = **inquire**, question, quiz, query, interrogate **OPPOSITE:** answer 2 = **request**, appeal to, plead with, demand, beg 3 = **invite**, bid, summon

asleep = **sleeping**, napping, dormant, dozing, slumbering, snoozing (*informal*), fast asleep, sound asleep

aspect 1 = **feature**, side, factor, angle, characteristic, facet 2 = **position**, view, situation, scene, prospect, point of view, outlook 3 = **appearance**, look, air, condition, quality, bearing, attitude, cast

aspiration = **aim**, plan, hope, goal, dream, wish, desire, objective

aspire to = **aim for**, desire, hope for, long for, seek out, wish for, dream about, set your heart on

ass 1 = **donkey**, moke (*slang*) 2 = **fool**, idiot, twit (*informal, chiefly Brit*), oaf, jackass, blockhead, halfwit, numbskull *or* numskull, dorba *or* dorb (*Austral slang*), bogan (*Austral slang*)

assassin = **murderer**, killer, slayer, liquidator, executioner, hit man (*slang*), hatchet man (*slang*)

assassinate = **murder**, kill, eliminate (*slang*), take out (*slang*), terminate, hit (*slang*), slay, liquidate

assault NOUN 1 = **attack**, raid, invasion, charge, offensive, onslaught, foray OPPOSITE: defence
▷ VERB 2 = **strike**, attack, beat, knock, bang, slap, smack, thump

assemble 1 = **gather**, meet, collect, rally, come together, muster, congregate OPPOSITE: scatter 2 = **bring together**, collect, gather, rally, come together, muster, amass, congregate 3 = **put together**, join, set up, build up, connect, construct, piece together, fabricate OPPOSITE: take apart

assembly 1 = **gathering**, group, meeting, council, conference, crowd, congress, collection, hui (*NZ*), runanga (*NZ*)
2 = **putting together**, setting up, construction, building up, connecting, piecing together

assert 1 = **state**, argue, maintain, declare, swear, pronounce, affirm, profess OPPOSITE: deny 2 = **insist upon**, stress, defend, uphold, put forward, press, stand up for OPPOSITE: retract

▷ PHRASES: **assert yourself** = **be forceful**, put your foot down (*informal*), put yourself forward, make your presence felt, exert your influence

assertion 1 = **statement**, claim, declaration, pronouncement
2 = **insistence**, stressing, maintenance

assertive = **confident**, positive, aggressive, forceful, emphatic, insistent, feisty (*informal, chiefly US & Canad*), pushy (*informal*) OPPOSITE: meek

assess 1 = **judge**, estimate, analyse, evaluate, rate, value, check out, weigh up
2 = **evaluate**, rate, tax, value, estimate, fix, impose, levy

assessment 1 = **judgment**, analysis, evaluation, valuation, appraisal, rating, opinion, estimate 2 = **evaluation**, rating, charge, fee, toll, levy, valuation

asset = **benefit**, help, service, aid, advantage, strength, resource, attraction OPPOSITE: disadvantage

assign 1 = **give**, set, grant, allocate, give out, consign, allot, apportion 2 = **select for**, post, commission, elect, appoint, delegate, nominate, name
3 = **attribute**, credit, put down, set down, ascribe, accredit

assignment = **task**, job, position, post, commission, exercise, responsibility, duty

assist 1 = **help**, support, aid, cooperate with, abet, lend a helping hand to 2 = **facilitate**, help, further, serve, aid, forward, speed up **OPPOSITE:** hinder

assistance = **help**, backing, support, aid, cooperation, helping hand **OPPOSITE:** hindrance

assistant = **helper**, ally, colleague, supporter, aide, second, attendant, accomplice

associate **VERB** 1 = **connect**, link, ally, identify, join, combine, attach, fasten **OPPOSITE:** separate 2 = **socialize**, mix, accompany, mingle, consort, hobnob **OPPOSITE:** avoid
▷ **NOUN** 3 = **partner**, friend, ally, colleague, mate (*informal*), companion, comrade, affiliate, cobber (*Austral & NZ old-fashioned informal*), E hoa (*NZ*)

association 1 = **group**, club, society, league, band, set, pack, collection, social network (*computing*) 2 = **connection**, union, joining, pairing, combination, mixture, blend, juxtaposition

assorted = **various**, different, mixed, varied, diverse, miscellaneous, sundry, motley **OPPOSITE:** similar

assume 1 = **presume**, think, believe, expect, suppose, imagine, fancy, take for granted **OPPOSITE:** know 2 = **take on**, accept, shoulder, take over, put on, enter upon 3 = **simulate**, affect, adopt, put on, imitate, mimic, feign, impersonate 4 = **take over**, take, appropriate, seize, commandeer **OPPOSITE:** give up

assumed = **false**, made-up, fake, bogus, counterfeit, fictitious, make-believe **OPPOSITE:** real

assumption 1 = **presumption**, belief, guess, hypothesis, inference, conjecture, surmise, supposition 2 = **taking on**, managing, handling, shouldering, putting on, taking up, takeover, acquisition 3 = **seizure**, taking, takeover, acquisition, appropriation, wresting, confiscation, commandeering

assurance 1 = **promise**, statement, guarantee, commitment, pledge, vow, declaration, assertion **OPPOSITE:** lie 2 = **confidence**, conviction, certainty, self-confidence, poise, faith, nerve, aplomb **OPPOSITE:** self-doubt

assure 1 = **convince**, encourage, persuade, satisfy, comfort, reassure, hearten, embolden 2 = **make certain**, ensure, confirm, guarantee, secure, make sure, complete, seal 3 = **promise to**, pledge to, vow to, guarantee to, swear to, confirm to, certify to, give your word to

a

assured 1 = confident, certain, positive, poised, fearless, self-confident, self-assured, dauntless **OPPOSITE:** self-conscious **2 = certain**, sure, ensured, confirmed, settled, guaranteed, fixed, secure, nailed-on (slang) **OPPOSITE:** doubtful

astonish = amaze, surprise, stun, stagger, bewilder, astound, daze, confound

astounding = amazing, surprising, brilliant, impressive, astonishing, staggering, sensational (informal), bewildering

astute = intelligent, sharp, clever, subtle, shrewd, cunning, canny, perceptive **OPPOSITE:** stupid

asylum 1 (Old-fashioned) **= mental hospital**, hospital, institution, psychiatric hospital, madhouse (informal) **2 = refuge**, haven, safety, protection, preserve, shelter, retreat, harbour

athlete = sportsperson, player, runner, competitor, sportsman, contestant, gymnast, sportswoman

athletic = fit, strong, powerful, healthy, active, trim, strapping, energetic **OPPOSITE:** feeble

athletics = sports, games, races, exercises, contests, sporting events, gymnastics, track and field events

atmosphere 1 = air, sky, heavens, aerosphere **2 = feeling**, character, environment, spirit, surroundings, tone, mood, climate

atom = particle, bit, spot, trace, molecule, dot, speck

atrocity 1 = act of cruelty, crime, horror, evil, outrage, abomination **2 = cruelty**, horror, brutality, savagery, wickedness, barbarity, viciousness, fiendishness

attach 1 = affix, stick, secure, add, join, couple, link, tie **OPPOSITE:** detach **2 = ascribe**, connect, attribute, assign, associate

attached = spoken for, married, partnered, engaged, accompanied
▷ **PHRASES: attached to = fond of**, devoted to, affectionate towards, full of regard for

attachment 1 = fondness, liking, feeling, relationship, regard, attraction, affection, affinity, aroha (NZ) **OPPOSITE:** aversion **2 = accessory**, fitting, extra, component, extension, supplement, fixture, accoutrement

attack VERB 1 = assault, strike (at), mug, ambush, tear into, set upon, lay into (informal) **OPPOSITE:** defend **2 = invade**, occupy, raid, infringe, storm, encroach **3 = criticize**, blame, abuse, condemn, knock (*informal*), put down, slate (*informal*), have a go (at) (*informal*)

▷ **NOUN 4 = assault**, charge, campaign, strike, raid, invasion, offensive, blitz **OPPOSITE:** defence **5 = criticism**, censure, disapproval, abuse, bad press, vilification, denigration, disparagement **6 = bout**, fit, stroke, seizure, spasm, convulsion, paroxysm

attacker = assailant, assaulter, raider, intruder, invader, aggressor, mugger

attain 1 = obtain, get, reach, complete, gain, achieve, acquire, fulfil **2 = reach**, achieve, acquire, accomplish

attempt VERB 1 = try, seek, aim, struggle, venture, undertake, strive, endeavour

▷ **NOUN 2 = try**, go (*informal*), shot (*informal*), effort, trial, bid, crack (*informal*), stab (*informal*) **3 = attack**

attend 1 = be present, go to, visit, frequent, haunt, appear at, turn up at, patronize **OPPOSITE:** be absent **2 = pay attention**, listen, hear, mark, note, observe, heed, pay heed **OPPOSITE:** ignore

▷ **PHRASES: attend to something = apply yourself to**, concentrate on, look after, take care of, see to, get to work on, devote yourself to, occupy yourself with

attendance 1 = presence, being there, attending, appearance **2 = turnout**, audience, gate, congregation, house, crowd, throng, number present

attendant NOUN 1 = assistant, guard, servant, companion, aide, escort, follower, helper

▷ **ADJECTIVE 2 = accompanying**, related, associated, accessory, consequent, resultant, concomitant

attention 1 = thinking, thought, mind, consideration, scrutiny, heed, deliberation, intentness **2 = care**, support, concern, treatment, looking after, succour, ministration **3 = awareness**, regard, notice, recognition, consideration, observation, consciousness **OPPOSITE:** inattention

attic = loft, garret, roof space

attitude 1 = opinion, view, position, approach, mood, perspective, point of view, stance **2 = position**, bearing, pose, stance, carriage, posture

attract 1 = allure, draw, persuade, charm, appeal to, win over, tempt, lure (*informal*) **OPPOSITE:** repel **2 = pull**, draw, magnetize

attraction 1 = appeal, pull (*informal*), charm, lure, temptation, fascination, allure, magnetism **2 = pull**, magnetism

attractive 1 = **seductive**, charming, tempting, pretty, fair, inviting, lovely, pleasant, hot (*informal*), fit (*Brit informal*), lush (*slang*) **OPPOSITE:** unattractive 2 = **appealing**, pleasing, inviting, tempting, irresistible **OPPOSITE:** unappealing

attribute VERB 1 = **ascribe**, credit, refer, trace, assign, charge, allocate, put down ▷ NOUN 2 = **quality**, feature, property, character, element, aspect, characteristic, distinction

audience 1 = **spectators**, company, crowd, gathering, gallery, assembly, viewers, listeners 2 = **interview**, meeting, hearing, exchange, reception, consultation

aura = **air**, feeling, quality, atmosphere, tone, mood, ambience

austerity 1 = **plainness**, simplicity, starkness 2 = **asceticism**, self-discipline, sobriety, puritanism, self-denial

authentic 1 = **real**, pure, genuine, valid, undisputed, lawful, bona fide, dinkum (*Austral & NZ informal*), true-to-life, live (~*of data*) **OPPOSITE:** fake 2 = **accurate**, legitimate, authoritative **OPPOSITE:** fictitious

authenticity 1 = **genuineness**, purity 2 = **accuracy**, certainty, validity, legitimacy, faithfulness, truthfulness

author 1 = **writer**, composer, novelist, hack, creator, scribbler, scribe, wordsmith 2 = **creator**, father, producer, designer, founder, architect, inventor, originator

authoritarian ADJECTIVE 1 = **strict**, severe, autocratic, dictatorial, dogmatic, tyrannical, doctrinaire **OPPOSITE:** lenient ▷ NOUN 2 = **disciplinarian**, dictator, tyrant, despot, autocrat, absolutist

authoritative 1 = **commanding**, masterly, imposing, assertive, imperious, self-assured **OPPOSITE:** timid 2 = **reliable**, accurate, valid, authentic, definitive, dependable, trustworthy **OPPOSITE:** unreliable

authority 1 *usually plural* = **powers that be**, government, police, officials, the state, management, administration, the system 2 = **prerogative**, influence, power, control, weight, direction, command, licence, mana (*NZ*) 3 = **expert**, specialist, professional, master, guru, virtuoso, connoisseur, fundi (*S African*) 4 = **command**, power, control, rule, management, direction, mastery

authorize 1 = **empower**, commission, enable, entitle, mandate, accredit, give authority to 2 = **permit**, allow, grant, approve, sanction, license, warrant, consent to **OPPOSITE:** forbid

automatic 1 = **mechanical**, automated, mechanized, push-button, self-propelling **OPPOSITE:** done by hand 2 = **involuntary**, natural, unconscious, mechanical, spontaneous, reflex, instinctive, unwilled **OPPOSITE:** conscious

autonomous = **self-ruling**, free, independent, sovereign, self-sufficient, self-governing, self-determining

autonomy = **independence**, freedom, sovereignty, self-determination, self-government, self-rule, self-sufficiency, home rule, rangatiratanga (NZ) **OPPOSITE:** dependency

availability = **accessibility**, readiness, handiness, attainability

available = **accessible**, ready, to hand, handy, at hand, free, to be had, achievable **OPPOSITE:** in use

avalanche 1 = **snow-slide**, landslide, landslip 2 = **large amount**, barrage, torrent, deluge, inundation

avant-garde = **progressive**, pioneering, experimental, innovative, unconventional, ground-breaking **OPPOSITE:** conservative

avenue = **street**, way, course, drive, road, approach, route, path

average NOUN 1 = **standard**, normal, usual, par, mode, mean, medium, norm
▷ ADJECTIVE 2 = **usual**, standard, general, normal, regular, ordinary, typical, commonplace **OPPOSITE:** unusual 3 = **mean**, middle, medium, intermediate, median **OPPOSITE:** minimum
▷ VERB 4 = **make on average**, be on average, even out to, do on average, balance out to
▷ PHRASES: **on average** = **usually**, generally, normally, typically, for the most part, as a rule

avert 1 = **ward off**, avoid, prevent, frustrate, fend off, preclude, stave off, forestall 2 = **turn away**, turn aside

avoid 1 = **prevent**, stop, frustrate, hamper, foil, inhibit, avert, thwart 2 = **refrain from**, bypass, dodge, eschew, escape, duck (out of) (informal), fight shy of, shirk from 3 = **keep away from**, dodge, evade, steer clear of, bypass

await 1 = **wait for**, expect, look for, look forward to, anticipate, stay for 2 = **be in store for**, wait for, be ready for, lie in wait for, be in readiness for

a

awake VERB 1 = **wake up**, come to, wake, stir, awaken, rouse 2 = **alert**, stimulate, provoke, revive, arouse, stir up, kindle 3 = **stimulate**, provoke, alert, stir up, kindle ▷ ADJECTIVE 4 = **not sleeping**, sleepless, wide-awake, aware, conscious, aroused, awakened, restless **OPPOSITE:** asleep

award VERB 1 = **present with**, give, grant, hand out, confer, endow, bestow 2 = **grant**, give, confer ▷ NOUN 3 = **prize**, gift, trophy, decoration, grant, bonsela (*S African*), koha (*NZ*)

aware = **informed**, enlightened, knowledgeable, learned, expert, versed, up to date, in the picture **OPPOSITE:** ignorant

awareness
▷ PHRASES: **awareness of** = **knowledge of**, understanding of, recognition of, perception of, consciousness of, realization of, familiarity with

away ADJECTIVE 1 = **absent**, out, gone, elsewhere, abroad, not here, not present, on vacation ▷ ADVERB 2 = **off**, elsewhere, abroad, hence, from here 3 = **aside**, out of the way, to one side 4 = **at a distance**, far, apart, remote, isolated 5 = **continuously**, repeatedly, relentlessly, incessantly, interminably, unremittingly, uninterruptedly

awe NOUN 1 = **wonder**, fear, respect, reverence, horror, terror, dread, admiration **OPPOSITE:** contempt ▷ VERB 2 = **impress**, amaze, stun, frighten, terrify, astonish, horrify, intimidate

awesome = **awe-inspiring**, amazing, stunning, impressive, astonishing, formidable, intimidating, breathtaking

awful 1 = **disgusting**, offensive, gross, foul, dreadful, revolting, sickening, frightful, festy (*Austral slang*), yucko (*Austral slang*) 2 = **bad**, poor, terrible, appalling, foul, rubbish (*slang*), dreadful, horrendous **OPPOSITE:** wonderful 3 = **shocking**, dreadful 4 = **unwell**, poorly (*informal*), ill, terrible, sick, crook (*Austral & NZ informal*), unhealthy, off-colour, under the weather (*informal*)

awfully 1 (*informal*) = **very**, extremely, terribly, exceptionally, greatly, immensely, exceedingly, dreadfully 2 = **badly**, woefully, dreadfully, disgracefully, wretchedly, unforgivably, reprehensibly

awkward 1 = **embarrassing**, difficult, sensitive, delicate, uncomfortable, humiliating, disconcerting, inconvenient, barro (*Austral slang*) **OPPOSITE:** comfortable 2 = **inconvenient**, difficult, troublesome, cumbersome, unwieldy, unmanageable, clunky (*informal*) **OPPOSITE:** convenient **3** = **clumsy**, lumbering, bumbling, unwieldy, ponderous, ungainly, gauche, gawky, unco (*Austral slang*) **OPPOSITE:** graceful

axe NOUN **1** = **hatchet**, chopper, tomahawk, cleaver, adze
▷ VERB **2** (*informal*) = **abandon**, end, eliminate, cancel, scrap, cut back, terminate, dispense with **3** (*informal*) = **dismiss**, fire (*informal*), sack (*informal*), remove, get rid of, kennet (*Austral slang*), jeff (*Austral slang*)
▷ PHRASES: **the axe** (*informal*) = **the sack** (*informal*), dismissal, the boot (*slang*), termination, the chop (*slang*)

axis = **pivot**, shaft, axle, spindle, centre line

baas (*S African*) = **master**, chief, ruler, commander, head, overlord, overseer

baby NOUN **1** = **child**, infant, babe, bairn (*Scot & Northern English*), newborn child, babe in arms, ankle biter (*Austral slang*), tacker (*Austral slang*)
▷ ADJECTIVE **2** = **small**, little, minute, tiny, mini, wee, miniature, petite

back NOUN **1** = **spine**, backbone, vertebrae, spinal column, vertebral column **2** = **rear** **OPPOSITE:** front **3** = **reverse**, rear, other side, wrong side, underside, flip side
▷ ADJECTIVE **4** = **rear OPPOSITE:** front **5** = **rearmost**, hind, hindmost **6** = **previous**, earlier, former, past, elapsed **OPPOSITE:** future **7** = **tail**, end, rear, posterior
▷ VERB **8** = **support**, help, aid, champion, defend, promote, assist, advocate **OPPOSITE:** oppose **9** = **subsidize**, help, support, sponsor, assist

b

backbone 1 = **spinal column**, spine, vertebrae, vertebral column 2 = **strength of character**, character, resolution, nerve, daring, courage, determination, pluck

backer 1 = **supporter**, second, angel (*informal*), patron, promoter, subscriber, helper, benefactor 2 = **advocate**, supporter, patron, sponsor, promoter

backfire = **fail**, founder, flop (*informal*), rebound, boomerang, miscarry, misfire

background 1 = **upbringing**, history, culture, environment, tradition, circumstances 2 = **experience**, grounding, education 3 = **circumstances**, history, conditions, situation, atmosphere, environment, framework, ambience

backing 1 = **support**, encouragement, endorsement, moral support 2 = **assistance**, support, help, aid, sponsorship, patronage

backlash = **reaction**, response, resistance, retaliation, repercussion, counterblast, counteraction

backward
1 = **underdeveloped**, undeveloped 2 (*old-fashioned or offens*) = **slow**, behind, underdeveloped, intellectually handicapped (*Austral*)

backwards *or* **backward** = **towards the rear**, behind you, in reverse, rearwards

bacteria = **microorganisms**, viruses, bugs (*slang*), germs, microbes, pathogens, bacilli

> **USAGE NOTE**
> *Bacteria* is a plural noun. It is therefore incorrect to talk about *a bacteria*, even though this is quite commonly heard, especially in the media. The correct singular is *a bacterium*.

bad 1 = **harmful**, damaging, dangerous, destructive, unhealthy, detrimental, hurtful, ruinous **OPPOSITE:** beneficial 2 = **unfavourable**, distressing, unfortunate, grim, unpleasant, gloomy, adverse 3 = **inferior**, poor, inadequate, faulty, unsatisfactory, defective, imperfect, substandard, bush-league (*Austral & NZ informal*), half-pie (*NZ informal*), bodger *or* bodgie (*Austral slang*) **OPPOSITE:** satisfactory 4 = **incompetent**, poor, useless, incapable, unfit, inexpert 5 = **grim**, severe, hard, tough 6 = **wicked**, criminal, evil, corrupt, immoral, sinful, depraved **OPPOSITE:** virtuous 7 = **naughty**, defiant, wayward, mischievous, wicked, unruly, impish, undisciplined **OPPOSITE:** well-behaved 8 = **rotten**, off, rank, sour, rancid, mouldy, putrid, festy (*Austral slang*)

badge 1 = **image**, brand, stamp, identification, crest, emblem, insignia 2 = **mark**, sign, token

badger = **pester**, harry, bother, bug (*informal*), bully, plague, hound, harass

badly 1 = **poorly**, incorrectly, carelessly, inadequately, imperfectly, ineptly **OPPOSITE:** well 2 = **severely**, greatly, deeply, seriously, desperately, intensely, exceedingly 3 = **unfavourably**, unsuccessfully

baffle = **puzzle**, confuse, stump, bewilder, confound, perplex, mystify, flummox **OPPOSITE:** explain

bag NOUN 1 = **sack**, container, sac, receptacle
▷ VERB 2 = **get**, land, score (*slang*), capture, acquire, procure 3 = **catch**, kill, shoot, capture, acquire, trap

baggage = **luggage**, things, cases, bags, equipment, gear, suitcases, belongings

baggy = **loose**, slack, bulging, sagging, sloppy, floppy, roomy, ill-fitting **OPPOSITE:** tight

bail (*Law*) = **security**, bond, guarantee, pledge, warranty, surety
▷ PHRASES: bail out = **escape**, withdraw, get away, retreat, make your getaway, break free *or* out ▶ bail something *or* someone out (*informal*)

= **save**, help, release, aid, deliver, recover, rescue, get out

bait NOUN 1 = **lure**, attraction, incentive, carrot (*informal*), temptation, snare, inducement, decoy
▷ VERB 2 = **tease**, annoy, irritate, bother, mock, wind up (*Brit slang*), hound, torment

baked = **dry**, desert, seared, scorched, barren, sterile, arid, torrid

bakkie (*S African*) = **truck**, pick-up, van, lorry, pick-up truck

balance VERB 1 = **stabilize**, level, steady **OPPOSITE:** overbalance 2 = **weigh**, consider, compare, estimate, contrast, assess, evaluate, set against 3 (*Accounting*) = **calculate**, total, determine, estimate, settle, count, square, reckon
▷ NOUN 4 = **equilibrium**, stability, steadiness, evenness **OPPOSITE:** instability 5 = **stability**, equanimity, steadiness 6 = **parity**, equity, fairness, impartiality, equality, correspondence, equivalence 7 = **remainder**, rest, difference, surplus, residue 8 = **composure**, stability, restraint, self-control, poise, self-discipline, equanimity, self-restraint

balcony 1 = **terrace**, veranda 2 = **upper circle**, gods, gallery

bald 1 = **hairless**, depilated, baldheaded 2 = **plain**, direct, frank, straightforward, blunt, rude, forthright, unadorned

ball = **sphere**, drop, globe, pellet, orb, globule, spheroid

balloon = **expand**, rise, increase, swell, blow up, inflate, bulge, billow

ballot = **vote**, election, voting, poll, polling, referendum, show of hands

ban VERB 1 = **prohibit**, bar, block, veto, forbid, boycott, outlaw, banish OPPOSITE: permit 2 = **bar**, prohibit, exclude, forbid, disqualify, preclude, debar, declare ineligible
▷ NOUN 3 = **prohibition**, restriction, veto, boycott, embargo, injunction, taboo, disqualification, rahui (NZ), restraining order (US law) OPPOSITE: permission

band¹ 1 = **ensemble**, group, orchestra, combo 2 = **gang**, company, group, party, team, body, crowd, pack

band² = **headband**, strip, ribbon

bandage NOUN 1 = **dressing**, plaster, compress, gauze
▷ VERB 2 = **dress**, cover, bind, swathe

bandit = **robber**, outlaw, raider, plunderer, mugger (informal), looter, highwayman, desperado

bang NOUN 1 = **explosion**, pop, clash, crack, blast, slam, discharge, thump 2 = **blow**, knock, stroke, punch, bump,

sock (slang), smack, thump
▷ VERB 3 = **resound**, boom, explode, thunder, thump, clang 4 = **bump**, knock, elbow, jostle 5 often with **on** = **hit**, strike, knock, belt (informal), slam, thump, clatter, beat or knock seven bells out of (informal)
▷ ADVERB 6 = **exactly**, straight, square, squarely, precisely, slap, smack, plumb (informal)

banish 1 = **exclude**, ban, dismiss, expel, throw out, eject, evict 2 = **expel**, exile, outlaw, deport OPPOSITE: admit 3 = **get rid of**, remove

bank¹ NOUN 1 = **financial institution**, repository, depository 2 = **store**, fund, stock, source, supply, reserve, pool, reservoir
▷ VERB 3 = **deposit**, keep, save

bank² NOUN 1 = **side**, edge, margin, shore, brink 2 = **mound**, banking, rise, hill, mass, pile, heap, ridge, kopje or koppie (S African)
▷ VERB 3 = **tilt**, tip, pitch, heel, slope, incline, slant, cant

bank³ = **row**, group, line, range, series, file, rank, sequence

bankrupt = **insolvent**, broke (informal), ruined, wiped out (informal), impoverished, in the red, destitute, gone bust (informal) OPPOSITE: solvent

bankruptcy = **insolvency**, failure, disaster, ruin, liquidation

banner 1 = **flag**, standard, colours, pennant, ensign, streamer 2 = **placard**

banquet = **feast**, spread (*informal*), dinner, meal, revel, repast, hakari (*NZ*)

bar NOUN 1 = **public house**, pub (*informal*, *chiefly Brit*), counter, inn, saloon, tavern, canteen, watering hole (*facetious slang*), beer parlour (*Canad*) 2 = **rod**, staff, stick, stake, rail, pole, paling, shaft 3 = **obstacle**, block, barrier, hurdle, hitch, barricade, snag, deterrent OPPOSITE: aid
▷ VERB 4 = **lock**, block, secure, attach, bolt, blockade, barricade, fortify 5 = **block**, restrict, restrain, hamper, thwart, hinder, obstruct, impede 6 = **exclude**, ban, forbid, prohibit, keep out of, disallow, shut out of, blackball OPPOSITE: admit

barbarian 1 = **savage**, monster, beast, brute, yahoo, swine, sadist 2 = **lout**, yahoo, bigot, philistine, hoon (*Austral & NZ*), cougan (*Austral slang*), scozza (*Austral slang*), bogan (*Austral slang*), boor, vulgarian

bare 1 = **naked**, nude, stripped, uncovered, undressed, unclothed, unclad, without a stitch on (*informal*) OPPOSITE: dressed 2 = **simple**, spare, stark, austere, spartan, unadorned, unembellished, unornamented, bare-bones OPPOSITE: adorned 3 = **plain**, simple, basic, obvious, sheer, patent, evident, stark

barely = **only just**, just, hardly, scarcely, at a push OPPOSITE: completely

bargain NOUN 1 = **good buy**, discount purchase, good deal, steal (*informal*), snip (*informal*), giveaway, cheap purchase 2 = **agreement**, deal (*informal*), promise, contract, arrangement, settlement, pledge, pact
▷ VERB 3 = **negotiate**, deal, contract, mediate, covenant, stipulate, transact, cut a deal

barge = **canal boat**, lighter, narrow boat, flatboat

bark¹ VERB 1 = **yap**, bay, howl, snarl, growl, yelp, woof
▷ NOUN 2 = **yap**, bay, howl, snarl, growl, yelp, woof

bark² = **covering**, casing, cover, skin, layer, crust, cortex (*anatomy*, *botany*), rind

barracks = **camp**, quarters, garrison, encampment, billet

barrage 1 = **bombardment**, attack, bombing, assault, shelling, battery, volley, blitz 2 = **torrent**, mass, burst, stream, hail, spate, onslaught, deluge

barren 1 = **desolate**, empty, desert, waste 2 (*Old-fashioned*) = **infertile**, sterile, childless, unproductive

b

barricade NOUN 1 = **barrier**, wall, fence, blockade, obstruction, rampart, bulwark, palisade
▷ VERB 2 = **bar**, block, defend, secure, lock, bolt, blockade, fortify

barrier = **barricade**, wall, bar, fence, boundary, obstacle, blockade, obstruction

base¹ NOUN 1 = **bottom**, floor, lowest part OPPOSITE: top
2 = **support**, stand, foot, rest, bed, bottom, foundation, pedestal 3 = **foundation**, institution, organization, establishment, starting point
4 = **centre**, post, station, camp, settlement, headquarters
5 = **home**, house, pad (slang), residence 6 = **essence**, source, basis, root, core
▷ VERB 7 = **ground**, found, build, establish, depend, construct, derive, hinge 8 = **place**, set, post, station, establish, locate, install

base² = **dishonourable**, evil, disgraceful, shameful, immoral, wicked, sordid, despicable, scungy (Austral & NZ) OPPOSITE: honourable

bash = **hit**, beat, strike, knock, smash, belt (informal), slap, sock (slang)

basic ADJECTIVE
1 = **fundamental**, main, essential, primary, vital, principal, cardinal, elementary
2 = **vital**, needed, important, key, necessary, essential, primary, crucial 3 = **essential**, key, vital, fundamental
OPPOSITE: secondary 4 = **main**, key, essential, primary
5 = **plain**, simple, classic, unfussy, unembellished, bare-bones, lo-fi
▷ PLURAL NOUN 6 = **essentials**, principles, fundamentals, nuts and bolts (informal), nitty-gritty (informal), rudiments, brass tacks (informal)

basically = **essentially**, mainly, mostly, principally, fundamentally, primarily, at heart, inherently

basis 1 = **arrangement**, way, system, footing, agreement
2 = **foundation**, support, base, ground, footing, bottom, groundwork

bask = **lie**, relax, lounge, sprawl, loaf, lie about, swim in, sunbathe, outspan (S African)

bass = **deep**, low, resonant, sonorous, low-pitched, deep-toned

bat
• See panel BATS

batch = **group**, set, lot, crowd, pack, collection, quantity, bunch

bath NOUN 1 = **wash**, cleaning, shower, soak, cleansing, scrub, scrubbing, douche
▷ VERB 2 = **clean**, wash, shower, soak, cleanse, scrub, bathe, rinse

---

BATS

barbastelle	insectivorous bat
false vampire	kalong
flying fox	noctule
fruit bat	pipistrelle
hammerhead	serotine
horseshoe bat	vampire bat

---

bathe 1 = **swim** 2 = **wash**, clean, bath, shower, soak, cleanse, scrub, rinse 3 = **cleanse**, clean, wash, soak, rinse 4 = **cover**, flood, steep, engulf, immerse, overrun, suffuse, wash over

baton = **stick**, club, staff, pole, rod, crook, cane, mace, mere (NZ), patu (NZ)

batter = **beat**, hit, strike, knock, bang, thrash, pound, buffet

battery = **artillery**, ordnance, gunnery, gun emplacement, cannonry

battle NOUN 1 = **fight**, attack, action, struggle, conflict, clash, encounter, combat, biffo (Austral slang), boilover (Austral) **OPPOSITE:** peace 2 = **conflict**, campaign, struggle, dispute, contest, crusade 3 = **campaign**, drive, movement, push, struggle ▷ VERB 4 = **wrestle**, war, fight, argue, dispute, grapple, clamour, lock horns 5 = **struggle**, work, labour, strain, strive, toil, go all out (informal), give it your best shot (informal)
• See panel **FAMOUS BATTLES**

battlefield = **battleground**, front, field, combat zone, field of battle

batty = **crazy**, odd, mad, eccentric, peculiar, daft (informal), touched, potty (Brit informal), off the air (Austral slang), porangi (NZ), daggy (Austral & NZ informal)

bay[1] = **inlet**, sound, gulf, creek, cove, fjord, bight, natural harbour

bay[2] = **recess**, opening, corner, niche, compartment, nook, alcove

bay[3] VERB 1 = **howl**, cry, roar (of a hound), bark, wail, growl, bellow, clamour
▷ NOUN 2 = **cry**, roar (of a hound), bark, howl, wail, growl, bellow, clamour

bazaar 1 = **market**, exchange, fair, marketplace 2 = **fair**, fête, gala, bring-and-buy

be = **be alive**, live, exist, survive, breathe, be present, endure

beach = **shore**, coast, sands, seaside, water's edge, seashore

FAMOUS BATTLES

Aboukir Bay or Abukir Bay	1798
Actium	31 B.C.
Agincourt	1415
Alamo	1836
Arnhem	1944
Atlantic	1939–45
Austerlitz	1805
Balaklava or Balaclava	1854
Bannockburn	1314
Barnet	1471
Bautzen	1813
Belleau Wood	1918
Blenheim	1704
Borodino	1812
Bosworth Field	1485
Boyne	1690
Britain	1940
Bulge	1944–45
Bull Run	1861; 1862
Bunker Hill	1775
Cannae	216 B.C.
Crécy	1346
Culloden	1746
Dien Bien Phu	1954
Edgehill	1642
El Alamein	1942
Falkirk	1298; 1746
Flodden	1513
Gettysburg	1863
Guadalcanal	1942–3
Hastings	1066
Hohenlinden	1800
Imphal	1944
Inkerman	1854
Issus	333 B.C.
Jemappes	1792
Jena	1806
Killiecrankie	1689
Kursk	1943
Ladysmith	1899–1900
Le Cateau	1914
Leipzig	1813
Lepanto	1571
Leyte Gulf	1944
Little Bighorn	1876
Lützen	1632
Manassas	1861; 1862
Mantinea or Mantineia	418 B.C.; 362 B.C.
Marathon	490 B.C.
Marengo	1800
Marston Moor	1644
Missionary Ridge	1863
Naseby	1645
Navarino	425 B.C.
Omdurman	1898
Passchendaele	1917
Philippi	42 B.C.
Plains of Abraham	1759
Plassey	1757
Plataea	479 B.C.
Poltava	1709
Prestonpans	1745
Pydna	168 B.C.
Quatre Bras	1815
Ramillies	1706
Roncesvalles	778
Sadowa or Sadová	1866
Saint-Mihiel	1918
Salamis	480 B.C.
Sedgemoor	1685

Sempach	1386	Tobruk	1941; 1942
Shiloh	1862	Trafalgar	1805
Shipka Pass	1877–78	Trenton	1776
Somme	1916; 1918	Verdun	1916
Stalingrad	1941–42	Vitoria	1813
Stamford Bridge	1066	Wagram	1809
Stirling Bridge	1297	Waterloo	1815
Tannenberg	1410; 1914	Ypres	1914; 1915;
Tewkesbury	1471		1917; 1918
Thermopylae	480 B.C.	Zama	202 B.C.

beached = **stranded**, grounded, abandoned, deserted, wrecked, ashore, marooned, aground

beacon 1 = **signal**, sign, beam, flare, bonfire 2 = **lighthouse**, watchtower

bead = **drop**, tear, bubble, pearl, dot, drip, blob, droplet

beam VERB 1 = **smile**, grin 2 = **transmit**, show, air, broadcast, cable, send out, relay, televise, stream 3 = **radiate**, flash, shine, glow, glitter, glare, gleam
▷ NOUN 4 = **ray**, flash, stream, glow, streak, shaft, gleam, glint 5 = **rafter**, support, timber, spar, plank, girder, joist 6 = **smile**, grin

bear 1 = **carry**, take, move, bring, transfer, conduct, transport, haul OPPOSITE: put down 2 = **support**, shoulder, sustain, endure, uphold, withstand OPPOSITE: give up 3 = **display**, have, show, hold, carry, possess 4 = **suffer**,

experience, go through, sustain, stomach, endure, brook, abide 5 = **bring yourself to**, allow, accept, permit, endure, tolerate 6 = **produce**, generate, yield, bring forth 7 = **give birth to**, produce, deliver, breed, bring forth, beget 8 = **exhibit**, hold, maintain 9 = **conduct**, carry, move, deport
▷ PHRASES: **bear something out** = **support**, prove, confirm, justify, endorse, uphold, substantiate, corroborate

bearer 1 = **agent**, carrier, courier, herald, envoy, messenger, conveyor, emissary 2 = **carrier**, runner, servant, porter

bearing NOUN 1 *usually with on or* **upon** = **relevance**, relation, application, connection, import, reference, significance, pertinence OPPOSITE: irrelevance 2 = **manner**, attitude, conduct, aspect, behaviour, posture, demeanour,

deportment
▷ **PLURAL NOUN 3 = way**, course, position, situation, track, aim, direction, location

beast 1 = animal, creature, brute **2 = brute**, monster, savage, barbarian, fiend, swine, ogre, sadist

beastly (*informal*) **= unpleasant**, mean, awful, nasty, rotten, horrid, disagreeable **OPPOSITE:** pleasant

beat VERB 1 = batter, hit, strike, knock, pound, smack, thrash, thump **2 = pound**, strike, hammer, batter, thrash **3 = throb**, thump, pound, quake, vibrate, pulsate, palpitate **4 = hit**, strike, bang **5 = flap**, thrash, flutter, wag **6 = defeat**, outdo, trounce, overcome, crush, overwhelm, conquer, surpass
▷ **NOUN 7 = throb**, pounding, pulse, thumping, vibration, pulsating, palpitation, pulsation **8 = route**, way, course, rounds, path, circuit
▷ **PHRASES: beat someone up** (*informal*) **= assault**, attack, batter, thrash, set about, set upon, lay into (*informal*), beat the living daylights out of (*informal*)

beaten 1 = stirred, mixed, whipped, blended, whisked, frothy, foamy **2 = defeated**, overcome, overwhelmed, cowed, thwarted, vanquished

beautiful = attractive, pretty, lovely, charming, tempting, pleasant, handsome, fetching, hot (*informal*), fit (*Brit informal*) **OPPOSITE:** ugly

beauty 1 = attractiveness, charm, grace, glamour, elegance, loveliness, handsomeness, comeliness **OPPOSITE:** ugliness **2 = good-looker**, lovely (*slang*), belle, stunner (*informal*), beaut (*Austral & NZ slang*)

because = since, as, in that
▷ **PHRASES: because of = as a result of**, on account of, by reason of, thanks to, owing to

> **USAGE NOTE**
> The phrase *on account of* can provide a useful alternative to *because of* in writing. It occurs relatively infrequently in spoken language, where it is sometimes followed by a clause, as in *on account of I don't do drugs*. However, this use is considered nonstandard.

beckon = gesture, sign, wave, indicate, signal, nod, motion, summon

become 1 = come to be, develop into, be transformed into, grow into, change into, alter to, mature into, ripen into **2 = suit**, fit, enhance, flatter, embellish, set off

becoming 1 = flattering, pretty, attractive, enhancing,

neat, graceful, tasteful, well-chosen **OPPOSITE:** unflattering **2** = **appropriate**, seemly, fitting, suitable, proper, worthy, in keeping, compatible **OPPOSITE:** inappropriate

bed 1 = **bedstead**, couch, berth, cot, divan **2** = **plot**, area, row, strip, patch, ground, land, garden **3** = **bottom**, ground, floor **4** = **base**, footing, basis, bottom, foundation, underpinning, groundwork, bedrock

bee
• See panel **ANTS, BEES, AND WASPS**

beer parlour (*Canad*) = **tavern**, inn, bar, pub (*informal, chiefly Brit*), public house, beverage room (*Canad*), hostelry, alehouse (*archaic*)

beetle
• See panel **BEETLES**

before PREPOSITION 1 = **earlier than**, ahead of, prior to, in advance of **OPPOSITE:** after **2** = **in front of**, ahead of, in advance of **3** = **in the presence of**, in front of **4** = **ahead of**, in front of, in advance of
▷ **ADVERB 5** = **previously**, earlier, sooner, in advance, formerly **OPPOSITE:** after **6** = **in the past**, earlier, once, previously, formerly, hitherto, beforehand

 RELATED WORDS
prefixes: ante-, fore-, pre-

beforehand = **in advance**, before, earlier, already, sooner, ahead, previously, in anticipation

beg 1 = **implore**, plead with, beseech, request, petition, solicit, entreat **2** = **scrounge**, bum (*informal*), touch (someone) for (*slang*), cadge, sponge on (someone) for, freeload (*slang*), seek charity, solicit charity **OPPOSITE:** give

beggar = **tramp**, bum (*informal*), derelict, drifter, down-and-out, pauper, vagrant, bag lady (*chiefly US*), derro (*Austral slang*)

begin 1 = **start**, commence, proceed **OPPOSITE:** stop **2** = **commence**, start, initiate, embark on, set about, instigate, institute, make a beginning **3** = **start talking**, start, initiate, commence **4** = **come into existence**, start, appear, emerge, arise, originate, come into being **5** = **emerge**, start, spring, stem, derive, originate **OPPOSITE:** end

beginner = **novice**, pupil, amateur, newcomer, starter, trainee, apprentice, learner **OPPOSITE:** expert

beginning 1 = **start**, opening, birth, origin, outset, onset, initiation, inauguration **OPPOSITE:** end **2** = **outset**, start, opening, birth, onset, commencement **3** = **origins**

BEETLES

ambrosia beetle
Asiatic beetle
bacon beetle
bark beetle
bee beetle
black beetle or (NZ) kekerengu or Māori bug
blister beetle
bloody-nosed beetle
boll weevil
bombardier beetle
burying beetle or sexton
cabinet beetle
cardinal beetle
carpet beetle or (US) carpet bug
carrion beetle
chafer
Christmas beetle or king beetle
churchyard beetle
click beetle, snapping beetle, or skipjack
cockchafer, May beetle, or May bug
Colorado beetle or potato beetle
curculio
deathwatch beetle
devil's coach-horse
diving beetle
dor
dung beetle or chafer
elater
firefly
flea beetle
furniture beetle
glow-worm
gold beetle or goldbug
goldsmith beetle
goliath beetle
ground beetle
Hercules beetle
huhu
Japanese beetle
June bug, June beetle, May bug, or May beetle
ladybird or (US & Canad) ladybug
larder beetle
leaf beetle
leather beetle
longicorn (beetle) or long-horned beetle
May beetle, cockchafer, or June bug
museum beetle
oil beetle
pill beetle
rhinoceros beetle
rose chafer or rose beetle
rove beetle
scarab
scavenger beetle
snapping beetle
snout beetle
soldier beetle
Spanish fly
stag beetle
tiger beetle
timberman beetle
tortoise beetle
vedalia
water beetle
weevil or snout beetle
weevil, pea weevil, or bean weevil
whirligig beetle

behave 1 = **act** 2 *often reflexive* = **be well-behaved**, mind your manners, keep your nose clean, act correctly, conduct yourself properly **OPPOSITE:** misbehave

behaviour 1 = **conduct**, ways, actions, bearing, attitude, manner, manners, demeanour 2 = **action**, performance, operation, functioning

behind PREPOSITION 1 = **at the rear of**, at the back of, at the heels of 2 = **after**, following 3 = **supporting**, for, backing, on the side of, in agreement with 4 = **causing**, responsible for, initiating, at the bottom of, instigating 5 = **later than**, after ▷ ADVERB 6 = **after**, next, following, afterwards, subsequently, in the wake (of) **OPPOSITE:** in advance of 7 = **behind schedule**, delayed, running late, behind time **OPPOSITE:** ahead 8 = **overdue**, in debt, in arrears, behindhand ▷ NOUN 9 (*informal*) = **bottom**, butt (*US & Canad informal*), buttocks, posterior

being 1 = **individual**, creature, human being, living thing 2 = **life**, reality **OPPOSITE:** nonexistence 3 = **soul**, spirit, substance, creature, essence, organism, entity

beleaguered 1 = **harassed**, troubled, plagued, hassled (*informal*), badgered, persecuted, pestered, vexed 2 = **besieged**, surrounded, blockaded, beset, encircled, assailed, hemmed in

belief 1 = **trust**, confidence, conviction **OPPOSITE:** disbelief 2 = **faith**, principles, doctrine, ideology, creed, dogma, tenet, credo 3 = **opinion**, feeling, idea, impression, assessment, notion, judgment, point of view

believe 1 = **think**, judge, suppose, estimate, imagine, assume, gather, reckon 2 = **accept**, trust, credit, depend on, rely on, have faith in, swear by, be certain of **OPPOSITE:** disbelieve

believer = **follower**, supporter, convert, disciple, devotee, apostle, adherent, zealot **OPPOSITE:** sceptic

bellow VERB 1 = **shout**, cry (out), scream, roar, yell, howl, shriek, bawl ▷ NOUN 2 = **shout**, cry, scream, roar, yell, howl, shriek, bawl

belly = **stomach**, insides (*informal*), gut, abdomen, tummy, paunch, potbelly, corporation (*informal*), puku (*NZ*)

belong = **go with**, fit into, be part of, relate to, be connected with, pertain to

belonging = **fellowship**, relationship, association, loyalty, acceptance, attachment, inclusion, affinity

b

belongings = possessions, goods, things, effects, property, stuff, gear, paraphernalia

beloved = **dear**, loved, valued, prized, admired, treasured, precious, darling

below PREPOSITION 1 = **under**, underneath, lower than
2 = **less than**, lower than
3 = **subordinate to**, subject to, inferior to, lesser than
▷ ADVERB 4 = **lower**, down, under, beneath, underneath
5 = **beneath**, following, at the end, underneath, at the bottom, further on

belt 1 = **waistband**, band, sash, girdle, girth, cummerbund
2 = **conveyor belt**, band, loop, fan belt, drive belt 3 (*Geography*) = **zone**, area, region, section, district, stretch, strip, layer

bemused = **puzzled**, confused, baffled, at sea, bewildered, muddled, perplexed, mystified

bench 1 = **seat**, stall, pew
2 = **worktable**, stand, table, counter, trestle table, workbench
▷ PHRASES: the bench = **court**, judges, magistrates, tribunal, judiciary, courtroom

benchmark = **reference point**, gauge, yardstick, measure, level, standard, model, par

bend VERB 1 = **twist**, turn, wind, lean, hook, bow, curve, arch
▷ NOUN 2 = **curve**, turn, corner, twist, angle, bow, loop, arc

beneath PREPOSITION
1 = **under**, below, underneath, lower than **OPPOSITE:** over 2 = **inferior to**, below
3 = **unworthy of**, unfitting for, unsuitable for, inappropriate for, unbefitting
▷ ADVERB 4 = **underneath**, below, in a lower place

RELATED WORD
prefix: sub-

beneficial = **favourable**, useful, valuable, helpful, profitable, benign, wholesome, advantageous **OPPOSITE:** harmful

beneficiary 1 = **recipient**, receiver, payee 2 = **heir**, inheritor

benefit NOUN 1 = **good**, help, profit, favour **OPPOSITE:** harm
2 = **advantage**, aid, favour, assistance
▷ VERB 3 = **profit from**, make the most of, gain from, do well out of, reap benefits from, turn to your advantage 4 = **help**, aid, profit, improve, enhance, assist, avail **OPPOSITE:** harm

benign 1 = **benevolent**, kind, kindly, warm, friendly, obliging, sympathetic, compassionate **OPPOSITE:** unkind 2 (*Medical*) = **harmless**, innocent, innocuous, curable, inoffensive, remediable **OPPOSITE:** malignant

bent ADJECTIVE 1 = **misshapen**, twisted, angled, bowed, curved,

arched, crooked, distorted
OPPOSITE: straight **2** = **stooped**,
bowed, arched, hunched
▷ **NOUN 3** = **inclination**, ability,
leaning, tendency, preference,
penchant, propensity, aptitude
▷ **PHRASES: bent on** = **intent on**,
set on, fixed on, predisposed to,
resolved on, insistent on

bequeath 1 = **leave**, will, give,
grant, hand down, endow,
bestow, entrust **2** = **give**,
accord, grant, afford, yield, lend,
pass on, confer

berth NOUN 1 = **bunk**, bed,
hammock, billet **2** (*Nautical*)
= **anchorage**, haven, port,
harbour, dock, pier, wharf, quay
▷ **VERB 3** (*Nautical*) = **anchor**,
land, dock, moor, tie up, drop
anchor

beside = **next to**, near, close
to, neighbouring, alongside,
adjacent to, at the side of,
abreast of
▷ **PHRASES: beside yourself**
= **distraught**, desperate,
distressed, frantic, frenzied,
demented, unhinged,
overwrought

USAGE NOTE
People occasionally confuse
beside and *besides*. *Besides*
is used for mentioning
something that adds to what
you have already said, for
example: *I didn't feel like going
and besides, I had nothing to
wear*. *Beside* usually means

*next to or at the side of something
or someone*, for example: *he
was standing beside me* (not
besides me).

besides PREPOSITION 1 = **apart
from**, barring, excepting, other
than, excluding, as well (as), in
addition to, over and above
▷ **ADVERB 2** = **also**, too, further,
otherwise, in addition, as well,
moreover, furthermore

besiege 1 = **harass**, harry,
plague, hound, hassle (*informal*),
badger, pester **2** = **surround**,
enclose, blockade, encircle, hem
in, shut in, lay siege to

best ADJECTIVE 1 = **finest**,
leading, supreme, principal,
foremost, pre-eminent,
unsurpassed, most
accomplished
▷ **ADVERB 2** = **most highly**, most
fully, most deeply
▷ **PHRASES: the best** = **the
finest**, the pick, the flower, the
cream, the elite, the crème de
la crème

bestow = **present**, give, award,
grant, commit, hand out, lavish,
impart **OPPOSITE:** obtain

bet VERB 1 = **gamble**, chance,
stake, venture, hazard,
speculate, wager, risk money
▷ **NOUN 2** = **gamble**, risk, stake,
venture, speculation, flutter
(*informal*), punt, wager

betray 1 = **be disloyal to**, dob
in (*Austral slang*), double-cross
(*informal*), stab in the back,

be unfaithful to, inform on *or*
against 2 = **give away**, reveal,
expose, disclose, uncover,
divulge, unmask, let slip

betrayal = **disloyalty**, sell-out
(*informal*), deception, treason,
treachery, trickery, double-cross
(*informal*), breach of trust
OPPOSITE: loyalty

better ADVERB 1 = **to a greater
degree**, more completely,
more thoroughly 2 = **in a
more excellent manner**, more
effectively, more attractively,
more advantageously, more
competently, in a superior way
OPPOSITE: worse
▷ ADJECTIVE 3 = **well**,
stronger, recovering, cured,
fully recovered, on the mend
(*informal*) **OPPOSITE:** worse
4 = **superior**, finer, higher-
quality, surpassing, preferable,
more desirable **OPPOSITE:**
inferior

between = **amidst**, among, mid,
in the middle of, betwixt

 RELATED WORD
 prefix: inter-

 USAGE NOTE
 After *distribute* and words
 with a similar meaning,
 among should be used rather
 than *between*: *share out the
 sweets among the children* (not
 between the children, unless
 there are only two children).

beverage = **drink**, liquid, liquor,
refreshment

beverage room (*Canad*)
= **tavern**, inn, bar, pub (*informal*,
chiefly Brit), public house, beer
parlour (*Canad*), hostelry,
alehouse (*archaic*)

beware 1 = **be careful**, look out,
watch out, be wary, be cautious,
take heed, guard against
something 2 = **avoid**, mind

bewilder = **confound**, confuse,
puzzle, baffle, perplex, mystify,
flummox, bemuse

bewildered = **confused**,
puzzled, baffled, at sea,
muddled, perplexed, at a loss,
mystified

beyond 1 = **on the other side
of** 2 = **after**, over, past, above
3 = **past** 4 = **except for**, but,
save, apart from, other than,
excluding, besides, aside from
5 = **exceeding**, surpassing,
superior to, out of reach of
6 = **outside**, over, above

bias NOUN 1 = **prejudice**,
leaning, tendency, inclination,
favouritism, partiality
OPPOSITE: impartiality
▷ VERB 2 = **influence**, colour,
weight, prejudice, distort, sway,
warp, slant

biased = **prejudiced**, weighted,
one-sided, partial, distorted,
slanted

bid NOUN 1 = **attempt**, try,
effort, go (*informal*), shot
(*informal*), stab (*informal*), crack
(*informal*) 2 = **offer**, price,
amount, advance, proposal,

sum, tender
▷ **VERB** 3 = **make an offer**,
offer, propose, submit, tender,
proffer 4 = **wish**, say, call, tell,
greet 5 = **tell**, ask, order, require,
direct, command, instruct
bidding = **order**, request,
command, instruction,
summons, beck and call
big 1 = **large**, great, huge,
massive, vast, enormous,
substantial, extensive,
supersize **OPPOSITE:** small
2 = **important**, significant,
urgent, far-reaching **OPPOSITE:**
unimportant 3 = **powerful**,
important, prominent,
dominant, influential, eminent,
skookum (*Canad*) 4 = **grown-up**,
adult, grown, mature, elder,
full-grown **OPPOSITE:** young
5 = **generous**, good, noble,
gracious, benevolent, altruistic,
unselfish, magnanimous
bill[1] **NOUN** 1 = **charges**,
rate, costs, score, account,
statement, reckoning, expense
2 = **act of parliament**, measure,
proposal, piece of legislation,
projected law 3 = **list**, listing,
programme, card, schedule,
agenda, catalogue, inventory
4 = **advertisement**, notice,
poster, leaflet, bulletin, circular,
handout, placard
▷ **VERB** 5 = **charge**, debit,
invoice, send a statement
to, send an invoice to
6 = **advertise**, post, announce,

promote, plug (*informal*),
tout, publicize, give advance
notice of
bill[2] = **beak**, nib, neb (*archaic
dialect*), mandible
bind VERB 1 = **oblige**, make,
force, require, engage, compel,
constrain, necessitate 2 = **tie**,
join, stick, secure, wrap, knot,
strap, lash **OPPOSITE:** untie
▷ **NOUN** 3 (*informal*) = **nuisance**,
inconvenience, hassle (*informal*),
drag (*informal*), spot (*informal*),
difficulty, bore, dilemma, uphill
(*S African*)
binding = **compulsory**,
necessary, mandatory,
obligatory, irrevocable,
unalterable, indissoluble
OPPOSITE: optional
binge (*informal*) = **bout**, spell,
fling, feast, stint, spree, orgy,
bender (*informal*)
biography = **life story**, life,
record, account, profile, memoir,
CV, curriculum vitae
bird = **feathered friend**, fowl,
songbird

> **RELATED WORDS**
> *male:* cock
> *female:* hen
> *young:* chick, fledgeling,
> fledgling, nestling
> *home:* nest

• *See panels* **BIRDS**, **SEA BIRDS**,
TYPES OF FOWL
birth 1 = **childbirth**, delivery,
nativity, parturition **OPPOSITE:**
death 2 = **ancestry**, stock,

b

BIRDS

accentor
amazon
amokura (*NZ*)
ani
apostle bird *or* happy family bird (*Austral*)
avadavat *or* amadavat
avocet
axebird (*Austral*)
babbler
Baltimore oriole
banded dotterel (*NZ*)
banded rail (*NZ*)
barbet
beccafico
bee-eater
bellbird *or* (*NZ*) koromako *or* makomako
bird of paradise
bishopbird
bittern
blackbird
blackcap
blackcock
black-fronted tern *or* tara (*NZ*)
black grouse
blackpoll
black robin (*NZ*)
bluebird
blue duck, mountain duck, whio, *or* whistling duck (*NZ*)
blue grouse
blue jay
bluethroat
bluetit
boatbill *or* boat-billed heron
bobolink
bobwhite
bokmakierie
boobook (*Austral*)
bowerbird
brain-fever bird *or* (*Austral*) pallid cuckoo
brambling
broadbill
brolga, Australian crane, *or* (*Austral*) native companion
brown creeper *or* pipipi (*NZ*)
brown duck (*NZ*)
brown kiwi (*NZ*)
budgerigar *or* (*Austral*) zebra parrot
bulbul
bullfinch
bunting
bush shrike
bushtit
bush wren (*NZ*)
bustard *or* (*Austral*) plain turkey, plains turkey, *or* wild turkey
button quail *or* (*Austral*) bustard quail
cacique
Californian quail (*NZ*)
canary
Cape Barren goose
Cape pigeon
capercaillie *or* capercailzie
Cape sparrow
capuchin
cardinal *or* cardinal grosbeak
carrion crow
cassowary
catbird

chaffinch
chat
chickadee
chicken or (Austral informal) chook
chiffchaff
chimney swallow or chimney swift
chipping sparrow
chough
chuck-will's-widow
chukar
cliff swallow
coal tit or coletit
cockatiel, cockateel, or cockatoo-parrot
cockatoo
cock-of-the-rock
collared dove
coly or mousebird
conure
coppersmith
coquette
corella
corn bunting
corncrake
cotinga or chatterer
coucal, pheasant coucal, or swamp pheasant
cowbird
crake
crane
crested tit
crocodile bird
crombec
crossbill
crow or (Scot) corbie
cuckoo

cuckoo-shrike
cumulet
curassow
curlew
currawong or bell magpie
dabchick
darter, anhinga, or snakebird
demoiselle (crane) or Numidian crane
diamond bird or pardalote
dipper or water ouzel
diver
dollarbird
dotterel or dottrel
dove or (archaic or poetic) culver
dowitcher
drongo
dunlin or red-backed sandpiper
egret
emperor penguin
emu
emu-wren
fantail or (NZ) piwakawaka
fernbird (NZ)
fieldfare
fig-bird
finch
finfoot
firebird
firecrest
flamingo
flower-pecker
flycatcher
francolin
friarbird
frogmouth
galah or (Austral) galar or gillar
gang-gang

BIRDS continued

gnatcatcher
go-away bird
godwit
goldcrest
golden oriole
goldfinch
Gouldian finch, painted finch, or purple-breasted finch
grackle or crow blackbird
grassfinch
grassquit
great crested grebe or loon
great northern diver
great tit
grebe
greenfinch
green leek
greenlet
greenshank
green woodpecker
grey-crowned babbler, happy family bird, Happy Jack, or parson bird (Austral)
grey warbler or riroriro (NZ)
grosbeak
grouse
guan
guinea fowl
hadedah
hawfinch
hazelhen
hedge sparrow or dunnock
helldiver, pie-billed grebe, or dabchick
hen harrier or (US & Canad) marsh harrier
heron

hill myna
hoatzin or hoactzin
homing pigeon
honey creeper
honeyeater
honey guide
honeysucker
hooded crow
hoopoe
hornbill
house martin
house sparrow
hummingbird or trochilus
ibis
jabiru or (Austral) policeman bird
jacamar
jaçana or lily-trotter
jackdaw
jacksnipe
Jacobin
jaeger (US & Canad)
Java sparrow
jay
junco
jungle fowl
kagu
kaka (NZ)
kakapo (NZ)
kakariki (NZ)
karoro or blackbacked gull (NZ)
kea (NZ)
killdeer
kingbird
kingfisher or (NZ) kotare
king penguin
kiwi or apteryx
knot

koel or (*Austral*) black cuckoo or cooee bird

kokako or blue-wattled crow (*NZ*)

kookaburra, laughing jackass, or (*Austral*) bushman's clock, settler's clock, goburra, or great brown kingfisher

kotuku or white heron (*NZ*)

Lahore

lapwing or green plover

lark

limpkin or courlan

linnet

locust bird

loggerhead shrike

longspur

long-tailed tit

lorikeet

lory

lourie

lovebird

lyrebird or (*Austral*) buln-buln

macaw

magpie or (*Austral*) piping shrike or piping crow-shrike

magpie lark or (*Austral*) mudlark, Murray magpie, mulga, or peewit

Major Mitchell or Leadbeater's cockatoo

makomako (*Austral*)

marabou

marsh tit

martin

meadowlark

meadow pipit

metallic starling or shining starling (*Austral*)

minivet

miromiro (*NZ*)

mistle thrush or missel thrush

mistletoe bird (*Austral*)

mockingbird

mohua or bush canary (*NZ*)

monal or monaul

motmot or sawbill

mourning dove

myna, mynah, or mina

New Zealand pigeon or kereru (*NZ*)

nighthawk, bullbat, or mosquito hawk

night heron

nightingale

nightjar, (*US & Canad*) goatsucker, or (*Austral*) nighthawk

noddy

noisy friarbird or leatherhead

noisy miner or (*Austral*) micky or soldier bird

notornis

nun

nutcracker

nuthatch

oil bird or guacharo

oriole

ortolan or ortolan bunting

ostrich

ouzel or ousel

ovenbird

oxpecker or tick-bird

paradise duck or putangitangi (*NZ*)

parakeet or parrakeet

pardalote (*Austral*)

b

BIRDS *continued*

parrot
partridge
peacock
peafowl
peewit
pelican
penguin
phalarope
pheasant
pied goose *or* magpie goose
pied wagtail
pigeon
pipit *or (NZ)* pihoihoi
pipiwharauroa *or* bronze-winged cuckoo *(NZ)*
pitta *(Austral)*
plover
pratincole
ptarmigan
puffbird
puffin
pukeko
purple gallinule
pyrrhuloxia
quail
quarrian *or* quarrion
quetzal
racket-tail
rail
rainbow bird
rainbow lorikeet
raven
red-backed shrike
redbreast
red grouse
red-legged partridge
redpoll

redshank
redstart
redwing
reedbird
reed bunting
reedling *or* bearded tit
reed warbler
regent-bird *or* regent bowerbird
regent honeyeater
rhea *or* American ostrich
ricebird
riflebird
rifleman *or (NZ)* titipounamu
ringed plover
ring-necked pheasant
ringneck parrot, Port Lincoln parrot, *or* buln-buln *(Austral)*
ring ouzel
roadrunner *or* chaparral cock
robin *or* robin redbreast
rock dove *or* rock pigeon
rockhopper
roller
rook
rosella
rosy finch
ruff
ruffed grouse
runt
saddleback
saddlebill *or* jabiru
sage grouse
sanderling
sandgrouse
sand martin
sandpiper

sapsucker
satin bowerbird
Scandaroon
scarlet tanager
scrub bird
sedge warbler
seriema
serin
sheathbill
shoebill
shore bird or (Brit) wader
shrike or butcherbird
sicklebill
silver-eye (Austral)
siskin or (formerly) aberdevine
sitella or tree-runner
skimmer
skylark
snipe
snow bunting
snowy egret
solitaire
song sparrow
song thrush or mavis
sora
sparrow
spoonbill
spotted crake or (Austral)
  water crake
spotted flycatcher
spotted sandpiper or (US)
  peetweet
squacco
starling
stilt
stint
stock dove
stonechat

stone curlew or thick-knee
stork
sugar bird
sulphur-crested cockatoo or
  white cockatoo
sunbird
sun bittern
superb blue wren (Austral)
superb lyrebird (Austral)
surfbird
swallow
swift
swiftlet
swordbill
tailorbird
takahe
tanager
tattler
tawny pippit
tern
thornbill
thrasher
thrush or (poetic) throstle
tit
titmouse
tody
topknot pigeon (Austral)
toucan
touraco, turaco, or
  plantain-eater
towhee
tragopan
tree creeper
tree sparrow
trochilus
trogon
tropicbird
troupial

BIRDS *continued*

trumpeter	white-fronted tern *or* kahawai bird (*NZ*)
tui *or* parson bird (*NZ*)	
turtledove	whitethroat
twite	whooping crane
umbrella bird	willet
veery	willow grouse
verdin	willow tit
wader *or* wading bird	willow warbler
wagtail	wonga-wonga *or* wonga pigeon
wall creeper	woodchat *or* woodchat shrike
warbler	woodcock
water rail	wood ibis
water thrush	woodlark
wattlebird	woodpecker
waxbill	wood pigeon, ringdove, cushat, (*Scot*) cushie-doo, *or* (*English dialect*) quist
waxwing	
weaverbird *or* weaver	
weka, weka rail, Māori hen, *or* wood hen (*NZ*)	woodswallow
	wood warbler
wheatear	wren
whimbrel	wrybill
whinchat	wryneck
whip bird	yellowhammer
whippoorwill	yellowtail *or* yellowtail kingfisher (*Austral*)
white-eye *or* (*NZ*) blighty, silvereye, tauhou, *or* waxeye	zebra finch

blood, background, breeding, pedigree, lineage, parentage

RELATED WORD
adjective: natal

bit¹ 1 = slice, fragment, crumb, morsel **2 = piece**, scrap **3 = jot**, iota **4 = part**

bit² = curb, check, brake, restraint, snaffle

bite VERB 1 = nip, cut, tear, wound, snap, pierce, pinch, chew
▷ **NOUN 2 = snack**, food, piece, taste, refreshment, mouthful, morsel, titbit **3 = wound**, sting, pinch, nip, prick

biting 1 = piercing, cutting, sharp, frozen, harsh,

penetrating, arctic, icy
2 = **sarcastic**, cutting, stinging, scathing, acrimonious, incisive, virulent, caustic

bitter 1 = **resentful**, angry, offended, sour, sore, acrimonious, sullen, miffed (*informal*) **OPPOSITE:** happy
2 = **freezing**, biting, severe, intense, raw, fierce, chill, stinging **OPPOSITE:** mild
3 = **sour**, sharp, acid, harsh, tart, astringent, acrid, unsweetened **OPPOSITE:** sweet

bitterness 1 = **resentment**, hostility, indignation, animosity, acrimony, rancour, ill feeling, bad blood 2 = **sourness**, acidity, sharpness, tartness, acerbity

bizarre = **strange**, unusual, extraordinary, fantastic, weird, peculiar, eccentric, ludicrous, daggy (*Austral & NZ informal*) **OPPOSITE:** normal

black 1 = **dark**, raven, ebony, sable, jet, dusky, pitch-black, swarthy **OPPOSITE:** light
2 = **gloomy**, sad, depressing, grim, bleak, hopeless, dismal, ominous **OPPOSITE:** happy
3 = **terrible**, bad, devastating, tragic, fatal, catastrophic, ruinous, calamitous 4 = **wicked**, bad, evil, corrupt, vicious, immoral, depraved, villainous **OPPOSITE:** good 5 = **angry**, cross, furious, hostile, sour, menacing, moody, resentful **OPPOSITE:** happy

USAGE NOTE
When referring to people with dark skin, the adjective *black* or *Black* is widely used. For people of the US whose origins lie in Africa, the preferred term is *African-American*. To use *a Black* or *Blacks* as a noun is considered offensive, and it is better to talk about *a Black person* and *Black people*.
• *See panel* **SHADES FROM BLACK TO WHITE**

blackmail NOUN 1 = **threat**, intimidation, ransom, extortion, hush money (*slang*)
▷ VERB 2 = **threaten**, squeeze, compel, intimidate, coerce, dragoon, extort, hold to ransom

blame VERB 1 = **hold responsible**, accuse, denounce, indict, impeach, incriminate, impute **OPPOSITE:** absolve
2 = **attribute to**, credit to, assign to, put down to, impute to 3 *used in negative constructions* = **criticize**, condemn, censure, reproach, chide, find fault with **OPPOSITE:** praise
▷ NOUN 4 = **responsibility**, liability, accountability, onus, culpability, answerability **OPPOSITE:** praise

bland 1 = **dull**, boring, plain, flat, dreary, run-of-the-mill, uninspiring, humdrum **OPPOSITE:** exciting

---

SHADES FROM BLACK TO WHITE

ash	pearl
black	pewter
charcoal	pitch-black
cream	platinum
ebony	putty
eggshell	raven
grey	sable
gunmetal	silver
iron	slate
ivory	steel grey
jet	stone
off-white	white
oyster white	

---

2 = **tasteless**, insipid, flavourless, thin

blank ADJECTIVE 1 = **unmarked**, white, clear, clean, empty, plain, bare, void OPPOSITE: marked 2 = **expressionless**, empty, vague, vacant, deadpan, impassive, poker-faced (*informal*) OPPOSITE: expressive
▷ NOUN 3 = **empty space**, space, gap 4 = **void**, vacuum, vacancy, emptiness, nothingness

blanket NOUN 1 = **cover**, rug, coverlet 2 = **covering**, sheet, coat, layer, carpet, cloak, mantle, thickness
▷ VERB 3 = **coat**, cover, hide, mask, conceal, obscure, cloak

blast NOUN 1 = **explosion**, crash, burst, discharge, eruption, detonation 2 = **gust**, rush, storm, breeze, puff, gale, tempest, squall 3 = **blare**, blow, scream, trumpet, wail, resound, clamour, toot
▷ VERB 4 = **blow up**, bomb, destroy, burst, ruin, break up, explode, shatter

blatant = **obvious**, clear, plain, evident, glaring, manifest, noticeable, conspicuous OPPOSITE: subtle

blaze VERB 1 = **burn**, glow, flare, be on fire, go up in flames, be ablaze, fire, flame 2 = **shine**, flash, beam, glow, flare, glare, gleam, radiate
▷ NOUN 3 = **inferno**, fire, flames, bonfire, combustion, conflagration 4 = **flash**, glow, glitter, flare, glare, gleam, brilliance, radiance

bleach = **lighten**, wash out, blanch, whiten

bleak 1 = **dismal**, dark, depressing, grim, discouraging, gloomy, hopeless, dreary **OPPOSITE:** cheerful 2 = **exposed**, empty, bare, barren, desolate, windswept, weather-beaten, unsheltered **OPPOSITE:** sheltered 3 = **stormy**, severe, rough, harsh, tempestuous, intemperate

bleed 1 = **lose blood**, flow, gush, spurt, shed blood 2 = **blend**, run, meet, unite, mix, combine, flow, fuse 3 (*informal*) = **extort**, milk, squeeze, drain, exhaust, fleece

blend VERB 1 = **mix**, join, combine, compound, merge, unite, mingle, amalgamate 2 = **go well**, match, fit, suit, go with, correspond, complement, coordinate 3 = **combine**, mix, link, integrate, merge, unite, amalgamate
▷ NOUN 4 = **mixture**, mix, combination, compound, brew, union, synthesis, alloy

bless 1 = **sanctify**, dedicate, ordain, exalt, anoint, consecrate, hallow **OPPOSITE:** curse 2 = **endow**, give to, provide for, grant, favour, grace, bestow to **OPPOSITE:** afflict

blessed = **holy**, sacred, divine, adored, revered, hallowed, sanctified, beatified

blessing 1 = **benefit**, help, service, favour, gift, windfall, kindness, good fortune **OPPOSITE:** disadvantage

2 = **approval**, backing, support, agreement, favour, sanction, permission, leave **OPPOSITE:** disapproval 3 = **benediction**, grace, dedication, thanksgiving, invocation, commendation, consecration, benison **OPPOSITE:** curse

blight NOUN 1 = **curse**, suffering, evil, corruption, pollution, plague, hardship, woe **OPPOSITE:** blessing 2 = **disease**, pest, fungus, mildew, infestation, pestilence, canker
▷ VERB 3 = **frustrate**, destroy, ruin, crush, mar, dash, wreck, spoil, crool or cruel (*Austral slang*)

blind 1 = **sightless**, unsighted, unseeing, eyeless, visionless **OPPOSITE:** sighted 2 *usually followed by* **to** = **unaware of**, unconscious of, ignorant of, indifferent to, insensitive to, oblivious of, unconcerned about, inconsiderate of **OPPOSITE:** aware 3 = **unquestioning**, prejudiced, wholesale, indiscriminate, uncritical, unreasoning, undiscriminating

blindly 1 = **thoughtlessly**, carelessly, recklessly, indiscriminately, senselessly, heedlessly 2 = **wildly**, aimlessly

blink 1 = **flutter**, wink, bat 2 = **flash**, flicker, wink, shimmer, twinkle, glimmer
▷ PHRASES: on the blink (*slang*) = **not working (properly)**, faulty, defective, playing up,

b

out of action, malfunctioning, out of order

bliss 1 = **joy**, ecstasy, euphoria, rapture, nirvana, felicity, gladness, blissfulness **OPPOSITE:** misery 2 = **beatitude**, blessedness

blister = **sore**, boil, swelling, cyst, pimple, carbuncle, pustule

blitz = **attack**, strike, assault, raid, offensive, onslaught, bombardment, bombing campaign

bloc = **group**, union, league, alliance, coalition, axis

block NOUN 1 = **piece**, bar, mass, brick, lump, chunk, hunk, ingot 2 = **obstruction**, bar, barrier, obstacle, impediment, hindrance
▷ VERB 3 = **obstruct**, close, stop, plug, choke, clog, stop up, bung up (*informal*) **OPPOSITE:** clear 4 = **obscure**, bar, obstruct 5 = **shut off**, stop, bar, hamper, obstruct

blockade = **stoppage**, block, barrier, restriction, obstacle, barricade, obstruction, impediment

blog = **weblog**, microblog, vlog, blook, website, forum, chatroom, column, newsletter, podcast, profile (*on a social networking site*), webcast, vodcast

bloke (*informal*) = **man**, person, individual, character (*informal*), guy (*informal*), fellow, chap

blonde *or* **blond** 1 = **fair**, light, flaxen 2 = **fair-haired**, golden-haired, tow-headed

blood 1 = **lifeblood**, gore, vital fluid 2 = **family**, relations, birth, descent, extraction, ancestry, lineage, kinship

bloodshed = **killing**, murder, massacre, slaughter, slaying, carnage, butchery, blood-letting

bloody 1 = **cruel**, fierce, savage, brutal, vicious, ferocious, cut-throat, warlike 2 = **bloodstained**, raw, bleeding, blood-soaked, blood-spattered

bloom NOUN 1 = **flower**, bud, blossom 2 = **prime**, flower, beauty, height, peak, flourishing, heyday, zenith 3 = **glow**, freshness, lustre, radiance **OPPOSITE:** pallor
▷ VERB 4 = **flower**, blossom, open, bud **OPPOSITE:** wither 5 = **grow**, develop, wax 6 = **succeed**, flourish, thrive, prosper, fare well **OPPOSITE:** fail

blossom NOUN 1 = **flower**, bloom, bud, efflorescence, floret
▷ VERB 2 = **develop**, bloom, grow, mature 3 = **succeed**, progress, thrive, flourish, prosper 4 = **flower**, bloom, bud

blow¹ 1 = **move**, carry, drive, sweep, fling, buffet, waft 2 = **be carried**, flutter 3 = **exhale**, breathe, pant, puff 4 = **play**, sound, pipe, trumpet, blare, toot
▷ PHRASES: blow something up

b

1 = **explode**, bomb, blast, detonate, blow sky-high 2 = **inflate**, pump up, fill, expand, swell, enlarge, puff up, distend 3 = **magnify**, increase, extend, expand, widen, broaden, amplify ▶ **blow up** 1 = **explode**, burst, shatter, erupt, detonate 2 = **lose your temper**, rage, erupt, see red (*informal*), become angry, hit the roof (*informal*), fly off the handle (*informal*), go crook (*Austral & NZ slang*), blow your top (*informal*)

blow² 1 = **knock**, stroke, punch, bang, sock (*slang*), smack, thump, clout (*informal*) 2 = **setback**, shock, disaster, reverse, disappointment, catastrophe, misfortune, bombshell

bludge (*Austral & NZ informal*) = **slack**, skive (*Brit informal*), idle, shirk

blue ADJECTIVE 1 = **depressed**, low, sad, unhappy, melancholy, dejected, despondent, downcast OPPOSITE: happy 2 = **smutty**, obscene, indecent, lewd, risqué, X-rated (*informal*) OPPOSITE: respectable ▷ PLURAL NOUN 3 = **depression**, gloom, melancholy, unhappiness, low spirits, the dumps (*informal*), the doldrums • *See panel* SHADES OF BLUE

SHADES OF BLUE

aqua	Nile blue
aquamarine	Oxford blue
azure	peacock blue
Cambridge blue	periwinkle
cerulean	perse
clear blue	petrol blue
cobalt blue	pewter
Copenhagen blue	royal blue
cyan	sapphire
duck-egg blue	saxe blue
electric blue	sky blue
gentian blue	steel blue
heliotrope	teal
indigo	turquoise
lapis lazuli	ultramarine
midnight blue	Wedgwood blue
navy blue	

b

blue-collar = **manual**, industrial, physical, manufacturing, labouring

blueprint 1 = **scheme**, plan, design, system, programme, proposal, strategy, pattern 2 = **plan**, scheme, pattern, draft, outline, sketch

bluff¹ NOUN 1 = **deception**, fraud, sham, pretence, deceit, bravado, bluster, humbug ▷ VERB 2 = **deceive**, trick, fool, pretend, cheat, con, fake, mislead

bluff² NOUN 1 = **precipice**, bank, peak, cliff, ridge, crag, escarpment, promontory ▷ ADJECTIVE 2 = **hearty**, open, blunt, outspoken, genial, ebullient, jovial, plain-spoken **OPPOSITE:** tactful

blunder NOUN 1 = **mistake**, slip, fault, error, oversight, gaffe, slip-up (*informal*), indiscretion, barry or Barry Crocker (*Austral slang*) **OPPOSITE:** correctness ▷ VERB 2 = **make a mistake**, blow it (*slang*), err, slip up (*informal*), foul up, put your foot in it (*informal*) **OPPOSITE:** be correct 3 = **stumble**, fall, reel, stagger, lurch

blunt ADJECTIVE 1 = **frank**, forthright, straightforward, rude, outspoken, bluff, brusque, plain-spoken **OPPOSITE:** tactful 2 = **dull**, rounded, dulled, edgeless, unsharpened **OPPOSITE:** sharp

▷ VERB 3 = **dull**, weaken, soften, numb, dampen, water down, deaden, take the edge off **OPPOSITE:** stimulate

blur NOUN 1 = **haze**, confusion, fog, obscurity, indistinctness ▷ VERB 2 = **become indistinct**, become vague, become hazy, become fuzzy 3 = **obscure**, make indistinct, mask, obfuscate, make vague, make hazy

blush VERB 1 = **turn red**, colour, glow, flush, redden, go red (as a beetroot), turn scarlet **OPPOSITE:** turn pale ▷ NOUN 2 = **reddening**, colour, glow, flush, pink tinge, rosiness, ruddiness, rosy tint

board NOUN 1 = **plank**, panel, timber, slat, piece of timber 2 = **council**, directors, committee, congress, advisers, panel, assembly, trustees 3 = **meals**, provisions, victuals, daily meals ▷ VERB 4 = **get on**, enter, mount, embark **OPPOSITE:** get off

boast VERB 1 = **brag**, crow, vaunt, talk big (*slang*), blow your own trumpet, show off, be proud of, congratulate yourself on, skite (*Austral & NZ informal*) **OPPOSITE:** cover up 2 = **possess**, exhibit ▷ NOUN 3 = **bragging OPPOSITE:** disclaimer

bob = **bounce**, duck, hop, oscillate

bodily = **physical**, material, actual, substantial, tangible, corporal, carnal, corporeal

body 1 = **physique**, build, form, figure, shape, frame, constitution 2 = **torso**, trunk 3 = **corpse**, dead body, remains, stiff (*slang*), carcass, cadaver 4 = **organization**, company, group, society, association, band, congress, institution 5 = **main part**, matter, material, mass, substance, bulk, essence 6 = **expanse**, mass (*informal*)

▌ **RELATED WORDS**
adjectives: corporal, physical

bog = **marsh**, swamp, slough, wetlands, fen, mire, quagmire, morass, pakihi (*NZ*), muskeg (*Canad*)

bogey = **bugbear**, bête noire, horror, nightmare, bugaboo

bogus = **fake**, false, artificial, forged, imitation, sham, fraudulent, counterfeit
OPPOSITE: genuine

Bohemian **ADJECTIVE** 1 *often not cap.* = **unconventional**, alternative, artistic, unorthodox, arty (*informal*), offbeat, left bank, nonconformist **OPPOSITE:** conventional
▷ **NOUN** 2 *often not cap.* = **nonconformist**, rebel, radical, eccentric, maverick, hippy, dropout, individualist

boil¹ = **simmer**, bubble, foam, seethe, fizz, froth, effervesce

boil² = **pustule**, gathering, swelling, blister, carbuncle

bold 1 = **fearless**, enterprising, brave, daring, heroic, adventurous, courageous, audacious **OPPOSITE:** timid 2 = **impudent**, forward, confident, rude, cheeky, feisty (*informal, chiefly US & Canad*), brazen, shameless, insolent **OPPOSITE:** shy

bolster = **support**, help, boost, strengthen, reinforce, shore up, augment

bolt **NOUN** 1 = **pin**, rod, peg, rivet 2 = **bar**, catch, lock, latch, fastener, sliding bar
▷ **VERB** 3 = **lock**, close, bar, secure, fasten, latch 4 = **dash**, fly 5 = **gobble**, stuff, wolf, cram, gorge, devour, gulp, guzzle

bomb **NOUN** 1 = **explosive**, mine, shell, missile, device, rocket, grenade, torpedo
▷ **VERB** 2 = **blow up**, attack, destroy, assault, shell, blitz, bombard, torpedo

bombard 1 = **attack**, assault, besiege, beset, assail 2 = **bomb**, shell, blitz, open fire, strafe, fire upon

bombardment = **bombing**, attack, assault, shelling, blitz, barrage, fusillade

bond **NOUN** 1 = **tie**, union, coupling, link, association, relation, connection, alliance 2 = **fastening**, tie, chain, cord, shackle, fetter, manacle

b

3 = **agreement**, word, promise, contract, guarantee, pledge, obligation, covenant
▷ VERB 4 = **form friendships**, connect 5 = **fix**, hold, bind, connect, glue, stick, paste, fasten

bonus 1 = **extra**, prize, gift, reward, premium, dividend 2 = **advantage**, benefit, gain, extra, plus, asset, icing on the cake

book NOUN 1 = **work**, title, volume, publication, tract, tome, e-book *or* ebook, blook 2 = **notebook**, album, journal, diary, pad, notepad, exercise book, jotter
▷ VERB 3 = **reserve**, schedule, engage, organize, charter, arrange for, make reservations, e-book *or* ebook
▷ PHRASES: book in = **register**, enter

booklet = **brochure**, leaflet, hand-out, pamphlet, folder, mailshot, handbill

boom NOUN 1 = **expansion**, increase, development, growth, jump, boost, improvement, upsurge **OPPOSITE:** decline 2 = **bang**, crash, clash, blast, burst, explosion, roar, thunder
▷ VERB 3 = **increase**, flourish, grow, develop, expand, strengthen, swell, thrive **OPPOSITE:** fall 4 = **bang**, roll, crash, blast, explode, roar, thunder, rumble

boon 1 = **benefit**, blessing, godsend, gift 2 (*archaic*) = **gift**, favour

boost VERB 1 = **increase**, develop, raise, expand, add to, heighten, enlarge, amplify **OPPOSITE:** decrease
▷ NOUN 2 = **rise**, increase, jump, addition, improvement, expansion, upsurge, upturn **OPPOSITE:** fall 3 = **encouragement**, help

boot = **kick**, punt, put the boot in(to) (*slang*), drop-kick

border NOUN 1 = **frontier**, line, limit, bounds, boundary, perimeter, borderline 2 = **edge**, margin, verge, rim
▷ VERB 3 = **edge**, bound, decorate, trim, fringe, rim, hem

bore¹ = **drill**, mine, sink, tunnel, pierce, penetrate, burrow, puncture

bore² VERB 1 = **tire**, fatigue, weary, wear out, jade, be tedious, pall on, send to sleep **OPPOSITE:** excite
▷ NOUN 2 = **nuisance**, pain (*informal*), yawn (*informal*), anorak (*informal*)

bored = **fed up**, tired, wearied, uninterested, sick and tired (*informal*), listless, brassed off (*Brit slang*), hoha (*NZ*)

boredom = **tedium**, apathy, weariness, monotony, sameness, ennui, flatness, world-weariness **OPPOSITE:** excitement

boring = **uninteresting**, dull, tedious, tiresome, monotonous, flat, humdrum, mind-numbing

borrow 1 = **take on loan**, touch (someone) for (*slang*), scrounge (*informal*), cadge, use temporarily **OPPOSITE:** lend **2** = **steal**, take, copy, adopt, pinch (*informal*)

boss = **manager**, head, leader, director, chief, master, employer, supervisor, baas (*S African*), sherang (*Austral & NZ*)
▷ **PHRASES: boss someone around** (*informal*) = **order around**, dominate, bully, oppress, push around (*slang*)

bother VERB 1 = **trouble**, concern, worry, alarm, disturb, disconcert, perturb **2** = **pester**, plague, harass, hassle (*informal*), inconvenience **OPPOSITE:** help
▷ **NOUN 3** = **trouble**, problem, worry, difficulty, fuss, irritation, hassle (*informal*), nuisance, uphill (*S African*) **OPPOSITE:** help

bottle shop (*Austral & NZ*) = **off-licence** (*Brit*), liquor store (*US & Canad*), bottle store (*S African*), package store (*US & Canad*), offie or offy (*Brit informal*)

bottle store (*S African*) = **off-licence** (*Brit*), liquor store (*US & Canad*), bottle shop (*Austral & NZ*), package store (*US & Canad*), offie or offy (*Brit informal*)

bottom NOUN 1 = **lowest part**, base, foot, bed, floor, foundation, depths **OPPOSITE:** top **2** = **underside**, sole, underneath, lower side **3** (*informal*) = **buttocks**, behind (*informal*), rear, backside, rump, seat, posterior
▷ **ADJECTIVE 4** = **lowest**, last **OPPOSITE:** higher

bounce VERB 1 = **rebound**, recoil, ricochet **2** = **bound**, spring, jump, leap, skip, gambol
▷ **NOUN 3** = **springiness**, give, spring, resilience, elasticity, recoil **4** (*informal*) = **life**, go (*informal*), energy, zip (*informal*), vigour, exuberance, dynamism, vivacity

bound¹ 1 = **compelled**, obliged, forced, committed, pledged, constrained, beholden, duty-bound **2** = **tied**, fixed, secured, attached, tied up, fastened, pinioned **3** = **certain**, sure, fated, doomed, destined

bound² VERB 1 = **leap**, bob, spring, jump, bounce, skip, vault
▷ **NOUN 2** = **leap**, bob, spring, jump, bounce, hurdle, skip, vault

bound³ 1 = **surround**, confine, enclose, encircle, hem in, demarcate **2** = **limit**, restrict, confine, restrain, circumscribe

boundary 1 = **frontier**, edge, border, barrier, margin, brink **2** = **edges**, limits, fringes, extremities **3** = **dividing line**, borderline

bounds = **boundary**, limit, edge, border, confines, verge, rim, perimeter

b

bouquet 1 = **bunch of flowers**, spray, garland, wreath, posy, buttonhole, corsage, nosegay 2 = **aroma**, smell, scent, perfume, fragrance, savour, odour, redolence

bourgeois = **middle-class**, traditional, conventional, materialistic, hidebound

bout 1 = **period**, term, fit, spell, turn, interval 2 = **round**, series, session, cycle, sequence, stint 3 = **fight**, match, competition, struggle, contest, set-to, encounter, engagement

bow¹ VERB 1 = **bend**, bob, nod, stoop, droop, genuflect ▷ NOUN 2 = **bending**, bob, nod, obeisance, kowtow, genuflection

bow³ (*Nautical*) = **prow**, head, stem, fore, beak

bowels 1 = **guts**, insides (*informal*), intestines, innards (*informal*), entrails, viscera, vitals 2 = **depths**, hold, inside, deep, interior, core, belly

bowl¹ = **basin**, plate, dish, vessel

bowl² = **throw**, hurl, launch, cast, pitch, toss, fling, chuck (*informal*)

box¹ NOUN 1 = **container**, case, chest, trunk, pack, package, carton, casket ▷ VERB 2 = **pack**, package, wrap, encase, bundle up

box² = **fight**, spar, exchange blows

boxer = **fighter**, pugilist, prizefighter

boy = **lad**, kid (*informal*), youth, fellow, youngster, schoolboy, junior, stripling

boycott = **embargo**, reject, snub, black **OPPOSITE:** support

boyfriend = **sweetheart**, man, lover, beloved, admirer, suitor, beau, date

brace VERB 1 = **steady**, support, secure, stabilize 2 = **support**, strengthen, steady, reinforce, bolster, fortify, buttress ▷ NOUN 3 = **support**, stay, prop, bolster, bracket, reinforcement, strut, truss

bracing = **refreshing**, fresh, stimulating, crisp, brisk, exhilarating, invigorating **OPPOSITE:** tiring

brain = **intelligence**, understanding, sense, intellect

brake NOUN 1 = **control**, check, curb, restraint, constraint, rein ▷ VERB 2 = **slow**, decelerate, reduce speed

branch 1 = **bough**, shoot, arm, spray, limb, sprig, offshoot 2 = **office**, department, unit, wing, chapter, bureau 3 = **division**, part, section, subdivision, subsection 4 = **discipline**, section, subdivision

brand NOUN 1 = **trademark** 2 = **label**, mark, sign, stamp, symbol, logo, trademark, marker ▷ VERB 3 = **stigmatize**, mark, expose, denounce, disgrace, discredit, censure 4 = **mark**, burn, label, stamp, scar

brash = **bold**, rude, cocky, pushy (*informal*), brazen, impertinent, insolent, impudent **OPPOSITE:** timid

brave ADJECTIVE

1 = **courageous**, daring, bold, heroic, adventurous, fearless, resolute, audacious **OPPOSITE:** timid

▷ VERB 2 = **confront**, face, suffer, tackle, endure, defy, withstand, stand up to **OPPOSITE:** give in to

bravery = **courage**, nerve, daring, pluck, spirit, fortitude, heroism, mettle **OPPOSITE:** cowardice

brawl NOUN 1 = **fight**, clash, fray, skirmish, scuffle, punch-up (*Brit informal*), fracas, altercation, biffo (*Austral slang*)

▷ VERB 2 = **fight**, scrap (*informal*), wrestle, tussle, scuffle

breach 1 = **nonobservance**, abuse, violation, infringement, trespass, transgression, contravention, infraction **OPPOSITE:** compliance

2 = **opening**, crack, split, gap, rift, rupture, cleft, fissure

bread 1 = **food**, fare, kai (*NZ informal*), nourishment, sustenance 2 (*slang*) = **money**, cash, dough (*slang*)

breadth 1 = **width**, spread, span, latitude, broadness,

wideness 2 = **extent**, range, scale, scope, compass, expanse

break VERB 1 = **shatter**, separate, destroy, crack, snap, smash, crush, fragment **OPPOSITE:** repair 2 = **fracture**, crack, smash 3 = **burst**, tear, split 4 = **disobey**, breach, defy, violate, disregard, flout, infringe, contravene **OPPOSITE:** obey 5 = **stop**, cut, suspend, interrupt, cut short, discontinue 6 = **disturb**, interrupt 7 = **end**, stop, cut, drop, give up, abandon, suspend, interrupt 8 = **weaken**, undermine, tame, subdue, demoralize, dispirit 9 = **be revealed**, be published, be announced, be made public, be proclaimed, be let out 10 = **reveal**, tell, announce, declare, disclose, proclaim, make known 11 = **beat**, top, better, exceed, go beyond, excel, surpass, outstrip

▷ NOUN 12 = **fracture**, opening, tear, hole, split, crack, gap, fissure 13 = **interval**, pause, interlude, intermission 14 = **holiday**, leave, vacation, time off, recess, awayday, schoolie (*Austral*), accumulated day off or ADO (*Austral*) 15 (*informal*) = **stroke of luck**, chance, opportunity, advantage, fortune, opening

▷ PHRASES: break off = **stop talking**, pause ▶ break out = **begin**, start, happen, occur,

b

arise, set in, commence, spring up ▸ **break something off** = **detach**, separate, divide, cut off, pull off, sever, part, remove ▸ **break something up** = **stop**, end, suspend, dismantle, terminate, disband, diffuse ▸ **break up 1** = **finish**, be suspended, adjourn **2** = **split up**, separate, part, divorce

breakdown = **collapse**

break-in = **burglary**, robbery, breaking and entering, home invasion (*Austral & NZ*)

breakthrough = **development**, advance, progress, discovery, find, invention, step forward, leap forwards

breast = **bosom**, boob (*slang*), tit (*slang*), booby (*slang*)

breath = **inhalation**, breathing, pant, gasp, gulp, wheeze, exhalation, respiration

breathe 1 = **inhale and exhale**, pant, gasp, puff, gulp, wheeze, respire, draw in breath **2** = **whisper**, sigh, murmur

breathless 1 = **out of breath**, panting, gasping, gulping, wheezing, short-winded **2** = **excited**, curious, eager, enthusiastic, impatient, on tenterhooks, in suspense

breathtaking = **amazing**, exciting, stunning (*informal*), impressive, thrilling, magnificent, astonishing, sensational

breed NOUN **1** = **variety**, race, stock, type, species, strain, pedigree **2** = **kind**, sort, type, variety, brand, stamp ▸ VERB **3** = **rear**, tend, keep, raise, maintain, farm, look after, care for **4** = **reproduce**, multiply, propagate, procreate, produce offspring, bear young, bring forth young **5** = **produce**, cause, create, generate, bring about, arouse, give rise to, stir up

breeding = **refinement**, culture, taste, manners, polish, courtesy, sophistication, cultivation

breeze NOUN **1** = **light wind**, air, draught, gust, waft, zephyr, breath of wind, current of air ▸ VERB **2** = **sweep**, move briskly, pass, sail, hurry, glide, flit

brew VERB **1** = **boil**, make, soak, steep, stew, infuse (~*tea*) **2** = **make**, ferment **3** = **start**, develop, gather, foment **4** = **develop**, form, gather, foment ▸ NOUN **5** = **drink**, preparation, mixture, blend, liquor, beverage, infusion, concoction

bribe NOUN **1** = **inducement**, pay-off (*informal*), sweetener (*slang*), kickback (*US*), backhander (*slang*), enticement, allurement ▸ VERB **2** = **buy off**, reward, pay off (*informal*), corrupt, suborn, grease the palm *or* hand of (*slang*)

bribery = **corruption**, inducement, buying off, payola (*informal*), palm-greasing (*slang*)

bridge NOUN 1 = **arch**, span, viaduct, flyover, overpass, fixed link (*Canad*)

▷ VERB 2 = **span**, cross 3 = **reconcile**, resolve OPPOSITE: divide

brief ADJECTIVE 1 = **short**, quick, fleeting, swift, short-lived, momentary, ephemeral, transitory OPPOSITE: long

▷ VERB 2 = **inform**, prime, prepare, advise, fill in (*informal*), instruct, put in the picture (*informal*), keep (someone) posted

▷ NOUN 3 = **summary**, résumé, outline, sketch, abstract, digest, epitome, rundown

briefing 1 = **conference**, priming 2 = **instructions**, information, priming, directions, preparation, guidance, rundown

briefly 1 = **quickly**, shortly, hastily, momentarily, hurriedly 2 = **in outline**, in brief, in a nutshell, concisely

brigade 1 = **corps**, company, force, unit, division, troop, squad, team 2 = **group**, band, squad, organization

bright 1 = **vivid**, rich, brilliant, glowing, colourful 2 = **shining**, glowing, dazzling, gleaming, shimmering, radiant, luminous, lustrous 3 (*informal*) = **intelligent**, smart, clever, aware, sharp, enlightened, astute, wide-awake OPPOSITE: stupid 4 (*informal*) = **clever**, smart, ingenious 5 = **sunny**, clear, fair, pleasant, lucid, cloudless, unclouded OPPOSITE: cloudy

brighten 1 = **light up**, shine, glow, gleam, lighten OPPOSITE: dim 2 = **enliven**, animate, make brighter, vitalize 3 = **become brighter**, light up, glow, gleam

brilliance *or* **brilliancy** 1 = **cleverness**, talent, wisdom, distinction, genius, excellence, greatness, inventiveness OPPOSITE: stupidity 2 = **brightness**, intensity, sparkle, dazzle, lustre, radiance, luminosity, vividness OPPOSITE: darkness 3 = **splendour**, glamour, grandeur, magnificence, éclat, illustriousness

brilliant 1 = **intelligent**, sharp, intellectual, clever, profound, penetrating, inventive, perspicacious OPPOSITE: stupid 2 = **expert**, masterly, talented, gifted, accomplished OPPOSITE: untalented 3 = **splendid**, famous, celebrated, outstanding, superb, magnificent, glorious, notable 4 = **bright**, shining, intense, sparkling, glittering, dazzling, vivid, radiant OPPOSITE: dark

brim NOUN 1 = **rim**, edge, border, lip, margin, verge, brink

▷ VERB 2 = **be full**, spill, well over, run over 3 = **fill**, well over, fill up, overflow

b

bring 1 = **fetch**, take, carry, bear, transfer, deliver, transport, convey **2** = **take**, guide, conduct, escort **3** = **cause**, produce, create, effect, occasion, result in, contribute to, inflict
▷ **PHRASES: bring someone up** = **rear**, raise, support, train, develop, teach, breed, foster
▶ **bring something about** = **cause**, produce, create, effect, achieve, generate, accomplish, give rise to ▶ **bring something off** = **accomplish**, achieve, perform, succeed, execute, pull off, carry off ▶ **bring something up** = **mention**, raise, introduce, point out, refer to, allude to, broach

brink = **edge**, limit, border, lip, margin, boundary, skirt, frontier

brisk 1 = **quick**, lively, energetic, active, vigorous, bustling, sprightly, spry **OPPOSITE:** slow **2** = **short**, brief, blunt, abrupt, terse, gruff, brusque, monosyllabic

briskly = **quickly**, smartly, promptly, rapidly, readily, actively, efficiently, energetically

bristle NOUN 1 = **hair**, spine, thorn, whisker, barb, stubble, prickle
▷ **VERB 2** = **stand up**, rise, stand on end **3** = **be angry**, rage, seethe, flare up, bridle, see red

brittle = **fragile**, delicate, crisp, crumbling, frail, crumbly, breakable, friable **OPPOSITE:** tough

broad 1 = **wide**, large, ample, generous, expansive **2** = **large**, huge, vast, extensive, ample, spacious, expansive, roomy **OPPOSITE:** narrow **3** = **full**, general, comprehensive, complete, wide, sweeping, wide-ranging, thorough **4** = **universal**, general, common, wide, sweeping, worldwide, widespread, wide-ranging **5** = **general**, loose, vague, approximate, indefinite, ill-defined, inexact, unspecific

broadcast NOUN 1 = **transmission**, show, programme, telecast, podcast, webcast, vodcast, mobcast
▷ **VERB 2** = **transmit**, show, air, radio, cable, beam, send out, relay, stream (~*videos*), podcast, open-line (*Canad*) **3** = **make public**, report, announce, publish, spread, advertise, proclaim, circulate

broaden = **expand**, increase, develop, spread, extend, stretch, swell, supplement **OPPOSITE:** restrict

brochure = **booklet**, advertisement, leaflet, hand-out, circular, pamphlet, folder, mailshot

broekies (*S African informal*) = **underpants**, pants, briefs, drawers, knickers, panties, boxer shorts, Y-fronts®, underdaks (*Austral slang*)

broke (*informal*) = **penniless**, short, ruined, bust (*informal*), bankrupt, impoverished, in the red, insolvent **OPPOSITE:** rich

broken 1 = **interrupted**, incomplete, erratic, intermittent, fragmentary, spasmodic, discontinuous 2 = **imperfect**, halting, hesitating, stammering, disjointed 3 = **smashed**, burst, shattered, fragmented, fractured, severed, ruptured, separated 4 = **defective**, not working, imperfect, out of order, on the blink (*slang*), kaput (*informal*)

broker = **dealer**, agent, trader, supplier, merchant, negotiator, mediator, intermediary

bronze = **reddish-brown**, copper, tan, rust, chestnut, brownish
• *See panel* **SHADES OF BROWN**

brood NOUN 1 = **offspring**, issue, clutch, litter, progeny 2 = **children**, family, nearest and dearest, flesh and blood, ainga (*NZ*)
▷ VERB 3 = **think**, obsess, muse, ponder, agonize, mull over, mope, ruminate

brook = **stream**, burn (*Scot & Northern English*), rivulet, beck, watercourse, rill

brother 1 = **male sibling** 2 = **monk**, cleric, friar, religious

▌ **RELATED WORD**
adjective: fraternal

brotherly = **fraternal**, friendly, neighbourly, sympathetic, benevolent, affectionate, kind, amicable

brown ADJECTIVE 1 = **brunette**, bay, coffee, chocolate, chestnut, hazel, dun, auburn 2 = **tanned**, bronze, tan, sunburnt
▷ VERB 3 = **fry**, cook, grill, sear, sauté
• *See panel* **SHADES OF BROWN**

browse 1 = **skim**, scan, glance at, survey, look through, look round, dip into, leaf through 2 = **graze**, eat, feed, nibble

bruise NOUN 1 = **discoloration**, mark, injury, blemish, contusion
▷ VERB 2 = **hurt**, injure, mark 3 = **damage**, mark, mar, discolour

brush¹ NOUN 1 = **broom**, sweeper, besom 2 = **conflict**, clash, confrontation, skirmish, tussle 3 = **encounter**, meeting, confrontation, rendezvous
▷ VERB 4 = **clean**, wash, polish, buff 5 = **touch**, sweep, kiss, stroke, glance, flick, scrape, graze
▷ PHRASES: brush someone off (*slang*) = **ignore**, reject, dismiss, snub, disregard, scorn, disdain, spurn ▶ brush something up *or* brush up on something = **revise**, study, go over, cram, polish up, read up on, relearn, bone up on (*informal*)

SHADES OF BROWN

almond	henna
amber	khaki
auburn	liver
bay	mahogany
beige	mocha
biscuit	mousy
bisque	mushroom
bistre	neutral
bronze	nutbrown
buff	nutmeg
burnt sienna	oatmeal
burnt umber	oxblood
butternut	russet
café au lait	rust
camel	sable
chestnut	sand
chocolate	seal brown
cinnabar	sepia
cinnamon	sienna
cocoa	sorrel
coffee	tan
copper	taupe
cream	tawny
drab	teak
dun	terracotta
ecru	tortoiseshell
fawn	umber
ginger	walnut
hazel	

brush² = **shrubs**, bushes, scrub, undergrowth, thicket, copse, brushwood

brutal 1 = **cruel**, savage, vicious, ruthless, callous, sadistic, heartless, inhuman **OPPOSITE:**

kind 2 = **harsh**, tough, severe, rough, rude, indifferent, insensitive, callous **OPPOSITE:** sensitive

brutality = **cruelty**, atrocity, ferocity, savagery, ruthlessness, barbarism, inhumanity, viciousness

bubble NOUN 1 = **air ball**, drop, bead, blister, blob, droplet, globule
▷ VERB 2 = **boil**, seethe 3 = **foam**, fizz, froth, percolate, effervesce 4 = **gurgle**, splash, murmur, trickle, ripple, babble, burble, lap

bubbly 1 = **lively**, happy, excited, animated, merry, bouncy, elated, sparky 2 = **frothy**, sparkling, fizzy, effervescent, carbonated, foamy

buckle NOUN 1 = **fastener**, catch, clip, clasp, hasp
▷ VERB 2 = **fasten**, close, secure, hook, clasp 3 = **distort**, bend, warp, crumple, contort 4 = **collapse**, bend, twist, fold, give way, subside, cave in, crumple

bud NOUN 1 = **shoot**, branch, sprout, sprig, offshoot
▷ VERB 2 = **develop**, grow, shoot, sprout, burgeon, burst forth

budding = **developing**, beginning, growing, promising, potential, burgeoning, fledgling, embryonic

budge 1 = **move**, stir 2 = **dislodge**, move, push, transfer, shift, stir

budget NOUN 1 = **allowance**, means, funds, income, finances, resources, allocation
▷ VERB 2 = **plan**, estimate, allocate, cost, ration, apportion

buff¹ ADJECTIVE 1 = **fawn**, tan, beige, yellowish, straw-coloured, sand-coloured, yellowish-brown
▷ VERB 2 = **polish**, smooth, brush, shine, rub, wax, brighten, burnish
• See panels SHADES OF BROWN, SHADES OF YELLOW

buff² (informal) = **expert**, fan, addict, enthusiast, admirer, devotee, connoisseur, aficionado, fundi (S African)

buffer = **safeguard**, screen, shield, cushion, intermediary, bulwark

buffet 1 = **smorgasbord** 2 = **snack bar**, café, cafeteria, brasserie, refreshment counter

bug NOUN 1 (informal) = **illness**, disease, virus, infection, disorder, sickness, ailment, affliction 2 = **fault**, error, defect, flaw, glitch, gremlin, malware
▷ VERB 3 = **tap**, eavesdrop, listen in on 4 (informal) = **annoy**, bother, disturb, irritate, hassle (informal), pester, vex, get on your nerves (informal)

build VERB 1 = **construct**, make, raise, put up, assemble, erect, fabricate, form OPPOSITE: demolish
▷ NOUN 2 = **physique**, form, body, figure, shape, structure, frame

building = **structure**, house, construction, dwelling, erection, edifice, domicile

build-up = **increase**, development, growth, expansion, accumulation, enlargement, escalation

bulge VERB 1 = **swell out**, project, expand, stick out, protrude, puff out, distend
2 = **stick out**, stand out, protrude
▷ NOUN 3 = **lump**, swelling, bump, projection, hump, protuberance, protrusion
OPPOSITE: hollow 4 = **increase**, rise, boost, surge, intensification

bulk 1 = **size**, volume, dimensions, magnitude, substance, immensity, largeness 2 = **weight**, size, mass, heaviness, poundage
3 = **majority**, mass, most, body, best part, lion's share, better part, preponderance

> **USAGE NOTE**
> The use of a plural noun after *bulk*, when it has the meaning 'majority', although common, is considered by some to be incorrect and should be avoided. This usage is most commonly encountered, according to the Bank of English, when referring to *funds* and *profits*: *the bulk of our profits stem from the sale of beer*. The synonyms *majority* and *most* would work better in this context.

bullet = **projectile**, ball, shot, missile, slug, pellet

bulletin = **report**, account, statement, message, communication, announcement, dispatch, communiqué

bully NOUN 1 = **persecutor**, tough, oppressor, tormentor, bully boy, browbeater, coercer, ruffian
▷ VERB 2 = **persecute**, intimidate, torment, oppress, pick on, victimize, terrorize, push around (*slang*) 3 = **force**, coerce, browbeat, hector, domineer

bump VERB 1 = **knock**, hit, strike, crash, smash, slam, bang
2 = **jerk**, shake, bounce, rattle, jog, lurch, jolt
▷ NOUN 3 = **knock**, blow, impact, collision, thump
4 = **thud**, crash, knock, bang, smack, thump 5 = **lump**, swelling, bulge, hump, nodule, protuberance, contusion

bumper = **exceptional**, excellent, exo (*Austral slang*), massive, jumbo (*informal*), abundant, whopping (*informal*), bountiful

bunch 1 (*informal*) = **group**, band, crowd, party, team, gathering, gang, flock 2 = **bouquet**, sheaf
3 = **cluster**, clump
▷ PHRASES: bunch together or up = **group**, mass, collect, assemble, cluster, huddle

bundle NOUN 1 = **bunch**, group, collection, mass, pile, stack,

heap, batch
▷ **VERB** 2 = **push**, thrust, shove, throw, rush, hurry, jostle, hustle
▷ **PHRASES: bundle someone up** = **wrap up**, swathe

bungle = **mess up**, blow (*slang*), ruin, spoil, blunder, botch, make a mess of, muff, crool *or* cruel (*Austral slang*) **OPPOSITE:** accomplish

bungling = **incompetent**, blundering, clumsy, inept, cack-handed (*informal*), maladroit, ham-fisted (*informal*), unco (*Austral slang*)

bunk *or* **bunkum** (*informal*) = **nonsense**, rubbish, garbage (*informal*), hot air (*informal*), twaddle, moonshine, malarkey, baloney (*informal*), hogwash, bizzo (*Austral slang*), bull's wool (*Austral & NZ slang*), kak (*S African taboo slang*)

buoy = **float**, guide, signal, marker, beacon

buoyant 1 = **cheerful**, happy, upbeat (*informal*), carefree, jaunty, chirpy (*informal*), light-hearted **OPPOSITE:** gloomy 2 = **floating**, light

burden NOUN 1 = **trouble**, worry, weight, responsibility, strain, affliction, onus, millstone 2 = **load**, weight, cargo, freight, consignment, encumbrance
▷ **VERB** 3 = **weigh down**, worry, load, tax, bother, handicap, oppress, inconvenience

bureau 1 = **agency** 2 = **office**, department, section, branch, station, unit, division, subdivision 3 = **desk**, writing desk

bureaucracy 1 = **government**, officials, authorities, administration, the system, civil service, corridors of power 2 = **red tape**, regulations, officialdom

bureaucrat = **official**, officer, administrator, civil servant, public servant, functionary, mandarin

burglar = **housebreaker**, thief, robber, pilferer, filcher, cat burglar, sneak thief

burglary = **breaking and entering**, housebreaking, break-in, home invasion (*Austral & NZ*)

burial = **funeral**, interment, obsequies, entombment, exequies

burn 1 = **be on fire**, blaze, be ablaze, smoke, flame, glow, flare, go up in flames 2 = **set on fire**, light, ignite, kindle, incinerate 3 = **scorch**, toast, sear, char, singe 4 = **be passionate**, be aroused, be inflamed 5 = **seethe**, fume, be angry, simmer, smoulder

burning 1 = **intense**, passionate, eager, ardent, fervent, impassioned, vehement **OPPOSITE:** mild 2 = **crucial**, important, pressing, significant, essential, vital, critical, acute

b

burrow NOUN 1 = **hole**, shelter, tunnel, den, lair, retreat
▷ VERB 2 = **dig**, tunnel, excavate 3 = **delve**, search, probe, ferret, rummage, forage, fossick (*Austral & NZ*)

burst VERB 1 = **explode**, blow up, break, split, crack, shatter, puncture, rupture 2 = **rush**, run, break, break out, erupt, spout, gush forth 3 = **barge**, charge, rush, shove
▷ NOUN 4 = **rush**, surge, outbreak, outburst, spate, gush, torrent, spurt 5 = **explosion**, crack, blast, bang, discharge

bury 1 = **inter**, lay to rest, entomb, consign to the grave, inhume OPPOSITE: dig up 2 = **hide**, cover, conceal, stash (*informal*), secrete, stow away OPPOSITE: uncover 3 = **sink**, embed, immerse, enfold 4 = **forget**

bush = **shrub**, plant, hedge, thicket, shrubbery
▷ PHRASES: the bush = **the wilds**, brush, scrub, woodland, backwoods, scrubland

business 1 = **trade**, selling, industry, manufacturing, commerce, dealings 2 = **establishment**, company, firm, concern, organization, corporation, venture, enterprise 3 = **profession**, work, job, line, trade, career, function, employment 4 = **matter**, issue, subject, point, problem, responsibility, task, duty 5 = **concern**, affair

businessman = **executive**, director, manager, merchant, capitalist, administrator, entrepreneur, tycoon

bust[1] = **bosom**, breasts, chest, front

bust[2] (*informal*) 1 = **break**, smash, split, burst, shatter, fracture, rupture 2 = **arrest**, catch, raid
▷ PHRASES: go bust = **go bankrupt**, fail, be ruined, become insolvent

bustle VERB 1 = **hurry**, rush, fuss, hasten, scuttle, scurry, scamper OPPOSITE: idle
▷ NOUN 2 = **activity**, to-do, stir, excitement, fuss, flurry, commotion, ado OPPOSITE: inactivity

bustling = **busy**, full, crowded, active, lively, buzzing, humming, swarming

busy 1 = **active**, industrious, rushed off your feet OPPOSITE: idle 2 = **occupied with**, working, engaged in, on duty, employed in, hard at work OPPOSITE: unoccupied 3 = **hectic**, full, exacting, energetic
▷ PHRASES: busy yourself = **occupy yourself**, be engrossed, immerse yourself, involve yourself, absorb yourself, employ yourself, engage yourself

but CONJUNCTION 1 = **however**, still, yet, nevertheless

▷ **PREPOSITION** 2 = **except (for)**, save, bar, barring, excepting, excluding, with the exception of
▷ **ADVERB** 3 = **only**, just, simply, merely

butcher NOUN 1 = **murderer**, killer, slaughterer, slayer, destroyer, executioner, cut-throat, exterminator
▷ **VERB** 2 = **slaughter**, prepare, carve, cut up, dress, cut, clean, joint 3 = **kill**, slaughter, massacre, destroy, cut down, assassinate, slay, liquidate

butt¹ 1 = **end**, handle, shaft, stock, shank, hilt, haft 2 = **stub**, tip, leftover, fag end (*informal*)

butt² = **target**, victim, dupe, laughing stock, Aunt Sally

butt³ = **knock**, push, bump, thrust, ram, shove, poke, prod
▷ **PHRASES: butt in** 1 = **interfere**, meddle, intrude, heckle, barge in (*informal*), stick your nose in, put your oar in 2 = **interrupt**, cut in, break in, chip in (*informal*)

butt⁴ = **cask**, barrel

butterfly

> **RELATED WORDS**
> *young*: caterpillar, chrysalis, chrysalid
> *enthusiast*: lepidopterist
> • *See panel* **BUTTERFLIES AND MOTHS**

buy VERB 1 = **purchase**, get, pay for, obtain, acquire, invest in, shop for, procure **OPPOSITE:** sell
▷ **NOUN** 2 = **purchase**, deal,

BUTTERFLIES AND MOTHS

apollo
argus
bag moth (*NZ*)
bagworm moth
bell moth
bogong *or* bugong (moth)
brimstone
brown-tail moth
buff-tip moth
cabbage white
cactoblastis
Camberwell beauty *or* (*US*) mourning cloak
cardinal
carpenter moth
carpet moth
cleopatra

comma butterfly
copper
cecropia moth
cinnabar
clearwing (moth)
Clifden nonpareil
codlin(g) moth
death's-head moth
drinker (moth)
egger *or* eggar
ermine (moth)
festoon
ghost moth
gipsy moth
goldtail moth *or* yellowtail (moth)
grass moth

BUTTERFLIES AND MOTHS *continued*

grayling	puss moth
hairstreak	red admiral
hawk moth, sphinx moth, *or* hummingbird moth	red underwing
	ringlet
herald moth	silver-Y
house moth	skipper
Io moth	small white
Kentish glory	snout
kitten moth	speckled wood
lackey moth	swallowtail
lappet moth	swift
large white *or* cabbage white	tapestry moth
leopard moth	thorn (moth)
lobster moth	tiger (moth)
luna moth	tussock moth
magpie moth	two-tailed pasha
marbled white	umber (moth)
monarch	vapourer moth
mother-of-pearl moth	wall brown
Mother Shipton	wave (moth)
old lady	wax moth, honeycomb moth, *or* bee moth
orange-tip	
painted lady	white
peacock butterfly	white admiral
peppered moth	winter moth
privet hawk	yellow
processionary moth	yellow underwing
purple emperor	

bargain, acquisition, steal (*informal*), snip (*informal*), giveaway

by PREPOSITION 1 = **through**, through the agency of 2 = **via**, over, by way of 3 = **near**, past, along, close to, closest to, neighbouring, next to, beside ▷ ADVERB 4 = **nearby**, close, handy, at hand, within reach

bypass 1 = **get round**, avoid 2 = **go round**, circumvent, depart from, deviate from, pass round, detour round OPPOSITE: cross

Cc

cab = **taxi**, minicab, taxicab, hackney carriage

cabin 1 = **room**, berth, quarters, compartment 2 = **hut**, shed, cottage, lodge, shack, chalet, shanty, whare (*NZ*)

cabinet 1 = **cupboard**, case, locker, dresser, closet, press, chiffonier 2 *often cap.* = **council**, committee, administration, ministry, assembly, board

cad (*Old-fashioned informal*) = **scoundrel** (*slang*), rat (*informal*), bounder (*Brit old-fashioned slang*), rotter (*slang, chiefly Brit*), heel, wrong 'un (*Austral slang*)

café = **snack bar**, restaurant, cafeteria, coffee shop, brasserie, coffee bar, tearoom, lunchroom

cage = **enclosure**, pen, coop, hutch, pound

cake = **block**, bar, slab, lump, cube, loaf, mass

calculated = **deliberate**, planned, considered, intended, intentional, designed, aimed, purposeful **OPPOSITE:** unplanned

calculating = **scheming**, sharp, shrewd, cunning, sly, devious, manipulative, crafty **OPPOSITE:** direct

calculation 1 = **computation**, working out, reckoning, estimate, forecast, judgment, result, answer 2 = **planning**, intention, deliberation, foresight, contrivance, forethought, premeditation

calibre *or* (*US*) **caliber** 1 = **worth**, quality, ability, talent, capacity, merit, distinction, stature 2 = **standard**, level, quality, grade 3 = **diameter**, bore, gauge, measure

call VERB 1 = **name**, entitle, dub, designate, term, style, label, describe as 2 = **cry**, shout, scream, yell, whoop **OPPOSITE:** whisper 3 = **phone**, telephone, ring (up) (*informal, chiefly Brit*), Skype®, video call 4 = **hail**, summon 5 = **summon**, gather, rally, assemble, muster, convene **OPPOSITE:** dismiss 6 = **waken**, arouse, rouse

▷ NOUN 7 = **telephone call**, bell (*informal*), phone call, buzz (*informal*), ring (*informal*), video call, Skype® 8 = **request**, order, demand, appeal, notice, command, invitation, plea 9 *used in negative constructions* = **need**, cause, reason, grounds, occasion, excuse, justification 10 = **attraction**, pull (*informal*), appeal, lure, allure, magnetism

c

11 = cry, shout, scream, yell, whoop **OPPOSITE:** whisper
▷ **PHRASES: call for someone = fetch**, pick up, collect ▶ **call for something 1 = demand**, order, request, insist on, cry out for **2 = require**, need, involve, demand, occasion, entail, necessitate

calling = profession, trade, career, mission, vocation, life's work

calm ADJECTIVE 1 = cool, relaxed, composed, sedate, collected, dispassionate, unemotional, self-possessed, chilled (*informal*) **OPPOSITE:** excited **2 = still**, quiet, smooth, mild, serene, tranquil, balmy, windless **OPPOSITE:** rough
▷ **NOUN 3 = peacefulness**, peace, serenity **4 = stillness**, peace, quiet, hush, serenity, tranquillity, repose, peacefulness **5 = peace**, calmness **OPPOSITE:** disturbance
▷ **VERB 6 = soothe**, quiet, relax, appease, still, allay, assuage, quieten **OPPOSITE:** excite **7 = placate**, hush, pacify, mollify **OPPOSITE:** aggravate

camouflage NOUN 1 = protective colouring 2 = disguise, cover, screen, blind, mask, cloak, masquerade, subterfuge
▷ **VERB 3 = disguise**, cover, screen, hide, mask, conceal, obscure, veil **OPPOSITE:** reveal

camp¹ 1 = camp site, tents, encampment, camping ground **2 = bivouac**, cantonment (*military*)

camp² (*informal***) 1 = effeminate 2 = affected**, mannered, artificial, posturing, ostentatious

campaign 1 = drive, appeal, movement, push (*informal*), offensive, crusade **2 = operation**, drive, attack, movement, push, offensive, expedition, crusade

canal = waterway, channel, passage, conduit, duct, watercourse

cancel 1 = call off, drop, forget about **2 = annul**, abolish, repeal, abort, do away with, revoke, eliminate
▷ **PHRASES: cancel something out = counterbalance**, offset, make up for, compensate for, neutralize, nullify, balance out

cancellation 1 = abandonment 2 = annulment, abolition, repeal, elimination, revocation

cancer 1 = growth, tumour, malignancy **2 = evil**, corruption, sickness, pestilence

candidate = contender, competitor, applicant, nominee, entrant, claimant, contestant, runner

cannabis = marijuana, pot (*slang*), dope (*slang*), grass (*slang*), hemp, dagga (*S African*)

cannon = **gun**, big gun, field gun, mortar

canon 1 = **rule**, standard, principle, regulation, formula, criterion, dictate, statute 2 = **list**, index, catalogue, roll

canopy = **awning**, covering, shade, sunshade

cap 1 (*informal*) = **beat**, top, better, exceed, eclipse, surpass, transcend, outstrip 2 = **top**, crown 3 = **complete**, crown

capability = **ability**, means, power, potential, capacity, qualification(s), competence, proficiency **OPPOSITE:** inability

capable 1 = **able**, suited **OPPOSITE:** incapable 2 = **accomplished**, qualified, talented, gifted, efficient, competent, proficient **OPPOSITE:** incompetent

capacity 1 = **ability**, facility, gift, genius, capability, aptitude, aptness, competence *or* competency 2 = **size**, room, range, space, volume, extent, dimensions, scope 3 = **function**, position, role, post, office

cape = **headland**, point, head, peninsula, promontory

capital NOUN 1 = **money**, funds, investment(s), cash, finances, resources, assets, wealth ▷ ADJECTIVE 2 (*Old-fashioned*) = **first-rate**, fine, excellent, superb

capitalism = **private enterprise**, free enterprise, private ownership, laissez faire *or* laisser faire

capsule 1 = **pill**, tablet, lozenge 2 (*Botany*) = **pod**, case, shell, vessel, sheath, receptacle, seed case

captain 1 = **leader**, boss, master, skipper, head, chief 2 = **commander**, skipper

captivate = **charm**, attract, fascinate, entrance, enchant, enthral, beguile, allure **OPPOSITE:** repel

captive ADJECTIVE 1 = **confined**, caged, imprisoned, locked up, enslaved, incarcerated, ensnared, subjugated ▷ NOUN 2 = **prisoner**, hostage, convict, prisoner of war, detainee, internee

captivity = **confinement**, custody, detention, imprisonment, incarceration, internment

capture VERB 1 = **catch**, arrest, take, bag, secure, seize, collar (*informal*), apprehend **OPPOSITE:** release ▷ NOUN 2 = **arrest**, catching, trapping, imprisonment, seizure, apprehension, taking, taking captive

car 1 = **vehicle**, motor, wheels (*informal*), auto (*US*), automobile, jalopy (*informal*), motor car, machine 2 (*US & Canad*) = **(railway) carriage**, coach, cable car, dining car, sleeping car, buffet car, van

cardinal = **principal**, first, leading, chief, main, central, key, essential **OPPOSITE:** secondary

care VERB 1 = **be concerned**, mind, bother, be interested, be bothered, give a damn, concern yourself
▷ NOUN 2 = **custody**, keeping, control, charge, management, protection, supervision, guardianship 3 = **caution**, attention, pains, consideration, heed, prudence, vigilance, forethought **OPPOSITE:** carelessness 4 = **worry**, concern, pressure, trouble, responsibility, stress, anxiety, disquiet **OPPOSITE:** pleasure
▷ PHRASES: **care for someone** 1 = **look after**, mind, tend, attend, nurse, minister to, watch over 2 = **love**, desire, be fond of, want, prize ▸ **care for something** or **someone** = **like**, enjoy, take to, relish, be fond of, be keen on, be partial to ▸ **take care of something** or **someone** 1 = **look after**, mind, watch, protect, tend, nurse, care for, provide for 2 = **deal with**, manage, cope with, see to, handle

career NOUN 1 = **occupation**, calling, employment, pursuit, vocation, livelihood, life's work
▷ VERB 2 = **rush**, race, speed, tear, dash, barrel (along) (*informal, chiefly US & Canad*), bolt, hurtle

careful 1 = **cautious**, scrupulous, circumspect, chary, thoughtful, discreet **OPPOSITE:** careless 2 = **thorough**, full, particular, precise, intensive, in-depth, meticulous, conscientious **OPPOSITE:** casual 3 = **prudent**, sparing, economical, canny, provident, frugal, thrifty

careless 1 = **slapdash**, irresponsible, sloppy (*informal*), cavalier, offhand, neglectful, slipshod, lackadaisical **OPPOSITE:** careful 2 = **negligent**, hasty, thoughtless, unthinking, forgetful, absent-minded, remiss **OPPOSITE:** careful 3 = **nonchalant**, casual, offhand, artless, unstudied **OPPOSITE:** careful

caretaker = **warden**, keeper, porter, superintendent, curator, custodian, watchman, janitor

cargo = **load**, goods, contents, shipment, freight, merchandise, baggage, consignment

caricature NOUN 1 = **parody**, cartoon, distortion, satire, send-up (*Brit informal*), travesty, takeoff (*informal*), lampoon
▷ VERB 2 = **parody**, take off (*informal*), mock, distort, ridicule, mimic, send up (*Brit informal*), lampoon

carnage = **slaughter**, murder, massacre, holocaust, havoc, bloodshed, shambles, mass murder

carnival = **festival**, fair, fête, celebration, gala, jubilee, jamboree, revelry

carnivore
• See panel **CARNIVORES**

carol = **song**, hymn, Christmas song

carp = **find fault**, complain, criticize, reproach, quibble, cavil, pick holes, nit-pick (informal)
OPPOSITE: praise

carpenter = **joiner**, cabinet-maker, woodworker

carriage 1 = **vehicle**, coach, trap, gig, cab, wagon, hackney, conveyance 2 = **bearing**, posture, gait, deportment, air

carry 1 = **convey**, take, move, bring, bear, transfer, conduct, transport 2 = **transport**, take, transfer 3 = **transmit**, transfer, spread, pass on 4 = **win**, gain, secure, capture, accomplish
▷ **PHRASES: carry on**
1 = **continue**, last, endure, persist, keep going, persevere, crack on (informal) 2 (informal) = **make a fuss**, misbehave, create (slang), raise Cain ▶ **carry something on** = **engage in**, conduct, carry out, undertake, embark on, enter into ▶ **carry something out** = **perform**, effect, achieve, realize, implement, fulfil, accomplish, execute

carry-on (informal, chiefly Brit) = **fuss**, disturbance, racket, commotion

carton = **box**, case, pack, package, container

cartoon 1 = **drawing**, parody, satire, caricature, comic strip, takeoff (informal), lampoon, sketch 2 = **animation**, animated film, animated cartoon

carve 1 = **sculpt**, cut, chip, whittle, chisel, hew, fashion 2 = **etch**, engrave

---

CARNIVORES

aardwolf	catamount, catamountain, or cat-o'-mountain
arctic fox	
badger	cheetah or chetah
bear	cinnamon bear
binturong	civet
black bear	corsac
bobcat	coyote or prairie wolf
brown bear	dhole
cacomistle or cacomixle	dingo or (Austral) native dog or warrigal
caracal or desert lynx	
cat	dog

CARNIVORES *continued*

ermine
fennec
ferret
fox
genet *or* genette
giant panda
grey fox (*US*)
grey wolf *or* timber wolf
grison
grizzly bear *or* grizzly
hog badger
hognosed skunk
hyena *or* hyaena
ichneumon
jackal
jaguar
jaguarondi, jaguarundi, *or* (*Austral*) eyra
kinkajou, honey bear, *or* potto
Kodiak bear
kolinsky
laughing hyena *or* spotted hyena
leopard *or* panther
linsang
lion
lynx
margay
marten
meerkat
mink
mongoose
mountain lion
ocelot
otter
otter shrew

palm civet
panda
panther
pine marten *or* sweet marten
polar bear *or* (*N Canad*) nanook
polecat
prairie dog
puma *or* cougar
raccoon, racoon, *or* coon
raccoon dog
rasse
ratel
red fox
rooikat
sable
sea otter
serval
silver fox
skunk
sloth bear
snow leopard *or* ounce
stoat
stone marten
strandwolf
sun bear
swift fox *or* kit fox
tayra
teledu
tiger
tiger cat
weasel
wolf
wolverine, glutton, *or* carcajou
zibeline
zibet
zorilla *or* zorille

cascade NOUN 1 = **waterfall**, falls, torrent, flood, shower, fountain, avalanche, deluge
▷ VERB 2 = **flow**, fall, flood, pour, plunge, surge, spill, tumble

case¹ 1 = **situation**, event, circumstance(s), state, position, condition, context, contingency 2 = **instance**, example, occasion, specimen, occurrence 3 (*Law*) = **lawsuit**, trial, suit, proceedings, dispute, action

case² 1 = **cabinet**, box, chest, holder 2 = **container**, carton, canister, casket, receptacle 3 = **suitcase**, bag, grip, holdall, portmanteau, valise 4 = **crate**, box 5 = **covering**, casing, shell, jacket, envelope, capsule, sheath, wrapper

cash = **money**, funds, notes, currency, silver, brass (*Northern English dialect*), dough (*slang*), coinage

cast NOUN 1 = **actors**, company, players, characters, troupe, dramatis personae 2 = **type**, sort, kind, style, stamp
▷ VERB 3 = **choose**, name, pick, select, appoint, assign, allot 4 = **bestow**, give, level, direct 5 = **give out**, spread, deposit, shed, distribute, scatter, emit, radiate 6 = **throw**, launch, pitch, toss, thrust, hurl, fling, sling 7 = **mould**, set, found, form, model, shape

caste = **class**, order, rank, status, stratum, social order

castle = **fortress**, keep, palace, tower, chateau, stronghold, citadel

casual 1 = **careless**, relaxed, unconcerned, blasé, offhand, nonchalant, lackadaisical OPPOSITE: serious 2 = **chance**, unexpected, random, accidental, incidental OPPOSITE: planned 3 = **informal**, leisure, sporty, non-dressy OPPOSITE: formal

casualty 1 = **fatality**, death, loss, wounded 2 = **victim**, sufferer

cat = **feline**, pussy (*informal*), moggy (*slang*), puss (*informal*), ballarat (*Austral informal*), tabby

> **RELATED WORDS**
> *adjective:* feline
> *male:* tom
> *female:* queen
> *young:* kitten

catalogue or (*US*) **catalog** NOUN 1 = **list**, record, schedule, index, register, directory, inventory, gazetteer
▷ VERB 2 = **list**, file, index, register, classify, inventory, tabulate, alphabetize

catastrophe = **disaster**, tragedy, calamity, cataclysm, trouble, adversity, fiasco

catch VERB 1 = **capture**, arrest, trap, seize, snare, apprehend, ensnare, entrap OPPOSITE: free 2 = **trap**, capture, snare, ensnare, entrap 3 = **seize**, get, grab, snatch 4 = **grab**,

take, grip, seize, grasp, clutch, lay hold of **OPPOSITE:** release **5** = **discover**, surprise, find out, expose, detect, catch in the act, take unawares **6** = **contract**, get, develop, suffer from, incur, succumb to, go down with **OPPOSITE:** escape
▷ **NOUN 7** = **fastener**, clip, bolt, latch, clasp **8** (informal) = **drawback**, trick, trap, disadvantage, hitch, snag, stumbling block, fly in the ointment **OPPOSITE:** advantage
▷ **PHRASES: catch on 1** (informal) = **understand**, see, find out, grasp, see through, comprehend, twig (Brit informal), get the picture **2** = **become popular**, take off, become trendy, come into fashion

catchcry (Austral) = **catch phrase**, slogan, saying, quotation, motto

catching = **infectious**, contagious, transferable, communicable, transmittable **OPPOSITE:** non-infectious

category = **class**, grouping, heading, sort, department, type, division, section

cater
▷ **PHRASES: cater for something** or **someone 1** = **provide for**, supply, purvey **2** = **take into account**, consider, bear in mind, make allowance for, have regard for

cattle = **cows**, stock, beasts, livestock, bovines

▌ **RELATED WORDS**
adjective: bovine
collective nouns: drove, herd

cause NOUN 1 = **origin**, source, spring, agent, maker, producer, root, beginning **OPPOSITE:** result **2** = **reason**, call, need, grounds, basis, incentive, motive, motivation **3** = **aim**, movement; principle, ideal, enterprise
▷ **VERB 4** = **produce**, create, lead to, result in, generate, induce, bring about, give rise to **OPPOSITE:** prevent

caution NOUN 1 = **care**, discretion, heed, prudence, vigilance, alertness, forethought, circumspection **OPPOSITE:** carelessness **2** = **reprimand**, warning, injunction, admonition
▷ **VERB 3** = **warn**, urge, advise, alert, tip off, forewarn **4** = **reprimand**, warn, admonish, give an injunction to

cautious = **careful**, guarded, wary, tentative, prudent, judicious, circumspect, cagey (informal) **OPPOSITE:** careless

cavalry = **horsemen**, horse, mounted troops **OPPOSITE:** infantrymen

cave = **hollow**, cavern, grotto, den, cavity

cavity = **hollow**, hole, gap, pit, dent, crater

cease 1 = **stop**, end, finish, come to an end **OPPOSITE:** start 2 = **discontinue**, end, stop, finish, conclude, halt, terminate, break off **OPPOSITE:** begin

celebrate 1 = **rejoice**, party, enjoy yourself, carouse, live it up (*informal*), make merry, put the flags out, kill the fatted calf 2 = **commemorate**, honour, observe, toast, drink to, keep 3 = **perform**, observe, preside over, officiate at, solemnize

celebrated = **renowned**, popular, famous, distinguished, well-known, prominent, acclaimed, notable **OPPOSITE:** unknown

celebration 1 = **party**, festival, gala, jubilee, festivity, revelry, red-letter day, merrymaking 2 = **commemoration**, honouring, remembrance 3 = **performance**, observance, solemnization

celebrity 1 = **personality**, star, superstar, big name, dignitary, luminary, big shot (*informal*), V.I.P. **OPPOSITE:** nobody 2 = **fame**, reputation, distinction, prestige, prominence, stardom, renown, repute **OPPOSITE:** obscurity

cell 1 = **room**, chamber, lock-up, compartment, cavity, cubicle, dungeon, stall 2 = **unit**, group, section, core, nucleus, caucus, coterie

cement NOUN 1 = **mortar**, plaster, paste 2 = **sealant**, glue, gum, adhesive
▷ VERB 3 = **stick**, join, bond, attach, seal, glue, plaster, weld

cemetery = **graveyard**, churchyard, burial ground, necropolis, God's acre

censor = **expurgate**, cut, blue-pencil, bowdlerize

censure VERB 1 = **criticize**, blame, condemn, denounce, rebuke, reprimand, reproach, scold **OPPOSITE:** applaud
▷ NOUN 2 = **disapproval**, criticism, blame, condemnation, rebuke, reprimand, reproach, stick (*slang*) **OPPOSITE:** approval

central 1 = **inner**, middle, mid, interior **OPPOSITE:** outer 2 = **main**, chief, key, essential, primary, principal, fundamental, focal **OPPOSITE:** minor

centre = **middle**, heart, focus, core, nucleus, hub, pivot, kernel **OPPOSITE:** edge
▷ PHRASES: centre on something *or* someone = **focus**, concentrate, cluster, revolve, converge

ceremonial ADJECTIVE 1 = **formal**, public, official, ritual, stately, solemn, liturgical, courtly **OPPOSITE:** informal
▷ NOUN 2 = **ritual**, ceremony, rite, formality, solemnity

ceremony 1 = **ritual**, service, rite, observance, commemoration, solemnities

C

2 = **formality**, ceremonial, propriety, decorum

certain 1 = **sure**, convinced, positive, confident, satisfied, assured **OPPOSITE:** unsure 2 = **bound**, sure, fated, destined **OPPOSITE:** unlikely 3 = **inevitable**, unavoidable, inescapable 4 = **known**, true, positive, conclusive, unequivocal, undeniable, irrefutable, unquestionable, nailed-on (*slang*) **OPPOSITE:** doubtful 5 = **fixed**, decided, established, settled, definite **OPPOSITE:** indefinite

certainly = **definitely**, surely, truly, undoubtedly, without doubt, undeniably, indisputably, assuredly

certainty 1 = **confidence**, trust, faith, conviction, assurance, sureness, positiveness **OPPOSITE:** doubt 2 = **inevitability OPPOSITE:** uncertainty 3 = **fact**, truth, reality, sure thing (*informal*), banker

certificate = **document**, licence, warrant, voucher, diploma, testimonial, authorization, credential(s)

certify = **confirm**, declare, guarantee, assure, testify, verify, validate, attest

chain NOUN 1 = **tether**, coupling, link, bond, shackle, fetter, manacle 2 = **series**, set, train, string, sequence,

succession, progression ▷ VERB 3 = **bind**, confine, restrain, handcuff, shackle, tether, fetter, manacle

chairman *or* **chairwoman** 1 = **director**, president, chief, executive, chairperson 2 = **master of ceremonies**, spokesman, chair, speaker, MC, chairperson

> **USAGE NOTE**
> The general trend of nonsexist language is to find a term which can apply to both sexes equally, as in the use of *actor* to refer to both men and women. *Chairman* can seem inappropriate when applied to a woman, while *chairwoman* specifies gender, therefore the terms *chair* and *chairperson* are often preferred as alternatives.

challenge NOUN 1 = **dare**, provocation, wero (*NZ*) 2 = **test**, trial, opposition, confrontation, ultimatum ▷ VERB 3 = **dispute**, question, tackle, confront, defy, object to, disagree with, take issue with 4 = **dare**, invite, defy, throw down the gauntlet 5 = **test** 6 = **question**, interrogate

chamber 1 = **hall**, room 2 = **council**, assembly, legislature, legislative body 3 = **room**, bedroom, apartment, enclosure, cubicle 4 = **compartment**

champion NOUN 1 = **winner**, hero, victor, conqueror, title holder 2 = **defender**, guardian, patron, backer, protector, upholder
▷ VERB 3 = **support**, back, defend, promote, advocate, fight for, uphold, espouse

chance NOUN 1 = **probability**, odds, possibility, prospect, likelihood OPPOSITE: certainty 2 = **opportunity**, opening, occasion, time 3 = **accident**, fortune, luck, fate, destiny, coincidence, providence OPPOSITE: design 4 = **risk**, speculation, gamble, hazard
▷ VERB 5 = **risk**, try, stake, venture, gamble, hazard, wager

change NOUN 1 = **alteration**, innovation, transformation, modification, mutation, metamorphosis, difference, revolution 2 = **variety**, break (informal), departure, variation, novelty, diversion OPPOSITE: monotony 3 = **exchange**, trade, conversion, swap, substitution, interchange
▷ VERB 4 = **alter**, reform, transform, adjust, revise, modify, reorganize, restyle OPPOSITE: keep 5 = **shift**, vary, transform, alter, modify, mutate OPPOSITE: stay 6 = **exchange**, trade, replace, substitute, swap, interchange

channel NOUN 1 = **means**, way, course, approach, medium, route, path, avenue 2 = **strait**, sound, route, passage, canal, waterway 3 = **duct**, artery, groove, gutter, furrow, conduit
▷ VERB 4 = **direct**, guide, conduct, transmit, convey

chant NOUN 1 = **song**, carol, chorus, melody, psalm
▷ VERB 2 = **sing**, chorus, recite, intone, carol

chaos = **disorder**, confusion, mayhem, anarchy, lawlessness, pandemonium, bedlam, tumult OPPOSITE: orderliness

chaotic = **disordered**, confused, uncontrolled, anarchic, tumultuous, lawless, riotous, topsy-turvy

chap (informal) = **fellow**, man, person, individual, character, guy (informal), bloke (Brit informal)

chapter 1 = **section**, part, stage, division, episode, topic, segment, instalment 2 = **period**, time, stage, phase

character 1 = **personality**, nature, attributes, temperament, complexion, disposition 2 = **nature**, kind, quality, calibre 3 = **reputation**, honour, integrity, good name, rectitude 4 = **role**, part, persona 5 = **eccentric**, card (informal), original, oddball (informal) 6 = **symbol**, mark, sign, letter, figure, device, rune, hieroglyph

characteristic NOUN
1 = **feature**, mark, quality,

property, attribute, faculty,
trait, quirk
▷ ADJECTIVE 2 = **typical**, special,
individual, representative,
distinguishing, distinctive,
peculiar, singular **OPPOSITE:** rare

characterize = **distinguish**,
mark, identify, brand, stamp,
typify

charge VERB 1 = **accuse**, indict,
impeach, incriminate, arraign
OPPOSITE: acquit 2 = **attack**,
assault, assail **OPPOSITE:** retreat
3 = **rush**, storm, stampede
4 = **fill**, load
▷ NOUN 5 = **price**, rate, cost,
amount, payment, expense, toll,
expenditure 6 = **accusation**,
allegation, indictment,
imputation **OPPOSITE:** acquittal
7 = **care**, trust, responsibility,
custody, safekeeping 8 = **duty**,
office, responsibility, remit
9 = **ward**, pupil, protégé,
dependant 10 = **attack**, rush,
assault, onset, onslaught,
stampede, sortie **OPPOSITE:**
retreat

charisma = **charm**, appeal,
personality, attraction, lure,
allure, magnetism, force of
personality, mojo (*slang*)

charismatic = **charming**,
appealing, attractive,
influential, magnetic, enticing,
alluring

charitable 1 = **benevolent**,
liberal, generous, lavish,
philanthropic, bountiful,

beneficent **OPPOSITE:** mean
2 = **kind**, understanding,
forgiving, sympathetic,
favourable, tolerant, indulgent,
lenient **OPPOSITE:** unkind

charity 1 = **charitable
organization**, fund,
movement, trust, endowment
2 = **donations**, help, relief,
gift, contributions, assistance,
hand-out, philanthropy, koha
(*NZ*) **OPPOSITE:** meanness
3 = **kindness**, humanity,
goodwill, compassion,
generosity, indulgence,
altruism, benevolence, aroha
(*NZ*) **OPPOSITE:** ill will

charm NOUN 1 = **attraction**,
appeal, fascination, allure,
magnetism **OPPOSITE:**
repulsiveness 2 = **trinket**
3 = **talisman**, amulet, fetish
4 = **spell**, magic, enchantment,
sorcery, makutu (*NZ*)
▷ VERB 5 = **attract**, delight,
fascinate, entrance, win over,
enchant, captivate, beguile
OPPOSITE: repel 6 = **persuade**,
seduce, coax, beguile, sweet-
talk (*informal*)

charming = **attractive**, pleasing,
appealing, fetching, delightful,
cute, seductive, captivating
OPPOSITE: unpleasant

chart NOUN 1 = **table**, diagram,
blueprint, graph, plan, map
▷ VERB 2 = **plot**, map out,
delineate, sketch, draft,
tabulate 3 = **monitor**, follow,

record, note, document, register, trace, outline

charter NOUN 1 = **document**, contract, permit, licence, deed, prerogative 2 = **constitution**, laws, rules, code
▷ VERB 3 = **hire**, commission, employ, rent, lease 4 = **authorize**, permit, sanction, entitle, license, empower, give authority

chase VERB 1 = **pursue**, follow, track, hunt, run after, course 2 = **drive away**, drive, expel, hound, send away, send packing, put to flight 3 (*informal*) = **rush**, run, race, shoot, fly, speed, dash, bolt
▷ NOUN 4 = **pursuit**, race, hunt, hunting

chat VERB 1 = **talk**, gossip, jaw (*slang*), natter, blather, blether (*Scot*)
▷ NOUN 2 = **talk**, tête-à-tête, conversation, gossip, heart-to-heart, natter, blather, blether (*Scot*), korero (*NZ*)

chatter VERB 1 = **prattle**, chat, rabbit on (*Brit informal*), babble, gab (*informal*), natter, blather, schmooze (*slang*)
▷ NOUN 2 = **prattle**, chat, gossip, babble, gab (*informal*), natter, blather, blether (*Scot*)

cheap 1 = **inexpensive**, reduced, keen, reasonable, bargain, low-priced, low-cost, cut-price **OPPOSITE:** expensive 2 = **inferior**, poor, worthless, second-rate, shoddy, tawdry, tatty, trashy, bodger *or* bodgie (*Austral slang*) **OPPOSITE:** good 3 (*informal*) = **despicable**, mean, contemptible, scungy (*Austral & NZ*) **OPPOSITE:** decent

cheat VERB 1 = **deceive**, trick, fool, con (*informal*), mislead, rip off (*slang*), fleece, defraud, scam (*slang*)
▷ NOUN 2 = **deceiver**, sharper, shark, charlatan, trickster, con man (*informal*), double-crosser (*informal*), swindler, rorter (*Austral slang*), rogue trader

check VERB 1 *often with* **out** = **examine**, test, study, look at, research, investigate, monitor, vet, parse (~*computer code*) **OPPOSITE:** overlook 2 = **stop**, limit, delay, halt, restrain, inhibit, hinder, obstruct **OPPOSITE:** further
▷ NOUN 3 = **examination**, test, research, investigation, inspection, scrutiny, once-over (*informal*) 4 = **control**, limitation, restraint, constraint, obstacle, curb, obstruction, stoppage

cheek (*informal*) = **impudence**, nerve, disrespect, audacity, lip (*slang*), temerity, chutzpah (*US & Canad informal*), insolence

cheeky = **impudent**, rude, forward, insulting, saucy, audacious, pert, disrespectful **OPPOSITE:** respectful

cheer VERB 1 = **applaud**, hail, acclaim, clap **OPPOSITE:** boo

C

2 = **hearten**, encourage, comfort, uplift, brighten, cheer up, buoy up, gladden **OPPOSITE:** dishearten
▷ **NOUN** 3 = **applause**, ovation
▷ **PHRASES: cheer someone up** = **comfort**, encourage, hearten, enliven, gladden, gee up, jolly along (*informal*) ▶ **cheer up** = **take heart**, rally, perk up, buck up (*informal*)

cheerful 1 = **happy**, optimistic, enthusiastic, jolly, merry, upbeat (*informal*), buoyant, cheery **OPPOSITE:** sad 2 = **pleasant** **OPPOSITE:** gloomy

chemical = **compound**, drug, substance, synthetic substance, potion

chemist = **pharmacist**, apothecary (*obsolete*), dispenser

cherish 1 = **cling to**, prize, treasure, hold dear, cleave to **OPPOSITE:** despise 2 = **care for**, love, support, comfort, look after, shelter, nurture, hold dear **OPPOSITE:** neglect 3 = **harbour**, nurse, sustain, foster, entertain

chest 1 = **breast**, front 2 = **box**, case, trunk, crate, coffer, casket, strongbox

> **RELATED WORD**
> *adjective:* pectoral

chew = **munch**, bite, grind, champ, crunch, gnaw, chomp, masticate

chic = **stylish**, smart, elegant, fashionable, trendy (*Brit informal*), schmick (*Austral informal*) **OPPOSITE:** unfashionable

chief NOUN 1 = **head**, leader, director, manager, boss (*informal*), captain, master, governor, baas (*S African*), ariki (*NZ*), sherang (*Austral & NZ*) **OPPOSITE:** subordinate
▷ **ADJECTIVE** 2 = **primary**, highest, leading, main, prime, key, premier, supreme **OPPOSITE:** minor

chiefly 1 = **especially**, essentially, principally, primarily, above all 2 = **mainly**, largely, usually, mostly, in general, on the whole, predominantly, in the main

child 1 = **youngster**, baby, kid (*informal*), infant, babe, juvenile, toddler, tot, littlie (*Austral informal*), ankle-biter (*Austral & US slang*), tacker (*Austral slang*) 2 = **offspring**

> **RELATED WORDS**
> *adjective:* filial
> *prefix:* paedo-

childbirth = **child-bearing**, labour, delivery, lying-in, confinement, parturition

childhood = **youth**, minority, infancy, schooldays, immaturity, boyhood *or* girlhood

childish 1 = **youthful**, young, boyish *or* girlish 2 = **immature**, juvenile, foolish, infantile, puerile **OPPOSITE:** mature

chill VERB 1 = **cool**, refrigerate, freeze 2 = **dishearten**, depress, discourage, dismay, dampen, deject

▷ NOUN 3 = **coldness**, bite, nip, sharpness, coolness, rawness, crispness, frigidity 4 = **shiver**, frisson

▷ ADJECTIVE 5 = **chilly**, biting, sharp, freezing, raw, bleak, wintry

chilly 1 = **cool**, fresh, sharp, crisp, penetrating, brisk, draughty, nippy **OPPOSITE:** warm 2 = **unfriendly**, hostile, unsympathetic, frigid, unresponsive, unwelcoming **OPPOSITE:** friendly

china¹ = pottery, ceramics, ware, porcelain, crockery, tableware, service

china² (*Brit & S African informal*) = **friend**, pal, mate (*informal*), buddy (*informal*), companion, best friend, intimate, comrade, cobber (*Austral & NZ old-fashioned informal*), E hoa (*NZ*)

chip NOUN 1 = **fragment**, shaving, wafer, sliver, shard 2 = **scratch**, nick, notch 3 = **counter**, disc, token
▷ VERB 4 = **nick**, damage, gash 5 = **chisel**, whittle

choice NOUN 1 = **range**, variety, selection, assortment 2 = **selection**, preference, pick 3 = **option**, say, alternative
▷ ADJECTIVE 4 = **best**, prime, select, excellent, exclusive, elite, booshit (*Austral slang*), exo (*Austral slang*), sik (*Austral slang*),

rad (*informal*), phat (*slang*), schmick (*Austral informal*)

choke 1 = **suffocate**, stifle, smother, overpower, asphyxiate 2 = **strangle**, throttle, asphyxiate 3 = **block**, clog, obstruct, bung, constrict, congest, stop, bar

choose 1 = **pick**, prefer, select, elect, adopt, opt for, designate, settle upon **OPPOSITE:** reject 2 = **wish**, want

chop = cut, fell, hack, sever, cleave, hew, lop

chore = task, job, duty, burden, hassle (*informal*), errand

chorus 1 = **refrain**, response, strain, burden 2 = **choir**, singers, ensemble, vocalists, choristers
▷ PHRASES: in chorus = in unison, as one, all together, in concert, in harmony, in accord, with one voice

christen 1 = **baptize**, name 2 = **name**, call, term, style, title, dub, designate

Christmas = the festive season, Noël, Xmas (*informal*), Yule (*archaic*), Yuletide (*archaic*)

chronicle VERB 1 = **record**, tell, report, enter, relate, register, recount, set down
▷ NOUN 2 = **record**, story, history, account, register, journal, diary, narrative, blog (*informal*)

chuck 1 (*informal*) = **throw**, cast, pitch, toss, hurl, fling, sling, heave 2 (*informal*) often with

away *or* **out** = **throw out**, dump
(*informal*), scrap, get rid of, ditch
(*slang*), dispose of, dispense
with, jettison 3 (*informal*) = **give
up** *or* **over**, leave, abandon,
cease, resign from, pack in
4 (*slang*) = **vomit**, throw up
(*informal*), spew, heave (*slang*),
puke (*slang*), barf (*US slang*),
chunder (*slang, chiefly Austral*)

chuckle VERB 1 = **laugh**, giggle,
snigger, chortle, titter
▷ NOUN 2 = **laugh**, giggle,
snigger, chortle, titter

chum (*informal*) = **friend**,
mate (*informal*), pal (*informal*),
companion, comrade, crony,
cobber (*Austral & NZ old-fashioned
informal*), E hoa (*NZ*)

chunk = **piece**, block, mass,
portion, lump, slab, hunk,
nugget

churn 1 = **stir up**, beat, disturb,
swirl, agitate 2 = **swirl**, toss

cinema 1 = **pictures**, movies,
picture-house, flicks (*slang*)
2 = **films**, pictures, movies, the
big screen (*informal*), motion
pictures, the silver screen

circle NOUN 1 = **ring**, disc, hoop,
halo 2 = **group**, company, set,
club, society, clique, coterie
▷ VERB 3 = **go round**, ring,
surround, enclose, envelop,
encircle, circumscribe,
circumnavigate 4 = **wheel**,
spiral

circuit 1 = **course**, tour, track,
route, journey 2 = **racetrack**,

course, track, racecourse
3 = **lap**, tour, revolution, orbit

circular ADJECTIVE 1 = **round**,
ring-shaped 2 = **circuitous**,
cyclical, orbital
▷ NOUN 3 = **advertisement**,
notice, ad (*informal*),
announcement, advert (*Brit
informal*), press release

circulate 1 = **spread**, issue,
publish, broadcast, distribute,
publicize, disseminate,
promulgate 2 = **flow**, revolve,
rotate, radiate

circulation 1 = **distribution**,
currency, readership
2 = **bloodstream**, blood
flow 3 = **flow**, circling,
motion, rotation 4 = **spread**,
distribution, transmission,
dissemination

circumstance 1 *usually
plural* = **condition**, situation,
contingency, state of affairs, lie of
the land 2 *usually plural* = **detail**,
event, particular, respect
3 *usually plural* = **situation**, state,
means, position, station, status
4 = **chance**, the times, accident,
fortune, luck, fate, destiny,
providence

cite = **quote**, name, advance,
mention, extract, specify, allude
to, enumerate

citizen = **inhabitant**, resident,
dweller, denizen, subject,
townsman

▌ **RELATED WORD**
▌ *adjective*: civil

city = **town**, metropolis, municipality, conurbation

RELATED WORD
adjective: civic

civic = **public**, municipal, communal, local

civil 1 = **civic**, political, domestic, municipal **OPPOSITE:** state
2 = **polite**, obliging, courteous, considerate, affable, well-mannered **OPPOSITE:** rude

civilization 1 = **society**, people, community, nation, polity
2 = **culture**, development, education, progress, enlightenment, sophistication, advancement, cultivation

civilize = **cultivate**, educate, refine, tame, enlighten, sophisticate

civilized 1 = **cultured**, educated, sophisticated, enlightened, humane **OPPOSITE:** primitive
2 = **polite**, mannerly, tolerant, gracious, courteous, well-behaved, well-mannered

claim VERB 1 = **assert**, insist, maintain, allege, uphold, profess
2 = **demand**, call for, ask for, insist on
▷ NOUN 3 = **assertion**, statement, allegation, declaration, pretension, affirmation, protestation 4 = **demand**, application, request, petition, call
5 = **right**, title, entitlement

clamour = **noise**, shouting, racket, outcry, din, uproar, commotion, hubbub

clamp NOUN 1 = **vice**, press, grip, bracket, fastener
▷ VERB 2 = **fasten**, fix, secure, brace, make fast

clan 1 = **family**, group, society, tribe, fraternity, brotherhood, ainga (*NZ*), ngai *or* ngati (*NZ*)
2 = **group**, set, circle, gang, faction, coterie, cabal

clap = **applaud**, cheer, acclaim **OPPOSITE:** boo

clarify = **explain**, interpret, illuminate, clear up, simplify, make plain, elucidate, throw *or* shed light on

clarity 1 = **clearness**, precision, simplicity, transparency, lucidity, straightforwardness **OPPOSITE:** obscurity
2 = **transparency**, clearness **OPPOSITE:** cloudiness

clash VERB 1 = **conflict**, grapple, wrangle, lock horns, cross swords, war, feud, quarrel
2 = **disagree**, conflict, vary, counter, differ, contradict, diverge, run counter to 3 = **not go**, jar, not match 4 = **crash**, bang, rattle, jar, clatter, jangle, clang, clank
▷ NOUN 5 = **conflict**, fight, brush, confrontation, collision, showdown (*informal*), boilover (*Austral*) 6 = **disagreement**, difference, argument, dispute, dissent, difference of opinion

clasp VERB 1 = **grasp**, hold, press, grip, seize, squeeze, embrace, clutch

▷ NOUN 2 = **grasp**, hold, grip, embrace, hug 3 = **fastening**, catch, grip, hook, pin, clip, buckle, brooch

class NOUN 1 = **group**, set, division, rank 2 = **type**, set, sort, kind, category, genre
▷ VERB 3 = **classify**, group, rate, rank, brand, label, grade, designate

classic ADJECTIVE 1 = **typical**, standard, model, regular, usual, ideal, characteristic, definitive, dinki-di (*Austral informal*) 2 = **masterly**, best, finest, world-class, consummate, first-rate **OPPOSITE**: second-rate 3 = **lasting**, enduring, abiding, immortal, undying, ageless, deathless
▷ NOUN 4 = **standard**, masterpiece, prototype, paradigm, exemplar, model

classification
1 = **categorization**, grading, taxonomy, sorting, analysis, arrangement, profiling
2 = **class**, grouping, heading, sort, department, type, division, section

classify = **categorize**, sort, rank, arrange, grade, catalogue, pigeonhole, tabulate

classy (*informal*) = **high-class**, exclusive, superior, elegant, stylish, posh (*informal*, *chiefly Brit*), up-market, top-drawer, schmick (*Austral informal*)

clause = **section**, condition, article, chapter, passage, part, paragraph

claw NOUN 1 = **nail**, talon
2 = **pincer**
▷ VERB 3 = **scratch**, tear, dig, rip, scrape, maul, mangulate (*Austral slang*), lacerate

clean ADJECTIVE 1 = **hygienic**, fresh, sterile, pure, purified, antiseptic, sterilized, uncontaminated **OPPOSITE**: contaminated 2 = **spotless**, fresh, immaculate, impeccable, flawless, unblemished, unsullied **OPPOSITE**: dirty
3 = **moral**, good, pure, decent, innocent, respectable, upright, honourable **OPPOSITE**: immoral
4 = **complete**, final, whole, total, perfect, entire, decisive, thorough
▷ VERB 5 = **cleanse**, wash, scrub, rinse, launder, scour, purify, disinfect **OPPOSITE**: dirty

cleanse 1 = **purify**, clear, purge
2 = **absolve**, clear, purge, purify
3 = **clean**, wash, scrub, rinse, scour

clear ADJECTIVE
1 = **comprehensible**, explicit, understandable **OPPOSITE**: confused 2 = **distinct OPPOSITE**: indistinct 3 = **obvious**, plain, apparent, evident, distinct, pronounced, manifest, blatant **OPPOSITE**: ambiguous
4 = **certain**, sure, convinced, positive, satisfied, resolved, definite, decided **OPPOSITE**:

confused 5 = **transparent**, see-through, translucent, crystalline, glassy, limpid, pellucid **OPPOSITE:** opaque 6 = **unobstructed**, open, free, empty, unhindered, unimpeded **OPPOSITE:** blocked 7 = **bright**, fine, fair, shining, sunny, luminous, cloudless, light **OPPOSITE:** cloudy 8 = **untroubled**, clean, pure, innocent, immaculate, unblemished, untarnished ▷ VERB 9 = **unblock**, free, loosen, extricate, open, disentangle 10 = **remove**, clean, wipe, cleanse, tidy (up), sweep away 11 = **brighten**, break up, lighten 12 = **pass over**, jump, leap, vault, miss 13 = **absolve**, acquit, vindicate, exonerate **OPPOSITE:** blame

clear-cut = **straightforward**, specific, plain, precise, black-and-white, explicit, definite, unequivocal

clearly 1 = **obviously**, undoubtedly, evidently, distinctly, markedly, overtly, undeniably, beyond doubt 2 = **legibly**, distinctly 3 = **audibly**, distinctly, intelligibly, comprehensibly

clergy = **priesthood**, ministry, clerics, clergymen, churchmen, the cloth, holy orders

clever 1 = **intelligent**, bright, talented, gifted, smart, knowledgeable, quick-witted

OPPOSITE: stupid 2 = **shrewd**, bright, ingenious, resourceful, canny **OPPOSITE:** unimaginative 3 = **skilful**, talented, gifted **OPPOSITE:** inept

cliché = **platitude**, stereotype, commonplace, banality, truism, hackneyed phrase

client = **customer**, consumer, buyer, patron, shopper, patient

cliff = **rock face**, overhang, crag, precipice, escarpment, scar, bluff

climate = **weather**, temperature

climax = **culmination**, top, summit, height, highlight, peak, high point, zenith

climb 1 = **ascend**, scale, mount, go up, clamber, shin up 2 = **clamber**, descend, scramble, dismount 3 = **rise**, go up, soar, ascend, fly up ▷ PHRASES: climb down = **back down**, withdraw, yield, concede, retreat, surrender, give in, cave in (*informal*)

clinch 1 = **secure**, close, confirm, conclude, seal, sew up (*informal*), set the seal on 2 = **settle**, decide, determine

cling 1 = **clutch**, grip, embrace, grasp, hug, hold on to, clasp 2 = **stick to**, adhere to

clinical = **unemotional**, cold, scientific, objective, detached, analytic, impersonal, dispassionate

clip¹ VERB 1 = **trim**, cut, crop, prune, shorten, shear, snip,

pare 2 (*informal*) = **smack**, strike, knock, punch, thump, clout (*informal*), cuff, whack
▷ NOUN 3 (*informal*) = **smack**, strike, knock, punch, thump, clout (*informal*), cuff, whack

clip² = **attach**, fix, secure, connect, pin, staple, fasten, hold

cloak NOUN 1 = **cape**, coat, wrap, mantle 2 = **covering**, layer, blanket, shroud
▷ VERB 3 = **cover**, coat, wrap, blanket, shroud, envelop
4 = **hide**, cover, screen, mask, disguise, conceal, obscure, veil

clog = **obstruct**, block, jam, hinder, impede, congest

close¹ 1 = **near**, neighbouring, nearby, handy, adjacent, adjoining, cheek by jowl
OPPOSITE: far 2 = **intimate**, loving, familiar, thick (*informal*), attached, devoted, confidential, inseparable OPPOSITE: distant
3 = **noticeable**, marked, strong, distinct, pronounced
4 = **careful**, detailed, intense, minute, thorough, rigorous, painstaking 5 = **even**, level, neck and neck, fifty-fifty (*informal*), evenly matched 6 = **imminent**, near, impending, at hand, nigh
OPPOSITE: far away 7 = **stifling**, oppressive, suffocating, stuffy, humid, sweltering, airless, muggy OPPOSITE: airy

close² VERB 1 = **shut**, lock, fasten, secure OPPOSITE: open
2 = **shut down**, finish, cease

3 = **wind up**, finish, shut down, terminate 4 = **block up**, bar, seal OPPOSITE: open 5 = **end**, finish, complete, conclude, wind up, terminate OPPOSITE: begin
6 = **clinch**, confirm, secure, conclude, seal, sew up (*informal*), set the seal on 7 = **come together**, join, connect
OPPOSITE: separate
▷ NOUN 8 = **end**, ending, finish, conclusion, completion, finale, culmination, denouement

closed 1 = **shut**, locked, sealed, fastened OPPOSITE: open
2 = **shut down**, out of service
3 = **exclusive**, select, restricted
4 = **finished**, over, ended, decided, settled, concluded, resolved, terminated

cloth = **fabric**, material, textiles

clothe = **dress**, array, robe, drape, swathe, attire, fit out, garb OPPOSITE: undress

clothes = **clothing**, wear, dress, gear (*informal*), outfit, costume, wardrobe, garments

clothing = **clothes**, wear, dress, gear (*informal*), outfit, costume, wardrobe, garments

cloud NOUN 1 = **mist**, haze, vapour, murk, gloom
▷ VERB 2 = **confuse**, distort, impair, muddle, disorient 3 = **darken**, dim, be overshadowed

clout (*informal*) VERB 1 = **hit**, strike, punch, slap, sock (*slang*), smack, thump, clobber (*slang*)

▷ NOUN 2 = **thump**, blow, punch, slap, sock (*slang*), wallop (*informal*) 3 = **influence**, power, authority, pull, weight, prestige, mana (*NZ*)

clown NOUN 1 = **comedian**, fool, harlequin, jester, buffoon 2 = **joker**, comic, prankster 3 = **fool**, idiot, twit (*informal, chiefly Brit*), imbecile (*informal*), ignoramus, dolt, blockhead, dorba *or* dorb (*Austral slang*), bogan (*Austral slang*)
▷ VERB 4 usually with **around** = **play the fool**, mess about, jest, act the fool

club NOUN 1 = **association**, company, group, union, society, lodge, guild, fraternity 2 = **stick**, bat, bludgeon, truncheon, cosh (*Brit*), cudgel
▷ VERB 3 = **beat**, strike, hammer, batter, bash, bludgeon, pummel, cosh (*Brit*)

clue = **indication**, lead, sign, evidence, suggestion, trace, hint, suspicion

clump NOUN 1 = **cluster**, group, bunch, bundle
▷ VERB 2 = **stomp**, thump, lumber, tramp, plod, thud

clumsy = **awkward**, lumbering, bumbling, ponderous, ungainly, gauche, gawky, uncoordinated, unco (*Austral slang*) OPPOSITE: skilful

cluster NOUN 1 = **gathering**, group, collection, bunch, knot, clump, assemblage

▷ VERB 2 = **gather**, group, collect, bunch, assemble, flock, huddle

clutch VERB 1 = **hold**, grip, embrace, grasp, cling to, clasp 2 = **seize**, catch, grab, grasp, snatch
▷ PLURAL NOUN 3 = **power**, hands, control, grip, possession, grasp, custody, sway

clutter NOUN 1 = **untidiness**, mess, disorder, confusion, litter, muddle, disarray, jumble OPPOSITE: order
▷ VERB 2 = **litter**, scatter, strew, mess up OPPOSITE: tidy

coach NOUN 1 = **instructor**, teacher, trainer, tutor, handler 2 = **bus**, charabanc
▷ VERB 3 = **instruct**, train, prepare, exercise, drill, tutor

coalition = **alliance**, union, association, combination, merger, conjunction, bloc, confederation

coarse 1 = **rough**, crude, unfinished, homespun, impure, unrefined, unprocessed, unpolished OPPOSITE: smooth 2 = **vulgar**, rude, indecent, improper, earthy, smutty, ribald, indelicate

coast NOUN 1 = **shore**, border, beach, seaside, coastline, seaboard
▷ VERB 2 = **cruise**, sail, drift, taxi, glide, freewheel

coat NOUN 1 = **fur**, hair, skin, hide, wool, fleece, pelt 2 = **layer**,

covering, coating, overlay
▷ **VERB** 3 = **cover**, spread, plaster, smear

coax = **persuade**, cajole, talk into, wheedle, sweet-talk (*informal*), prevail upon, entice, allure **OPPOSITE:** bully

cobber (*Austral & NZ old-fashioned informal*) = **friend**, pal, mate (*informal*), buddy (*informal*), china (*Brit & S African informal*), best friend, intimate, comrade, E hoa (*NZ*)

cocktail = **mixture**, combination, compound, blend, mix

cocky *or* **cockie** = **farmer**, smallholder, crofter (*Scot*), grazier, agriculturalist, rancher

code 1 = **principles**, rules, manners, custom, convention, ethics, maxim, etiquette, kawa (*NZ*), tikanga (*NZ*) 2 = **cipher**, cryptograph

coherent 1 = **consistent**, reasoned, organized, rational, logical, meaningful, systematic, orderly **OPPOSITE:** inconsistent 2 = **articulate**, lucid, comprehensible, intelligible **OPPOSITE:** unintelligible

coil 1 = **wind**, twist, curl, loop, spiral, twine 2 = **curl**, wind, twist, snake, loop, twine, wreathe

coin **NOUN** 1 = **money**, change, cash, silver, copper, specie, kembla (*Austral slang*)
▷ **VERB** 2 = **invent**, create, make up, forge, originate, fabricate

coincide 1 = **occur simultaneously**, coexist, synchronize, be concurrent 2 = **agree**, match, accord, square, correspond, tally, concur, harmonize **OPPOSITE:** disagree

coincidence = **chance**, accident, luck, fluke, stroke of luck, happy accident

cold **ADJECTIVE** 1 = **chilly**, freezing, bleak, arctic, icy, frosty, wintry, frigid **OPPOSITE:** hot 2 = **distant**, reserved, indifferent, aloof, frigid, undemonstrative, standoffish **OPPOSITE:** emotional 3 = **unfriendly**, indifferent, frigid **OPPOSITE:** friendly ▷ **NOUN** 4 = **coldness**, chill, frigidity, frostiness, iciness

collaborate 1 = **work together**, team up, join forces, cooperate, play ball (*informal*), participate 2 = **conspire**, cooperate, collude, fraternize

collaboration 1 = **teamwork**, partnership, cooperation, association, alliance 2 = **conspiring**, cooperation, collusion, fraternization

collaborator 1 = **co-worker**, partner, colleague, associate, team-mate, confederate 2 = **traitor**, turncoat, quisling, fraternizer

collapse **VERB** 1 = **fall down**, fall, give way, subside, cave in, crumple, fall apart at the seams

2 = **fail**, fold, founder, break down, fall through, come to nothing, go belly-up (*informal*)
▷ NOUN 3 = **falling down**, ruin, falling apart, cave-in, disintegration, subsidence
4 = **failure**, slump, breakdown, flop, downfall 5 = **faint**, breakdown, blackout, prostration

collar (*informal*) = **seize**, catch, arrest, grab, capture, nail (*informal*), nab (*informal*), apprehend

colleague = **fellow worker**, partner, ally, associate, assistant, team-mate, comrade, helper

collect 1 = **gather**, save, assemble, heap, accumulate, amass, stockpile, hoard
OPPOSITE: scatter 2 = **assemble**, meet, rally, cluster, come together, convene, converge, congregate **OPPOSITE:** disperse

collected = **calm**, cool, composed, poised, serene, unperturbed, unruffled, self-possessed, chilled (*informal*)
OPPOSITE: nervous

collection 1 = **accumulation**, set, store, mass, pile, heap, stockpile, hoard
2 = **compilation**, accumulation, anthology 3 = **group**, company, crowd, assembly, cluster, assortment 4 = **gathering**
5 = **contribution**, donation, alms 6 = **offering**, offertory

collective 1 = **joint**, united, shared, combined, corporate, unified **OPPOSITE:** individual
2 = **combined**, aggregate, composite, cumulative
OPPOSITE: separate

collide 1 = **crash**, clash, meet head-on, come into collision 2 = **conflict**, clash, be incompatible, be at variance

collision 1 = **crash**, impact, accident, smash, bump, pile-up (*informal*), prang (*informal*)
2 = **conflict**, opposition, clash, encounter, disagreement, incompatibility

colony = **settlement**, territory, province, possession, dependency, outpost, dominion, satellite state

colour or (US) **color** NOUN
1 = **hue**, tone, shade, tint, colourway 2 = **paint**, stain, dye, tint, pigment, colorant
▷ VERB 3 = **blush**, flush, redden
• See panels **SHADES FROM BLACK TO WHITE**, **SHADES OF BLUE**, **SHADES OF BROWN**, **SHADES OF GREEN**, **SHADES OF PURPLE**, **SHADES OF RED**, **SHADES OF YELLOW**

colourful 1 = **bright**, brilliant, psychedelic, variegated, multicoloured **OPPOSITE:** drab 2 = **interesting**, rich, graphic, lively, distinctive, vivid, picturesque **OPPOSITE:** boring

column 1 = **pillar**, support, post, shaft, upright, obelisk 2 = **line**,

c

row, file, rank, procession, cavalcade

coma = **unconsciousness**, trance, oblivion, stupor

comb 1 = **untangle**, arrange, groom, dress 2 = **search**, hunt through, rake, sift, scour, rummage, ransack, forage, fossick (*Austral & NZ*)

combat NOUN 1 = **fight**, war, action, battle, conflict, engagement, warfare, skirmish **OPPOSITE:** peace ▷ VERB 2 = **fight**, oppose, resist, defy, withstand, do battle with **OPPOSITE:** support

combination 1 = **mixture**, mix, blend, composite, amalgamation, coalescence 2 = **association**, union, alliance, coalition, federation, consortium, syndicate, confederation

combine 1 = **amalgamate**, mix, blend, integrate, merge **OPPOSITE:** separate 2 = **join together**, link, connect, integrate, merge, amalgamate 3 = **unite**, associate, team up, get together, collaborate, join forces, join together, pool resources **OPPOSITE:** split up

come 1 = **approach**, near, advance, move towards, draw near 2 = **arrive**, turn up (*informal*), show up (*informal*) 3 = **reach**, extend 4 = **happen**, fall, occur, take place, come about, come to pass 5 = **be**

available, be made, be offered, be produced, be on offer (*slang*) ▷ PHRASES: **come across as something** *or* **someone** = **seem**, look, seem to be, appear to be, give the impression of being ▶ **come across someone** = **meet**, encounter, run into, bump into (*informal*) ▶ **come across something** = **find**, discover, notice, unearth, stumble upon, chance upon

comeback 1 (*informal*) = **return**, revival, rebound, resurgence, rally, recovery, triumph 2 = **response**, reply, retort, retaliation, riposte, rejoinder

comedian = **comic**, wit, clown, funny man, humorist, wag, joker, jester, dag (*NZ informal*)

comedy 1 = **light entertainment**, soap opera (*slang*), soapie *or* soapy (*Austral*) **OPPOSITE:** tragedy 2 = **humour**, fun, joking, farce, jesting, hilarity **OPPOSITE:** seriousness

comfort NOUN 1 = **ease**, luxury, wellbeing, opulence 2 = **consolation**, succour, help, support, relief, compensation **OPPOSITE:** annoyance ▷ VERB 3 = **console**, reassure, soothe, hearten, commiserate with **OPPOSITE:** distress

comfortable 1 = **pleasant**, homely, relaxing, cosy, agreeable, restful **OPPOSITE:** unpleasant 2 = **at ease**, happy, at home, contented, relaxed, serene **OPPOSITE:** uncomfortable 3 (*informal*) = **well-off**, prosperous, affluent, well-to-do, comfortably-off, in clover (*informal*)

comforting = **consoling**, encouraging, cheering, reassuring, soothing, heart-warming **OPPOSITE:** upsetting

comic ADJECTIVE 1 = **funny**, amusing, witty, humorous, farcical, comical, droll, jocular **OPPOSITE:** sad
▷ NOUN 2 = **comedian**, funny man, humorist, wit, clown, wag, jester, dag (*NZ informal*), buffoon

coming ADJECTIVE
1 = **approaching**, near, forthcoming, imminent, in store, impending, at hand, nigh
▷ NOUN 2 = **arrival**, approach, advent

command VERB 1 = **order**, tell, charge, demand, require, direct, bid, compel **OPPOSITE:** beg
2 = **have authority over**, lead, head, control, rule, manage, handle, dominate **OPPOSITE:** be subordinate to
▷ NOUN 3 = **order**, demand, instruction, requirement, decree, directive, ultimatum, commandment 4 = **domination**, control, rule, mastery, power, government 5 = **management**, power, control, charge, authority, supervision

commander = **leader**, chief, officer, boss, head, captain,

baas (*S African*), ruler, sherang (*Austral & NZ*)

commanding = **dominant**, controlling, dominating, superior, decisive, advantageous

commemorate = **celebrate**, remember, honour, recognize, salute, pay tribute to, immortalize **OPPOSITE:** ignore

commence 1 = **embark on**, start, open, begin, initiate, originate, instigate, enter upon **OPPOSITE:** stop 2 = **start**, open, begin, go ahead **OPPOSITE:** end

commend 1 = **praise**, acclaim, applaud, compliment, extol, approve, speak highly of **OPPOSITE:** criticize
2 = **recommend**, suggest, approve, advocate, endorse

comment VERB 1 = **remark**, say, note, mention, point out, observe, utter 2 *usually with* **on** = **remark on**, explain, talk about, discuss, speak about, say something about, allude to, elucidate
▷ NOUN 3 = **remark**, statement, observation 4 = **note**, explanation, illustration, commentary, exposition, annotation, elucidation

commentary 1 = **narration**, report, review, explanation, description, voice-over
2 = **analysis**, notes, review, critique, treatise

commentator 1 = **reporter**, special correspondent,

sportscaster 2 = **critic**,
interpreter, annotator
commercial 1 = **mercantile**,
trading 2 = **materialistic**,
mercenary, profit-making
commission VERB 1 = **appoint**,
order, contract, select, engage,
delegate, nominate, authorize
▷ NOUN 2 = **duty**, task, mission,
mandate, errand 3 = **fee**,
cut, percentage, royalties,
rake-off (*slang*) 4 = **committee**,
board, representatives,
commissioners, delegation,
deputation
commit 1 = **do**, perform, carry
out, execute, enact, perpetrate
2 = **put in custody**, confine,
imprison **OPPOSITE:** release
commitment 1 = **dedication**,
loyalty, devotion
2 = **responsibility**, tie,
duty, obligation, liability,
engagement
common 1 = **usual**, standard,
regular, ordinary, familiar,
conventional, routine, frequent
OPPOSITE: rare 2 = **popular**,
general, accepted, standard,
routine, widespread, universal,
prevailing 3 = **shared**,
collective 4 = **ordinary**,
average, typical, dinki-di
(*Austral informal*) **OPPOSITE:**
important 5 = **vulgar**, inferior,
coarse, plebeian **OPPOSITE:**
refined 6 = **collective**, public,
community, social, communal
OPPOSITE: personal

commonplace ADJECTIVE
1 = **everyday**, common,
ordinary, widespread, mundane,
banal, run-of-the-mill,
humdrum **OPPOSITE:** rare
▷ NOUN 2 = **cliché**, platitude,
banality, truism
common sense = **good
sense**, sound judgment,
level-headedness, prudence,
gumption (*Brit informal*), horse
sense, native intelligence, wit
communal = **public**, shared,
general, joint, collective
OPPOSITE: private
commune = **community**,
collective, cooperative, kibbutz
communicate 1 = **contact**,
talk, speak, make contact, get in
contact, e-mail, text 2 = **make
known**, declare, disclose, pass
on, proclaim, transmit, convey,
impart **OPPOSITE:** keep secret
3 = **pass on**, transfer, spread,
transmit
communication 1 = **contact**,
conversation, correspondence,
link, relations 2 = **passing
on**, circulation, transmission,
disclosure, imparting,
dissemination, conveyance
3 = **message**, news, report,
word, information, statement,
announcement, disclosure,
e-mail, text
communism *usually cap.*
= **socialism**, Marxism,
collectivism, Bolshevism, state
socialism

communist *often cap.*
= **socialist**, Red (*informal*),
Marxist, Bolshevik, collectivist

community = **society**, people,
public, residents, commonwealth,
general public, populace, state

commuter = **daily traveller**,
passenger, suburbanite

compact¹ ADJECTIVE 1 = **closely
packed**, solid, thick, dense,
compressed, condensed, pressed
together OPPOSITE: loose
2 = **concise**, brief, to the point,
succinct, terse OPPOSITE: lengthy
▷ VERB 3 = **pack closely**, stuff,
cram, compress, condense, tamp
OPPOSITE: loosen

compact² = **agreement**, deal,
understanding, contract, bond,
arrangement, treaty, bargain

companion 1 = **friend**, partner,
ally, colleague, associate, mate
(*informal*), comrade, accomplice,
plus-one (*informal*), cobber
(*Austral & NZ old-fashioned
informal*) 2 = **assistant**, aide,
escort, attendant

company 1 = **business**, firm,
association, corporation,
partnership, establishment,
syndicate, house 2 = **group**,
set, community, band, crowd,
collection, gathering, assembly
3 = **troop**, unit, squad, team
4 = **companionship**, society,
presence, fellowship 5 = **guests**,
party, visitors, callers

comparable 1 = **equal**,
equivalent, on a par,
tantamount, a match,
proportionate, commensurate,
as good OPPOSITE: unequal
2 = **similar**, related, alike,
corresponding, akin, analogous,
of a piece, cognate

comparative = **relative**,
qualified, by comparison

compare = **contrast**, balance,
weigh, set against, juxtapose
▷ PHRASES: compare to
something = **liken to**, parallel,
identify with, equate to,
correlate to, mention in the
same breath as ▶ compare
with something = **be as good
as**, match, approach, equal,
compete with, be on a par with,
be the equal of, hold a candle to

comparison 1 = **contrast**,
distinction, differentiation,
juxtaposition 2 = **similarity**,
analogy, resemblance,
correlation, likeness,
comparability

compartment 1 = **section**,
carriage, berth 2 = **bay**, booth,
locker, niche, cubicle, alcove,
pigeonhole, cubbyhole

compass = **range**, field, area,
reach, scope, limit, extent,
boundary

compassion = **sympathy**,
understanding, pity, humanity,
mercy, sorrow, kindness,
tenderness, aroha (*NZ*)
OPPOSITE: indifference

compassionate
= **sympathetic**, understanding,

pitying, humanitarian, charitable, humane, benevolent, merciful **OPPOSITE:** uncaring

compatible 1 = **consistent**, in keeping, congruous **OPPOSITE:** inappropriate **2** = **like-minded**, harmonious, in harmony **OPPOSITE:** incompatible

compel = **force**, make, railroad (*informal*), oblige, constrain, coerce, impel, dragoon

compelling 1 = **convincing**, telling, powerful, forceful, conclusive, weighty, cogent, irrefutable **2** = **fascinating**, gripping, irresistible, enchanting, enthralling, hypnotic, spellbinding, mesmeric **OPPOSITE:** boring

compensate 1 = **recompense**, repay, refund, reimburse, remunerate, make good **2** = **make amends for**, make up for, atone for, pay for, do penance for, cancel out, make reparation for **3** = **balance**, cancel (out), offset, make up for, redress, counteract, counterbalance

compensation
1 = **reparation**, damages, recompense, remuneration, restitution, reimbursement **2** = **recompense**, amends, reparation, restitution, atonement

compete 1 = **contend**, fight, vie, challenge, struggle, contest, strive **2** = **take part**, participate, be in the running, be a competitor, be a contestant, play

competence 1 = **ability**, skill, talent, capacity, expertise, proficiency, capability **OPPOSITE:** incompetence **2** = **fitness**, suitability, adequacy, appropriateness **OPPOSITE:** inadequacy

competent 1 = **able**, skilled, capable, proficient **OPPOSITE:** incompetent **2** = **fit**, qualified, suitable, adequate **OPPOSITE:** unqualified

competition 1 = **rivalry**, opposition, struggle, strife **2** = **opposition**, field, rivals, challengers **3** = **contest**, event, championship, tournament, head-to-head

competitive 1 = **cut-throat**, aggressive, fierce, ruthless, relentless, antagonistic, dog-eat-dog **2** = **ambitious**, pushing, opposing, aggressive, vying, contentious, combative

competitor 1 = **rival**, adversary, antagonist **2** = **contestant**, participant, contender, challenger, entrant, player, opponent

compilation = **collection**, treasury, accumulation, anthology, assortment, assemblage

compile = **put together**, collect, gather, organize, accumulate, marshal, garner, amass

complacency = **smugness**,
satisfaction, contentment, self-
congratulation, self-satisfaction

complacent = **smug**,
self-satisfied, pleased with
yourself, resting on your laurels,
contented, satisfied, serene,
unconcerned **OPPOSITE:** insecure

complain = **find fault**, moan,
grumble, whinge (*informal*),
carp, groan, lament, whine,
nit-pick (*informal*)

complaint 1 = **protest**,
objection, grievance, charge
2 = **grumble**, criticism, moan,
lament, grievance, grouse, gripe
(*informal*) 3 = **disorder**, problem,
disease, upset, illness, sickness,
ailment, affliction

complement VERB
1 = **enhance**, complete,
improve, boost, crown, add to,
set off, heighten
▷ NOUN 2 = **accompaniment**,
companion, accessory,
completion, finishing touch,
rounding-off, adjunct,
supplement 3 = **total**, capacity,
quota, aggregate, contingent,
entirety

> **USAGE NOTE**
> This is sometimes confused
> with *compliment* but the
> two words have very
> different meanings. As
> the synonyms show, the
> verb form of *complement*
> means 'to enhance' and 'to
> complete' something. In

> contrast, common synonyms
> of *compliment* as a verb are
> *praise*, *commend*, and *flatter*.

complementary = **matching**,
companion, corresponding,
compatible, reciprocal,
interrelating, interdependent,
harmonizing **OPPOSITE:**
incompatible

complete ADJECTIVE
1 = **total**, perfect, absolute,
utter, outright, thorough,
consummate, out-and-
out 2 = **whole**, full, entire
OPPOSITE: partial 3 = **entire**,
full, whole, intact, unbroken,
faultless **OPPOSITE:** incomplete
4 = **unabridged**, full, entire
5 = **finished**, done, ended,
achieved, concluded, fulfilled,
accomplished **OPPOSITE:**
unfinished
▷ VERB 6 = **perfect**, finish off,
round off, crown **OPPOSITE:**
spoil 7 = **finish**, conclude, end,
close, settle, wrap up (*informal*),
finalize **OPPOSITE:** start

completely = **totally**, entirely,
wholly, utterly, perfectly, fully,
absolutely, altogether

completion = **finishing**, end,
close, conclusion, fulfilment,
culmination, fruition

complex ADJECTIVE
1 = **compound**, multiple,
composite, manifold,
heterogeneous, multifarious
2 = **complicated**, difficult,
involved, elaborate, tangled,

C

intricate, tortuous, convoluted
OPPOSITE: simple
▷ **NOUN 3** = **structure**, system, scheme, network, organization, aggregate, composite
4 (*informal*) = **obsession**, preoccupation, phobia, fixation, fixed idea, idée fixe (*French*)

> **USAGE NOTE**
> Although *complex* and *complicated* are close in meaning, care should be taken when using one as a synonym of the other. *Complex* should be used to say that something consists of several parts rather than that it is difficult to understand, analyse, or deal with, which is what *complicated* inherently means. In the following real example a clear distinction is made between the two words: *the British benefits system is phenomenally complex and is administered by a complicated range of agencies.*

complexion 1 = **skin**, colour, colouring, hue, skin tone, pigmentation **2** = **nature**, character, make-up
complexity = **complication**, involvement, intricacy, entanglement
complicate = **make difficult**, confuse, muddle, entangle, involve **OPPOSITE:** simplify
complicated 1 = **involved**, difficult, puzzling, troublesome, problematic, perplexing
OPPOSITE: simple **2** = **complex**, involved, elaborate, intricate
OPPOSITE: understandable
complication 1 = **problem**, difficulty, obstacle, drawback, snag, uphill (*S African*)
2 = **complexity**, web, confusion, intricacy, entanglement
compliment NOUN 1 = **praise**, honour, tribute, bouquet, flattery, eulogy **OPPOSITE:** criticism
▷ **PLURAL NOUN 2** = **greetings**, regards, respects, good wishes, salutation **OPPOSITE:** insult
3 = **congratulations**, praise, commendation
▷ **VERB 4** = **praise**, flatter, salute, congratulate, pay tribute to, commend, extol, wax lyrical about **OPPOSITE:** criticize

> **USAGE NOTE**
> *Compliment* is sometimes confused with *complement*.

complimentary 1 = **flattering**, approving, appreciative, congratulatory, commendatory
OPPOSITE: critical **2** = **free**, donated, courtesy, honorary, on the house, gratuitous, gratis
comply = **obey**, follow, observe, submit to, conform to, adhere to, abide by, acquiesce with
OPPOSITE: defy
component NOUN 1 = **part**, piece, unit, item, element, ingredient, constituent
▷ **ADJECTIVE 2** = **constituent**, inherent, intrinsic

compose 1 = **put together**, make up, constitute, comprise, make, build, form, fashion
OPPOSITE: destroy 2 = **create**, write, produce, invent, devise, contrive 3 = **arrange**, make up, construct, put together, order, organize
▷ **PHRASES:** compose yourself = **calm yourself**, control yourself, collect yourself, pull yourself together

composed = **calm**, cool, collected, relaxed, poised, at ease, serene, sedate, chilled (*informal*), grounded **OPPOSITE:** agitated

composition 1 = **design**, structure, make-up, organization, arrangement, formation, layout, configuration 2 = **creation**, work, piece, production, opus, masterpiece 3 = **essay**, exercise, treatise, literary work 4 = **production**, creation, making, fashioning, formation, putting together, compilation, formulation

compound NOUN
1 = **combination**, mixture, blend, composite, fusion, synthesis, alloy, medley
OPPOSITE: element
▷ **ADJECTIVE** 2 = **complex**, multiple, composite, intricate
OPPOSITE: simple
▷ **VERB** 3 = **intensify**, add to, complicate, worsen, heighten, exacerbate, aggravate, magnify

OPPOSITE: lessen 4 = **combine**, unite, mix, blend, synthesize, amalgamate, intermingle
OPPOSITE: divide

comprehend = **understand**, see, take in, perceive, grasp, conceive, make out, fathom
OPPOSITE: misunderstand

comprehension
= **understanding**, grasp, conception, realization, intelligence, perception, discernment **OPPOSITE:** incomprehension

comprehensive = **broad**, full, complete, blanket, thorough, inclusive, exhaustive, all-inclusive **OPPOSITE:** limited

compress 1 = **squeeze**, crush, squash, press 2 = **condense**, contract, concentrate, shorten, abbreviate, zip (~*data*)

comprise 1 = **be composed of**, include, contain, consist of, take in, embrace, encompass 2 = **make up**, form, constitute, compose

> **USAGE NOTE**
> The use of *of* after *comprise* should be avoided: *the library comprises* (not *comprises of*) *6,500,000 books and manuscripts. Consist*, however, should be followed by *of* when used in this way: *Her crew consisted of children from Devon and Cornwall*.

compromise NOUN 1 = **give-and-track**, agreement,

settlement, accommodation, concession, adjustment, trade-off **OPPOSITE:** disagreement
▷ **VERB** 2 = **meet halfway**, concede, make concessions, give and take, strike a balance, strike a happy medium, go fifty-fifty (*informal*) **OPPOSITE:** disagree 3 = **undermine**, expose, embarrass, weaken, prejudice, discredit, jeopardize, dishonour **OPPOSITE:** support

compulsive 1 = **obsessive**, confirmed, chronic, persistent, addictive, uncontrollable, incurable, inveterate
2 = **fascinating**, gripping, absorbing, compelling, captivating, enthralling, hypnotic, engrossing
3 = **irresistible**, overwhelming, compelling, urgent, neurotic, uncontrollable, driving

compulsory = **obligatory**, forced, required, binding, mandatory, imperative, requisite, de rigueur (*French*) **OPPOSITE:** voluntary

compute = **calculate**, total, count, reckon, figure out, add up, tally, enumerate

comrade = **companion**, friend, partner, ally, colleague, associate, fellow, co-worker, cobber (*Austral & NZ old-fashioned informal*)

con (*informal*) **VERB** 1 = **swindle**, trick, cheat, rip off (*slang*), deceive, defraud, dupe, hoodwink, scam (*slang*)
▷ **NOUN** 2 = **swindle**, trick, fraud, deception, scam (*slang*), sting (*informal*), fastie (*Austral slang*)

conceal 1 = **hide**, bury, cover, screen, disguise, obscure, camouflage **OPPOSITE:** reveal
2 = **keep secret**, hide, disguise, mask, suppress, veil **OPPOSITE:** show

concede 1 = **admit**, allow, accept, acknowledge, own, grant, confess **OPPOSITE:** deny
2 = **give up**, yield, hand over, surrender, relinquish, cede **OPPOSITE:** conquer

conceive 1 = **imagine**, envisage, comprehend, visualize, think, believe, suppose, fancy
2 = **think up**, create, design, devise, formulate, contrive
3 = **become pregnant**, get pregnant, become impregnated

concentrate 1 = **focus your attention**, focus, pay attention, be engrossed, apply yourself **OPPOSITE:** pay no attention
2 = **focus**, centre, converge, bring to bear 3 = **gather**, collect, cluster, accumulate, congregate **OPPOSITE:** scatter

concentrated 1 = **condensed**, rich, undiluted, reduced, evaporated, thickened, boiled down 2 = **intense**, hard, deep, intensive, all-out (*informal*)

concentration 1 = **attention**, application, absorption, single-mindedness, intentness **OPPOSITE:** inattention 2 = **focusing**, centring, consolidation, convergence, bringing to bear, intensification, centralization 3 = **convergence**, collection, mass, cluster, accumulation, aggregation **OPPOSITE:** scattering

concept = **idea**, view, image, theory, notion, conception, hypothesis, abstraction

conception 1 = **idea**, plan, design, image, concept, notion 2 = **impregnation**, insemination, fertilization, germination

concern NOUN 1 = **anxiety**, fear, worry, distress, unease, apprehension, misgiving, disquiet 2 = **worry**, care, anxiety 3 = **affair**, issue, matter, consideration 4 = **care**, interest, attentiveness 5 = **business**, job, affair, responsibility, task 6 = **company**, business, firm, organization, corporation, enterprise, establishment 7 = **importance**, interest, bearing, relevance ▷ VERB 8 = **worry**, trouble, bother, disturb, distress, disquiet, perturb, make anxious 9 = **be about**, cover, deal with, go into, relate to, have to do with 10 = **be relevant to**, involve, affect, regard, apply to, bear on, have something to do with, pertain to

concerned 1 = **involved**, interested, active, mixed up, implicated, privy to 2 = **worried**, troubled, upset, bothered, disturbed, anxious, distressed, uneasy **OPPOSITE:** indifferent

concerning = **regarding**, about, re, touching, respecting, relating to, on the subject of, with reference to

concession 1 = **compromise**, agreement, settlement, accommodation, adjustment, trade-off, give-and-take 2 = **privilege**, right, permit, licence, entitlement, indulgence, prerogative 3 = **reduction**, saving, grant, discount, allowance 4 = **surrender**, yielding, conceding, renunciation, relinquishment

conclude 1 = **decide**, judge, assume, gather, work out, infer, deduce, surmise 2 = **come to an end**, end, close, finish, wind up **OPPOSITE:** begin 3 = **bring to an end**, end, close, finish, complete, wind up, terminate, round off **OPPOSITE:** begin 4 = **accomplish**, effect, bring about, carry out, pull off

conclusion 1 = **decision**, opinion, conviction, verdict, judgment, deduction, inference 2 = **end**, ending, close, finish, completion, finale, termination, bitter end 3 = **outcome**, result, upshot, consequence, culmination, end result

c

concrete 1 = **specific**, precise, explicit, definite, clear-cut, unequivocal **OPPOSITE:** vague 2 = **real**, material, actual, substantial, sensible, tangible, factual **OPPOSITE:** abstract

condemn 1 = **denounce**, damn, criticize, disapprove, censure, reprove, upbraid, blame **OPPOSITE:** approve 2 = **sentence**, convict, damn, doom, pass sentence on **OPPOSITE:** acquit

condemnation = **denunciation**, blame, censure, disapproval, reproach, stricture, reproof

condition NOUN 1 = **state**, order, shape, nick (*Brit informal*), trim 2 = **situation**, state, position, status, circumstances 3 = **requirement**, terms, rider, restriction, qualification, limitation, prerequisite, proviso 4 = **health**, shape, fitness, trim, form, kilter, state of health, fettle 5 = **ailment**, problem, complaint, weakness, malady, infirmity
▷ PLURAL NOUN 6 = **circumstances**, situation, environment, surroundings, way of life, milieu
▷ VERB 7 = **train**, teach, adapt, accustom

conditional = **dependent**, limited, qualified, contingent, provisional, with reservations **OPPOSITE:** unconditional

condone = **overlook**, excuse, forgive, pardon, turn a blind eye to, look the other way, make allowance for, let pass **OPPOSITE:** condemn

conduct VERB 1 = **carry out**, run, control, manage, direct, handle, organize, administer 2 = **accompany**, lead, escort, guide, steer, convey, usher
▷ NOUN 3 = **management**, running, control, handling, administration, direction, organization, guidance 4 = **behaviour**, ways, bearing, attitude, manners, demeanour, deportment
▷ PHRASES: conduct yourself = **behave yourself**, act, carry yourself, acquit yourself, deport yourself, comport yourself

confer 1 = **discuss**, talk, consult, deliberate, discourse, converse 2 = **grant**, give, present, accord, award, hand out, bestow

conference = **meeting**, congress, discussion, convention, forum, consultation, seminar, symposium, hui (*NZ*)

confess 1 = **admit**, acknowledge, disclose, confide, own up, come clean (*informal*), divulge **OPPOSITE:** cover up 2 = **declare**, allow, reveal, confirm, concede, assert, affirm, profess

confession = **admission**, revelation, disclosure,

acknowledgment, exposure, unbosoming

confidant or **confidante**
= **close friend**, familiar, intimate, crony, alter ego, bosom friend

confide = **tell**, admit, reveal, confess, whisper, disclose, impart, divulge

confidence 1 = **trust**, belief, faith, dependence, reliance, credence **OPPOSITE:** distrust 2 = **self-assurance**, courage, assurance, aplomb, boldness, self-possession, nerve **OPPOSITE:** shyness 3 = **secret**
▷ **PHRASES: in confidence**
= **in secrecy**, privately, confidentially, between you and me (and the gatepost), (just) between ourselves

confident 1 = **certain**, sure, convinced, positive, secure, satisfied, counting on **OPPOSITE:** unsure 2 = **self-assured**, positive, assured, bold, self-confident, self-reliant, sure of yourself **OPPOSITE:** insecure

confidential 1 = **secret**, private, intimate, classified, privy, off the record, hush-hush (*informal*), closed or closed source (*computing*), protected (*computing*) 2 = **secretive**, low, soft, hushed

confine VERB 1 = **imprison**, enclose, shut up, intern, incarcerate, hem in, keep, cage 2 = **restrict**, limit

▷ **PLURAL NOUN** 3 = **limits**, bounds, boundaries, compass, precincts, circumference, edge

confirm 1 = **prove**, support, establish, back up, verify, validate, bear out, substantiate 2 = **ratify**, establish, sanction, endorse, authorize 3 = **strengthen**, establish, fix, secure, reinforce, fortify

confirmation 1 = **proof**, evidence, testimony, verification, ratification, validation, corroboration, authentication **OPPOSITE:** repudiation 2 = **affirmation**, approval, acceptance, endorsement, ratification, assent, agreement **OPPOSITE:** disapproval

confirmed = **long-established**, seasoned, chronic, hardened, habitual, ingrained, inveterate, dyed-in-the-wool

confiscate = **seize**, appropriate, impound, commandeer, sequester **OPPOSITE:** give back

conflict NOUN 1 = **dispute**, difference, opposition, hostility, disagreement, friction, strife, fighting, cyberwar **OPPOSITE:** agreement 2 = **struggle**, battle, clash, strife 3 = **battle**, war, fight, clash, contest, encounter, combat, strife, boilover (*Austral*) **OPPOSITE:** peace
▷ **VERB** 4 = **be incompatible**, clash, differ, disagree, collide, be at variance **OPPOSITE:** agree

C

conflicting = incompatible, opposing, clashing, contrary, contradictory, inconsistent, paradoxical, discordant **OPPOSITE:** agreeing

conform 1 = **fit in**, follow, adjust, adapt, comply, obey, fall in, toe the line 2 *with* **with** = **fulfil**, meet, match, suit, satisfy, agree with, obey, abide by

confound = bewilder, baffle, confuse, astound, perplex, mystify, flummox, dumbfound

confront 1 = **tackle**, deal with, cope with, meet head-on 2 = **trouble**, face, perturb, bedevil 3 = **challenge**, face, oppose, tackle, encounter, defy, stand up to, accost **OPPOSITE:** evade

confrontation = conflict, fight, contest, set-to (*informal*), encounter, showdown (*informal*), head-to-head, boilover (*Austral*)

confuse 1 = **mix up with**, take for, muddle with 2 = **bewilder**, puzzle, baffle, perplex, mystify, fluster, faze, flummox 3 = **obscure**, cloud, make more difficult

confused 1 = **bewildered**, puzzled, baffled, at sea, muddled, perplexed, taken aback, disorientated **OPPOSITE:** enlightened 2 = **disorderly**, disordered, chaotic, mixed up, jumbled, untidy, in disarray, topsy-turvy **OPPOSITE:** tidy

confusing = bewildering, puzzling, misleading, unclear, baffling, contradictory, perplexing **OPPOSITE:** clear

confusion 1 = **bewilderment**, doubt, uncertainty **OPPOSITE:** enlightenment 2 = **disorder**, chaos, turmoil, upheaval, muddle, shambles, commotion **OPPOSITE:** order

congestion = overcrowding, crowding, jam, clogging, bottleneck

congratulate = compliment, pat on the back, wish joy to

congratulations PLURAL NOUN 1 = **good wishes**, greetings, compliments, best wishes, felicitations
▷ INTERJECTION 2 = **good wishes**, greetings, compliments, best wishes, felicitations

congregation = parishioners, brethren, crowd, assembly, flock, fellowship, multitude, throng

congress 1 = **meeting**, council, conference, assembly, convention, conclave, hui (*NZ*), runanga (*NZ*) 2 = **legislature**, council, parliament, House of Representatives (*NZ*)

conjure = produce, generate, bring about, give rise to, make, create, effect, produce as if by magic
▷ PHRASES: conjure something up = **bring to mind**, recall, evoke, recreate, recollect

connect 1 = **link**, join, couple, attach, fasten, affix, unite **OPPOSITE:** separate
2 = **associate**, join, link, identify, lump together

connected = **linked**, united, joined, coupled, related, allied, associated, combined

connection 1 = **association**, relationship, link, bond, relevance, tie-in
2 = **communication**, alliance, attachment, liaison, affinity, union 3 = **link**, coupling, junction, fastening, tie, portal (*computing*), USB port
4 = **contact**, friend, ally, associate, acquaintance

conquer 1 = **seize**, obtain, acquire, occupy, overrun, annex, win 2 = **defeat**, overcome, overthrow, beat, master, crush, overpower, quell **OPPOSITE:** lose to 3 = **overcome**, beat, defeat, master, overpower

conquest 1 = **takeover**, coup, invasion, occupation, annexation, subjugation
2 = **defeat**, victory, triumph, overthrow, rout, mastery

conscience 1 = **principles**, scruples, moral sense, sense of right and wrong, still small voice
2 = **guilt**, shame, regret, remorse, contrition, self-reproach

conscious 1 *often with of* = **aware of**, alert to, responsive to, sensible of **OPPOSITE:** unaware 2 = **deliberate**,

knowing, studied, calculated, self-conscious, intentional, wilful, premeditated **OPPOSITE:** unintentional 3 = **awake**, wide-awake, sentient, alive **OPPOSITE:** asleep

consciousness = **awareness**, understanding, knowledge, recognition, sensibility, realization, apprehension

consecutive = **successive**, running, succeeding, in turn, uninterrupted, sequential, in sequence

consensus = **agreement**, general agreement, unanimity, common consent, unity, harmony, assent, concord, kotahitanga (*NZ*)

> **USAGE NOTE**
> The original meaning of the word *consensus* is *a collective opinion*. Because the concept of 'opinion' is contained within this word, a few people argue that the phrase *a consensus of opinion* is incorrect and should be avoided. However, this common use of the word is unlikely to jar with the majority of speakers.

consent NOUN 1 = **agreement**, sanction, approval, go-ahead (*informal*), permission, compliance, assent, acquiescence **OPPOSITE:** refusal
▷ VERB 2 = **agree**, approve, permit, concur, assent, acquiesce **OPPOSITE:** refuse

consequence 1 = **result**, effect, outcome, repercussion, issue, sequel, end result, upshot 2 = **importance**, concern, moment, value, account, weight, import, significance

consequently = **as a result**, thus, therefore, hence, subsequently, accordingly, for that reason, thence

conservation
1 = **preservation**, saving, protection, maintenance, safeguarding, upkeep, guardianship, safekeeping
2 = **economy**, saving, thrift, husbandry

Conservative ADJECTIVE
1 = **Tory**, Republican (US), right-wing
▷ NOUN 2 = **Tory**, Republican (US), right-winger

conservative ADJECTIVE
1 = **traditional**, conventional, cautious, sober, reactionary, die-hard, hidebound OPPOSITE: radical
▷ NOUN 2 = **traditionalist**, reactionary, die-hard, stick-in-the-mud (informal) OPPOSITE: radical

conserve 1 = **save**, husband, take care of, hoard, store up, use sparingly OPPOSITE: waste
2 = **protect**, keep, save, preserve

consider 1 = **think**, see, believe, rate, judge, suppose, deem, view as 2 = **think about**, reflect on, weigh, contemplate, deliberate, ponder, meditate, ruminate 3 = **bear in mind**, remember, respect, think about, take into account, reckon with, take into consideration, make allowance for

considerable = **large**, goodly, great, marked, substantial, noticeable, plentiful, appreciable OPPOSITE: small

considerably = **greatly**, very much, significantly, remarkably, substantially, markedly, noticeably, appreciably

consideration 1 = **thought**, review, analysis, examination, reflection, scrutiny, deliberation
2 = **thoughtfulness**, concern, respect, kindness, tact, considerateness 3 = **factor**, point, issue, concern, element, aspect 4 = **payment**, fee, reward, remuneration, recompense, tip

considering = **taking into account**, in the light of, bearing in mind, in view of, keeping in mind, taking into consideration

consist
▷ PHRASES: consist in something = **lie in**, involve, reside in, be expressed by, subsist in, be found or contained in ▶ consist of something = **be made up of**, include, contain, incorporate, amount to, comprise, be composed of

consistency 1 = **agreement**, regularity, uniformity,

constancy, steadiness,
steadiness, evenness
2 = **texture**, density,
thickness, firmness, viscosity,
compactness

consistent 1 = **steady**, even,
regular, stable, constant,
persistent, dependable,
unchanging **OPPOSITE:** erratic
2 = **compatible**, agreeing,
in keeping, harmonious,
in harmony, consonant, in
accord, congruous **OPPOSITE:**
incompatible 3 = **coherent**,
logical, compatible,
harmonious, consonant
OPPOSITE: contradictory

consolation = **comfort**,
help, support, relief, cheer,
encouragement, solace, succour

console = **comfort**, cheer,
soothe, support, encourage,
calm, succour, express
sympathy for **OPPOSITE:**
distress

consolidate 1 = **strengthen**,
secure, reinforce, fortify,
stabilize 2 = **combine**, unite,
join, merge, unify, amalgamate,
federate

conspicuous = **obvious**, clear,
patent, evident, noticeable,
blatant, salient **OPPOSITE:**
inconspicuous

conspiracy = **plot**, scheme,
intrigue, collusion, machination

conspire 1 = **plot**, scheme,
intrigue, manoeuvre, contrive,
machinate, plan 2 = **work**

together, combine, contribute,
cooperate, concur, tend

constant 1 = **continuous**,
sustained, perpetual,
interminable, unrelenting,
incessant, ceaseless, nonstop
OPPOSITE: occasional
2 = **unchanging**, even, fixed,
permanent, stable, steady,
uniform, invariable **OPPOSITE:**
changing 3 = **faithful**, true,
devoted, loyal, stalwart,
staunch, trustworthy, trusty
OPPOSITE: undependable

constantly = **continuously**,
always, all the time, invariably,
continually, endlessly,
perpetually, incessantly
OPPOSITE: occasionally

constituent NOUN 1 = **voter**,
elector, member of the electorate
2 = **component**, element,
ingredient, part, unit, factor
▷ ADJECTIVE 3 = **component**,
basic, essential, integral,
elemental

constitute 1 = **represent**, be,
consist of, embody, exemplify,
be equivalent to 2 = **make up**,
form, compose, comprise

constitution 1 = **state of
health**, build, body, frame,
physique, physical condition
2 = **structure**, form, nature,
make-up, composition,
character, disposition

constitutional = **legitimate**,
official, legal, chartered,
statutory, vested

constrain 1 = **restrict**, confine, curb, restrain, constrict, straiten, check 2 = **force**, bind, compel, oblige, necessitate, coerce, impel, pressurize

constraint 1 = **restriction**, limitation, curb, rein, deterrent, hindrance, check 2 = **force**, pressure, necessity, restraint, compulsion, coercion

construct 1 = **build**, make, form, create, fashion, shape, manufacture, assemble **OPPOSITE:** demolish 2 = **create**, make, form, compose, put together

construction 1 = **building**, creation, composition 2 (*Formal*) = **interpretation**, reading, explanation, rendering, inference

constructive = **helpful**, positive, useful, practical, valuable, productive **OPPOSITE:** unproductive

consult 1 = **ask**, refer to, turn to, take counsel, pick (someone's) brains, question 2 = **confer**, talk, compare notes 3 = **refer to**, check in, look in

consultant = **specialist**, adviser, counsellor, authority

consultation 1 = **discussion**, talk, council, conference, dialogue 2 = **meeting**, interview, session, appointment, examination, deliberation, hearing

consume 1 = **eat**, swallow, devour, put away, gobble (up),

eat up 2 = **use up**, spend, waste, absorb, exhaust, squander, dissipate, expend 3 = **destroy**, devastate, demolish, ravage, annihilate, lay waste 4 *often passive* = **obsess**, dominate, absorb, preoccupy, eat up, monopolize, engross

consumer = **buyer**, customer, user, shopper, purchaser

consumption 1 = **using up**, use, loss, waste, expenditure, exhaustion, depletion, dissipation 2 (*Old-fashioned*) = **tuberculosis**, T.B.

contact NOUN
1 = **communication**, link, association, connection, correspondence 2 = **touch**, contiguity 3 = **connection**, colleague, associate, liaison, acquaintance, confederate ▷ VERB 4 = **get** *or* **be in touch with**, call, reach, approach, write to, speak to, communicate with, e-mail, text

contain 1 = **hold**, incorporate, accommodate, enclose, have capacity for 2 = **include**, consist of, embrace, comprise, embody, comprehend 3 = **restrain**, control, hold in, curb, suppress, hold back, stifle, repress

container = **holder**, vessel, repository, receptacle

contaminate = **pollute**, infect, stain, corrupt, taint, defile, adulterate, befoul **OPPOSITE:** purify

contamination = **pollution**, infection, corruption, poisoning, taint, impurity, contagion, defilement

contemplate 1 = **consider**, plan, think of, intend, envisage, foresee 2 = **think about**, consider, ponder, reflect upon, ruminate (upon), muse over, deliberate over 3 = **look at**, examine, inspect, gaze at, eye up, view, study, regard

contemporary ADJECTIVE
1 = **modern**, recent, current, up-to-date, present-day, à la mode, newfangled, present **OPPOSITE:** old-fashioned 2 = **coexisting**, concurrent, contemporaneous
▷ NOUN 3 = **peer**, fellow, equal

> **USAGE NOTE**
> Since *contemporary* can mean either 'of the present period' or 'of the same period', it is best to avoid it where ambiguity might arise, as in *a production of Othello in contemporary dress*. A synonym such as *modern* or *present-day* would clarify if the sense 'of the present period' were being used, while a specific term, such as *Elizabethan*, would be appropriate if the sense 'of the same period' were being used.

contempt = **scorn**, disdain, mockery, derision, disrespect, disregard **OPPOSITE:** respect

contend 1 = **argue**, hold, maintain, allege, assert, affirm

2 = **compete**, fight, struggle, clash, contest, strive, vie, jostle

content[1] NOUN 1 = **subject matter**, material, theme, substance, essence, gist
2 = **amount**, measure, size, load, volume, capacity
▷ PLURAL NOUN
3 = **constituents**, elements, load, ingredients

content[2] ADJECTIVE
1 = **satisfied**, happy, pleased, contented, comfortable, fulfilled, at ease, gratified
▷ NOUN 2 = **satisfaction**, ease, pleasure, comfort, peace of mind, gratification, contentment
▷ PHRASES: content yourself with something = **satisfy yourself with**, be happy with, be satisfied with, be content with

contented = **satisfied**, happy, pleased, content, comfortable, glad, thankful, gratified **OPPOSITE:** discontented

contentious = **argumentative**, wrangling, bickering, quarrelsome, querulous, cavilling, disputatious, captious

contest NOUN 1 = **competition**, game, match, trial, tournament
2 = **struggle**, fight, battle, conflict, dispute, controversy, combat
▷ VERB 3 = **compete in**, take part in, fight in, go in for, contend for, vie in 4 = **oppose**, question, challenge, argue,

debate, dispute, object to, call in *or* into question

contestant = competitor, candidate, participant, contender, entrant, player

context 1 = circumstances, conditions, situation, ambience 2 = frame of reference, background, framework, relation, connection

contingency = possibility, happening, chance, event, incident, accident, emergency, eventuality

continual 1 = constant, interminable, incessant, unremitting OPPOSITE: erratic 2 = frequent, regular, repeated, recurrent OPPOSITE: occasional

continually 1 = constantly, always, all the time, forever, incessantly, nonstop, interminably 2 = repeatedly, often, frequently, many times, over and over, persistently

continuation 1 = continuing, lasting, carrying on, keeping up, endurance, perpetuation, prolongation 2 = addition, extension, supplement, sequel, resumption, postscript

continue 1 = keep on, go on, maintain, sustain, carry on, persist in, persevere, stick at OPPOSITE: stop 2 = go on, progress, proceed, carry on, keep going, crack on (*informal*) 3 = resume, return to, take up again, proceed, carry on,

recommence, pick up where you left off OPPOSITE: stop 4 = remain, last, stay, survive, carry on, live on, endure, persist OPPOSITE: quit

continuing = lasting, sustained, enduring, ongoing, in progress

continuity = cohesion, flow, connection, sequence, succession, progression

continuous = constant, extended, prolonged, unbroken, uninterrupted, unceasing OPPOSITE: occasional

contract NOUN 1 = agreement, commitment, arrangement, settlement, bargain, pact, covenant
▷ VERB 2 = agree, negotiate, pledge, bargain, undertake, come to terms, covenant, make a deal OPPOSITE: refuse 3 = constrict, confine, tighten, shorten, compress, condense, shrivel 4 = tighten, narrow, shorten OPPOSITE: stretch 5 = lessen, reduce, shrink, diminish, decrease, dwindle OPPOSITE: increase 6 = catch, get, develop, acquire, incur, be infected with, go down with, be afflicted with OPPOSITE: avoid

contraction 1 = tightening, narrowing, shortening, constricting, shrinkage 2 = abbreviation, reduction, shortening, compression

contradict 1 = **dispute**, deny, challenge, belie, fly in the face of, be at variance with 2 = **negate**, deny, rebut, controvert **OPPOSITE:** confirm

contradiction 1 = **conflict**, inconsistency, contravention, incongruity 2 = **negation**, opposite, denial

contradictory = **inconsistent**, conflicting, opposed, opposite, contrary, incompatible, paradoxical

contrary ADJECTIVE
1 = **opposite**, different, opposed, clashing, counter, reverse, adverse, contradictory **OPPOSITE:** in agreement
2 = **perverse**, difficult, awkward, intractable, obstinate, stroppy (Brit slang), cantankerous, disobliging **OPPOSITE:** cooperative
▷ NOUN 3 = **opposite**, reverse, converse, antithesis

contrast NOUN 1 = **difference**, opposition, comparison, distinction, foil, disparity, divergence, dissimilarity
▷ VERB 2 = **differentiate**, compare, oppose, distinguish, set in opposition 3 = **differ**, be contrary, be at variance, be dissimilar

contribute = **give**, provide, supply, donate, subscribe, chip in (informal), bestow
▷ PHRASES: **contribute to something** = **be partly responsible for**, lead to, be instrumental in, be conducive to, help

contribution = **gift**, offering, grant, donation, input, subscription, koha (NZ)

contributor = **donor**, supporter, patron, subscriber, giver

contrive 1 = **devise**, plan, fabricate, create, design, scheme, manufacture, plot
2 = **manage**, succeed, arrange, manoeuvre

contrived = **forced**, planned, laboured, strained, artificial, elaborate, unnatural, overdone **OPPOSITE:** natural

control NOUN 1 = **power**, authority, management, command, guidance, supervision, supremacy, charge
2 = **restraint**, check, regulation, brake, limitation, curb 3 = **self-discipline**, self-restraint, restraint, self-command
4 = **switch**, instrument, button, dial, lever, knob
▷ PLURAL NOUN
5 = **instruments**, dash, dials, console, dashboard, control panel
▷ VERB 6 = **have power over**, manage, direct, handle, command, govern, administer, supervise 7 = **limit**, restrict, curb 8 = **restrain**, limit, check, contain, curb, hold back, subdue, repress

controversial = **disputed**, contentious, at issue, debatable, under discussion, open to question, disputable

controversy = **argument**, debate, row, dispute, quarrel, squabble, wrangling, altercation

convene 1 = **call**, gather, assemble, summon, bring together, convoke 2 = **meet**, gather, assemble, come together, congregate

convenience 1 = **benefit**, good, advantage 2 = **suitability**, fitness, appropriateness 3 = **usefulness**, utility **OPPOSITE:** uselessness 4 = **accessibility**, availability, nearness 5 = **appliance**, facility, comfort, amenity, labour-saving device, help

convenient 1 = **suitable**, fit, handy, satisfactory 2 = **useful**, practical, handy, serviceable, labour-saving **OPPOSITE:** useless 3 = **nearby**, available, accessible, handy, at hand, within reach, close at hand, just round the corner **OPPOSITE:** inaccessible 4 = **appropriate**, timely, suitable, helpful

convention 1 = **custom**, practice, tradition, code, usage, protocol, etiquette, propriety, kawa (*NZ*), tikanga (*NZ*) 2 = **agreement**, contract, treaty, bargain, pact, protocol 3 = **assembly**, meeting, council, conference, congress, convocation, hui (*NZ*), runanga (*NZ*)

conventional 1 = **proper**, conservative, respectable, genteel, conformist 2 = **ordinary**, standard, normal, regular, usual 3 = **traditional**, accepted, orthodox, customary 4 = **unoriginal**, routine, stereotyped, banal, prosaic, run-of-the-mill, hackneyed **OPPOSITE:** unconventional

converge = **come together**, meet, join, combine, gather, merge, coincide, intersect ▷ **PHRASES:** converge on something = **close in on**, arrive at, move towards, home in on, come together at

conversation = **talk**, discussion, dialogue, tête-à-tête, conference, chat, gossip, discourse, korero (*NZ*)

❙ **RELATED WORD**
❙ *adjective*: colloquial

conversion 1 = **change**, transformation, metamorphosis 2 = **adaptation**, reconstruction, modification, alteration, remodelling, reorganization

convert VERB 1 = **change**, turn, transform, alter, transpose 2 = **adapt**, modify, remodel, reorganize, customize, restyle 3 = **reform**, convince, proselytize ▷ **NOUN** 4 = **neophyte**, disciple, proselyte

convey 1 = **communicate**, impart, reveal, relate, disclose, make known, tell 2 = **carry**, transport, move, bring, bear, conduct, fetch

convict VERB 1 = **find guilty**, sentence, condemn, imprison, pronounce guilty
▷ NOUN 2 = **prisoner**, criminal, lag (*slang*), felon, jailbird

conviction 1 = **belief**, view, opinion, principle, faith, persuasion, creed, tenet, kaupapa (*NZ*) 2 = **certainty**, confidence, assurance, firmness, certitude

convince 1 = **assure**, persuade, satisfy, reassure 2 = **persuade**, induce, coax, talk into, prevail upon, bring round to the idea of

> USAGE NOTE
> The use of *convince* to talk about persuading someone to do something is considered by many British speakers to be wrong or unacceptable. It would be preferable to use an alternative such as *persuade* or *talk into*.

convincing = **persuasive**, credible, conclusive, telling, powerful, impressive, plausible, cogent **OPPOSITE**: unconvincing

cool ADJECTIVE 1 = **cold**, chilled, refreshing, chilly, nippy **OPPOSITE**: warm 2 = **calm**, collected, relaxed, composed, sedate, self-controlled, unruffled, unemotional, chilled

(*informal*) **OPPOSITE**: agitated 3 = **unfriendly**, distant, indifferent, aloof, lukewarm, offhand, unenthusiastic, unwelcoming **OPPOSITE**: friendly 4 = **unenthusiastic**, indifferent, lukewarm, unwelcoming
▷ VERB 5 = **lose heat**, cool off **OPPOSITE**: warm (up) 6 = **make cool**, freeze, chill, refrigerate, cool off **OPPOSITE**: warm (up)
▷ NOUN 7 = **coldness**, chill, coolness 8 (*slang*) = **calmness**, control, temper, composure, self-control, poise, self-discipline, self-possession

cooperate = **work together**, collaborate, coordinate, join forces, conspire, pull together, pool resources, combine your efforts **OPPOSITE**: conflict

cooperation = **teamwork**, unity, collaboration, give-and-take, combined effort, esprit de corps, kotahitanga (*NZ*) **OPPOSITE**: opposition

cooperative 1 = **shared**, joint, combined, collective, collaborative 2 = **helpful**, obliging, accommodating, supportive, responsive, onside (*informal*)

cope = **manage**, get by (*informal*), struggle through, survive, carry on, make the grade, hold your own
▷ PHRASES: cope with something = **deal with**, handle,

c

struggle with, grapple with, wrestle with, contend with, weather

copy NOUN 1 = **reproduction**, duplicate, replica, imitation, forgery, counterfeit, likeness, facsimile **OPPOSITE:** original
▷ VERB 2 = **reproduce**, replicate, duplicate, transcribe, counterfeit **OPPOSITE:** create 3 = **imitate**, act like, emulate, behave like, follow, repeat, mirror, ape

cord = **rope**, line, string, twine

cordon = **chain**, line, ring, barrier, picket line
▷ PHRASES: **cordon something off** = **surround**, isolate, close off, fence off, separate, enclose, picket, encircle

core 1 = **centre** 2 = **heart**, essence, nucleus, kernel, crux, gist, nub, pith

corner NOUN 1 = **angle**, joint, crook 2 = **bend**, curve 3 = **space**, hideaway, nook, hide-out
▷ VERB 4 = **trap**, catch, run to earth 5 (~a market) = **monopolize**, take over, dominate, control, hog (slang), engross

corporation 1 = **business**, company, concern, firm, society, association, organization, enterprise 2 = **town council**, council, municipal authorities, civic authorities

corps = **team**, unit, regiment, detachment, company, band, division, troop

corpse = **body**, remains, carcass, cadaver, stiff (slang)

correct ADJECTIVE 1 = **accurate**, right, true, exact, precise, flawless, faultless, O.K. or okay (informal) **OPPOSITE:** inaccurate 2 = **right**, standard, appropriate, acceptable, proper, precise 3 = **proper**, seemly, standard, fitting, kosher (informal) **OPPOSITE:** inappropriate
▷ VERB 4 = **rectify**, remedy, redress, right, reform, cure, adjust, amend **OPPOSITE:** spoil 5 = **rebuke**, discipline, reprimand, chide, admonish, chastise, chasten, reprove **OPPOSITE:** praise

correction 1 = **rectification**, improvement, amendment, adjustment, modification, alteration, emendation 2 = **punishment**, discipline, reformation, admonition, chastisement, reproof, castigation

correctly = **rightly**, right, perfectly, properly, precisely, accurately

correctness 1 = **truth**, accuracy, precision, exactitude, exactness, faultlessness 2 = **decorum**, propriety, good manners, civility, good breeding

correspond 1 = **be consistent**, match, agree, accord, fit, square, tally, conform **OPPOSITE:** differ 2 = **communicate**, write, keep in touch, exchange letters, e-mail, text

correspondence
1 = **communication**, writing, contact 2 = **letters**, post, mail
3 = **relation**, match, agreement, comparison, harmony, coincidence, similarity, correlation

correspondent 1 = **reporter**, journalist, contributor, hack
2 = **letter writer**, pen friend *or* pen pal

corresponding = **equivalent**, matching, similar, related, complementary, reciprocal, analogous

corridor = **passage**, alley, aisle, hallway, passageway

corrupt ADJECTIVE
1 = **dishonest**, bent (*slang*), crooked (*informal*), fraudulent, unscrupulous, venal, unprincipled OPPOSITE: honest 2 = **depraved**, vicious, degenerate, debased, profligate, dissolute 3 = **distorted**, doctored, altered, falsified
▷ VERB 4 = **bribe**, fix (*informal*), buy off, suborn, grease (someone's) palm (*slang*)
5 = **deprave**, pervert, subvert, debauch OPPOSITE: reform
6 = **distort**, doctor, tamper with

corruption 1 = **dishonesty**, fraud, bribery, extortion, venality, shady dealings (*informal*) 2 = **depravity**, vice, evil, perversion, decadence,

wickedness, immorality
3 = **distortion**, doctoring, falsification

cosmetic = **superficial**, surface, nonessential

cosmic 1 = **extraterrestrial**, stellar 2 = **universal**, general, overarching

cosmopolitan = **sophisticated**, cultured, refined, cultivated, urbane, well-travelled, worldly-wise OPPOSITE: unsophisticated

cost NOUN 1 = **price**, worth, expense, charge, damage (*informal*), amount, payment, outlay 2 = **loss**, suffering, damage, injury, penalty, hurt, expense, harm
▷ PLURAL NOUN 3 = **expenses**, spending, expenditure, overheads, outgoings, outlay, budget
▷ VERB 4 = **sell at**, come to, set (someone) back (*informal*), be priced at, command a price of
5 = **lose**, deprive of, cheat of

costly 1 = **expensive**, dear, stiff, steep (*informal*), highly-priced, exorbitant, extortionate OPPOSITE: inexpensive
2 = **damaging**, disastrous, harmful, catastrophic, loss-making, ruinous, deleterious

costume = **outfit**, dress, clothing, uniform, ensemble, livery, apparel, attire

cosy 1 = **comfortable**, homely, warm, intimate, snug, comfy (*informal*), sheltered 2 = **snug**,

warm, comfortable, sheltered, comfy (*informal*), tucked up
3 = **intimate**, friendly, informal
cottage = **cabin**, lodge, hut, shack, chalet, whare (*NZ*)
cough VERB 1 = **clear your throat**, bark, hack
▷ NOUN 2 = **frog** *or* **tickle in your throat**, bark, hack
council 1 = **committee**, governing body, board
2 = **governing body**, parliament, congress, cabinet, panel, assembly, convention, conference, runanga (*NZ*)
counsel NOUN 1 = **advice**, information, warning, direction, suggestion, recommendation, guidance 2 = **legal adviser**, lawyer, attorney, solicitor, advocate, barrister
▷ VERB 3 = **advise**, recommend, advocate, warn, urge, instruct, exhort
count VERB 1 *often with* **up** = **add (up)**, total, reckon (up), tot up, calculate, compute, tally, number 2 = **matter**, be important, carry weight, tell, rate, weigh, signify
3 = **consider**, judge, regard, deem, think of, rate, look upon 4 = **include**, number among, take into account *or* consideration
▷ NOUN 5 = **calculation**, poll, reckoning, sum, tally, numbering, computation, enumeration

▷ PHRASES: **count on** *or* **upon something** *or* **someone** = **depend on**, trust, rely on, bank on, take for granted, lean on, reckon on, take on trust
counter VERB 1 = **oppose**, meet, block, resist, parry, deflect, repel, rebuff OPPOSITE: yield
2 = **retaliate**, answer, reply, respond, retort, hit back, rejoin, strike back
▷ ADVERB 3 = **opposite to**, against, versus, conversely, in defiance of, at variance with, contrariwise OPPOSITE: in accordance with
counterpart = **opposite number**, equal, twin, equivalent, match, fellow, mate
countless = **innumerable**, legion, infinite, myriad, untold, limitless, incalculable, immeasurable OPPOSITE: limited
country 1 = **nation**, state, land, commonwealth, kingdom, realm, people 2 = **people**, community, nation, society, citizens, inhabitants, populace, public 3 = **countryside**, provinces, sticks (*informal*), farmland, outback (*Austral & NZ*), green belt, backwoods, bush (*NZ & S African*) OPPOSITE: town
countryside = **country**, rural areas, outback (*Austral & NZ*), green belt, sticks (*informal*)
county = **province**, district, shire

coup = **masterstroke**, feat, stunt, action, exploit, manoeuvre, deed, accomplishment

couple = **pair**, two, brace, duo, twosome

▷ **PHRASES: couple something to something** = **link to**, connect to, pair with, unite with, join to, hitch to, yoke to

coupon = **slip**, ticket, certificate, token, voucher, card

courage = **bravery**, nerve, resolution, daring, pluck, heroism, mettle, gallantry **OPPOSITE:** cowardice

courageous = **brave**, daring, bold, gritty, fearless, gallant, intrepid, valiant **OPPOSITE:** cowardly

courier 1 = **messenger**, runner, carrier, bearer, envoy 2 = **guide**, representative, escort, conductor

course NOUN 1 = **route**, way, line, road, track, direction, path, passage 2 = **procedure**, plan, policy, programme, method, conduct, behaviour, manner 3 = **progression**, order, unfolding, development, movement, progress, flow, sequence 4 = **classes**, programme, schedule, lectures, curriculum 5 = **racecourse**, circuit 6 = **period**, time, duration, term, passing

▷ **VERB** 7 = **run**, flow, stream, gush, race, speed, surge 8 = **hunt**, follow, chase, pursue

▷ **PHRASES: of course** = **naturally**, certainly, obviously, definitely, undoubtedly, needless to say, without a doubt, indubitably

court NOUN 1 = **law court**, bar, bench, tribunal 2 = **palace**, hall, castle, manor 3 = **royal household**, train, suite, attendants, entourage, retinue, cortege

▷ **VERB** 4 = **cultivate**, seek, flatter, solicit, pander to, curry favour with, fawn upon 5 = **invite**, seek, attract, prompt, provoke, bring about, incite 6 = **woo**, go (out) with, date, take out, run after, walk out with, set your cap at, step out with (*informal*)

courtesy 1 = **politeness**, good manners, civility, gallantry, graciousness, affability, urbanity 2 = **favour**, kindness, indulgence

courtyard = **yard**, square, piazza, quadrangle, plaza, enclosure, cloister, quad (*informal*)

cove = **bay**, sound, inlet, anchorage

covenant = **promise**, contract, agreement, commitment, arrangement, pledge, pact

cover VERB 1 = **conceal**, hide, mask, disguise, obscure, veil, cloak, shroud **OPPOSITE:** reveal 2 = **clothe**, dress, wrap, envelop **OPPOSITE:** uncover 3 = **overlay**, blanket 4 = **coat**, cake, plaster,

smear, envelop, spread, encase, daub **5 = submerge**, flood, engulf, overrun, wash over **6 = travel over**, cross, traverse, pass through *or* over **7 = protect**, guard, defend, shield **8 = consider**, deal with, investigate, describe, tell of **9 = report on**, write about, commentate on, relate, tell of, narrate, write up **10 = pay for**, fund, provide for, offset, be enough for
▷ NOUN **11 = protection**, shelter, shield, defence, guard, camouflage, concealment **12 = insurance**, protection, compensation, indemnity, reimbursement **13 = covering**, case, top, coating, envelope, lid, canopy, wrapper **14 = bedclothes**, bedding, sheet, blanket, quilt, duvet, eiderdown **15 = jacket**, case, wrapper **16 = disguise**, front, screen, mask, veil, façade, pretext, smoke screen

covering NOUN **1 = cover**, coating, casing, wrapping, layer, blanket
▷ ADJECTIVE **2 = explanatory**, accompanying, introductory, descriptive

covet = long for, desire, envy, crave, aspire to, yearn for, lust after, set your heart on

coward = wimp, chicken (*slang*), scaredy-cat (*informal*), yellow-belly (*slang*)

cowardly = faint-hearted, scared, spineless, soft, yellow (*informal*), weak, chicken (*slang*), fearful, sookie (*NZ*) **OPPOSITE:** brave

cowboy = cowhand, drover, rancher, stockman, cattleman, herdsman, gaucho

crack VERB **1 = break**, split, burst, snap, fracture, splinter **2 = snap**, ring, crash, burst, explode, pop, detonate **3** (*informal*) **= hit**, clip (*informal*), slap, smack, clout (*informal*), cuff, whack **4 = cleave**, break **5 = solve**, work out, resolve, clear up, fathom, decipher, suss (out) (*slang*), get to the bottom of **6 = break down**, collapse, yield, give in, give way, succumb, lose control, be overcome
▷ NOUN **7 = break**, chink, gap, fracture, rift, cleft, crevice, fissure **8 = split**, break, fracture **9 = snap**, pop, crash, burst, explosion, clap, report **10** (*informal*) **= blow**, slap, smack, clout (*informal*), cuff, whack, clip (*informal*) **11** (*informal*) **= joke**, dig, gag (*informal*), quip, jibe, wisecrack, witticism, funny remark
▷ ADJECTIVE **12** (*slang*) **= first-class**, choice, excellent, ace, elite, superior, world-class, first-rate

crackdown = clampdown, crushing, repression, suppression

cracked = **broken**, damaged, split, chipped, flawed, faulty, defective, imperfect

cradle NOUN 1 = **crib**, cot, Moses basket, bassinet 2 = **birthplace**, beginning, source, spring, origin, fount, fountainhead, wellspring
▷ VERB 3 = **hold**, support, rock, nurse, nestle

craft 1 = **vessel**, boat, ship, plane, aircraft, spacecraft 2 = **occupation**, work, business, trade, employment, pursuit, vocation, handicraft 3 = **skill**, art, ability, technique, know-how (informal), expertise, aptitude, artistry

craftsman = **skilled worker**, artisan, master, maker, wright, technician, smith

cram 1 = **stuff**, force, jam, shove, compress 2 = **pack**, fill, stuff 3 = **squeeze**, press, pack in 4 = **study**, revise, swot, bone up (informal), mug up (slang)

cramp¹ = **spasm**, pain, ache, contraction, pang, stitch, convulsion, twinge

cramp² = **restrict**, hamper, inhibit, hinder, handicap, constrain, obstruct, impede

cramped = **restricted**, confined, overcrowded, crowded, packed, uncomfortable, closed in, congested OPPOSITE: spacious

crash NOUN 1 = **collision**, accident, smash, wreck, prang (informal), bump, pile-up

(informal) 2 = **smash**, clash, boom, bang, thunder, racket, din, clatter 3 = **collapse**, failure, depression, ruin, downfall
▷ VERB 4 = **fall**, plunge, topple, lurch, hurtle, overbalance, fall headlong 5 = **plunge**, hurtle 6 = **collapse**, fail, go under, be ruined, go bust (informal), fold up, go to the wall, go belly up (informal)
▷ PHRASES: **crash into** = **collide with**, hit, bump into, drive into, plough into

crate = **container**, case, box, packing case, tea chest

crater = **hollow**, hole, depression, dip, cavity

crave 1 = **long for**, yearn for, hanker after, want, desire, hope for, lust after 2 (informal) = **beg**, ask for, seek, petition, pray for, plead for, solicit, implore

craving = **longing**, hope, desire, yen (informal), hunger, appetite, yearning, thirst

crawl 1 = **creep**, slither, inch, wriggle, writhe, worm your way, advance slowly OPPOSITE: run 2 = **grovel**, creep, humble yourself
▷ PHRASES: **crawl to someone** = **fawn on**, toady to

craze = **fad**, fashion, trend, rage, enthusiasm, vogue, mania, infatuation

crazed = **mad**, crazy, raving, insane, lunatic,

berko (*Austral slang*), off the air (*Austral slang*), porangi (*NZ*)

crazy 1 (*informal*) = **ridiculous**, absurd, foolish, ludicrous, senseless, preposterous, idiotic, nonsensical, porangi (*NZ*) **OPPOSITE:** sensible 2 = **insane**, mad, unbalanced, deranged, nuts (*slang*), crazed, demented, off the air (*Austral slang*), out of your mind, porangi (*NZ*) **OPPOSITE:** sane 3 = **fanatical**, wild (*informal*), mad, devoted, enthusiastic, passionate, infatuated **OPPOSITE:** uninterested

cream NOUN 1 = **lotion**, ointment, oil, essence, cosmetic, paste, emulsion, salve 2 = **best**, elite, prime, pick, flower, the crème de la crème ▷ ADJECTIVE 3 = **off-white**, ivory, yellowish-white • *See panel* SHADES FROM BLACK TO WHITE

creamy 1 = **milky**, buttery 2 = **smooth**, soft, velvety, rich

crease NOUN 1 = **fold**, line, ridge, groove, corrugation 2 = **wrinkle**, line, crow's-foot ▷ VERB 3 = **crumple**, rumple, fold, double up, corrugate 4 = **wrinkle**, crumple, screw up

create 1 = **cause**, lead to, occasion, bring about 2 = **make**, produce, invent, compose, devise, originate, formulate, spawn **OPPOSITE:** destroy 3 = **appoint**, make, establish, set up, invest, install, constitute

creation 1 = **universe**, world, nature, cosmos 2 = **invention**, production, achievement, brainchild (*informal*), concoction, handiwork, pièce de résistance (*French*), magnum opus 3 = **making**, generation, formation, conception, genesis 4 = **setting up**, development, production, institution, foundation, establishment, formation, inception

creative = **imaginative**, gifted, artistic, inventive, original, inspired, clever, ingenious

creativity = **imagination**, inspiration, ingenuity, originality, inventiveness, cleverness

creator 1 = **maker**, father, author, designer, architect, inventor, originator 2 *usually with cap.* = **God**, Maker

creature 1 = **living thing**, being, animal, beast, brute 2 = **person**, man, woman, individual, soul, human being, mortal

credentials 1 = **qualifications**, ability, skill, fitness, attribute, capability, eligibility, aptitude 2 = **certification**, document, reference(s), papers, licence, passport, testimonial, authorization

credibility = **believability**, reliability, plausibility, trustworthiness

credible 1 = **believable**, possible, likely, reasonable, probable, plausible, conceivable, imaginable **OPPOSITE:** unbelievable 2 = **reliable**, honest, dependable, trustworthy, sincere, trusty **OPPOSITE:** unreliable

credit NOUN 1 = **praise**, honour, recognition, approval, tribute, acclaim, acknowledgment, kudos 2 = **source of satisfaction** *or* **pride**, asset, honour, feather in your cap 3 = **prestige**, reputation, standing, position, influence, regard, status, esteem 4 = **belief**, trust, confidence, faith, reliance, credence ▷ VERB 5 = **believe**, rely on, have faith in, trust, accept ▷ PHRASES: credit someone with something = **attribute to**, assign to, ascribe to, impute to

creed = **belief**, principles, doctrine, dogma, credo, catechism, articles of faith

creek 1 = **inlet**, bay, cove, bight, firth *or* frith (*Scot*) 2 (*US, Canad, Austral & NZ*) = **stream**, brook, tributary, bayou, rivulet, watercourse, runnel

creep VERB 1 = **sneak**, steal, tiptoe, slink, skulk, approach unnoticed ▷ NOUN 2 (*slang*) = **bootlicker** (*informal*), sneak, sycophant, crawler (*slang*), toady ▷ PHRASES: give someone the creeps (*informal*) = **disgust**, frighten, scare, repel, repulse,

make your hair stand on end, make you squirm

crescent = **meniscus**, sickle, new moon

crest 1 = **top**, summit, peak, ridge, highest point, pinnacle, apex, crown 2 = **tuft**, crown, comb, plume, mane 3 = **emblem**, badge, symbol, insignia, bearings, device

crew 1 = **(ship's) company**, hands, (ship's) complement 2 = **team**, squad, gang, corps, posse 3 (*informal*) = **crowd**, set, bunch (*informal*), band, pack, gang, mob, horde

crime 1 = **offence**, violation, trespass, felony, misdemeanour, misdeed, transgression, unlawful act 2 = **lawbreaking**, corruption, illegality, vice, misconduct, wrongdoing, e-crime *or* ecrime, cybercrime

criminal NOUN 1 = **lawbreaker**, convict, offender, crook (*informal*), villain, culprit, sinner, felon, rorter (*Austral slang*), skelm (*S African*), rogue trader, perp (*US & Canad informal*) ▷ ADJECTIVE 2 = **unlawful**, illicit, lawless, wrong, illegal, corrupt, crooked (*informal*), immoral **OPPOSITE:** lawful 3 (*informal*) = **disgraceful**, ridiculous, foolish, senseless, scandalous, preposterous, deplorable

cripple 1 = **disable**, paralyse, lame, maim, incapacitate, weaken, hamstring

c

2 = **damage**, destroy, ruin, spoil, impair, put paid to, put out of action **OPPOSITE:** help

crippled = **damaged**, destroyed, impaired, paralysed, incapacitated

crisis 1 = **emergency**, plight, predicament, trouble, deep water, meltdown (*informal*), dire straits 2 = **critical point**, climax, height, crunch (*informal*), turning point, culmination, crux, moment of truth, tipping point

crisp 1 = **firm**, crunchy, crispy, crumbly, fresh, brittle, unwilted **OPPOSITE:** soft 2 = **bracing**, fresh, refreshing, brisk, invigorating **OPPOSITE:** warm 3 = **clean**, smart, trim, neat, tidy, spruce, well-groomed, well-pressed

criterion = **standard**, test, rule, measure, principle, gauge, yardstick, touchstone

> **USAGE NOTE**
> The word *criteria* is the plural of *criterion* and it is incorrect to use it as an alternative singular form; *these criteria are not valid* is correct, and so is *this criterion is not valid*, but not *this criteria is not valid*.

critic 1 = **judge**, authority, expert, analyst, commentator, pundit, reviewer, connoisseur 2 = **fault-finder**, attacker, detractor, knocker (*informal*)

critical 1 = **crucial**, decisive, pressing, serious, vital, urgent, all-important, pivotal **OPPOSITE:** unimportant 2 = **grave**, serious, acute, precarious **OPPOSITE:** safe 3 = **disparaging**, disapproving, scathing, derogatory, nit-picking (*informal*), censorious, fault-finding, captious, nit-picky (*informal*) **OPPOSITE:** complimentary 4 = **analytical**, penetrating, discriminating, discerning, perceptive, judicious **OPPOSITE:** undiscriminating

criticism 1 = **fault-finding**, censure, disapproval, disparagement, stick (*slang*), flak (*informal*), bad press, character assassination 2 = **analysis**, assessment, judgment, commentary, evaluation, appreciation, appraisal, critique

criticize = **find fault with**, censure, disapprove of, knock (*informal*), condemn, carp, put down, slate (*informal*), nit-pick (*informal*) **OPPOSITE:** praise

crook NOUN 1 (*informal*) = **criminal**, rogue, cheat, thief, shark, villain, robber, racketeer, skelm (*S African*)

▷ ADJECTIVE 2 (*Austral & NZ informal*) = **ill**, sick, poorly (*informal*), unhealthy, seedy (*informal*), unwell, queasy, out of sorts (*informal*)

▷ PHRASES: go (off) crook (*Austral & NZ informal*) = **lose your temper**, be furious, rage, go mad, lose it (*informal*), crack up (*informal*), see red (*informal*), blow your top

crooked 1 = **bent**, twisted, curved, irregular, warped, out of shape, misshapen **OPPOSITE:** straight 2 = **deformed**, distorted 3 = **at an angle**, uneven, slanting, squint, awry, lopsided, askew, off-centre 4 (*informal*) = **dishonest**, criminal, illegal, corrupt, unlawful, shady (*informal*), fraudulent, bent (*slang*) **OPPOSITE:** honest

crop NOUN 1 = **yield**, produce, gathering, fruits, harvest, vintage, reaping
▷ **VERB** 2 = **graze**, eat, browse, feed on, nibble 3 = **cut**, trim, clip, prune, shear, snip, pare, lop
▷ **PHRASES: crop up** (*informal*) = **happen**, appear, emerge, occur, arise, turn up, spring up

cross VERB 1 = **go across**, pass over, traverse, cut across, move across, travel across 2 = **span**, bridge, go across, extend over 3 = **intersect**, intertwine, crisscross 4 = **oppose**, interfere with, obstruct, block, resist, impede 5 = **interbreed**, mix, blend, cross-pollinate, crossbreed, hybridize, cross-fertilize, intercross
▷ **NOUN** 6 = **crucifix** 7 = **trouble**, worry, trial, load, burden, grief, woe, misfortune 8 = **mixture**, combination, blend, amalgam, amalgamation

▷ **ADJECTIVE** 9 = **angry**, annoyed, put out, grumpy, short, ill-tempered, irascible, tooshie (*Austral slang*), in a bad mood, hoha (*NZ*) **OPPOSITE:** good-humoured
▷ **PHRASES: cross something out** *or* **off** = **strike off** *or* **out**, eliminate, cancel, delete, blue-pencil, score off *or* out

crouch = **bend down**, kneel, squat, stoop, bow, duck, hunch

crow = **gloat**, triumph, boast, swagger, brag, exult, blow your own trumpet

crowd NOUN 1 = **multitude**, mass, throng, army, host, pack, mob, swarm 2 = **group**, set, lot, circle, gang, bunch (*informal*), clique 3 = **audience**, spectators, house, gate, attendance
▷ **VERB** 4 = **flock**, mass, collect, gather, stream, surge, swarm, throng 5 = **squeeze**, pack, pile, bundle, cram 6 = **congest**, pack, cram

crowded = **packed**, full, busy, cramped, swarming, teeming, congested, jam-packed

crown NOUN 1 = **coronet**, tiara, diadem, circlet 2 = **laurel wreath**, trophy, prize, honour, garland, laurels, wreath 3 = **high point**, top, tip, summit, crest, pinnacle, apex
▷ **VERB** 4 = **install**, honour, dignify, ordain, inaugurate 5 = **top**, cap, be on top of, surmount 6 = **cap**, finish,

c

complete, perfect, round off, put the finishing touch to, be the climax *or* culmination of **7** (*slang*) = **strike**, belt (*informal*), bash, hit over the head, box, punch, cuff, biff (*slang*)
▷ **PHRASES: the Crown**
1 = **monarch**, ruler, sovereign, emperor *or* empress, king *or* queen **2** = **monarchy**, sovereignty, royalty

crucial 1 (*informal*) = **vital**, important, pressing, essential, urgent, momentous, high-priority **2** = **critical**, central, key, psychological, decisive, pivotal

crude 1 = **rough**, basic, makeshift **2** = **simple**, rudimentary, basic, primitive, coarse, clumsy, rough-and-ready **3** = **vulgar**, dirty, rude, obscene, coarse, indecent, tasteless, smutty **OPPOSITE:** tasteful **4** = **unrefined**, natural, raw, unprocessed **OPPOSITE:** processed

crudely 1 = **roughly**, basically **2** = **simply**, roughly, basically, coarsely **3** = **vulgarly**, rudely, coarsely, crassly, obscenely, lewdly, impolitely, tastelessly

cruel 1 = **brutal**, ruthless, callous, sadistic, inhumane, vicious, monstrous, unkind **OPPOSITE:** kind **2** = **bitter**, ruthless, traumatic, grievous, unrelenting, merciless, pitiless

cruelly 1 = **brutally**, severely, mercilessly, in cold blood,

callously, monstrously, sadistically, pitilessly **2** = **bitterly**, deeply, severely, ruthlessly, mercilessly, grievously, pitilessly, traumatically

cruelty = **brutality**, ruthlessness, depravity, inhumanity, barbarity, callousness, spitefulness, mercilessness

cruise NOUN 1 = **sail**, voyage, boat trip, sea trip
▷ **VERB 2** = **sail**, coast, voyage **3** = **travel along**, coast, drift, keep a steady pace

crumb 1 = **bit**, grain, fragment, shred, morsel **2** = **morsel**, scrap, shred, snippet, soupçon (*French*)

crumble 1 = **disintegrate**, collapse, deteriorate, decay, fall apart, degenerate, tumble down, go to pieces **2** = **crush**, fragment, pulverize, pound, grind, powder, granulate **3** = **collapse**, deteriorate, decay, fall apart, degenerate, go to pieces, go to rack and ruin

crumple 1 = **crush**, squash, screw up, scrumple **2** = **crease**, wrinkle, rumple, ruffle, pucker **3** = **collapse**, sink, go down, fall **4** = **break down**, fall, collapse, give way, cave in, go to pieces **5** = **screw up**

crunch = **chomp**, champ, munch, chew noisily, grind
▷ **PHRASES: the crunch** (*informal*) = **critical point**, test,

crisis, emergency, crux, moment of truth

crusade NOUN 1 = **campaign**, drive, movement, cause, push
2 = **holy war**
▷ VERB 3 = **campaign**, fight, push, struggle, lobby, agitate, work

crush VERB 1 = **squash**, break, squeeze, compress, press, pulverize 2 = **crease**, wrinkle, crumple 3 = **overcome**, overwhelm, put down, subdue, overpower, quash, quell, stamp out 4 = **demoralize**, depress, devastate, discourage, humble, put down (*slang*), humiliate, squash
▷ NOUN 5 = **crowd**, mob, horde, throng, pack, mass, jam, huddle

crust = **layer**, covering, coating, skin, surface, shell

crustacean
• *See panel* **CRUSTACEANS**

cry VERB 1 = **weep**, sob, shed tears, blubber, snivel **OPPOSITE:** laugh 2 = **shout**, scream, roar, yell, howl, call out, exclaim, shriek **OPPOSITE:** whisper
▷ NOUN 3 = **weep**, sob, bawl, blubber 4 = **shout**, call, scream, roar, yell, howl, shriek, bellow 5 = **weeping**, sobbing, blubbering, snivelling
▷ PHRASES: cry off (*informal*) = **back out**, withdraw, quit, excuse yourself

cuddle 1 = **hug**, embrace, fondle, cosset 2 = **pet**, hug, bill and coo
▷ PHRASES: cuddle up = **snuggle**

CRUSTACEANS

barnacle	Norway lobster
crab	opossum shrimp
craw (*Austral & NZ*)	oyster crab
crayfish *or* crawfish (*US*)	prawn
Dublin Bay prawn	robber crab
freshwater shrimp	sand hopper, beach flea, *or*
goose barnacle	sand flea
gribble	sand shrimp
hermit crab	scorpion
horseshoe crab *or* king crab	sea spider
king prawn	shrimp
koura (*NZ*)	soft-shell crab
krill	spider crab
land crab	spiny lobster, rock lobster,
langoustine	crawfish, *or* langouste
lobster	water flea

cue = **signal**, sign, hint, prompt, reminder, suggestion

culminate = **end up**, close, finish, conclude, wind up, climax, come to a head, come to a climax

culprit = **offender**, criminal, felon, guilty party, wrongdoer, miscreant, evildoer, transgressor, perp (*US & Canad informal*)

cult 1 = **sect**, faction, school, religion, clique, hauhau (*NZ*) 2 = **craze**, fashion, trend, fad 3 = **obsession**, worship, devotion, idolization

cultivate 1 = **farm**, work, plant, tend, till, plough 2 = **develop**, establish, foster 3 = **court**, seek out, run after, dance attendance upon 4 = **improve**, refine

cultural 1 = **ethnic**, national, native, folk, racial 2 = **artistic**, educational, aesthetic, enriching, enlightening, civilizing, edifying

culture 1 = **the arts** 2 = **civilization**, society, customs, way of life 3 = **lifestyle**, habit, way of life, mores 4 = **refinement**, education, enlightenment, sophistication, good taste, urbanity

cultured = **refined**, intellectual, educated, sophisticated, enlightened, well-informed, urbane, highbrow **OPPOSITE:** uneducated

cunning ADJECTIVE 1 = **crafty**, sly, devious, artful, sharp, wily, Machiavellian, shifty **OPPOSITE:** frank 2 = **ingenious**, imaginative, sly, devious, artful, Machiavellian 3 = **skilful**, clever **OPPOSITE:** clumsy ▷ NOUN 4 = **craftiness**, guile, trickery, deviousness, artfulness, slyness **OPPOSITE:** candour 5 = **skill**, subtlety, ingenuity, artifice, cleverness **OPPOSITE:** clumsiness

cup 1 = **mug**, goblet, chalice, teacup, beaker, bowl 2 = **trophy**

cupboard = **cabinet**, press

curb VERB 1 = **restrain**, control, check, restrict, suppress, inhibit, hinder, retard ▷ NOUN 2 = **restraint**, control, check, brake, limitation, rein, deterrent, bridle

cure VERB 1 = **make better**, correct, heal, relieve, remedy, mend, ease 2 = **restore to health**, restore, heal 3 = **preserve**, smoke, dry, salt, pickle ▷ NOUN 4 = **remedy**, treatment, antidote, panacea, nostrum

curiosity 1 = **inquisitiveness**, interest, prying, snooping (*informal*), nosiness (*informal*), infomania 2 = **oddity**, wonder, sight, phenomenon, spectacle, freak, novelty, rarity

curious 1 = **inquisitive**, interested, questioning, searching, inquiring, meddling,

prying, nosy (*informal*)
OPPOSITE: uninterested
2 = **strange**, unusual, bizarre,
odd, novel, rare, extraordinary,
unexpected **OPPOSITE:** ordinary
curl NOUN 1 = **ringlet**, lock
2 = **twist**, spiral, coil, kink, whorl
▷ **VERB** 3 = **crimp**, wave, perm
4 = **twirl**, turn, bend, twist,
curve, loop, spiral, coil 5 = **wind**
curly = **wavy**, curled, curling,
fuzzy, frizzy
currency 1 = **money**, coinage,
legal tender, notes, coins
2 = **acceptance**, popularity,
circulation, vogue, prevalence
current NOUN 1 = **flow**, course,
undertow, jet, stream, tide,
progression, river 2 = **draught**,
flow, breeze, puff 3 = **mood**,
feeling, spirit, atmosphere,
trend, tendency, undercurrent
▷ **ADJECTIVE** 4 = **present**,
fashionable, up-to-date,
contemporary, trendy (*Brit
informal*), topical, present-day, in
fashion, live (~*data*) **OPPOSITE:**
out-of-date 5 = **prevalent**,
common, accepted, popular,
widespread, customary, in
circulation
curse VERB 1 = **swear**, cuss
(*informal*), blaspheme, take the
Lord's name in vain 2 = **abuse**,
damn, scold, vilify
▷ **NOUN** 3 = **oath**, obscenity,
blasphemy, expletive,
profanity, imprecation,
swearword 4 = **malediction**,

jinx, anathema, hoodoo
(*informal*), excommunication
5 = **affliction**, plague, scourge,
trouble, torment, hardship,
bane
cursed = **under a curse**,
damned, doomed, jinxed,
bedevilled, accursed, ill-fated
curtail = **reduce**, diminish,
decrease, dock, cut back,
shorten, lessen, cut short
curtain = **hanging**, drape (*chiefly
US*), portière
curve NOUN 1 = **bend**, turn,
loop, arc, curvature
▷ **VERB** 2 = **bend**, turn, wind,
twist, arch, snake, arc, coil
curved = **bent**, rounded,
twisted, bowed, arched,
serpentine, sinuous
cushion NOUN 1 = **pillow**, pad,
bolster, headrest, beanbag,
hassock
▷ **VERB** 2 = **protect** 3 = **soften**,
dampen, muffle, mitigate,
deaden, suppress, stifle
custody 1 = **care**, charge,
protection, supervision,
safekeeping, keeping
2 = **imprisonment**, detention,
confinement, incarceration
custom 1 = **tradition**, practice,
convention, ritual, policy, rule,
usage, kaupapa (*NZ*) 2 = **habit**,
way, practice, procedure,
routine, wont 3 = **customers**,
business, trade, patronage
customary 1 = **usual**, common,
accepted, established,

traditional, normal, ordinary, conventional **OPPOSITE:** unusual 2 = **accustomed**, regular, usual

customer = **client**, consumer, regular (*informal*), buyer, patron, shopper, purchaser

customs = **import charges**, tax, duty, toll, tariff

cut VERB 1 = **slit**, score, slice, slash, pierce, penetrate 2 = **chop**, split, slice, dissect 3 = **carve**, slice 4 = **sever**, cut in two 5 = **shape**, carve, engrave, chisel, form, score, fashion, whittle 6 = **slash**, wound 7 = **clip**, mow, trim, prune, snip, pare, lop 8 = **trim**, shave, snip 9 = **reduce**, lower, slim (down), diminish, slash, decrease, cut back, kennet (*Austral slang*), jeff (*Austral slang*) **OPPOSITE:** increase 10 = **abridge**, edit, shorten, curtail, condense, abbreviate **OPPOSITE:** extend 11 = **delete**, take out, expurgate 12 = **hurt**, wound, upset, sting, hurt someone's feelings 13 (*informal*) = **ignore**, avoid, slight, blank (*slang*), snub, spurn, cold-shoulder, turn your back on **OPPOSITE:** greet 14 = **cross**, bisect
▷ NOUN 15 = **incision**, nick, stroke, slash, slit 16 = **gash**, nick, wound, slash, laceration 17 = **reduction**, fall, lowering, slash, decrease, cutback 18 (*informal*) = **share**, piece, slice,

percentage, portion 19 = **style**, look, fashion, shape

cutback = **reduction**, cut, retrenchment, economy, decrease, lessening

cute = **appealing**, sweet, attractive, engaging, charming, delightful, lovable, winsome

cutting = **hurtful**, wounding, bitter, malicious, scathing, acrimonious, barbed, sarcastic **OPPOSITE:** kind

cycle = **series of events**, circle, revolution, rotation

cynic = **sceptic**, doubter, pessimist, misanthrope, misanthropist, scoffer

cynical 1 = **sceptical**, mocking, pessimistic, scoffing, contemptuous, scornful, distrustful, derisive **OPPOSITE:** trusting 2 = **unbelieving**, sceptical, disillusioned, pessimistic, disbelieving, mistrustful **OPPOSITE:** optimistic

cynicism 1 = **scepticism**, pessimism, misanthropy 2 = **disbelief**, doubt, scepticism, mistrust

Dd

dab VERB 1 = **pat**, touch, tap
2 = **apply**, daub, stipple
▷ NOUN 3 = **spot**, bit, drop,
pat, smudge, speck 4 = **touch**,
stroke, flick

daft (*informal, chiefly Brit*)
1 = **stupid**, crazy, silly, absurd,
foolish, idiotic, witless, crackpot
(*informal*), off the air (*Austral
slang*) 2 (*slang*) = **crazy**, mad,
touched, nuts (*slang*), crackers
(*Brit slang*), insane, demented,
deranged, off the air (*Austral
slang*), porangi (*NZ*)

dag (*NZ informal*) = **joker**, comic,
wag, wit, comedian, clown,
humorist, prankster
▷ PHRASES: **rattle your dags** (*NZ
informal*) = **hurry up**, get a move
on, step on it (*informal*), get your
skates on (*informal*), make haste

dagga (*S African*) = **cannabis**,
marijuana, pot (*slang*), dope
(*slang*), hash (*slang*), grass
(*slang*), weed (*slang*), hemp

daily ADJECTIVE 1 = **everyday**,
diurnal, quotidian
▷ ADVERB 2 = **every day**, day by
day, once a day

dam NOUN 1 = **barrier**,
wall, barrage, obstruction,
embankment
▷ VERB 2 = **block up**, restrict,
hold back, barricade, obstruct

damage NOUN 1 = **destruction**,
harm, loss, injury, suffering,
hurt, ruin, devastation
OPPOSITE: improvement
2 (*informal*) = **cost**, price, charge,
bill, amount, payment, expense,
outlay
▷ VERB 3 = **spoil**, hurt, injure,
harm, ruin, crush, devastate,
wreck OPPOSITE: fix
▷ PLURAL NOUN 4 (*Law*)
= **compensation**, fine,
satisfaction, amends,
reparation, restitution,
reimbursement, atonement

damaging = **harmful**,
detrimental, hurtful, ruinous,
deleterious, injurious,
disadvantageous OPPOSITE:
helpful

dame *with cap.* = **lady**, baroness,
dowager, grande dame (*French*),
noblewoman, peeress

damn = **criticize**, condemn,
blast, denounce, put down,
censure OPPOSITE: praise

damned (*slang*) = **infernal**,
detestable, confounded,
hateful, loathsome

damp ADJECTIVE 1 = **moist**, wet,
soggy, humid, dank, sopping,
clammy, dewy OPPOSITE: dry
▷ NOUN 2 = **moisture**, liquid,
drizzle, dampness, wetness,

d

dankness **OPPOSITE:** dryness
▷ **VERB** 3 = **moisten**, wet, soak, dampen, moisturize
▷ **PHRASES:** damp something down = **curb**, reduce, check, diminish, inhibit, stifle, allay, pour cold water on

dampen 1 = **reduce**, check, moderate, dull, restrain, stifle, lessen 2 = **moisten**, wet, spray, make damp

dance **VERB** 1 = **prance**, trip, hop, skip, sway, whirl, caper, jig 2 = **caper**, trip, spring, jump, bound, skip, frolic, cavort
▷ **NOUN** 3 = **ball**, social, hop (*informal*), disco, knees-up (*Brit informal*), discotheque, B and S (*Austral informal*)

dancer = **ballerina**, Terpsichorean

danger 1 = **jeopardy**, vulnerability 2 = **hazard**, risk, threat, menace, peril, pitfall

dangerous = **perilous**, risky, hazardous, vulnerable, insecure, unsafe, precarious, breakneck **OPPOSITE:** safe

dangerously = **perilously**, alarmingly, precariously, recklessly, riskily, hazardously, unsafely

dangle 1 = **hang**, swing, trail, sway, flap, hang down 2 = **offer**, flourish, brandish, flaunt

dare 1 = **risk doing**, venture, presume, make bold (*archaic*), hazard doing 2 = **challenge**, provoke, defy, taunt, goad, throw down the gauntlet

daring **ADJECTIVE** 1 = **brave**, bold, adventurous, reckless, fearless, audacious, intrepid, daredevil **OPPOSITE:** timid
▷ **NOUN** 2 = **bravery**, nerve (*informal*), courage, spirit, bottle (*Brit slang*), pluck, audacity, boldness **OPPOSITE:** timidity

dark **ADJECTIVE** 1 = **dim**, murky, shady, shadowy, grey, dingy, unlit, poorly lit 2 = **black**, brunette, ebony, dark-skinned, sable, dusky, swarthy **OPPOSITE:** fair 3 = **evil**, foul, sinister, vile, wicked, infernal 4 = **secret**, hidden, mysterious, concealed 5 = **gloomy**, sad, grim, miserable, bleak, dismal, pessimistic, melancholy **OPPOSITE:** cheerful
▷ **NOUN** 6 = **darkness**, shadows, gloom, dusk, obscurity, murk, dimness, semi-darkness 7 = **night**, twilight, evening, evo (*Austral slang*), dusk, night-time, nightfall

darken 1 = **cloud**, obscure, dim, overshadow, blacken **OPPOSITE:** brighten 2 = **make dark**, blacken

darkness = **dark**, shadows, shade, gloom, blackness, murk, duskiness

darling **NOUN** 1 = **beloved**, love, dear, dearest, angel, treasure, precious, sweetheart
▷ **ADJECTIVE** 2 = **beloved**, dear, treasured, precious, adored, cherished

dart = **dash**, run, race, shoot, fly, speed, spring, tear

dash VERB 1 = **rush**, run, race, shoot, fly, career, speed, tear **OPPOSITE:** dawdle 2 = **throw**, cast, pitch, slam, toss, hurl, fling, chuck (*informal*) 3 = **crash**, break, smash, shatter, splinter ▷ NOUN 4 = **rush**, run, race, sprint, dart, spurt, sortie 5 = **drop**, little, bit, shot (*informal*), touch, spot, trace, hint **OPPOSITE:** lot 6 = **style**, spirit, flair, flourish, verve, panache, élan, brio

dashing (*Old-fashioned*) = **stylish**, smart, elegant, flamboyant, sporty, jaunty, showy

data 1 = **details**, facts, figures, intelligence, statistics 2 (*Computing*) = **information**

date NOUN 1 = **time**, stage, period 2 = **appointment**, meeting, arrangement, commitment, engagement, rendezvous, tryst, assignation 3 = **partner**, escort, friend ▷ VERB 4 = **put a date on**, assign a date to, fix the period of 5 = **become dated**, become old-fashioned ▷ PHRASES: **date from** *or* **date back to** = **come from**, belong to, originate in, exist from, bear a date of

dated = **old-fashioned**, outdated, out of date, obsolete, unfashionable, outmoded, passé, old hat **OPPOSITE:** modern

daunting = **intimidating**, alarming, frightening, discouraging, unnerving, disconcerting, demoralizing, off-putting (*Brit informal*) **OPPOSITE:** reassuring

dawn NOUN 1 = **daybreak**, morning, sunrise, daylight, aurora (*poetic*), crack of dawn, sunup, cockcrow 2 (*literary*) = **beginning**, start, birth, rise, origin, emergence, advent, genesis ▷ VERB 3 = **begin**, start, rise, develop, emerge, unfold, originate 4 = **grow light**, break, brighten, lighten ▷ PHRASES: **dawn on** *or* **upon someone** = **hit**, strike, occur to, register (*informal*), become apparent, come to mind, come into your head

day 1 = **twenty-four hours** 2 = **daytime**, daylight 3 = **date** 4 = **time**, age, era, period, epoch

daylight = **sunlight**, sunshine, light of day

daze VERB 1 = **stun**, shock, paralyse, numb, stupefy, benumb ▷ NOUN 2 = **shock**, confusion, distraction, trance, bewilderment, stupor, trancelike state

dazzle VERB 1 = **impress**, amaze, overwhelm, astonish, overpower, bowl over (*informal*),

take your breath away **2** = **blind**, confuse, daze, bedazzle
▷ **NOUN 3** = **splendour**, sparkle, glitter, brilliance, magnificence, razzmatazz (*slang*)

dazzling = **splendid**, brilliant, stunning, glorious, sparkling, glittering, sensational (*informal*), virtuoso **OPPOSITE:** ordinary

dead ADJECTIVE **1** = **deceased**, departed, late, perished, extinct, defunct, passed away **OPPOSITE:** alive **2** = **boring**, dull, dreary, flat, plain, humdrum, uninteresting **3** = **not working**, useless, inactive, inoperative **OPPOSITE:** working **4** = **numb**, frozen, paralysed, insensitive, inert, deadened, immobilized, unfeeling **5** (*of a centre, silence, or a stop*) = **total**, complete, absolute, utter, outright, thorough, unqualified **6** (*informal*) = **exhausted**, tired, worn out, spent, done in (*informal*), all in (*slang*), drained, knackered (*slang*)
▷ **NOUN 7** = **middle**, heart, depth, midst
▷ **ADVERB 8** = **exactly**, completely, totally, directly, fully, entirely, absolutely, thoroughly

deadline = **time limit**, cutoff point, target date or time, limit

deadlock 1 = **impasse**, stalemate, standstill, gridlock, standoff **2** = **tie**, draw, stalemate, impasse, standstill, gridlock, standoff, dead heat

deadly 1 = **lethal**, fatal, deathly, dangerous, devastating, mortal, murderous, malignant **2** (*informal*) = **boring**, dull, tedious, flat, monotonous, uninteresting, mind-numbing, wearisome

deaf 1 = **hard of hearing**, without hearing, stone deaf **2** = **oblivious**, indifferent, unmoved, unconcerned, unsympathetic, impervious, unhearing

deal 1 (*informal*) = **agreement**, understanding, contract, arrangement, bargain, transaction, pact **2** = **amount**, quantity, measure, degree, mass, volume, share, portion
▷ **PHRASES: deal in something** = **sell**, trade in, stock, traffic in, buy and sell ▶ **deal something out** = **distribute**, give, share, assign, allocate, dispense, allot, mete out ▶ **deal with something** = **be concerned with**, involve, concern, touch, regard, apply to, bear on, pertain to ▶ **deal with something or someone** = **handle**, manage, treat, cope with, take care of, see to, attend to, get to grips with

dealer = **trader**, merchant, supplier, wholesaler, purveyor, tradesman

dear ADJECTIVE **1** = **beloved**, close, valued, favourite, prized, treasured, precious,

intimate **OPPOSITE:** hated
2 = **expensive**, costly, high-priced, pricey (*informal*), at a premium, overpriced, exorbitant **OPPOSITE:** cheap
▷ **NOUN** 3 = **darling**, love, dearest, angel, treasure, precious, beloved, loved one

dearly 1 = **very much**, greatly, extremely, profoundly 2 = **at great cost**, at a high price

death 1 = **dying**, demise, end, passing, departure **OPPOSITE:** birth 2 = **destruction**, finish, ruin, undoing, extinction, downfall **OPPOSITE:** beginning

> **RELATED WORDS**
> *adjectives*: fatal, lethal, mortal

deathly = **deathlike**, white, pale, ghastly, wan, pallid, ashen

debacle *or* **débâcle** = **disaster**, catastrophe, fiasco

debate **NOUN** 1 = **discussion**, talk, argument, dispute, analysis, conversation, controversy, dialogue
▷ **VERB** 2 = **discuss**, question, talk about, argue about, dispute, examine, deliberate 3 = **consider**, reflect, think about, weigh, contemplate, deliberate, ponder, ruminate

debris = **remains**, bits, waste, ruins, fragments, rubble, wreckage, detritus

debt = **debit**, commitment, obligation, liability
▷ **PHRASES:** in debt = **owing**, liable, in the red (*informal*), in arrears

debtor = **borrower**, mortgagor

debut 1 = **entrance**, beginning, launch, introduction, first appearance 2 = **presentation**, coming out, introduction, first appearance, initiation

decay **VERB** 1 = **rot**, spoil, crumble, deteriorate, perish, decompose, moulder, go bad 2 = **decline**, diminish, crumble, deteriorate, fall off, dwindle, lessen, wane **OPPOSITE:** grow
▷ **NOUN** 3 = **rot**, corruption, mould, blight, decomposition, gangrene, canker, caries 4 = **decline**, collapse, deterioration, failing, fading, degeneration **OPPOSITE:** growth

deceased = **dead**, late, departed, expired, defunct, lifeless

deceive = **take in**, trick, fool (*informal*), cheat, con (*informal*), mislead, dupe, swindle, scam (*slang*)

decency 1 = **propriety**, correctness, decorum, respectability, etiquette 2 = **courtesy**, politeness, civility, graciousness, urbanity, courteousness

decent 1 = **satisfactory**, fair, all right, reasonable, sufficient, good enough, adequate, ample **OPPOSITE:** unsatisfactory 2 = **proper**, becoming, seemly, fitting, appropriate, suitable, respectable, befitting **OPPOSITE:** improper **3** (*informal*) = **good**, kind, friendly, neighbourly, generous, helpful, obliging, accommodating **4** = **respectable**, pure, proper, modest, chaste, decorous

deception 1 = **trickery**, fraud, deceit, cunning, treachery, guile, legerdemain **OPPOSITE:** honesty **2** = **trick**, lie, bluff, hoax, decoy, ruse, subterfuge, fastie (*Austral slang*)

decide 1 = **make a decision**, make up your mind, reach *or* come to a decision, choose, determine, conclude **OPPOSITE:** hesitate **2** = **resolve**, answer, determine, conclude, clear up, ordain, adjudicate, adjudge **3** = **settle**, determine, resolve

decidedly = **definitely**, clearly, positively, distinctly, downright, unequivocally, unmistakably

decision 1 = **judgment**, finding, ruling, sentence, resolution, conclusion, verdict, decree **2** = **decisiveness**, purpose, resolution, resolve, determination, firmness, forcefulness, strength of mind *or* will

decisive 1 = **crucial**, significant, critical, influential, momentous, conclusive, fateful **OPPOSITE:** uncertain **2** = **resolute**, decided, firm, determined, forceful, incisive, trenchant, strong-minded **OPPOSITE:** indecisive

deck = **decorate**, dress, clothe, array, adorn, embellish, festoon, beautify

declaration 1 = **announcement**, proclamation, decree, notice, notification, edict, pronouncement **2** = **affirmation**, profession, assertion, revelation, disclosure, acknowledgment, protestation, avowal **3** = **statement**, testimony

declare 1 = **state**, claim, announce, voice, express, maintain, assert, proclaim **2** = **testify**, state, swear, assert, affirm, bear witness, vouch **3** = **make known**, reveal, show, broadcast, confess, communicate, disclose

decline VERB 1 = **fall**, drop, lower, sink, fade, shrink, diminish, decrease **OPPOSITE:** rise **2** = **deteriorate**, weaken, pine, decay, worsen, languish, degenerate, droop **OPPOSITE:** improve **3** = **refuse**, reject, turn down, avoid, spurn, abstain, say 'no' **OPPOSITE:** accept ▷ **NOUN 4** = **depression**, recession, slump, falling off, downturn, dwindling, lessening **OPPOSITE:** rise **5** = **deterioration**, failing, weakening, decay, worsening, degeneration **OPPOSITE:** improvement

decor *or* **décor** = **decoration**, colour scheme, ornamentation, furnishing style

decorate 1 = **adorn**, trim, embroider, ornament, embellish, festoon, beautify, grace 2 = **do up**, paper, paint, wallpaper, renovate (*informal*), furbish 3 = **pin a medal on**, cite, confer an honour on *or* upon

decoration 1 = **adornment**, trimming, enhancement, elaboration, embellishment, ornamentation, beautification 2 = **ornament**, trimmings, garnish, frill, bauble 3 = **medal**, award, star, ribbon, badge

decorative = **ornamental**, fancy, pretty, attractive, for show, embellishing, showy, beautifying

decrease VERB 1 = **drop**, decline, lessen, lower, shrink, diminish, dwindle, subside 2 = **reduce**, cut, lower, moderate, weaken, diminish, cut down, shorten **OPPOSITE:** increase
▷ NOUN 3 = **lessening**, decline, reduction, loss, falling off, dwindling, contraction, cutback **OPPOSITE:** growth

decree NOUN 1 = **law**, order, ruling, act, command, statute, proclamation, edict 2 = **judgment**, finding, ruling, decision, verdict, arbitration
▷ VERB 3 = **order**, rule, command, demand, proclaim, prescribe, pronounce, ordain

dedicate 1 = **devote**, give, apply, commit, pledge, surrender,

give over to 2 = **offer**, address, inscribe

dedicated = **committed**, devoted, enthusiastic, single-minded, zealous, purposeful, wholehearted **OPPOSITE:** indifferent

dedication 1 = **commitment**, loyalty, devotion, allegiance, adherence, single-mindedness, faithfulness, wholeheartedness **OPPOSITE:** indifference 2 = **inscription**, message, address

deduct = **subtract**, remove, take off, take away, reduce by, knock off (*informal*), decrease by **OPPOSITE:** add

deduction 1 = **conclusion**, finding, verdict, judgment, assumption, inference 2 = **reasoning**, thinking, thought, analysis, logic 3 = **discount**, reduction, cut, concession, decrease, rebate, diminution 4 = **subtraction**, reduction, concession

deed 1 = **action**, act, performance, achievement, exploit, feat 2 (*Law*) = **document**, title, contract

deep ADJECTIVE 1 = **big**, wide, broad, profound, yawning, bottomless, unfathomable **OPPOSITE:** shallow 2 = **intense**, great, serious (*informal*), acute, extreme, grave, profound, heartfelt **OPPOSITE:** superficial 3 = **sound**,

profound, unbroken, undisturbed, untroubled **4** *with* **in = absorbed in**, lost in, gripped by, preoccupied with, immersed in, engrossed in, rapt by **5 = dark**, strong, rich, intense, vivid **OPPOSITE:** light **6 = low**, booming, bass, resonant, sonorous, low-pitched **OPPOSITE:** high **7 = secret**, hidden, mysterious, obscure, abstract, esoteric, mystifying, arcane
▷ NOUN **8 = middle**, heart, midst, dead
▷ ADVERB **9 = far**, a long way, a good way, miles, a great distance
▷ PHRASES: **the deep** (*poetic*) **= the ocean**, the sea, the waves, the main, the high seas, the briny (*informal*)

deepen 1 = intensify, increase, grow, strengthen, reinforce, escalate, magnify **2 = dig out**, excavate, scoop out, hollow out

deeply = thoroughly, completely, seriously, sadly, severely, gravely, profoundly, intensely

de facto ADVERB **1 = in fact**, really, actually, in effect, in reality
▷ ADJECTIVE **2 = actual**, real, existing

default NOUN **1 = failure**, neglect, deficiency, lapse, omission, dereliction
2 = nonpayment, evasion

▷ VERB **3 = fail to pay**, dodge, evade, neglect

defeat VERB **1 = beat**, crush, overwhelm, conquer, master, rout, trounce, vanquish **OPPOSITE:** surrender
2 = frustrate, foil, thwart, ruin, baffle, confound, balk, get the better of
▷ NOUN **3 = conquest**, beating, overthrow, rout **OPPOSITE:** victory **4 = frustration**, failure, reverse, setback, thwarting

defect NOUN **1 = deficiency**, failing, fault, error, flaw, imperfection
▷ VERB **2 = desert**, rebel, quit, revolt, change sides

defence *or* (*US*) **defense** NOUN **1 = protection**, cover, security, guard, shelter, safeguard, immunity **2 = armaments**, weapons **3 = argument**, explanation, excuse, plea, justification, vindication, rationalization **4 = plea** (*law*), testimony, denial, alibi, rebuttal
▷ PLURAL NOUN **5 = shield**, barricade, fortification, buttress, rampart, bulwark, fortified pa (*NZ*)

defend 1 = protect, cover, guard, screen, preserve, look after, shelter, shield **2 = support**, champion, justify, endorse, uphold, vindicate, stand up for, speak up for

defendant = accused, respondent, prisoner at the bar

defender 1 = **supporter**, champion, advocate, sponsor, follower 2 = **protector**, guard, guardian, escort, bodyguard

defensive 1 = **protective**, watchful, on the defensive, on guard 2 = **oversensitive**, uptight (*informal*)

defer = **postpone**, delay, put off, suspend, shelve, hold over, procrastinate, put on ice (*informal*)

defiance = **resistance**, opposition, confrontation, contempt, disregard, disobedience, insolence, insubordination **OPPOSITE:** obedience

defiant = **resisting**, rebellious, daring, bold, provocative, audacious, antagonistic, insolent **OPPOSITE:** obedient

deficiency 1 = **lack**, want, deficit, absence, shortage, scarcity, dearth **OPPOSITE:** sufficiency 2 = **failing**, fault, weakness, defect, flaw, drawback, shortcoming, imperfection

deficit = **shortfall**, shortage, deficiency, loss, arrears

define 1 = **mark out**, outline, limit, bound, delineate, circumscribe, demarcate 2 = **describe**, interpret, characterize, explain, spell out, expound 3 = **establish**, specify, designate

definite 1 = **specific**, exact, precise, clear, particular, fixed, black-and-white, cut-and-dried (*informal*) **OPPOSITE:** vague 2 = **clear**, black-and-white, unequivocal, unambiguous, guaranteed, cut-and-dried (*informal*) 3 = **noticeable**, marked, clear, decided, striking, particular, distinct, conspicuous 4 = **certain**, decided, sure, settled, convinced, positive, confident, assured **OPPOSITE:** uncertain

definitely = **certainly**, clearly, surely, absolutely, positively, without doubt, unquestionably, undeniably

definition 1 = **description**, interpretation, explanation, clarification, exposition, elucidation, statement of meaning 2 = **sharpness**, focus, clarity, contrast, precision, distinctness

definitive 1 = **final**, convincing, absolute, clinching, decisive, definite, conclusive, irrefutable 2 = **authoritative**, greatest, ultimate, reliable, exhaustive, superlative

deflect = **turn aside**, bend

defy = **resist**, oppose, confront, brave, disregard, stand up to, spurn, flout

degenerate VERB 1 = **decline**, slip, sink, decrease, deteriorate, worsen, decay, lapse ▷ ADJECTIVE 2 = **depraved**, corrupt, low, perverted, immoral, decadent, debauched, dissolute

degrade = **demean**, disgrace, humiliate, shame, humble, discredit, debase, dishonour **OPPOSITE:** ennoble

degree = **amount**, stage, grade

delay VERB 1 = **put off**, suspend, postpone, shelve, defer, hold over 2 = **hold up**, detain, hold back, hinder, obstruct, impede, bog down, set back **OPPOSITE:** speed (up)
▷ NOUN 3 = **hold-up**, wait, setback, interruption, stoppage, impediment, hindrance

delegate NOUN
1 = **representative**, agent, deputy, ambassador, commissioner, envoy, proxy, legate
▷ VERB 2 = **entrust**, transfer, hand over, give, pass on, assign, consign, devolve 3 = **appoint**, commission, select, contract, engage, nominate, designate, mandate

delegation 1 = **deputation**, envoys, contingent, commission, embassy, legation 2 = **commissioning**, assignment, devolution, committal

delete = **remove**, cancel, erase, strike out, obliterate, efface, cross out, expunge

deliberate ADJECTIVE
1 = **intentional**, meant, planned, intended, conscious, calculated, wilful, purposeful **OPPOSITE:** accidental 2 = **careful**, measured, slow, cautious, thoughtful, circumspect, methodical, unhurried **OPPOSITE:** hurried
▷ VERB 3 = **consider**, think, ponder, discuss, debate, reflect, consult, weigh

deliberately = **intentionally**, on purpose, consciously, knowingly, wilfully, by design, in cold blood, wittingly

deliberation 1 = **consideration**, thought, reflection, calculation, meditation, forethought, circumspection 2 *usually plural* = **discussion**, talk, conference, debate, analysis, conversation, dialogue, consultation

delicacy 1 = **fragility**, flimsiness 2 = **daintiness**, charm, grace, elegance, neatness, prettiness, slenderness, exquisiteness
3 = **difficulty** 4 = **sensitivity**, understanding, consideration, diplomacy, discretion, tact, thoughtfulness, sensitiveness
5 = **treat**, luxury, savoury, dainty, morsel, titbit
6 = **lightness**, accuracy, precision, elegance, sensibility, purity, subtlety, refinement

delicate 1 = **fine**, elegant, exquisite, graceful 2 = **subtle**, fine, delicious, faint, refined, understated, dainty 3 = **fragile**, weak, frail, brittle, tender, flimsy, dainty, breakable **4 = skilled**, precise, deft **5 = diplomatic**, sensitive, thoughtful, discreet, considerate, tactful **OPPOSITE:** insensitive

delicious = delectable, tasty, choice, savoury, dainty, mouthwatering, scrumptious (*informal*), appetizing, lekker (*S African slang*), yummo (*Austral slang*) **OPPOSITE:** unpleasant

delight VERB **1 = please**, satisfy, thrill, charm, cheer, amuse, enchant, gratify **OPPOSITE:** displease
▷ NOUN **2 = pleasure**, joy, satisfaction, happiness, ecstasy, enjoyment, bliss, glee **OPPOSITE:** displeasure
▷ PHRASES: delight in *or* take a delight in something *or* someone = **like**, love, enjoy, appreciate, relish, savour, revel in, take pleasure in

delightful = pleasant, charming, thrilling, enjoyable, enchanting, agreeable, pleasurable, rapturous **OPPOSITE:** unpleasant

deliver 1 = bring, carry, bear, transport, distribute, convey, cart **2** *sometimes with* **over** *or* **up = hand over**, commit, give up, yield, surrender, turn over, relinquish, make over **3 = give**, read, present, announce, declare, utter **4 = strike**, give, deal, launch, direct, aim, administer, inflict **5 = release**, free, save, rescue, loose, liberate, ransom, emancipate

delivery 1 = handing over, transfer, distribution, transmission, dispatch, consignment, conveyance **2 = consignment**, goods, shipment, batch **3 = speech**, utterance, articulation, intonation, elocution, enunciation **4 = childbirth**, labour, confinement, parturition

delusion = misconception, mistaken idea, misapprehension, fancy, illusion, hallucination, fallacy, false impression

demand VERB **1 = request**, ask (for), order, expect, claim, seek, insist on, exact **2 = challenge**, ask, question, inquire **3 = require**, want, need, involve, call for, entail, necessitate, cry out for **OPPOSITE:** provide
▷ NOUN **4 = request**, order **5 = need**, want, call, market, claim, requirement

demanding = difficult, trying, hard, taxing, wearing, challenging, tough, exacting **OPPOSITE:** easy

demise 1 = failure, end, fall, defeat, collapse, ruin, breakdown, overthrow **2** (*euphemistic*) **= death**, end, dying, passing, departure, decease

democracy = self-government, republic, commonwealth

Democrat = left-winger
democratic = self-governing,
  popular, representative,
  autonomous, populist,
  egalitarian
demolish 1 = **knock down**, level,
  destroy, dismantle, flatten, tear
  down, bulldoze, raze **OPPOSITE:**
  build 2 = **destroy**, wreck,
  overturn, overthrow, undo
demolition = **knocking down**,
  levelling, destruction, explosion,
  wrecking, tearing down,
  bulldozing, razing
demon 1 = **evil spirit**, devil,
  fiend, goblin, ghoul, malignant
  spirit, atua (*NZ*), wairua
  (*NZ*) 2 = **wizard**, master, ace
  (*informal*), fiend
demonstrate 1 = **prove**, show,
  indicate, make clear, manifest,
  testify to, flag up 2 = **show**,
  express, display, indicate,
  exhibit, manifest, flag up
  3 = **march**, protest, rally, object,
  parade, picket, remonstrate,
  express disapproval, hikoi (*NZ*)
  4 = **describe**, show, explain,
  teach, illustrate
demonstration 1 = **march**,
  protest, rally, sit-in, parade,
  picket, mass lobby, hikoi (*NZ*)
  2 = **display**, show, performance,
  explanation, description,
  presentation, exposition
  3 = **indication**, proof, testimony,
  confirmation, substantiation
  4 = **exhibition**, display,
  expression, illustration

den 1 = **lair**, hole, shelter, cave,
  haunt, cavern, hide-out 2 (*chiefly
  US*) = **study**, retreat, sanctuary,
  hideaway, sanctum, cubbyhole
denial 1 = **negation**,
  contradiction, dissent,
  retraction, repudiation
  OPPOSITE: admission
  2 = **refusal**, veto, rejection,
  prohibition, rebuff, repulse
denomination 1 = **religious
  group**, belief, sect, persuasion,
  creed, school, hauhau (*NZ*)
  2 = **unit**, value, size, grade
denounce 1 = **condemn**, attack,
  censure, revile, vilify, stigmatize
  2 = **report**, dob in (*Austral slang*)
dense 1 = **thick**, heavy,
  solid, compact, condensed,
  impenetrable, close-knit
  OPPOSITE: thin 2 = **heavy**,
  thick, opaque, impenetrable
  3 = **stupid**, thick, dull, dumb
  (*informal*), dozy (*Brit informal*),
  stolid, dopey (*informal*), moronic
  OPPOSITE: bright
density 1 = **tightness**,
  thickness, compactness,
  impenetrability, denseness
  2 = **mass**, bulk, consistency,
  solidity
dent NOUN 1 = **hollow**, chip,
  indentation, depression,
  impression, pit, dip, crater, ding
  (*Austral & NZ obsolete informal*)
  ▷ VERB 2 = **make a dent in**,
  press in, gouge, hollow, push in
deny 1 = **contradict**, disagree
  with, rebuff, negate, rebut,

refute **OPPOSITE:** admit
2 = **renounce**, reject, retract,
repudiate, disown, recant,
disclaim 3 = **refuse**, forbid,
reject, rule out, turn down,
prohibit, withhold, preclude
OPPOSITE: permit

depart 1 = **leave**, go, withdraw,
retire, disappear, quit, retreat,
exit, rack off (*Austral & NZ slang*)
OPPOSITE: arrive 2 = **deviate**,
vary, differ, stray, veer, swerve,
diverge, digress

department = **section**, office,
unit, station, division, branch,
bureau, subdivision

departure 1 = **leaving**, going,
retirement, withdrawal,
exit, going away, removal,
exodus **OPPOSITE:** arrival
2 = **retirement**, going,
withdrawal, exit, going
away, removal 3 = **shift**,
change, difference, variation,
innovation, novelty, deviation,
divergence

dependent *or* (*sometimes US*)
dependant 1 = **reliant**,
vulnerable, helpless, powerless,
weak, defenceless **OPPOSITE:**
independent 2 = **determined
by**, depending on, subject to,
influenced by, conditional on,
contingent on
▷ **PHRASES: dependent on** *or*
upon = **reliant on**, relying on

depend on 1 = **be determined
by**, be based on, be subject to,
hang on, rest on, revolve around,
hinge on, be subordinate to
2 = **count on**, turn to, trust in,
bank on, lean on, rely upon,
reckon on

depict 1 = **illustrate**, portray,
picture, paint, outline, draw,
sketch, delineate 2 = **describe**,
present, represent, outline,
characterize

deplete = **use up**, reduce, drain,
exhaust, consume, empty,
lessen, impoverish **OPPOSITE:**
increase

deplore = **disapprove of**,
condemn, object to, denounce,
censure, abhor, take a dim
view of

deploy (*~troops or military
resources*) = **use**, station,
position, arrange, set out, utilize

deployment (*of troops or military
resources*) = **use**, stationing,
spread, organization,
arrangement, positioning,
utilization

deport = **expel**, exile, throw
out, oust, banish, expatriate,
extradite, evict

depose = **oust**, dismiss, displace,
demote, dethrone, remove
from office

deposit VERB 1 = **put**, place, lay,
drop 2 = **store**, keep, put, bank,
lodge, entrust, consign
▷ **NOUN** 3 = **down payment**,
security, stake, pledge,
instalment, retainer, part
payment 4 = **accumulation**,
mass, build-up, layer

d

5 = **sediment**, grounds, residue, lees, precipitate, silt, dregs

depot 1 = **arsenal**, warehouse, storehouse, repository, depository 2 (*US & Canad*) = **bus station**, station, garage, terminus

depreciation = **devaluation**, fall, drop, depression, slump, deflation

depress 1 = **sadden**, upset, distress, discourage, grieve, oppress, weigh down, make sad, harsh someone's mellow *or* buzz (*slang*) **OPPOSITE:** cheer 2 = **lower**, cut, reduce, diminish, decrease, lessen **OPPOSITE:** raise 3 = **devalue**, depreciate, cheapen 4 = **press down**, push, squeeze, lower, flatten, compress, push down

depressed 1 = **sad**, blue, unhappy, discouraged, fed up, mournful, dejected, despondent 2 = **poverty-stricken**, poor, deprived, disadvantaged, rundown, impoverished, needy 3 = **lowered**, devalued, weakened, depreciated, cheapened 4 = **sunken**, hollow, recessed, indented, concave

depressing = **bleak**, sad, discouraging, gloomy, dismal, harrowing, saddening, dispiriting

depression 1 = **despair**, misery, sadness, the dumps (*informal*), the blues, melancholy, unhappiness, despondency

2 = **recession**, slump, economic decline, credit crunch, stagnation, inactivity, hard *or* bad times 3 = **hollow**, pit, dip, bowl, valley, dent, cavity, indentation

deprivation 1 = **lack**, denial, withdrawal, removal, expropriation, dispossession 2 = **want**, need, hardship, suffering, distress, privation, destitution

deprive = **dispossess**, rob, strip, despoil, bereave

deprived = **poor**, disadvantaged, needy, in need, lacking, bereft, destitute, down at heel **OPPOSITE:** prosperous

depth 1 = **deepness**, drop, measure, extent 2 = **insight**, wisdom, penetration, profundity, discernment, sagacity, astuteness, profoundness **OPPOSITE:** superficiality 3 = **breadth**

deputy = **substitute**, representative, delegate, lieutenant, proxy, surrogate, second-in-command, legate

derelict ADJECTIVE 1 = **abandoned**, deserted, ruined, neglected, discarded, forsaken, dilapidated ▷ NOUN 2 = **tramp**, outcast, drifter, down-and-out, vagrant, bag lady, derro (*Austral slang*)

descend 1 = **fall**, drop, sink, go down, plunge, dive, tumble, plummet **OPPOSITE:** rise

2 = **get off** 3 = **go down**, come down, walk down, move down, climb down 4 = **slope**, dip, incline, slant
▷ **PHRASES:** be descended from = **originate from**, derive from, spring from, proceed from, issue from

descent 1 = **fall**, drop, plunge, coming down, swoop 2 = **slope**, drop, dip, incline, slant, declivity 3 = **decline**, deterioration, degeneration 4 = **origin**, extraction, ancestry, lineage, family tree, parentage, genealogy, derivation

describe 1 = **relate**, tell, report, explain, express, recount, recite, narrate 2 = **portray**, depict 3 = **trace**, draw, outline, mark out, delineate

description 1 = **account**, report, explanation, representation, sketch, narrative, portrayal, depiction 2 = **calling**, naming, branding, labelling, dubbing, designation 3 = **kind**, sort, type, order, class, variety, brand, category

desert¹ = **wilderness**, waste, wilds, wasteland

desert² 1 = **abandon**, leave, quit (*informal*), forsake 2 = **leave**, abandon, strand, maroon, walk out on (*informal*), forsake, jilt, leave stranded **OPPOSITE:** take care of 3 = **abscond**

deserted 1 = **empty**, abandoned, desolate, neglected, vacant, derelict, unoccupied 2 = **abandoned**, neglected, forsaken

deserve = **merit**, warrant, be entitled to, have a right to, rate, earn, justify, be worthy of

deserved = **well-earned**, fitting, due, earned, justified, merited, proper, warranted

deserving = **worthy**, righteous, commendable, laudable, praiseworthy, meritorious, estimable **OPPOSITE:** undeserving

desiccate = **dry**, drain, evaporate, dehydrate, parch, exsiccate

design VERB 1 = **plan**, draw, draft, trace, outline, devise, sketch, formulate 2 = **create**, plan, fashion, propose, invent, conceive, originate, fabricate 3 = **intend**, mean, plan, aim, purpose
▷ NOUN 4 = **pattern**, form, style, shape, organization, arrangement, construction 5 = **plan**, drawing, model, scheme, draft, outline, sketch, blueprint 6 = **intention**, end, aim, goal, target, purpose, object, objective

designate 1 = **name**, call, term, style, label, entitle, dub 2 = **choose**, reserve, select, label, flag, assign, allocate, set aside 3 = **appoint**, name, choose, commission, select, elect, delegate, nominate

designer 1 = **couturier**
2 = **producer**, architect, deviser, creator, planner, inventor, originator

desirable 1 = **advantageous**, useful, valuable, helpful, profitable, of service, convenient, worthwhile **OPPOSITE:** disadvantageous 2 = **popular OPPOSITE:** unpopular 3 = **attractive**, appealing, pretty, fair, inviting, lovely, charming, sexy (*informal*) **OPPOSITE:** unattractive

desire VERB 1 = **want**, long for, crave, hope for, ache for, wish for, yearn for, thirst for
▷ **NOUN** 2 = **wish**, want, longing, hope, urge, aspiration, craving, thirst 3 = **lust**, passion, libido, appetite, lasciviousness

despair VERB 1 = **lose hope**, give up, lose heart
▷ **NOUN** 2 = **despondency**, depression, misery, gloom, desperation, anguish, hopelessness, dejection

despatch ▷ *See* **DISPATCH**

desperate 1 = **grave**, pressing, serious, severe, extreme, urgent, drastic 2 = **last-ditch**, daring, furious, risky, frantic, audacious

desperately = **gravely**, badly, seriously, severely, dangerously, perilously

desperation 1 = **misery**, worry, trouble, despair, agony, anguish, unhappiness, hopelessness
2 = **recklessness**, madness, frenzy, impetuosity, rashness, foolhardiness

despise = **look down on**, loathe, scorn, detest, revile, abhor **OPPOSITE:** admire

despite = **in spite of**, in the face of, regardless of, even with, notwithstanding, in the teeth of, undeterred by

destination = **stop**, station, haven, resting-place, terminus, journey's end

destined = **fated**, meant, intended, certain, bound, doomed, predestined

destiny 1 = **fate**, fortune, lot, portion, doom, nemesis 2 *usually cap.* = **fortune**, chance, karma, providence, kismet, predestination, divine will

destroy 1 = **ruin**, crush, devastate, wreck, shatter, wipe out, demolish, eradicate 2 = **slaughter**, kill

destruction 1 = **ruin**, havoc, wreckage, demolition, devastation, annihilation 2 = **slaughter**, extermination, eradication

destructive = **devastating**, fatal, deadly, lethal, harmful, damaging, catastrophic, ruinous

detach 1 = **separate**, remove, divide, cut off, sever, disconnect, tear off, disengage **OPPOSITE:** attach 2 = **free**, remove, separate, isolate, cut off, disengage

detached 1 = **objective**, neutral, impartial, reserved, impersonal, disinterested, unbiased, dispassionate **OPPOSITE:** subjective 2 = **separate**, disconnected, discrete, unconnected, undivided

detachment 1 = **indifference**, fairness, neutrality, objectivity, impartiality, coolness, remoteness, nonchalance 2 (*Military*) = **unit**, party, force, body, squad, patrol, task force

detail NOUN 1 = **point**, fact, feature, particular, respect, factor, element, aspect 2 = **fine point**, particular, nicety, triviality 3 (*Military*) = **party**, force, body, duty, squad, assignment, fatigue, detachment ▷ VERB 4 = **list**, relate, catalogue, recount, rehearse, recite, enumerate, itemize

detailed = **comprehensive**, full, complete, minute, particular, thorough, exhaustive, all-embracing **OPPOSITE:** brief

detain 1 = **hold**, arrest, confine, restrain, imprison, intern, take prisoner, hold in custody 2 = **delay**, hold up, hamper, hinder, retard, impede, keep back, slow up *or* down

detect 1 = **discover**, find, uncover, track down, unmask 2 = **notice**, see, spot, note, identify, observe, recognize, perceive

detective = **investigator**, cop (*slang*), private eye, sleuth (*informal*), private investigator, gumshoe (*US slang*)

detention = **imprisonment**, custody, quarantine, confinement, incarceration **OPPOSITE:** release

deter 1 = **discourage**, inhibit, put off, frighten, intimidate, dissuade, talk out of 2 = **prevent**, stop

deteriorate = **decline**, worsen, degenerate, slump, go downhill **OPPOSITE:** improve

determination = **resolution**, purpose, resolve, dedication, fortitude, persistence, tenacity, perseverance **OPPOSITE:** indecision

determine 1 = **affect**, decide, regulate, ordain 2 = **settle**, learn, establish, discover, find out, work out, detect, verify 3 = **decide on**, choose, elect, resolve 4 = **decide**, conclude, resolve, make up your mind

determined = **resolute**, firm, dogged, intent, persistent, persevering, single-minded, tenacious

deterrent = **discouragement**, obstacle, curb, restraint, impediment, check, hindrance, disincentive **OPPOSITE:** incentive

devastate = **destroy**, ruin, sack, wreck, demolish, level, ravage, raze

devastation = **destruction**, ruin, havoc, demolition, desolation

develop 1 = **grow**, advance, progress, mature, evolve, flourish, ripen 2 = **establish**, set up, promote, generate, undertake, initiate, embark on, cultivate 3 = **form**, establish, breed, generate, originate 4 = **expand**, extend, work out, elaborate, unfold, enlarge, broaden, amplify

development 1 = **growth**, increase, advance, progress, spread, expansion, evolution, enlargement 2 = **establishment**, forming, generation, institution, invention, initiation, inauguration, instigation 3 = **event**, happening, result, incident, improvement, evolution, unfolding, occurrence

deviant ADJECTIVE
1 = **perverted**, sick (*informal*), twisted, warped, kinky (*slang*)
OPPOSITE: normal
▷ NOUN 2 = **pervert**, freak, misfit

device 1 = **gadget**, machine, tool, instrument, implement, appliance, apparatus, contraption 2 = **smartphone**, tablet, laptop, iPad®, iPhone®, Kindle®, BlackBerry® 3 = **ploy**, scheme, plan, trick, manoeuvre, gambit, stratagem, wile

devil 1 = **evil spirit**, demon, fiend, atua (*NZ*), wairua (*NZ*)

2 = **brute**, monster, beast, barbarian, fiend, terror, swine, ogre 3 = **person**, individual, soul, creature, thing, beggar 4 = **scamp**, rogue, rascal, scoundrel, scallywag (*informal*), nointer (*Austral slang*)
▷ PHRASES: the Devil = **Satan**, Lucifer, Prince of Darkness, Mephistopheles, Evil One, Beelzebub, Old Nick (*informal*)

devise = **work out**, design, construct, invent, conceive, formulate, contrive, dream up

devoid with of = **lacking in**, without, free from, wanting in, bereft of, empty of, deficient in

devote = **dedicate**, give, commit, apply, reserve, pledge, surrender, assign

devoted = **dedicated**, committed, true, constant, loyal, faithful, ardent, staunch
OPPOSITE: disloyal

devotee = **enthusiast**, fan, supporter, follower, admirer, buff (*informal*), fanatic, adherent

devotion NOUN 1 = **love**, passion, affection, attachment, fondness 2 = **dedication**, commitment, loyalty, allegiance, fidelity, adherence, constancy, faithfulness
OPPOSITE: indifference
3 = **worship**, reverence, spirituality, holiness, piety, godliness, devoutness
OPPOSITE: irreverence

▷ PLURAL NOUN 4 = **prayers**, religious observance, church service, divine office

devour 1 = **eat**, consume, swallow, wolf, gulp, gobble, guzzle, polish off (informal) 2 = **enjoy**, take in, read compulsively or voraciously

devout = **religious**, godly, pious, pure, holy, saintly, reverent **OPPOSITE:** irreverent

diagnose = **identify**, determine, recognize, distinguish, interpret, pronounce, pinpoint

diagnosis = **identification**, discovery, recognition, detection

diagram = **plan**, figure, drawing, chart, representation, sketch, graph

dialogue 1 = **discussion**, conference, exchange, debate 2 = **conversation**, discussion, communication, discourse

diary 1 = **journal**, chronicle, blog (informal) 2 = **engagement book**, Filofax®, appointment book

dictate VERB 1 = **speak**, say, utter, read out
▷ NOUN 2 = **command**, order, decree, demand, direction, injunction, fiat, edict 3 = **principle**, law, rule, standard, code, criterion, maxim
▷ PHRASES: dictate to someone = **order (about)**, direct, lay down the law, pronounce to

dictator = **absolute ruler**, tyrant, despot, oppressor, autocrat, absolutist, martinet

dictatorship = **absolute rule**, tyranny, totalitarianism, authoritarianism, despotism, autocracy, absolutism

dictionary = **wordbook**, vocabulary, glossary, lexicon

die 1 = **pass away**, expire, perish, croak (slang), give up the ghost, snuff it (slang), peg out (informal), kick the bucket (slang), cark it (Austral & NZ slang) **OPPOSITE:** live 2 = **stop**, fail, halt, break down, run down, stop working, peter out, fizzle out 3 = **dwindle**, decline, sink, fade, diminish, decrease, decay, wither **OPPOSITE:** increase
▷ PHRASES: be dying for something = **long for**, want, desire, crave, yearn for, hunger for, pine for, hanker after

diet¹ NOUN 1 = **food**, provisions, fare, rations, kai (NZ informal), nourishment, sustenance, victuals 2 = **fast**, regime, abstinence, regimen
▷ VERB 3 = **slim**, fast, lose weight, abstain, eat sparingly **OPPOSITE:** overindulge

diet² often cap. = **council**, meeting, parliament, congress, chamber, convention, legislature

differ 1 = **be dissimilar**, contradict, contrast with, vary, belie, depart from, diverge,

negate **OPPOSITE:** accord
2 = **disagree**, clash, dispute,
dissent **OPPOSITE:** agree

difference 1 = **dissimilarity**,
contrast, variation, change,
variety, diversity, alteration,
discrepancy **OPPOSITE:**
similarity 2 = **remainder**,
rest, balance, remains, excess
3 = **disagreement**, conflict,
argument, clash, dispute,
quarrel, contretemps **OPPOSITE:**
agreement

different 1 = **dissimilar**,
opposed, contrasting, changed,
unlike, altered, inconsistent,
disparate 2 = **various**,
varied, diverse, assorted,
miscellaneous, sundry
3 = **unusual**, special, strange,
extraordinary, distinctive,
peculiar, uncommon, singular

> **USAGE NOTE**
> On the whole, *different from* is
> preferable to *different to* and
> *different than*, both of which
> are considered unacceptable
> by some people. *Different to* is
> often heard in British English,
> but is thought by some people
> to be incorrect; and *different
> than*, though acceptable in
> American English, is often
> regarded as unacceptable
> in British English. This
> makes *different from* the
> safest option: *this result is
> only slightly different from that
> obtained in the US* – or you can

> rephrase the sentence: *this
> result differs only slightly from
> that obtained in the US.*

differentiate 1 = **distinguish**,
separate, discriminate, contrast,
mark off, make a distinction,
tell apart, set off *or* apart
2 = **make different**, separate,
distinguish, characterize, single
out, segregate, individualize,
mark off 3 = **become different**,
change, convert, transform,
alter, adapt, modify

difficult 1 = **hard**, tough, taxing,
demanding, challenging,
exacting, formidable,
uphill **OPPOSITE:** easy
2 = **problematical**, involved,
complex, complicated,
obscure, baffling, intricate,
knotty **OPPOSITE:** simple
3 = **troublesome**, demanding,
perverse, fussy, fastidious,
hard to please, refractory,
unaccommodating **OPPOSITE:**
cooperative

difficulty 1 = **problem**, trouble,
obstacle, hurdle, dilemma,
complication, snag, uphill (*S
African*) 2 = **hardship**, strain,
awkwardness, strenuousness,
arduousness, laboriousness

dig VERB 1 = **hollow out**, mine,
quarry, excavate, scoop out
2 = **delve**, tunnel, burrow
3 = **turn over** 4 = **search**, hunt,
root, delve, forage, dig down,
fossick (*Austral & NZ*) 5 = **poke**,
drive, push, stick, punch, stab,

thrust, shove
▷ **NOUN 6 = cutting remark**,
crack (*slang*), insult, taunt, sneer,
jeer, barb, wisecrack (*informal*)
7 = poke, thrust, nudge, prod,
jab, punch

digest VERB **1 = ingest**, absorb,
incorporate, dissolve, assimilate
2 = take in, absorb, grasp,
soak up
▷ **NOUN 3 = summary**, résumé,
abstract, epitome, synopsis,
précis, abridgment

dignity 1 = decorum,
gravity, majesty, grandeur,
respectability, nobility,
solemnity, courtliness **2 = self-
importance**, pride, self-esteem,
self-respect

dilemma = predicament,
problem, difficulty, spot
(*informal*), mess, puzzle, plight,
quandary

> **USAGE NOTE**
> The use of *dilemma* to refer
> to a problem that seems
> incapable of solution is
> considered by some people
> to be incorrect. To avoid
> this misuse of the word, an
> appropriate alternative such
> as *predicament* could be used.

dilute 1 = water down, thin
(out), weaken, adulterate, make
thinner, cut (*informal*) **OPPOSITE:**
condense **2 = reduce**, weaken,
diminish, temper, decrease,
lessen, diffuse, mitigate
OPPOSITE: intensify

dim ADJECTIVE **1 = poorly lit**,
dark, gloomy, murky, shady,
shadowy, dusky, tenebrous
2 = cloudy, grey, gloomy, dismal,
overcast, leaden **OPPOSITE:**
bright **3 = unclear**, obscured,
faint, blurred, fuzzy, shadowy,
hazy, bleary **OPPOSITE:** distinct
4 (*informal*) **= stupid**, thick, dull,
dense, dumb (*informal*), daft
(*informal*), dozy (*Brit informal*),
obtuse **OPPOSITE:** bright
▷ VERB **5 = turn down**, fade,
dull **6 = grow or become faint**,
fade, dull, grow or become dim
7 = darken, dull, cloud over

dimension 1 = aspect, side,
feature, angle, facet **2 = extent**,
size

diminish 1 = decrease, decline,
lessen, shrink, dwindle, wane,
recede, subside **OPPOSITE:**
grow **2 = reduce**, cut, decrease,
lessen, lower, curtail **OPPOSITE:**
increase

din = noise, row, racket, crash,
clamour, clatter, uproar,
commotion **OPPOSITE:** silence

dine = eat, lunch, feast, sup

dinkum (*Austral & NZ informal*)
= genuine, honest, natural,
frank, sincere, candid, upfront
(*informal*), artless

dinner 1 = meal, main meal,
spread (*informal*), repast
2 = banquet, feast, repast,
hakari (*NZ*)

dinosaur
• *See panel* **DINOSAURS**

d

DINOSAURS

allosaur(us)	megalosaur(us)
ankylosaur(us)	mosasaur(us)
apatosaur(us)	oviraptor
atlantosaur(us)	plesiosaur(us)
brachiosaur(us)	pteranodon
brontosaur(us)	pterodactyl or pterosaur
ceratosaur(us)	protoceratops
compsognathus	stegodon or stegodont
dimetrodon	stegosaur(us)
diplodocus	theropod
dolichosaur(us)	titanosaur(us)
dromiosaur(us)	trachodon
elasmosaur(us)	triceratops
hadrosaur(us)	tyrannosaur(us)
ichthyosaur(us)	velociraptor
iguanodon or iguanodont	

dip VERB 1 = **plunge**, immerse, bathe, duck, douse, dunk 2 = **drop (down)**, fall, lower, sink, descend, subside 3 = **slope**, drop (down), descend, fall, decline, sink, incline, drop away ▷ NOUN 4 = **plunge**, ducking, soaking, drenching, immersion, douche 5 = **nod**, drop, lowering, slump, sag 6 = **hollow**, hole, depression, pit, basin, trough, concavity
▷ PHRASES: dip into something = **sample**, skim, glance at, browse, peruse, surf (computing)

diplomacy 1 = **statesmanship**, statecraft, international negotiation 2 = **tact**, skill, sensitivity, craft, discretion, subtlety, delicacy, finesse OPPOSITE: tactlessness

diplomat = **official**, ambassador, envoy, statesman, consul, attaché, emissary, chargé d'affaires

diplomatic 1 = **consular**, official, foreign-office, ambassadorial, foreign-politic 2 = **tactful**, politic, sensitive, subtle, delicate, polite, discreet, prudent OPPOSITE: tactless

dire = **desperate**, pressing, critical, terrible, crucial, extreme, awful, urgent

direct VERB 1 = **aim**, point, level, train, focus 2 = **guide**, show, lead, point the way, point in the direction of 3 = **control**, run,

manage, lead, guide, handle, conduct, oversee 4 = **order**, command, instruct, charge, demand, require, bid 5 = **address**, send, mail, route, label
▷ ADJECTIVE 6 = **quickest**, shortest 7 = **straight**, through **OPPOSITE:** circuitous 8 = **first-hand**, personal, immediate **OPPOSITE:** indirect 9 = **clear**, specific, plain, absolute, definite, explicit, downright, point-blank **OPPOSITE:** ambiguous 10 = **straightforward**, open, straight, frank, blunt, honest, candid, forthright **OPPOSITE:** indirect 11 = **verbatim**, exact, word-for-word, strict, accurate, faithful, letter-for-letter
▷ ADVERB 12 = **non-stop**, straight

direction 1 = **way**, course, line, road, track, bearing, route, path 2 = **management**, control, charge, administration, leadership, command, guidance, supervision

directions = **instructions**, rules, information, plan, briefing, regulations, recommendations, guidelines

directive = **order**, ruling, regulation, command, instruction, decree, mandate, injunction

directly 1 = **straight**, unswervingly, without deviation, by the shortest route, in a beeline 2 = **immediately**, promptly, right

away, straightaway 3 = **at once**, as soon as possible, straightaway, forthwith 4 = **honestly**, openly, frankly, plainly, point-blank, unequivocally, truthfully, unreservedly

director = **controller**, head, leader, manager, chief, executive, governor, administrator, baas (S African), sherang (Austral & NZ)

dirt 1 = **filth**, muck, grime, dust, mud, impurity, kak (S African taboo slang) 2 = **soil**, ground, earth, clay, turf, loam

dirty ADJECTIVE 1 = **filthy**, soiled, grubby, foul, muddy, polluted, messy, grimy, festy (Austral slang) **OPPOSITE:** clean 2 = **dishonest**, illegal, unfair, cheating, crooked, fraudulent, treacherous, unscrupulous **OPPOSITE:** honest 3 = **obscene**, indecent, blue, offensive, filthy, pornographic, sleazy, lewd **OPPOSITE:** decent
▷ VERB 4 = **soil**, foul, stain, spoil, muddy, pollute, blacken, defile **OPPOSITE:** clean

disability = **condition**, affliction, disorder, incapacity, infirmity

disable = **handicap**, cripple, damage, paralyse, impair, incapacitate, immobilize, enfeeble

disabled = **differently abled**, physically challenged, handicapped (old-fashioned or offens), challenged, weakened, crippled (*old-fashioned or offens*), paralysed, incapacitated **OPPOSITE:** able-bodied

> **USAGE NOTE**
> Referring to people with disabilities as *the disabled* can cause offence and should be avoided. Instead, refer to them as people *with disabilities* or *who are physically challenged*, or, possibly, *disabled people* or *differently abled people*. In general, the terms used for disabilities or medical conditions should be avoided as collective nouns for people who have them – so, for example, instead of *the blind*, it is preferable to refer to *sightless people*, *vision-impaired people*, or *partially-sighted people*, depending on the degree of their condition.

disadvantage 1 = drawback, trouble, handicap, nuisance, snag, inconvenience, downside **OPPOSITE:** advantage **2 = harm**, loss, damage, injury, hurt, prejudice, detriment, disservice **OPPOSITE:** benefit

disagree 1 = differ (in opinion), argue, clash, dispute, dissent, quarrel, take issue with, cross swords **OPPOSITE:** agree **2 = make ill**, upset, sicken, trouble, hurt, bother, distress, discomfort

disagreement = argument, row, conflict, clash, dispute, dissent, quarrel, squabble **OPPOSITE:** agreement

disappear 1 = vanish, recede, evanesce **OPPOSITE:** appear **2 = pass**, fade away **3 = cease**, dissolve, evaporate, perish, die out, pass away, melt away, leave no trace

disappearance 1 = vanishing, going, passing, melting, eclipse, evaporation, evanescence **2 = flight**, departure **3 = loss**, losing, mislaying

disappoint = let down, dismay, fail, disillusion, dishearten, disenchant, dissatisfy, disgruntle

disappointment 1 = regret, discontent, dissatisfaction, disillusionment, chagrin, disenchantment, dejection, despondency **2 = letdown**, blow, setback, misfortune, calamity, choker (*informal*) **3 = frustration**

disapproval = displeasure, criticism, objection, condemnation, dissatisfaction, censure, reproach, denunciation

disapprove = condemn, object to, dislike, deplore, frown on, take exception to, take a dim view of, find unacceptable **OPPOSITE:** approve

disarm 1 = demilitarize, disband, demobilize, deactivate **2 = win over**, persuade

disarmament = arms reduction, demobilization, arms

limitation, demilitarization, de-escalation

disarming = **charming**, winning, irresistible, persuasive, likable *or* likeable

disarray 1 = **confusion**, disorder, indiscipline, disunity, disorganization, unruliness **OPPOSITE:** order 2 = **untidiness**, mess, chaos, muddle, clutter, shambles, jumble, hotchpotch **OPPOSITE:** tidiness

disaster 1 = **catastrophe**, trouble, tragedy, ruin, misfortune, adversity, calamity, cataclysm 2 = **failure**, mess, flop (*informal*), catastrophe, debacle, cock-up (*Brit slang*), washout (*informal*)

disastrous 1 = **terrible**, devastating, tragic, fatal, catastrophic, ruinous, calamitous, cataclysmic 2 = **unsuccessful**

disbelief = **scepticism**, doubt, distrust, mistrust, incredulity, unbelief, dubiety **OPPOSITE:** belief

discard = **get rid of**, drop, throw away *or* out, reject, abandon, dump (*informal*), dispose of, dispense with **OPPOSITE:** keep

discharge VERB 1 = **release**, free, clear, liberate, pardon, allow to go, set free 2 = **dismiss**, sack (*informal*), fire (*informal*), remove, expel, discard, oust, cashier, kennet (*Austral slang*), jeff (*Austral slang*) 3 = **carry out**,

perform, fulfil, accomplish, do, effect, realize, observe 4 = **pay**, meet, clear, settle, square (up), honour, satisfy, relieve 5 = **pour forth**, release, leak, emit, dispense, ooze, exude, give off 6 = **fire**, shoot, set off, explode, let off, detonate, let loose (*informal*)
▷ NOUN 7 = **release**, liberation, clearance, pardon, acquittal 8 = **dismissal**, notice, removal, the boot (*slang*), expulsion, the push (*slang*), the sack (*informal*), marching orders (*informal*), ejection 9 = **emission**, ooze, secretion, excretion, pus, seepage, suppuration 10 = **firing**, report, shot, blast, burst, explosion, volley, salvo

disciple 1 = **apostle** 2 = **follower**, student, supporter, pupil, devotee, apostle, adherent **OPPOSITE:** teacher

discipline NOUN 1 = **control**, authority, regulation, supervision, orderliness, strictness 2 = **self-control**, control, restraint, self-discipline, willpower, self-restraint, orderliness 3 = **training**, practice, exercise, method, regulation, drill, regimen 4 = **field of study**, area, subject, theme, topic, course, curriculum, speciality
▷ VERB 5 = **punish**, correct, reprimand, castigate, chastise,

chasten, penalize, bring to book
6 = **train**, educate
disclose 1 = **make known**,
reveal, publish, relate,
broadcast, confess,
communicate, divulge
OPPOSITE: keep secret **2** = **show**,
reveal, expose, unveil, uncover,
lay bare, bring to light **OPPOSITE:**
hide
disclosure 1 = **revelation**,
announcement, publication,
leak, admission, declaration,
confession, acknowledgment
2 = **uncovering**, publication,
revelation, divulgence
discomfort 1 = **pain**,
hurt, ache, throbbing,
irritation, tenderness, pang,
malaise **OPPOSITE:** comfort
2 = **uneasiness**, worry, anxiety,
doubt, distress, misgiving,
qualms, trepidation **OPPOSITE:**
reassurance **3** = **inconvenience**,
trouble, difficulty, bother,
hardship, irritation, nuisance,
uphill (S African)
discontent = **dissatisfaction**,
unhappiness, displeasure,
regret, envy, restlessness,
uneasiness
discontented = **dissatisfied**,
unhappy, fed up, disgruntled,
disaffected, vexed, displeased
OPPOSITE: satisfied
discount VERB 1 = **mark down**,
reduce, lower **2** = **disregard**,
reject, ignore, overlook, discard,
set aside, dispel, pass over

▷ **NOUN 3** = **deduction**, cut,
reduction, concession, rebate
discourage 1 = **dishearten**,
depress, intimidate, overawe,
demoralize, put a damper
on, dispirit, deject **OPPOSITE:**
hearten **2** = **put off**, deter,
prevent, dissuade, talk out of
OPPOSITE: encourage
discourse 1 = **conversation**,
talk, discussion, speech,
communication, chat, dialogue
2 = **speech**, essay, lecture,
sermon, treatise, dissertation,
homily, oration, whaikorero (NZ)
discover 1 = **find out**, learn,
notice, realize, recognize,
perceive, detect, uncover
2 = **find**, come across, uncover,
unearth, turn up, dig up, come
upon
discovery 1 = **finding out**,
news, revelation, disclosure,
realization **2** = **invention**,
launch, institution, pioneering,
innovation, inauguration
3 = **breakthrough**, find,
development, advance, leap,
invention, step forward,
quantum leap **4** = **finding**,
revelation, uncovering,
disclosure, detection
discredit VERB 1 = **disgrace**,
shame, smear, humiliate,
taint, disparage, vilify, slander
OPPOSITE: honour **2** = **dispute**,
question, challenge, deny,
reject, discount, distrust,
mistrust

▷ NOUN 3 = **disgrace**, scandal, shame, disrepute, stigma, ignominy, dishonour, ill-repute
OPPOSITE: honour

discreet = **tactful**, diplomatic, guarded, careful, cautious, wary, prudent, considerate
OPPOSITE: tactless

discrepancy = **disagreement**, difference, variation, conflict, contradiction, inconsistency, disparity, divergence

discretion 1 = **tact**, consideration, caution, diplomacy, prudence, wariness, carefulness, judiciousness
OPPOSITE: tactlessness
2 = **choice**, will, pleasure, preference, inclination, volition

discriminate = **differentiate**, distinguish, separate, tell the difference, draw a distinction
▷ PHRASES: discriminate against someone = **treat differently**, single out, victimize, treat as inferior, show bias against, show prejudice against

discriminating = **discerning**, particular, refined, cultivated, selective, tasteful, fastidious
OPPOSITE: undiscriminating

discrimination 1 = **prejudice**, bias, injustice, intolerance, bigotry, favouritism, unfairness
2 = **discernment**, taste, judgment, perception, subtlety, refinement

discuss = **talk about**, consider, debate, examine, argue about, deliberate about, converse about, confer about

discussion 1 = **talk**, debate, argument, conference, conversation, dialogue, consultation, discourse, korero (*NZ*) 2 = **examination**, investigation, analysis, scrutiny, dissection

disdain NOUN 1 = **contempt**, scorn, arrogance, derision, haughtiness, superciliousness
▷ VERB 2 = **scorn**, reject, slight, disregard, spurn, deride, look down on, sneer at

disease = **illness**, condition, complaint, infection, disorder, sickness, ailment, affliction

diseased = **unhealthy**, sick, infected, rotten, ailing, sickly, unwell, crook (*Austral & NZ informal*), unsound

disgrace NOUN 1 = **shame**, degradation, disrepute, ignominy, dishonour, infamy, opprobrium, odium **OPPOSITE:** honour 2 = **scandal**, stain, stigma, blot, blemish
▷ VERB 3 = **shame**, humiliate, discredit, degrade, taint, sully, dishonour, bring shame upon
OPPOSITE: honour

disgraceful = **shameful**, shocking, scandalous, unworthy, ignominious, disreputable, contemptible, dishonourable

disgruntled = **discontented**, dissatisfied, annoyed, irritated, put out, grumpy, vexed, displeased, hoha (*NZ*)

disguise VERB 1 = **hide**, cover, conceal, screen, mask, suppress, withhold, veil
▷ NOUN 2 = **costume**, mask, camouflage

disguised 1 = **in disguise**, masked, camouflaged, undercover, incognito 2 = **false**, artificial, forged, fake, mock, imitation, sham, counterfeit

disgust VERB 1 = **sicken**, offend, revolt, put off, repel, nauseate OPPOSITE: delight
▷ NOUN 2 = **outrage**, shock, anger, hurt, fury, resentment, wrath, indignation

disgusting 1 = **sickening**, foul, revolting, gross, repellent, nauseating, repugnant, loathsome, festy (*Austral slang*), yucko (*Austral slang*) 2 = **appalling**, shocking, awful, offensive, dreadful, horrifying

dish 1 = **bowl**, plate, platter, salver 2 = **food**, fare, recipe

dishonest = **deceitful**, corrupt, crooked (*informal*), lying, bent (*slang*), false, cheating, treacherous OPPOSITE: honest

disintegrate = **break up**, crumble, fall apart, separate, shatter, splinter, break apart, go to pieces

dislike VERB 1 = **hate**, object to, loathe, despise, disapprove of, detest, recoil from, take a dim view of OPPOSITE: like

▷ NOUN 2 = **hatred**, hostility, disapproval, distaste, animosity, aversion, displeasure, antipathy OPPOSITE: liking

dismal 1 = **bad**, awful, dreadful, rotten (*informal*), terrible, poor, dire, abysmal 2 = **sad**, gloomy, dark, depressing, discouraging, bleak, dreary, sombre OPPOSITE: happy 3 = **gloomy**, depressing, dull, dreary OPPOSITE: cheerful

dismantle = **take apart**, strip, demolish, disassemble, take to pieces *or* bits

dismay VERB 1 = **alarm**, frighten, scare, panic, distress, terrify, appal, startle 2 = **disappoint**, upset, discourage, daunt, disillusion, let down, dishearten, dispirit
▷ NOUN 3 = **alarm**, fear, horror, anxiety, dread, apprehension, nervousness, consternation 4 = **disappointment**, frustration, dissatisfaction, disillusionment, chagrin, disenchantment, discouragement

dismiss 1 = **reject**, disregard 2 = **banish**, dispel, discard, set aside, cast out, lay aside, put out of your mind 3 = **sack**, fire (*informal*), remove (*informal*), axe (*informal*), discharge, lay off, cashier, give (someone) notice, kennet (*Austral slang*), jeff (*Austral slang*) 4 = **let go**, free, release, discharge, dissolve, liberate, disperse, send away

dismissal = **the sack** (*informal*), removal, notice, the boot (*slang*), expulsion, the push (*slang*), marching orders (*informal*)

disobey 1 = **defy**, ignore, rebel, disregard, refuse to obey 2 = **infringe**, defy, refuse to obey, flout, violate, contravene, overstep, transgress

disorder 1 = **illness**, disease, complaint, condition, sickness, ailment, affliction, malady 2 = **untidiness**, mess, confusion, chaos, muddle, clutter, shambles, disarray 3 = **disturbance**, riot, turmoil, unrest, uproar, commotion, unruliness, biffo (*Austral slang*)

disorderly 1 = **untidy**, confused, chaotic, messy, jumbled, shambolic (*informal*), disorganized, higgledy-piggledy (*informal*) **OPPOSITE:** tidy 2 = **unruly**, disruptive, rowdy, turbulent, tumultuous, lawless, riotous, ungovernable

dispatch *or* **despatch** VERB 1 = **send**, consign 2 = **kill**, murder, destroy, execute, slaughter, assassinate, slay, liquidate 3 = **carry out**, perform, fulfil, effect, finish, achieve, settle, dismiss
▷ **NOUN** 4 = **message**, news, report, story, account, communication, bulletin, communiqué

dispel = **drive away**, dismiss, eliminate, expel, disperse, banish, chase away

dispense 1 = **distribute**, assign, allocate, allot, dole out, share out, apportion, deal out 2 = **prepare**, measure, supply, mix 3 = **administer**, operate, carry out, implement, enforce, execute, apply, discharge
▷ **PHRASES:** dispense with something *or* someone 1 = **do away with**, give up, cancel, abolish, brush aside, forgo, relinquish 2 = **do without**, get rid of, dispose of

disperse 1 = **scatter**, spread, distribute, strew, diffuse, disseminate, throw about 2 = **break up**, separate, scatter, dissolve, disband **OPPOSITE:** gather 3 = **dissolve**, break up

displace 1 = **replace**, succeed, supersede, oust, usurp, supplant, take the place of 2 = **move**, shift, disturb, budge, misplace

display VERB 1 = **show**, present, exhibit, put on view **OPPOSITE:** conceal 2 = **expose**, show, reveal, exhibit, uncover 3 = **demonstrate**, show, reveal, register, expose, disclose, manifest 4 = **show off**, parade, exhibit, sport (*informal*), flash (*informal*), flourish, brandish, flaunt
▷ **NOUN** 5 = **proof**, exhibition, demonstration, evidence,

expression, illustration, revelation, testimony
6 = exhibition, show, demonstration, presentation, array **7 = ostentation**, show, flourish, fanfare, pomp
8 = show, exhibition, parade, spectacle, pageant
disposable 1 = throwaway, nonreturnable **2 = available**, expendable, consumable
disposal = throwing away, dumping (*informal*), scrapping, removal, discarding, jettisoning, ejection, riddance
▷ **PHRASES: at your disposal = available**, ready, to hand, accessible, handy, at hand, on tap, expendable
dispose = arrange, put, place, group, order, distribute, array
▷ **PHRASES: dispose of someone = kill**, murder, destroy, execute, slaughter, assassinate, slay, liquidate ▶ **dispose of something 1 = get rid of**, destroy, dump (*informal*), scrap, discard, unload, jettison, throw out *or* away **2 = deal with**, manage, treat, handle, settle, cope with, take care of, see to
disposition 1 = character, nature, spirit, make-up, constitution, temper, temperament **2 = tendency**, inclination, propensity, habit, leaning, bent, bias, proclivity **3** (*archaic*) **= arrangement**, grouping, ordering,

organization, distribution, placement
dispute VERB 1 = contest, question, challenge, deny, doubt, oppose, object to, contradict **2 = argue**, fight, clash, disagree, fall out (*informal*), quarrel, squabble, bicker
▷ **NOUN 3 = disagreement**, conflict, argument, dissent, altercation **4 = argument**, row, clash, controversy, contention, feud, quarrel, squabble
disqualify = ban, rule out, prohibit, preclude, debar, declare ineligible
disregard VERB 1 = ignore, discount, overlook, neglect, pass over, turn a blind eye to, make light of, pay no heed to **OPPOSITE:** pay attention to
▷ **NOUN 2 = ignoring**, neglect, contempt, indifference, negligence, disdain, disrespect
disrupt 1 = interrupt, stop, upset, hold up, interfere with, unsettle, obstruct, cut short **2 = disturb**, upset, confuse, disorder, spoil, disorganize, disarrange
disruption = disturbance, interference, interruption, stoppage
disruptive = disturbing, upsetting, disorderly, unsettling, troublesome, unruly **OPPOSITE:** well-behaved
dissatisfaction = discontent, frustration, resentment,

disappointment, irritation,
unhappiness, annoyance,
displeasure
dissatisfied = **discontented**,
frustrated, unhappy,
disappointed, fed up,
disgruntled, displeased,
unsatisfied **OPPOSITE:** satisfied
dissent = **disagreement**,
opposition, protest, resistance,
refusal, objection, discord,
demur **OPPOSITE:** assent
dissident ADJECTIVE
1 = **dissenting**, disagreeing,
nonconformist, heterodox
▷ **NOUN** 2 = **protester**, rebel,
dissenter, demonstrator, agitator
dissolve 1 = **melt**, soften, thaw,
liquefy, deliquesce 2 = **end**,
suspend, break up, wind
up, terminate, discontinue,
dismantle, disband
distance 1 = **space**, length,
extent, range, stretch, gap,
interval, span 2 = **aloofness**,
reserve, detachment, restraint,
stiffness, coolness, coldness,
standoffishness
distant 1 = **far-off**, far, remote,
abroad, out-of-the-way,
far-flung, faraway, outlying
OPPOSITE: close 2 = **remote**
3 = **reserved**, withdrawn,
cool, remote, detached, aloof,
unfriendly, reticent **OPPOSITE:**
friendly 4 = **faraway**, blank,
vague, distracted, vacant,
preoccupied, oblivious, absent-
minded

distinct 1 = **different**, individual,
separate, discrete, unconnected
OPPOSITE: similar 2 = **striking**,
dramatic, outstanding,
noticeable, well-defined
3 = **definite**, marked, clear,
decided, obvious, evident,
noticeable, conspicuous
OPPOSITE: vague
distinction 1 = **difference**,
contrast, variation, differential,
discrepancy, disparity,
dissimilarity 2 = **excellence**,
importance, fame, merit,
prominence, greatness,
eminence, repute 3 = **feature**,
quality, characteristic, mark,
individuality, peculiarity,
distinctiveness, particularity
4 = **merit**, honour, integrity,
excellence, rectitude
distinctive = **characteristic**,
special, individual, unique,
typical, peculiar, singular,
idiosyncratic **OPPOSITE:**
ordinary
distinctly 1 = **definitely**, clearly,
obviously, plainly, patently,
decidedly, markedly, noticeably
2 = **clearly**, plainly
distinguish 1 = **differentiate**,
determine, separate,
discriminate, decide, judge,
ascertain, tell the difference
2 = **characterize**, mark,
separate, single out, set apart
3 = **make out**, recognize,
perceive, know, see, tell, pick
out, discern

distinguished = eminent, noted, famous, celebrated, well-known, prominent, esteemed, acclaimed **OPPOSITE**: unknown

distort 1 = **misrepresent**, twist, bias, disguise, pervert, slant, colour, misinterpret 2 = **deform**, bend, twist, warp, buckle, mangle, mangulate (*Austral slang*), disfigure, contort

distortion
1 = **misrepresentation**, bias, slant, perversion, falsification
2 = **deformity**, bend, twist, warp, buckle, contortion, malformation, crookedness

distract 1 = **divert**, sidetrack, draw away, turn aside, lead astray, draw *or* lead away from 2 = **amuse**, occupy, entertain, beguile, engross

distracted = **agitated**, troubled, puzzled, at sea, perplexed, flustered, in a flap (*informal*)

distraction 1 = **disturbance**, interference, diversion, interruption 2 = **entertainment**, recreation, amusement, diversion, pastime

distraught = **frantic**, desperate, distressed, distracted, worked-up, agitated, overwrought, out of your mind

distress VERB 1 = **upset**, worry, trouble, disturb, grieve, torment, harass, agitate
▷ NOUN 2 = **suffering**, pain, worry, grief, misery, torment, sorrow, heartache 3 = **need**, trouble, difficulties, poverty, hard times, hardship, misfortune, adversity

distressed 1 = **upset**, worried, troubled, distracted, tormented, distraught, agitated, wretched 2 = **poverty-stricken**, poor, impoverished, needy, destitute, indigent, down at heel, straitened

distressing = **upsetting**, worrying, disturbing, painful, sad, harrowing, heart-breaking

distribute 1 = **hand out**, pass round 2 = **circulate**, deliver, convey 3 = **share**, deal, allocate, dispense, allot, dole out, apportion

distribution 1 = **delivery**, mailing, transportation, handling 2 (*Economics*) = **sharing**, division, assignment, rationing, allocation, allotment, apportionment 3 = **spread**, organization, arrangement, placement

district = **area**, region, sector, quarter, parish, neighbourhood, vicinity, locality

distrust VERB 1 = **suspect**, doubt, be wary of, mistrust, disbelieve, be suspicious of **OPPOSITE**: trust
▷ NOUN 2 = **suspicion**, question, doubt, disbelief, scepticism, mistrust, misgiving, wariness **OPPOSITE**: trust

disturb 1 = **interrupt**, trouble, bother, plague, disrupt, interfere

with, hassle, inconvenience
2 = upset, concern, worry,
trouble, alarm, distress,
unsettle, unnerve **OPPOSITE:**
calm **3 = muddle**, disorder,
mix up, mess up, jumble up,
disarrange, muss (*US & Canad*)

disturbance 1 = disorder,
fray, brawl, fracas, commotion,
rumpus **2 = upset**, bother,
distraction, intrusion,
interruption, annoyance

disturbed 1 (*Psychiatry*)
= unbalanced, troubled,
disordered, unstable, neurotic,
upset, deranged, maladjusted
OPPOSITE: balanced
2 = worried, concerned,
troubled, upset, bothered,
nervous, anxious, uneasy
OPPOSITE: calm

disturbing = worrying,
upsetting, alarming,
frightening, distressing,
startling, unsettling, harrowing

ditch NOUN 1 = channel, drain,
trench, dyke, furrow, gully,
moat, watercourse
▷ **VERB 2** (*slang*) **= get rid of**,
dump (*informal*), scrap, discard,
dispose of, dispense with,
jettison, throw out *or* overboard
3 (*slang*) **= leave**, drop, abandon,
dump (*informal*), get rid of,
forsake

dive VERB 1 = plunge, drop,
duck, dip, descend, plummet
**2 = go underwater 3 = nose-
dive**, plunge, crash, swoop,
plummet
▷ **NOUN 4 = plunge**, spring,
jump, leap, lunge, nose dive

diverse 1 = various, mixed,
varied, assorted, miscellaneous,
several, sundry, motley
2 = different, unlike, varying,
separate, distinct, disparate,
discrete, dissimilar

diversify = vary, change,
expand, spread out, branch out

diversion 1 = distraction,
deviation, digression
2 = pastime, game, sport,
entertainment, hobby,
relaxation, recreation,
distraction **3** (*chiefly Brit*)
= detour, roundabout way,
indirect course **4** (*chiefly
Brit*) **= deviation**, departure,
straying, divergence, digression

diversity 1 = difference,
multiplicity, heterogeneity,
diverseness **2 = range**, variety,
scope, sphere

divert 1 = redirect, switch,
avert, deflect, deviate, turn
aside **2 = distract**, sidetrack,
lead astray, draw *or* lead away
from **3 = entertain**, delight,
amuse, please, charm, gratify,
beguile, regale

divide 1 = separate, split,
segregate, bisect **OPPOSITE:** join
2 = share, distribute, allocate,
dispense, allot, mete, deal
out **3 = split**, break up, come
between, estrange, cause to
disagree

d

d

dividend = **bonus**, share, cut (*informal*), gain, extra, plus, portion, divvy (*informal*)

divine ADJECTIVE 1 = **heavenly**, spiritual, holy, immortal, supernatural, celestial, angelic, superhuman 2 = **sacred**, religious, holy, spiritual, blessed, revered, hallowed, consecrated 3 (*informal*) = **wonderful**, perfect, beautiful, excellent, lovely, glorious, marvellous, splendid ▷ **VERB** 4 = **guess**, suppose, perceive, discern, infer, deduce, apprehend, surmise

division 1 = **separation**, dividing, splitting up, partition, cutting up 2 = **sharing**, distribution, assignment, rationing, allocation, allotment, apportionment 3 = **disagreement**, split, rift, rupture, abyss, chasm, variance, discord **OPPOSITE:** unity 4 = **department**, group, branch 5 = **part**, bit, piece, section, class, category, fraction

divorce NOUN 1 = **separation**, split, break-up, parting, split-up, rift, dissolution, annulment ▷ **VERB** 2 = **split up**, separate, part company, dissolve your marriage

dizzy 1 = **giddy**, faint, light-headed, swimming, reeling, shaky, wobbly, off balance 2 = **confused**, dazzled, at sea, bewildered, muddled, bemused, dazed, disorientated

do VERB 1 = **perform**, achieve, carry out, complete, accomplish, execute, pull off 2 = **make**, prepare, fix, arrange, look after, see to, get ready 3 = **solve**, work out, resolve, figure out, decode, decipher, puzzle out 4 = **be adequate**, be sufficient, satisfy, suffice, pass muster, cut the mustard, meet requirements 5 = **produce**, make, create, develop, manufacture, construct, invent, fabricate ▷ **NOUN** 6 (*informal, chiefly Brit & NZ*) = **party**, gathering, function, event, affair, occasion, celebration, reception ▷ **PHRASES: do away with something** = **get rid of**, remove, eliminate, abolish, discard, put an end to, dispense with, discontinue ▶ **do without something** *or* **someone** = **manage without**, give up, dispense with, forgo, kick (*informal*), abstain from, get along without

dock¹ NOUN 1 = **port**, haven, harbour, pier, wharf, quay, waterfront, anchorage ▷ **VERB** 2 = **moor**, land, anchor, put in, tie up, berth, drop anchor 3 (*of a spacecraft*) = **link up**, unite, join, couple, rendezvous, hook up

dock² 1 = **cut**, reduce, decrease, diminish, lessen **OPPOSITE:** increase 2 = **deduct**, subtract

3 = **cut off**, crop, clip, shorten, curtail, cut short

doctor NOUN 1 = **physician**, medic (*informal*), general practitioner, medical practitioner, G.P.
▷ VERB 2 = **change**, alter, interfere with, disguise, pervert, tamper with, tinker with, misrepresent 3 = **add to**, spike, cut, mix something with something, dilute, water down, adulterate

doctrine = **teaching**, principle, belief, opinion, conviction, creed, dogma, tenet, kaupapa (*NZ*)

document NOUN 1 = **paper**, form, certificate, report, record, testimonial, authorization
▷ VERB 2 = **support**, certify, verify, detail, validate, substantiate, corroborate, authenticate

dodge VERB 1 = **duck**, dart, swerve, sidestep, shoot, turn aside 2 = **evade**, avoid, escape, get away from, elude 3 = **avoid**, evade, shirk
▷ NOUN 4 = **trick**, scheme, ploy, trap, device, fraud, manoeuvre, deception, fastie (*Austral slang*)

dodgy 1 (*Brit, Austral & NZ informal*) = **nasty**, offensive, unpleasant, revolting, distasteful, repellent, obnoxious, repulsive, shonky (*Austral & NZ informal*) 2 (*Brit, Austral & NZ informal*) = **risky**,

difficult, tricky, dangerous, delicate, uncertain, dicey (*informal, chiefly Brit*), chancy (*informal*), shonky (*Austral & NZ informal*)

dog NOUN 1 = **hound**, canine, pooch (*slang*), cur, man's best friend, kuri *or* goorie (*NZ*), brak (*S African*)
▷ VERB 2 = **plague**, follow, trouble, haunt, hound, torment 3 = **pursue**, follow, track, chase, trail, hound, stalk

| **RELATED WORDS**
| *adjective:* canine
| *female:* bitch
| *young:* pup, puppy

dogged = **determined**, persistent, stubborn, resolute, tenacious, steadfast, obstinate, indefatigable OPPOSITE: irresolute

dole = **share**, grant, gift, allowance, handout, koha (*NZ*)
▷ PHRASES: dole something out = **give out**, distribute, assign, allocate, hand out, dispense, allot, apportion

dolphin

| **RELATED WORD**
| *collective noun:* school
• See panel WHALES AND DOLPHINS

domestic ADJECTIVE 1 = **home**, internal, native, indigenous 2 = **household**, home, family, private 3 = **home-loving**, homely, housewifely, stay-at-home, domesticated

4 = **domesticated**, trained, tame, pet, house-trained
▷ NOUN 5 = **servant**, help, maid, daily, char (*informal*), charwoman

dominant 1 = **main**, chief, primary, principal, prominent, predominant, pre-eminent **OPPOSITE:** minor 2 = **controlling**, ruling, commanding, supreme, governing, superior, authoritative

dominate 1 = **control**, rule, direct, govern, monopolize, tyrannize, have the whip hand over 2 = **tower above**, overlook, survey, stand over, loom over, stand head and shoulders above

domination = **control**, power, rule, authority, influence, command, supremacy, ascendancy

don = **put on**, get into, dress in, pull on, change into, get dressed in, clothe yourself in, slip on *or* into

donate = **give**, present, contribute, grant, subscribe, endow, entrust, impart

donation = **contribution**, gift, subscription, offering, present, grant, hand-out, koha (*NZ*)

donor = **giver**, contributor, benefactor, philanthropist, donator **OPPOSITE:** recipient

doom NOUN 1 = **destruction**, ruin, catastrophe, downfall
▷ VERB 2 = **condemn**, sentence, consign, destine

doomed = **hopeless**, condemned, ill-fated, fated, unhappy, unfortunate, cursed, unlucky

door = **opening**, entry, entrance, exit, doorway

dope NOUN 1 (*slang*) = **drugs**, narcotics, opiates, dadah (*Austral slang*) 2 (*informal*) = **idiot**, fool, twit (*informal*, *chiefly Brit*), dunce, simpleton, dimwit (*informal*), nitwit (*informal*), dumb-ass (*slang*), dorba *or* dorb (*Austral slang*), bogan (*Austral slang*), mampara (*S African informal*)
▷ VERB 3 = **drug**, knock out, sedate, stupefy, anaesthetize, narcotize

dorp (*S African*) = **town**, village, settlement, municipality, kainga *or* kaika (*NZ*)

dose 1 (*Medical*) = **measure**, amount, allowance, portion, prescription, ration, draught, dosage 2 = **quantity**, measure, supply, portion

dot NOUN 1 = **spot**, point, mark, fleck, jot, speck, speckle
▷ VERB 2 = **spot**, stud, fleck, speckle
▷ PHRASES: **on the dot** = **on time**, promptly, precisely, exactly (*informal*), to the minute, on the button (*informal*), punctually

double ADJECTIVE 1 = **matching**, coupled, paired, twin, duplicate, in pairs 2 = **dual**, enigmatic, twofold

▷ NOUN 3 = **twin**, lookalike, spitting image, clone, replica, dead ringer (*slang*), Doppelgänger, duplicate

▷ VERB 4 = **multiply by two**, duplicate, increase twofold, enlarge, magnify 5 = **fold up** *or* **over** 6 *with* **as** = **function as**, serve as

▷ PHRASES **at** *or* **on the double** = **at once**, now, immediately, directly, quickly, promptly, straight away, right away

doubt NOUN 1 = **uncertainty**, confusion, hesitation, suspense, indecision, hesitancy, lack of conviction, irresolution **OPPOSITE:** certainty 2 = **suspicion**, scepticism, distrust, apprehension, mistrust, misgivings, qualms **OPPOSITE:** belief

▷ VERB 3 = **be uncertain**, be sceptical, be dubious 4 = **waver**, hesitate, vacillate, fluctuate 5 = **disbelieve**, question, suspect, query, distrust, mistrust, lack confidence in **OPPOSITE:** believe

doubtful 1 = **unlikely**, unclear, dubious, questionable, improbable, debatable, equivocal **OPPOSITE:** certain 2 = **unsure**, uncertain, hesitant, suspicious, hesitating, sceptical, tentative, wavering **OPPOSITE:** certain

doubtless = **probably**, presumably, most likely

down ADJECTIVE 1 = **depressed**, low, sad, unhappy, discouraged, miserable, fed up, dejected

▷ VERB 2 (*informal*) = **swallow**, drink (down), drain, gulp (down), put away (*informal*), toss off

downfall = **ruin**, fall, destruction, collapse, disgrace, overthrow, undoing, comeuppance (*slang*)

downgrade = **demote**, degrade, take down a peg (*informal*), lower *or* reduce in rank **OPPOSITE:** promote

downright = **complete**, absolute, utter, total, plain, outright, unqualified, out-and-out

down-to-earth = **sensible**, practical, realistic, matter-of-fact, sane, no-nonsense, unsentimental, plain-spoken, grounded

downward = **descending**, declining, heading down, earthward

draft NOUN 1 = **outline**, plan, sketch, version, rough, abstract 2 = **money order**, bill (of exchange), cheque, postal order

▷ VERB 3 = **outline**, write, plan, produce, create, design, draw, compose

drag VERB 1 = **pull**, draw, haul, trail, tow, tug, jerk, lug

▷ NOUN 2 (*informal*) = **nuisance**, bore, bother, pest, hassle (*informal*), inconvenience, annoyance

drain NOUN 1 = **sewer**, channel, pipe, sink, ditch, trench, conduit, duct 2 = **reduction**, strain, drag, exhaustion, sapping, depletion
▷ VERB 3 = **remove**, draw, empty, withdraw, tap, pump, bleed 4 = **empty** 5 = **flow out**, leak, trickle, ooze, seep, exude, well out, effuse 6 = **drink up**, swallow, finish, put away (*informal*), quaff, gulp down 7 = **exhaust**, wear out, strain, weaken, fatigue, debilitate, tire out, enfeeble 8 = **consume**, exhaust, empty, use up, sap, dissipate

drama 1 = **play**, show, stage show, dramatization 2 = **theatre**, acting, stagecraft, dramaturgy 3 = **excitement**, crisis, spectacle, turmoil, histrionics

dramatic 1 = **exciting**, thrilling, tense, sensational, breathtaking, electrifying, melodramatic, climactic 2 = **theatrical**, Thespian, dramaturgical 3 = **expressive** 4 = **powerful**, striking, impressive, vivid, jaw-dropping
OPPOSITE: ordinary

drape = **cover**, wrap, fold, swathe

drastic = **extreme**, strong, radical, desperate, severe, harsh

draught *or* (US) **draft** 1 = **breeze**, current, movement, flow, puff, gust, current of air 2 = **drink**

draw VERB 1 = **sketch**, design, outline, trace, portray, paint, depict, mark out 2 = **pull**, drag, haul, tow, tug 3 = **extract**, take, remove 4 = **deduce**, make, take, derive, infer 5 = **attract** 6 = **entice**
▷ NOUN 7 = **tie**, deadlock, stalemate, impasse, dead heat 8 (*informal*) = **appeal**, pull (*informal*), charm, attraction, lure, temptation, fascination, allure
▷ PHRASES: **draw on** *or* **upon something** = **make use of**, use, employ, rely on, exploit, extract, take from, fall back on

drawback = **disadvantage**, difficulty, handicap, deficiency, flaw, hitch, snag, downside
OPPOSITE: advantage

drawing = **picture**, illustration, representation, cartoon, sketch, portrayal, depiction, study

drawn = **tense**, worn, stressed, tired, pinched, haggard

dread VERB 1 = **fear**, shrink from, cringe at the thought of, quail from, shudder to think about, have cold feet about (*informal*), tremble to think about
▷ NOUN 2 = **fear**, alarm, horror, terror, dismay, fright, apprehension, trepidation

dreadful 1 = **terrible**, shocking, awful, appalling, horrible, fearful, hideous, atrocious

2 = **serious**, terrible, awful, horrendous, monstrous, abysmal 3 = **awful**, terrible, horrendous, frightful

dream NOUN 1 = **vision**, illusion, delusion, hallucination 2 = **ambition**, wish, fantasy, desire, pipe dream 3 = **daydream** 4 = **delight**, pleasure, joy, beauty, treasure, gem, marvel, pearler (*Austral slang*), beaut (*Austral & NZ slang*)
▷ VERB 5 = **have dreams**, hallucinate 6 = **daydream**, stargaze, build castles in the air *or* in Spain
▷ ADJECTIVE
▷ PHRASES: **dream of something** *or* **someone** = **daydream about**, fantasize about

dreamer = **idealist**, visionary, daydreamer, utopian, escapist, Walter Mitty, fantasist

dreary = **dull**, boring, tedious, drab, tiresome, monotonous, humdrum, uneventful
OPPOSITE: exciting

drench = **soak**, flood, wet, drown, steep, swamp, saturate, inundate

dress NOUN 1 = **frock**, gown, robe 2 = **clothing**, clothes, costume, garments, apparel, attire, garb, togs
▷ VERB 3 = **put on clothes**, don clothes, slip on *or* into something OPPOSITE: undress 4 = **clothe** 5 = **bandage**, treat, plaster, bind up 6 = **arrange**, prepare, get ready

dribble 1 = **run**, drip, trickle, drop, leak, ooze, seep, fall in drops 2 = **drool**, drivel, slaver, slobber

drift VERB 1 = **float**, go (aimlessly), bob, coast, slip, sail, slide, glide 2 = **wander**, stroll, stray, roam, meander, rove, range 3 = **stray**, wander, digress, get off the point 4 = **pile up**, gather, accumulate, amass, bank up
▷ NOUN 5 = **pile**, bank, mass, heap, mound, accumulation 6 = **meaning**, point, gist, direction, import, intention, tendency, significance

drill NOUN 1 = **bit**, borer, gimlet, boring tool 2 = **training**, exercise, discipline, instruction, preparation, repetition 3 (*informal*) = **practice**
▷ VERB 4 = **bore**, pierce, penetrate, sink in, puncture, perforate 5 = **train**, coach, teach, exercise, discipline, practise, instruct, rehearse

drink VERB 1 = **swallow**, sip, suck, gulp, sup, guzzle, imbibe, quaff 2 = **booze** (*informal*), tipple, tope, hit the bottle (*informal*)
▷ NOUN 3 = **glass**, cup, draught 4 = **beverage**, refreshment, potion, liquid 5 = **alcohol**, booze (*informal*), liquor, spirits, the bottle (*informal*), hooch *or*

d

hootch (*informal, chiefly US & Canad*)

drip VERB 1 = **drop**, splash, sprinkle, trickle, dribble, exude, plop
▷ NOUN 2 = **drop**, bead, trickle, dribble, droplet, globule, pearl
3 (*informal*) = **weakling**, wet (*Brit informal*), weed (*informal*), softie (*informal*), mummy's boy (*informal*), namby-pamby

drive VERB 1 = **go (by car)**, ride (by car), motor, travel by car
2 = **operate**, manage, direct, guide, handle, steer 3 = **push**, propel 4 = **thrust**, push, hammer, ram 5 = **herd**, urge, impel 6 = **force**, press, prompt, spur, prod, constrain, coerce, goad
▷ NOUN 7 = **run**, ride, trip, journey, spin (*informal*), outing, excursion, jaunt 8 = **initiative**, energy, enterprise, ambition, motivation, zip (*informal*), vigour, get-up-and-go (*informal*)
9 = **campaign**, push (*informal*), crusade, action, effort, appeal
10 (*Computing*) = **storage device**, flash drive, key drive, keyring drive, microdrive, pen drive, thumb drive, USB drive, USB key

drop VERB 1 = **fall**, decline, diminish 2 *often with* **away**
= **decline**, fall, sink 3 = **plunge**, fall, tumble, descend, plummet
4 = **drip**, trickle, dribble, fall in drops 5 = **sink**, fall, descend
6 = **quit**, give up, axe (*informal*),

kick (*informal*), relinquish, discontinue
▷ NOUN 7 = **decrease**, fall, cut, lowering, decline, reduction, slump, fall-off 8 = **droplet**, bead, globule, bubble, pearl, drip
9 = **dash**, shot (*informal*), spot, trace, sip, tot, trickle, mouthful
10 = **fall**, plunge, descent
▷ PHRASES: **drop off** (*informal*)
1 = **fall asleep**, nod (off), doze (off), snooze (*informal*), have forty winks (*informal*)
2 = **decrease**, lower, decline, shrink, diminish, dwindle, lessen, subside ▶ **drop out**
= **leave**, stop, give up, withdraw, quit, pull out, fall by the wayside
▶ **drop out of something**
= **discontinue**, give up, quit

dross = **nonsense**, garbage (*chiefly US*), twaddle, rot, trash, hot air (*informal*), tripe (*informal*), claptrap (*informal*), bizzo (*Austral slang*), bull's wool (*Austral & NZ slang*)

drought = **water shortage**, dryness, dry spell, aridity
OPPOSITE: flood

drove *often plural* = **herd**, company, crowds, collection, mob, flocks, swarm, horde

drown 1 = **go down**, go under
2 = **drench**, flood, soak, steep, swamp, saturate, engulf, submerge 3 *often with* **out**
= **overwhelm**, overcome, wipe out, overpower, obliterate, swallow up

drug NOUN 1 = **medication**, medicine, remedy, physic, medicament 2 = **dope** (*slang*), narcotic (*slang*), stimulant, opiate, dadah (*Austral slang*)
▷ VERB 3 = **knock out**, dope (*slang*), numb, deaden, stupefy, anaesthetize

drum = **pound**, beat, tap, rap, thrash, tattoo, throb, pulsate
▷ PHRASES: **drum something into someone** = **drive**, hammer, instil, din, harp on about

drunk ADJECTIVE

1 = **intoxicated**, plastered (*slang*), drunken, merry (*Brit informal*), under the influence (*informal*), tipsy, legless (*informal*), inebriated, out to it (*Austral & NZ slang*), babalas (*S African*)
▷ NOUN 2 = **drunkard**, alcoholic, lush (*slang*), boozer (*informal*), wino (*informal*), inebriate, alko or alco (*Austral slang*)

dry ADJECTIVE 1 = **dehydrated**, dried-up, arid, parched, desiccated OPPOSITE: wet 2 = **thirsty**, parched 3 = **sarcastic**, cynical, low-key, sly, sardonic, deadpan, droll, ironical 4 = **dull**, boring, tedious, dreary, tiresome, monotonous, run-of-the-mill, humdrum OPPOSITE: interesting 5 = **plain**, simple, bare, basic, stark, unembellished
▷ VERB 6 = **drain**, make dry 7 *often with* **out** = **dehydrate**, make dry, desiccate, sear, parch, dehumidify OPPOSITE: wet
▷ PHRASES: **dry out** *or* **up** = **become dry**, harden, wither, shrivel up, wizen

dual = **twofold**, double, twin, matched, paired, duplicate, binary, duplex

dubious 1 = **suspect**, suspicious, crooked, dodgy (*Brit, Austral & NZ informal*), questionable, unreliable, fishy (*informal*), disreputable OPPOSITE: trustworthy 2 = **unsure**, uncertain, suspicious, hesitating, doubtful, sceptical, tentative, wavering OPPOSITE: sure

duck VERB 1 = **bob**, drop, lower, bend, bow, dodge, crouch, stoop 2 (*informal*) = **dodge**, avoid, escape, evade, elude, sidestep, shirk 3 = **dunk**, wet, plunge, dip, submerge, immerse, douse, souse

due ADJECTIVE 1 = **expected**, scheduled 2 = **fitting**, deserved, appropriate, justified, suitable, merited, proper, rightful 3 = **payable**, outstanding, owed, owing, unpaid, in arrears
▷ NOUN 4 = **right(s)**, privilege, deserts, merits, comeuppance (*informal*)
▷ ADVERB 5 = **directly**, dead, straight, exactly, undeviatingly

duel NOUN 1 = **single combat**, affair of honour 2 = **contest**, fight, competition, clash,

encounter, engagement, rivalry
▷ **VERB 3 = fight**, struggle, clash, compete, contest, contend, vie with, lock horns

dues = membership fee, charges, fee, contribution, levy

duff (*Brit*, *Austral & NZ informal*) = **bad**, poor, useless, inferior, unsatisfactory, defective, imperfect, substandard, bodger or bodgie (*Austral slang*)

dull ADJECTIVE 1 = boring, tedious, dreary, flat, plain, monotonous, run-of-the-mill, humdrum **OPPOSITE:** exciting **2 = lifeless**, indifferent, apathetic, listless, unresponsive, passionless **OPPOSITE:** lively **3 = cloudy**, dim, gloomy, dismal, overcast, leaden **OPPOSITE:** bright **4 = blunt**, blunted, unsharpened **OPPOSITE:** sharp
▷ **VERB 5 = relieve**, blunt, lessen, moderate, soften, alleviate, allay, take the edge off

duly 1 = properly, fittingly, correctly, appropriately, accordingly, suitably, deservedly, rightfully **2 = on time**, promptly, punctually, at the proper time

dumb 1 = unable to speak, mute **OPPOSITE:** articulate **2 = silent**, mute, speechless, tongue-tied, wordless, voiceless, soundless, mum **3** (*informal*) **= stupid**, thick, dull, foolish, dense, unintelligent, asinine, dim-witted (*informal*) **OPPOSITE:** clever

dummy NOUN 1 = model, figure, mannequin, form, manikin **2 = imitation**, copy, duplicate, sham, counterfeit, replica **3** (*slang*) **= fool**, idiot, dunce, oaf, simpleton, nitwit (*informal*), blockhead, dumb-ass (*slang*), dorba or dorb (*Austral slang*), mampara (*S African informal*)
▷ **ADJECTIVE 4 = imitation**, false, fake, artificial, mock, bogus, simulated, sham

dump VERB 1 = drop, deposit, throw down, let fall, fling down **2 = get rid of**, tip, dispose of, unload, jettison, empty out, throw away or out **3 = scrap**, get rid of, abolish, put an end to, discontinue, jettison, put paid to
▷ **NOUN 4 = rubbish tip**, tip, junkyard, rubbish heap, refuse heap **5** (*informal*) **= pigsty**, hole (*informal*), slum, hovel

dunny (*Austral & NZ old-fashioned informal*) **= toilet**, lavatory, bathroom, loo (*Brit informal*), W.C., bog (*slang*), Gents or Ladies, can (*US & Canad slang*), bogger (*Austral slang*), brasco (*Austral slang*)

duplicate ADJECTIVE 1 = identical, matched, matching, twin, corresponding, twofold
▷ **NOUN 2 = copy**, facsimile **3 = photocopy**, copy, reproduction, replica, carbon copy

▷ VERB 4 = **repeat**, reproduce, copy, clone, replicate 5 = **copy**

durable 1 = **hard-wearing**, strong, tough, reliable, resistant, sturdy, long-lasting **OPPOSITE:** fragile 2 = **enduring**, continuing, dependable, unwavering, unfaltering

duration = **length**, time, period, term, stretch, extent, spell, span, time frame, timeline

dusk = **twilight**, evening, evo (*Austral slang*), nightfall, sunset, dark, sundown, eventide, gloaming (*Scot poetic*) **OPPOSITE:** dawn

dust NOUN 1 = **grime**, grit 2 = **particles**, powder ▷ VERB 3 = **sprinkle**, cover, powder, spread, spray, scatter, sift, dredge

dusty = **dirty**, grubby, unclean, unswept

duty 1 = **responsibility**, job, task, work, role, function, obligation, assignment 2 = **tax**, toll, levy, tariff, excise ▷ PHRASES: **on duty** = **at work**, busy, engaged, on active service

dwarf NOUN 1 = **gnome**, midget, Lilliputian, Tom Thumb, pygmy *or* pigmy ▷ ADJECTIVE 2 = **miniature**, small, baby, tiny, diminutive, bonsai, undersized ▷ VERB 3 = **tower above** *or* **over**, dominate, overlook, stand over, loom over, stand head and shoulders above 4 = **eclipse**, tower above *or* over, put in the shade, diminish

dwell (*Formal, literary*) = **live**, reside, lodge, abide

dwelling (*Formal, literary*) = **home**, house, residence, abode, quarters, lodging, habitation, domicile, whare (*NZ*)

dwindle = **lessen**, decline, fade, shrink, diminish, decrease, wane, subside **OPPOSITE:** increase

dye NOUN 1 = **colouring**, colour, pigment, stain, tint, tinge, colorant ▷ VERB 2 = **colour**, stain, tint, tinge, pigment

dying 1 = **near death**, moribund, in extremis (*Latin*), at death's door, not long for this world 2 = **final**, last, parting, departing 3 = **failing**, declining, foundering, diminishing, decreasing, dwindling, subsiding

dynamic = **energetic**, powerful, vital, go-ahead, lively, animated, high-powered, forceful **OPPOSITE:** apathetic

dynasty = **empire**, house, rule, regime, sovereignty

Ee

each ADJECTIVE 1 = **every**, every single

▷ PRONOUN 2 = **every one**, all, each one, each and every one, one and all

▷ ADVERB 3 = **apiece**, individually, for each, to each, respectively, per person, per head, per capita

> **USAGE NOTE**
> *Each* is a singular pronoun and should be used with a singular verb – for example, *each of the candidates was interviewed separately* (not *were interviewed separately*).

eager 1 *often with* **to** *or* **for** = **anxious**, keen, hungry, impatient, itching, thirsty **OPPOSITE:** unenthusiastic 2 = **keen**, interested, intense, enthusiastic, passionate, avid (*informal*), fervent **OPPOSITE:** uninterested

ear = **sensitivity**, taste, discrimination, appreciation

early ADVERB 1 = **in good time**, beforehand, ahead of schedule, in advance, with time to spare **OPPOSITE:** late 2 = **too soon**, before the usual time, prematurely, ahead of time **OPPOSITE:** late

▷ ADJECTIVE 3 = **first**, opening, initial, introductory 4 = **premature**, forward, advanced, untimely, unseasonable **OPPOSITE:** belated 5 = **primitive**, first, earliest, young, original, undeveloped, primordial, primeval **OPPOSITE:** developed

earmark 1 = **set aside**, reserve, label, flag, allocate, designate, mark out 2 = **mark out**, identify, designate

earn 1 = **be paid**, make, get, receive, gain, net, collect, bring in 2 = **deserve**, win, gain, attain, justify, merit, warrant, be entitled to

earnest 1 = **serious**, grave, intense, dedicated, sincere, thoughtful, solemn, ardent **OPPOSITE:** frivolous 2 = **determined**, dogged, intent, persistent, persevering, resolute, wholehearted **OPPOSITE:** half-hearted

earnings = **income**, pay, wages, revenue, proceeds, salary, receipts, remuneration

earth 1 = **world**, planet, globe, sphere, orb, earthly sphere 2 = **ground**, land, dry land, terra firma 3 = **soil**, ground, land, dust, clay, dirt, turf, silt

earthly 1 = **worldly**, material, secular, mortal, temporal, human **OPPOSITE:** spiritual 2 = **sensual**, worldly, physical, fleshly, bodily, carnal 3 (*informal*) = **possible**, likely, practical, feasible, conceivable, imaginable

ease NOUN
1 = **straightforwardness**, simplicity, readiness
2 = **comfort**, luxury, leisure, relaxation, prosperity, affluence, rest, repose **OPPOSITE:** hardship
3 = **peace of mind**, peace, content, quiet, comfort, happiness, serenity, tranquillity **OPPOSITE:** agitation
▷ VERB 4 = **relieve**, calm, soothe, lessen, alleviate, lighten, lower, relax **OPPOSITE:** aggravate 5 *often with* **off** *or* **up** = **reduce**, diminish, lessen, slacken 6 = **move carefully**, edge, slip, inch, slide, creep, manoeuvre

easily = **without difficulty**, smoothly, readily, comfortably, effortlessly, with ease, straightforwardly

easy 1 = **simple**, straightforward, no trouble, not difficult, effortless, painless, uncomplicated, child's play (*informal*) **OPPOSITE:** hard
2 = **untroubled**, relaxed, peaceful, serene, tranquil, quiet
3 = **carefree**, comfortable, leisurely, trouble-free, untroubled, cushy (*informal*) **OPPOSITE:** difficult 4 = **tolerant**, soft, mild, laid-back (*informal*), indulgent, easy-going, lenient, permissive **OPPOSITE:** strict

eat 1 = **consume**, swallow, chew, scoff (*slang*), devour, munch, tuck into (*informal*), put away 2 = **have a meal**, lunch, breakfast, dine, snack, feed, graze (*informal*), have lunch

ebb VERB 1 = **flow back**, go out, withdraw, retreat, wane, recede 2 = **decline**, flag, diminish, decrease, dwindle, lessen, subside, fall away
▷ NOUN 3 = **flowing back**, going out, withdrawal, retreat, wane, low water, low tide, outgoing tide

e-book *or* **ebook** NOUN
1 = **electronic book**, iBook®, book
▷ VERB 2 = **reserve**, book, schedule, engage, organize, arrange (for), procure, e-procure

eccentric ADJECTIVE 1 = **odd**, strange, peculiar, irregular, quirky, unconventional, idiosyncratic, outlandish, daggy (*Austral & NZ informal*) **OPPOSITE:** normal
▷ NOUN 2 = **crank** (*informal*), character (*informal*), oddball (*informal*), nonconformist, weirdo *or* weirdie (*informal*), gink (*slang*)

echo NOUN 1 = **reverberation**, ringing, repetition, answer,

e

resonance, resounding
2 = **copy**, reflection, clone,
reproduction, imitation,
duplicate, double, reiteration
▷ **VERB 3** = **reverberate**,
repeat, resound, ring, resonate
4 = **recall**, reflect, copy, mirror,
resemble, imitate, ape
eclipse NOUN **1** = **obscuring**,
covering, blocking, shading,
dimming, extinction, darkening,
blotting out
▷ **VERB 2** = **surpass**, exceed,
overshadow, excel, transcend,
outdo, outclass, outshine
economic 1 = **financial**,
industrial, commercial **2** (*Brit*)
= **profitable**, successful,
commercial, rewarding,
productive, lucrative,
worthwhile, viable **3** (*informal*)
= **economical**, cheap,
reasonable, modest, low-priced,
inexpensive
economical 1 = **thrifty**,
sparing, careful, prudent,
provident, frugal, parsimonious,
scrimping **OPPOSITE:**
extravagant **2** = **efficient**,
sparing, cost-effective, money-
saving, time-saving **OPPOSITE:**
wasteful
economy 1 = **financial system**,
financial state **2** = **thrift**,
restraint, prudence, husbandry,
frugality, parsimony
ecstasy = **rapture**, delight, joy,
bliss, euphoria, fervour, elation
OPPOSITE: agony

ecstatic = **rapturous**,
entranced, joyous, elated,
overjoyed, blissful, euphoric,
enraptured, stoked (*Austral &
NZ informal*)
edge NOUN **1** = **border**, side,
limit, outline, boundary, fringe,
verge, brink **2** = **verge**, point,
brink, threshold **3** = **advantage**,
lead, dominance, superiority,
upper hand, head start,
ascendancy, whip hand
4 = **power**, force, bite,
effectiveness, incisiveness,
powerful quality **5** = **sharpness**,
point, bitterness, keenness
▷ **VERB 6** = **inch**, ease, creep,
slink, steal, sidle, move slowly
7 = **border**, fringe, hem, pipe
▷ **PHRASES: on edge** = **tense**,
nervous, impatient, irritable,
apprehensive, edgy, ill at ease,
on tenterhooks, adrenalized
edit = **revise**, improve, correct,
polish, adapt, rewrite,
condense, redraft
edition 1 = **printing**, publication
2 = **copy**, impression
3 = **version**, volume, issue
4 = **programme** (*TV, Radio*)
educate = **teach**, school, train,
develop, improve, inform,
discipline, tutor
educated 1 = **cultured**,
intellectual, learned,
sophisticated, refined,
cultivated, enlightened,
knowledgeable **OPPOSITE:**
uncultured **2** = **taught**,

schooled, coached, informed, tutored, instructed, nurtured, well-informed **OPPOSITE:** uneducated

education 1 = **teaching**, schooling, training, development, discipline, instruction, nurture, tuition, e-learning or elearning 2 = **learning**, schooling, cultivation, refinement

educational 1 = **academic**, school, learning, teaching, scholastic, pedagogical, pedagogic 2 = **instructive**, useful, cultural, illuminating, enlightening, informative, instructional, edifying

eerie = **uncanny**, strange, frightening, ghostly, weird, mysterious, scary (*informal*), sinister

effect NOUN 1 = **result**, consequence, conclusion, outcome, event, end result, upshot 2 = **impression**, feeling, impact, influence 3 = **purpose**, impression, sense, intent, essence, thread, tenor ▷ VERB 4 = **bring about**, produce, complete, achieve, perform, fulfil, accomplish, execute

USAGE NOTE

It is quite common for the verb *effect* to be mistakenly used where *affect* is intended. *Effect* is relatively uncommon and rather formal, and is a synonym of 'bring about'. Conversely, the noun *effect* is quite often mistakenly written with an initial *a*. The following are correct: *the group is still recovering from the effects of the recession; they really are powerless to effect any change*. The next two examples are incorrect: *the full affects of the shutdown won't be felt for several more days; men whose lack of hair doesn't effect their self-esteem*.

effective 1 = **efficient**, successful, useful, active, capable, valuable, helpful, adequate **OPPOSITE:** ineffective 2 = **powerful**, strong, convincing, persuasive, telling, impressive, compelling, forceful **OPPOSITE:** weak 3 = **virtual**, essential, practical, implied, implicit, tacit, unacknowledged 4 = **in operation**, official, current, legal, active, in effect, valid, operative **OPPOSITE:** inoperative

effects = **belongings**, goods, things, property, stuff, gear, possessions, paraphernalia

efficiency 1 = **effectiveness**, power, economy, productivity, organization, cost-effectiveness, orderliness 2 = **competence**, expertise, capability, professionalism, proficiency, adeptness

efficient 1 = **effective**, successful, structured, productive, systematic, streamlined, cost-effective, methodical **OPPOSITE:** inefficient 2 = **competent**, professional, capable, organized, productive, proficient, businesslike, well-organized **OPPOSITE:** incompetent

effort 1 = **attempt**, try, endeavour, shot (*informal*), bid, essay, go (*informal*), stab (*informal*) 2 = **exertion**, work, trouble, energy, struggle, application, graft, toil

egg = **ovum**, gamete, germ cell ▷ **PHRASES: egg someone on** = **incite**, push, encourage, urge, prompt, spur, provoke, prod

eject 1 = **throw out**, remove, turn out, expel (*slang*), oust, banish, drive out, evict 2 = **bail out**, escape, get out

elaborate ADJECTIVE 1 = **complicated**, detailed, studied, complex, precise, thorough, intricate, painstaking 2 = **ornate**, involved, complex, fancy, complicated, intricate, baroque, ornamented **OPPOSITE:** plain ▷ **VERB** 3 = **develop**, flesh out 4 *usually with* **on** *or* **upon** = **expand upon**, extend upon, enlarge on, amplify upon, embellish, flesh out, add detail to **OPPOSITE:** simplify

elastic 1 = **flexible**, supple, rubbery, pliable, plastic, springy, pliant, tensile **OPPOSITE:** rigid 2 = **adaptable**, yielding, variable, flexible, accommodating, tolerant, adjustable, supple **OPPOSITE:** inflexible

elbow = **joint**, angle, curve

elder ADJECTIVE 1 = **older**, first, senior, first-born ▷ **NOUN** 2 = **older person**, senior

elect 1 = **vote for**, choose, pick, determine, select, appoint, opt for, settle on 2 = **choose**, decide, prefer, select, opt

election 1 = **vote**, poll, ballot, referendum, franchise, plebiscite, show of hands 2 = **appointment**, picking, choice, selection

electric 1 = **electric-powered**, powered, cordless, battery-operated, electrically-charged, mains-operated 2 = **charged**, exciting, stirring, thrilling, stimulating, dynamic, tense, rousing, adrenalized

elegance = **style**, taste, grace, dignity, sophistication, grandeur, refinement, gracefulness

elegant = **stylish**, fine, sophisticated, delicate, handsome, refined, chic, exquisite, schmick (*Austral informal*) **OPPOSITE:** inelegant

element NOUN 1 = **component**, part, unit, section, factor,

principle, aspect, foundation
2 = group, faction, clique, set, party, circle **3 = trace**, suggestion, hint, dash, suspicion, tinge, smattering, soupçon
▷ **PLURAL NOUN 4 = weather conditions**, climate, the weather, wind and rain, atmospheric conditions, powers of nature
▷ **PHRASES: in your element = in a situation you enjoy**, in your natural environment, in familiar surroundings

elementary = simple, clear, easy, plain, straightforward, rudimentary, uncomplicated, undemanding **OPPOSITE:** complicated

elevate 1 = promote, raise, advance, upgrade, exalt, kick upstairs (*informal*), aggrandize, give advancement to
2 = increase, lift, raise, step up, intensify, move up, hoist, raise high **3 = raise**, lift, heighten, uplift, hoist, lift up, raise up, hike up

elevated 1 = exalted, important, august, grand, superior, noble, dignified, high-ranking **2 = high-minded**, fine, grand, noble, inflated, dignified, sublime, lofty **OPPOSITE:** humble **3 = raised**, high, lifted up, upraised

elicit 1 = bring about, cause, derive, bring out, evoke, give

rise to, draw out, bring forth
2 = obtain, extract, exact, evoke, wrest, draw out, extort

eligible 1 = entitled, fit, qualified, suitable **OPPOSITE:** ineligible **2 = available**, free, single, unmarried, unattached

eliminate = remove, end, stop, withdraw, get rid of, abolish, cut out, dispose of

elite = aristocracy, best, pick, cream, upper class, nobility, the crème de la crème, flower **OPPOSITE:** rabble

eloquent 1 = silver-tongued, moving, powerful, effective, stirring, articulate, persuasive, forceful **OPPOSITE:** inarticulate **2 = expressive**, telling, pointed, significant, vivid, meaningful, indicative, suggestive

elsewhere = in *or* to another place, away, abroad, hence (*archaic*), somewhere else, not here, in other places, in *or* to a different place

elude 1 = evade, escape, lose, avoid, flee, duck (*informal*), dodge, get away from
2 = escape, baffle, frustrate, puzzle, stump, be beyond (someone)

▌ **USAGE NOTE**
Elude is sometimes wrongly used where *allude* is meant: *he was alluding* (not *eluding*) *to his previous visit to the city*.

elusive 1 = difficult to catch, tricky, slippery, difficult to find,

e

evasive, shifty **2 = indefinable**, fleeting, subtle, indefinite, transient, intangible, indescribable, transitory

> **USAGE NOTE**
> The spelling of *elusive*, as in *a shy, elusive character*, should be noted. This adjective derives from the verb *elude*, and should not be confused with the rare word *illusive* meaning 'not real' or 'based on illusion'.

email *or* **e-mail** NOUN **= mail**, electronic mail, webmail

emanate *often with* **from = flow**, emerge, spring, proceed, arise, stem, derive, originate

embargo NOUN **1 = ban**, bar, restriction, boycott, restraint, prohibition, moratorium, stoppage, rahui (*NZ*)
▷ VERB **2 = block**, stop, bar, ban, restrict, boycott, prohibit, blacklist

embark = go aboard, climb aboard, board ship, step aboard, go on board, take ship
OPPOSITE: get off
▷ PHRASES: embark on something **= begin**, start, launch, enter, take up, set out, set about, plunge into

embarrass = shame, distress, show up (*informal*), humiliate, disconcert, fluster, mortify, discomfit

embarrassed = ashamed, shamed, uncomfortable, awkward, abashed, humiliated, uneasy, unsettled

embarrassing = humiliating, upsetting, compromising, delicate, uncomfortable, awkward, sensitive, troublesome, barro (*Austral slang*)

embarrassment 1 = shame, distress, showing up (*informal*), humiliation, discomfort, unease, self-consciousness, awkwardness **2 = problem**, difficulty, nuisance, source of trouble, thorn in your flesh **3 = predicament**, problem, difficulty (*informal*), mess, jam (*informal*), plight, scrape (*informal*), pickle (*informal*)

embodiment = personification, example, type, symbol, representation, manifestation, incarnation, epitome, paragon, exemplar, quintessence, avatar

embody 1 = personify, represent, stand for, manifest, exemplify, symbolize, typify, actualize **2** *often with* **in = incorporate**, include, contain, combine, collect, take in, encompass

embrace VERB **1 = hug**, hold, cuddle, seize, squeeze, clasp, envelop, canoodle (*slang*) **2 = accept**, support, welcome, adopt, take up, seize, espouse, take on board **3 = include**, involve, cover, contain, take

in, incorporate, comprise,
encompass
▷ **NOUN 4 = hug**, hold, cuddle,
squeeze, clinch (*slang*), clasp
embroil = involve, mix up,
implicate, entangle, mire,
ensnare, enmesh
embryo 1 = fetus, unborn
child, fertilized egg **2 = germ**,
beginning, source, root, seed,
nucleus, rudiment
emerge 1 = come out, appear,
surface, rise, arise, turn up,
spring up, emanate **OPPOSITE:**
withdraw **2 = become
apparent**, come out, become
known, come to light, crop up,
transpire, become evident,
come out in the wash
emergence 1 = coming,
development, arrival, surfacing,
rise, appearance, arising,
turning up **2 = disclosure**,
publishing, broadcasting,
broadcast, publication,
declaration, revelation,
becoming known
emergency NOUN 1 = crisis,
danger, difficulty, accident,
disaster, necessity, plight, scrape
(*informal*)
▷ **ADJECTIVE 2 = urgent**, crisis,
immediate **3 = alternative**,
extra, additional, substitute,
replacement, temporary,
makeshift, stopgap
emigrate = move abroad,
move, relocate, migrate,
resettle, leave your country

eminent = prominent, noted,
respected, famous, celebrated,
distinguished, well-known,
esteemed **OPPOSITE:** unknown
emission = giving off *or*
out, release, shedding,
leak, radiation, discharge,
transmission, ejaculation
emit 1 = give off, release, leak,
transmit, discharge, send out,
radiate, eject **OPPOSITE:** absorb
2 = utter, produce, voice, give
out, let out
emotion 1 = feeling, spirit, soul,
passion, excitement, sensation,
sentiment, fervour **2 = instinct**,
sentiment, sensibility, intuition,
tenderness, gut feeling, soft-
heartedness
emotional 1 = psychological,
private, personal, hidden,
spiritual, inner **2 = moving**,
touching, affecting, stirring,
sentimental, poignant, emotive,
heart-rending **3 = emotive**,
sensitive, controversial,
delicate, contentious,
heated, inflammatory, touchy
4 = passionate, sentimental,
temperamental, excitable,
demonstrative, hot-blooded
OPPOSITE: dispassionate
emphasis 1 = importance,
attention, weight, significance,
stress, priority, prominence
2 = stress, accent, force, weight
emphasize 1 = highlight,
stress, underline, draw
attention to, dwell on, play up,

make a point of, give priority to
OPPOSITE: minimize 2 = **stress**,
accentuate, lay stress on

emphatic 1 = **forceful**,
positive, definite, vigorous,
unmistakable, insistent,
unequivocal, vehement
OPPOSITE: hesitant
2 = **significant**, pronounced,
decisive, resounding, conclusive
OPPOSITE: insignificant

empire 1 = **kingdom**,
territory, province, federation,
commonwealth, realm, domain
2 = **organization**, company,
business, firm, concern,
corporation, consortium,
syndicate

▌ **RELATED WORD**
adjective: imperial

empirical = **first-hand**, direct,
observed, practical, actual,
experimental, pragmatic,
factual **OPPOSITE:** hypothetical

employ 1 = **hire**, commission,
appoint, take on, retain,
engage, recruit, sign up 2 = **use**,
apply, exercise, exert, make
use of, utilize, ply, bring to bear
3 = **spend**, fill, occupy, involve,
engage, take up, make use of,
use up

employed 1 = **working**, in work,
having a job, in employment,
in a job, earning your living
OPPOSITE: out of work 2 = **busy**,
active, occupied, engaged, hard
at work, in harness, rushed off
your feet **OPPOSITE:** idle

employee or (*sometimes US*)
employe = **worker**, labourer,
workman, staff member,
member of staff, hand, wage-
earner, white-collar worker

employer 1 = **boss** (*informal*),
manager, head, leader, director,
chief, owner, master, baas (*S
African*), sherang (*Austral & NZ*)
2 = **company**, business, firm,
organization, establishment,
outfit (*informal*)

employment 1 = **job**,
work, position, trade,
post, situation, profession,
occupation 2 = **taking on**,
commissioning, appointing,
hire, hiring, retaining, engaging,
appointment 3 = **use**,
application, exertion, exercise,
utilization

empower 1 = **authorize**, allow,
commission, qualify, permit,
sanction, entitle, delegate
2 = **enable**, equip, emancipate,
give means to, enfranchise

empty ADJECTIVE 1 = **bare**,
clear, abandoned, deserted,
vacant, free, void, desolate
OPPOSITE: full 2 = **meaningless**,
cheap, hollow, vain, idle, futile,
insincere 3 = **worthless**,
meaningless, hollow, pointless,
futile, senseless, fruitless, inane
OPPOSITE: meaningful
▷ VERB 4 = **clear**, drain, void,
unload, pour out, unpack,
remove the contents of
OPPOSITE: fill 5 = **exhaust**,

consume the contents of, void, deplete, use up **OPPOSITE:** replenish 6 = **evacuate**, clear, vacate

emulate = **imitate**, follow, copy, mirror, echo, mimic, model yourself on

enable 1 = **allow**, permit, empower, give someone the opportunity, give someone the means **OPPOSITE:** prevent 2 = **authorize**, allow, permit, qualify, sanction, entitle, license, warrant **OPPOSITE:** stop

enact 1 = **establish**, order, command, approve, sanction, proclaim, decree, authorize 2 = **perform**, play, present, stage, represent, put on, portray, depict

enchant = **fascinate**, delight, charm, entrance, dazzle, captivate, enthral, beguile

enclose *or* **inclose** 1 = **surround**, circle, bound, fence, confine, close in, wall in, encircle 2 = **send with**, include, put in, insert

encompass 1 = **include**, hold, cover, admit, deal with, contain, take in, embrace 2 = **surround**, circle, enclose, close in, envelop, encircle, fence in, ring

encounter **VERB** 1 = **experience**, meet, face, suffer, have, go through, sustain, endure 2 = **meet**, confront, come across, bump into (*informal*), run across, come

upon, chance upon, meet by chance ▷ **NOUN** 3 = **meeting**, brush, confrontation, rendezvous, chance meeting 4 = **battle**, conflict, clash, contest, run-in (*informal*), confrontation, head-to-head

encourage 1 = **inspire**, comfort, cheer, reassure, console, hearten, cheer up, embolden **OPPOSITE:** discourage 2 = **urge**, persuade, prompt, spur, coax, egg on **OPPOSITE:** dissuade 3 = **promote**, back, support, increase, foster, advocate, stimulate, endorse **OPPOSITE:** prevent

encouragement 1 = **inspiration**, support, comfort, comforting, cheer, cheering, reassurance, morale boosting 2 = **urging**, prompting, stimulus, persuasion, coaxing, egging on, incitement 3 = **promotion**, backing, support, endorsement, stimulation, furtherance

end **NOUN** 1 = **close**, ending, finish, expiry, expiration **OPPOSITE:** beginning 2 = **conclusion**, ending, climax, completion, finale, culmination, denouement, consummation **OPPOSITE:** start 3 = **finish**, close, stop, resolution, conclusion, closure, completion, termination 4 = **extremity**, limit, edge, border, extent, extreme, margin, boundary **5 = tip**, point, head, peak, extremity **6 = purpose**, point, reason, goal, target, aim, object, mission **7 = outcome**, resolution, conclusion **8 = death**, dying, ruin, destruction, passing on, doom, demise, extinction **9 = remnant**, butt, stub, scrap, fragment, stump, remainder, leftover ▷ **VERB 10 = stop**, finish, halt, cease, wind up, terminate, call off, discontinue **OPPOSITE:** start **11 = finish**, close, conclude, wind up, culminate, terminate, come to an end, draw to a close **OPPOSITE:** begin

▎**RELATED WORDS**
adjectives: final, terminal, ultimate

endanger = put at risk, risk, threaten, compromise, jeopardize, imperil, put in danger, expose to danger **OPPOSITE:** save

endearing = attractive, winning, pleasing, appealing, sweet, engaging, charming, pleasant

endeavour (*Formal*) **VERB 1 = try**, labour, attempt, aim, struggle, venture, strive, aspire ▷ **NOUN 2 = attempt**, try, effort, trial, bid, venture, enterprise, undertaking

ending = finish, end, close, conclusion, summing up, completion, finale, culmination **OPPOSITE:** start

endless = eternal, infinite, continual, unlimited, interminable, incessant, boundless, everlasting **OPPOSITE:** temporary

endorse 1 = approve, back, support, champion, promote, recommend, advocate, uphold **2 = sign**, initial, countersign, sign on the back of

endorsement = approval, backing, support, favour, recommendation, acceptance, agreement, upholding

endow 1 = finance, fund, pay for, award, confer, bestow, bequeath, donate money to **2 = imbue**

endowed *usually with* **with = provided**, favoured, graced, blessed, supplied, furnished

endowment = provision, funding, award, grant, gift, contribution, subsidy, donation, koha (*NZ*)

endurance 1 = staying power, strength, resolution, determination, patience, stamina, fortitude, persistence **2 = permanence**, stability, continuity, duration, longevity, durability, continuance

endure 1 = experience, suffer, bear, meet, encounter, cope with, sustain, undergo **2 = last**, continue, remain, stay, stand, go on, survive, live on

enemy = **foe**, rival, opponent, the opposition, competitor, the other side, adversary, antagonist **OPPOSITE:** friend

energetic 1 = **forceful**, determined, active, aggressive, dynamic, vigorous, hard-hitting, strenuous 2 = **lively**, active, dynamic, vigorous, animated, tireless, bouncy, indefatigable **OPPOSITE:** lethargic 3 = **strenuous**, hard, taxing, demanding, tough, exhausting, vigorous, arduous

energy 1 = **strength**, might, stamina, forcefulness 2 = **liveliness**, drive, determination, pep, vitality, vigour, verve, resilience 3 = **power**

enforce 1 = **carry out**, apply, implement, fulfil, execute, administer, put into effect, put into action 2 = **impose**, force, insist on

engage 1 = **participate in**, join in, take part in, undertake, embark on, enter into, become involved in, set about 2 = **captivate**, catch, arrest, fix, capture 3 = **occupy**, involve, draw, grip, absorb, preoccupy, immerse, engross 4 = **employ**, appoint, take on, hire, retain, recruit, enlist, enrol **OPPOSITE:** dismiss 5 = **set going**, apply, trigger, activate, switch on, energize, bring into operation 6 (*Military*) = **begin battle with**, attack, take on, encounter, fall on, battle with, meet, assail

engaged 1 = **occupied**, working, employed, busy, tied up 2 = **betrothed**, promised, pledged, affianced, promised in marriage **OPPOSITE:** unattached 3 = **in use**, busy, tied up, unavailable **OPPOSITE:** free

engagement 1 = **appointment**, meeting, interview, date, commitment, arrangement, rendezvous 2 = **betrothal**, marriage contract, troth (*archaic*), agreement to marry 3 = **battle**, fight, conflict, action, struggle, clash, encounter, combat 4 = **participation**, joining, taking part, involvement

engaging = **charming**, interesting, pleasing, attractive, lovely, entertaining, winning, fetching (*informal*) **OPPOSITE:** unpleasant

engine = **machine**, motor, mechanism, generator, dynamo

engineer NOUN 1 = **designer**, producer, architect, developer, deviser, creator, planner, inventor 2 = **worker**, specialist, operator, practitioner, operative, driver, conductor, technician
▷ VERB 3 = **design**, plan, create, construct, devise 4 = **bring about**, plan, effect, set up (*informal*), scheme, arrange, plot, mastermind

engraving = **print**, carving, etching, inscription, plate, woodcut, dry point

engulf 1 = **immerse**, swamp, submerge, overrun, inundate, envelop, swallow up
2 = **overwhelm**, overcome, crush, swamp

enhance = **improve**, better, increase, lift, boost, add to, strengthen, reinforce **OPPOSITE:** reduce

enjoy 1 = **take pleasure in** or **from**, like, love, appreciate, relish, delight in, be pleased with, be fond of **OPPOSITE:** hate
2 = **have**, use, own, experience, possess, have the benefit of, reap the benefits of, be blessed or favoured with

enjoyable = **pleasurable**, good, great, fine, nice, satisfying, lovely, entertaining **OPPOSITE:** unpleasant

enjoyment 1 = **pleasure**, liking, fun, delight, entertainment, joy, happiness, relish **2** = **benefit**, use, advantage, favour, possession, blessing

enlarge 1 = **expand**, increase, extend, add to, build up, widen, intensify, broaden **OPPOSITE:** reduce **2** = **grow**, increase, extend, expand, swell, become bigger, puff up, grow larger
▷ **PHRASES:** enlarge on something = **expand on**, develop, add to, fill out, elaborate on, flesh out,

expatiate on, give further details about

enlighten = **inform**, tell, teach, advise, counsel, educate, instruct, illuminate

enlightened = **informed**, aware, reasonable, educated, sophisticated, cultivated, open-minded, knowledgeable **OPPOSITE:** ignorant

enlightenment = **understanding**, learning, education, knowledge, instruction, awareness, wisdom, insight

enlist 1 = **join up**, join, enter (into), register, volunteer, sign up, enrol **2** = **obtain**, get, gain, secure, engage, procure

enormous = **huge**, massive, vast, extensive, tremendous, gross, immense, gigantic, supersize **OPPOSITE:** tiny

enough ADJECTIVE
1 = **sufficient**, adequate, ample, abundant, as much as you need, as much as is necessary
▷ **PRONOUN 2** = **sufficiency**, plenty, sufficient, abundance, adequacy, right amount, ample supply
▷ **ADVERB 3** = **sufficiently**, amply, reasonably, adequately, satisfactorily, abundantly, tolerably

enquire ▷ See **INQUIRE**
enquiry ▷ See **INQUIRY**
enrage = **anger**, infuriate, incense, madden, inflame,

exasperate, antagonize, make you angry **OPPOSITE:** calm

enrich 1 = **enhance**, develop, improve, boost, supplement, refine, heighten, augment 2 = **make rich**, make wealthy, make affluent, make prosperous, make well-off

enrol or (US) **enroll** 1 = **enlist**, register, be accepted, be admitted, join up, put your name down for, sign up or on 2 = **recruit**, take on, enlist

en route = **on** or **along the way**, travelling, on the road, in transit, on the journey

ensemble 1 = **group**, company, band, troupe, cast, orchestra, chorus 2 = **collection**, set, body, whole, total, sum, combination, entity 3 = **outfit**, suit, get-up (informal), costume

ensue = **follow**, result, develop, proceed, arise, stem, derive, issue **OPPOSITE:** come first

ensure 1 = **make certain**, guarantee, secure, make sure, confirm, warrant, certify 2 = **protect**, defend, secure, safeguard, guard, make safe

entail = **involve**, require, produce, demand, call for, occasion, need, bring about

enter 1 = **come** or **go in** or **into**, arrive, set foot in somewhere, cross the threshold of somewhere, make an entrance **OPPOSITE:** exit 2 = **penetrate**, get in, pierce, pass into,

perforate 3 = **join**, start work at, begin work at, enrol in, enlist in **OPPOSITE:** leave 4 = **participate in**, join (in), be involved in, get involved in, play a part in, partake in, associate yourself with, start to be in 5 = **begin**, start, take up, move into, commence, set out on, embark upon 6 = **compete in**, contest, join in, fight, sign up for, go in for 7 = **record**, note, register, log, list, write down, take down, inscribe

enterprise 1 = **firm**, company, business, concern, operation, organization, establishment, commercial undertaking 2 = **venture**, operation, project, adventure, undertaking, programme, pursuit, endeavour 3 = **initiative**, energy, daring, enthusiasm, imagination, drive, ingenuity, originality

enterprising = **resourceful**, original, spirited, daring, bold, enthusiastic, imaginative, energetic

entertain 1 = **amuse**, interest, please, delight, charm, enthral, cheer, regale 2 = **show hospitality to**, receive, accommodate, treat, put up, lodge, be host to, have company of 3 = **consider**, imagine, think about, contemplate, conceive of, bear in mind, keep in mind, give thought to

entertainment
1 = **enjoyment**, fun, pleasure, leisure, relaxation, recreation, amusement 2 = **pastime**, show, sport, performance, treat, presentation, leisure activity

enthusiasm = **keenness**, interest, passion, motivation, relish, zeal, zest, fervour

enthusiast = **fan**, supporter, lover, follower, addict, buff (*informal*), fanatic, devotee

enthusiastic = **keen**, committed, eager, passionate, vigorous, avid, fervent, zealous **OPPOSITE:** apathetic

entice = **lure**, attract, invite, persuade, tempt, induce, seduce, lead on

entire = **whole**, full, complete, total

entirely = **completely**, totally, absolutely, fully, altogether, thoroughly, wholly, utterly **OPPOSITE:** partly

entitle 1 = **give the right to**, allow, enable, permit, sanction, license, authorize, empower 2 = **call**, name, title, term, label, dub, christen, give the title of

entity = **thing**, being, individual, object, substance, creature, organism

entrance¹ 1 = **way in**, opening, door, approach, access, entry, gate, passage **OPPOSITE:** exit 2 = **appearance**, coming in, entry, arrival, introduction **OPPOSITE:** exit 3 = **admission**, access, entry, entrée, admittance, permission to enter, right of entry

entrance² 1 = **enchant**, delight, charm, fascinate, dazzle, captivate, enthral, beguile **OPPOSITE:** bore 2 = **mesmerize**, bewitch, hypnotize, put a spell on, cast a spell on, put in a trance

entrant = **competitor**, player, candidate, entry, participant, applicant, contender, contestant

entrenched *or* **intrenched** = **fixed**, set, rooted, well-established, ingrained, deep-seated, deep-rooted, unshakeable *or* unshakable

entrepreneur = **businessman** *or* **businesswoman**, tycoon, executive, industrialist, speculator, magnate, impresario, business executive

entrust *or* **intrust** 1 = **give custody of**, deliver, commit, delegate, hand over, turn over, confide 2 *usually with* **with** = **assign**

entry 1 = **admission**, access, entrance, admittance, entrée, permission to enter, right of entry 2 = **coming in**, entering, appearance, arrival, entrance **OPPOSITE:** exit 3 = **introduction**, presentation, initiation, inauguration, induction, debut, investiture 4 = **record**, listing, account, note, statement, item 5 = **way in**, opening, door, approach, access, gate, passage, entrance

envelope = **wrapping**, casing, case, covering, cover, jacket, sleeve, wrapper

environment

1 = **surroundings**, setting, conditions, situation, medium, circumstances, background, atmosphere 2 (*Ecology*) = **habitat**, home, surroundings, territory, terrain, locality, natural home

environmental = **ecological**, green, eco-friendly

environmentalist = **conservationist**, ecologist, green

envisage 1 = **imagine**, contemplate, conceive (of), visualize, picture, fancy, think up, conceptualize 2 = **foresee**, see, expect, predict, anticipate, envision

envoy 1 = **ambassador**, diplomat, emissary 2 = **messenger**, agent, representative, delegate, courier, intermediary, emissary

envy NOUN 1 = **covetousness**, resentment, jealousy, bitterness, resentfulness, enviousness (*informal*)
▷ VERB 2 = **be jealous (of)**, resent, begrudge, be envious (of) 3 = **covet**, desire, crave, aspire to, yearn for, hanker after

epidemic 1 = **outbreak**, plague, growth, spread, scourge,

contagion 2 = **spate**, plague, outbreak, wave, rash, eruption, upsurge

episode 1 = **event**, experience, happening, matter, affair, incident, adventure, occurrence 2 = **instalment**, part, act, scene, section, chapter, passage, webisode

equal ADJECTIVE 1 *often with* **to** *or* **with** = **identical**, the same, matching, equivalent, uniform, alike, corresponding OPPOSITE: unequal 2 = **fair**, just, impartial, egalitarian, unbiased, even-handed OPPOSITE: unfair 3 = **even**, balanced, fifty-fifty (*informal*), evenly matched OPPOSITE: uneven
▷ NOUN 4 = **match**, equivalent, twin, counterpart
▷ VERB 5 = **amount to**, make, come to, total, level, parallel, tie with, equate OPPOSITE: be unequal to 6 = **be equal to**, match, reach 7 = **be as good as**, match, compare with, equate with, measure up to, be as great as

equality 1 = **fairness**, equal opportunity, equal treatment, egalitarianism, fair treatment, justness OPPOSITE: inequality 2 = **sameness**, balance, identity, similarity, correspondence, parity, likeness, uniformity OPPOSITE: disparity

equate 1 = **identify**, associate,

equation | 208

connect, compare, relate,
mention in the same breath,
think of in connection with
2 = **make equal**, match,
even up

equation = **equating**,
comparison, parallel,
correspondence

equilibrium = **stability**,
balance, symmetry,
steadiness, evenness,
equipoise

equip 1 = **supply**, provide,
stock, arm, array, furnish,
fit out, kit out 2 = **prepare**,
qualify, educate, get ready

equipment = **apparatus**,
stock, supplies, stuff, tackle,
gear, tools, provisions

equitable = **even-handed**,
just, fair, reasonable, proper,
honest, impartial, unbiased

equivalent ADJECTIVE
1 = **equal**, same, comparable,
parallel, identical, alike,
corresponding, tantamount
OPPOSITE: different
▷ NOUN 2 = **equal**, counterpart,
twin, parallel, match, opposite
number

era = **age**, time, period, date,
generation, epoch, day or
days

eradicate = **wipe out**,
eliminate, remove, destroy,
get rid of, erase, extinguish,
obliterate

erase 1 = **delete**, cancel out,
wipe out, remove, eradicate,
obliterate, blot out, expunge
2 = **rub out**, remove, wipe out,
delete

e-reader or **eReader**
= **electronic book**, e-book or
ebook, book
• See panel TYPES OF E-READER

erect ADJECTIVE 1 = **upright**,
straight, stiff, vertical, elevated,
perpendicular, pricked-up
OPPOSITE: bent
▷ VERB 2 = **build**, raise, set up,
construct, put up, assemble,
put together **OPPOSITE:**
demolish 3 = **found**, establish,
form, create, set up, institute,
organize, put up

erode 1 = **disintegrate**,
crumble, deteriorate,
corrode, break up, grind
down, waste away, wear
down or away 2 = **destroy**,
consume, crumble, eat away,
corrode, break up, grind down,
abrade 3 = **weaken**, destroy,
undermine, diminish, impair,
lessen, wear away

TYPES OF E-READER

Cybook®	Papyrus®
Kindle®	Reader®
Nook®	

erosion 1 = **disintegration**, deterioration, wearing down or away, grinding down 2 = **deterioration**, undermining, destruction, weakening, attrition, eating away, abrasion, grinding down

erotic = **sexual**, sexy (informal), crude, explicit, sensual, seductive, vulgar, voluptuous

erratic = **unpredictable**, variable, unstable, irregular, inconsistent, uneven, unreliable, wayward **OPPOSITE:** regular

error = **mistake**, slip, blunder, oversight, howler (informal), bloomer (Brit informal), miscalculation, solecism, barry or Barry Crocker (Austral slang)

erupt 1 = **explode**, blow up, emit lava 2 = **gush**, burst out, pour forth, belch forth, spew forth or out 3 = **start**, break out, begin, explode, flare up, burst out, boil over 4 (Medical) = **break out**, appear, flare up

escalate 1 = **grow**, increase, extend, intensify, expand, surge, mount, heighten **OPPOSITE:** decrease 2 = **increase**, develop, extend, intensify, expand, build up, heighten **OPPOSITE:** lessen

escape VERB 1 = **get away**, flee, take off, fly, bolt, slip away, abscond, make a break for it, do a Skase (Austral informal) 2 = **avoid**, miss, evade, dodge, shun, elude, duck, steer clear of

3 usually with **from** = **leak out**, flow out, gush out, emanate, seep out, exude, spill out, pour forth ▷ NOUN 4 = **getaway**, break, flight, break-out 5 = **avoidance**, evasion, circumvention 6 = **relaxation**, recreation, distraction, diversion, pastime 7 = **leak**, emission, outpouring, seepage, issue, emanation

escort NOUN 1 = **guard**, bodyguard, train, convoy, entourage, retinue, cortege 2 = **companion**, partner, attendant, guide, beau, chaperon ▷ VERB 3 = **accompany**, lead, partner, conduct, guide, shepherd, usher, chaperon

especially 1 = **notably**, mostly, strikingly, conspicuously, outstandingly 2 = **very**, specially, extremely, remarkably, unusually, exceptionally, markedly, uncommonly

espionage = **spying**, intelligence, surveillance, counter-intelligence, undercover work

essay NOUN 1 = **composition**, study, paper, article, piece, assignment, discourse, tract ▷ VERB 2 (Formal) = **attempt**, try, undertake, endeavour

essence 1 = **fundamental nature**, nature, being, heart, spirit, soul, core, substance

e

2 = **concentrate**, spirits, extract, tincture, distillate

essential ADJECTIVE

1 = **vital**, important, needed, necessary, critical, crucial, key, indispensable **OPPOSITE:** unimportant 2 = **fundamental**, main, basic, principal, cardinal, elementary, innate, intrinsic **OPPOSITE:** secondary
▷ NOUN 3 = **prerequisite**, fundamental, necessity, must, basic, sine qua non (*Latin*), rudiment, must-have

establish 1 = **set up**, found, create, institute, constitute, inaugurate 2 = **prove**, confirm, demonstrate, certify, verify, substantiate, corroborate, authenticate 3 = **secure**, form, ground, settle

Establishment
▷ PHRASES: the Establishment = **the authorities**, the system, the powers that be, the ruling class

establishment 1 = **creation**, founding, setting up, foundation, institution, organization, formation, installation 2 = **organization**, company, business, firm, concern, operation, institution, corporation

estate 1 = **lands**, property, area, grounds, domain, manor, holdings, homestead (*US & Canad*) 2 (*chiefly Brit*) = **area**, centre, park, development, site, zone, plot 3 (*Law*) = **property**, capital, assets, fortune, goods, effects, wealth, possessions

esteem VERB 1 = **respect**, admire, think highly of, love, value, prize, treasure, revere
▷ NOUN 2 = **respect**, regard, honour, admiration, reverence, estimation, veneration

estimate VERB 1 = **calculate roughly**, value, guess, judge, reckon, assess, evaluate, gauge 2 = **think**, believe, consider, rate, judge, hold, rank, reckon
▷ NOUN 3 = **approximate calculation**, guess, assessment, judgment, valuation, guesstimate (*informal*), rough calculation, ballpark figure (*informal*)
4 = **assessment**, opinion, belief, appraisal, evaluation, judgment, estimation

estuary = **inlet**, mouth, creek, firth, fjord

etch 1 = **engrave**, cut, impress, stamp, carve, imprint, inscribe
2 = **corrode**, eat into, burn into

etching = **print**, carving, engraving, imprint, inscription

eternal 1 = **everlasting**, lasting, permanent, enduring, endless, perpetual, timeless, unending **OPPOSITE:** transitory
2 = **interminable**, endless, infinite, continual, immortal, never-ending, everlasting
OPPOSITE: occasional

eternity 1 = **the afterlife**, heaven, paradise, the next world, the hereafter 2 = **perpetuity**, immortality, infinity, timelessness, endlessness 3 = **ages**

ethical 1 = **moral**, behavioural 2 = **right**, morally acceptable, good, just, fair, responsible, principled **OPPOSITE:** unethical

ethics = **moral code**, standards, principles, morals, conscience, morality, moral values, moral principles, tikanga (*NZ*)

ethnic *or* **ethnical** = **cultural**, national, traditional, native, folk, racial, genetic, indigenous

euphoria = **elation**, joy, ecstasy, rapture, exhilaration, jubilation **OPPOSITE:** despondency

euthanasia = **mercy killing**, assisted suicide

evacuate 1 = **remove**, clear, withdraw, expel, move out, send to a safe place 2 = **abandon**, leave, clear, desert, quit, withdraw from, pull out of, move out of

evade 1 = **avoid**, escape, dodge, get away from, elude, steer clear of, sidestep, duck **OPPOSITE:** face 2 = **avoid answering**, parry, fend off, fudge, hedge, equivocate

evaluate = **assess**, rate, judge, estimate, reckon, weigh, calculate, gauge

evaporate 1 = **disappear**, vaporize, dematerialize, vanish, dissolve, dry up, fade away, melt away 2 = **dry up**, dry, dehydrate, vaporize, desiccate 3 = **fade away**, disappear, vanish, dissolve, melt away

eve 1 = **night before**, day before, vigil 2 = **brink**, point, edge, verge, threshold

even 1 = **regular**, stable, constant, steady, smooth, uniform, unbroken, uninterrupted **OPPOSITE:** variable 2 = **level**, straight, flat, smooth, true, steady, uniform, parallel **OPPOSITE:** uneven 3 = **equal**, like, matching, similar, identical, comparable **OPPOSITE:** unequal 4 = **equally matched**, level, tied, on a par, neck and neck, fifty-fifty (*informal*), all square **OPPOSITE:** ill-matched 5 = **square**, quits, on the same level, on an equal footing 6 = **calm**, composed, cool, well-balanced, placid, unruffled, imperturbable, even-tempered **OPPOSITE:** excitable

evening = **dusk** (*archaic*), night, sunset, twilight, sundown, gloaming (*Scot poetic*), close of day, evo (*Austral slang*)

event 1 = **incident**, happening, experience, affair, occasion, proceeding, business, circumstance 2 = **competition**, game, tournament, contest, bout

eventual = **final**, overall, concluding, ultimate

eventually = **in the end**, finally, one day, after all, some time, ultimately, at the end of the day, when all is said and done

ever 1 = **at any time**, at all, in any case, at any point, by any chance, on any occasion, at any period 2 = **always**, for ever, at all times, evermore 3 = **constantly**, continually, perpetually

every = **each**, each and every, every single

everybody = **everyone**, each one, the whole world, each person, every person, all and sundry, one and all

everyday = **ordinary**, common, usual, routine, stock, customary, mundane, run-of-the-mill **OPPOSITE:** unusual

everyone = **everybody**, each one, the whole world, each person, every person, all and sundry, one and all

> **USAGE NOTE**
> *Everyone* and *everybody* are interchangeable, and can be used as synonyms of each other in any context. Care should be taken, however, to distinguish between *everyone* as a single word and *every one* as two words, the latter form correctly being used to refer to each individual person or thing in a particular group: *every one of them is wrong*.

everything = **all**, the lot, the whole lot, each thing

everywhere 1 = **all over**, all around, the world over, high and low, in every nook and cranny, far and wide *or* near, to *or* in every place 2 = **all around**, all over, in every nook and cranny, ubiquitously, far and wide *or* near, to *or* in every place

evidence NOUN 1 = **proof**, grounds, demonstration, confirmation, verification, corroboration, authentication, substantiation 2 = **sign(s)**, suggestion, trace, indication 3 (*Law*) = **testimony**, statement, submission, avowal
▷ VERB 4 = **show**, prove, reveal, display, indicate, witness, demonstrate, exhibit

evident = **obvious**, clear, plain, apparent, visible, manifest, noticeable, unmistakable **OPPOSITE:** hidden

evidently 1 = **obviously**, clearly, plainly, undoubtedly, manifestly, without question, unmistakably 2 = **apparently**, seemingly, outwardly, ostensibly, so it seems, to all appearances

evil ADJECTIVE 1 = **wicked**, bad, malicious, immoral, sinful, malevolent, depraved, villainous 2 = **harmful**, disastrous, destructive, dire, catastrophic, pernicious, ruinous 3 = **demonic**, satanic, diabolical, hellish, devilish, infernal, fiendish 4 = **offensive**, nasty, foul, unpleasant, vile, noxious,

disagreeable, pestilential
5 = **unfortunate**, unfavourable, ruinous, calamitous
▷ NOUN 6 = **wickedness**, bad, vice, sin, wrongdoing, depravity, badness, villainy 7 = **harm**, suffering, hurt, woe 8 = **act of cruelty**, crime, ill, horror, outrage, misfortune, mischief, affliction

evoke = **arouse**, cause, induce, awaken, give rise to, stir up, rekindle, summon up **OPPOSITE:** suppress

evolution 1 (*Biology*) = **rise**, development, adaptation, natural selection, Darwinism, survival of the fittest
2 = **development**, growth, advance, progress, working out, expansion, extension, unfolding

evolve 1 = **develop**, metamorphose, adapt yourself
2 = **grow**, develop, advance, progress, mature 3 = **work out**, develop, progress, expand, unfold

exact ADJECTIVE 1 = **accurate**, correct, true, right, specific, precise, definite, faultless
OPPOSITE: approximate
▷ VERB 2 = **demand**, claim, force, command, extract, compel, extort 3 = **inflict**, apply, administer, mete out, deal out

exacting 1 = **demanding**, hard, taxing, difficult, tough
OPPOSITE: easy 2 = **strict**, severe, harsh, rigorous, stringent

exactly 1 = **accurately**, correctly, precisely, faithfully, explicitly, scrupulously, truthfully, unerringly
2 = **precisely**, specifically, bang on (*informal*), to the letter

exaggerate = **overstate**, enlarge, embroider, amplify, embellish, overestimate, overemphasize, pile it on about (*informal*)

examination 1 (*Medical*) = **checkup**, analysis, going-over (*informal*), exploration, health check, check 2 = **exam**, test, research, paper, investigation, practical, assessment, quiz

examine 1 = **inspect**, study, survey, investigate, explore, analyse, scrutinize, peruse
2 (*Medical*) = **check**, analyse, check over 3 (*Education*) = **test**, question, assess, quiz, evaluate, appraise 4 (*Law*) = **question**, quiz, interrogate, cross-examine, grill (*informal*), give the third degree to (*informal*)

example 1 = **instance**, specimen, case, sample, illustration, particular case, particular instance, typical case 2 = **illustration**, model, ideal, standard, prototype, paradigm, archetype, paragon
3 = **warning**, lesson, caution, deterrent

e

exceed 1 = **surpass**, better, pass, eclipse, beat, cap (*informal*), top, be over 2 = **go over the limit of**, go beyond, overstep

excel = **be superior**, eclipse, beat, surpass, transcend, outdo, outshine
▷ **PHRASES: excel in** *or* **at something** = **be good at**, shine at, be proficient in, show talent in, be skilful at, be talented at

excellence = **high quality**, merit, distinction, goodness, superiority, greatness, supremacy, eminence

excellent = **outstanding**, good, great, fine, cool (*informal*), brilliant, very good, superb, booshit (*Austral slang*), exo (*Austral slang*), sik (*Austral slang*), rad (*informal*), phat (*slang*), schmick (*Austral informal*) **OPPOSITE:** terrible

except **PREPOSITION** 1 *often with* **for** = **apart from**, but for, saving, barring, excepting, other than, excluding, omitting
▷ **VERB** 2 = **exclude**, leave out, omit, disregard, pass over

exception = **special case**, freak, anomaly, inconsistency, deviation, oddity, peculiarity, irregularity

exceptional 1 = **remarkable**, special, excellent, extraordinary, outstanding, superior, first-class, marvellous **OPPOSITE:** average 2 = **unusual**, special, odd, strange, extraordinary, unprecedented, peculiar, abnormal **OPPOSITE:** ordinary

excerpt = **extract**, part, piece, section, selection, passage, fragment, quotation

excess 1 = **surfeit**, surplus, overload, glut, superabundance, superfluity **OPPOSITE:** shortage 2 = **overindulgence**, extravagance, profligacy, debauchery, dissipation, intemperance, indulgence, prodigality **OPPOSITE:** moderation

excessive 1 = **immoderate**, too much, extreme, exaggerated, unreasonable, disproportionate, undue, uncontrolled 2 = **inordinate**, unfair, unreasonable, disproportionate, undue, unwarranted, exorbitant, extortionate

exchange **VERB**
1 = **interchange**, change, trade, switch, swap, barter, give to each other, give to one another
▷ **NOUN** 2 = **conversation**, talk, word, discussion, chat, dialogue, natter, powwow
3 = **interchange**, trade, switch, swap, trafficking, swapping, substitution, barter

excite 1 = **thrill**, inspire, stir, provoke, animate, rouse, exhilarate, inflame 2 = **arouse**, provoke, rouse, stir up

3 = **titillate**, thrill, stimulate, turn on (*slang*), arouse, get going (*informal*), electrify

excitement = **exhilaration**, action, activity, passion, thrill, animation, furore, agitation

exciting 1 = **stimulating**, dramatic, gripping, stirring, thrilling, sensational, rousing, exhilarating **OPPOSITE:** boring 2 = **titillating**, stimulating, arousing, erotic

exclaim = **cry out**, declare, shout, proclaim, yell, utter, call out

exclude 1 = **keep out**, bar, ban, refuse, forbid, boycott, prohibit, disallow **OPPOSITE:** let in 2 = **omit**, reject, eliminate, rule out, miss out, leave out **OPPOSITE:** include 3 = **eliminate**, reject, ignore, rule out, leave out, set aside, omit, pass over

exclusion 1 = **ban**, bar, veto, boycott, embargo, prohibition, disqualification 2 = **elimination**, missing out, rejection, leaving out, omission

exclusive 1 = **select**, fashionable, stylish, restricted, posh (*informal, chiefly Brit*), chic, high-class, up-market **OPPOSITE:** unrestricted 2 = **sole**, full, whole, complete, total, entire, absolute, undivided **OPPOSITE:** shared 3 = **entire**, full, whole, complete, total, absolute, undivided 4 = **limited**,

unique, restricted, confined, peculiar

excursion = **trip**, tour, journey, outing, expedition, ramble, day trip, jaunt

excuse VERB 1 = **justify**, explain, defend, vindicate, mitigate, apologize for, make excuses for **OPPOSITE:** blame 2 = **forgive**, pardon, overlook, tolerate, acquit, turn a blind eye to, exonerate, make allowances for 3 = **free**, relieve, exempt, release, spare, discharge, let off, absolve **OPPOSITE:** convict ▷ NOUN 4 = **justification**, reason, explanation, defence, grounds, plea, apology, vindication **OPPOSITE:** accusation

execute 1 = **put to death**, kill, shoot, hang, behead, decapitate, guillotine, electrocute 2 = **carry out**, effect, implement, accomplish, discharge, administer, prosecute, enact 3 = **perform**, carry out, accomplish

execution 1 = **killing**, hanging, the death penalty, the rope, capital punishment, beheading, the electric chair, the guillotine 2 = **carrying out**, performance, operation, administration, prosecution, enforcement, implementation, accomplishment

executive NOUN 1 = **administrator**, official,

director, manager, chairman, managing director, controller, chief executive officer **2 = administration**, government, directors, management, leadership, hierarchy, directorate
▷ ADJECTIVE **3 = administrative**, controlling, directing, governing, regulating, decision-making, managerial

exemplify = **show**, represent, display, demonstrate, illustrate, exhibit, embody, serve as an example of

exempt VERB **1 = grant immunity**, free, excuse, release, spare, relieve, discharge, let off
▷ ADJECTIVE **2 = immune**, free, excepted, excused, released, spared, not liable to OPPOSITE: liable

exemption = **immunity**, freedom, relief, exception, discharge, release, dispensation, absolution

exercise VERB **1 = put to use**, use, apply, employ, exert, utilize, bring to bear, avail yourself of **2 = train**, work out, practise, keep fit, do exercises
▷ NOUN **3 = use**, practice, application, operation, discharge, implementation, fulfilment, utilization
4 = exertion, training, activity, work, labour, effort, movement, toil **5** (*Military*) = **manoeuvre**, campaign, operation,

movement, deployment
6 = task, problem, lesson, assignment, practice

exert = **apply**, use, exercise, employ, wield, make use of, utilize, bring to bear
▷ PHRASES: exert yourself
= **make an effort**, work, labour, struggle, strain, strive, endeavour, toil

exhaust 1 = tire out, fatigue, drain, weaken, weary, sap, wear out, debilitate **2 = use up**, spend, consume, waste, go through, run through, deplete, squander

exhausted 1 = worn out, tired out, drained, spent, bushed (*informal*), done in (*informal*), all in (*slang*), fatigued OPPOSITE: invigorated **2 = used up**, consumed, spent, finished, depleted, dissipated, expended OPPOSITE: replenished

exhaustion 1 = tiredness, fatigue, weariness, debilitation **2 = depletion**, emptying, consumption, using up

exhibit 1 = show, reveal, display, demonstrate, express, indicate, manifest **2 = display**, show, set out, parade, unveil, put on view

exhibition 1 = show, display, representation, presentation, spectacle, showcase, exposition, ex (*Canad informal*) **2 = display**, show, performance, demonstration, revelation

exile NOUN 1 = **banishment**, expulsion, deportation, eviction, expatriation 2 = **expatriate**, refugee, outcast, émigré, deportee
▷ VERB 3 = **banish**, expel, throw out, deport, drive out, eject, expatriate, cast out

exist 1 = **live**, be present, survive, endure, be in existence, be, have breath 2 = **occur**, be present 3 = **survive**, stay alive, make ends meet, subsist, eke out a living, scrape by, scrimp and save, support yourself

existence 1 = **reality**, being, life, subsistence, actuality 2 = **life**, situation, way of life, lifestyle

existent = **in existence**, living, existing, surviving, standing, present, alive, extant

exit NOUN 1 = **way out**, door, gate, outlet, doorway, gateway, escape route OPPOSITE: entry 2 = **departure**, withdrawal, retreat, farewell, going, goodbye, exodus, decamping
▷ VERB 3 = **depart**, leave, go out, withdraw, retire, quit, retreat, go away OPPOSITE: enter

exodus = **departure**, withdrawal, retreat, leaving, flight, exit, migration, evacuation

exotic 1 = **unusual**, striking, strange, fascinating, mysterious, colourful, glamorous, unfamiliar OPPOSITE: ordinary 2 = **foreign**, alien, tropical, external, naturalized

expand 1 = **get bigger**, increase, grow, extend, swell, widen, enlarge, become bigger OPPOSITE: contract 2 = **make bigger**, increase, develop, extend, widen, enlarge, broaden, magnify OPPOSITE: reduce 3 = **spread (out)**, stretch (out), unfold, unravel, diffuse, unfurl, unroll
▷ PHRASES: expand on something = **go into detail about**, embellish, elaborate on, develop, flesh out, expound on, enlarge on, expatiate on

expansion 1 = **increase**, development, growth, spread, magnification, amplification 2 = **enlargement**, increase, growth, opening out

expatriate ADJECTIVE 1 = **exiled**, refugee, banished, emigrant, émigré, expat
▷ NOUN 2 = **exile**, refugee, emigrant, émigré

expect 1 = **think**, believe, suppose, assume, trust, imagine, reckon, presume 2 = **anticipate**, look forward to, predict, envisage, await, hope for, contemplate 3 = **require**, demand, want, call for, ask for, hope for, insist on

expectation 1 *usually plural* = **projection**, supposition, assumption, belief, forecast, likelihood, probability, presumption 2 = **anticipation**, hope, promise, excitement, expectancy, apprehension, suspense

expedition = **journey**, mission, voyage, tour, quest, trek

expel 1 = **throw out**, exclude, ban, dismiss, kick out (*informal*), ask to leave, turf out (*informal*), debar **OPPOSITE:** let in 2 = **banish**, exile, deport, evict, force to leave **OPPOSITE:** take in 3 = **drive out**, discharge, force out, let out, eject, issue, spew, belch

expenditure 1 = **spending**, payment, expense, outgoings, cost, outlay 2 = **consumption**, using, output

expense = **cost**, charge, expenditure, payment, spending, outlay

expensive = **costly**, high-priced, lavish, extravagant, dear, stiff, steep (*informal*), pricey **OPPOSITE:** cheap

experience NOUN 1 = **knowledge**, practice, skill, contact, expertise, involvement, exposure, participation 2 = **event**, affair, incident, happening, encounter, episode, adventure, occurrence ▷ VERB 3 = **undergo**, feel, face, taste, go through, sample, encounter, endure

experienced = **knowledgeable**, skilled, tried, tested, seasoned, expert, veteran, practised **OPPOSITE:** inexperienced

experiment NOUN 1 = **test**, trial, investigation, examination, procedure, demonstration, observation, try-out 2 = **research**, investigation, analysis, observation, research and development, experimentation ▷ VERB 3 = **test**, investigate, trial, research, try, examine, pilot, sample

experimental 1 = **test**, trial, pilot, preliminary, provisional, tentative, speculative, exploratory 2 = **innovative**, new, original, radical, creative, ingenious, avant-garde, inventive

expert NOUN 1 = **specialist**, authority, professional, master, genius, guru, pundit, maestro, fundi (*S African*), geek (*computing informal*) **OPPOSITE:** amateur ▷ ADJECTIVE 2 = **skilful**, experienced, professional, masterly, qualified, talented, outstanding, practised, leet (*computing slang*) **OPPOSITE:** unskilled

expertise = **skill**, knowledge, know-how (*informal*), facility, judgment, mastery, proficiency, adroitness

expire 1 = **become invalid**, end, finish, conclude, close, stop, run out, cease 2 = **die**, depart, perish, kick the bucket (*informal*), depart this life, meet your maker, cark it (*Austral & NZ slang*), pass away or on

explain 1 = **make clear** or **plain**, describe, teach, define, resolve, clarify, clear up, simplify 2 = **account for**, excuse, justify, give a reason for

explanation 1 = **reason**, answer, account, excuse, motive, justification, vindication 2 = **description**, report, definition, teaching, interpretation, illustration, clarification, simplification

explicit 1 = **clear**, obvious, specific, direct, precise, straightforward, definite, overt **OPPOSITE:** vague 2 = **frank**, specific, graphic, unambiguous, unrestricted, unrestrained, uncensored **OPPOSITE:** indirect

explode 1 = **blow up**, erupt, burst, go off, shatter 2 = **detonate**, set off, discharge, let off 3 = **lose your temper**, rage, erupt, become angry, hit the roof (*informal*), go crook (*Austral & NZ slang*) 4 = **increase**, grow, develop, extend, advance, shoot up, soar, boost 5 = **disprove**, discredit, refute, demolish, repudiate, put paid to, invalidate, debunk

exploit NOUN 1 = **feat**, act, achievement, enterprise, adventure, stunt, deed, accomplishment ▷ VERB 2 = **take advantage of**, abuse, use, manipulate, milk, misuse, ill-treat, play on or upon 3 = **make the best use of**, use, make use of, utilize, cash in on (*informal*), capitalize on, use to good advantage, profit by or from

exploitation = **misuse**, abuse, manipulation, using, ill-treatment

exploration 1 = **expedition**, tour, trip, survey, travel, journey, reconnaissance 2 = **investigation**, research, survey, search, inquiry, analysis, examination, inspection

explore 1 = **travel around**, tour, survey, scout, reconnoitre 2 = **investigate**, consider, research, survey, search, examine, probe, look into

explosion 1 = **blast**, crack, burst, bang, discharge, report, blowing up, clap 2 = **increase**, rise, development, growth, boost, expansion, enlargement, escalation 3 = **outburst**, fit, storm, attack, surge, flare-up, eruption 4 = **outbreak**, flare-up, eruption, upsurge

explosive ADJECTIVE 1 = **unstable**, dangerous, volatile, hazardous, unsafe, perilous, combustible, inflammable 2 = **fiery**, violent, volatile, stormy, touchy, vehement ▷ NOUN 3 = **bomb**, mine, shell, missile, rocket, grenade, charge, torpedo

expose 1 = **uncover**, show, reveal, display, exhibit, present, unveil, lay bare **OPPOSITE:** hide 2 = **make vulnerable**, subject, leave open, lay open

exposure 1 = **hypothermia**, frostbite, extreme cold, intense cold 2 = **uncovering**, showing, display, exhibition, revelation, presentation, unveiling

express VERB 1 = **state**, communicate, convey, articulate, say, word, voice, declare 2 = **show**, indicate, exhibit, demonstrate, reveal, intimate, convey, signify ▷ ADJECTIVE 3 = **explicit**, clear, plain, distinct, definite, unambiguous, categorical 4 = **specific**, exclusive, particular, sole, special, singular, clear-cut, especial 5 = **fast**, direct, rapid, priority, prompt, swift, high-speed, speedy

expression 1 = **statement**, declaration, announcement, communication, utterance, articulation 2 = **indication**, demonstration, exhibition, display, showing, show, sign, symbol 3 = **look**, countenance, face, air, appearance, aspect 4 = **phrase**, saying, word, term, remark, maxim, idiom, adage

expressive = **vivid**, striking, telling, moving, poignant, eloquent **OPPOSITE:** impassive

expulsion 1 = **ejection**, exclusion, dismissal, removal,

eviction, banishment 2 = **discharge**, emission, spewing, secretion, excretion, ejection, seepage, suppuration

exquisite 1 = **beautiful**, elegant, graceful, pleasing, attractive, lovely, charming, comely **OPPOSITE:** unattractive 2 = **fine**, beautiful, lovely, elegant, precious, delicate, dainty 3 = **intense**, acute, severe, sharp, keen, extreme

extend 1 = **spread out**, reach, stretch 2 = **stretch**, stretch out, spread out, straighten out 3 = **last**, continue, go on, stretch, carry on 4 = **protrude**, project, stand out, bulge, stick out, hang, overhang, jut out 5 = **widen**, increase, expand, add to, enhance, supplement, enlarge, broaden **OPPOSITE:** reduce 6 = **make longer**, prolong, lengthen, draw out, spin out, drag out **OPPOSITE:** shorten 7 = **offer**, present, confer, stick out, impart, proffer **OPPOSITE:** withdraw

extension 1 = **annexe**, addition, supplement, appendix, appendage 2 = **lengthening**, extra time, continuation, additional period of time 3 = **development**, expansion, widening, increase, broadening, enlargement, diversification

extensive 1 = **large**, considerable, substantial, spacious, wide, broad,

expansive **OPPOSITE:** confined
2 = comprehensive, complete,
wide, pervasive **OPPOSITE:**
restricted **3 = great**, vast,
widespread, large-scale, far-
reaching, far-flung, voluminous
OPPOSITE: limited

extent 1 = magnitude, amount,
scale, level, stretch, expanse
2 = size, area, length, width,
breadth

exterior NOUN 1 = outside,
face, surface, covering, skin,
shell, coating, façade
▷ **ADJECTIVE 2 = outer**, outside,
external, surface, outward,
outermost **OPPOSITE:** inner

external 1 = outer, outside,
surface, outward, exterior,
outermost **OPPOSITE:** internal
2 = foreign, international, alien,
extrinsic **OPPOSITE:** domestic
3 = outside, visiting **OPPOSITE:**
inside

extinct = dead, lost, gone,
vanished, defunct **OPPOSITE:**
living

extinction = dying out,
destruction, abolition, oblivion,
extermination, annihilation,
eradication, obliteration

extra ADJECTIVE 1 = additional,
more, added, further,
supplementary, auxiliary,
ancillary **OPPOSITE:** vital
2 = surplus, excess, spare,
redundant, unused, leftover,
superfluous
▷ **NOUN 3 = addition**, bonus,

supplement, accessory
OPPOSITE: necessity
▷ **ADVERB 4 = in addition**,
additionally, over and above
5 = exceptionally, very,
specially, especially, particularly,
extremely, remarkably,
unusually

extract VERB 1 = take out,
draw, pull, remove, withdraw,
pull out, bring out **2 = pull out**,
remove, take out, draw, uproot,
pluck out **3 = elicit**, obtain,
force, draw, derive, glean, coerce
▷ **NOUN 4 = passage**, selection,
excerpt, cutting, clipping,
quotation, citation **5 = essence**,
solution, concentrate, juice,
distillation

| **USAGE NOTE**
People sometimes use
extract where *extricate*
would be better. Although
both words can refer to a
physical act of removal from
a place, *extract* has a more
general sense than *extricate*.
Extricate has additional
overtones of 'difficulty', and
is most commonly used with
reference to getting a person
– particularly *yourself* – out of
a situation. So, for example,
you might say *he will find it
difficult to extricate himself*
(not *extract himself*) *from this
situation*.

extraordinary 1 = remarkable,
outstanding, amazing,

fantastic, astonishing,
exceptional, phenomenal,
extremely good **OPPOSITE:**
unremarkable **2** = **unusual**,
strange, remarkable,
uncommon **OPPOSITE:** ordinary

extravagant 1 = **wasteful**,
lavish, prodigal, profligate,
spendthrift **OPPOSITE:**
economical **2** = **excessive**,
outrageous, over the top (*slang*),
unreasonable, preposterous
OPPOSITE: moderate

extreme ADJECTIVE 1 = **great**,
highest, supreme, acute, severe,
maximum, intense, ultimate
OPPOSITE: mild **2** = **severe**,
radical, strict, harsh, rigid,
drastic, uncompromising
3 = **radical**, excessive, fanatical,
immoderate **OPPOSITE:**
moderate **4** = **farthest**, furthest,
far, remotest, far-off, outermost,
most distant **OPPOSITE:** nearest
▷ **NOUN 5** = **limit**, end, edge,
opposite, pole, boundary,
antithesis, extremity

extremely = **very**, particularly,
severely, terribly, unusually,
exceptionally, extraordinarily,
tremendously

extremist NOUN 1 = **radical**,
activist, militant, fanatic, die-
hard, bigot, zealot
▷ **ADJECTIVE 2** = **extreme**, wild,
passionate, frenzied, obsessive,
fanatical, fervent, zealous

eye NOUN 1 = **eyeball**, optic
(*informal*), organ of vision,
organ of sight **2** *often plural*
= **eyesight**, sight, vision,
perception, ability to see, power
of seeing **3** = **appreciation**,
taste, recognition, judgment,
discrimination, perception,
discernment **4** = **observance**,
observation, surveillance, vigil,
watch, lookout **5** = **centre**,
heart, middle, mid, core, nucleus
▷ **VERB 6** = **look at**, view,
study, watch, survey, observe,
contemplate, check out
(*informal*)

Ff

fable 1 = **legend**, myth, parable, allegory, story, tale 2 = **fiction**, fantasy, myth, invention, yarn (*informal*), fabrication, urban myth, tall story (*informal*) **OPPOSITE:** fact

fabric 1 = **cloth**, material, stuff, textile, web 2 = **framework**, structure, make-up, organization, frame, foundations, construction, constitution 3 = **structure**, foundations, construction, framework

fabulous 1 (*informal*) = **wonderful**, excellent, brilliant, superb, spectacular, fantastic (*informal*), marvellous, sensational (*informal*) **OPPOSITE:** ordinary 2 = **astounding**, amazing, extraordinary, remarkable, incredible, astonishing, unbelievable, breathtaking 3 = **legendary**, imaginary, mythical, fictitious, made-up, fantastic, invented, unreal

façade 1 = **front**, face, exterior 2 = **show**, front, appearance, mask, exterior, guise, pretence, semblance

face NOUN 1 = **countenance**, features, profile, mug (*slang*), visage 2 = **expression**, look, air, appearance, aspect, countenance 3 = **side**, front, outside, surface, exterior, elevation, vertical surface ▷ VERB 4 *often with* **to**, **towards**, *or* **on** = **look onto**, overlook, be opposite, look out on, front onto 5 = **confront**, meet, encounter, deal with, oppose, tackle, experience, brave

face up to = **accept**, deal with, tackle, acknowledge, cope with, confront, come to terms with, meet head-on

facilitate = **further**, help, forward, promote, speed up, pave the way for, make easy, expedite **OPPOSITE:** hinder

facility 1 *often plural* = **amenity**, means, aid, opportunity, advantage, resource, equipment, provision 2 = **opportunity**, possibility, convenience 3 = **ability**, skill, efficiency, fluency, proficiency, dexterity, adroitness 4 = **ease**, fluency, effortlessness **OPPOSITE:** difficulty

fact 1 = **truth**, reality, certainty, verity **OPPOSITE:** fiction 2 (*Criminal law*) = **event**, happening, act, performance, incident, deed, occurrence, fait accompli (*French*)

faction 1 = **group**, set, party, gang, bloc, contingent, clique, coterie, public-interest group (*US & Canad*) 2 = **dissension**, division, conflict, rebellion, disagreement, variance, discord, infighting **OPPOSITE:** agreement

factor = **element**, part, cause, influence, item, aspect, characteristic, consideration (*Scot*)

> **USAGE NOTE**
> In strict usage, *factor* should only be used to refer to something which contributes to a result. It should not be used to refer to a part of something, such as a plan or arrangement; more appropriate alternatives in this sense are words such as *component* or *element*.

factory = **works**, plant, mill, workshop, assembly line, shop floor

factual = **true**, authentic, real, correct, genuine, exact, precise, dinkum (*Austral & NZ informal*), true-to-life **OPPOSITE:** fictitious

faculty 1 = **ability**, power, skill, facility, capacity, propensity, aptitude **OPPOSITE:** failing 2 = **department**, school 3 = **teaching staff**, staff, teachers, professors, lecturers (*chiefly US*) 4 = **power**, reason, sense, intelligence, mental ability, physical ability

fad = **craze**, fashion, trend, rage, vogue, whim, mania

fade 1 = **become pale**, bleach, wash out, discolour, lose colour, decolour 2 = **make pale**, dim, bleach, wash out, blanch, discolour, decolour 3 = **grow dim**, fade away, become less loud 4 *usually with* **away** *or* **out** = **dwindle**, disappear, vanish, melt away, decline, dissolve, wane, die away

fail 1 = **be unsuccessful**, founder, fall, break down, flop (*informal*), fizzle out (*informal*), come unstuck, miscarry **OPPOSITE:** succeed 2 = **disappoint**, abandon, desert, neglect, omit, let down, forsake, be disloyal to 3 = **stop working**, stop, die, break down, stall, cut out, malfunction, conk out (*informal*), crash (*of a computer*) 4 = **wither**, perish, sag, waste away, shrivel up 5 = **go bankrupt**, collapse, fold (*informal*), close down, go under, go bust (*informal*), go out of business, be wound up 6 = **decline**, deteriorate, degenerate 7 = **give out**, dim, peter out, die away, grow dim
▷ **PHRASES: without fail** = **without exception**, regularly, constantly, invariably, religiously, unfailingly, conscientiously, like clockwork

failing NOUN 1 = **shortcoming**, fault, weakness, defect, deficiency, flaw, drawback,

blemish **OPPOSITE:** strength
▷ **PREPOSITION 2 = in the
absence of**, lacking, in default of
failure 1 = lack of success,
defeat, collapse, breakdown,
overthrow, miscarriage, fiasco,
downfall **OPPOSITE:** success
2 = loser, disappointment,
flop (*informal*), write-off,
no-hoper (*chiefly Austral*),
dud (*informal*), black sheep,
washout (*informal*), dead duck
(*slang*) **3 = bankruptcy**, crash,
collapse, ruin, closure, winding
up, downfall, going under
OPPOSITE: prosperity
faint ADJECTIVE **1 = dim**, low,
soft, faded, distant, vague,
unclear, muted **OPPOSITE:**
clear **2 = slight**, weak, feeble,
unenthusiastic, remote, slim,
vague, slender **3 = dizzy**, giddy,
light-headed, weak, exhausted,
wobbly, muzzy, woozy (*informal*)
OPPOSITE: energetic
▷ VERB **4 = pass out**, black out,
lose consciousness, keel over
(*informal*), go out, collapse,
swoon (*literary*), flake out
(*informal*)
▷ NOUN **5 = blackout**, collapse,
coma, swoon (*literary*),
unconsciousness
faintly 1 = slightly, rather,
a little, somewhat, dimly
2 = softly, weakly, feebly, in a
whisper, indistinctly, unclearly
fair¹ 1 = unbiased, impartial,
even-handed, unprejudiced,

just, reasonable, proper,
legitimate **OPPOSITE:** unfair
2 = respectable, average,
reasonable, decent, acceptable,
moderate, adequate,
satisfactory **3 = light**, golden,
blonde, blond, yellowish, fair-
haired, light-coloured, flaxen-
haired **4 = fine**, clear, dry, bright,
pleasant, sunny, cloudless,
unclouded **5 = beautiful**, pretty,
attractive, lovely, handsome,
good-looking, bonny, comely, fit
(*Brit informal*) **OPPOSITE:** ugly
fair² 1 = carnival, fête, gala,
bazaar **2 = exhibition**, show,
festival, mart
fairly 1 = equitably, objectively,
legitimately, honestly,
justly, lawfully, without
prejudice, dispassionately
2 = moderately, rather,
quite, somewhat, reasonably,
adequately, pretty well,
tolerably **3 = positively**,
really, simply, absolutely
4 = deservedly, objectively,
honestly, justifiably, justly,
impartially, equitably, without
fear or favour
fairness = impartiality, justice,
equity, legitimacy, decency,
disinterestedness, rightfulness,
equitableness
fairy = sprite, elf, brownie, pixie,
puck, imp, leprechaun, peri
fairy tale *or* **fairy story**
1 = folk tale, romance,
traditional story **2 = lie**, fiction,

invention, fabrication, untruth, urban myth, tall story, urban legend

faith 1 = **confidence**, trust, credit, conviction, assurance, dependence, reliance, credence **OPPOSITE:** distrust 2 = **religion**, church, belief, persuasion, creed, communion, denomination, dogma **OPPOSITE:** agnosticism

faithful 1 = **loyal**, true, committed, constant, devoted, dedicated, reliable, staunch **OPPOSITE:** disloyal 2 = **accurate**, close, true, strict, exact, precise

fake VERB 1 = **forge**, copy, reproduce, fabricate, counterfeit, falsify 2 = **sham**, put on, pretend, simulate, feign, go through the motions of ▷ NOUN 3 = **forgery**, copy, fraud, reproduction, dummy, imitation, hoax, counterfeit 4 = **charlatan**, deceiver, sham, quack ▷ ADJECTIVE 5 = **artificial**, false, forged, counterfeit, put-on, pretend (*informal*), mock, imitation **OPPOSITE:** genuine

fall VERB 1 = **drop**, plunge, tumble, plummet, collapse, sink, go down, come down **OPPOSITE:** rise 2 = **decrease**, drop, decline, go down, slump, diminish, dwindle, lessen **OPPOSITE:** increase 3 = **be overthrown**, surrender, succumb, submit, capitulate, be conquered, pass into enemy

hands **OPPOSITE:** triumph 4 = **be killed**, die, perish, meet your end **OPPOSITE:** survive 5 = **occur**, happen, come about, chance, take place, befall, come to pass ▷ NOUN 6 = **drop**, slip, plunge, dive, tumble, descent, plummet, nose dive 7 = **decrease**, drop, lowering, decline, reduction, slump, dip, lessening 8 = **collapse**, defeat, downfall, ruin, destruction, overthrow, submission, capitulation

false 1 = **incorrect**, wrong, mistaken, misleading, faulty, inaccurate, invalid, erroneous **OPPOSITE:** correct 2 = **untrue**, fraudulent, trumped up, fallacious, untruthful **OPPOSITE:** true 3 = **artificial**, forged, fake, reproduction, replica, imitation, bogus, simulated **OPPOSITE:** real

falter 1 = **hesitate**, delay, waver, vacillate **OPPOSITE:** persevere 2 = **tumble**, totter 3 = **stutter**, pause, stumble, hesitate, stammer

fame = **prominence**, glory, celebrity, stardom, reputation, honour, prestige, stature **OPPOSITE:** obscurity

familiar 1 = **well-known**, recognized, common, ordinary, routine, frequent, accustomed, customary **OPPOSITE:** unfamiliar 2 = **friendly**, close, dear, intimate, amicable **OPPOSITE:** formal 3 = **relaxed**, easy, friendly, comfortable, intimate, casual, amicable **4** = **disrespectful**, forward, bold, intrusive, presumptuous, impudent, overfamiliar

familiarity 1 = **acquaintance**, experience, understanding, knowledge, awareness, grasp **OPPOSITE:** unfamiliarity **2** = **friendliness**, intimacy, ease, openness, informality, sociability **OPPOSITE:** formality **3** = **disrespect**, forwardness, overfamiliarity, cheek, presumption, boldness **OPPOSITE:** respect

family 1 = **relations**, relatives, household, folk (*informal*), kin, nuclear family, next of kin, kith and kin, ainga (*NZ*), cuzzies or cuzzie-bros (*NZ*), rellies (*Austral slang*) **2** = **children**, kids (*informal*), offspring, little ones, littlies (*Austral informal*) **3** = **ancestors**, house, race, tribe, clan, dynasty, line of descent **4** = **species**, group, class, system, order, network, genre, subdivision

> **USAGE NOTE**
> Some careful writers insist that a singular verb should always be used with collective nouns such as *government*, *team*, *family*, *committee*, and *class*, for example: *the class is doing a project on Vikings*; *the company is mounting a big sales campaign*. In British usage, however, a plural verb is often used with a collective noun, especially where the emphasis is on a collection of individual objects or people rather than a group regarded as a unit: *the family are all on holiday*. The most important thing to remember is never to treat the same collective noun as both singular and plural in the same sentence: *the family is well and sends its best wishes* or *the family are well and send their best wishes*, but not *the family is well and send their best wishes*.

famine = **hunger**, want, starvation, deprivation, scarcity, dearth

famous = **well-known**, celebrated, acclaimed, noted, distinguished, prominent, legendary, renowned **OPPOSITE:** unknown

fan¹ NOUN **1** = **blower**, ventilator, air conditioner
▷ VERB **2** = **blow**, cool, refresh, air-condition, ventilate

fan² **1** = **supporter**, lover, follower, enthusiast, admirer **2** = **devotee**, buff (*informal*), aficionado, groupie (*slang*)

fanatic = **extremist**, activist, militant, bigot, zealot

fancy ADJECTIVE **1** = **elaborate**, decorative, extravagant, intricate, baroque, ornamental, ornate, embellished

OPPOSITE: plain

▷ **NOUN 2 = whim**, thought, idea, desire, urge, notion, humour, impulse **3 = delusion**, dream, vision, fantasy, daydream, chimera

▷ **VERB 4** (*informal*) **= wish for**, want, desire, hope for, long for, crave, yearn for, thirst for **5** (*Brit informal*) **= be attracted to**, find attractive, lust after, like, take to, be captivated by, have a thing about (*informal*), have eyes for **6 = suppose**, think, believe, imagine, reckon, conjecture, think likely

fantastic 1 (*informal*) **= wonderful**, great, excellent, very good, smashing (*informal*), superb, tremendous (*informal*), magnificent, booshit (*Austral slang*), exo (*Austral slang*), sik (*Austral slang*), rad (*informal*), phat (*slang*), schmick (*Austral informal*) **OPPOSITE:** ordinary **2 = strange**, bizarre, grotesque, fanciful, outlandish **3 = implausible**, unlikely, incredible, absurd, preposterous, cock-and-bull (*informal*)

fantasy *or* **phantasy 1 = daydream**, dream, wish, reverie, flight of fancy, pipe dream **2 = imagination**, fancy, invention, creativity, originality

far 1 = a long way, miles, deep, a good way, afar, a great distance **2 = much**, greatly, very much, extremely, significantly, considerably, decidedly, markedly **3** *often with* **off = remote**, distant, far-flung, faraway, out-of-the-way, outlying, off the beaten track **OPPOSITE:** near

farce 1 = comedy, satire, slapstick, burlesque, buffoonery **2 = mockery**, joke, nonsense, parody, shambles, sham, travesty

fare NOUN 1 = charge, price, ticket price, ticket money **2 = food**, provisions, board, rations, kai (*NZ informal*), nourishment, sustenance, victuals, nutriment

▷ **VERB 3 = get on**, do, manage, make out, prosper, get along

farewell INTERJECTION 1 = goodbye, bye (*informal*), so long, see you, take care, good morning, bye-bye (*informal*), good day, haere ra (*NZ*)

▷ **NOUN 2 = goodbye**, parting, departure, leave-taking, adieu, valediction, sendoff (*informal*)

farm NOUN 1 = smallholding, ranch (*chiefly US & Canad*), farmstead, station (*Austral & NZ*), vineyard, plantation, croft (*Scot*), grange, homestead

▷ **VERB 2 = cultivate**, work, plant, grow crops on, keep animals on

fascinate = entrance, absorb, intrigue, rivet, captivate,

enthral, beguile, transfix
OPPOSITE: bore

fascinating = **captivating**, engaging, gripping, compelling, intriguing, very interesting, irresistible, enticing **OPPOSITE:** boring

fascination = **attraction**, pull, magic, charm, lure, allure, magnetism, enchantment

fashion 1 = **style**, look, trend, rage, custom, mode, vogue, craze 2 = **method**, way, style, manner, mode
▷ 3 = **make**, shape, cast, construct, form, create, manufacture, forge

fashionable = **popular**, in fashion, trendy (*Brit informal*), in (*informal*), modern, with it (*informal*), stylish, chic, schmick (*Austral informal*), funky **OPPOSITE:** unfashionable

fast¹ ADJECTIVE 1 = **quick**, flying, rapid, fleet, swift, speedy, brisk, hasty **OPPOSITE:** slow 2 = **fixed**, firm, sound, stuck, secure, tight, jammed, fastened **OPPOSITE:** unstable 3 = **dissipated**, wild, exciting, loose, extravagant, reckless, self-indulgent, wanton 4 = **close**, firm, devoted, faithful, steadfast
▷ ADVERB 5 = **quickly**, rapidly, swiftly, hastily, hurriedly, speedily, in haste, at full speed **OPPOSITE:** slowly 6 = **securely**, firmly, tightly, fixedly

7 = **fixedly**, firmly, soundly, deeply, securely, tightly

fast² VERB 1 = **go hungry**, abstain, go without food, deny yourself
▷ NOUN 2 = **fasting**, diet, abstinence

fasten 1 = **secure**, close, do up 2 = **tie**, bind, tie up 3 = **fix**, join, link, connect, attach, affix

fat NOUN 1 = **fatness**, flesh, bulk, obesity, flab, blubber, paunch, fatty tissue
▷ ADJECTIVE 2 = **overweight**, large, heavy, plump, stout, obese, tubby, portly **OPPOSITE:** thin 3 = **fatty**, greasy, adipose, oleaginous, oily **OPPOSITE:** lean

fatal 1 = **disastrous**, devastating, crippling, catastrophic, ruinous, calamitous, baleful, baneful **OPPOSITE:** minor 2 = **lethal**, deadly, mortal, causing death, final, killing, terminal, malignant **OPPOSITE:** harmless

fate 1 = **destiny**, chance, fortune, luck, the stars, providence, nemesis, kismet 2 = **fortune**, destiny, lot, portion, cup, horoscope

fated = **destined**, doomed, predestined, preordained, foreordained

Father = **priest**, minister, vicar, parson, pastor, cleric, churchman, padre (*informal*)

father NOUN 1 = **daddy** (*informal*), dad (*informal*),

male parent, pop (*US informal*), old man (*Brit informal*), pa (*informal*), papa (*old-fashioned informal*), pater **2 = founder**, author, maker, architect, creator, inventor, originator, prime mover **3** *often plural* **= forefather**, predecessor, ancestor, forebear, progenitor, tupuna *or* tipuna (*NZ*)
▷ VERB **4 = sire**, parent, conceive, bring to life, beget, procreate, bring into being, give life to

RELATED WORD
adjective: paternal

fatherly = paternal, kindly, protective, supportive, benign, affectionate, patriarchal, benevolent

fatigue NOUN **1 = tiredness**, lethargy, weariness, heaviness, languor, listlessness **OPPOSITE:** freshness
▷ VERB **2 = tire**, exhaust, weaken, weary, drain, wear out, take it out of (*informal*), tire out **OPPOSITE:** refresh

fatty = greasy, fat, creamy, oily, adipose, oleaginous, suety, rich

faucet (*US & Canad*) **= tap**, spout, spigot, stopcock, valve

fault NOUN **1 = responsibility**, liability, guilt, accountability, culpability **2 = mistake**, slip, error, blunder, lapse, oversight, indiscretion, howler (*informal*), barry *or* Barry Crocker (*Austral slang*) **3 = failing**,

weakness, defect, deficiency, flaw, shortcoming, blemish, imperfection **OPPOSITE:** strength
▷ VERB **4 = criticize**, blame, complain, condemn, moan about, censure, hold (someone) responsible, find fault with
▷ PHRASES: **find fault with something** *or* **someone = criticize**, complain about, whinge about (*informal*), whine about (*informal*), quibble, carp at, take to task, pick holes in, nit-pick (*informal*) ▶ **to a fault = excessively**, unduly, in the extreme, overmuch, immoderately

faulty 1 = defective, damaged, malfunctioning, broken, flawed, impaired, imperfect, out of order, buggy (*of a computer*) **2 = incorrect**, flawed, unsound

favour *or* (*US*) **favor** NOUN **1 = approval**, goodwill, commendation, approbation **OPPOSITE:** disapproval **2 = favouritism**, preferential treatment **3 = support**, backing, aid, assistance, patronage, good opinion **4 = good turn**, service, benefit, courtesy, kindness, indulgence, boon, good deed **OPPOSITE:** wrong
▷ VERB **5 = prefer**, opt for, like better, incline towards, choose, pick, desire, go for **OPPOSITE:** object to **6 = indulge**,

reward, side with, smile
upon 7 = **support**, champion,
encourage, approve, advocate,
subscribe to, commend, stand
up for **OPPOSITE:** oppose
8 = **help**, benefit

favourable or (US) **favorable**
1 = **positive**, encouraging,
approving, praising, reassuring,
enthusiastic, sympathetic,
commending **OPPOSITE:**
disapproving 2 = **affirmative**,
agreeing, confirming, positive,
assenting, corroborative
3 = **advantageous**, promising,
encouraging, suitable,
helpful, beneficial, auspicious,
opportune **OPPOSITE:**
disadvantageous

favourite or (US) **favorite**
ADJECTIVE 1 = **preferred**,
favoured, best-loved, most-
liked, special, choice, dearest,
pet
▷ NOUN 2 = **darling**, pet, blue-
eyed boy (*informal*), beloved,
idol, fave (*informal*), teacher's
pet, the apple of your eye

fear NOUN 1 = **dread**, horror,
panic, terror, fright, alarm,
trepidation, fearfulness
2 = **bugbear**, bête noire, horror,
nightmare, anxiety, terror,
dread, spectre
▷ VERB 3 = **be afraid of**, dread,
shudder at, be fearful of, tremble
at, be terrified by, take fright
at, shake in your shoes about
4 = **regret**, feel, suspect, have

a feeling, have a hunch, have a
sneaking suspicion, have a funny
feeling
▷ PHRASES: **fear for something**
or **someone** = **worry about**, be
anxious about, feel concern for

fearful 1 = **scared**, afraid,
alarmed, frightened, nervous,
terrified, petrified **OPPOSITE:**
unafraid 2 = **timid**, afraid,
frightened, scared, alarmed,
nervous, uneasy, jumpy
OPPOSITE: brave 3 (*informal*)
= **frightful**, terrible, awful,
dreadful, horrific, dire,
horrendous, gruesome

feasible = **practicable**, possible,
reasonable, viable, workable,
achievable, attainable, likely
OPPOSITE: impracticable

feast NOUN 1 = **banquet**, repast,
spread (*informal*), dinner, treat,
hakari (*NZ*) 2 = **festival**, holiday,
fête, celebration, holy day,
red-letter day, religious festival,
saint's day
▷ VERB 3 = **eat your fill**, wine
and dine, overindulge, consume,
indulge, gorge, devour, pig out
(*slang*)

feat = **accomplishment**, act,
performance, achievement,
enterprise, undertaking, exploit,
deed

feather = **plume**

feature NOUN 1 = **aspect**,
quality, characteristic, property,
factor, trait, hallmark, facet
2 = **article**, report, story, piece,

item, column **3 = highlight**, attraction, speciality, main item
▷ **PLURAL NOUN 4 = face**, countenance, physiognomy, lineaments
▷ **VERB 5 = spotlight**, present, emphasize, play up, foreground, give prominence to **6 = star**, appear, participate, play a part

federation = union, league, association, alliance, combination, coalition, partnership, consortium

fed up = cheesed off, depressed, bored, tired, discontented, dissatisfied, glum, sick and tired (*informal*), hoha (*NZ*)

fee = charge, price, cost, bill, payment, wage, salary, toll

feeble 1 = weak, frail, debilitated, sickly, puny, weedy (*informal*), infirm, effete **OPPOSITE:** strong **2 = inadequate**, pathetic, insufficient, lame **3 = unconvincing**, poor, thin, tame, pathetic, lame, flimsy, paltry **OPPOSITE:** effective

feed VERB 1 = cater for, provide for, nourish, provide with food, supply, sustain, cook for, wine and dine **2 = graze**, eat, browse, pasture **3 = eat**, drink milk
▷ **NOUN 4 = food**, fodder, provender, pasturage
5 (*informal*) **= meal**, spread (*informal*), dinner, lunch, tea, breakfast, feast, supper

feel VERB 1 = experience, bear **2 = touch**, handle, manipulate, finger, stroke, paw, caress, fondle **3 = be aware of 4 = perceive**, detect, discern, experience, notice, observe **5 = sense**, be aware, be convinced, have a feeling, intuit **6 = believe**, consider, judge, deem, think, hold
▷ **NOUN 7 = texture**, finish, touch, surface, surface quality **8 = impression**, feeling, air, sense, quality, atmosphere, mood, aura

feeling 1 = emotion, sentiment **2 = opinion**, view, attitude, belief, point of view, instinct, inclination **3 = passion**, emotion, intensity, warmth **4 = ardour**, love, care, warmth, tenderness, fervour **5 = sympathy**, understanding, concern, pity, sensitivity, compassion, sorrow, sensibility **6 = sensation**, sense, impression, awareness **7 = sense of touch**, perception, sensation **8 = impression**, idea, sense, notion, suspicion, hunch, inkling, presentiment **9 = atmosphere**, mood, aura, ambience, feel, air, quality

feisty (*informal*) **= fiery**, spirited, bold, plucky, vivacious, (as) game as Ned Kelly (*Austral slang*)

fell 1 = cut down, cut, level, demolish, knock down, hew **2 = knock down**

fellow 1 (*Old-fashioned*) **= man**, person, individual, character,

guy (*informal*), bloke (*Brit informal*), chap (*informal*), boykie (*S African informal*)
2 = **associate**, colleague, peer, partner, companion, comrade, crony

fellowship 1 = **society**, club, league, association, organization, guild, fraternity, brotherhood 2 = **camaraderie**, brotherhood, companionship, sociability

feminine = **womanly**, pretty, soft, gentle, tender, delicate, ladylike **OPPOSITE:** masculine

fence NOUN 1 = **barrier**, wall, defence, railings, hedge, barricade, hedgerow, rampart
▷ VERB 2 *with* in *or* off = **enclose**, surround, bound, protect, pen, confine, encircle

ferocious 1 = **fierce**, violent, savage, ravening, predatory, rapacious, wild **OPPOSITE:** gentle 2 = **cruel**, bitter, brutal, vicious, ruthless, bloodthirsty

ferry NOUN 1 = **ferry boat**, boat, ship, passenger boat, packet boat, packet
▷ VERB 2 = **transport**, bring, carry, ship, take, run, shuttle, convey

fertile = **productive**, rich, lush, prolific, abundant, plentiful, fruitful, teeming **OPPOSITE:** barren

fertility = **fruitfulness**, abundance, richness, fecundity, luxuriance, productiveness

fertilizer = **compost**, muck, manure, dung, bone meal, dressing, toad juice (*Austral*)

festival 1 = **celebration**, fair, carnival, gala, fête, entertainment, jubilee, fiesta
2 = **holy day**, holiday, feast, commemoration, feast day, red-letter day, saint's day, fiesta

festive = **celebratory**, happy, merry, jubilant, cheery, joyous, joyful, jovial **OPPOSITE:** mournful

fetch 1 = **bring**, pick up, collect, go and get, get, carry, deliver, transport 2 = **sell for**, make, raise, earn, realize, go for, yield, bring in

fetching (*informal*) = **attractive**, charming, cute, enticing, captivating, alluring, winsome

feud NOUN 1 = **hostility**, row, conflict, argument, disagreement, rivalry, quarrel, vendetta
▷ VERB 2 = **quarrel**, row, clash, dispute, fall out, contend, war, squabble

fever = **excitement**, frenzy, ferment, agitation, fervour, restlessness, delirium

few = **not many**, one or two, scarcely any, rare, meagre, negligible, sporadic, sparse **OPPOSITE:** many

fiasco = **flop**, failure, disaster, mess (*informal*), catastrophe, debacle, cock-up (*Brit slang*), washout (*informal*)

f

fibre or (US) **fiber** = **thread**, strand, filament, tendril, pile, texture, wisp

fiction 1 = **tale**, story, novel, legend, myth, romance, narration, creative writing 2 = **lie**, invention, fabrication, falsehood, untruth, urban myth, tall story, urban legend

fictional = **imaginary**, made-up, invented, legendary, unreal, nonexistent

fiddle NOUN 1 (Brit informal) = **fraud**, racket, scam (slang), fix, swindle 2 (informal) = **violin** ▷ VERB 3 (informal) often with **with** = **fidget**, play, finger, tamper, mess about or around 4 (informal) often with **with** = **tinker**, adjust, interfere, mess about or around 5 (informal) = **cheat**, cook (informal), fix, diddle (informal), wangle (informal)

fiddling = **trivial**, small, petty, trifling, insignificant, unimportant, pettifogging, futile

fidelity 1 = **loyalty**, devotion, allegiance, constancy, faithfulness, dependability, trustworthiness, staunchness **OPPOSITE:** disloyalty 2 = **accuracy**, precision, correspondence, closeness, faithfulness, exactness, scrupulousness **OPPOSITE:** inaccuracy

field NOUN 1 = **meadow**, land, green, lea (poetic), pasture 2 = **speciality**, line, area, department, territory, discipline, province, sphere 3 = **line**, reach, sweep 4 = **competitors**, competition, candidates, runners, applicants, entrants, contestants ▷ VERB 5 (informal) = **deal with**, answer, handle, respond to, reply to, deflect, turn aside 6 (Sport) = **retrieve**, return, stop, catch, pick up

fierce 1 = **ferocious**, wild, dangerous, cruel, savage, brutal, aggressive, menacing, aggers (Austral slang), biffo (Austral slang) **OPPOSITE:** gentle 2 = **intense**, strong, keen, relentless, cut-throat 3 = **stormy**, strong, powerful, violent, intense, raging, furious, howling **OPPOSITE:** tranquil

fiercely = **ferociously**, savagely, passionately, furiously, viciously, tooth and nail, tigerishly, with no holds barred

fiery 1 = **burning**, flaming, blazing, on fire, ablaze, aflame, afire 2 = **excitable**, fierce, passionate, irritable, impetuous, irascible, hot-headed

fight VERB 1 = **oppose**, campaign against, dispute, contest, resist, defy, contend, withstand 2 = **battle**, combat, do battle 3 = **engage in**, conduct, wage, pursue, carry on ▷ NOUN 4 = **battle**, campaign,

movement, struggle
5 = conflict, clash, contest,
encounter **6 = brawl**, scrap
(*informal*), confrontation,
rumble (*US & NZ slang*), duel,
skirmish, tussle, biffo (*Austral
slang*), boilover (*Austral
slang*) **7 = row**,
argument, dispute, quarrel,
squabble **8 = resistance**, spirit,
pluck, militancy, belligerence,
pluckiness

fighter 1 = **boxer**, wrestler,
pugilist, prize fighter
2 = **soldier**, warrior, fighting
man, man-at-arms

figure NOUN 1 = **digit**,
character, symbol, number,
numeral 2 = **shape**, build,
body, frame, proportions,
physique 3 = **personage**,
person, individual, character,
personality, celebrity, big
name, dignitary 4 = **diagram**,
drawing, picture, illustration,
representation, sketch
5 = **design**, shape, pattern
6 = **price**, cost, value, amount,
total, sum
▷ VERB 7 *usually with* **in**
= **feature**, act, appear,
contribute to, play a part, be
featured 8 = **calculate**, work
out, compute, tot up, total,
count, reckon, tally
▷ PHRASES: **figure something**
or **someone out** = **understand**,
make out, fathom, see, solve,
comprehend, make sense of,
decipher

figurehead = **nominal head**,
titular head, front man, puppet,
mouthpiece

file¹ NOUN 1 = **folder**, case,
portfolio, binder 2 = **dossier**,
record, information, data,
documents, case history,
report, case 3 = **line**, row,
chain, column, queue,
procession
▷ VERB 4 = **arrange**, order,
classify, put in place, categorize,
pigeonhole, put in order
5 = **register**, record, enter,
log, put on record 6 = **march**,
troop, parade, walk in line, walk
behind one another

file² = **smooth**, shape, polish, rub,
scrape, rasp, abrade

fill 1 = **top up**, fill up, make
full, become full, brim over
2 = **swell**, expand, become
bloated, extend, balloon, fatten
3 = **pack**, crowd, squeeze, cram,
throng 4 = **stock**, supply, pack,
load 5 = **plug**, close, stop, seal,
cork, bung, block up, stop up
6 = **saturate**, charge, pervade,
permeate, imbue, impregnate,
suffuse 7 = **fulfil**, hold, perform,
carry out, occupy, execute,
discharge 8 *often with* **up**
= **satisfy**, stuff, glut

filling NOUN 1 = **stuffing**,
padding, filler, wadding, inside,
insides, contents
▷ ADJECTIVE 2 = **satisfying**,
heavy, square, substantial,
ample

film NOUN 1 = **movie**, picture, flick (*slang*), motion picture, MPEG, MP4 2 = **cinema**, the movies 3 = **layer**, covering, cover, skin, coating, dusting, tissue, membrane
▷ VERB 4 = **photograph**, record, shoot, video, videotape, take 5 = **adapt for the screen**, make into a film

filter NOUN 1 = **sieve**, mesh, gauze, strainer, membrane, riddle, sifter
▷ VERB 2 = **trickle**, seep, percolate, escape, leak, penetrate, ooze, dribble 3 *with* **through** = **purify**, treat, strain, refine, riddle, sift, sieve, winnow

filthy 1 = **dirty**, foul, polluted, squalid, slimy, unclean, putrid, festy (*Austral slang*) 2 = **grimy**, muddy, blackened, grubby, begrimed, festy (*Austral slang*) 3 = **obscene**, corrupt, indecent, pornographic, lewd, depraved, impure, smutty

final 1 = **last**, latest, closing, finishing, concluding, ultimate, terminal **OPPOSITE:** first 2 = **irrevocable**, absolute, definitive, decided, settled, definite, conclusive, irrefutable

finale = **climax**, ending, close, conclusion, culmination, denouement, last part, epilogue **OPPOSITE:** opening

finally 1 = **eventually**, at last, in the end, ultimately, at length, at long last, after a long time 2 = **lastly**, in the end, ultimately 3 = **in conclusion**, lastly, in closing, to conclude, to sum up, in summary

finance NOUN 1 = **economics**, business, money, banking, accounts, investment, commerce
▷ PLURAL NOUN 2 = **resources**, money, funds, capital, cash, affairs, budgeting, assets
▷ VERB 3 = **fund**, back, support, pay for, guarantee, invest in, underwrite, endow

financial = **economic**, business, commercial, monetary, fiscal, pecuniary, pocketbook

find VERB 1 = **discover**, uncover, spot, locate, detect, come across, hit upon, put your finger on **OPPOSITE:** lose 2 = **encounter**, meet, recognize 3 = **observe**, learn, note, discover, notice, realize, come up with, perceive
▷ NOUN 4 = **discovery**, catch, asset, bargain, acquisition, good buy

fine¹ 1 = **excellent**, good, striking, masterly, very good, impressive, outstanding, magnificent **OPPOSITE:** poor 2 = **satisfactory**, good, all right, suitable, acceptable, convenient, fair, O.K. *or* okay (*informal*) 3 = **thin**, light, narrow, wispy 4 = **delicate**, light, thin, sheer, flimsy, wispy, gossamer, diaphanous **OPPOSITE:** coarse

5 = **stylish**, expensive, elegant, refined, tasteful, quality, schmick (*Austral informal*)
6 = **exquisite**, delicate, fragile, dainty **7** = **minute**, exact, precise, nice **8** = **keen**, minute, nice, sharp, acute, subtle, precise, hairsplitting
9 = **brilliant**, quick, keen, alert, clever, penetrating, astute
10 = **sunny**, clear, fair, dry, bright, pleasant, clement, balmy **OPPOSITE:** cloudy

fine² NOUN **1** = **penalty**, damages, punishment, forfeit, financial penalty
▷ VERB **2** = **penalize**, charge, punish

finger = **touch**, feel, handle, play with, manipulate, paw (*informal*), maul, toy with

finish VERB **1** = **stop**, close, complete, conclude, cease, wrap up (*informal*), terminate, round off **OPPOSITE:** start
2 = **get done**, complete, conclude **3** = **end**, stop, conclude, wind up, terminate
4 = **consume**, dispose of, devour, polish off, eat, get through **5** = **use up**, empty, exhaust **6** = **coat**, polish, stain, texture, wax, varnish, gild, veneer **7** *often with* **off** = **destroy**, defeat, overcome, bring down, ruin, dispose of, rout, put an end to **8** *often with* **off** = **kill**, murder, destroy, massacre, butcher, slaughter, slay, exterminate

▷ NOUN **9** = **end**, close, conclusion, run-in, completion, finale, culmination, cessation **OPPOSITE:** beginning
10 = **surface**, polish, shine, texture, glaze, veneer, lacquer, lustre

finished 1 = **over**, done, through, ended, closed, complete, executed, finalized **OPPOSITE:** begun **2** = **ruined**, done for (*informal*), doomed, through, lost, defeated, wiped out, undone

fire NOUN **1** = **flames**, blaze, combustion, inferno, conflagration, holocaust
2 = **passion**, energy, spirit, enthusiasm, excitement, intensity, sparkle, vitality
3 = **bombardment**, shooting, firing, shelling, hail, volley, barrage, gunfire
▷ VERB **4** = **let off**, shoot, shell, set off, discharge, detonate
5 = **shoot**, explode, discharge, detonate, pull the trigger
6 (*informal*) = **dismiss**, sack (*informal*), get rid of, discharge, lay off, make redundant, cashier, give notice, kennet (*Austral slang*), jeff (*Austral slang*) **7** = **inspire**, excite, stir, stimulate, motivate, awaken, animate, rouse

fireworks 1 = **pyrotechnics**, illuminations, feux d'artifice
2 (*informal*) = **trouble**, row, storm, rage, uproar, hysterics

firm¹ 1 = hard, solid, dense, set, stiff, compacted, rigid, inflexible **OPPOSITE:** soft
2 = secure, fixed, rooted, stable, steady, fast, embedded, immovable **OPPOSITE:** unstable
3 = strong, close, tight, steady
4 = strict, unshakeable, resolute, inflexible, unyielding, unbending **5 = determined**, resolved, definite, set on, adamant, resolute, inflexible, unyielding **OPPOSITE:** wavering
6 = definite, hard, clear, confirmed, settled, fixed, hard-and-fast, cut-and-dried (*informal*)

firm² = company, business, concern, association, organization, corporation, venture, enterprise

firmly 1 = securely, safely, tightly **2 = immovably**, securely, steadily, like a rock, unflinchingly, unshakeably
3 = steadily, securely, tightly, unflinchingly **4 = resolutely**, staunchly, steadfastly, definitely, unwaveringly, unchangeably

first ADJECTIVE 1 = earliest, initial, opening, introductory, original, maiden, primordial
2 = top, best, winning, premier
3 = elementary, key, basic, primary, fundamental, cardinal, rudimentary, elemental
4 = foremost, highest, greatest, leading, head, ruling, chief, prime

▷ **NOUN 5 = novelty**, innovation, originality, new experience
▷ **ADVERB 6 = to begin with**, firstly, initially, at the beginning, in the first place, beforehand, to start with, at the outset
▷ **PHRASES: from the first = start**, from the beginning, from the outset, from the very beginning, from the introduction, from the starting point, from the inception, from the commencement

fish = angle, net, cast, trawl
• *See panels* **FISH, SHARKS**

fit¹ VERB 1 = adapt, shape, arrange, alter, adjust, modify, tweak (*informal*), customize
2 = place, insert **3 = suit**, meet, match, belong to, conform to, correspond to, accord with, be appropriate to **4 = equip**, provide, arm, prepare, fit out, kit out
▷ **ADJECTIVE 5 = appropriate**, suitable, right, becoming, seemly, fitting, skilled, correct **OPPOSITE:** inappropriate
6 = healthy, strong, robust, sturdy, well, trim, strapping, hale **OPPOSITE:** unfit

fit² 1 (*Pathology*) **= seizure**, attack, bout, spasm, convulsion, paroxysm **2 = bout**, burst, outbreak, outburst, spell

fitness 1 = appropriateness, competence, readiness, eligibility, suitability, propriety, aptness **2 = health**, strength,

FISH
Types of Fish

ahi
ahuru (*NZ*)
albacore
alewife
alfonsino
amberjack
anabantid
anabas
anableps
anchoveta
anchovy
angelfish
arapaima
archerfish
argentine
aua (*NZ*)
Australian salmon, native salmon, salmon trout, bay trout, *or* kahawai (*NZ & Austral*)
barbel
barracouta *or* (*Austral*) hake
barracuda
barramunda
barramundi *or* (*Austral*) barra *or* giant perch
bass
batfish
beluga
bib, pout, *or* whiting pout
bigeye
billfish
bitterling
black bass
black bream
black cod *or* Māori chief (*NZ*)
blackfish *or* (*Austral*) nigger

bleak
blenny
blindfish
bloodfin
blowfish *or* (*Austral*) toado
blue cod, rock cod, *or* (*NZ*) rawaru, pakirikiri, *or* patutuki
bluefin tuna
bluefish *or* snapper
bluegill
blue nose (*NZ*)
boarfish
bonefish
bonito *or* (*Austral*) horse mackerel
bony bream (*Austral*)
bowfin *or* dogfish
bream *or* (*Austral*) brim
brill
brook trout *or* speckled trout
brown trout
buffalo fish
bullhead
bull trout
bully *or* (*NZ*) pakoko, titarakura, *or* toitoi
burbot, eelpout, *or* ling
butterfish
butterfish, greenbone, *or* (*NZ*) koaea *or* marari
butterfly fish
cabezon *or* cabezone
cabrilla
callop
candlefish *or* eulachon
capelin *or* caplin

Types of Fish *continued*

carp
catfish
cavalla *or* cavally
cavefish
cero
characin *or* characid
chimaera
Chinook salmon, quinnat salmon, *or* king salmon
chub
chum
cichlid
cisco *or* lake herring
climbing fish *or* climbing perch
clingfish
clownfish
coalfish *or* (Brit) saithe *or* coley
cobia, black kingfish, *or* sergeant fish
cockabully
cod *or* codfish
coelacanth
coho *or* silver salmon
coley
conger
coral trout
crappie
croaker
crucian
dab
dace
damselfish
danio
dart (Austral)
darter
dealfish
dentex

dollarfish
dorado
dory
dragonet
eel *or* (NZ) tuna
eelpout
electric eel
fallfish
father lasher *or* short-spined sea scorpion
fighting fish *or* betta
filefish
flatfish *or* (NZ) flattie
flathead
flounder *or* (NZ) patiki
flying fish
flying gurnard
four-eyed fish
frogfish
garpike, garfish, gar, *or* (Austral) ballahoo
geelbek
gemfish *or* (Austral) hake
gilthead
goby
golden perch, freshwater bream, Murray perch, *or* yellow-belly (Austral)
goldeye
goldfish
goldsinny *or* goldfinny
gourami
grayling *or* (Austral) yarra herring
greenling
grenadier *or* rat-tail
groper *or* grouper
grunion

grunt
gudgeon
guitarfish
gunnel
guppy
gurnard or gurnet
gwyniad
haddock
hagfish, hag, or blind eel
hairtail or (US) cutlass fish
hake
halfbeak
halibut
hapuku (Austral & NZ)
herring
hogfish
hoki (NZ)
horned pout or brown bullhead
horse mackerel
houndfish
houting
ice fish
jacksmelt
javelin fish or Queensland trumpeter
jewelfish
jewfish or (Austral informal) jewie
John Dory
jurel
kelpfish or (Austral informal) kelpie
killifish
kingfish
kingklip (S African)
kokanee
kokopu (NZ)
labyrinth fish
lampern or river lamprey

lamprey or lamper eel
lancet fish
lantern fish
largemouth bass
latimeria
leatherjacket
lemon sole
lepidosiren
ling or (Austral) beardie
lingcod
lionfish
loach
louvar
luderick or (NZ) parore
lumpfish or lumpsucker
lungfish
mackerel or (colloquial) shiner
mangrove Jack (Austral)
manta, manta ray, devilfish, or devil ray
maomao (NZ)
marlin or spearfish
megrim
menhaden
milkfish
miller's thumb
minnow or (Scot) baggie minnow
mirror carp
moki or blue moki (NZ)
molly
monkfish or (US) goosefish
mooneye
moonfish
Moorish idol
moray
morwong, black perch, or (NZ) porae
mudcat

Types of Fish continued

mudfish
mudskipper
opah, moonfish, or kingfish
orange chromide
orange roughy (Austral)
orfe
ouananiche
ox-eye herring (Austral)
paddlefish
panchax
pandora
paradise fish
parore, blackfish, black rockfish,
   or mangrove fish (NZ)
parrotfish
pearl perch (Austral)
perch or (Austral) redfin
pickerel
pigfish or hogfish
pike, luce, or jackfish
pikeperch
pilchard or (Austral informal) pillie
pilot fish
pinfish or sailor's choice
pipefish or needlefish
piranha or piraña
plaice
platy
pogge or armed bullhead
pollack or pollock
pollan
pomfret
pompano
porae (NZ)
porcupine fish or globefish
porgy or pogy
pout

powan or lake herring
puffer or globefish
pumpkinseed
Queensland halibut
Queensland lungfish
rabbitfish
rainbow trout
ray
red cod
red emperor
redfin
redfish
red mullet or (US) goatfish
red salmon
red snapper
remora
ribbonfish
roach
robalo
rock bass
rock cod
rockfish or (formerly) rock salmon
rockling
rosefish
rudd
ruffe, ruff, or pope
runner
salmon
salmon trout
sand dab
sand eel, sand lance, or launce
sardine
sauger
saury or skipper
sawfish
scabbard fish
scad

scaldfish
scat
scorpion fish
sculpin (US & Canad)
scup or northern porgy
sea bass
sea bream
sea horse
sea lamprey
sea perch
sea raven
sea robin
sea scorpion
sea snail or snailfish
sea trout
Sergeant Baker
sergeant major
shad
shanny
sheepshead
shiner
shovelnose
Siamese fighting fish
sild
silver belly (NZ)
silverfish
silverside or silversides
skate
skelly
skipjack or skipjack tuna
sleeper or sleeper goby
smallmouth bass
smelt
smooth hound
snapper, red bream, or (Austral)
  wollomai or wollamai
snipefish or bellows fish
snoek

snook
sockeye or red salmon
sole
solenette
spadefish
Spanish mackerel or Queensland
  kingfish
spotted mackerel or school
  mackerel
sprat
squeteague
squirrelfish
steelhead
sterlet
stickleback
stingray
stone bass or wreckfish
stonefish
stone roller
sturgeon
sucker
sunfish
surfperch or sea perch
surgeonfish
swordfish
swordtail
tailor
tarakihi or terakihi (NZ)
tarpon
tarwhine
tautog or blackfish
tench
teraglin
tetra
thornback
threadfin
tilapia
tilefish

f

f

Types of Fish *continued*

toadfish	warehou (*NZ*)
tommy rough *or* tommy ruff (*Austral*)	weakfish
	weever
topminnow	whitebait
torsk *or* (*US & Canadian*) cusk	whitefish
trevalla (*Austral*)	whiting
trevally, araara, *or* samson fish (*Austral & NZ*)	wirrah
	witch
triggerfish	wobbegong, wobbygong, *or* wobegong
tripletail	
trout	wolffish *or* catfish
trunkfish, boxfish, *or* cowfish	wrasse
tuna *or* tunny	yellowfin (*NZ*)
turbot	yellowfin tuna
vendace	yellow jack
wahoo	yellowtail
walleye, walleyed pike, *or* dory	zander

---

good health, vigour, good condition, wellness, robustness

fitting ADJECTIVE
1 = **appropriate**, suitable, proper, apt, right, becoming, seemly, correct OPPOSITE: unsuitable
▷ NOUN **2** = **accessory**, part, piece, unit, component, attachment

fix VERB **1** = **place**, join, stick, attach, set, position, plant, link **2** *often with* **up** = **decide**, set, choose, establish, determine, settle, arrange, arrive at **3** *often with* **up** = **arrange**, organize, sort out, see to, make arrangements for **4** = **repair**, mend, service,

correct, restore, see to, overhaul, patch up **5** = **focus**, direct at, fasten on **6** (*informal*) = **rig**, set up (*informal*), influence, manipulate, fiddle (*informal*)
▷ NOUN **7** (*informal*) = **mess**, corner, difficulty, dilemma, embarrassment, plight, pickle (*informal*), uphill (*S African*)
▷ PHRASES: **fix someone up** *often with* **with** = **provide**, supply, bring about, lay on, arrange for ▶ **fix something up** = **arrange**, plan, settle, fix, organize, sort out, agree on, make arrangements for

fixed 1 = **inflexible**, set, steady, resolute, unwavering OPPOSITE:

wavering 2 = **immovable**, set, established, secure, rooted, permanent, rigid **OPPOSITE:** mobile 3 = **agreed**, set, planned, decided, established, settled, arranged, resolved

fizz 1 = **bubble**, froth, fizzle, effervesce, produce bubbles 2 = **sputter**, buzz, sparkle, hiss, crackle

flag¹ NOUN 1 = **banner**, standard, colours, pennant, ensign, streamer, pennon
▷ VERB 2 = **mark**, identify, indicate, label, pick out, note 3 *often with* **down** = **hail**, stop, signal, wave down

flag² = **weaken**, fade, weary, falter, wilt, wane, sag, languish

flagging = **weakening**, declining, waning, fading, deteriorating, wearying, faltering, wilting

flair 1 = **ability**, feel, talent, gift, genius, faculty, mastery, knack 2 (*informal*) = **style**, taste, dash, chic, elegance, panache, discernment, stylishness

flake NOUN 1 = **chip**, scale, layer, peeling, shaving, wafer, sliver
▷ VERB 2 = **chip**, peel (off), blister

flamboyant 1 = **camp** (*informal*), dashing, theatrical 2 = **showy**, elaborate, extravagant, ornate, ostentatious 3 = **colourful**, striking, brilliant, glamorous, stylish, dazzling, glitzy (*slang*), showy, bling (*slang*)

flame NOUN 1 = **fire**, light, spark, glow, blaze, brightness, inferno 2 (*informal*) = **sweetheart**, partner, lover, girlfriend, boyfriend, heart-throb (*Brit*), beau
▷ VERB 3 = **burn**, flash, shine, glow, blaze, flare, glare

flank 1 = **side**, hip, thigh, loin 2 = **wing**, side, sector, aspect

flap VERB 1 = **flutter**, wave, flail 2 = **beat**, wave, thrash, flutter, wag, vibrate, shake
▷ NOUN 3 = **flutter**, beating, waving, shaking, swinging, swish 4 (*informal*) = **panic**, state (*informal*), agitation, commotion, sweat (*informal*), dither (*chiefly Brit*), fluster, tizzy (*informal*)

flare VERB 1 = **blaze**, flame, glare, flicker, burn up 2 = **widen**, spread, broaden, spread out, dilate, splay
▷ NOUN 3 = **flame**, burst, flash, blaze, glare, flicker

flash NOUN 1 = **blaze**, burst, spark, beam, streak, flare, dazzle, glare
▷ VERB 2 = **blaze**, shine, beam, sparkle, flare, glare, gleam, light up 3 = **speed**, race, shoot, fly, tear, dash, whistle, streak 4 (*informal*) = **show quickly**, display, expose, exhibit, flourish, show off, flaunt
▷ ADJECTIVE 5 (*informal*)

= **ostentatious**, smart, trendy, showy, bling (*slang*)

flat¹ ADJECTIVE 1 = **even**, level, levelled, smooth, horizontal OPPOSITE: uneven 2 = **punctured**, collapsed, burst, blown out, deflated, empty 3 = **used up**, finished, empty, drained, expired 4 = **absolute**, firm, positive, explicit, definite, outright, downright, unequivocal 5 = **dull**, dead, empty, boring, depressing, tedious, lacklustre, tiresome OPPOSITE: exciting 6 = **without energy**, empty, weak, tired, depressed, drained, weary, worn out 7 = **monotonous**, boring, dull, tedious, tiresome, unchanging

▷ ADVERB 8 = **completely**, directly, absolutely, categorically, precisely, exactly, utterly, outright

▷ PHRASES: flat out (*informal*) = **at full speed**, all out, to the full, hell for leather (*informal*), as hard as possible, at full tilt, for all you are worth

flat² = **apartment**, rooms, quarters, digs, suite, penthouse, living quarters, duplex (*US & Canad*), bachelor apartment (*Canad*)

flatly = **absolutely**, completely, positively, categorically, unequivocally, unhesitatingly

flatten 1 *sometimes with* **out** = **level**, squash, compress, trample, iron out, even out, smooth off 2 *sometimes with* **out** = **destroy**, level, ruin, demolish, knock down, pull down, raze, kennet (*Austral slang*), jeff (*Austral slang*)

flatter 1 = **praise**, compliment, pander to, sweet-talk (*informal*), wheedle, soft-soap (*informal*), butter up 2 = **suit**, become, enhance, set off, embellish, do something for, show to advantage

flattering 1 = **becoming**, kind, effective, enhancing, well-chosen OPPOSITE: unflattering 2 = **ingratiating**, complimentary, fawning, fulsome, laudatory, adulatory OPPOSITE: uncomplimentary

flavour or (*US*) **flavor** NOUN 1 = **taste**, seasoning, flavouring, savour, relish, smack, aroma, zest OPPOSITE: blandness 2 = **quality**, feeling, feel, style, character, tone, essence, tinge

▷ VERB 3 = **season**, spice, add flavour to, enrich, infuse, imbue, pep up, leaven

flaw = **weakness**, failing, defect, weak spot, fault, blemish, imperfection, chink in your armour

flawed 1 = **damaged**, defective, imperfect, blemished, faulty 2 = **erroneous**, incorrect, invalid, wrong, mistaken, false, faulty, unsound

flee = **run away**, escape, bolt, fly, take off (*informal*), depart, run off, take flight

fleet = **navy**, task force, flotilla, armada

fleeting = **momentary**, passing, brief, temporary, short-lived, transient, ephemeral, transitory
OPPOSITE: lasting

flesh 1 = **fat**, muscle, tissue, brawn 2 (*informal*) = **fatness**, fat, adipose tissue, corpulence, weight 3 = **meat** 4 = **physical nature**, carnality, human nature, flesh and blood, sinful nature
▷ **PHRASES: your own flesh and blood** = **family**, blood, relations, relatives, kin, kith and kin, blood relations, kinsfolk, ainga (*NZ*), rellies (*Austral slang*)

flexibility 1 = **elasticity**, pliability, springiness, pliancy, give (*informal*) 2 = **adaptability**, openness, versatility, adjustability 3 = **complaisance**, accommodation, give and take, amenability

flexible 1 = **pliable**, plastic, elastic, supple, lithe, springy, pliant, stretchy **OPPOSITE:** rigid 2 = **adaptable**, open, variable, adjustable, discretionary
OPPOSITE: inflexible

flick 1 = **jerk**, pull, tug, lurch, jolt 2 = **strike**, tap, remove quickly, hit, touch, stroke, flip, whisk
▷ **PHRASES: flick through something** = **browse**, glance at, skim, leaf through, flip through, thumb through, skip through

flicker VERB 1 = **twinkle**, flash, sparkle, flare, shimmer, gutter, glimmer 2 = **flutter**, waver, quiver, vibrate
▷ NOUN 3 = **glimmer**, flash, spark, flare, gleam 4 = **trace**, breath, spark, glimmer, iota

flight[1] 1 = **journey**, trip, voyage 2 = **aviation**, flying, aeronautics 3 = **flock**, group, unit, cloud, formation, squadron, swarm, flying group

flight[2] = **escape**, fleeing, departure, retreat, exit, running away, exodus, getaway

fling VERB 1 = **throw**, toss, hurl, launch, cast, propel, sling, catapult
▷ NOUN 2 = **binge**, good time, bash, party, spree, night on the town, rave-up (*Brit slang*)

flip VERB 1 = **flick**, switch, snap, click 2 = **spin**, turn, overturn, turn over, roll over 3 = **toss**, throw, flick, fling, sling
▷ NOUN 4 = **toss**, throw, spin, snap, flick

flirt VERB 1 = **chat up**, lead on (*informal*), make advances at, make eyes at, philander, make sheep's eyes at 2 *usually with* **with** = **toy with**, consider, entertain, play with, dabble in, trifle with, give a thought to, expose yourself to
▷ NOUN 3 = **tease**, philanderer, coquette, heart-breaker

float 1 = **glide**, sail, drift, move gently, bob, coast, slide, be carried 2 = **be buoyant**, hang, hover **OPPOSITE:** sink 3 = **launch**, offer, sell, set up, promote, get going **OPPOSITE:** dissolve

floating 1 = **uncommitted**, wavering, undecided, indecisive, vacillating, sitting on the fence (*informal*), unaffiliated, independent 2 = **free**, wandering, variable, fluctuating, unattached, movable

flock NOUN 1 = **herd**, group, flight, drove, colony, gaggle, skein 2 = **crowd**, company, group, host, collection, mass, gathering, herd ▷ **VERB** 3 = **stream**, crowd, mass, swarm, throng 4 = **gather**, crowd, mass, collect, assemble, herd, huddle, converge

flog = **beat**, whip, lash, thrash, whack, scourge, hit hard, trounce

flood NOUN 1 = **deluge**, downpour, inundation, tide, overflow, torrent, spate 2 = **torrent**, flow, rush, stream, tide, abundance, glut, profusion 3 = **series**, stream, avalanche, barrage, spate, torrent 4 = **outpouring**, rush, stream, surge, torrent ▷ **VERB** 5 = **immerse**, swamp, submerge, inundate, drown, cover with water 6 = **pour over**, swamp, run over, overflow, inundate 7 = **engulf**, sweep into, overwhelm, surge into, swarm into, pour into 8 = **saturate**, fill, choke, swamp, glut, oversupply, overfill 9 = **stream**, flow, rush, pour, surge

floor NOUN 1 = **ground** 2 = **storey**, level, stage, tier ▷ **VERB** 3 (*informal*) = **disconcert**, stump, baffle, confound, throw (*informal*), defeat, puzzle, bewilder 4 = **knock down**, fell, knock over, prostrate, deck (*slang*)

flop VERB 1 = **slump**, fall, drop, collapse, sink 2 = **hang down**, hang, dangle, sag, droop 3 (*informal*) = **fail**, fold (*informal*), founder, fall flat, come unstuck, misfire, go belly-up (*slang*) **OPPOSITE:** succeed ▷ **NOUN** 4 (*informal*) = **failure**, disaster, fiasco, debacle, washout (*informal*), nonstarter **OPPOSITE:** success

floppy = **droopy**, soft, loose, limp, sagging, baggy, flaccid, pendulous

floral = **flowery**, flower-patterned

flounder 1 = **falter**, struggle, stall, slow down, run into trouble, come unstuck (*informal*), be in difficulties, hit a bad patch 2 = **dither**, struggle, blunder, be confused, falter, be in the dark, be out of your depth 3 = **struggle**, toss, thrash, stumble, fumble, grope

> **USAGE NOTE**
> *Flounder* is sometimes wrongly used where *founder* is meant: *the project foundered* (not *floundered*) *because of lack of funds*.

flourish VERB 1 = **thrive**, increase, advance, progress, boom, bloom, blossom, prosper **OPPOSITE:** fail 2 = **succeed**, move ahead, go places (*informal*) 3 = **grow**, thrive, flower, succeed, bloom, blossom, prosper 4 = **wave**, brandish, display, shake, wield, flaunt
> NOUN 5 = **wave**, sweep, brandish, swish, swing, twirl 6 = **show**, display, parade, fanfare 7 = **curlicue**, sweep, decoration, swirl, plume, embellishment, ornamentation

flourishing = **thriving**, successful, blooming, prospering, rampant, going places, in the pink

flow VERB 1 = **run**, course, rush, sweep, move, pass, roll, flood 2 = **pour**, move, sweep, flood, stream 3 = **issue**, follow, result, emerge, spring, proceed, arise, derive
> NOUN 4 = **stream**, current, movement, motion, course, flood, drift, tide

flower NOUN 1 = **bloom**, blossom, efflorescence 2 = **elite**, best, prime, finest, pick, choice, cream, the crème de la crème 3 = **height**, prime, peak
> VERB 4 = **bloom**, open, mature, flourish, unfold, blossom 5 = **blossom**, grow, develop, progress, mature, thrive, flourish, bloom

> **RELATED WORD**
> *adjective:* floral

fluctuate 1 = **change**, swing, vary, alternate, waver, veer, seesaw 2 = **shift**, oscillate

fluent = **effortless**, natural, articulate, well-versed, voluble

fluid NOUN 1 = **liquid**, solution, juice, liquor, sap
> ADJECTIVE 2 = **liquid**, flowing, watery, molten, melted, runny, liquefied **OPPOSITE:** solid

flurry 1 = **commotion**, stir, bustle, flutter, excitement, fuss, disturbance, ado 2 = **gust**, shower, gale, swirl, squall, storm

flush¹ VERB 1 = **blush**, colour, glow, redden, turn red, go red 2 = **cleanse**, wash out, rinse out, flood, swill, hose down 3 = **expel**, drive, dislodge
> NOUN 4 = **blush**, colour, glow, reddening, redness, rosiness

flush² 1 = **level**, even, true, flat, square 2 (*informal*) = **wealthy**, rich, well-off, in the money (*informal*), well-heeled (*informal*), replete, moneyed, minted (*Brit slang*)

flutter VERB 1 = **beat**, flap, tremble, ripple, waver, quiver, vibrate, palpitate 2 = **flit**

▷ NOUN 3 = **tremor**, tremble, shiver, shudder, palpitation
4 = **vibration**, twitching, quiver
5 = **agitation**, state (*informal*), confusion, excitement, flap (*informal*), dither (*chiefly Brit*), commotion, fluster

fly¹ 1 = **take wing**, soar, glide, wing, sail, hover, flutter, flit
2 = **pilot**, control, operate, steer, manoeuvre, navigate 3 = **airlift**, send by plane, take by plane, take in an aircraft 4 = **flutter**, wave, float, flap 5 = **display**, show, flourish, brandish
6 = **rush**, race, shoot, career, speed, tear, dash, hurry 7 = **pass swiftly**, pass, glide, slip away, roll on, flit, elapse, run its course
8 = **leave**, get away, escape, flee, run for it, skedaddle (*informal*), take to your heels

fly²
• See panel **FLIES**

flying = **hurried**, brief, rushed, fleeting, short-lived, hasty, transitory

foam NOUN 1 = **froth**, spray, bubbles, lather, suds, spume, head
▷ VERB 2 = **bubble**, boil, fizz, froth, lather, effervesce

focus NOUN 1 = **centre**, focal point, central point 2 = **focal point**, heart, target, hub
▷ VERB 3 *often with* **on**
= **concentrate**, centre, spotlight, direct, aim, pinpoint, zoom in 4 = **fix**, train, direct, aim

foe (*Formal*, *literary*) = **enemy**, rival, opponent, adversary, antagonist **OPPOSITE:** friend

fog = **mist**, gloom, haze, smog, murk, miasma, peasouper (*informal*)

foil¹ = **thwart**, stop, defeat, disappoint, counter, frustrate, hamper, balk

foil² = **complement**, relief, contrast, antithesis

fold VERB 1 = **bend**, crease, double over 2 (*informal*) *often with* **up** = **go bankrupt**, fail, crash, collapse, founder, shut down, go under, go bust (*informal*)
▷ NOUN 3 = **crease**, gather, bend, overlap, wrinkle, pleat, ruffle, furrow

folk 1 = **people**, persons, individuals, men and women, humanity, inhabitants, mankind, mortals 2 (*informal*) *usually plural* = **family**, parents, relations, relatives, tribe, clan, kin, kindred, ainga (*NZ*), rellies (*Austral slang*)

follow 1 = **accompany**, attend, escort, go behind, tag along behind, come behind
2 = **pursue**, track, dog, hunt, chase, shadow, trail, hound **OPPOSITE:** avoid 3 = **come after**, go after, come next **OPPOSITE:** precede 4 = **result**, issue, develop, spring, flow, proceed, arise, ensue 5 = **obey**, observe, adhere to, stick to,

FLIES

antlion or antlion fly
aphid or plant louse
aphis
apple blight or American blight
bee fly
beetfly or mangold fly
blackfly or bean aphid
blowfly, bluebottle, or (Austral informal) blowie
botfly
buffalo gnat or black fly
bulb fly
bushfly
carrot fly
chalcid or chalcid fly
cluster fly
crane fly or (Brit) daddy-longlegs
damselfly
dobsonfly
dragonfly or (colloquial) devil's darning-needle
drosophila, fruit fly, or vinegar fly
fly
frit fly
fruit fly
gadfly
gallfly
gnat
grannom
green blowfly or (Austral informal) blue-arsed fly
greenbottle
greenfly
horsefly or cleg
housefly
hover fly
lacewing
lantern fly
mayfly or dayfly
Mediterranean fruit fly or Medfly
needle fly
onion fly
robber fly, bee killer, or assassin fly
sandfly
scorpion fly
screwworm fly
silverhorn
snake fly
stable fly
stonefly
tachina fly
tsetse fly or tzetze fly
vinegar fly
warble fly
whitefly
willow fly

heed, conform to, keep to, pay attention to **OPPOSITE:** ignore **6 = succeed**, replace, come after, take over from, come next, supersede, supplant, take the place of **7 = understand**, realize, appreciate, take in, grasp, catch on (informal), comprehend, fathom **8 = keep up with**, support, be interested in, cultivate, be a fan of, keep abreast of

follower = **supporter**, fan, disciple, devotee, apostle, pupil, adherent, groupie (*slang*)
OPPOSITE: leader

following ADJECTIVE 1 = **next**, subsequent, successive, ensuing, later, succeeding, consequent 2 = **coming**, about to be mentioned ▷ NOUN 3 = **supporters**, backing, train, fans, suite, clientele, entourage, coterie

folly = **foolishness**, nonsense, madness, stupidity, indiscretion, lunacy, imprudence, rashness
OPPOSITE: wisdom

fond 1 = **loving**, caring, warm, devoted, tender, adoring, affectionate, indulgent
OPPOSITE: indifferent
2 = **unrealistic**, empty, naive, vain, foolish, deluded, overoptimistic, delusive
OPPOSITE: sensible
▷ PHRASES: fond of
1 = **attached to**, in love with, keen on, attracted to, having a soft spot for, enamoured of
2 = **keen on**, into (*informal*), hooked on, partial to, having a soft spot for, addicted to

fondly 1 = **lovingly**, tenderly, affectionately, amorously, dearly, possessively, with affection, indulgently 2 = **unrealistically**, stupidly, vainly, foolishly, naively, credulously

food = **nourishment**, fare, diet, tucker (*Austral & NZ informal*), rations, nutrition, cuisine, refreshment, nibbles, kai (*NZ informal*)

fool NOUN 1 = **simpleton**, idiot, mug (*Brit slang*), dummy (*slang*), git (*Brit slang*), twit (*informal, chiefly Brit*), dunce, imbecile (*informal*), dorba *or* dorb (*Austral slang*), bogan (*Austral slang*), mampara (*S African informal*)
OPPOSITE: genius 2 = **dupe**, mug (*Brit slang*), sucker (*slang*), stooge (*slang*), laughing stock, pushover (*informal*), fall guy (*informal*) 3 = **jester**, clown, harlequin, buffoon, court jester
▷ VERB 4 = **deceive**, mislead, delude, trick, take in, con (*informal*), dupe, beguile, scam (*slang*)

foolish = **unwise**, silly, absurd, rash, senseless, foolhardy, ill-judged, imprudent **OPPOSITE:** sensible

footing 1 = **basis**, foundation, base position, groundwork
2 = **relationship**, position, basis, standing, rank, status, grade

footpath (*Austral & NZ*) = **pavement**, sidewalk (*US & Canad*)

footstep = **step**, tread, footfall

foray = **raid**, sally, incursion, inroad, attack, assault, invasion, swoop

forbid = **prohibit**, ban, disallow, exclude, rule out, veto, outlaw, preclude
OPPOSITE: permit

USAGE NOTE
Traditionally, it has been considered more correct to talk about *forbidding someone to do something*, rather than *forbidding someone from doing something*. Recently, however, the *from* option has become generally more acceptable, so that *he was forbidden to come in* and *he was forbidden from coming in* may both now be considered correct.

forbidden = prohibited, banned, vetoed, outlawed, taboo, out of bounds, proscribed

forbidding = threatening, severe, frightening, hostile, menacing, sinister, daunting, ominous **OPPOSITE:** inviting

force NOUN 1 = compulsion, pressure, violence, constraint, oppression, coercion, duress, arm-twisting (*informal*)
2 = power, might, pressure, energy, strength, momentum, impulse, vigour **OPPOSITE:** weakness 3 = intensity, vigour, vehemence, fierceness, emphasis 4 = army, unit, company, host, troop, squad, patrol, regiment
▷ VERB 5 = compel, make, drive, press, oblige, constrain, coerce, impel 6 = push, thrust, propel 7 = break open, blast, wrench, prise, wrest **OPPOSITE:** coax

▷ PHRASES: in force 1 = valid, working, current, effective, binding, operative, operational, in operation 2 = in great numbers, all together, in full strength

forced 1 = compulsory, enforced, mandatory, obligatory, involuntary, conscripted **OPPOSITE:** voluntary 2 = false, affected, strained, wooden, stiff, artificial, contrived, unnatural **OPPOSITE:** natural

forceful 1 = dynamic, powerful, assertive **OPPOSITE:** weak 2 = powerful, strong, convincing, effective, compelling, persuasive, cogent

forecast VERB 1 = predict, anticipate, foresee, foretell, divine, prophesy, augur, forewarn
▷ NOUN 2 = prediction, prognosis, guess, prophecy, conjecture, forewarning

forefront = lead, centre, front, fore, spearhead, prominence, vanguard, foreground

foreign = alien, exotic, unknown, strange, imported, remote, external, unfamiliar **OPPOSITE:** native

foreigner = alien, incomer, immigrant, non-native, stranger, settler

foremost = leading, best, highest, chief, prime, primary, supreme, most important

foresee = **predict**, forecast, anticipate, envisage, prophesy, foretell

forever or **for ever**
1 = **evermore**, always, ever, for good, for keeps, for all time, in perpetuity, till the cows come home (*informal*)
2 = **constantly**, always, all the time, continually, endlessly, persistently, eternally, perpetually

> **USAGE NOTE**
> *Forever* and *for ever* can both be used to say that something is without end. For all other meanings, *forever* is the preferred form.

forfeit NOUN 1 = **penalty**, fine, damages, forfeiture, loss, mulct
▷ VERB 2 = **relinquish**, lose, give up, surrender, renounce, be deprived of, say goodbye to, be stripped of

forge 1 = **form**, build, create, establish, set up, fashion, shape, frame 2 = **fake**, copy, reproduce, imitate, counterfeit, feign, falsify 3 = **create**, make, work, found, form, model, fashion, shape

forget 1 = **neglect**, overlook, omit, not remember, be remiss, fail to remember 2 = **leave behind**, lose, lose sight of, mislay

forgive = **excuse**, pardon, not hold something against, understand, acquit, condone, let off (*informal*), turn a blind eye to **OPPOSITE:** blame

forgiveness = **pardon**, mercy, absolution, exoneration, amnesty, acquittal, remission

fork = **branch**, part, separate, split, divide, diverge, subdivide, bifurcate

forked = **branching**, split, branched, divided, angled, pronged, zigzag, Y-shaped

form NOUN 1 = **type**, sort, kind, variety, class, style 2 = **shape**, formation, configuration, structure, pattern, appearance 3 = **condition**, health, shape, nick (*informal*), fitness, trim, fettle 4 = **document**, paper, sheet, questionnaire, application 5 = **procedure**, etiquette, use, custom, convention, usage, protocol, wont, kawa (*NZ*), tikanga (*NZ*) 6 (*Education, chiefly Brit*) = **class**, year, set, rank, grade, stream
▷ VERB 7 = **arrange**, combine, line up, organize, assemble, draw up 8 = **make**, produce, fashion, build, create, shape, construct, forge 9 = **constitute**, make up, compose, comprise 10 = **establish**, start, launch 11 = **take shape**, grow, develop, materialize, rise, appear, come into being, crystallize 12 = **draw up**, devise, formulate, organize 13 = **develop**, pick up, acquire, cultivate, contract

formal 1 = **serious**, stiff, detached, official, correct, conventional, remote, precise **OPPOSITE:** informal 2 = **official**, authorized, endorsed, certified, solemn 3 = **ceremonial**, traditional, solemn, ritualistic, dressy 4 = **conventional**, established, traditional

formality 1 = **correctness**, seriousness, decorum, protocol, etiquette 2 = **convention**, procedure, custom, ritual, rite

format = **arrangement**, form, style, make-up, look, plan, design, type

formation 1 = **establishment**, founding, forming, setting up, starting, production, generation, manufacture 2 = **development**, shaping, constitution, moulding, genesis 3 = **arrangement**, grouping, design, structure, pattern, organization, array, configuration

former = **previous**, one-time, erstwhile, earlier, prior, sometime, foregoing **OPPOSITE:** current

formerly = **previously**, earlier, in the past, at one time, before, lately, once

formidable 1 = **impressive**, great, powerful, tremendous, mighty, terrific, awesome, invincible 2 = **intimidating**, threatening, terrifying, menacing, dismaying, fearful, daunting, frightful **OPPOSITE:** encouraging

formula = **method**, plan, policy, rule, principle, procedure, recipe, blueprint

formulate 1 = **devise**, plan, develop, prepare, work out, invent, forge, draw up 2 = **express**, detail, frame, define, specify, articulate, set down, put into words

fort = **fortress**, keep, camp, tower, castle, garrison, stronghold, citadel, fortified pa (NZ)
▷ **PHRASES: hold the fort** (informal) = **take responsibility**, cover, stand in, carry on, take over the reins, deputize, keep things on an even keel

forte = **speciality**, strength, talent, strong point, métier, long suit (informal), gift **OPPOSITE:** weak point

forth 1 (Formal, old-fashioned) = **forward**, out, away, ahead, onward, outward 2 = **out**

forthcoming 1 = **approaching**, coming, expected, future, imminent, prospective, impending, upcoming 2 = **available**, ready, accessible, at hand, in evidence, obtainable, on tap (informal) 3 = **communicative**, open, free, informative, expansive, sociable, chatty, talkative

fortify 1 = **protect**, defend, strengthen, reinforce, support,

shore up, augment, buttress
2 = **strengthen**, add alcohol to
fortitude = **courage**, strength,
resolution, grit, bravery,
backbone, perseverance, valour
fortress = **castle**, fort,
stronghold, citadel, redoubt,
fastness, fortified pa (*NZ*)
fortunate 1 = **lucky**,
favoured, jammy (*Brit slang*),
in luck **OPPOSITE:** unfortunate
2 = **providential**, fortuitous,
felicitous, timely, helpful,
convenient, favourable,
advantageous
fortunately = **luckily**,
happily, as luck would have it,
providentially, by good luck, by a
happy chance
fortune 1 = **wealth**, means,
property, riches, resources,
assets, possessions, treasure
OPPOSITE: poverty 2 = **luck**,
fluke (*informal*), stroke of luck,
serendipity, twist of fate, run of
luck 3 = **chance**, fate, destiny,
providence, the stars, Lady Luck,
kismet 4 *often plural* = **destiny**, lot,
experiences, history, condition,
success, means, adventures
forwards 1 = **forth**, on,
ahead, onwards **OPPOSITE:**
backward(s) 2 = **on**, onward,
onwards
fossick (*Austral & NZ*) = **search**,
hunt, explore, ferret, check,
forage, rummage
foster 1 = **bring up**, mother,
raise, nurse, look after, rear, care

for, take care of 2 = **develop**,
support, further, encourage,
feed, promote, stimulate,
uphold **OPPOSITE:** suppress
foul ADJECTIVE 1 = **dirty**,
unpleasant, stinking, filthy,
grubby, repellent, squalid,
repulsive, festy (*Austral slang*),
yucko (*Austral slang*) **OPPOSITE:**
clean 2 = **obscene**, crude,
indecent, blue, abusive, coarse,
vulgar, lewd 3 = **unfair**, illegal,
crooked, shady (*informal*),
fraudulent, dishonest,
unscrupulous, underhand
4 = **offensive**, bad, wrong, evil,
corrupt, disgraceful, shameful,
immoral **OPPOSITE:** admirable
▷ VERB 5 = **dirty**, stain,
contaminate, pollute, taint,
sully, defile, besmirch **OPPOSITE:**
clean
found = **establish**, start, set
up, begin, create, institute,
organize, constitute
foundation 1 = **basis** 2 *often
plural* = **substructure**,
underpinning, groundwork,
bedrock, base, footing, bottom
3 = **setting up**, institution,
instituting, organization,
settlement, establishment,
initiating, originating
founder¹ = **initiator**, father,
author, architect, creator,
beginner, inventor, originator
founder² 1 = **fail**, collapse,
break down, fall through, be
unsuccessful, come unstuck,

miscarry, misfire 2 = **sink**, go down, be lost, submerge, capsize, go to the bottom

USAGE NOTE
Founder is sometimes wrongly used where *flounder* is meant: *this unexpected turn of events left him floundering* (not *foundering*).

fountain 1 = **font**, spring, reservoir, spout, fount, water feature, well 2 = **jet**, stream, spray, gush 3 = **source**, fount, wellspring, cause, origin, derivation, fountainhead

fowl = **poultry**
• *See panel* **TYPES OF FOWL**

foyer = **entrance hall**, lobby, reception area, vestibule, anteroom, antechamber

fraction = **percentage**, share, section, slice, portion

fracture NOUN 1 = **break**, split, crack 2 = **cleft**, opening, split, crack, rift, rupture, crevice, fissure
▷ VERB 3 = **break**, crack
4 = **split**, separate, divide, rend, fragment, splinter, rupture

fragile 1 = **unstable**, weak, vulnerable, delicate, uncertain, insecure, precarious, flimsy
2 = **fine**, weak, delicate, frail, brittle, flimsy, dainty, easily broken **OPPOSITE:** durable
3 = **unwell**, poorly, weak, delicate, crook (*Austral & NZ informal*), shaky, frail, feeble, sickly

fragment NOUN 1 = **piece**, bit, scrap, particle, portion, shred, speck, sliver
▷ VERB 2 = **break**, shatter, crumble, disintegrate, splinter, come apart, break into pieces, come to pieces **OPPOSITE:** fuse
3 = **break up**, split up

fragrance *or* **fragrancy**
1 = **scent**, smell, perfume, bouquet, aroma, sweet smell, sweet odour, redolence **OPPOSITE:** stink 2 = **perfume**, scent, cologne, eau de toilette, eau de Cologne, toilet water, Cologne water

fragrant = **aromatic**, perfumed, balmy, redolent, sweet-smelling, sweet-scented, odorous **OPPOSITE:** stinking

frail 1 = **feeble**, weak, puny, infirm **OPPOSITE:** strong
2 = **flimsy**, weak, vulnerable, delicate, fragile, insubstantial

frame NOUN 1 = **casing**, framework, structure, shell, construction, skeleton, chassis
2 = **physique**, build, form, body, figure, anatomy, carcass
▷ VERB 3 = **mount**, case, enclose
4 = **surround**, ring, enclose, encompass, envelop, encircle, hem in 5 = **devise**, draft, compose, sketch, put together, draw up, formulate, map out
▷ PHRASES: **frame of mind**
= **mood**, state, attitude, humour, temper, outlook, disposition, mind-set

TYPES OF FOWL

American wigeon or baldpate
Ancona chicken
Andalusian chicken
Australorp chicken
bantam chicken
barnacle goose
Bewick's swan
black swan
blue duck
blue goose
Brahma chicken
brush turkey or scrub turkey
bufflehead
Campine chicken
Canada goose
canvasback
chicken or (Austral slang) chook
Cochin chicken
cock or cockerel
Dorking chicken
duck
eider or eider duck
Faverolle chicken
gadwall
goldeneye
goosander
goose
greylag or greylag goose
Hamburg chicken
harlequin duck
hen
Houdan chicken
Leghorn chicken
magpie goose
mallard
mallee fowl or (Austral) gnow
mandarin duck

marsh hen
megapode
merganser or sawbill
Minorca chicken
moorhen
Muscovy duck or musk duck
mute swan
nene
New Hampshire chicken
Orpington chicken
paradise duck
pintail
Plymouth Rock chicken
pochard
redhead
Rhode Island Red chicken
ruddy duck
scaup or scaup duck
screamer
sea duck
shelduck
shoveler
smew
snow goose
sultan
Sumatra chicken
Sussex chicken
swan
teal
trumpeter swan
turkey
velvet scoter
whistling swan
whooper or whooper swan
wigeon or widgeon
wood duck
Wyandotte chicken

framework 1 = **system**, plan, order, scheme, arrangement, the bare bones 2 = **structure**, body, frame, foundation, shell, skeleton

frank = **candid**, open, direct, straightforward, blunt, sincere, outspoken, honest **OPPOSITE:** secretive

frankly 1 = **honestly**, sincerely, in truth, candidly, to tell (you) the truth, to be frank (with you), to be honest 2 = **openly**, freely, directly, plainly, bluntly, candidly, without reserve

frantic 1 = **frenzied**, wild, furious, distracted, distraught, berserk, at the end of your tether, beside yourself, berko (*Austral slang*) **OPPOSITE:** calm 2 = **hectic**, desperate, frenzied, fraught (*informal*), frenetic

fraternity 1 = **companionship**, fellowship, brotherhood, kinship, camaraderie 2 = **circle**, company, guild 3 (*US & Canad*) = **brotherhood**, club, union, society, league, association

fraud 1 = **deception**, deceit, treachery, swindling, trickery, duplicity, double-dealing, chicanery **OPPOSITE:** honesty 2 = **scam**, deception (*slang*) 3 = **hoax**, trick, con (*informal*), deception, sham, spoof (*informal*), prank, swindle, fastie (*Austral slang*) 4 (*informal*) = **impostor**, fake, hoaxer, pretender, charlatan, fraudster, swindler, phoney or phony (*informal*)

fraudulent = **deceitful**, crooked (*informal*), untrue, sham, treacherous, dishonest, swindling, double-dealing **OPPOSITE:** genuine

fray = **wear thin**, wear, rub, wear out, chafe

freak MODIFIER 1 = **abnormal**, chance, unusual, exceptional, unparalleled ▷ NOUN 2 (*informal*) = **enthusiast**, fan, nut (*slang*), addict, buff (*informal*), fanatic, devotee, fiend (*informal*) 3 = **aberration**, eccentric, anomaly, oddity, monstrosity, malformation 4 (*informal*) = **weirdo** or **weirdie** (*informal*), eccentric, character (*informal*), oddball (*informal*), nonconformist

free ADJECTIVE 1 = **complimentary**, for free (*informal*), for nothing, unpaid, for love, free of charge, on the house, without charge, open or open source (*computing*) 2 = **allowed**, permitted, unrestricted, unimpeded, clear, able 3 = **at liberty**, loose, liberated, at large, on the loose **OPPOSITE:** confined 4 = **independent**, unfettered, footloose 5 = **available**, empty, spare, vacant, unused, unoccupied, untaken 6 *often with* **of** *or* **with** = **generous**, liberal, lavish, unstinting, unsparing **OPPOSITE:** mean

▷ VERB **7** *often with* **of** *or* **from** = **clear**, disengage, cut loose, release, rescue, extricate

8 = **release**, liberate, let out, set free, deliver, loose, untie, unchain **OPPOSITE:** confine

9 = **disentangle**, extricate, disengage, loose, unravel, disconnect, untangle

freedom 1 = **independence**, democracy, sovereignty, self-determination, emancipation, autarchy, rangatiratanga (*NZ*) **2** = **liberty**, release, discharge, emancipation, deliverance **OPPOSITE:** captivity **3** = **licence**, latitude, free rein, opportunity, discretion, carte blanche, blank cheque **OPPOSITE:** restriction

freely 1 = **abundantly**, liberally, lavishly, extravagantly, copiously, unstintingly, amply **2** = **openly**, frankly, plainly, candidly, unreservedly, straightforwardly, without reserve **3** = **willingly**, readily, voluntarily, spontaneously, without prompting, of your own free will, of your own accord

freeway (*US & Austral*) = **motorway** (*Brit*), autobahn (*German*), autoroute (*French*), autostrada (*Italian*)

freeze 1 = **ice over** *or* **up**, harden, stiffen, solidify, become solid **2** = **chill 3** = **fix**, hold, limit, hold up **4** = **suspend**, stop, shelve, curb, cut short, discontinue

freezing (*informal*) **1** = **icy**, biting, bitter, raw, chill, arctic, frosty, glacial **2** = **frozen**, very cold

freight 1 = **transportation**, traffic, delivery, carriage, shipment, haulage, conveyance, transport **2** = **cargo**, goods, load, delivery, burden, shipment, merchandise, consignment

French = **Gallic**

frenzied = **uncontrolled**, wild, crazy, furious, frantic, frenetic, feverish, rabid

frenzy = **fury**, passion, rage, seizure, hysteria, paroxysm, derangement **OPPOSITE:** calm

frequent ADJECTIVE
1 = **common**, repeated, usual, familiar, everyday, persistent, customary, recurrent **OPPOSITE:** infrequent

▷ VERB **2** = **visit**, attend, haunt, be found at, patronize, hang out at (*informal*), visit often, go to regularly **OPPOSITE:** keep away

frequently = **often**, commonly, repeatedly, many times, habitually, not infrequently, much **OPPOSITE:** infrequently

fresh 1 = **additional**, more, new, other, added, further, extra, supplementary **2** = **natural**, unprocessed, unpreserved **OPPOSITE:** preserved **3** = **new**, original, novel, different, recent, modern, up-to-date, unorthodox **OPPOSITE:** old

4 = **invigorating**, clean, pure, crisp, bracing, refreshing, brisk, unpolluted **OPPOSITE:** stale 5 = **cool**, cold, refreshing, brisk, chilly, nippy 6 = **lively**, keen, alert, refreshed, vigorous, energetic, sprightly, spry **OPPOSITE:** weary 7 (*informal*) = **cheeky** (*informal*), impertinent, forward, familiar, audacious, disrespectful, presumptuous, insolent **OPPOSITE:** well-mannered

fret = **worry**, brood, agonize, obsess, lose sleep, upset yourself, distress yourself

friction 1 = **conflict**, hostility, resentment, disagreement, animosity, discord, bad blood, dissension 2 = **resistance**, rubbing, scraping, grating, rasping, chafing, abrasion

friend NOUN 1 = **companion**, pal, mate (*informal*), buddy (*informal*), best friend, close friend, comrade, chum (*informal*), cobber (*Austral & NZ*), cuzzie or cuzzie-bro (*NZ*), E hoa (*NZ old-fashioned informal*) **OPPOSITE:** foe 2 = **supporter**, ally, associate, sponsor, patron, well-wisher
▷ VERB 3 (*Computing*) = **add**, follow **OPPOSITE:** defriend

friendly 1 = **amiable**, welcoming, warm, neighbourly, pally (*informal*), helpful, sympathetic, affectionate 2 = **amicable**, warm, familiar, pleasant, intimate, informal, cordial, congenial **OPPOSITE:** unfriendly

friendship 1 = **attachment**, relationship, bond, link, association, tie, bromance (*informal*) 2 = **friendliness**, affection, harmony, goodwill, intimacy, familiarity, rapport, companionship **OPPOSITE:** unfriendliness

fright 1 = **fear**, shock, alarm, horror, panic, dread, consternation, trepidation **OPPOSITE:** courage 2 = **scare**, start, turn, surprise, shock, jolt, the creeps (*informal*), the willies (*slang*)

frighten = **scare**, shock, alarm, terrify, startle, intimidate, unnerve, petrify **OPPOSITE:** reassure

frightened = **afraid**, alarmed, scared, terrified, shocked, startled, petrified, flustered

frightening = **terrifying**, shocking, alarming, startling, horrifying, menacing, scary (*informal*), fearful

fringe NOUN 1 = **border**, edging, edge, trimming, hem, frill, flounce 2 = **edge**, limits, border, margin, outskirts, perimeter, periphery, borderline
▷ MODIFIER 3 = **unofficial**, alternative, radical, innovative, avant-garde, unconventional, unorthodox

frog
• *See panel* **AMPHIBIANS**

front NOUN 1 = **head**, start, lead, forefront 2 = **exterior**, face, façade, frontage 3 = **foreground**, fore, forefront, nearest part 4 (*Military*) = **front line**, trenches, vanguard, firing line 5 (*informal*) = **disguise**, cover, blind, mask, cover-up, cloak, façade, pretext ▷ ADJECTIVE 6 = **foremost**, at the front **OPPOSITE:** back 7 = **leading**, first, lead, head, foremost, topmost ▷ VERB 8 *often with* **on** *or* **onto** = **face onto**, overlook, look out on, have a view of, look over *or* onto

frontier = **border**, limit, edge, boundary, verge, perimeter, borderline, dividing line

frost = **hoarfrost**, freeze, rime

frown VERB 1 = **scowl**, glare, glower, make a face, look daggers, knit your brows, lour *or* lower ▷ NOUN 2 = **scowl**, glare, glower, dirty look

frozen 1 = **icy**, hard, solid, frosted, arctic, ice-covered, icebound 2 = **chilled**, cold, iced, refrigerated, ice-cold 3 = **ice-cold**, freezing, numb, very cold, frigid, frozen stiff

fruit 1 (*Botany*) = **produce**, crop, yield, harvest 2 *often plural* = **result**, reward, outcome, end result, return, effect, benefit, profit

frustrate = **thwart**, stop, check, block, defeat, disappoint, counter, spoil, crool *or* cruel (*Austral slang*) **OPPOSITE:** further

frustrated = **disappointed**, discouraged, infuriated, exasperated, resentful, embittered, disheartened

frustration 1 = **annoyance**, disappointment, resentment, irritation, grievance, dissatisfaction, exasperation, vexation 2 = **obstruction**, blocking, foiling, spoiling, thwarting, circumvention

fudge = **misrepresent**, hedge, stall, flannel (*Brit informal*), equivocate

fuel = **incitement**, ammunition, provocation, incentive

fugitive = **runaway**, refugee, deserter, escapee

fulfil *or* (*US*) **fulfill** 1 = **carry out**, perform, complete, achieve, accomplish **OPPOSITE:** neglect 2 = **achieve**, realize, satisfy, attain, consummate, bring to fruition 3 = **satisfy**, please, content, cheer, refresh, gratify, make happy 4 = **comply with**, meet, fill, satisfy, observe, obey, conform to, answer

fulfilment *or* (*US*) **fulfillment** = **achievement**, implementation, completion, accomplishment, realization, attainment, consummation

full 1 = **filled**, stocked, brimming, replete, complete, loaded, saturated 2 = **satiated**, having had enough, replete

3 = **extensive**, complete, generous, adequate, ample, abundant, plentiful **OPPOSITE:** incomplete 4 = **comprehensive**, complete, exhaustive, all-embracing 5 = **rounded**, strong, rich, powerful, intense, pungent 6 = **plump**, rounded, voluptuous, shapely, well-rounded, buxom, curvaceous 7 = **voluminous**, large, loose, baggy, billowing, puffy, capacious, loose-fitting **OPPOSITE:** tight 8 (*Music*) = **rich**, strong, deep, loud, distinct, resonant, sonorous, clear **OPPOSITE:** thin

full-scale = **major**, wide-ranging, all-out, sweeping, comprehensive, thorough, in-depth, exhaustive

fully 1 = **completely**, totally, perfectly, entirely, altogether, thoroughly, wholly, utterly 2 = **in all respects**, completely, totally, entirely, altogether, thoroughly, wholly

fumble *often with* **for** *or* **with** = **grope**, flounder, scrabble, feel around

fume VERB 1 = **rage**, seethe, see red (*informal*), storm, rant, smoulder, get hot under the collar (*informal*)
▷ NOUN 2 *often plural* = **smoke**, gas, exhaust, pollution, vapour, smog

fun NOUN 1 = **amusement**, sport, pleasure, entertainment, recreation, enjoyment, merriment, jollity 2 = **enjoyment**, pleasure, mirth **OPPOSITE:** gloom
▷ MODIFIER 3 = **enjoyable**, entertaining, pleasant, amusing, lively, diverting, witty, convivial
▷ PHRASES: **make fun of something** *or* **someone** = **mock**, tease, ridicule, poke fun at, laugh at, mimic, parody, send up (*Brit informal*)

function NOUN 1 = **purpose**, business, job, use, role, responsibility, task, duty 2 = **reception**, party, affair, gathering, bash (*informal*), social occasion, soiree, do (*informal*)
▷ VERB 3 = **work**, run, operate, perform, go 4 *with* **as** = **act**, operate, perform, behave, do duty, have the role of

functional 1 = **practical**, utilitarian, serviceable, hard-wearing, useful 2 = **working**, operative, operational, going, prepared, ready, viable, up and running

fund NOUN 1 = **reserve**, stock, supply, store, collection, pool
▷ VERB 2 = **finance**, back, support, pay for, subsidize, provide money for, put up the money for

fundamental 1 = **central**, key, basic, essential, primary, principal, cardinal **OPPOSITE:** incidental 2 = **basic**, essential,

underlying, profound,
elementary, rudimentary
fundamentally 1 = basically,
at heart, at bottom
2 = essentially, radically,
basically, primarily, profoundly,
intrinsically
fundi (*S African*) **= expert**
funds = money, capital, cash,
finance, means, savings,
resources, assets
funeral = burial, committal,
laying to rest, cremation,
interment, obsequies,
entombment
funny 1 = humorous, amusing,
comical, entertaining, comic,
witty, hilarious, riotous
OPPOSITE: unfunny **2 = comic**,
comical **3 = peculiar**, odd,
strange, unusual, bizarre,
curious, weird, mysterious
4 (*informal*) **= ill**, poorly (*informal*),
sick, odd, crook (*Austral & NZ
informal*), ailing, unhealthy,
unwell, off-colour (*informal*)
furious 1 = angry, raging,
fuming, infuriated, incensed,
enraged, inflamed, very angry,
tooshie (*Austral slang*) **OPPOSITE:**
pleased **2 = violent**, intense,
fierce, savage, turbulent,
vehement, unrestrained
furnish 1 = decorate, fit out,
stock, equip **2 = supply**, give,
offer, provide, present, grant,
hand out
furniture = household goods,
furnishings, fittings, house

fittings, goods, things (*informal*),
possessions, appliances
furore *or* (*US*)**furor**
= commotion, to-do, stir,
disturbance, outcry, uproar,
hullabaloo
further ADVERB 1 = in addition,
moreover, besides, furthermore,
also, to boot, additionally, into
the bargain
▷ **ADJECTIVE 2 = additional**,
more, new, other, extra, fresh,
supplementary
▷ **VERB 3 = promote**, help,
develop, forward, encourage,
advance, work for, assist
OPPOSITE: hinder
furthermore = moreover,
further, in addition, besides, too,
as well, to boot, additionally
furthest = most distant,
extreme, ultimate, remotest,
furthermost, outmost
fury 1 = anger, passion, rage,
madness, frenzy, wrath,
impetuosity **OPPOSITE:**
calmness **2 = violence**, force,
intensity, severity, ferocity,
savagery, vehemence, fierceness
OPPOSITE: peace
fuss NOUN 1 = commotion,
to-do, bother, stir, excitement,
ado, hue and cry, palaver
2 = bother, trouble, struggle,
hassle (*informal*), nuisance,
inconvenience, hindrance
3 = complaint, row, protest,
objection, trouble, argument,
squabble, furore

▷ **VERB 4** = **worry**, flap (*informal*), fret, fidget, take pains, be agitated, get worked up

futile = **useless**, vain, unsuccessful, pointless, worthless, fruitless, ineffectual, unprofitable **OPPOSITE:** useful

future NOUN 1 = **time to come**, hereafter, what lies ahead
2 = **prospect**, expectation, outlook
▷ **ADJECTIVE 3** = **forthcoming**, coming, later, approaching, to come, succeeding, fated, subsequent **OPPOSITE:** past

fuzzy 1 = **frizzy**, fluffy, woolly, downy **2** = **indistinct**, blurred, vague, distorted, unclear, bleary, out of focus, ill-defined
OPPOSITE: distinct

Gg

gadget = **device**, thing, appliance, machine, tool, implement, invention, instrument

gag¹ NOUN 1 = **muzzle**, tie, restraint
▷ **VERB 2** = **suppress**, silence, muffle, curb, stifle, muzzle, quieten **3** = **retch**, heave

gag² (*informal*) = **joke**, crack (*slang*), funny (*informal*), quip, pun, jest, wisecrack (*informal*), witticism

gain VERB 1 = **acquire**, get, receive, pick up, secure, collect, gather, obtain **2** = **profit**, get, land, secure, collect, gather, capture, acquire **OPPOSITE:** lose
3 = **put on**, increase in, gather, build up **4** = **attain**, get, reach, get to, secure, obtain, acquire, arrive at
▷ **NOUN 5** = **rise**, increase, growth, advance, improvement, upsurge, upturn, upswing
6 = **profit**, return, benefit, advantage, yield, dividend
OPPOSITE: loss
▷ **PLURAL NOUN 7** = **profits**,

earnings, revenue, proceeds, winnings, takings

▷ PHRASES: **gain on something** *or* **someone** = **get nearer to**, close in on, approach, catch up with, narrow the gap on

gala = **festival**, fête, celebration, carnival, festivity, pageant, jamboree

gale 1 = **storm**, hurricane, tornado, cyclone, blast, typhoon, tempest, squall **2** (*informal*) = **outburst**, scream, roar, fit, storm, shout, burst, explosion

gall = **annoy**, provoke, irritate, trouble, disturb, madden, exasperate, vex

gallop 1 = **run**, race, career, speed, bolt **2** = **dash**, run, race, career, speed, rush, sprint

gamble NOUN **1** = **risk**, chance, venture, lottery, speculation, uncertainty, leap in the dark **OPPOSITE:** certainty **2** = **bet**, flutter (*informal*), punt (*chiefly Brit*), wager

▷ VERB **3** *often with* **on** = **take a chance**, speculate, stick your neck out (*informal*) **4** = **risk**, chance, hazard, wager **5** = **bet**, play, game, speculate, punt, wager, have a flutter (*informal*)

game NOUN **1** = **pastime**, sport, activity, entertainment, recreation, distraction, amusement, diversion **OPPOSITE:** job **2** = **match**, meeting, event, competition,

tournament, clash, contest, head-to-head **3** = **amusement**, joke, entertainment, diversion **4** = **wild animals** *or* **birds**, prey, quarry **5** = **scheme**, plan, design, trick, plot, tactic, manoeuvre, ploy, fastie (*Austral slang*)

▷ ADJECTIVE **6** = **willing**, prepared, ready, keen, eager, interested, desirous **7** = **brave**, courageous, spirited, daring, persistent, gritty, feisty (*informal, chiefly US & Canad*), intrepid, plucky, (as) game as Ned Kelly (*Austral slang*) **OPPOSITE:** cowardly

gang = **group**, crowd, pack, company, band, bunch, mob

gangster = **hoodlum** (*chiefly US*), crook (*informal*), bandit, hood (*US slang*), robber, mobster (*US slang*), racketeer, ruffian, tsotsi (*S African*)

gap 1 = **opening**, space, hole, break, crack, slot, aperture, cleft **2** = **interval**, pause, interruption, respite, lull, interlude, breathing space, hiatus **3** = **difference**, gulf, contrast, disagreement, discrepancy, inconsistency, disparity, divergence

gape 1 = **stare**, wonder, goggle, gawp (*Brit slang*), gawk **2** = **open**, split, crack, yawn

gaping = **wide**, great, open, broad, vast, yawning, wide open, cavernous

garland NOUN 1 = **wreath**, band, bays, crown, honours, laurels, festoon, chaplet
▷ VERB 2 = **adorn**, crown, deck, festoon, wreathe

garment *often plural* = **clothes**, dress, clothing, gear (*slang*), uniform, outfit, costume, apparel

garnish NOUN 1 = **decoration**, embellishment, adornment, ornamentation, trimming
▷ VERB 2 = **decorate**, adorn, ornament, embellish, trim
OPPOSITE: strip

garrison NOUN 1 = **troops**, group, unit, section, command, armed force, detachment
2 = **fort**, fortress, camp, base, post, station, stronghold, fortification, fortified pa (*NZ*)
▷ VERB 3 = **station**, position, post, install, assign, put on duty

gas 1 = **fumes**, vapour 2 (*US, Canad & NZ*) = **petrol**, gasoline

gasp VERB 1 = **pant**, blow, puff, choke, gulp, catch your breath
▷ NOUN 2 = **pant**, puff, gulp, sharp intake of breath

gate = **barrier**, opening, door, entrance, exit, gateway, portal

gather 1 = **congregate**, assemble, collect, meet, mass, come together, muster, converge **OPPOSITE:** scatter
2 = **assemble**, collect, bring together, muster, call together
OPPOSITE: disperse 3 = **collect**, assemble, accumulate, mass,

muster, garner, amass, stockpile
4 = **pick**, harvest, pluck, reap, garner, glean 5 = **build up**, rise, increase, grow, expand, swell, intensify, heighten
6 = **understand**, believe, hear, learn, assume, conclude, presume, infer 7 = **fold**, tuck, pleat

gathering = **assembly**, group, crowd, meeting, conference, company, congress, mass, hui (*NZ*), runanga (*NZ*)

gauge VERB 1 = **measure**, calculate, evaluate, value, determine, count, weigh, compute 2 = **judge**, estimate, guess, assess, evaluate, rate, appraise, reckon
▷ NOUN 3 = **meter**, dial, measuring instrument

gay ADJECTIVE 1 = **homosexual**, lesbian, queer (*informal offens*), moffie (*S African offens slang*)
2 = **cheerful**, lively, sparkling, merry, upbeat (*informal*), buoyant, cheery, carefree
OPPOSITE: sad 3 = **colourful**, rich, bright, brilliant, vivid, flamboyant, flashy, showy
OPPOSITE: drab
▷ NOUN 4 = **homosexual**, lesbian, auntie *or* aunty (*Austral offens slang*) **OPPOSITE:** heterosexual

> **USAGE NOTE**
> By far the most common and up-to-date use of the word *gay* is in reference to being

homosexual. Other senses of the word have become uncommon and dated.

gaze VERB 1 = **stare**, look, view, watch, regard, gape
▷ NOUN 2 = **stare**, look, fixed look

gazette = **newspaper**, paper, journal, periodical, news-sheet

g'day or **gidday** (Austral & NZ) = **hello**, hi (informal), greetings, how do you do?, good morning, good evening, good afternoon, welcome, kia ora (NZ)

gear NOUN 1 = **mechanism**, works, machinery, cogs, cogwheels, gearwheels
2 = **equipment**, supplies, tackle, tools, instruments, apparatus, paraphernalia, accoutrements
3 = **clothing**, wear, dress, clothes, outfit, costume, garments, togs
▷ VERB 4 with **to** or **towards** = **equip**, fit, adjust, adapt

geek (informal) 1 = **nerd** or **nurd**, anorak (informal), dork (slang)
2 (Computing) = **techie**, nerd or nurd, gamer, programmer, whiz, netizen, alpha geek, genius, e-type, digital native OPPOSITE: newbie, noob or noob

gem 1 = **precious stone**, jewel, stone 2 = **treasure**, prize, jewel, pearl, masterpiece, humdinger (slang), taonga (NZ)

general 1 = **widespread**, accepted, popular, public, common, broad, extensive, universal OPPOSITE: individual

2 = **overall**, complete, total, global, comprehensive, blanket, inclusive, all-embracing OPPOSITE: restricted 3 = **universal**, overall, widespread, collective, across-the-board OPPOSITE: exceptional 4 = **vague**, loose, blanket, sweeping, unclear, approximate, woolly, indefinite OPPOSITE: specific

generally 1 = **usually**, commonly, typically, normally, on the whole, by and large, ordinarily, as a rule OPPOSITE: occasionally 2 = **commonly**, widely, publicly, universally, extensively, popularly, conventionally, customarily OPPOSITE: individually

generate = **produce**, create, make, cause, give rise to, engender OPPOSITE: end

generation 1 = **age group**, peer group 2 = **age**, period, era, time, lifetime, span, epoch

generic = **collective**, general, common, wide, comprehensive, universal, blanket, inclusive OPPOSITE: specific

generosity 1 = **liberality**, charity, bounty, munificence, beneficence, largesse or largess
2 = **magnanimity**, goodness, kindness, selflessness, charity, unselfishness, high-mindedness, nobleness

generous 1 = **liberal**, lavish, charitable,

hospitable, bountiful, open-handed, unstinting, beneficent **OPPOSITE:** mean 2 = **magnanimous**, kind, noble, good, high-minded, unselfish, big-hearted 3 = **plentiful**, lavish, ample, abundant, full, rich, liberal, copious **OPPOSITE:** meagre

genesis = **beginning**, origin, start, birth, creation, formation, inception **OPPOSITE:** end

genius 1 = **brilliance**, ability, talent, capacity, gift, bent, excellence, flair 2 = **master**, expert, mastermind, maestro, virtuoso, whiz (*informal*), hotshot (*informal*), brainbox, fundi (*S African*) **OPPOSITE:** dunce

genre = **type**, group, order, sort, kind, class, style, species

gentle 1 = **kind**, kindly, tender, mild, humane, compassionate, meek, placid **OPPOSITE:** unkind 2 = **slow**, easy, slight, moderate, gradual, imperceptible 3 = **moderate**, light, soft, slight, mild, soothing **OPPOSITE:** violent

gentlemanly = **chivalrous**, refined, polite, civil, courteous, gallant, genteel, well-mannered

genuine 1 = **authentic**, real, actual, true, valid, legitimate, veritable, bona fide, dinkum (*Austral & NZ informal*) **OPPOSITE:** counterfeit 2 = **heartfelt**, sincere, honest, earnest, real, true, frank, unaffected

OPPOSITE: affected 3 = **sincere**, honest, frank, candid, dinkum (*Austral & NZ informal*), guileless **OPPOSITE:** hypocritical

germ 1 = **microbe**, virus, bug (*informal*), bacterium, bacillus, microorganism 2 = **beginning**, root, seed, origin, spark, embryo, rudiment

gesture NOUN 1 = **sign**, action, signal, motion, indication, gesticulation
▷ VERB 2 = **signal**, sign, wave, indicate, motion, beckon, gesticulate

get 1 = **become**, grow, turn, come to be 2 = **persuade**, convince, induce, influence, entice, incite, impel, prevail upon 3 (*informal*) = **annoy**, upset, anger, disturb, trouble, bug (*informal*), irritate, gall 4 = **obtain**, receive, gain, acquire, win, land, net, pick up 5 = **fetch**, bring, collect 6 = **understand**, follow, catch, see, realize, take in, perceive, grasp 7 = **catch**, develop, contract, succumb to, fall victim to, go down with, come down with 8 = **arrest**, catch, grab, capture, seize, take, nab (*informal*), apprehend
▷ PHRASES: get at someone = **criticize**, attack, blame, put down, knock (*informal*), nag, pick on, disparage ▶ get at something 1 = **reach**, touch, grasp, get (a) hold of, stretch to

2 = find out, learn, reach, reveal, discover, acquire, detect, uncover **3 = imply**, mean, suggest, hint, intimate, lead up to, insinuate ▶ **get by = manage**, survive, cope, fare, exist, get along, make do, muddle through ▶ **get something across = communicate**, pass on, transmit, convey, impart, bring home, make known, put over

ghastly = horrible, shocking, terrible, awful, dreadful, horrendous, hideous, frightful **OPPOSITE:** lovely

ghost 1 = spirit, soul, phantom, spectre, spook (*informal*), apparition, wraith, atua (*NZ*), kehua (*NZ*), wairua (*NZ*) **2 = trace**, shadow, suggestion, hint, suspicion, glimmer, semblance

> **RELATED WORD**
> *adjective:* spectral

ghostly = unearthly, phantom, eerie, supernatural, spooky (*informal*), spectral

giant ADJECTIVE 1 = huge, vast, enormous, tremendous, immense, titanic, gigantic, monumental, supersize **OPPOSITE:** tiny
▷ **NOUN 2 = ogre**, monster, titan, colossus

gift 1 = donation, offering, present, contribution, grant, legacy, hand-out, endowment, bonsela (*S African*), koha (*NZ*)

2 = talent, ability, capacity, genius, power, capability, flair, knack

gifted = talented, able, skilled, expert, masterly, brilliant, capable, clever **OPPOSITE:** talentless

gigantic = huge, large, giant, massive, enormous, tremendous, immense, titanic, supersize **OPPOSITE:** tiny

giggle VERB 1 = laugh, chuckle, snigger, chortle, titter, twitter
▷ **NOUN 2 = laugh**, chuckle, snigger, chortle, titter, twitter

girl = female child, lass, lassie (*informal*), miss, maiden (*archaic*), maid (*archaic*)

give 1 = perform, do, carry out, execute **2 = communicate**, announce, transmit, pronounce, utter, issue **3 = produce**, make, cause, occasion, engender **4 = present**, contribute, donate, provide, supply, award, grant, deliver **OPPOSITE:** take **5 = concede**, allow, grant **6 = surrender**, yield, devote, hand over, relinquish, part with
▷ **PHRASES: give in = admit defeat**, yield, concede, collapse, quit, submit, surrender, succumb ▶ **give something away = reveal**, expose, leak, disclose, betray, uncover, let out, divulge ▶ **give something off** *or* **out = emit**, produce, release, discharge, send out, throw out, exude ▶ **give something up**

= **abandon**, stop, quit, cease, renounce, leave off, desist

glad 1 = **happy**, pleased, delighted, contented, gratified, joyful, overjoyed **OPPOSITE:** unhappy 2 (*archaic*) = **pleasing**, happy, cheering, pleasant, cheerful, gratifying

gladly 1 = **happily**, cheerfully, gleefully 2 = **willingly**, freely, happily, readily, cheerfully, with pleasure **OPPOSITE:** reluctantly

glamorous 1 = **attractive**, elegant, dazzling **OPPOSITE:** unglamorous 2 = **exciting**, glittering, prestigious, glossy, bling (*slang*) **OPPOSITE:** unglamorous

glamour 1 = **charm**, appeal, beauty, attraction, fascination, allure, enchantment 2 = **excitement**, magic, thrill, romance, prestige, glitz (*slang*)

glance VERB 1 = **peek**, look, view, glimpse, peep **OPPOSITE:** scrutinize

▷ NOUN 2 = **peek**, look, glimpse, peep, dekko (*slang*) **OPPOSITE:** good look

> **USAGE NOTE**
> Care should be taken not to confuse *glance* and *glimpse*: *he caught a glimpse* (not *glance*) *of her making her way through the crowd; he gave a quick glance* (not *glimpse*) *at his watch*. A *glance* is a deliberate action, while a *glimpse* seems opportunistic.

glare VERB 1 = **scowl**, frown, glower, look daggers, lour or lower 2 = **dazzle**, blaze, flare, flame

▷ NOUN 3 = **scowl**, frown, glower, dirty look, black look, lour or lower 4 = **dazzle**, glow, blaze, flame, brilliance

glaring = **obvious**, gross, outrageous, manifest, blatant, conspicuous, flagrant, unconcealed **OPPOSITE:** inconspicuous

glaze NOUN 1 = **coat**, finish, polish, shine, gloss, varnish, enamel, lacquer

▷ VERB 2 = **coat**, polish, gloss, varnish, enamel, lacquer

gleam VERB 1 = **shine**, flash, glow, sparkle, glitter, shimmer, glint, glimmer

▷ NOUN 2 = **glimmer**, flash, beam, glow, sparkle 3 = **trace**, suggestion, hint, flicker, glimmer, inkling

glide = **slip**, sail, slide

glimpse NOUN 1 = **look**, sighting, sight, glance, peep, peek

▷ VERB 2 = **catch sight of**, spot, sight, view, spy, espy

glitter VERB 1 = **shine**, flash, sparkle, glare, gleam, shimmer, twinkle, glint

▷ NOUN 2 = **glamour**, show, display, splendour, tinsel, pageantry, gaudiness, showiness 3 = **sparkle**, flash, shine, glare, gleam, sheen, shimmer, brightness

global 1 = **worldwide**, world, international, universal
2 = **comprehensive**, general, total, unlimited, exhaustive, all-inclusive **OPPOSITE:** limited

globe = **planet**, world, earth, sphere, orb

gloom 1 = **darkness**, dark, shadow, shade, twilight, dusk, obscurity, blackness **OPPOSITE:** light 2 = **depression**, sorrow, woe, melancholy, unhappiness, despondency, dejection, low spirits **OPPOSITE:** happiness

gloomy 1 = **dark**, dull, dim, dismal, black, grey, murky, dreary **OPPOSITE:** light
2 = **miserable**, sad, pessimistic, melancholy, glum, dejected, dispirited, downcast **OPPOSITE:** happy 3 = **depressing**, bad, dreary, sombre, dispiriting, disheartening, cheerless

glorious 1 = **splendid**, beautiful, brilliant, shining, superb, gorgeous, dazzling **OPPOSITE:** dull 2 = **delightful**, fine, wonderful, excellent, marvellous, gorgeous
3 = **illustrious**, famous, celebrated, distinguished, honoured, magnificent, renowned, eminent **OPPOSITE:** ordinary

glory NOUN 1 = **honour**, praise, fame, distinction, acclaim, prestige, eminence, renown **OPPOSITE:** shame
2 = **splendour**, majesty, greatness, grandeur, nobility, pomp, magnificence, pageantry
▷ VERB 3 = **triumph**, boast, relish, revel, exult, take delight, pride yourself

gloss[1] = **shine**, gleam, sheen, polish, brightness, veneer, lustre, patina

gloss[2] NOUN 1 = **interpretation**, comment, note, explanation, commentary, translation, footnote, elucidation
▷ VERB 2 = **interpret**, explain, comment, translate, annotate, elucidate

glossy = **shiny**, polished, shining, glazed, bright, silky, glassy, lustrous **OPPOSITE:** dull

glow NOUN 1 = **light**, gleam, splendour, glimmer, brilliance, brightness, radiance, luminosity **OPPOSITE:** dullness
▷ VERB 2 = **shine**, burn, gleam, brighten, glimmer, smoulder
3 = **be pink**

glowing = **complimentary**, enthusiastic, rave (*informal*), ecstatic, rhapsodic, laudatory, adulatory **OPPOSITE:** scathing

glue NOUN 1 = **adhesive**, cement, gum, paste
▷ VERB 2 = **stick**, fix, seal, cement, gum, paste, affix

go VERB 1 = **move**, travel, advance, journey, proceed, pass, set off **OPPOSITE:** stay
2 = **leave**, withdraw, depart, move out, slope off, make tracks
3 = **elapse**, pass, flow, fly by,

g

expire, lapse, slip away **4 = be given**, be spent, be awarded, be allotted **5 = function**, work, run, move, operate, perform **OPPOSITE:** fail **6 = match**, blend, correspond, fit, suit, chime, harmonize **7 = serve**, help, tend ▷ **NOUN 8 = attempt**, try, effort, bid, shot (*informal*), crack (*informal*) **9 = turn**, shot (*informal*), stint **10** (*informal*) **= energy**, life, drive, spirit, vitality, vigour, verve, force ▷ **PHRASES: go off 1 = depart**, leave, quit, go away, move out, decamp, slope off, rack off (*Austral & NZ slang*) **2 = explode**, fire, blow up, detonate **3 = take place**, come about **4 = go bad**, turn, spoil, rot, go stale ▶ **go out = be extinguished**, die out, fade out ▶ **go out with = see someone**, court, date (*informal, chiefly US*), woo, go steady (*informal*), be romantically involved with, step out with (*informal*) ▶ **go through something 1 = suffer**, experience, bear, endure, brave, undergo, tolerate, withstand **2 = search**, look through, rummage through, rifle through, hunt through, fossick through (*Austral & NZ*), ferret about in **3 = examine**, check, search, explore, look through

goal = aim, end, target, purpose, object, intention, objective, ambition

god = deity, immortal, divinity, divine being, supreme being, atua (*NZ*)
• *See panel* **GODS AND GODDESSES**

godly = devout, religious, holy, righteous, pious, good, saintly, god-fearing

gogga (*S African*) **= insect**, bug, creepy-crawly (*Brit informal*)

golden 1 = yellow, blonde, blond, flaxen **OPPOSITE:** dark **2 = successful**, glorious, prosperous, rich, flourishing, halcyon **OPPOSITE:** worst **3 = promising**, excellent, favourable, opportune **OPPOSITE:** unfavourable
• *See panel* **SHADES OF YELLOW**

gone 1 = missing, lost, away, vanished, absent, astray **2 = past**, over, ended, finished, elapsed

good ADJECTIVE 1 = excellent, great, fine, pleasing, acceptable, first-class, splendid, satisfactory, booshit (*Austral slang*), exo (*Austral slang*), sik (*Austral slang*), rad (*informal*), phat (*slang*), schmick (*Austral informal*) **OPPOSITE:** bad **2 = proficient**, able, skilled, expert, talented, clever, accomplished, first-class **OPPOSITE:** bad **3 = beneficial**, useful, helpful, favourable, wholesome, advantageous **OPPOSITE:** harmful **4 = honourable**, moral, worthy, ethical, upright, admirable, honest, righteous **OPPOSITE:**

GODS AND GODDESSES
Greek

Aeolus	winds
Aphrodite	love and beauty
Apollo	light, youth, and music
Ares	war
Artemis	hunting and the moon
Asclepius	healing
Athene *or* Pallas Athene	wisdom
Bacchus	wine
Boreas	north wind
Cronos	fertility of the earth
Demeter	agriculture
Dionysus	wine
Eos	dawn
Eris	discord
Eros	love
Fates	destiny
Gaea *or* Gaia	the earth
Graces	charm and beauty
Hades	underworld
Hebe	youth and spring
Hecate	underworld
Helios	sun
Hephaestus	fire and metalworking
Hera	queen of the gods
Hermes	messenger of the gods
Horae *or* the Hours	seasons
Hymen	marriage
Hyperion	sun
Hypnos	sleep
Iris	rainbows
Momus	blame and mockery
Morpheus	sleep and dreams
Nemesis	vengeance
Nike	victory
Pan	woods and shepherds
Poseidon	seas and earthquakes

Rhea	fertility
Selene	moon
Uranus	sky
Zephyrus	west wind
Zeus	king of the gods

Roman

Aesculapius	medicine
Apollo	light, youth, and music
Aurora	dawn
Bacchus	wine
Bellona	war
Bona Dea	fertility
Ceres	agriculture
Cupid	love
Cybele	nature
Diana	hunting and the moon
Faunus	forests
Flora	flowers
Janus	doors and beginnings
Juno	queen of the gods
Jupiter *or* Jove	king of the gods
Lares	household
Luna	moon
Mars	war
Mercury	messenger of the gods
Minerva	wisdom
Neptune	sea
Penates	storeroom
Phoebus	sun
Pluto	underworld
Quirinus	war
Saturn	agriculture and vegetation
Sol	sun
Somnus	sleep
Trivia	crossroads
Venus	love

g

GODS AND GODDESSES *continued*	
Victoria	victory
Vulcan	fire and metalworking

bad 5 = **well-behaved**, polite, orderly, obedient, dutiful, well-mannered **OPPOSITE:** naughty 6 = **kind**, kindly, friendly, obliging, charitable, humane, benevolent, merciful **OPPOSITE:** unkind 7 = **true**, real, genuine, proper, dinkum (*Austral & NZ informal*) 8 = **full**, complete, extensive **OPPOSITE:** scant 9 = **considerable**, large, substantial, sufficient, adequate, ample 10 = **valid**, convincing, compelling, legitimate, authentic, persuasive, bona fide **OPPOSITE:** invalid 11 = **convenient**, timely, fitting, appropriate, suitable **OPPOSITE:** inconvenient ▷ NOUN 12 = **benefit**, interest, gain, advantage, use, profit, welfare, usefulness **OPPOSITE:** disadvantage 13 = **virtue**, goodness, righteousness, worth, merit, excellence, morality, rectitude **OPPOSITE:** evil ▷ PHRASES: **for good** = **permanently**, finally, for ever, once and for all, irrevocably

goodbye NOUN 1 = **farewell**, parting, leave-taking ▷ INTERJECTION 2 = **farewell**, see you, see you later, ciao (*Italian*), cheerio, adieu, ta-ta, au revoir (*French*), haere ra (*NZ*)

goodness 1 = **virtue**, honour, merit, integrity, morality, honesty, righteousness, probity **OPPOSITE:** badness 2 = **excellence**, value, quality, worth, merit, superiority 3 = **nutrition**, benefit, advantage, wholesomeness, salubriousness 4 = **kindness**, charity, humanity, goodwill, mercy, compassion, generosity, friendliness

goods 1 = **merchandise**, stock, products, stuff, commodities, wares 2 = **property**, things, effects, gear, possessions, belongings, trappings, paraphernalia

goodwill = **friendliness**, friendship, benevolence, amity, kindliness

gore[1] = **blood**, slaughter, bloodshed, carnage, butchery

gore[2] = **pierce**, wound, transfix, impale

gorge NOUN 1 = **ravine**, canyon, pass, chasm, cleft, fissure, defile, gulch (*US & Canad*) ▷ VERB 2 = **overeat**, devour, gobble, wolf, gulp, guzzle

3 *usually reflexive* = **stuff**, feed, cram, glut

gorgeous 1 = **magnificent**, beautiful, superb, spectacular, splendid, dazzling, sumptuous **OPPOSITE:** shabby **2** (*informal*) = **beautiful**, lovely, stunning (*informal*), elegant, handsome, exquisite, ravishing, hot (*informal*) **OPPOSITE:** ugly

gospel 1 = **doctrine**, news, teachings, message, revelation, creed, credo, tidings **2** = **truth**, fact, certainty, the last word

gossip NOUN 1 = **idle talk**, scandal, hearsay, tittle-tattle, goss (*informal*), small talk, chitchat, blether, chinwag (*Brit informal*) **2** = **busybody**, chatterbox (*informal*), chatterer, scandalmonger, gossipmonger, tattletale (*chiefly US & Canad*)
▷ **VERB 3** = **chat**, chatter, jaw (*slang*), blether

gourmet = **connoisseur**, foodie (*informal*), bon vivant (*French*), epicure, gastronome

govern 1 = **rule**, lead, control, command, manage, direct, guide, handle **2** = **restrain**, control, check, master, discipline, regulate, curb, tame

government
1 = **administration**, executive, ministry, regime, powers-that-be, e-government *or* egovernment **2** = **rule**, authority, administration, sovereignty, governance, statecraft

governor = **leader**, administrator, ruler, head, director, manager, chief, executive, baas (*S African*)

gown = **dress**, costume, garment, robe, frock, garb, habit

grab = **snatch**, catch, seize, capture, grip, grasp, clutch, snap up

grace NOUN 1 = **elegance**, poise, ease, polish, refinement, fluency, suppleness, gracefulness **OPPOSITE:** ungainliness **2** = **manners**, decency, etiquette, consideration, propriety, tact, decorum **OPPOSITE:** bad manners **3** = **indulgence**, mercy, pardon, reprieve **4** = **benevolence**, favour, goodness, goodwill, generosity, kindness, kindliness **OPPOSITE:** ill will **5** = **prayer**, thanks, blessing, thanksgiving, benediction **6** = **favour**, regard, respect, approval, approbation, good opinion **OPPOSITE:** disfavour
▷ **VERB 7** = **adorn**, enhance, decorate, enrich, set off, ornament, embellish **8** = **honour**, favour, dignify **OPPOSITE:** insult

graceful = **elegant**, easy, pleasing, beautiful **OPPOSITE:** inelegant

gracious = **courteous**, polite, civil, accommodating, kind, friendly, cordial, well-mannered **OPPOSITE:** ungracious

grade VERB 1 = **classify**, rate, order, class, group, sort, range, rank
▷ NOUN 2 = **class** 3 = **mark**, degree 4 = **level**, rank, group, class, stage, category, echelon

gradual = **steady**, slow, regular, gentle, progressive, piecemeal, unhurried **OPPOSITE:** sudden

gradually = **steadily**, slowly, progressively, gently, step by step, little by little, by degrees, unhurriedly

graduate 1 = **mark off**, grade, proportion, regulate, gauge, calibrate, measure out 2 = **classify**, rank, grade, group, order, sort, arrange

graft¹ NOUN 1 = **shoot**, bud, implant, sprout, splice, scion
▷ VERB 2 = **join**, insert, transplant, implant, splice, affix

graft² (*informal*) NOUN 1 = **labour**, work, effort, struggle, sweat, toil, slog, exertion
▷ VERB 2 = **work**, labour, struggle, sweat (*informal*), slave, strive, toil

grain 1 = **seed**, kernel, grist 2 = **cereal**, corn 3 = **bit**, piece, trace, scrap, particle, fragment, speck, morsel 4 = **texture**, pattern, surface, fibre, weave, nap

grand 1 = **impressive**, great, large, magnificent, imposing,

splendid, regal, stately **OPPOSITE:** unimposing 2 = **ambitious**, great, grandiose 3 = **superior**, great, dignified, stately 4 = **excellent**, great (*informal*), fine, wonderful, outstanding, smashing (*informal*), first-class, splendid **OPPOSITE:** bad

grandeur = **splendour**, glory, majesty, nobility, pomp, magnificence, sumptuousness, sublimity

grant NOUN 1 = **award**, allowance, donation, endowment, gift, subsidy, hand-out
▷ VERB 2 = **give**, allow, present, award, permit, assign, allocate, hand out 3 = **accept**, allow, admit, acknowledge, concede

graphic 1 = **vivid**, clear, detailed, striking, explicit, expressive **OPPOSITE:** vague 2 = **pictorial**, visual, diagrammatic **OPPOSITE:** impressionistic

grapple 1 = **deal**, tackle, struggle, take on, confront, get to grips, address yourself to 2 = **struggle**, fight, combat, wrestle, battle, clash, tussle, scuffle

grasp VERB 1 = **grip**, hold, catch, grab, seize, snatch, clutch, clinch 2 = **understand**, realize, take in, get, see, catch on, comprehend, catch *or* get the drift of
▷ NOUN 3 = **grip**, hold, possession, embrace, clutches,

clasp 4 = **understanding**, knowledge, grip, awareness, mastery, comprehension
5 = **reach**, power, control, scope

grasping = **greedy**, acquisitive, rapacious, avaricious, covetous, snoep (S African informal) **OPPOSITE:** generous

grate 1 = **shred**, mince, pulverize 2 = **scrape**, grind, rub, scratch, creak, rasp

grateful = **thankful**, obliged, in (someone's) debt, indebted, appreciative, beholden

grating[1] = **grille**, grid, grate, lattice, trellis, gridiron

grating[2] = **irritating**, harsh, annoying, jarring, unpleasant, raucous, strident, discordant **OPPOSITE:** pleasing

gratitude = **thankfulness**, thanks, recognition, obligation, appreciation, indebtedness, gratefulness **OPPOSITE:** ingratitude

grave[1] = **tomb**, vault, crypt, mausoleum, sepulchre, pit, burying place

grave[2] 1 = **serious**, important, critical, pressing, threatening, dangerous, acute, severe **OPPOSITE:** trifling 2 = **solemn**, sober, sombre, dour, unsmiling **OPPOSITE:** carefree

graveyard = **cemetery**, churchyard, burial ground, charnel house, necropolis

gravity 1 = **seriousness**, importance, significance, urgency, severity, acuteness, weightiness, momentousness **OPPOSITE:** triviality
2 = **solemnity**, seriousness, gravitas **OPPOSITE:** frivolity

graze[1] = **feed**, crop, browse, pasture

graze[2] VERB 1 = **scratch**, skin, scrape, chafe, abrade 2 = **touch**, brush, rub, scrape, shave, skim, glance off
▷ NOUN 3 = **scratch**, scrape, abrasion

greasy = **fatty**, slippery, oily, slimy, oleaginous

great 1 = **large**, big, huge, vast, enormous, immense, gigantic, prodigious, supersize **OPPOSITE:** small 2 = **important**, serious, significant, critical, crucial, momentous **OPPOSITE:** unimportant 3 = **famous**, outstanding, remarkable, prominent, renowned, eminent, illustrious, noteworthy
4 (informal) = **excellent**, fine, wonderful, superb, fantastic (informal), tremendous (informal), marvellous (informal), terrific (informal), booshit (Austral slang), exo (Austral slang), sik (Austral slang), rad (informal), phat (slang), schmick (Austral informal) **OPPOSITE:** poor 5 = **very**, really, extremely, exceedingly

greatly = **very much**, hugely, vastly, considerably, remarkably, enormously, immensely, tremendously

greatness 1 = **grandeur**, glory, majesty, splendour, pomp, magnificence 2 = **fame**, glory, celebrity, distinction, eminence, note, renown, illustriousness

greed or **greediness** 1 = **gluttony**, voracity 2 = **avarice**, longing, desire, hunger, craving, selfishness, acquisitiveness, covetousness **OPPOSITE:** generosity

greedy 1 = **gluttonous**, insatiable, voracious, ravenous, piggish 2 = **avaricious**, grasping, selfish, insatiable, acquisitive, rapacious, materialistic, desirous **OPPOSITE:** generous

green 1 = **verdant**, leafy, grassy 2 = **ecological**, conservationist, environment-friendly, ozone-friendly, non-polluting, green-collar 3 = **inexperienced**, new, raw, naive, immature, gullible, untrained, wet behind the ears (informal) 4 = **jealous**, grudging, resentful, envious, covetous 5 = **lawn**, common, turf, sward
• See panel **SHADES OF GREEN**

greet 1 = **salute**, hail, say hello to, address, accost 2 = **welcome**, meet, receive, karanga (NZ), mihi (NZ), haeremai (NZ) 3 = **receive**, take, respond to, react to

greeting = **welcome**, reception, salute, address, salutation, hongi (NZ), kia ora (NZ)

grey 1 = **dull**, dark, dim, gloomy, drab 2 = **boring**, dull, anonymous, faceless, colourless, nondescript, characterless 3 = **pale**, wan, pallid, ashen 4 = **ambiguous**, uncertain, neutral, unclear, debatable
• See panel **SHADES FROM BLACK TO WHITE**

grief = **sadness**, suffering, regret, distress, misery, sorrow, woe, anguish **OPPOSITE:** joy

SHADES OF GREEN	
almond green	jade
apple green	lime green
aqua	Lincoln green
aquamarine	Nile green
avocado	olive
celadon	pea green
chartreuse	pine green
citron	pistachio
cyan	sea green
eau de nil	teal
emerald green	turquoise

grievance = **complaint**, gripe
(*informal*), axe to grind
grieve 1 = **mourn**, suffer, weep,
lament 2 = **sadden**, hurt, injure,
distress, wound, pain, afflict,
upset **OPPOSITE:** gladden
grim = **terrible**, severe, harsh,
forbidding, formidable, sinister
grind VERB 1 = **crush**, mill,
powder, grate, pulverize, pound,
abrade, granulate 2 = **press**,
push, crush, jam, mash, force
down 3 = **grate**, scrape, gnash
4 = **sharpen**, polish, sand,
smooth, whet
▷ NOUN 5 = **hard work**
(*informal*), labour, sweat
(*informal*), chore, toil, drudgery
grip VERB 1 = **grasp**, hold, catch,
seize, clutch, clasp, take hold of
2 = **engross**, fascinate, absorb,
entrance, hold, compel, rivet,
enthral
▷ NOUN 3 = **clasp**, hold, grasp
4 = **control**, rule, influence,
command, power, possession,
domination, mastery 5 = **hold**,
purchase, friction, traction
6 = **understanding**, sense,
command, awareness,
grasp, appreciation, mastery,
comprehension
gripping = **fascinating**,
exciting, thrilling, entrancing,
compelling, riveting,
enthralling, engrossing
grit NOUN 1 = **gravel**, sand, dust,
pebbles 2 = **courage**, spirit,
resolution, determination, guts

(*informal*), backbone, fortitude,
tenacity
▷ VERB 3 = **clench**, grind, grate,
gnash
gritty 1 = **rough**, sandy, dusty,
rasping, gravelly, granular
2 = **courageous**, dogged,
determined, spirited, brave,
feisty (*informal, chiefly US &
Canad*), resolute, tenacious,
plucky, (as) game as Ned Kelly
(*Austral slang*)
groan VERB 1 = **moan**, cry, sigh
2 (*informal*) = **complain**, object,
moan, grumble, gripe (*informal*),
carp, lament, whine
▷ NOUN 3 = **moan**, cry, sigh,
whine 4 (*informal*) = **complaint**,
protest, objection, grumble,
grouse, gripe (*informal*)
groom NOUN 1 = **stableman**,
stableboy, hostler *or* ostler
(*archaic*) 2 = **newly-wed**,
husband, bridegroom, marriage
partner
▷ VERB 3 = **brush**, clean, tend,
rub down, curry 4 = **smarten
up**, clean, tidy, preen, spruce up,
primp 5 = **train**, prime, prepare,
coach, ready, educate, drill,
nurture
groove = **indentation**, cut,
hollow, channel, trench, flute,
trough, furrow
grope = **feel**, search, fumble,
flounder, fish, scrabble, cast
about, fossick (*Austral & NZ*)
gross ADJECTIVE 1 = **flagrant**,
blatant, rank, sheer, utter,

grievous, heinous, unmitigated **OPPOSITE:** qualified 2 = **vulgar**, offensive, crude, obscene, coarse, indelicate **OPPOSITE:** decent 3 = **fat**, obese, overweight, hulking, corpulent **OPPOSITE:** slim 4 = **total**, whole, entire, aggregate, before tax, before deductions **OPPOSITE:** net
▷ **VERB** 5 = **earn**, make, take, bring in, rake in (*informal*)

grotesque 1 = **unnatural**, bizarre, strange, fantastic, distorted, deformed, outlandish, freakish **OPPOSITE:** natural 2 = **absurd**, preposterous **OPPOSITE:** natural

ground NOUN 1 = **earth**, land, dry land, terra firma 2 = **arena**, pitch, stadium, park, field, enclosure
▷ **PLURAL NOUN** 3 = **estate**, land, fields, gardens, territory 4 = **reason**, cause, basis, occasion, foundation, excuse, motive, justification 5 = **dregs**, lees, deposit, sediment
▷ **VERB** 6 = **base**, found, establish, set, settle, fix 7 = **instruct**, train, teach, initiate, tutor, acquaint with, familiarize with

group NOUN 1 = **crowd**, party, band, pack, gang, bunch
▷ **VERB** 2 = **arrange**, order, sort, class, classify, marshal, bracket

grove = **wood**, plantation, covert, thicket, copse, coppice, spinney

grow 1 = **develop**, get bigger **OPPOSITE:** shrink 2 = **get bigger**, spread, swell, stretch, expand, enlarge, multiply 3 = **cultivate**, produce, raise, farm, breed, nurture, propagate 4 = **become**, get, turn, come to be 5 = **originate**, spring, arise, stem, issue 6 = **improve**, advance, progress, succeed, thrive, flourish, prosper

grown-up NOUN 1 = **adult**, man, woman
▷ **ADJECTIVE** 2 = **mature**, adult, of age, fully-grown

growth 1 = **increase**, development, expansion, proliferation, enlargement, multiplication **OPPOSITE:** decline 2 = **progress**, success, improvement, expansion, advance, prosperity **OPPOSITE:** failure 3 (*Medical*) = **tumour**, cancer, swelling, lump, carcinoma (*pathology*), sarcoma (*medical*)

grudge NOUN 1 = **resentment**, bitterness, grievance, dislike, animosity, antipathy, enmity, rancour **OPPOSITE:** goodwill
▷ **VERB** 2 = **resent**, mind, envy, covet, begrudge **OPPOSITE:** welcome

gruelling = **exhausting**, demanding, tiring, taxing, severe, punishing, strenuous, arduous **OPPOSITE:** easy

gruesome = **horrific**, shocking, terrible, horrible, grim, ghastly, grisly, macabre **OPPOSITE:** pleasant

grumble VERB 1 = **complain**, moan, gripe (*informal*), whinge (*informal*), carp, whine, grouse, bleat 2 = **rumble**, growl, gurgle
▷ NOUN 3 = **complaint**, protest, objection, moan, grievance, grouse, gripe (*informal*), grouch (*informal*) 4 = **rumble**, growl, gurgle

guarantee VERB 1 = **ensure**, secure, assure, warrant, make certain 2 = **promise**, pledge, undertake
▷ NOUN 3 = **promise**, pledge, assurance, certainty, word of honour 4 = **warranty**, contract, bond

guard VERB 1 = **protect**, defend, secure, mind, preserve, shield, safeguard, watch over
▷ NOUN 2 = **sentry**, warder, warden, custodian, watch, lookout, watchman, sentinel 3 = **shield**, security, defence, screen, protection, safeguard, buffer

guarded = **cautious**, reserved, careful, suspicious, wary, prudent, reticent, circumspect

guardian = **keeper**, champion, defender, guard, warden, curator, protector, custodian

guerrilla = **freedom fighter**, partisan, underground fighter

guess VERB 1 = **estimate**, predict, work out, speculate, conjecture, postulate,

hypothesize **OPPOSITE:** know 2 = **suppose**, think, believe, suspect, judge, imagine, reckon, fancy
▷ NOUN 3 = **estimate**, speculation, judgment, hypothesis, conjecture, shot in the dark **OPPOSITE:** certainty 4 = **supposition**, idea, theory, hypothesis

guest = **visitor**, company, caller, manu(w)hiri (*NZ*)

guidance = **advice**, direction, leadership, instruction, help, management, teaching, counselling

guide NOUN 1 = **handbook**, manual, guidebook, instructions, catalogue 2 = **directory**, street map 3 = **escort**, leader, usher 4 = **pointer**, sign, landmark, marker, beacon, signpost, guiding light, lodestar 5 = **model**, example, standard, ideal, inspiration, paradigm
▷ VERB 6 = **lead**, direct, escort, conduct, accompany, shepherd, usher, show the way 7 = **steer**, control, manage, direct, handle, command, manoeuvre 8 = **supervise**, train, teach, influence, advise, counsel, instruct, oversee

guild = **society**, union, league, association, company, club, order, organization

guilt 1 = **shame**, regret, remorse, contrition, guilty conscience,

self-reproach **OPPOSITE:**
pride 2 = **culpability**, blame,
responsibility, misconduct,
wickedness, sinfulness,
guiltiness **OPPOSITE:** innocence

guilty 1 = **ashamed**, sorry,
rueful, sheepish, contrite,
remorseful, regretful,
shamefaced **OPPOSITE:** proud
2 = **culpable**, responsible,
to blame, offending, erring,
at fault, reprehensible,
blameworthy **OPPOSITE:**
innocent

guise 1 = **form**, appearance,
shape, aspect, mode, semblance
2 = **pretence**, disguise, aspect,
semblance

gulch (*US & Canad*) = **ravine**,
canyon, defile, gorge, gully, pass

gulf 1 = **bay**, bight, sea inlet
2 = **chasm**, opening, split, gap,
separation, void, rift, abyss

gum NOUN 1 = **glue**, adhesive,
resin, cement, paste
▷ VERB 2 = **stick**, glue, affix,
cement, paste

gun = **firearm**, shooter (*slang*),
piece (*slang*), handgun

gunman = **armed man**,
gunslinger (*US slang*)

guru 1 = **authority**, expert,
leader, master, pundit, Svengali,
fundi (*S African*) 2 = **teacher**,
mentor, sage, master, tutor

gush VERB 1 = **flow**, run, rush,
flood, pour, stream, cascade,
spurt 2 = **enthuse**, rave, spout,
overstate, effuse

▷ NOUN 3 = **stream**, flow, rush,
flood, jet, cascade, torrent, spurt

gut NOUN 1 = **paunch** (*informal*),
belly, spare tyre (*Brit slang*),
potbelly, puku (*NZ*)
▷ VERB 2 = **disembowel**, clean
3 = **ravage**, empty, clean out,
despoil
▷ ADJECTIVE 4 = **instinctive**,
natural, basic, spontaneous,
intuitive, involuntary, heartfelt,
unthinking

guts 1 = **intestines**, insides
(*informal*), stomach, belly,
bowels, innards (*informal*),
entrails 2 (*informal*) = **courage**,
spirit, nerve, daring, pluck,
backbone, bottle (*slang*),
audacity

gutter = **drain**, channel, ditch,
trench, trough, conduit, sluice

guy (*informal*) = **man**, person,
fellow, lad, bloke (*Brit informal*),
chap

Gypsy *or* **Gipsy** = **traveller**,
roamer, wanderer, Bohemian,
rover, rambler, nomad, Romany

Hh

habit 1 = **mannerism**, custom, way, practice, characteristic, tendency, quirk, propensity 2 = **addiction**, dependence, compulsion

hack¹ 1 *sometimes with* **away** = **cut**, chop, slash, mutilate, mangle, mangulate (*Austral slang*), hew, lacerate 2 (~*a computer, phone, etc*) = **manipulate**, exploit, attack, hijack, access, spoof, bluejack, pharm, bluesnarf, phish, phreak, spear-phish

hack² = **reporter**, writer, correspondent, journalist, scribbler, contributor, literary hack

hacker = **fraudster**, black hat, white hat, cybercriminal, script kiddie, hacktivist (*informal*), intruder

haemorrhage NOUN 1 = **drain**, outpouring, rapid loss ▷ VERB 2 = **drain**, bleed, flow rapidly

hail¹ NOUN 1 = **hailstones**, sleet, hailstorm, frozen rain 2 = **shower**, rain, storm, battery, volley, barrage, bombardment, downpour ▷ VERB 3 = **rain**, shower, pelt 4 = **batter**, rain, bombard, pelt, rain down on, beat down upon

hail² 1 = **acclaim**, honour, acknowledge, cheer, applaud **OPPOSITE:** condemn 2 = **salute**, greet, address, welcome, say hello to, halloo **OPPOSITE:** snub 3 = **flag down**, summon, signal to, wave down ▷ PHRASES: **hail from somewhere** = **come from**, be born in, originate in, be a native of, have your roots in

hair = **locks**, mane, tresses, shock, mop, head of hair

hairdresser = **stylist**, barber, coiffeur *or* coiffeuse

hairy 1 = **shaggy**, woolly, furry, stubbly, bushy, unshaven, hirsute 2 (*slang*) = **dangerous**, risky, unpredictable, hazardous, perilous

hale (*Old-fashioned*) = **healthy**, well, strong, sound, fit, flourishing, robust, vigorous

half NOUN 1 = **fifty per cent**, equal part ▷ ADJECTIVE 2 = **partial**, limited, moderate, halved ▷ ADVERB 3 = **partially**, partly, in part

> RELATED WORDS
> *prefixes*: bi-, demi-, hemi-, semi-

halfway ADVERB 1 = **midway**, to *or* in the middle

▷ **ADJECTIVE** 2 = **midway**, middle, mid, central, intermediate, equidistant

hall 1 = **passage**, lobby, corridor, hallway, foyer, entry, passageway, entrance hall 2 = **meeting place**, chamber, auditorium, concert hall, assembly room

hallmark 1 = **trademark**, sure sign, telltale sign 2 (*Brit*) = **mark**, sign, device, stamp, seal, symbol

halt **VERB** 1 = **stop**, break off, stand still, wait, rest **OPPOSITE:** continue 2 = **come to an end**, stop, cease 3 = **hold back**, end, check, block, curb, terminate, cut short, bring to an end **OPPOSITE:** aid
▷ **NOUN** 4 = **stop**, end, close, pause, standstill, stoppage **OPPOSITE:** continuation

halting = **faltering**, stumbling, awkward, hesitant, laboured, stammering, stuttering

halve 1 = **cut in half**, reduce by fifty per cent, decrease by fifty per cent, lessen by fifty per cent 2 = **split in two**, cut in half, bisect, divide in two, share equally, divide equally

hammer 1 = **hit**, drive, knock, beat, strike, tap, bang 2 (*informal*) = **defeat**, beat, thrash, trounce, run rings around (*informal*), wipe the floor with (*informal*), drub

hamper = **hinder**, handicap, prevent, restrict, frustrate, hamstring, interfere with, obstruct **OPPOSITE:** help

hand **NOUN** 1 = **palm**, fist, paw (*informal*), mitt (*slang*) 2 = **worker**, employee, labourer, workman, operative, craftsman, artisan, hired man 3 = **round of applause**, clap, ovation, big hand 4 = **writing**, script, handwriting, calligraphy
▷ **VERB** 5 = **give**, pass, hand over, present to, deliver

handbook = **guidebook**, guide, manual, instruction book

handcuff **VERB** 1 = **shackle**, secure, restrain, fetter, manacle
▷ **PLURAL NOUN** 2 = **shackles**, cuffs (*informal*), fetters, manacles

handful = **few**, sprinkling, small amount, smattering, small number **OPPOSITE:** a lot

handicap **NOUN** 1 (*old-fashioned or offens*) = **disability**, condition, disorder 2 = **disadvantage**, barrier, restriction, obstacle, limitation, drawback, stumbling block, impediment **OPPOSITE:** advantage 3 = **advantage**, head start
▷ **VERB** 4 = **hinder**, limit, restrict, burden, hamstring, hamper, hold back, impede **OPPOSITE:** help

handle **NOUN** 1 = **grip**, hilt, haft, stock
▷ **VERB** 2 = **manage**, deal with, tackle, cope with 3 = **control**, manage, direct,

h

guide, manipulate, manoeuvre
4 = hold, feel, touch, pick up,
finger, grasp

handsome 1 = good-looking,
attractive, gorgeous, elegant,
personable, dishy (*informal*,
chiefly Brit), comely, hot
(*informal*), fit (*Brit informal*)
OPPOSITE: ugly **2 = generous**,
large, princely, liberal,
considerable, lavish, ample,
abundant **OPPOSITE:** mean

handy 1 = useful, practical,
helpful, neat, convenient,
easy to use, manageable,
user-friendly **OPPOSITE:** useless
2 = convenient, close, available,
nearby, accessible, on hand, at
hand, within reach **OPPOSITE:**
inconvenient **3 = skilful**, skilled,
expert, adept, deft, proficient,
adroit, dexterous **OPPOSITE:**
unskilled

hang 1 = dangle, swing, suspend
2 = lower, suspend, dangle
3 = lean 4 = execute, lynch,
string up (*informal*)
▷ **PHRASES: get the hang
of something = grasp**,
understand, learn, master,
comprehend, catch on to,
acquire the technique of ▶ **hang
back = be reluctant**, hesitate,
hold back, recoil, demur

hangover = aftereffects,
morning after (*informal*)

hang-up (*informal*)
= preoccupation, thing
(*informal*), problem, block,

difficulty, obsession, mania,
inhibition

hank = coil, roll, length, bunch,
piece, loop, clump, skein

happen 1 = occur, take place,
come about, result, develop,
transpire (*informal*), come to pass
2 = chance, turn out (*informal*)

happening = event, incident,
experience, affair, proceeding,
episode, occurrence

happily 1 = luckily, fortunately,
providentially, opportunely
2 = joyfully, cheerfully, gleefully,
blithely, merrily, gaily, joyously
3 = willingly, freely, gladly, with
pleasure

happiness = pleasure, delight,
joy, satisfaction, ecstasy, bliss,
contentment, elation **OPPOSITE:**
unhappiness

happy 1 = pleased, delighted,
content, thrilled, glad, cheerful,
merry, ecstatic, stoked (*Austral
& NZ informal*) **OPPOSITE:**
sad **2 = contented**, joyful,
blissful **3 = fortunate**, lucky,
timely, favourable, auspicious,
propitious, advantageous
OPPOSITE: unfortunate

harass = annoy, trouble, bother,
harry, plague, hound, hassle
(*informal*), persecute

harassed = hassled (*informal*),
worried, troubled, strained,
under pressure, tormented,
distraught, vexed

harassment = hassle (*informal*),
trouble, bother, irritation,

persecution, nuisance, annoyance, pestering

harbour NOUN 1 = **port**, haven, dock, mooring, marina, pier, wharf, anchorage
▷ VERB 2 = **hold**, bear, maintain, nurse, retain, foster, entertain, nurture 3 = **shelter**, protect, hide, shield, provide refuge, give asylum to

hard ADJECTIVE 1 = **tough**, strong, firm, solid, stiff, rigid, resistant, compressed **OPPOSITE:** soft 2 = **difficult**, involved, complicated, puzzling, intricate, perplexing, impenetrable, thorny **OPPOSITE:** easy 3 = **exhausting**, tough, exacting, rigorous, gruelling, strenuous, arduous, laborious **OPPOSITE:** easy 4 = **harsh**, cold, cruel, stern, callous, unkind, unsympathetic, pitiless **OPPOSITE:** kind 5 = **grim**, painful, distressing, harsh, unpleasant, intolerable, grievous, disagreeable
▷ ADVERB 6 = **strenuously**, steadily, persistently, doggedly, diligently, energetically, industriously, untiringly, flatstick (S African slang) 7 = **intently**, closely, carefully, sharply, keenly 8 = **forcefully**, strongly, heavily, sharply, severely, fiercely, vigorously, intensely **OPPOSITE:** softly

harden 1 = **solidify**, set, freeze, cake, bake, clot, thicken, stiffen

2 = **accustom**, season, toughen, train, inure, habituate

hardened 1 = **habitual**, chronic, shameless, inveterate, incorrigible **OPPOSITE:** occasional 2 = **seasoned**, experienced, accustomed, toughened, inured, habituated **OPPOSITE:** naive

hardly = **barely**, only just, scarcely, just, with difficulty, with effort **OPPOSITE:** completely

hardship = **suffering**, need, difficulty, misfortune, adversity, tribulation, privation **OPPOSITE:** ease

hardy = **strong**, tough, robust, sound, rugged, sturdy, stout **OPPOSITE:** frail

hare

> **RELATED WORDS**
> *adjective:* leporine
> *male:* buck
> *female:* doe
> *young:* leveret
> *home:* down, husk

harm VERB 1 = **injure**, hurt, wound, abuse, ill-treat, maltreat **OPPOSITE:** heal 2 = **damage**, hurt, ruin, spoil
▷ NOUN 3 = **injury**, suffering, damage, ill, hurt, distress 4 = **damage**, loss, ill, hurt, misfortune, mischief **OPPOSITE:** good

harmful = **damaging**, dangerous, negative, destructive, hazardous,

unhealthy, detrimental, hurtful
OPPOSITE: harmless
harmless 1 = **safe**, benign,
wholesome, innocuous,
nontoxic **OPPOSITE:** dangerous
2 = **inoffensive**, innocent,
innocuous, gentle, tame,
unobjectionable
harmony 1 = **accord**, peace,
agreement, friendship,
sympathy, cooperation, rapport,
compatibility **OPPOSITE:**
conflict 2 = **tune**, melody,
unison, tunefulness, euphony
OPPOSITE: discord
harness VERB 1 = **exploit**,
control, channel, employ, utilize,
mobilize
▷ NOUN 2 = **equipment**, tackle,
gear, tack
harrowing = **distressing**,
disturbing, painful, terrifying,
traumatic, tormenting,
agonizing, nerve-racking
harry = **pester**, bother, plague,
harass, hassle (informal), badger,
chivvy
harsh 1 = **severe**, hard, tough,
stark, austere, inhospitable,
bare-bones 2 = **bleak**, freezing,
severe, icy 3 = **cruel**, savage,
ruthless, barbarous, pitiless
4 = **hard**, severe, cruel, stern,
pitiless **OPPOSITE:** kind
5 = **drastic**, punitive, Draconian
6 = **raucous**, rough, grating,
strident, rasping, discordant,
guttural, dissonant **OPPOSITE:**
soft

harshly = **severely**, roughly,
cruelly, strictly, sternly, brutally
harvest NOUN 1 = **harvesting**,
picking, gathering, collecting,
reaping, harvest-time 2 = **crop**,
yield, year's growth, produce
▷ VERB 3 = **gather**, pick, collect,
bring in, pluck, reap
hassle (informal) NOUN
1 = **trouble**, problem, difficulty,
bother, grief (informal), uphill (S
African), inconvenience
▷ VERB 2 = **bother**, bug
(informal), annoy, hound, harass,
badger, pester
hasten = **rush**, race, fly, speed,
dash, hurry (up), scurry, make
haste **OPPOSITE:** dawdle
hastily 1 = **quickly**,
rapidly, promptly, speedily
2 = **hurriedly**, rashly,
precipitately, impetuously
hatch 1 = **incubate**, breed,
sit on, brood, bring forth
2 = **devise**, design, invent,
put together, conceive, brew,
formulate, contrive
hate VERB 1 = **detest**,
loathe, despise, dislike,
abhor, recoil from, not be
able to bear **OPPOSITE:** love
2 = **dislike**, detest, shrink
from, recoil from, not be able
to bear **OPPOSITE:** like 3 = **be
unwilling**, regret, be reluctant,
hesitate, be sorry, be loath, feel
disinclined
▷ NOUN 4 = **dislike**, hostility,
hatred, loathing, animosity,

aversion, antipathy, enmity **OPPOSITE:** love

hatred = **hate**, dislike, animosity, aversion, revulsion, antipathy, enmity, repugnance **OPPOSITE:** love

haul VERB 1 = **drag**, draw, pull, heave
▷ NOUN 2 = **yield**, gain, spoils, catch, harvest, loot, takings, booty

haunt VERB 1 = **plague**, trouble, obsess, torment, possess, stay with, recur, prey on
▷ NOUN 2 = **meeting place**, hangout (*informal*), rendezvous, stamping ground

haunted 1 = **possessed**, ghostly, cursed, eerie, spooky (*informal*), jinxed 2 = **preoccupied**, worried, troubled, plagued, obsessed, tormented

haunting = **evocative**, poignant, unforgettable

have 1 = **own**, keep, possess, hold, retain, boast, be the owner of 2 = **get**, obtain, take, receive, accept, gain, secure, acquire 3 = **suffer**, experience, undergo, sustain, endure, be suffering from 4 = **give birth to**, bear, deliver, bring forth, beget 5 = **experience**, go through, undergo, meet with, come across, run into, be faced with
▷ PHRASES: **have someone on** = **tease**, kid (*informal*), wind up (*Brit slang*), trick, deceive, take the mickey, pull someone's leg

▶ **have something on** = **wear**, be wearing, be dressed in, be clothed in, be attired in ▶ **have to** = **must**, should, be forced, ought, be obliged, be bound, have got to, be compelled

haven = **sanctuary**, shelter, retreat, asylum, refuge, oasis, sanctum

havoc 1 = **devastation**, damage, destruction, ruin 2 (*informal*) = **disorder**, confusion, chaos, disruption, mayhem, shambles

hazard NOUN 1 = **danger**, risk, threat, problem, menace, peril, jeopardy, pitfall
▷ VERB 2 = **jeopardize**, risk, endanger, threaten, expose, imperil, put in jeopardy
▷ PHRASES: **hazard a guess** = **guess**, conjecture, presume, take a guess

hazardous = **dangerous**, risky, difficult, insecure, unsafe, precarious, perilous, dicey (*informal, chiefly Brit*) **OPPOSITE:** safe

haze = **mist**, cloud, fog, obscurity, vapour

head NOUN 1 = **skull**, crown, pate, nut (*slang*), loaf (*slang*) 2 = **mind**, reasoning, understanding, thought, sense, brain, brains (*informal*), intelligence 3 = **top**, crown, summit, peak, crest, pinnacle 4 (*informal*) = **head teacher**, principal 5 = **leader**, president, director, manager, chief,

boss (*informal*), captain, master, sherang (*Austral & NZ*)
▷ **ADJECTIVE 6 = chief**, main, leading, first, prime, premier, supreme, principal
▷ **VERB 7 = lead**, precede, be the leader of, be *or* go first, be *or* go at the front of, lead the way
8 = top, lead, crown, cap **9 = be in charge of**, run, manage, lead, control, direct, guide, command
▷ **PHRASES: go to your head 1 = intoxicate 2 = make someone conceited**, puff someone up, make someone full of themselves ▶ **head over heels = completely**, thoroughly, utterly, intensely, wholeheartedly, uncontrollably

headache 1 = migraine, head (*informal*), neuralgia **2** (*informal*) **= problem**, worry, trouble, bother, nuisance, inconvenience, bane, vexation

heading = title, name, caption, headline, rubric

heady 1 = exciting, thrilling, stimulating, exhilarating, intoxicating **2 = intoxicating**, strong, potent, inebriating

heal 1 *sometimes with* **up = mend**, get better, get well, regenerate, show improvement **2 = cure**, restore, mend, make better, remedy, make good, make well **OPPOSITE:** injure

health 1 = condition, state, shape, constitution, fettle **2 = wellbeing**, strength, fitness, vigour, good condition, soundness, robustness, healthiness **OPPOSITE:** illness

healthy 1 = well, fit, strong, active, robust, in good shape (*informal*), in the pink, in fine fettle **OPPOSITE:** ill **2 = wholesome**, beneficial, nourishing, nutritious, salutary, hygienic, salubrious **OPPOSITE:** unwholesome **3 = invigorating**, beneficial, salutary, salubrious

heap NOUN 1 = pile, lot, collection, mass, stack, mound, accumulation, hoard **2** (*informal*) *often plural* **= a lot**, lots, plenty, masses, load(s) (*informal*), great deal, tons (*informal*), stack(s)
▷ **VERB 3** *sometimes with* **up = pile**, collect, gather, stack, accumulate, amass, hoard
▷ **PHRASES: heap something on someone = load with**, confer on, assign to, bestow on, shower upon

hear 1 = overhear, catch, detect **2 = listen to 3** (*Law*) **= try**, judge, examine, investigate **4 = learn**, discover, find out, pick up, gather, ascertain, get wind of (*informal*)

hearing = inquiry, trial, investigation, industrial tribunal

heart 1 = emotions, feelings, love, affection **2 = nature**, character, soul, constitution, essence, temperament, disposition **3 = root**, core,

centre, nucleus, hub, gist, nitty-gritty (*informal*), nub
4 = **courage**, will, spirit, purpose, bottle (*Brit informal*), resolution, resolve, stomach
▷ **PHRASES: by heart** = **from** *or* **by memory**, verbatim, word for word, pat, word-perfect, by rote, off by heart, off pat

| **RELATED WORDS**
adjectives: cardiac, cardiothoracic

heat VERB **1** *sometimes with up* = **warm (up)**, cook, boil, roast, reheat, make hot **OPPOSITE:** chill
▷ NOUN **2** = **warmth**, hotness, temperature **OPPOSITE:** cold
3 = **hot weather**, warmth, closeness, high temperature, heatwave, warm weather, hot climate, mugginess
4 = **passion**, excitement, intensity, fury, fervour, vehemence **OPPOSITE:** calmness

heated 1 = **impassioned**, intense, spirited, excited, angry, furious, fierce, lively **OPPOSITE:** calm **2** = **wound up**, worked up, keyed up, het up (*informal*)

heaven 1 = **paradise**, next world, hereafter, nirvana (*Buddhism*, *Hinduism*), bliss, Zion (*Christianity*), life everlasting, Elysium *or* Elysian fields (*Greek myth*) **2** (*informal*) = **happiness**, paradise, ecstasy, bliss, utopia, rapture, seventh heaven
▷ **PHRASES: the heavens**

(*Old-fashioned*) = **sky**, ether, firmament

heavenly 1 = **celestial**, holy, divine, blessed, immortal, angelic **OPPOSITE:** earthly
2 (*informal*) = **wonderful**, lovely, delightful, beautiful, divine (*informal*), exquisite, sublime, blissful **OPPOSITE:** awful

heavily 1 = **excessively**, to excess, very much, a great deal, considerably, copiously, without restraint, immoderately
2 = **densely**, closely, thickly, compactly **3** = **hard**, clumsily, awkwardly, weightily

heavy 1 = **weighty**, large, massive, hefty, bulky, ponderous **OPPOSITE:** light **2** = **intensive**, severe, serious, concentrated, fierce, excessive, relentless
3 = **considerable**, large, huge, substantial, abundant, copious, profuse **OPPOSITE:** slight

hectic = **frantic**, chaotic, heated, animated, turbulent, frenetic, feverish **OPPOSITE:** peaceful

hedge = **prevaricate**, evade, sidestep, duck, dodge, flannel (*Brit informal*), equivocate, temporize
▷ **PHRASES: hedge against something** = **protect**, insure, guard, safeguard, shield, cover

heed VERB **1** = **pay attention to**, listen to, take notice of, follow, consider, note, observe, obey **OPPOSITE:** ignore
▷ NOUN **2** = **thought**, care,

mind, attention, regard, respect, notice **OPPOSITE:** disregard

heel (*slang*) = **swine**, cad (*Brit informal*), bounder (*Brit old-fashioned slang*), rotter (*slang, chiefly Brit*), wrong 'un (*Austral slang*)

hefty (*informal*) = **big**, strong, massive, strapping, robust, muscular, burly, hulking **OPPOSITE:** small

height 1 = **tallness**, stature, highness, loftiness **OPPOSITE:** shortness 2 = **altitude**, measurement, highness, elevation, tallness **OPPOSITE:** depth 3 = **peak**, top, crown, summit, crest, pinnacle, apex **OPPOSITE:** valley 4 = **culmination**, climax, zenith, limit, maximum, ultimate **OPPOSITE:** low point

heighten = **intensify**, increase, add to, improve, strengthen, enhance, sharpen, magnify

heir = **successor**, beneficiary, inheritor, heiress (*fem.*), next in line

hell 1 = **the underworld**, the abyss, Hades (*Greek myth*), hellfire, the inferno, fire and brimstone, the nether world, the bad fire (*informal*) 2 (*informal*) = **torment**, suffering, agony, nightmare, misery, ordeal, anguish, wretchedness

hello = **hi** (*informal*), greetings, how do you do?, good morning, good evening, good afternoon,

welcome, kia ora (*NZ*), gidday or g'day (*Austral & NZ*)

helm (*Nautical*) = **tiller**, wheel, rudder

help VERB 1 *sometimes with* **out** = **aid**, support, assist, cooperate with, abet, lend a hand, succour **OPPOSITE:** hinder 2 = **improve**, ease, relieve, facilitate, alleviate, mitigate, ameliorate **OPPOSITE:** make worse 3 = **assist**, aid, support 4 = **resist**, refrain from, avoid, prevent, keep from ▷ NOUN 5 = **assistance**, aid, support, advice, guidance, cooperation, helping hand **OPPOSITE:** hindrance

helper = **assistant**, ally, supporter, mate, second, aide, attendant, collaborator

helpful 1 = **cooperative**, accommodating, kind, friendly, neighbourly, sympathetic, supportive, considerate 2 = **useful**, practical, profitable, constructive 3 = **beneficial**, advantageous

helping = **portion**, serving, ration, piece, dollop (*informal*), plateful

helpless = **powerless**, weak, disabled, incapable, challenged, paralysed, impotent, infirm **OPPOSITE:** powerful

hem = **edge**, border, margin, trimming, fringe ▷ PHRASES: hem something or someone in 1 = **surround**, confine, enclose, shut in

2 = **restrict**, confine, beset, circumscribe

hence = **therefore**, thus, consequently, for this reason, in consequence, ergo, on that account

herald VERB 1 = **indicate**, promise, usher in, presage, portend, foretoken
▷ NOUN 2 (*often literary*) = **forerunner**, sign, signal, indication, token, omen, precursor, harbinger
3 = **messenger**, courier, proclaimer, announcer, crier, town crier

herd = **flock**, crowd, collection, mass, drove, mob, swarm, horde

hereditary 1 = **genetic**, inborn, inbred, transmissible, inheritable 2 (*Law*) = **inherited**, passed down, traditional, ancestral

heritage = **inheritance**, legacy, birthright, tradition, endowment, bequest

hero 1 = **protagonist**, leading man 2 = **star**, champion, victor, superstar, conqueror 3 = **idol**, favourite, pin-up (*slang*), fave (*informal*)

heroic = **courageous**, brave, daring, fearless, gallant, intrepid, valiant, lion-hearted OPPOSITE: cowardly

heroine 1 = **protagonist**, leading lady, diva, prima donna 2 = **idol**, favourite, pin-up (*slang*), fave (*informal*)

USAGE NOTE
Note that the word *heroine*, meaning 'a female hero', has an *e* at the end. The drug *heroin* is spelled without a final *e*.

---

hesitate 1 = **waver**, delay, pause, wait, doubt, falter, dither (*chiefly Brit*), vacillate OPPOSITE: be decisive 2 = **be reluctant**, be unwilling, shrink from, think twice, scruple, demur, hang back, be disinclined OPPOSITE: be determined

hesitation = **reluctance**, reservation(s), misgiving(s), ambivalence, qualm(s), unwillingness, scruple(s), compunction

hidden 1 = **secret**, veiled, latent 2 = **concealed**, secret, covert, unseen, clandestine, secreted, under wraps

hide¹ 1 = **conceal**, stash (*informal*), secrete, put out of sight OPPOSITE: display 2 = **go into hiding**, take cover, keep out of sight, hole up, lie low, go underground, go to ground, go to earth 3 = **keep secret**, suppress, withhold, keep quiet about, hush up, draw a veil over, keep dark, keep under your hat OPPOSITE: disclose 4 = **obscure**, cover, mask, disguise, conceal, veil, cloak, shroud OPPOSITE: reveal

hide² = **skin**, leather, pelt

hideous = **ugly**, revolting, ghastly, monstrous, grotesque, gruesome, grisly, unsightly **OPPOSITE:** beautiful

hiding (*informal*) = **beating**, whipping, thrashing, licking (*informal*), spanking, walloping (*informal*), drubbing

hierarchy = **grading**, ranking, social order, pecking order, class system, social stratum

high ADJECTIVE 1 = **tall**, towering, soaring, steep, elevated, lofty **OPPOSITE:** short 2 = **extreme**, great, acute, severe, extraordinary, excessive **OPPOSITE:** low 3 = **strong**, violent, extreme, blustery, squally, sharp 4 = **important**, chief, powerful, superior, eminent, exalted, skookum (*Canad*) **OPPOSITE:** lowly 5 = **high-pitched**, piercing, shrill, penetrating, strident, sharp, acute, piping **OPPOSITE:** deep 6 (*informal*) = **intoxicated**, stoned (*slang*), tripping (*informal*) ▷ ADVERB 7 = **way up**, aloft, far up, to a great height

high-flown = **extravagant**, elaborate, pretentious, exaggerated, inflated, lofty, grandiose, overblown **OPPOSITE:** straightforward

highlight VERB 1 = **emphasize**, stress, accent, show up, underline, spotlight, accentuate, flag, call attention to **OPPOSITE:** play down ▷ NOUN 2 = **high point**, peak, climax, feature, focus, focal point, high spot **OPPOSITE:** low point

highly = **extremely**, very, greatly, vastly, exceptionally, immensely, tremendously

hijack *or* **highjack** = **seize**, take over, commandeer, expropriate

hike NOUN 1 = **walk**, march, trek, ramble, tramp, traipse ▷ VERB 2 = **walk**, march, trek, ramble, tramp, back-pack

hilarious 1 = **funny**, entertaining, amusing, hysterical, humorous, comical, side-splitting 2 = **merry**, uproarious, rollicking **OPPOSITE:** serious

hill = **mount**, fell, height, mound, hilltop, tor, knoll, hillock, kopje *or* koppie (*S African*)

hinder = **obstruct**, stop, check, block, delay, frustrate, handicap, interrupt **OPPOSITE:** help

hint NOUN 1 = **clue**, suggestion, implication, indication, pointer, allusion, innuendo, intimation 2 = **advice**, help, tip(s), suggestion(s), pointer(s) 3 = **trace**, touch, suggestion, dash, suspicion, tinge, undertone ▷ VERB 4 *sometimes with* **at** = **suggest**, indicate, imply, intimate, insinuate

hire VERB 1 = **employ**, commission, take on, engage, appoint, sign up, enlist 2 = **rent**, charter, lease, let, engage ▷ NOUN 3 = **rental**, hiring, rent, lease 4 = **charge**, rental, price, cost, fee

hiss VERB 1 = **whistle**, wheeze, whiz, whirr, sibilate 2 = **jeer**, mock, deride
▷ NOUN 3 = **fizz**, buzz, hissing, fizzing, sibilation

historic = **significant**, notable, momentous, famous, extraordinary, outstanding, remarkable, ground-breaking **OPPOSITE:** unimportant

> **USAGE NOTE**
> Although *historic* and *historical* are similarly spelt they are very different in meaning and should not be used interchangeably. A distinction is usually made between *historic*, which means 'important' or 'significant', and *historical*, which means 'pertaining to history': *a historic decision; a historical perspective*.

historical = **factual**, real, documented, actual, authentic, attested **OPPOSITE:** contemporary

history 1 = **the past**, antiquity, yesterday, yesteryear, olden days 2 = **chronicle**, record, story, account, narrative, recital, annals

hit VERB 1 = **strike**, beat, knock, bang, slap, smack, thump, clout (*informal*) 2 = **collide with**, run into, bump into, clash with, smash into, crash against, bang into 3 = **affect**, damage, harm, ruin, devastate, overwhelm, touch, impact on 4 = **reach**, gain, achieve, arrive at, accomplish, attain
▷ NOUN 5 = **shot**, blow 6 = **blow**, knock, stroke, belt (*informal*), rap, slap, smack, clout (*informal*) 7 = **success**, winner, triumph, smash (*informal*), sensation
▷ PHRASES: hit it off (*informal*) = **get on (well) with**, click (*slang*), be on good terms, get on like a house on fire (*informal*) ▶ hit on *or* upon something = **think up**, discover, arrive at, invent, stumble on, light upon, strike upon

hitch NOUN 1 = **problem**, catch, difficulty, hold-up, obstacle, drawback, snag, uphill (*S African*), impediment
▷ VERB 2 (*informal*) = **hitchhike**, thumb a lift 3 = **fasten**, join, attach, couple, tie, connect, harness, tether
▷ PHRASES: hitch something up = **pull up**, tug, jerk, yank

hitherto (*Formal*) = **previously**, so far, until now, thus far, heretofore

hobby = **pastime**, relaxation, leisure pursuit, diversion, avocation, (leisure) activity

hoist VERB 1 = **raise**, lift, erect, elevate, heave
▷ NOUN 2 = **lift**, crane, elevator, winch

hold VERB 1 = **embrace**, grasp, clutch, hug, squeeze, cradle, clasp, enfold
2 = **restrain** OPPOSITE: release
3 = **detain**, confine, imprison, impound OPPOSITE: release
4 = **accommodate**, take, contain, seat, have a capacity for 5 = **consider**, think, believe, judge, regard, assume, reckon, deem OPPOSITE: deny
6 = **occupy**, have, fill, maintain, retain, possess, hold down (*informal*) 7 = **conduct**, convene, call, run, preside over OPPOSITE: cancel
▷ NOUN 8 = **grip**, grasp, clasp 9 = **foothold**, footing
10 = **control**, influence, mastery, mana (*NZ*)

holder 1 = **owner**, bearer, possessor, keeper, proprietor
2 = **case**, cover, container

hold-up 1 = **robbery**, theft, mugging (*informal*), stick-up (*slang, chiefly US*) 2 = **delay**, wait, hitch, setback, snag, traffic jam, stoppage, bottleneck

hole 1 = **cavity**, pit, hollow, chamber, cave, cavern
2 = **opening**, crack, tear, gap, breach, vent, puncture, aperture
3 = **burrow**, den, earth, shelter, lair 4 (*informal*) = **hovel**, dump (*informal*), dive (*slang*), slum
5 (*informal*) = **predicament**, spot (*informal*), fix (*informal*), mess, jam (*informal*), dilemma, scrape (*informal*), hot water (*informal*)

holiday 1 = **vacation**, leave, break, time off, recess, schoolie (*Austral*), accumulated day off or ADO (*Austral*), staycation or stacation (*informal*) 2 = **festival**, fête, celebration, feast, gala

hollow ADJECTIVE 1 = **empty**, vacant, void, unfilled OPPOSITE: solid 2 = **worthless**, useless, vain, meaningless, pointless, futile, fruitless OPPOSITE: meaningful 3 = **dull**, low, deep, muted, toneless, reverberant OPPOSITE: vibrant
▷ NOUN 4 = **cavity**, hole, bowl, depression, pit, basin, crater, trough OPPOSITE: mound
5 = **valley**, dale, glen, dell, dingle OPPOSITE: hill
▷ VERB 6 *often followed by* out = **scoop out**, dig out, excavate, gouge out

holocaust 1 = **devastation**, destruction, genocide, annihilation, conflagration
2 = **genocide**, massacre, annihilation

holy 1 = **sacred**, blessed, hallowed, venerable, consecrated, sacrosanct, sanctified OPPOSITE: unsanctified 2 = **devout**, godly, religious, pure, righteous, pious, virtuous, saintly OPPOSITE: sinful

homage = **respect**, honour, worship, devotion, reverence, deference, adulation, adoration OPPOSITE: contempt

home NOUN 1 = **dwelling**, house, residence, abode, habitation, pad (*slang*), domicile 2 = **birthplace**, homeland, home town, native land, Godzone (*Austral informal*)
▷ ADJECTIVE 3 = **domestic**, local, internal, native
▷ PHRASES: **at home** 1 = **in**, present, available 2 = **at ease**, relaxed, comfortable, content, at peace ▶ **bring something home to someone** = **make clear**, emphasize, drive home, press home, impress upon

homeland = **native land**, birthplace, motherland, fatherland, country of origin, mother country, Godzone (*Austral informal*)

homeless = **destitute**, displaced, dispossessed, down-and-out

homely 1 = **comfortable**, welcoming, friendly, cosy, homespun 2 = **plain**, simple, ordinary, modest **OPPOSITE:** elaborate

homicide = **murder**, killing, manslaughter, slaying, bloodshed

hone 1 = **improve**, better, enhance, upgrade, refine, sharpen, help 2 = **sharpen**, point, grind, edge, file, polish, whet

| **USAGE NOTE**
| *Hone* is sometimes wrongly used where *home* is meant:

| this device makes it easier to
| home in on (not *hone in on*)
| the target.

honest 1 = **trustworthy**, upright, ethical, honourable, reputable, truthful, virtuous, law-abiding **OPPOSITE:** dishonest 2 = **open**, direct, frank, plain, sincere, candid, forthright, upfront (*informal*) **OPPOSITE:** secretive

honestly 1 = **ethically**, legally, lawfully, honourably, by fair means 2 = **frankly**, plainly, candidly, straight (out), truthfully, to your face, in all sincerity

honesty 1 = **integrity**, honour, virtue, morality, probity, rectitude, truthfulness, trustworthiness 2 = **frankness**, openness, sincerity, candour, bluntness, outspokenness, straightforwardness

honorary = **nominal**, unofficial, titular, in name *or* title only

honour NOUN 1 = **integrity**, morality, honesty, goodness, fairness, decency, probity, rectitude **OPPOSITE:** dishonour 2 = **prestige**, credit, reputation, glory, fame, distinction, dignity, renown **OPPOSITE:** disgrace 3 = **reputation**, standing, prestige, image, status, stature, good name, cachet 4 = **acclaim**, praise, recognition, compliments, homage, accolades, commendation

OPPOSITE: contempt
5 = **privilege**, credit, pleasure, compliment
▷ **VERB** 6 = **acclaim**, praise, decorate, commemorate, commend 7 = **respect**, value, esteem, prize, appreciate, adore
OPPOSITE: scorn 8 = **fulfil**, keep, carry out, observe, discharge, live up to, be true to 9 = **pay**, take, accept, pass, acknowledge
OPPOSITE: refuse

honourable 1 = **principled**, moral, ethical, fair, upright, honest, virtuous, trustworthy
2 = **proper**, respectable, virtuous, creditable

hook NOUN 1 = **fastener**, catch, link, peg, clasp
▷ **VERB** 2 = **fasten**, fix, secure, clasp 3 = **catch**, land, trap, entrap

hooked 1 = **bent**, curved, aquiline, hook-shaped
2 (*informal*) = **obsessed**, addicted, taken, devoted, turned on (*slang*), enamoured
3 (*informal*) = **addicted**, dependent, using (*informal*), having a habit

hooligan = **delinquent**, vandal, hoon (*Austral & NZ*), ruffian, lager lout, yob *or* yobbo (*Brit slang*), cougan (*Austral slang*), scozza (*Austral slang*), bogan (*Austral slang*), hoodie (*informal*)

hoop = **ring**, band, loop, wheel, round, girdle, circlet

hop VERB 1 = **jump**, spring, bound, leap, skip, vault, caper
▷ **NOUN** 2 = **jump**, step, spring, bound, leap, bounce, skip, vault

hope VERB 1 = **believe**, look forward to, cross your fingers
▷ **NOUN** 2 = **belief**, confidence, expectation, longing, dream, desire, ambition, assumption
OPPOSITE: despair

hopeful 1 = **optimistic**, confident, looking forward to, buoyant, sanguine, expectant **OPPOSITE:** despairing
2 = **promising**, encouraging, bright, reassuring, rosy, heartening, auspicious
OPPOSITE: unpromising

hopefully = **optimistically**, confidently, expectantly, with anticipation

> **USAGE NOTE**
> Some people object to the use of *hopefully* as a synonym for the phrase 'it is hoped that' in a sentence such as *hopefully I'll be able to attend the meeting*. This use of the adverb first appeared in America in the 1960s, but it has rapidly established itself elsewhere. There are really no strong grounds for objecting to it, since we accept other sentence adverbials that fulfil a similar function, for example *unfortunately*, which means 'it is unfortunate that' in a sentence such as *unfortunately I won't be able to attend the meeting*.

h

hopeless = **impossible**, pointless, futile, useless, vain, no-win, unattainable

horde = **crowd**, mob, swarm, host, band, pack, drove, gang

horizon = **skyline**, view, vista

horizontal = **level**, flat, parallel

horrible 1 (*informal*) = **dreadful**, terrible, awful, nasty, cruel, mean, unpleasant, horrid **OPPOSITE:** wonderful 2 = **terrible**, appalling, terrifying, shocking, grim, dreadful, revolting, ghastly

horrific = **horrifying**, shocking, appalling, awful, terrifying, dreadful, horrendous, ghastly

horrify 1 = **terrify**, alarm, frighten, scare, intimidate, petrify, make your hair stand on end **OPPOSITE:** comfort 2 = **shock**, appal, dismay, sicken, outrage **OPPOSITE:** delight

horror 1 = **terror**, fear, alarm, panic, dread, fright, consternation, trepidation 2 = **hatred**, disgust, loathing, aversion, revulsion, repugnance, odium, detestation **OPPOSITE:** love

horse = **nag**, mount, mare, colt, filly, stallion, steed (*archaic literary*), moke (*Austral slang*), yarraman *or* yarramin (*Austral*), gee-gee (*slang*)

> **RELATED WORDS**
> *male:* stallion
> *female:* mare
> *young:* foal, colt, filly

hospitality = **welcome**, warmth, kindness, friendliness, sociability, conviviality, neighbourliness, cordiality

host¹ NOUN 1 = **master of ceremonies**, proprietor, innkeeper, landlord *or* landlady 2 = **presenter**, compere (*Brit*), anchorman *or* anchorwoman ▷ VERB 3 = **present**, introduce, compere (*Brit*), front (*informal*)

host² 1 = **multitude**, lot, load (*informal*), wealth, array, myriad, great quantity, large number 2 = **crowd**, army, pack, drove, mob, herd, legion, swarm

hostage = **captive**, prisoner, pawn

hostile 1 = **antagonistic**, opposed, contrary, ill-disposed 2 = **unfriendly**, belligerent, antagonistic, rancorous, ill-disposed **OPPOSITE:** friendly 3 = **inhospitable**, adverse, uncongenial, unsympathetic, unwelcoming **OPPOSITE:** hospitable

hostility NOUN 1 = **unfriendliness**, hatred, animosity, spite, bitterness, malice, venom, enmity **OPPOSITE:** friendliness 2 = **opposition**, resentment, antipathy, aversion, antagonism, ill feeling, ill-will, animus **OPPOSITE:** approval ▷ PLURAL NOUN 3 = **warfare**, war, fighting, conflict, combat, armed conflict **OPPOSITE:** peace

h

hot 1 = **heated**, boiling, steaming, roasting, searing, scorching, scalding 2 = **warm**, close, stifling, humid, torrid, sultry, sweltering, balmy **OPPOSITE:** cold 3 = **spicy**, pungent, peppery, piquant, biting, sharp **OPPOSITE:** mild 4 = **intense**, passionate, heated, spirited, fierce, lively, animated, ardent 5 = **new**, latest, fresh, recent, up to date, just out, up to the minute, bang up to date (*informal*) **OPPOSITE:** old 6 = **popular**, hip, fashionable, cool, in demand, sought-after, must-see, in vogue **OPPOSITE:** unpopular 7 = **fierce**, intense, strong, keen, competitive, cut-throat 8 = **fiery**, violent, raging, passionate, stormy **OPPOSITE:** calm

hound = **harass**, harry, bother, provoke, annoy, torment, hassle (*informal*), badger

house NOUN 1 = **home**, residence, dwelling, pad (*slang*), homestead, abode, habitation, domicile, whare (*NZ*) 2 = **household**, family 3 = **firm**, company, business, organization, outfit (*informal*) 4 = **assembly**, parliament, Commons, legislative body 5 = **dynasty**, tribe, clan ▷ VERB 6 = **accommodate**, quarter, take in, put up, lodge, harbour, billet 7 = **contain**, keep, hold, cover, store, protect, shelter 8 = **take**, accommodate, sleep, provide shelter for, give a bed to ▷ PHRASES: on the house = **free**, for free (*informal*), for nothing, free of charge, gratis

household = **family**, home, house, family circle, ainga (*NZ*)

housing 1 = **accommodation**, homes, houses, dwellings, domiciles 2 = **case**, casing, covering, cover, shell, jacket, holder, container

hover 1 = **float**, fly, hang, drift, flutter 2 = **linger**, loiter, hang about *or* around (*informal*) 3 = **waver**, fluctuate, dither (*chiefly Brit*), oscillate, vacillate

however = **but**, nevertheless, still, though, yet, nonetheless, notwithstanding, anyhow

howl VERB 1 = **bay**, cry 2 = **cry**, scream, roar, weep, yell, wail, shriek, bellow ▷ NOUN 3 = **baying**, cry, bay, bark, barking, yelping 4 = **cry**, scream, roar, bay, wail, shriek, clamour, bawl

hub = **centre**, heart, focus, core, middle, focal point, nerve centre

huddle VERB 1 = **curl up**, crouch, hunch up 2 = **crowd**, press, gather, collect, squeeze, cluster, flock, herd ▷ NOUN 3 (*informal*) = **discussion**, conference, meeting, hui (*NZ*), powwow, confab (*informal*), korero (*NZ*)

hue = **colour**, tone, shade, dye, tint, tinge

hug VERB 1 = **embrace**, cuddle, squeeze, clasp, enfold, hold close, take in your arms
▷ NOUN 2 = **embrace**, squeeze, bear hug, clinch (*slang*), clasp

huge = **enormous**, large, massive, vast, tremendous, immense, gigantic, monumental **OPPOSITE**: tiny

hui (*NZ*) = **meeting**, gathering, assembly, conference, congress, rally, convention, get-together (*informal*)

hull = **framework**, casing, body, covering, frame

hum 1 = **drone**, buzz, murmur, throb, vibrate, purr, thrum, whir 2 (*informal*) = **be busy**, buzz, bustle, stir, pulse, pulsate

human ADJECTIVE 1 = **mortal**, manlike **OPPOSITE**: nonhuman
▷ NOUN 2 = **human being**, person, individual, creature, mortal, man *or* woman
OPPOSITE: nonhuman

humane = **kind**, compassionate, understanding, forgiving, tender, sympathetic, benign, merciful **OPPOSITE**: cruel

humanitarian ADJECTIVE 1 = **compassionate**, charitable, humane, benevolent, altruistic 2 = **charitable**, philanthropic, public-spirited
▷ NOUN 3 = **philanthropist**, benefactor, Good Samaritan, altruist

humanity 1 = **the human race**, man, mankind, people, mortals, humankind, Homo sapiens 2 = **human nature**, mortality 3 = **kindness**, charity, compassion, sympathy, mercy, philanthropy, fellow feeling, kind-heartedness

humble ADJECTIVE 1 = **modest**, meek, unassuming, unpretentious, self-effacing, unostentatious **OPPOSITE**: proud 2 = **lowly**, poor, mean, simple, ordinary, modest, obscure, undistinguished **OPPOSITE**: distinguished
▷ VERB 3 = **humiliate**, disgrace, crush, subdue, chasten, put (someone) in their place, take down a peg (*informal*) **OPPOSITE**: exalt

humidity = **damp**, moisture, dampness, wetness, moistness, dankness, clamminess, mugginess

humiliate = **embarrass**, shame, humble, crush, put down, degrade, chasten, mortify **OPPOSITE**: honour

humiliating = **embarrassing**, shaming, humbling, mortifying, crushing, degrading, ignominious, barro (*Austral slang*)

humiliation = **embarrassment**, shame, disgrace, humbling, put-down, degradation, indignity, ignominy

humorous = **funny**, comic, amusing, entertaining, witty, comical, droll, jocular **OPPOSITE:** serious

humour NOUN 1 = **comedy**, funniness, fun, amusement, funny side, jocularity, facetiousness, ludicrousness **OPPOSITE:** seriousness
2 = **mood**, spirits, temper, disposition, frame of mind
3 = **joking**, comedy, wit, farce, jesting, wisecracks (*informal*), witticisms
▷ VERB 4 = **indulge**, accommodate, go along with, flatter, gratify, pander to, mollify **OPPOSITE:** oppose

hunch NOUN 1 = **feeling**, idea, impression, suspicion, intuition, premonition, inkling, presentiment
▷ VERB 2 = **crouch**, bend, curve, arch, draw in

hunger 1 = **appetite**, emptiness, hungriness, ravenousness 2 = **starvation**, famine, malnutrition, undernourishment 3 = **desire**, appetite, craving, ache, lust, yearning, itch, thirst
▷ PHRASES: hunger for *or* after something = **want**, desire, crave, long for, wish for, yearn for, hanker after, ache for

hungry 1 = **starving**, ravenous, famished, starved, empty, voracious, peckish (*informal, chiefly Brit*) 2 = **eager**, keen, craving, yearning, greedy, avid, desirous, covetous

hunk = **lump**, piece, chunk, block, mass, wedge, slab, nugget

hunt VERB 1 = **stalk**, track, chase, pursue, trail, hound
▷ NOUN 2 = **search**, hunting, investigation, chase, pursuit, quest
▷ PHRASES: hunt for something *or* someone = **search for**, look for, seek for, forage for, scour for, fossick for (*Austral & NZ*), ferret about for

hurdle 1 = **obstacle**, difficulty, barrier, handicap, hazard, uphill (*S African*), obstruction, stumbling block 2 = **fence**, barrier, barricade

hurl = **throw**, fling, launch, cast, pitch, toss, propel, sling

hurricane = **storm**, gale, tornado, cyclone, typhoon, tempest, twister (*US informal*), willy-willy (*Austral*)

hurried 1 = **hasty**, quick, brief, rushed, short, swift, speedy
2 = **rushed**, perfunctory, speedy, hasty, cursory

hurry VERB 1 = **rush**, fly, dash, scurry, scoot **OPPOSITE:** dawdle
2 = **make haste**, rush, get a move on (*informal*), step on it (*informal*), crack on (*informal*)
▷ NOUN 3 = **rush**, haste, speed, urgency, flurry, quickness **OPPOSITE:** slowness

hurt VERB 1 = **injure**, damage, wound, cut, disable, bruise, scrape, impair **OPPOSITE:** heal

2 = **ache**, be sore, be painful, burn, smart, sting, throb, be tender **3** = **harm**, injure, ill-treat, maltreat **4** = **upset**, distress, pain, wound, annoy, grieve, sadden
▷ NOUN **5** = **distress**, suffering, pain, grief, misery, sorrow, heartache, wretchedness **OPPOSITE:** happiness
▷ ADJECTIVE **6** = **injured**, wounded, damaged, harmed, cut, bruised, scarred **OPPOSITE:** healed **7** = **upset**, wounded, crushed, offended, aggrieved, tooshie (*Austral slang*) **OPPOSITE:** calmed
hurtle = **rush**, charge, race, shoot, fly, speed, tear, crash
husband NOUN **1** = **partner**, spouse, mate, better half (*humorous*)
▷ VERB **2** = **conserve**, budget, save, store, hoard, economize on, use economically **OPPOSITE:** squander
hush VERB **1** = **quieten**, silence, mute, muzzle, shush
▷ NOUN **2** = **quiet**, silence, calm, peace, tranquillity, stillness
hut 1 = **cabin**, shack, shanty, hovel, whare (*NZ*) **2** = **shed**, outhouse, lean-to, lockup
hybrid 1 = **crossbreed**, cross, mixture, compound, composite, amalgam, mongrel, half-breed **2** = **mixture**, compound, composite, amalgam

hygiene = **cleanliness**, sanitation, disinfection, sterility
hymn 1 = **religious song**, song of praise, carol, chant, anthem, psalm, paean **2** = **song of praise**, anthem, paean
hype = **publicity**, promotion, plugging (*informal*), razzmatazz (*slang*), brouhaha, ballyhoo (*informal*)
hypocrisy = **insincerity**, pretence, deception, cant, duplicity, deceitfulness **OPPOSITE:** sincerity
hypothesis = **theory**, premise, proposition, assumption, thesis, postulate, supposition
hysteria = **frenzy**, panic, madness, agitation, delirium, hysterics
hysterical 1 = **frenzied**, frantic, raving, distracted, distraught, crazed, overwrought, berko (*Austral slang*) **OPPOSITE:** calm **2** (*informal*) = **hilarious**, uproarious, side-splitting, comical **OPPOSITE:** serious

h

icon = **representation**, image, likeness, avatar, favicon (*computing*)

icy 1 = **cold**, freezing, bitter, biting, raw, chill, chilly, frosty **OPPOSITE:** hot 2 = **slippery**, glassy, slippy (*informal dialect*), like a sheet of glass 3 = **unfriendly**, cold, distant, aloof, frosty, frigid, unwelcoming **OPPOSITE:** friendly

idea 1 = **notion**, thought, view, teaching, opinion, belief, conclusion, hypothesis 2 = **understanding**, thought, view, opinion, concept, impression, perception 3 = **intention**, aim, purpose, object, plan, objective

> **USAGE NOTE**
> It is usually considered correct to say that someone has *the idea of doing something*, rather than *the idea to do something*. For example, you would say *he had the idea of taking a holiday*, not *he had the idea to take a holiday*.

ideal NOUN 1 = **epitome**, standard, dream, pattern, perfection, last word, paragon 2 = **model**, prototype, paradigm ▷ ADJECTIVE 3 = **perfect**, best, model, classic, supreme, ultimate, archetypal, exemplary **OPPOSITE:** imperfect

ideally = **in a perfect world**, all things being equal, if you had your way

identical = **alike**, matching, twin, duplicate, indistinguishable, interchangeable **OPPOSITE:** different

identification 1 = **discovery**, recognition, determining, establishment, diagnosis, confirmation, divination 2 = **recognition**, naming, distinguishing, confirmation, pinpointing 3 = **connection**, relationship, association 4 = **understanding**, relationship, involvement, unity, sympathy, empathy, rapport, fellow feeling 5 = **ID**, identity card, proof of identity, photocard, electronic signature

identify 1 = **recognize**, place, name, remember, spot, diagnose, make out, pinpoint 2 = **establish**, spot, confirm, demonstrate, pick out, certify, verify, mark out, flag up ▷ PHRASES: **identify something or someone with something or someone** = **equate with**, associate with ▸ **identify with someone** = **relate to**, respond to, feel for, empathize with

identity = **individuality**, self, character, personality, existence, originality, separateness

idiot = **fool**, moron, twit (*informal, chiefly Brit*), chump, imbecile, cretin, simpleton, halfwit, galah (*Austral & NZ informal*), dorba *or* dorb (*Austral slang*), bogan (*Austral slang*), dill (*Austral & NZ informal*), mampara (*S African informal*)

idle ADJECTIVE 1 = **unoccupied**, unemployed, redundant, inactive OPPOSITE: occupied 2 = **unused**, inactive, out of order, out of service 3 = **lazy**, slow, slack, sluggish, lax, negligent, inactive, inert OPPOSITE: busy 4 = **useless**, vain, pointless, unsuccessful, ineffective, worthless, futile, fruitless OPPOSITE: useful ▷ VERB 5 *often with* **away** = **fritter**, lounge, potter, loaf, dally, loiter, dawdle, laze

idol 1 = **hero**, pin-up, favourite, pet, darling, beloved (*slang*), fave (*informal*) 2 = **graven image**, god, deity

if 1 = **provided**, assuming, given that, providing, supposing, presuming, on condition that, as long as 2 = **when**, whenever, every time, any time

ignite 1 = **catch fire**, burn, burst into flames, inflame, flare up,

take fire 2 = **set fire to**, light, set alight, torch, kindle

ignorance 1 = **lack of education**, stupidity, foolishness OPPOSITE: knowledge 2 *with* **of** = **unawareness of**, inexperience of, unfamiliarity with, innocence of, unconsciousness of

ignorant 1 = **uneducated**, illiterate OPPOSITE: educated 2 = **insensitive**, rude, crass 3 *with* **of** = **uninformed of**, unaware of, oblivious to, innocent of, unconscious of, inexperienced of, uninitiated about, unenlightened about OPPOSITE: informed

ignore 1 = **pay no attention to**, neglect, disregard, slight, overlook, scorn, spurn, rebuff OPPOSITE: pay attention to 2 = **overlook**, discount, disregard, reject, neglect, shrug off, pass over, brush aside 3 = **snub**, slight, rebuff

ill ADJECTIVE 1 = **unwell**, sick, poorly (*informal*), diseased, weak, crook (*Austral & NZ slang*), ailing, frail OPPOSITE: healthy 2 = **harmful**, bad, damaging, evil, foul, unfortunate, destructive, detrimental OPPOSITE: favourable ▷ NOUN 3 = **problem**, trouble, suffering, worry, injury, hurt, strain, harm ▷ ADVERB 4 = **badly**, unfortunately, unfavourably, inauspiciously 5 = **hardly**, barely, scarcely, just, only just, by no means, at a push **OPPOSITE:** well

illegal = **unlawful**, banned, forbidden, prohibited, criminal, outlawed, illicit, unlicensed **OPPOSITE:** legal

illicit 1 = **illegal**, criminal, prohibited, unlawful, illegitimate, unlicensed, unauthorized, felonious **OPPOSITE:** legal 2 = **forbidden**, improper, immoral, guilty, clandestine, furtive

illness = **sickness**, disease, infection, disorder, bug (*informal*), ailment, affliction, malady

illuminate 1 = **light up**, brighten **OPPOSITE:** darken 2 = **explain**, interpret, make clear, clarify, clear up, enlighten, shed light on, elucidate **OPPOSITE:** obscure

illuminating = **informative**, revealing, enlightening, helpful, explanatory, instructive **OPPOSITE:** confusing

illusion 1 = **delusion**, misconception, misapprehension, fancy, fallacy, false impression, false belief 2 = **false impression**, appearance, impression, deception, fallacy **OPPOSITE:** reality 3 = **fantasy**, vision, hallucination, trick, spectre, mirage, daydream, apparition

illustrate 1 = **demonstrate**, emphasize 2 = **explain**, sum up, summarize, bring home, point up, elucidate

illustrated = **pictured**, decorated, pictorial

illustration 1 = **example**, case, instance, sample, specimen, exemplar 2 = **picture**, drawing, painting, image, print, plate, figure, portrait

image 1 = **thought**, idea, vision, concept, impression, perception, mental picture, conceptualization 2 = **figure of speech** 3 = **reflection**, likeness, mirror image 4 = **figure**, idol, icon, fetish, talisman, avatar 5 = **replica**, copy, reproduction, counterpart, clone, facsimile, spitting image (*informal*), Doppelgänger 6 = **picture**, photo, photograph, representation, reproduction, snapshot, TIFF, JPEG, avatar, thumbnail

imaginary = **fictional**, made-up, invented, imagined, unreal, hypothetical, fictitious, illusory **OPPOSITE:** real

imagination 1 = **creativity**, vision, invention, ingenuity, enterprise, originality, inventiveness, resourcefulness 2 = **mind's eye**, fancy

imaginative = **creative**, original, inspired, enterprising, clever, ingenious, inventive **OPPOSITE:** unimaginative

i

imagine 1 = **envisage**,
see, picture, plan, think of,
conjure up, envision, visualize
2 = **believe**, think, suppose,
assume, suspect, guess
(*informal, chiefly US & Canad*), take
it, reckon

imitate 1 = **copy**, follow, repeat,
echo, emulate, ape, simulate,
mirror 2 = **do an impression of**,
mimic, copy

imitation NOUN 1 = **replica**,
fake, reproduction, sham,
forgery, counterfeiting,
likeness, duplication
2 = **copying**, resemblance,
mimicry 3 = **impression**,
impersonation
▷ ADJECTIVE 4 = **artificial**,
mock, reproduction, dummy,
synthetic, man-made,
simulated, sham **OPPOSITE**: real

immaculate 1 = **clean**,
spotless, neat, spruce,
squeaky-clean, spick-and-span
OPPOSITE: dirty 2 = **pure**,
perfect, impeccable, flawless,
faultless, above reproach
OPPOSITE: corrupt 3 = **perfect**,
flawless, impeccable, faultless,
unblemished, untarnished,
unexceptionable **OPPOSITE**:
tainted

immediate 1 = **instant**,
prompt, instantaneous, quick,
on-the-spot, split-second
OPPOSITE: later 2 = **nearest**,
next, direct, close, near
OPPOSITE: far

immediately = **at once**, now,
instantly, straight away, directly,
promptly, right away, without
delay

immense = **huge**, great,
massive, vast, enormous,
extensive, tremendous, very big,
supersize **OPPOSITE**: tiny

immerse 1 = **engross**, involve,
absorb, busy, occupy, engage
2 = **plunge**, dip, submerge, sink,
duck, bathe, douse, dunk

immigrant = **settler**, incomer,
alien, stranger, outsider,
newcomer, migrant, emigrant

imminent = **near**, coming,
close, approaching, gathering,
forthcoming, looming,
impending **OPPOSITE**: remote

immoral = **wicked**, bad, wrong,
corrupt, indecent, sinful,
unethical, depraved **OPPOSITE**:
moral

immortal ADJECTIVE
1 = **timeless**, eternal,
everlasting, lasting, traditional,
classic, enduring, perennial
OPPOSITE: ephemeral
2 = **undying**, eternal,
imperishable, deathless
OPPOSITE: mortal
▷ NOUN 3 = **hero**, genius, great
4 = **god**, goddess, deity, divine
being, immortal being, atua (*NZ*)

immune
▷ PHRASES: immune from
= **exempt from**, free from
▶ immune to 1 = **resistant to**,
free from, protected from,

safe from, not open to, spared from, secure against, invulnerable to **2 = unaffected by**, invulnerable to

immunity 1 = **exemption**, amnesty, indemnity, release, freedom, invulnerability 2 *with* **to = resistance**, protection, resilience, inoculation, immunization **OPPOSITE:** susceptibility

impact NOUN 1 = **effect**, influence, consequences, impression, repercussions, ramifications **2 = collision**, contact, crash, knock, stroke, smash, bump, thump
▷ VERB 3 = **hit**, strike, crash, clash, crush, ram, smack, collide

impair = **worsen**, reduce, damage, injure, harm, undermine, weaken, diminish **OPPOSITE:** improve

impaired = **damaged**, flawed, faulty, defective, imperfect, unsound

impasse = **deadlock**, stalemate, standstill, dead end, standoff

impatient 1 = **cross**, annoyed, irritated, prickly, touchy, bad-tempered, intolerant, ill-tempered **2 = eager**, longing, keen, anxious, hungry, enthusiastic, restless, avid **OPPOSITE:** calm

impeccable = **faultless**, perfect, immaculate, flawless, squeaky-clean, unblemished,

unimpeachable, irreproachable **OPPOSITE:** flawed

impending = **looming**, coming, approaching, near, forthcoming, imminent, upcoming, in the pipeline

imperative = **urgent**, essential, pressing, vital, crucial **OPPOSITE:** unnecessary

imperial = **royal**, regal, kingly, queenly, princely, sovereign, majestic, monarchial

impetus 1 = **incentive**, push, spur, motivation, impulse, stimulus, catalyst, goad **2 = force**, power, energy, momentum

implant 1 = **insert**, fix, graft **2 = instil**, infuse, inculcate

implement VERB 1 = **carry out**, effect, carry through, complete, apply, perform, realize, fulfil **OPPOSITE:** hinder
▷ NOUN 2 = **tool**, machine, device, instrument, appliance, apparatus, gadget, utensil

implicate = **incriminate**, involve, embroil, entangle, inculpate **OPPOSITE:** dissociate
▷ PHRASES: implicate something *or* someone in something = **involve in**, associate with

implication 1 = **suggestion**, hint, inference, meaning, significance, presumption, overtone, innuendo **2 = consequence**, result, development, upshot

implicit 1 = **implied**, understood, suggested, hinted at, taken for granted, unspoken, inferred, tacit **OPPOSITE:** explicit 2 = **inherent**, underlying, intrinsic, latent, ingrained, inbuilt 3 = **absolute**, full, complete, firm, fixed, constant, utter, outright

implied = **suggested**, indirect, hinted at, implicit, unspoken, tacit, undeclared, unstated

imply 1 = **suggest**, hint, insinuate, indicate, intimate, signify 2 = **involve**, mean, entail, require, indicate, point to, signify, presuppose

import VERB 1 = **bring in**, buy in, ship in, introduce
▷ NOUN 2 (Formal) = **significance**, concern, value, weight, consequence, substance, moment, magnitude 3 = **meaning**, implication, significance, sense, intention, substance, drift, thrust

importance 1 = **significance**, interest, concern, moment, value, weight, import, consequence 2 = **prestige**, standing, status, rule, authority, influence, distinction, esteem, mana (NZ)

important 1 = **significant**, critical, substantial, urgent, serious, far-reaching, momentous, seminal **OPPOSITE:** unimportant 2 = **powerful**, prominent, commanding,

dominant, influential, eminent, high-ranking, authoritative, skookum (Canad)

impose
▷ PHRASES: impose something on or upon someone 1 = **levy**, introduce, charge, establish, fix, institute, decree, ordain 2 = **inflict**, force, enforce, visit, press, apply, thrust, saddle (someone) with

imposing = **impressive**, striking, grand, powerful, commanding, awesome, majestic, dignified **OPPOSITE:** unimposing

imposition 1 = **application**, introduction, levying 2 = **intrusion**, liberty, presumption

impossible 1 = **not possible**, out of the question, impracticable, unfeasible 2 = **unachievable**, out of the question, vain, unthinkable, inconceivable, far-fetched, unworkable, implausible **OPPOSITE:** possible 3 = **absurd**, crazy (informal), ridiculous, outrageous, ludicrous, unreasonable, preposterous, farcical

impotence = **powerlessness**, inability, helplessness, weakness, incompetence, paralysis, frailty, incapacity **OPPOSITE:** powerfulness

impoverish 1 = **bankrupt**, ruin, beggar, break 2 = **deplete**, drain, exhaust, diminish, use up, sap, wear out, reduce

impoverished = poor, needy, destitute, bankrupt, poverty-stricken, impecunious, penurious **OPPOSITE:** rich

impress = excite, move, strike, touch, affect, inspire, amaze, overcome

▷ **PHRASES: impress something on** or **upon someone** = stress, bring home to, instil in, drum into, knock into, emphasize to, fix in, inculcate in

impression 1 = idea, feeling, thought, sense, view, assessment, judgment, reaction 2 = effect, influence, impact 3 = imitation, parody, impersonation, send-up (Brit informal), takeoff (informal) 4 = mark, imprint, stamp, outline, hollow, dent, indentation

impressive = grand, striking, splendid, good, great (informal), fine, powerful, exciting **OPPOSITE:** unimpressive

imprint NOUN 1 = mark, impression, stamp, indentation ▷ **VERB** 2 = engrave, print, stamp, impress, etch, emboss

imprison = jail, confine, detain, lock up, put away, intern, incarcerate, send down (informal) **OPPOSITE:** free

imprisoned = jailed, confined, locked up, inside (slang), in jail, captive, behind bars, incarcerated

imprisonment = confinement, custody, detention, captivity, incarceration

improbable 1 = doubtful, unlikely, dubious, questionable, fanciful, far-fetched, implausible **OPPOSITE:** probable 2 = unconvincing, weak, unbelievable, preposterous **OPPOSITE:** convincing

improper 1 = inappropriate, unfit, unsuitable, out of place, unwarranted, uncalled-for **OPPOSITE:** appropriate 2 = indecent, vulgar, suggestive, unseemly, untoward, risqué, smutty, unbecoming **OPPOSITE:** decent

improve 1 = enhance, better, add to, upgrade, touch up, ameliorate **OPPOSITE:** worsen 2 = get better, pick up, develop, advance

improvement 1 = enhancement, advancement, betterment 2 = advance, development, progress, recovery, upswing

improvise 1 = devise, contrive, concoct, throw together 2 = ad-lib, invent, busk, wing it (informal), play it by ear (informal), extemporize, speak off the cuff (informal)

impulse = urge, longing, wish, notion, yearning, inclination, itch, whim

inaccurate = **incorrect**, wrong, mistaken, faulty, unreliable, defective, erroneous, unsound **OPPOSITE:** accurate

inadequacy 1 = **shortage**, poverty, dearth, paucity, insufficiency, meagreness, scantiness 2 = **incompetence**, inability, deficiency, incapacity, ineffectiveness 3 = **shortcoming**, failing, weakness, defect, imperfection

inadequate 1 = **insufficient**, meagre, poor, lacking, scant, sparse, sketchy **OPPOSITE:** adequate 2 = **incapable**, incompetent, faulty, deficient, unqualified, not up to scratch (*informal*) **OPPOSITE:** capable

inadvertently = **unintentionally**, accidentally, by accident, mistakenly, unwittingly, by mistake, involuntarily **OPPOSITE:** deliberately

inaugural = **first**, opening, initial, maiden, introductory

incarnation = **embodiment**, manifestation, epitome, type, personification, avatar

incense = **anger**, infuriate, enrage, irritate, madden, inflame, rile (*informal*), make your blood boil (*informal*)

incensed = **angry**, furious, fuming, infuriated, enraged, maddened, indignant, irate, tooshie (*Austral slang*), off the air (*Austral slang*)

incentive = **inducement**, encouragement, spur, lure, bait, motivation, carrot (*informal*), stimulus **OPPOSITE:** disincentive

incident 1 = **disturbance**, scene, clash, disorder, confrontation, brawl, fracas, commotion 2 = **happening**, event, affair, business, fact, matter, occasion, episode 3 = **adventure**, drama, excitement, crisis, spectacle

incidentally = **by the way**, in passing, en passant, parenthetically, by the bye

inclination 1 = **desire**, longing, aspiration, craving, hankering 2 = **tendency**, liking, disposition, penchant, propensity, predisposition, predilection, proclivity **OPPOSITE:** aversion

incline VERB 1 = **predispose**, influence, persuade, prejudice, sway, dispose
▷ NOUN 2 = **slope**, rise, dip, grade, descent, ascent, gradient

inclined 1 = **disposed**, given, prone, likely, liable, apt, predisposed 2 = **willing**, minded, disposed

include 1 = **contain**, involve, incorporate, cover, consist of, take in, embrace, comprise **OPPOSITE:** exclude 2 = **count** 3 = **add**, enter, put in, insert

inclusion = **addition**, incorporation, introduction, insertion **OPPOSITE:** exclusion

inclusive = comprehensive, general, global, sweeping, blanket, umbrella, across-the-board, all-embracing **OPPOSITE:** limited

income = revenue, earnings, pay, returns, profits, wages, yield, proceeds

incoming 1 = arriving, landing, approaching, entering, returning, homeward **OPPOSITE:** departing 2 = new

incompatible = inconsistent, conflicting, contradictory, incongruous, unsuited, mismatched **OPPOSITE:** compatible

incompetence = ineptitude, inability, inadequacy, incapacity, ineffectiveness, uselessness, unfitness, incapability

incompetent = inept, useless, incapable, floundering, bungling, unfit, ineffectual, inexpert **OPPOSITE:** competent

incomplete = unfinished, partial, wanting, deficient, imperfect, fragmentary, half-pie (NZ informal) **OPPOSITE:** complete

inconsistency 1 = unreliability, instability, unpredictability, fickleness, unsteadiness 2 = incompatibility, discrepancy, disparity, disagreement, variance, divergence, incongruity

inconsistent 1 = changeable, variable, unpredictable, unstable, erratic, fickle, capricious, unsteady **OPPOSITE:** consistent 2 = incompatible, conflicting, at odds, contradictory, incongruous, discordant, out of step, irreconcilable **OPPOSITE:** compatible

inconvenience NOUN 1 = trouble, difficulty, bother, fuss, disadvantage, disturbance, disruption, nuisance, uphill (S African) ▷ VERB 2 = trouble, bother, disturb, upset, disrupt, put out, discommode

incorporate 1 = include, contain, take in, embrace, integrate, encompass, assimilate, comprise of 2 = integrate, include, absorb, merge, fuse, assimilate, subsume 3 = blend, combine, compound, mingle

incorrect = false, wrong, mistaken, flawed, faulty, inaccurate, untrue, erroneous **OPPOSITE:** correct

increase VERB 1 = raise, extend, boost, expand, develop, advance, strengthen, widen **OPPOSITE:** decrease 2 = grow, develop, spread, expand, swell, enlarge, escalate, multiply **OPPOSITE:** shrink ▷ NOUN 3 = growth, rise, development, gain, expansion, extension, proliferation, enlargement

increasingly = **progressively**, more and more

incredible 1 (*informal*) = **amazing**, wonderful, stunning, extraordinary, overwhelming, astonishing, staggering, sensational (*informal*) 2 = **unbelievable**, unthinkable, improbable, inconceivable, preposterous, unconvincing, unimaginable, far-fetched

incumbent NOUN 1 = **holder**, keeper, bearer
▷ ADJECTIVE 2 (*Formal*) = **obligatory**, required, necessary, essential, binding, compulsory, mandatory, imperative

incur = **sustain**, experience, suffer, gain, earn, collect, meet with, provoke

indecent 1 = **obscene**, lewd, dirty, inappropriate, rude, crude, filthy, improper OPPOSITE: decent 2 = **unbecoming**, unsuitable, vulgar, unseemly, undignified, indecorous OPPOSITE: proper

indeed 1 = **certainly**, yes, definitely, surely, truly, undoubtedly, without doubt, indisputably 2 = **really**, actually, in fact, certainly, genuinely, in truth, in actuality

indefinitely = **endlessly**, continually, for ever, ad infinitum

independence = **freedom**, liberty, autonomy, sovereignty, self-rule, self-sufficiency, self-reliance, rangatiratanga (*NZ*) OPPOSITE: subjugation

independent 1 = **separate**, unattached, uncontrolled, unconstrained OPPOSITE: controlled 2 = **self-sufficient**, free, liberated, self-contained, self-reliant, self-supporting 3 = **self-governing**, free, autonomous, liberated, sovereign, self-determining, nonaligned OPPOSITE: subject

independently = **separately**, alone, solo, on your own, by yourself, unaided, individually, autonomously

indicate 1 = **show**, suggest, reveal, display, demonstrate, point to, imply, manifest, flag up 2 = **imply**, suggest, hint, intimate, signify, insinuate 3 = **point to**, point out, specify, gesture towards, designate 4 = **register**, show, record, read, express, display, demonstrate

indication = **sign**, mark, evidence, suggestion, symptom, hint, clue, manifestation

indicator = **sign**, mark, measure, guide, signal, symbol, meter, gauge

indict = **charge**, accuse, prosecute, summon, impeach, arraign

indictment = **charge**, allegation, prosecution, accusation, impeachment, summons, arraignment

indifference = disregard, apathy, negligence, detachment, coolness, coldness, nonchalance, aloofness **OPPOSITE:** concern

indifferent 1 = **unconcerned**, detached, cold, cool, callous, aloof, unmoved, unsympathetic **OPPOSITE:** concerned
2 = **mediocre**, ordinary, moderate, so-so (*informal*), passable, undistinguished, no great shakes (*informal*), half-pie (*NZ informal*) **OPPOSITE:** excellent

indignation = resentment, anger, rage, exasperation, pique, umbrage

indirect 1 = **related**, secondary, subsidiary, incidental, unintended 2 = **circuitous**, roundabout, curving, wandering, rambling, deviant, meandering, tortuous **OPPOSITE:** direct

indispensable = essential, necessary, needed, key, vital, crucial, imperative, requisite **OPPOSITE:** dispensable

individual ADJECTIVE
1 = **separate**, independent, isolated, lone, solitary **OPPOSITE:** collective 2 = **unique**, special, fresh, novel, exclusive, singular, idiosyncratic, unorthodox **OPPOSITE:** conventional
▷ NOUN 3 = **person**, being, human, unit, character, soul, creature

individually = separately, independently, singly, one by one, one at a time

induce 1 = **cause**, produce, create, effect, lead to, occasion, generate, bring about **OPPOSITE:** prevent
2 = **persuade**, encourage, influence, convince, urge, prompt, sway, entice **OPPOSITE:** dissuade

indulge 1 = **gratify**, satisfy, feed, give way to, yield to, pander to, gladden 2 = **spoil**, pamper, cosset, humour, give in to, coddle, mollycoddle, overindulge
▷ PHRASES: indulge yourself = **treat yourself**, splash out, spoil yourself, luxuriate in something, overindulge yourself

indulgence 1 = **luxury**, treat, extravagance, favour, privilege
2 = **gratification**, satisfaction, fulfilment, appeasement, satiation

industrialist = capitalist, tycoon, magnate, manufacturer, captain of industry, big businessman

industry 1 = **business**, production, manufacturing, trade, commerce 2 = **trade**, world, business, service, line, field, profession, occupation
3 = **diligence**, effort, labour, hard work, trouble, activity, application, endeavour

ineffective 1 = **unproductive**, useless, futile, vain, unsuccessful, pointless, fruitless, ineffectual **OPPOSITE:** effective 2 = **inefficient**, useless, poor, powerless, unfit, worthless, inept, impotent

inefficient 1 = **wasteful**, uneconomical, profligate 2 = **incompetent**, inept, weak, bungling, ineffectual, disorganized **OPPOSITE:** efficient

inequality = **disparity**, prejudice, difference, bias, diversity, irregularity, unevenness, disproportion

inevitable = **unavoidable**, inescapable, inexorable, sure, certain, fixed, assured, fated **OPPOSITE:** avoidable

inevitably = **unavoidably**, naturally, necessarily, surely, certainly, as a result, automatically, consequently

inexpensive = **cheap**, reasonable, budget, bargain, modest, economical **OPPOSITE:** expensive

inexperienced = **new**, green, raw, callow, immature, untried, unpractised, unversed **OPPOSITE:** experienced

infamous = **notorious**, ignominious, disreputable, ill-famed **OPPOSITE:** esteemed

infancy = **beginnings**, start, birth, roots, seeds, origins, dawn, outset **OPPOSITE:** end

infant = **baby**, child, babe, toddler, tot, bairn (*Scot*), littlie (*Austral informal*), ankle-biter (*Austral slang*), tacker (*Austral slang*)

infect 1 = **contaminate** 2 = **pollute**, poison, corrupt, contaminate, taint, defile 3 = **affect**, move, upset, overcome, stir, disturb

infection = **disease**, condition, complaint, illness, virus, disorder, corruption, poison

infectious = **catching**, spreading, contagious, communicable, virulent, transmittable

inferior ADJECTIVE 1 = **lower**, minor, secondary, subsidiary, lesser, humble, subordinate, lowly **OPPOSITE:** superior ▷ NOUN 2 = **underling**, junior, subordinate, lesser, menial, minion

infertility = **sterility**, barrenness, unproductiveness, infecundity

infiltrate = **penetrate**, pervade, permeate, percolate, filter through to, make inroads into, sneak into (*informal*), insinuate yourself

infinite 1 = **vast**, enormous, immense, countless, measureless 2 = **limitless**, endless, unlimited, eternal, never-ending, boundless, everlasting, inexhaustible **OPPOSITE:** finite

inflame = **enrage**, stimulate, provoke, excite, anger, arouse, rouse, infuriate **OPPOSITE:** calm

inflamed = **swollen**, sore, red, hot, infected, fevered

inflate 1 = **blow up**, pump up, swell, dilate, distend, bloat, puff up *or* out **OPPOSITE:** deflate 2 = **increase**, expand, enlarge **OPPOSITE:** diminish 3 = **exaggerate**, embroider, embellish, enlarge, amplify, overstate, overestimate, overemphasize

inflated = **exaggerated**, swollen, overblown

inflation = **increase**, expansion, extension, swelling, escalation, enlargement

inflict = **impose**, administer, visit, apply, deliver, levy, wreak, mete *or* deal out

influence NOUN 1 = **control**, power, authority, direction, command, domination, supremacy, mastery, mana (*NZ*) 2 = **power**, authority, pull (*informal*), importance, prestige, clout (*informal*), leverage 3 = **spell**, hold, power, weight, magic, sway, allure, magnetism ▷ VERB 4 = **affect**, have an effect on, have an impact on, control, concern, direct, guide, bear upon 5 = **persuade**, prompt, urge, induce, entice, coax, incite, instigate

influential 1 = **important**, powerful, telling, leading,

inspiring, potent, authoritative, weighty **OPPOSITE:** unimportant 2 = **instrumental**, important, significant, crucial

influx = **arrival**, rush, invasion, incursion, inundation, inrush

inform = **tell**, advise, notify, instruct, enlighten, communicate to, tip someone off ▷ **PHRASES: inform on someone** = **betray**, denounce, shop (*slang, chiefly Brit*), give someone away, incriminate, blow the whistle on (*informal*), grass on (*Brit slang*), double-cross (*informal*), dob someone in (*Austral & NZ slang*)

informal 1 = **natural**, relaxed, casual, familiar, unofficial, laid-back, easy-going, colloquial 2 = **relaxed**, easy, comfortable, simple, natural, casual, cosy, laid-back (*informal*) **OPPOSITE:** formal 3 = **casual**, comfortable, leisure, everyday, simple 4 = **unofficial**, irregular **OPPOSITE:** official

information = **facts**, news, report, message, notice, knowledge, data, intelligence, drum (*Austral informal*), heads up (*US & Canad*)

informative = **instructive**, revealing, educational, forthcoming, illuminating, enlightening, chatty, communicative

informed = **knowledgeable**, up to date, enlightened, learned, expert, familiar, versed, in the picture

infuriate = **enrage**, anger, provoke, irritate, incense, madden, exasperate, rile **OPPOSITE:** soothe

infuriating = **annoying**, irritating, provoking, galling, maddening, exasperating, vexatious

ingenious = **creative**, original, brilliant, clever, bright, shrewd, inventive, crafty **OPPOSITE:** unimaginative

ingredient = **component**, part, element, feature, piece, unit, item, aspect

inhabit = **live in**, occupy, populate, reside in, dwell in, abide in

inhabitant = **occupant**, resident, citizen, local, native, tenant, inmate, dweller

inhabited = **populated**, peopled, occupied, developed, settled, tenanted, colonized

inhale = **breathe in**, gasp, draw in, suck in, respire **OPPOSITE:** exhale

inherent = **intrinsic**, natural, essential, native, fundamental, hereditary, instinctive, innate **OPPOSITE:** extraneous

inherit = **be left**, come into, be willed, succeed to, fall heir to

inheritance = **legacy**, heritage, bequest, birthright, patrimony

inhibit 1 = **hinder**, check, frustrate, curb, restrain, constrain, obstruct, impede **OPPOSITE:** further 2 = **prevent**, stop, frustrate **OPPOSITE:** allow

inhibited = **shy**, reserved, guarded, subdued, repressed, constrained, self-conscious, reticent **OPPOSITE:** uninhibited

initial = **opening**, first, earliest, beginning, primary, maiden, introductory, embryonic **OPPOSITE:** final

initially = **at first**, first, firstly, originally, primarily, in the beginning, at or in the beginning

initiate VERB 1 = **begin**, start, open, launch, kick off (*informal*), embark on, originate, set about 2 = **introduce**, admit, enlist, enrol, launch, establish, invest, recruit

▷ NOUN 3 = **novice**, member, pupil, convert, amateur, newcomer, beginner, trainee

▷ PHRASES: initiate someone into something = **instruct in**, train in, coach in, acquaint with, drill in, make aware of, teach about, tutor in

initiative 1 = **advantage**, start, lead, upper hand 2 = **enterprise**, drive, energy, leadership, ambition, daring, enthusiasm, dynamism

inject 1 = **vaccinate**, administer, inoculate 2 = **introduce**, bring in, insert, instil, infuse, breathe

injection 1 = **vaccination**, shot (*informal*), jab (*informal*), dose, booster, immunization, inoculation 2 = **introduction**, investment, insertion, advancement, dose, infusion

injunction = **order**, ruling, command, instruction, mandate, precept, exhortation

injure 1 = **hurt**, wound, harm, damage, smash, crush, mar, shatter, mangulate (*Austral slang*) 2 = **damage**, harm, ruin, wreck, spoil, impair, crool *or* cruel (*Austral slang*) 3 = **undermine**, damage

injured = **hurt**, damaged, wounded, broken, cut, crushed, disabled, challenged, weakened, crook (*Austral & NZ slang*)

injury 1 = **wound**, cut, damage, trauma (*pathology*), gash, lesion, laceration 2 = **harm**, suffering, damage, ill, hurt, disability, misfortune, affliction 3 = **wrong**, offence, insult, detriment, disservice

injustice 1 = **unfairness**, discrimination, prejudice, bias, inequality, oppression, intolerance, bigotry **OPPOSITE:** justice 2 = **wrong**, injury, crime, error, offence, sin, misdeed, transgression

inland = **interior**, internal, upcountry

inner 1 = **inside**, internal, interior, inward **OPPOSITE:** outer 2 = **central**, middle, internal, interior 3 = **hidden**, deep, secret, underlying, obscure, repressed, unrevealed **OPPOSITE:** obvious

innocence 1 = **naiveté**, simplicity, inexperience, credulity, gullibility, ingenuousness, artlessness, unworldliness **OPPOSITE:** worldliness 2 = **blamelessness**, clean hands, uprightness, irreproachability, guiltlessness **OPPOSITE:** guilt 3 = **chastity**, virtue, purity, modesty, celibacy, continence, maidenhood

innocent 1 = **not guilty**, in the clear, blameless, clean, honest, uninvolved, irreproachable, guiltless **OPPOSITE:** guilty 2 = **naive**, open, trusting, simple, childlike, gullible, unsophisticated, unworldly **OPPOSITE:** worldly 3 = **harmless**, innocuous, inoffensive, well-meant, unobjectionable, well-intentioned **OPPOSITE:** malicious

innovation 1 = **change**, revolution, departure, introduction, variation, transformation, upheaval, alteration 2 = **newness**, novelty, originality, freshness, modernization, uniqueness

inoculation = **injection**, shot (*informal*), jab (*informal*), vaccination, dose, vaccine, booster, immunization

inquest = **inquiry**, investigation, probe, inquisition

inquire *or* **enquire** = ask, question, query, quiz
▷ **PHRASES: inquire into** = **investigate**, study, examine, research, explore, look into, probe into, make inquiries into

inquiry *or* **enquiry**
1 = **question**, query, investigation 2 = **investigation**, study, review, survey, examination, probe, inspection, exploration 3 = **research**, investigation, analysis, inspection, exploration, interrogation

insane 1 = **mad**, crazy, crazed, demented, deranged, out of your mind, off the air (*Austral slang*), porangi (*NZ*)
OPPOSITE: sane 2 = **stupid**, foolish, daft (*informal*), irresponsible, irrational, senseless, preposterous, impractical **OPPOSITE:** reasonable

insect = **bug**, creepy-crawly (*Brit informal*), gogga (*S African informal*)
• *See panels* **ANTS, BEES, AND WASPS, BEETLES, BUTTERFLIES AND MOTHS, FLIES, INSECTS**

insecure 1 = **unconfident**, worried, anxious, afraid, shy, uncertain, unsure, timid **OPPOSITE:** confident
2 = **unsafe**, exposed, vulnerable, wide-open, unprotected, defenceless, unguarded
OPPOSITE: safe

insecurity = **anxiety**, fear, worry, uncertainty **OPPOSITE:** confidence

insert = **put**, place, position, slip, slide, slot, thrust, stick in

inside NOUN 1 = **interior**, contents, core, nucleus
▷ **PLURAL NOUN 2** (*informal*) = **stomach**, guts, belly, bowels, innards (*informal*), entrails, viscera, vitals
▷ **ADJECTIVE 3** = **inner**, internal, interior, inward **OPPOSITE:** outside 4 = **confidential**, private, secret, internal, exclusive, restricted, privileged, classified
▷ **ADVERB 5** = **indoors**, in, within, under cover

insight 1 = **perception**, understanding, sense, knowledge, vision, judgment, awareness, grasp 2 *with* **into** = **understanding**, perception, awareness, experience, description, introduction, observation, judgment

insignificant = **unimportant**, minor, irrelevant, petty, trivial, meaningless, trifling, paltry
OPPOSITE: important

insist 1 = **persist**, lay down the law, put your foot down (*informal*) 2 = **demand**, order, require, command, dictate, entreat 3 = **assert**, state, maintain, claim, declare, repeat, vow, swear

insistence 1 = **demand**, command, dictate, entreaty,

INSECTS
Types of Insect

apple maggot
body louse, cootie (*US & NZ*), or (*NZ slang*) kutu
bollworm
booklouse
bookworm
bristletail
cabbageworm
caddis worm *or* caseworm
cankerworm
cochineal *or* cochineal insect
cockroach
cotton stainer
crab (louse)
cricket
dust mite
earwig *or* (*Scot dialect*) clipshears, *or* clipshear
flea
German cockroach *or* (*US*) Croton bug
grasshopper
katydid
lac insect
locust
louse *or* (*NZ*) kutu

mantis *or* praying mantis
measuring worm, looper, *or* inchworm
midge
mole cricket
mosquito
nit
phylloxera
scale insect
seventeen-year locust *or* periodical cicada
sheep ked *or* sheep tick
silkworm
silverfish
stick insect *or* (*US & Canad*) walking stick
sucking louse
tent caterpillar
thrips
treehopper
wax insect
web spinner
weta (*NZ*)
wheel bug
wireworm
woodworm

importunity 2 = **assertion**, claim, statement, declaration, persistence, pronouncement
inspect 1 = examine, check, look at, view, survey, look over, scrutinize, go over *or* through
2 = **check**, examine, investigate, look at, survey, vet, look over, go over *or* through
inspection 1 = examination, investigation, scrutiny, once-over (*informal*) 2 = **check**, search, investigation, review, survey, examination, scrutiny, once-over (*informal*)

inspector = examiner, investigator, supervisor, monitor, superintendent, auditor, censor, surveyor

inspiration 1 = **imagination**, creativity, ingenuity, insight, originality, inventiveness, cleverness 2 = **motivation**, example, model, boost, spur, incentive, revelation, stimulus **OPPOSITE:** deterrent 3 = **influence**, spur, stimulus, muse

inspire 1 = **motivate**, stimulate, encourage, influence, spur, animate, enliven, galvanize **OPPOSITE:** discourage 2 = **give rise to**, produce, result in, engender

inspired 1 = **brilliant**, wonderful, impressive, outstanding, thrilling, memorable, dazzling, superlative 2 = **stimulated**, uplifted, exhilarated, enthused, elated

inspiring = **uplifting**, exciting, moving, stirring, stimulating, rousing, exhilarating, heartening **OPPOSITE:** uninspiring

instability 1 = **uncertainty**, insecurity, vulnerability, volatility, unpredictability, fluctuation, impermanence, unsteadiness **OPPOSITE:** stability 2 = **imbalance**, variability, unpredictability, unsteadiness, changeableness

install 1 = **set up**, put in, place, position, station, establish, lay, fix 2 = **institute**, establish, introduce, invest, ordain, inaugurate, induct 3 = **settle**, position, plant, establish, lodge, ensconce

installation 1 = **setting up**, fitting, instalment, placing, positioning, establishment 2 = **appointment**, ordination, inauguration, induction, investiture

instalment 1 = **payment**, repayment, part payment 2 = **part**, section, chapter, episode, portion, division

instance NOUN 1 = **example**, case, occurrence, occasion, sample, illustration ▷ VERB 2 = **name**, mention, identify, point out, advance, quote, refer to, point to

instant NOUN 1 = **moment**, second, flash, split second, jiffy (*informal*), trice, twinkling of an eye (*informal*) 2 = **time**, point, hour, moment, stage, occasion, phase, juncture ▷ ADJECTIVE 3 = **immediate**, prompt, instantaneous, direct, quick, on-the-spot, split-second 4 = **ready-made**, fast, convenience, ready-mixed, ready-cooked, precooked

instantly = **immediately**, at once, straight away, now, directly, right away, instantaneously, this minute

instead = **rather**, alternatively, preferably, in preference, in lieu, on second thoughts
▷ **PHRASES: instead of** = **in place of**, rather than, in preference to, in lieu of, in contrast with

instinct 1 = **natural inclination**, talent, tendency, faculty, inclination, knack, predisposition, proclivity
2 = **talent**, skill, gift, capacity, bent, genius, faculty, knack
3 = **intuition**, impulse

instinctive = **natural**, inborn, automatic, unconscious, inherent, spontaneous, reflex, innate **OPPOSITE:** acquired

instinctively = **intuitively**, naturally, automatically, without thinking, involuntarily, by instinct

institute NOUN
1 = **establishment**, body, centre, school, university, society, association, college
▷ **VERB** 2 = **establish**, start, found, launch, set up, introduce, fix, organize **OPPOSITE:** end

institution 1 = **establishment**, body, centre, school, university, society, association, college
2 = **custom**, practice, tradition, law, rule, procedure, convention, ritual

institutional = **conventional**, accepted, established, formal, routine, orthodox, procedural

instruct 1 = **order**, tell, direct, charge, bid, command, mandate, enjoin
2 = **teach**, school, train, coach, educate, drill, tutor

instruction NOUN 1 = **order**, ruling, command, rule, demand, regulation, dictate, decree
2 = **teaching**, schooling, training, grounding, education, coaching, lesson(s), guidance
▷ **PLURAL NOUN**
3 = **information**, rules, advice, directions, recommendations, guidance, specifications

instructor = **teacher**, coach, guide, adviser, trainer, demonstrator, tutor, mentor

instrument 1 = **tool**, device, implement, mechanism, appliance, apparatus, gadget, contraption (*informal*)
2 = **agent**, means, medium, agency, vehicle, mechanism, organ

instrumental = **active**, involved, influential, useful, helpful, contributory

insufficient = **inadequate**, scant, meagre, short, sparse, deficient, lacking **OPPOSITE:** ample

insulate = **isolate**, protect, screen, defend, shelter, shield, cut off, cushion

insult VERB 1 = **offend**, abuse, wound, slight, put down, snub, malign, affront **OPPOSITE:** praise
▷ **NOUN** 2 = **jibe**, slight, put-down, abuse, snub, barb, affront, abusive remark

3 = **offence**, slight, snub, slur, affront, slap in the face (*informal*), kick in the teeth (*informal*), insolence

insulting = **offensive**, rude, abusive, degrading, contemptuous, disparaging, scurrilous, insolent **OPPOSITE:** complimentary

insurance 1 = **assurance**, cover, security, protection, safeguard, indemnity **2** = **protection**, security, guarantee, shelter, safeguard, warranty

insure 1 = **assure**, cover, protect, guarantee, warrant, underwrite, indemnify **2** = **protect**, cover, safeguard

intact = **undamaged**, whole, complete, sound, perfect, entire, unscathed, unbroken **OPPOSITE:** damaged

integral = **essential**, basic, fundamental, necessary, component, constituent, indispensable, intrinsic **OPPOSITE:** inessential

integrate = **join**, unite, combine, blend, incorporate, merge, fuse, assimilate **OPPOSITE:** separate

integrity 1 = **honesty**, principle, honour, virtue, goodness, morality, purity, probity **OPPOSITE:** dishonesty **2** = **unity**, unification, cohesion, coherence, wholeness, soundness, completeness **OPPOSITE:** fragility

intellect = **intelligence**, mind, reason, understanding, sense, brains (*informal*), judgment

intellectual ADJECTIVE **1** = **scholarly**, learned, academic, lettered, intelligent, cerebral, erudite, scholastic **OPPOSITE:** stupid ▷ NOUN **2** = **academic**, expert, genius, thinker, master, mastermind, maestro, highbrow, fundi (*S African*), acca (*Austral slang*) **OPPOSITE:** idiot

intelligence 1 = **intellect**, understanding, brains (*informal*), sense, knowledge, judgment, wit, perception **OPPOSITE:** stupidity **2** = **information**, news, facts, report, findings, knowledge, data, notification, heads up (*US & Canad*) **OPPOSITE:** misinformation

intelligent = **clever**, bright, smart, sharp, enlightened, knowledgeable, well-informed, brainy (*informal*) **OPPOSITE:** stupid

intend = **plan**, mean, aim, propose, purpose, have in mind or view

intense 1 = **extreme**, great, severe, fierce, deep, powerful, supreme, acute **OPPOSITE:** mild **2** = **fierce**, tough **3** = **passionate**, emotional, fierce, heightened, ardent, fanatical, fervent, heartfelt **OPPOSITE:** indifferent

intensify 1 = **increase**, raise, add to, strengthen, reinforce, widen, heighten, sharpen **OPPOSITE:** decrease 2 = **escalate**, increase, widen, deepen

intensity 1 = **force**, strength, fierceness 2 = **passion**, emotion, fervour, force, strength, fanaticism, ardour, vehemence

intensive = **concentrated**, thorough, exhaustive, full, demanding, detailed, complete, serious

intent ADJECTIVE 1 = **absorbed**, intense, fascinated, preoccupied, enthralled, attentive, watchful, engrossed **OPPOSITE:** indifferent ▷ NOUN 2 = **intention**, aim, purpose, meaning, end, plan, goal, design **OPPOSITE:** chance

intention = **aim**, plan, idea, goal, end, design, target, wish

inter = **bury**, lay to rest, entomb, consign to the grave

intercept = **catch**, stop, block, seize, cut off, interrupt, head off, obstruct

intercourse 1 = **sexual intercourse**, sex (*informal*), copulation, coitus, carnal knowledge 2 = **contact**, communication, commerce, dealings

interest NOUN 1 *often plural* = **hobby**, activity, pursuit, entertainment, recreation, amusement, preoccupation, diversion 2 *often plural* = **advantage**, good, benefit, profit 3 = **stake**, investment ▷ VERB 4 = **arouse your curiosity**, fascinate, attract, grip, entertain, intrigue, divert, captivate **OPPOSITE:** bore

interested 1 = **curious**, attracted, excited, drawn, keen, gripped, fascinated, captivated **OPPOSITE:** uninterested 2 = **involved**, concerned, affected, implicated

interesting = **intriguing**, absorbing, appealing, attractive, engaging, gripping, entrancing, stimulating **OPPOSITE:** uninteresting

interface = **connection**, link, boundary, border, frontier

interfere = **meddle**, intervene, intrude, butt in, tamper, pry, encroach, stick your oar in (*informal*) ▷ PHRASES: interfere with something *or* someone = **conflict with**, check, clash, handicap, hamper, disrupt, inhibit, thwart

interference = intrusion, intervention, meddling, opposition, conflict, obstruction, prying

interim = temporary, provisional, makeshift, acting, caretaker, improvised, stopgap

interior NOUN 1 = inside, centre, heart, middle, depths, core, nucleus
▷ ADJECTIVE 2 = inside, internal, inner OPPOSITE: exterior 3 = mental, emotional, psychological, private, personal, secret, hidden, spiritual

intermediary = mediator, agent, middleman, broker, go-between

intermediate = middle, mid, halfway, in-between (informal), midway, intervening, transitional, median

internal 1 = domestic, home, national, local, civic, in-house, intramural 2 = inner, inside, interior OPPOSITE: external

international = global, world, worldwide, universal, cosmopolitan, intercontinental

internet
▷ PHRASES: the internet = the information superhighway, the net (informal), the web (informal), the World Wide Web, cyberspace, the cloud, blogosphere, the interweb (facetious), blogostream, extranet, podosphere

interpret 1 = take, understand, explain, construe 2 = translate, transliterate 3 = explain, make sense of, decode, decipher, elucidate 4 = understand, read, crack, solve, figure out (informal), comprehend, decode, deduce 5 = portray, present, perform, render, depict, enact, act out

interpretation
1 = explanation, analysis, exposition, elucidation
2 = performance, portrayal, presentation, reading, rendition
3 = reading, study, review, version, analysis, explanation, examination, evaluation

interpreter = translator

interrogation = questioning, inquiry, examination, grilling (informal), cross-examination, inquisition, third degree (informal)

interrupt 1 = intrude, disturb, intervene, interfere (with), break in, heckle, butt in, barge in (informal) 2 = suspend, stop, end, delay, cease, postpone, shelve, put off

interruption 1 = disruption, break, disturbance, hitch, intrusion 2 = stoppage, pause, suspension

interval 1 = period, spell, space, stretch, pause, span 2 = break, interlude, intermission, rest, gap, pause, respite, lull 3 = delay, gap, hold-up, stoppage 4 = stretch, space

intervene 1 = **step in** (*informal*), interfere, mediate, intrude, intercede, arbitrate, take a hand (*informal*) 2 = **interrupt**, involve yourself 3 = **happen**, occur, take place, follow, arise, ensue, befall, materialize

intervention = **mediation**, interference, intrusion, arbitration, conciliation, agency

interview NOUN 1 = **meeting** 2 = **audience**, talk, conference, exchange, dialogue, consultation, press conference ▷ VERB 3 = **examine**, talk to 4 = **question**, interrogate, examine, investigate, pump, grill (*informal*), quiz, cross-examine

interviewer = **questioner**, reporter, investigator, examiner, interrogator

intimacy = **familiarity**, closeness, confidentiality **OPPOSITE:** aloofness

intimate¹ ADJECTIVE 1 = **close**, dear, loving, near, familiar, thick (*informal*), devoted, confidential **OPPOSITE:** distant 2 = **private**, personal, confidential, special, individual, secret, exclusive **OPPOSITE:** public 3 = **detailed**, minute, full, deep, particular, immediate, comprehensive, profound 4 = **cosy**, relaxed, friendly, informal, harmonious, snug, comfy (*informal*), warm ▷ NOUN 5 = **friend**, close friend, crony, cobber (*Austral & NZ*

old-fashioned informal), confidant *or* confidante, (constant) companion, E hoa (*NZ*) **OPPOSITE:** stranger

intimate² 1 = **suggest**, indicate, hint, imply, insinuate 2 = **announce**, state, declare, communicate, make known

intimately 1 = **closely**, personally, warmly, familiarly, tenderly, affectionately, confidentially, confidingly 2 = **fully**, very well, thoroughly, in detail, inside out

intimidate = **frighten**, pressure, threaten, scare, bully, plague, hound, daunt

intimidation = **bullying**, pressure, threat(s), menaces, coercion, arm-twisting (*informal*), browbeating, terrorization

intricate = **complicated**, involved, complex, fancy, elaborate, tangled, tortuous, convoluted **OPPOSITE:** simple

intrigue NOUN 1 = **plot**, scheme, conspiracy, manoeuvre, collusion, stratagem, chicanery, wile 2 = **affair**, romance, intimacy, liaison, amour ▷ VERB 3 = **interest**, fascinate, attract, rivet, titillate 4 = **plot**, scheme, manoeuvre, conspire, connive, machinate

intriguing = **interesting**, fascinating, absorbing, exciting, engaging, gripping, stimulating, compelling

introduce 1 = bring in, establish, set up, start, found, launch, institute, pioneer **2 = present**, acquaint, make known, familiarize **3 = suggest**, air, advance, submit, bring up, put forward, broach, moot **4 = add**, insert, inject, throw in (*informal*), infuse

introduction 1 = launch, institution, pioneering, inauguration **OPPOSITE:** elimination **2 = opening**, prelude, preface, lead-in, preamble, foreword, prologue, intro (*informal*) **OPPOSITE:** conclusion

introductory 1 = preliminary, first, initial, inaugural, preparatory **OPPOSITE:** concluding **2 = starting**, opening, initial

introverted = introspective, withdrawn, inward-looking, self-contained, self-centred, indrawn, inner-directed

intruder = trespasser, invader, prowler, interloper, infiltrator, gate-crasher (*informal*)

intrusion 1 = interruption, interference, infringement, trespass, encroachment **2 = invasion**, breach, infringement, encroachment, infraction, usurpation

intuition 1 = instinct, perception, insight, sixth sense **2 = feeling**, idea, impression, suspicion, premonition, inkling, presentiment

invade 1 = attack, storm, assault, capture, occupy, seize, raid, overwhelm **2 = infest**, swarm, overrun, ravage, beset, pervade, permeate

invader = attacker, raider, plunderer, aggressor, trespasser

invalid¹ NOUN 1 = patient, sufferer, convalescent, valetudinarian ▷ **ADJECTIVE 2 = disabled**, challenged, ill, sick, ailing, frail, infirm, bedridden

invalid² 1 = null and void, void, worthless, inoperative **OPPOSITE:** valid **2 = unfounded**, false, illogical, irrational, unsound, fallacious **OPPOSITE:** sound

invaluable = precious, valuable, priceless, inestimable, worth your *or* its weight in gold **OPPOSITE:** worthless

invariably = always, regularly, constantly, repeatedly, consistently, continually, eternally, habitually

invasion 1 = attack, assault, capture, takeover, raid, offensive, occupation, conquering **2 = intrusion**, breach, violation, disturbance, disruption, infringement, encroachment, infraction

invent 1 = create, make, produce, design, discover, manufacture, devise, conceive

2 = **make up**, devise, concoct, forge, fake, fabricate, feign, falsify

invention 1 = **creation**, machine, device, design, instrument, discovery, innovation, gadget
2 = **development**, design, production, setting up, foundation, construction, creation, discovery 3 = **fiction**, fantasy, lie, yarn, fabrication, falsehood, untruth
4 = **creativity**, imagination, initiative, enterprise, genius, ingenuity, originality, inventiveness

inventive = **creative**, original, innovative, imaginative, inspired, fertile, ingenious, resourceful **OPPOSITE:** uninspired

inventor = **creator**, maker, author, designer, architect, coiner, originator

inventory = **list**, record, catalogue, listing, account, roll, file, register

invertebrate
  • See panels **CRUSTACEANS**, **INVERTEBRATES**, **SNAILS, SLUGS AND OTHER GASTROPODS**, **SPIDERS AND OTHER ARACHNIDS**

invest 1 = **spend**, expend, advance, venture, put in, devote, lay out, sink in
2 = **empower**, provide, charge, sanction, license, authorize, vest (archaic)

▷ **PHRASES: invest in something** = **buy**, get, purchase, pay for, obtain, acquire, procure

investigate = **examine**, study, research, go into, explore, look into, inspect, probe into

investigation = **examination**, study, inquiry, review, search, survey, probe, inspection

investigator = **examiner**, researcher, monitor, detective, analyser, explorer, scrutinizer, inquirer

investment 1 = **investing**, backing, funding, financing, contribution, speculation, transaction, expenditure
2 = **stake**, interest, share, concern, portion, ante (informal)
3 = **buy**, asset, acquisition, venture, risk, gamble

invisible = **unseen**, imperceptible, indiscernible, unseeable **OPPOSITE:** visible

invitation = **request**, call, invite (informal), summons

invite 1 = **ask** 2 = **request**, look for, bid for, appeal for
3 = **encourage**, attract, cause, court, ask for (informal), generate, foster, tempt

inviting = **tempting**, appealing, attractive, welcoming, enticing, seductive, alluring, mouthwatering **OPPOSITE:** uninviting

invoke 1 = **apply**, use, implement, initiate, resort to,

INVERTEBRATES
Types of Invertebrate

amoeba or (US) ameba
animalcule or animalculum
arrowworm
arthropod
Balmain bug
bardy, bardie, or bardi (Austral)
bivalve
bladder worm
blue-ringed octopus (Austral)
Bluff oyster (NZ)
box jellyfish or (Austral) sea wasp
brachiopod or lamp shell
brandling
bryozoan or (colloquial) sea mat
catworm, white worm, or
  white cat
centipede
chicken louse
chiton or coat-of-mail shell
clam
clappy-doo or clabby-doo (Scot)
cockle
cone (shell)
coral
crown-of-thorns (starfish)
ctenophore or comb jelly
cunjevoi or cunje (Austral)
cuttlefish or cuttle
daphnia
earthworm
eelworm
gaper
gapeworm
gastropod
Guinea worm
horseleech

jellyfish or (Austral slang) blubber
kina (NZ)
lancelet or amphioxus
leech
liver fluke
lugworm, lug, or lobworm
lungworm
millipede, millepede, or milleped
mollusc
mussel
octopus or devilfish
otter shell
oyster
paddle worm
paper nautilus, nautilus, or
  argonaut
pearly nautilus, nautilus, or
  chambered nautilus
piddock
pipi or ugari (Austral)
Portuguese man-of-war or
  (Austral) bluebottle
quahog, hard-shell clam, hard-
  shell, or round clam
ragworm or (US) clamworm
razor-shell or (US) razor clam
red coral or precious coral
roundworm
sandworm or (Austral)
  pumpworm
scallop
sea anemone
sea cucumber
sea lily
sea mouse
sea pen

sea slater	tube worm
sea squirt	tubifex
sea urchin	tusk shell *or* tooth shell
seed oyster	Venus's flower basket
soft-shell (clam)	Venus's-girdle
sponge	Venus shell
squid	vinegar eel, vinegar worm, *or*
starfish	eelworm
stomach worm	water louse *or* water slater
stony coral	water measurer
sunstar	water stick insect
tapeworm	wheatworm
tardigrade *or* water bear	whipworm
tellin	woodborer
teredo *or* shipworm	worm
trepang *or* bêche-de-mer	

put into effect **2 = call upon**, appeal to, pray to, petition, beseech, entreat, supplicate

involve 1 = entail, mean, require, occasion, imply, give rise to, necessitate **2 = concern**, draw in, bear on

involved = complicated, complex, intricate, hard, confused, confusing, elaborate, tangled **OPPOSITE:** straightforward

involvement = connection, interest, association, commitment, attachment

inward 1 = incoming, entering, inbound, ingoing **2 = internal**, inner, private, personal, inside, secret, hidden, interior **OPPOSITE:** outward

iron MODIFIER **1 = ferrous**, ferric
▷ ADJECTIVE **2 = inflexible**, hard, strong, tough, rigid, adamant, unconditional, steely **OPPOSITE:** weak
▷ PHRASES: **iron something out = settle**, resolve, sort out, get rid of, reconcile, clear up, put right, straighten out

RELATED WORDS
adjectives: ferric, ferrous

ironic *or* **ironical 1 = sarcastic**, dry, acid, bitter, mocking, wry, satirical, tongue-in-cheek **2 = paradoxical**, contradictory, puzzling, baffling, confounding, enigmatic, incongruous

irony 1 = sarcasm, mockery, ridicule, satire, cynicism,

derision 2 = **paradox**, incongruity

irrational = **illogical**, crazy, absurd, unreasonable, preposterous, nonsensical **OPPOSITE:** rational

irregular 1 = **variable**, erratic, occasional, random, casual, shaky, sporadic, haphazard **OPPOSITE:** steady 2 = **uneven**, rough, ragged, crooked, jagged, bumpy, contorted, lopsided **OPPOSITE:** even 3 = **inappropriate**, unconventional, unethical, unusual, extraordinary, exceptional, peculiar, unofficial 4 = **unofficial**, underground, guerrilla, resistance, partisan, rogue, paramilitary, mercenary

irrelevant = **unconnected**, unrelated, unimportant, inappropriate, peripheral, immaterial, extraneous, beside the point **OPPOSITE:** relevant

irresistible = **overwhelming**, compelling, overpowering, urgent, compulsive

irresponsible = **thoughtless**, reckless, careless, unreliable, untrustworthy, shiftless, scatterbrained **OPPOSITE:** responsible

irritate 1 = **annoy**, anger, bother, needle (*informal*), infuriate, exasperate, nettle, irk **OPPOSITE:** placate 2 = **inflame**, pain, rub, scratch, scrape, chafe

irritated = **annoyed**, cross, angry, bothered, put out, exasperated, nettled, vexed, tooshie (*Austral slang*), hoha (*NZ*)

irritating = **annoying**, trying, infuriating, disturbing, nagging, troublesome, maddening, irksome **OPPOSITE:** pleasing

irritation 1 = **annoyance**, anger, fury, resentment, gall, indignation, displeasure, exasperation **OPPOSITE:** pleasure 2 = **nuisance**, irritant, drag (*informal*), pain in the neck (*informal*), thorn in your flesh

island = **isle**, atoll, islet, ait *or* eyot (*dialect*), cay *or* key

RELATED WORD
adjective: insular

isolate 1 = **separate**, break up, cut off, detach, split up, insulate, segregate, disconnect 2 = **quarantine**

isolated = **remote**, far, distant, lonely, out-of-the-way, hidden, secluded, inaccessible

isolation = **separation**, segregation, detachment, solitude, seclusion, remoteness

issue NOUN 1 = **topic**, point, matter, problem, question, subject, theme 2 = **point**, question, bone of contention 3 = **edition**, printing, copy, publication, number, version 4 = **children**, offspring, babies, kids (*informal*), heirs, descendants, progeny **OPPOSITE:** parent

▷ VERB 5 = **give out**, release, publish, announce, deliver, spread, broadcast, distribute
▷ PHRASES: **take issue with something** *or* **someone** = **disagree with**, question, challenge, oppose, dispute, object to, argue with, take exception to

itch VERB 1 = **prickle**, tickle, tingle 2 = **long**, ache, crave, pine, hunger, lust, yearn, hanker
▷ NOUN 3 = **irritation**, tingling, prickling, itchiness 4 = **desire**, longing, craving, passion, yen (*informal*), hunger, lust, yearning

item 1 = **article**, thing, object, piece, unit, component 2 = **matter**, point, issue, case, question, concern, detail, subject 3 = **report**, story, piece, account, note, feature, notice, article

itinerary = **schedule**, programme, route, timetable

jab VERB 1 = **poke**, dig, punch, thrust, tap, stab, nudge, prod
▷ NOUN 2 = **poke**, dig, punch, thrust, tap, stab, nudge, prod

jacket = **covering**, casing, case, cover, skin, shell, coat, wrapping

jackpot = **prize**, winnings, award, reward, bonanza

jail NOUN 1 = **prison**, penitentiary (*US*), confinement, dungeon, nick (*Brit slang*), slammer (*slang*), reformatory, boob (*Austral slang*)
▷ VERB 2 = **imprison**, confine, detain, lock up, put away, intern, incarcerate, send down

jam NOUN 1 (*informal*) = **predicament**, tight spot, situation, trouble, hole (*slang*), fix (*informal*), mess, pinch
▷ VERB 2 = **pack**, force, press, stuff, squeeze, ram, wedge, cram 3 = **crowd**, throng, crush, mass, surge, flock, swarm, congregate 4 = **congest**, block, clog, stick, stall, obstruct

jar¹ = **pot**, container, drum, vase, jug, pitcher, urn, crock

jar² 1 *usually with* **on** = **irritate**, annoy, offend, nettle, irk, grate on, get on your nerves (*informal*) 2 = **jolt**, rock, shake, bump, rattle, vibrate, convulse

jargon = **parlance**, idiom, usage, argot, leetspeak, l33tspeak *or* 1337speak (*computing*), netspeak (*computing*)

jaw PLURAL NOUN 1 = **opening**, entrance, mouth
▷ VERB 2 (*slang*) = **talk**, chat, gossip, chatter, spout, natter

jealous 1 = **suspicious**, protective, wary, doubtful, sceptical, vigilant, watchful, possessive OPPOSITE: trusting 2 = **envious**, grudging, resentful, green, green with envy, desirous, covetous OPPOSITE: satisfied

jealousy = **suspicion**, mistrust, possessiveness, doubt, spite, resentment, wariness, dubiety

jeer VERB 1 = **mock**, deride, heckle, barrack, ridicule, taunt, scoff, gibe OPPOSITE: cheer
▷ NOUN 2 = **mockery**, abuse, ridicule, taunt, boo, derision, gibe, catcall OPPOSITE: applause

jeopardy = **danger**, risk, peril, vulnerability, insecurity

jerk VERB 1 = **jolt**, bang, bump, lurch
▷ NOUN 2 = **lurch**, movement, thrust, twitch, jolt

jet NOUN 1 = **stream**, current, spring, flow, rush, flood, burst, spray
▷ VERB 2 = **fly**, wing, cruise, soar, zoom

jewel 1 = **gemstone**, gem, ornament, sparkler (*informal*), rock (*slang*) 2 = **treasure**, wonder, darling, pearl, gem, paragon, pride and joy, taonga (*NZ*)

jewellery = **jewels**, treasure, gems, trinkets, ornaments, finery, regalia, bling (*slang*)

job 1 = **position**, work, calling, business, field, career, employment, profession 2 = **task**, duty, work, venture, enterprise, undertaking, assignment, chore

jobless = **unemployed**, redundant, out of work, inactive, unoccupied, idle

jog 1 = **run**, trot, canter, lope 2 = **nudge**, push, shake, prod 3 = **stimulate**, stir, prod

join 1 = **enrol in**, enter, sign up for, enlist in 2 = **connect**, unite, couple, link, combine, attach, fasten, add OPPOSITE: detach

joint ADJECTIVE 1 = **shared**, mutual, collective, communal, united, joined, allied, combined
▷ NOUN 2 = **junction**, connection, brace, bracket, hinge, intersection, node, nexus

jointly = **collectively**, together, in conjunction, as one, in common, mutually, in partnership, in league OPPOSITE: separately

joke NOUN 1 = **jest**, gag (*informal*), wisecrack (*informal*),

witticism, crack (*informal*), quip, pun, one-liner (*informal*) **2 = laugh**, jest, jape **3 = prank**, trick, practical joke, lark (*informal*), escapade, jape **4 = laughing stock**, clown, buffoon
▷ VERB **5 = jest**, kid (*informal*), mock, tease, taunt, quip, banter, play the fool

joker = comedian, comic, wit, clown, wag, jester, prankster, buffoon

jolly = happy, cheerful, merry, upbeat (*informal*), playful, cheery, genial, chirpy (*informal*)
OPPOSITE: miserable

jolt VERB **1 = jerk**, push, shake, knock, jar, shove, jog, jostle **2 = surprise**, stun, disturb, stagger, startle, perturb, discompose
▷ NOUN **3 = jerk**, start, jump, shake, bump, jar, jog, lurch **4 = surprise**, blow, shock, setback, bombshell, bolt from the blue

journal 1 = magazine, publication, gazette, periodical **2 = newspaper**, paper, daily, weekly, monthly **3 = diary**, record, history, log, notebook, chronicle, annals, yearbook, blog (*informal*)

journalist = reporter, writer, correspondent, newsman *or* newswoman, commentator, broadcaster, hack (*derogatory*), columnist

journey NOUN **1 = trip**, drive, tour, flight, excursion, trek, expedition, voyage **2 = progress**, voyage, pilgrimage, odyssey
▷ VERB **3 = travel**, go, move, tour, progress, proceed, wander, trek, go walkabout (*Austral*)

joy = delight, pleasure, satisfaction, ecstasy, enjoyment, bliss, glee, rapture
OPPOSITE: sorrow

jubilee = celebration, holiday, festival, festivity

judge NOUN **1 = magistrate**, justice, beak (*Brit slang*), His, Her *or* Your Honour **2 = referee**, expert, specialist, umpire, umpie (*Austral slang*), mediator, examiner, connoisseur, assessor **3 = critic**, assessor, arbiter
▷ VERB **4 = adjudicate**, referee, umpire, mediate, officiate, arbitrate **5 = evaluate**, rate, consider, view, value, esteem **6 = estimate**, guess, assess, calculate, evaluate, gauge

▌ **RELATED WORD**
▌ *adjective:* judicial

judgment 1 = opinion, view, estimate, belief, assessment, diagnosis, valuation, appraisal **2 = verdict**, finding, ruling, decision, sentence, decree, arbitration, adjudication **3 = sense**, good sense, understanding, discrimination, perception, wisdom, wit, prudence

judicial = **legal**, official

jug = **container**, pitcher, urn, carafe, creamer (*US & Canad*), vessel, jar, crock

juggle = **manipulate**, change, alter, modify, manoeuvre

juice 1 = **liquid**, extract, fluid, liquor, sap, nectar 2 = **secretion**

juicy 1 = **moist**, lush, succulent 2 = **interesting**, colourful, sensational, vivid, provocative, spicy (*informal*), suggestive, racy

jumble NOUN 1 = **muddle**, mixture, mess, disorder, confusion, clutter, disarray, mishmash
▷ VERB 2 = **mix**, mistake, confuse, disorder, shuffle, muddle, disorganize

jumbo = **giant**, large, huge, immense, gigantic, oversized, supersize **OPPOSITE:** tiny

jump VERB 1 = **leap**, spring, bound, bounce, hop, skip 2 = **vault**, hurdle, go over, sail over, hop over 3 = **spring**, bound, bounce 4 = **recoil**, start, jolt, flinch, shake, jerk, quake, shudder 5 = **increase**, rise, climb, escalate, advance, soar, surge, spiral 6 = **miss**, avoid, skip, omit, evade
▷ NOUN 7 = **leap**, spring, skip, bound, hop, vault 8 = **rise**, increase, upswing, advance, upsurge, upturn, increment

jumped-up (*informal*) = **conceited**, arrogant, pompous, overbearing, presumptuous, insolent

jumper = **sweater**, top, jersey, cardigan, woolly, pullover

junior 1 = **minor**, lower, secondary, lesser, subordinate, inferior 2 = **younger OPPOSITE:** senior

junk = **rubbish**, refuse, waste, scrap, litter, debris, garbage (*chiefly US*), trash

jurisdiction 1 = **authority**, power, control, rule, influence, command, mana (*NZ*)
2 = **range**, area, field, bounds, province, scope, sphere, compass

just ADVERB 1 = **recently**, lately, only now 2 = **merely**, only, simply, solely 3 = **barely**, hardly, by a whisker, by the skin of your teeth 4 = **exactly**, really, quite, completely, totally, perfectly, entirely, truly
▷ ADJECTIVE 5 = **fair**, good, legitimate, upright, honest, equitable, conscientious, virtuous **OPPOSITE:** unfair
6 = **fitting**, due, correct, deserved, appropriate, justified, decent, merited **OPPOSITE:** inappropriate

USAGE NOTE

The expression *just exactly* is considered to be poor style because, since both words mean the same thing, only one or the other is needed. Use *just* – *it's just what they want* - or *exactly* - *it's exactly what they want*, but not both together.

justice 1 = **fairness**, equity, integrity, honesty, decency, rightfulness, right **OPPOSITE:** injustice 2 = **justness**, fairness, legitimacy, right, integrity, honesty, legality, rightfulness 3 = **judge**, magistrate, beak (*Brit slang*), His, Her *or* Your Honour

justification = **reason**, grounds, defence, basis, excuse, warrant, rationale, vindication

justify = **explain**, support, warrant, defend, excuse, uphold, vindicate, exonerate

juvenile NOUN 1 = **child**, youth, minor, girl, boy, teenager, infant, adolescent **OPPOSITE:** adult ▷ ADJECTIVE 2 = **young**, junior, adolescent, youthful, immature **OPPOSITE:** adult 3 = **immature**, childish, infantile, puerile, young, youthful, inexperienced, callow

Kk

kai (*NZ informal*) = **food**, grub (*slang*), provisions, fare, tucker (*Austral & NZ informal*), refreshment, foodstuffs

kak (*S African taboo*) 1 = **faeces**, excrement, manure, dung, droppings, waste matter 2 = **rubbish**, nonsense, garbage (*informal*), rot, drivel, tripe (*informal*), bizzo (*Austral slang*), bull's wool (*Austral & NZ slang*)

keen 1 = **eager**, intense, enthusiastic, passionate, ardent, avid, fervent, impassioned **OPPOSITE:** unenthusiastic 2 = **earnest**, fierce, intense, vehement, passionate, heightened, ardent, fanatical 3 = **sharp**, incisive, cutting, edged, razor-like **OPPOSITE:** dull 4 = **perceptive**, quick, sharp, acute, smart, wise, clever, shrewd **OPPOSITE:** obtuse 5 = **intense**, strong, fierce, relentless, cut-throat

keep VERB 1 *usually with* **from** = **prevent**, restrain, hinder, keep back 2 = **hold on to**, maintain, retain, save, preserve, nurture,

k

cherish, conserve **OPPOSITE:** lose **3** = **store**, put, place, house, hold, deposit, stack, stow **4** = **carry**, stock, sell, supply, handle **5** = **support**, maintain, sustain, provide for, mind, fund, finance, feed **6** = **raise**, own, maintain, tend, farm, breed, look after, rear **7** = **manage**, run, administer, be in charge (of), direct, handle, supervise **8** = **delay**, detain, hinder, impede, obstruct, set back **OPPOSITE:** release ▷ NOUN **9** = **board**, food, maintenance, living, kai (*NZ informal*) **10** = **tower**, castle ▷ PHRASES: **keep something up 1** = **continue**, make, maintain, carry on, persist in, persevere with **2** = **maintain**, sustain, perpetuate, retain, preserve, prolong ▶ **keep up** = **keep pace**

keeper = **curator**, guardian, steward, attendant, caretaker, preserver

keeping = **care**, charge, protection, possession, custody, guardianship, safekeeping ▷ PHRASES: **in keeping with** = **in agreement with**, in harmony with, in accord with, in compliance with, in conformity with, in balance with, in correspondence with, in proportion with

key NOUN **1** = **opener**, door key, latchkey **2** = **answer** ▷ MODIFIER **3** = **essential**, leading, major, main, important, necessary, vital, crucial **OPPOSITE:** minor

kia ora (*NZ*) = **hello**, hi (*informal*), greetings, gidday *or* g'day (*Austral & NZ*), how do you do?, good morning, good evening, good afternoon

kick VERB **1** = **boot**, knock, punt **2** (*informal*) = **give up**, break, stop, abandon, quit, cease, eschew, leave off ▷ NOUN **3** (*informal*) = **thrill**, buzz (*slang*), tingle, high (*informal*) ▷ PHRASES: **kick someone out** (*informal*) = **dismiss**, remove, get rid of, expel, eject, evict, sack (*informal*), kennet (*Austral slang*), jeff (*Austral slang*) ▶ **kick something off** (*informal*) = **begin**, start, open, commence, initiate, get on the road

kid[1] (*informal*) = **child**, baby, teenager, youngster, infant, adolescent, juvenile, toddler, littlie (*Austral informal*), ankle-biter (*Austral slang*), tacker (*Austral slang*)

kid[2] = **tease**, joke, trick, fool, pretend, wind up (*Brit slang*), hoax, delude

kidnap = **abduct**, capture, seize, snatch (*slang*), hijack, hold to ransom

kill 1 = **slay**, murder, execute, slaughter, destroy, massacre, butcher, cut down **2** (*informal*) = **destroy**, crush, scotch, stop, halt, wreck, shatter, suppress

killer = **murderer**, slayer,
hit man (*slang*), butcher,
gunman, assassin, terminator,
executioner

killing NOUN 1 = **murder**,
massacre, slaughter, dispatch,
manslaughter, elimination,
slaying, homicide
▷ ADJECTIVE 2 (*informal*) = **tiring**,
taxing, exhausting, punishing,
fatiguing, gruelling, sapping,
debilitating (*informal*)
▷ PHRASES: **make a killing**
(*informal*) = **profit**, gain, clean
up (*informal*), be lucky, be
successful, make a fortune,
strike it rich (*informal*), make a
bomb (*slang*)

kind¹ = **considerate**, kindly,
concerned, friendly, generous,
obliging, charitable, benign
OPPOSITE: unkind

kind² 1 = **class**, sort, type,
variety, brand, category, genre
2 = **sort**, set, type, family,
species, breed

> USAGE NOTE
>
> It is common in informal
> speech to combine singular
> and plural in sentences like
> *children enjoy those kind of
> stories*. However, this is not
> acceptable in careful writing,
> where the plural must be used
> consistently: *children enjoy
> those kinds of stories*.

kindly ADJECTIVE
1 = **benevolent**, kind, caring,
warm, helpful, pleasant,
sympathetic, benign OPPOSITE:
cruel
▷ ADVERB 2 = **benevolently**,
politely, generously,
thoughtfully, tenderly, lovingly,
cordially, affectionately
OPPOSITE: unkindly

kindness = **goodwill**,
understanding, charity,
humanity, compassion,
generosity, philanthropy,
benevolence OPPOSITE: malice

king = **ruler**, monarch, sovereign,
leader, lord, Crown, emperor,
head of state

kingdom = **country**, state,
nation, territory, realm

kiss VERB 1 = **peck** (*informal*),
osculate, neck (*informal*)
2 = **brush**, touch, shave, scrape,
graze, glance off, stroke
▷ NOUN 3 = **peck** (*informal*), snog
(*Brit slang*), smacker (*slang*),
French kiss, osculation

kit 1 = **equipment**, materials,
tackle, tools, apparatus,
paraphernalia 2 = **gear**, things,
stuff, equipment, uniform
▷ PHRASES: **kit something or
someone out** *or* **up** = **equip**, fit,
supply, provide with, arm, stock,
costume, furnish

knack = **skill**, art, ability, facility,
talent, gift, capacity, trick
OPPOSITE: ineptitude

kneel = **genuflect**, stoop

knickers = **underwear**, smalls,
briefs, drawers, panties,
bloomers

k

knife NOUN 1 = **blade**, carver, cutter
▷ VERB 2 = **cut**, wound, stab, slash, thrust, pierce, spear, jab
knit 1 = **join**, unite, link, tie, bond, combine, bind, weave 2 = **heal**, unite, join, link, bind, fasten, intertwine 3 = **furrow**, tighten, knot, wrinkle, crease, screw up, pucker, scrunch up
knob = **ball**, stud, knot, lump, bump, projection, hump, protrusion
knock VERB 1 = **bang**, strike, tap, rap, thump, pummel 2 = **hit**, strike, punch, belt (*informal*), smack, thump, cuff 3 (*informal*) = **criticize**, condemn, put down, run down, abuse, slate (*informal*), censure, denigrate, nit-pick (*informal*)
▷ NOUN 4 = **knocking**, pounding, beating, tap, bang, banging, rap, thump 5 = **bang**, blow, impact, jar, collision, jolt, smash 6 = **blow**, hit, punch, crack, clip, slap, bash, smack 7 (*informal*) = **setback**, check, defeat, blow, reverse, disappointment, hold-up, hitch (*informal*)
▷ PHRASES: knock about *or* around = **wander**, travel, roam, rove, range, drift, stray, ramble, go walkabout (*Austral*) ▶ knock about *or* around with someone = **mix with**, associate with, mingle with, consort with, hobnob with, socialize

with, accompany ▶ knock off (*informal*) = **stop work**, get out, call it a day (*informal*), finish work, clock off, clock out ▶ knock someone about *or* around = **hit**, attack, beat, strike, abuse, injure, assault, batter ▶ knock someone down = **run over**, hit, run down, knock over, mow down ▶ knock something down = **demolish**, destroy, flatten, tear down, level, fell, dismantle, bulldoze, kennet (*Austral slang*), jeff (*Austral slang*) ▶ knock something off = **steal**, take, nick (*slang, chiefly Brit*), thieve, rob, pinch
knockout 1 = **killer blow**, coup de grâce (*French*), KO *or* K.O. (*slang*) 2 (*informal*) = **success**, hit, winner, triumph, smash, sensation, smash hit **OPPOSITE:** failure
knot NOUN 1 = **connection**, tie, bond, joint, loop, ligature
▷ VERB 2 = **tie**, secure, bind, loop, tether
know 1 = **have knowledge of**, see, understand, recognize, perceive, be aware of, be conscious of 2 = **be acquainted with**, recognize, be familiar with, be friends with, be friendly with, have knowledge of, have dealings with, socialize with **OPPOSITE:** be unfamiliar with 3 *sometimes with* **about** *or* **of** = **be familiar with**, understand,

comprehend, have knowledge of, be acquainted with, feel certain of, have dealings in, be versed in **OPPOSITE:** be ignorant of

know-how (*informal*) = **expertise**, ability, skill, knowledge, facility, talent, command, capability

knowing = **meaningful**, significant, expressive, enigmatic, suggestive

knowledge 1 = **understanding**, sense, judgment, perception, awareness, insight, grasp, appreciation 2 = **learning**, education, intelligence, instruction, wisdom, scholarship, enlightenment, erudition **OPPOSITE:** ignorance 3 = **acquaintance**, intimacy, familiarity **OPPOSITE:** unfamiliarity

knowledgeable 1 = **well-informed**, conversant, au fait (*French*), experienced, aware, familiar, in the know (*informal*), cognizant, leet (*computing slang*) 2 = **intelligent**, learned, educated, scholarly, erudite

known = **famous**, well-known, celebrated, noted, acknowledged, recognized, avowed **OPPOSITE:** unknown

koppie *or* **kopje** (*S African*) = **hill**, down (*archaic*), fell, mount, hilltop, knoll, hillock, brae (*Scot*)

label NOUN 1 = **tag**, ticket, tab, marker, sticker
▷ VERB 2 = **tag**, mark, stamp, ticket, tab

labour NOUN 1 = **workers**, employees, workforce, labourers, hands 2 = **work**, effort, employment, toil, industry 3 = **childbirth**, birth, delivery, parturition
▷ VERB 4 = **work**, toil, strive, work hard, sweat (*informal*), slave, endeavour, slog away (*informal*) **OPPOSITE:** rest 5 = **struggle**, work, strain, work hard, strive, grapple, toil, make an effort 6 = **overemphasize**, stress, elaborate, exaggerate, strain, dwell on, overdo, go on about 7 *usually with* **under** = be **disadvantaged by**, suffer from, be a victim of, be burdened by

laboured = **difficult**, forced, strained, heavy, awkward

labourer = **worker**, manual worker, hand, blue-collar worker, drudge, navvy (*Brit informal*)

Labour Party = **left-wing**, Democrat (*US*)

lace NOUN 1 = **netting**, net, filigree, meshwork, openwork 2 = **cord**, tie, string, lacing, shoelace, bootlace
▷ VERB 3 = **fasten**, tie, tie up, do up, secure, bind, thread 4 = **mix**, drug, doctor, add to, spike, contaminate, fortify, adulterate 5 = **intertwine**, interweave, entwine, twine, interlink

lack NOUN 1 = **shortage**, want, absence, deficiency, need, inadequacy, scarcity, dearth **OPPOSITE:** abundance
▷ VERB 2 = **miss**, want, need, require, not have, be without, be short of, be in need of **OPPOSITE:** have

lad = **boy**, kid (*informal*), guy (*informal*), youth, fellow, youngster, juvenile, nipper (*informal*)

laden = **loaded**, burdened, full, charged, weighed down, encumbered

lady 1 = **gentlewoman**, duchess, noble, dame, baroness, countess, aristocrat, viscountess 2 = **woman**, female, girl, damsel, charlie (*Austral slang*), chook (*Austral slang*), wahine (*NZ*)

lag = **hang back**, delay, trail, linger, loiter, straggle, dawdle, tarry

laid-back = **relaxed**, calm, casual, easy-going, unflappable (*informal*), unhurried, free and easy, chilled (*informal*) **OPPOSITE:** tense

lake = **pond**, pool, reservoir, loch (*Scot*), lagoon, mere, lough (*Irish*), tarn

lame 1 = **limping**, hobbling, game 2 = **unconvincing**, poor, pathetic, inadequate, thin, weak, feeble, unsatisfactory

lament VERB 1 = **bemoan**, grieve, mourn, weep over, complain about, regret, wail about, deplore
▷ NOUN 2 = **complaint**, moan, wailing, lamentation 3 = **dirge**, requiem, elegy, threnody

land NOUN 1 = **ground**, earth, dry land, terra firma 2 = **soil**, ground, earth, clay, dirt, sod, loam 3 = **countryside**, farmland 4 (*Law*) = **property**, grounds, estate, real estate, realty, acreage, homestead (*US & Canad*) 5 = **country**, nation, region, state, district, territory, province, kingdom
▷ VERB 6 = **arrive**, dock, put down, moor, alight, touch down, disembark, come to rest 7 (*informal*) = **gain**, get, win, secure, acquire
▷ PHRASES: **land up** = **end up**, turn up, wind up, finish up, fetch up (*informal*)

▌ **RELATED WORD**
adjective: terrestrial

landlord 1 = **owner**, landowner, proprietor, freeholder, lessor, landholder 2 = **innkeeper**, host, hotelier

landmark 1 = **feature**, spectacle, monument 2 = **milestone**, turning point, watershed, critical point, tipping point

landscape = **scenery**, country, view, land, scene, prospect, countryside, outlook

landslide = **landslip**, avalanche, mudslide, rockfall

lane = **road**, street, track, path, way, passage, trail, pathway

language 1 = **tongue**, dialect, vernacular, patois 2 = **speech**, communication, expression, speaking, talk, talking, discourse, parlance

languish 1 = **decline**, fade away, wither away, flag, weaken, wilt **OPPOSITE**: flourish 2 (*literary*) = **waste away**, suffer, rot, be abandoned, be neglected **OPPOSITE**: thrive 3 *often with* **for** = **pine**, long, desire, hunger, yearn, hanker

lap[1] = **circuit**, tour, leg, stretch, circle, orbit, loop

lap[2] 1 = **ripple**, wash, splash, swish, gurgle, slosh, purl, plash 2 = **drink**, sip, lick, swallow, gulp, sup
▷ **PHRASES: lap something up** = **relish**, like, enjoy, delight in, savour, revel in, wallow in, accept eagerly

lapse NOUN 1 = **decline**, fall, drop, deterioration 2 = **mistake**, failing, fault, failure, error, slip, negligence, omission 3 = **interval**, break, gap, pause, interruption, lull, breathing space, intermission
▷ **VERB** 4 = **slip**, fall, decline, sink, drop, slide, deteriorate, degenerate 5 = **end**, stop, run out, expire, terminate

lapsed = **expired**, ended, finished, run out, invalid, out of date, discontinued

large 1 = **big**, great, huge, heavy, massive, vast, enormous, tall, supersize **OPPOSITE**: small 2 = **massive**, great, big, huge, vast, enormous, considerable, substantial, supersize **OPPOSITE**: small
▷ **PHRASES: at large** 1 = **in general**, generally, chiefly, mainly, as a whole, in the main 2 = **free**, on the run, fugitive, at liberty, on the loose, unchained, unconfined ▶ **by and large** = **on the whole**, generally, mostly, in general, all things considered, predominantly, in the main, all in all

largely = **mainly**, generally, chiefly, mostly, principally, primarily, predominantly, by and large

large-scale = **wide-ranging**, global, sweeping, broad, wide, vast, extensive, wholesale

lash¹ VERB 1 = **pound**, beat, strike, hammer, drum, smack (*dialect*) 2 = **censure**, attack, blast, put down, criticize, slate (*informal, chiefly Brit*), scold, tear into (*informal*) 3 = **whip**, beat, thrash, birch, flog, scourge
▷ NOUN 4 = **blow**, hit, strike, stroke, stripe, swipe (*informal*)

lash² = **fasten**, tie, secure, bind, strap, make fast

last¹ ADJECTIVE 1 = **most recent**, latest, previous 2 = **hindmost**, final, at the end, remotest, furthest behind, most distant, rearmost **OPPOSITE:** foremost 3 = **final**, closing, concluding, ultimate **OPPOSITE:** first
▷ ADVERB 4 = **in** *or* **at the end**, after, behind, in the rear, bringing up the rear
▷ PHRASES: **the last word** 1 = **final decision**, final say, final statement, conclusive comment 2 = **leading**, finest, cream, supreme, elite, foremost, pre-eminent, unsurpassed

> **USAGE NOTE**
> Since *last* can mean either *after all others* or *most recent*, it is better to avoid using this word where ambiguity might arise, as in *her last novel*. *Final* or *latest* should be used as alternatives in such contexts to avoid any possible confusion.

last² = **continue**, remain, survive, carry on, endure, persist, keep on, abide **OPPOSITE:** end

lasting = **continuing**, long-term, permanent, enduring, remaining, abiding, long-standing, perennial **OPPOSITE:** passing

latch NOUN 1 = **fastening**, catch, bar, lock, hook, bolt, hasp
▷ VERB 2 = **fasten**, bar, secure, bolt, make fast

late ADJECTIVE 1 = **overdue**, delayed, last-minute, belated, tardy, behind time, behindhand **OPPOSITE:** early 2 = **dead**, deceased, departed, passed on, former, defunct **OPPOSITE:** alive 3 = **recent**, new, advanced, fresh **OPPOSITE:** old
▷ ADVERB 4 = **behind time**, belatedly, tardily, behindhand, dilatorily **OPPOSITE:** early

lately = **recently**, of late, just now, in recent times, not long ago, latterly

later ADVERB 1 = **afterwards**, after, eventually, in time, subsequently, later on, thereafter, in a while
▷ ADJECTIVE 2 = **subsequent**, next, following, ensuing

latest = **up-to-date**, current, fresh, newest, modern, most recent, up-to-the-minute

latitude = **scope**, liberty, freedom, play, space, licence, leeway, laxity

latter NOUN 1 = **second**, last, last-mentioned, second-mentioned

▷ ADJECTIVE 2 = **last**, ending, closing, final, concluding
OPPOSITE: earlier

> **USAGE NOTE**
>
> *The latter* should only be used to specify the second of two items, for example in *if I had to choose between the hovercraft and the ferry, I would opt for the latter.* Where there are three or more items, the last can be referred to as *the last-named*, but not *the latter.*

laugh VERB 1 = **chuckle**, giggle, snigger, cackle, chortle, guffaw, titter, be in stitches

▷ NOUN 2 = **chortle**, giggle, chuckle, snigger, guffaw, titter 3 (*informal*) = **joke**, scream (*informal*), hoot (*informal*), lark, prank 4 (*informal*) = **clown**, character (*informal*), scream (*informal*), entertainer, card (*informal*), joker, hoot (*informal*)

▷ PHRASES: **laugh something off** = **disregard**, ignore, dismiss, overlook, shrug off, minimize, brush aside, make light of

laughter = **amusement**, entertainment, humour, glee, fun, mirth, hilarity, merriment

launch 1 = **propel**, fire, dispatch, discharge, project, send off, set in motion, send into orbit 2 = **begin**, start, open, initiate, introduce, found, set up, originate

▷ PHRASES: **launch into something** = **start enthusiastically**, begin, initiate, embark on, instigate, inaugurate, embark upon

laurel

▷ PHRASES: **rest on your laurels** = **sit back**, relax, take it easy, relax your efforts

lavatory = **toilet**, bathroom, loo (*Brit informal*), privy, cloakroom (*Brit*), urinal, latrine, washroom, dunny (*Austral & NZ old-fashioned informal*), bogger (*Austral slang*), brasco (*Austral slang*)

lavish ADJECTIVE 1 = **grand**, magnificent, splendid, abundant, copious, profuse OPPOSITE: stingy 2 = **extravagant**, wild, excessive, exaggerated, wasteful, prodigal, unrestrained, immoderate
OPPOSITE: thrifty 3 = **generous**, free, liberal, bountiful, open-handed, unstinting, munificent
OPPOSITE: stingy

▷ VERB 4 = **shower**, pour, heap, deluge, dissipate OPPOSITE: stint

law 1 = **constitution**, code, legislation, charter 2 = **statute**, act, bill, rule, order, command, regulation, resolution
3 = **principle**, code, canon, precept, axiom, kaupapa (*NZ*)
4 = **the legal profession**, the bar, barristers

lawsuit = **case**, action, trial, suit, proceedings, dispute, prosecution, legal action

lawyer = **legal adviser**, attorney, solicitor, counsel, advocate, barrister, counsellor, legal representative

lay¹ 1 = **place**, put, set, spread, plant, leave, deposit, put down 2 = **devise**, plan, design, prepare, work out, plot, hatch, contrive 3 = **produce**, bear, deposit 4 = **arrange**, prepare, make, organize, position, set out, devise, put together 5 = **attribute**, assign, allocate, allot, ascribe, impute 6 = **put forward**, offer, present, advance, lodge, submit, bring forward 7 = **bet**, stake, venture, gamble, chance, risk, hazard, wager

▷ **PHRASES: lay someone off** = **dismiss**, fire (*informal*), release, sack (*informal*), pay off, discharge, let go, make redundant, kennet (*Austral slang*), jeff (*Austral slang*) ▶ **lay someone out** (*informal*) = **knock out**, fell, floor, knock unconscious, knock for six ▶ **lay something out** 1 = **arrange**, order, design, display, exhibit, put out, spread out 2 = **spend**, pay, invest, fork out (*slang*), expend, shell out (*informal*), disburse (*informal*)

> **USAGE NOTE**
> In standard English, the verb *to lay* (meaning 'to put something somewhere') always needs an object, for example *the Queen laid a wreath*. By contrast, the verb *to lie* is always used without an object, for example *he was just lying there*.

lay² 1 = **nonclerical**, secular, non-ordained 2 = **nonspecialist**, amateur, unqualified, untrained, inexpert, nonprofessional

layer = **tier**, level, seam, stratum

layout = **arrangement**, design, outline, format, plan, formation

lazy 1 = **idle**, inactive, indolent, slack, negligent, inert, workshy, slothful **OPPOSITE**: industrious 2 = **lethargic**, languorous, slow-moving, languid, sleepy, sluggish, drowsy, somnolent **OPPOSITE**: quick

leach = **extract**, strain, drain, filter, seep, percolate

lead VERB 1 = **go in front (of)**, head, be in front, be at the head (of), walk in front (of) 2 = **guide**, conduct, steer, escort, precede, usher, pilot, show the way 3 = **connect to**, link, open onto 4 = **be ahead (of)**, be first, exceed, be winning, excel, surpass, come first, transcend 5 = **command**, rule, govern, preside over, head, control, manage, direct 6 = **live**, have, spend, experience, pass, undergo 7 = **result in**, cause, produce, contribute, generate, bring about, bring on, give rise to 8 = **cause**, prompt, persuade, move, draw, influence, motivate, prevail

▷ **NOUN** 9 = **first place**, winning position, primary position, vanguard 10 = **advantage**, start, edge, margin, winning margin 11 = **example**, direction, leadership, guidance, model, pattern 12 = **clue**, suggestion, hint, indication, pointer, tip-off 13 = **leading role**, principal, protagonist, title role, principal part 14 = **leash**, line, cord, rein, tether

▷ **ADJECTIVE** 15 = **main**, prime, top, leading, first, head, chief, premier

▷ **PHRASES: lead someone on** = **entice**, tempt, lure, mislead, draw on, seduce, deceive, beguile ▶ **lead up to something** = **introduce**, prepare for, pave the way for

leader = **principal**, president, head, chief, boss (*informal*), director, manager, chairman, baas (*S African*), sherang (*Austral & NZ*) **OPPOSITE:** follower

leadership 1 = **authority**, control, influence, command, premiership, captaincy, governance, headship 2 = **guidance**, government, authority, management, direction, supervision, domination, superintendency

leading = **principal**, top, major, main, first, highest, greatest, chief **OPPOSITE:** minor

leaf NOUN 1 = **frond**, blade, cotyledon 2 = **page**, sheet, folio

▷ **PHRASES: leaf through something** = **skim**, glance, scan, browse, look through, dip into, flick through, flip through

leaflet = **booklet**, notice, brochure, circular, flyer, tract, pamphlet, handout

leafy = **green**, shaded, shady, verdant

league 1 = **association**, union, alliance, coalition, group, corporation, partnership, federation 2 = **class**, group, level, category

leak VERB 1 = **escape**, pass, spill, release, drip, trickle, ooze, seep 2 = **disclose**, tell, reveal, pass on, give away, make public, divulge, let slip

▷ **NOUN** 3 = **leakage**, discharge, drip, seepage, percolation 4 = **hole**, opening, crack, puncture, aperture, chink, crevice, fissure 5 = **disclosure**, exposé, exposure, admission, revelation, uncovering, betrayal, unearthing

lean¹ 1 = **bend**, tip, slope, incline, tilt, heel, slant 2 = **rest**, prop, be supported, recline, repose 3 = **tend**, prefer, favour, incline, be prone to, be disposed to

▷ **PHRASES: lean on someone** = **depend on**, trust, rely on, cling to, count on, have faith in (*informal*)

lean² = **thin**, slim, slender, skinny, angular, trim, spare, gaunt **OPPOSITE:** fat

leaning = **tendency**, bias, inclination, bent, disposition, penchant, propensity, predilection

leap VERB 1 = **jump**, spring, bound, bounce, hop, skip
▷ NOUN 2 = **jump**, spring, bound, vault 3 = **rise**, change, increase, soaring, surge, escalation, upsurge, upswing
▷ PHRASES: leap at something = **accept eagerly**, seize on, jump at

learn 1 = **master**, grasp, pick up, take in, familiarize yourself with 2 = **discover**, hear, understand, find out about, become aware, discern, ascertain, come to know 3 = **memorize**, commit to memory, learn by heart, learn by rote, learn parrot-fashion, get off pat

learned = **scholarly**, academic, intellectual, versed, well-informed, erudite, highbrow, well-read **OPPOSITE:** uneducated

learner = **student**, novice, beginner, apprentice, neophyte, tyro **OPPOSITE:** expert

learning = **knowledge**, study, education, scholarship, enlightenment, e-learning *or* elearning

lease = **hire**, rent, let, loan, charter, rent out, hire out

least = **smallest**, meanest, fewest, lowest, tiniest, minimum, slightest, minimal

leave¹ 1 = **depart from**, withdraw from, go from, escape from, quit, flee, exit, pull out of **OPPOSITE:** arrive 2 = **quit**, give up, get out of, resign from, drop out of 3 = **give up**, abandon, dump (*informal*), drop, surrender, ditch (*informal*), chuck (*informal*), discard **OPPOSITE:** stay with 4 = **entrust**, commit, delegate, refer, hand over, assign, consign, allot 5 = **bequeath**, will, transfer, endow, confer, hand down 6 = **forget**, leave behind, mislay 7 = **cause**, produce, result in, generate, deposit
▷ PHRASES: leave something *or* someone out = **omit**, exclude, miss out, forget, reject, ignore, overlook, neglect

leave² 1 = **holiday**, break, vacation, time off, sabbatical, leave of absence, furlough, schoolie (*Austral*), accumulated day off *or* ADO (*Austral*) 2 = **permission**, freedom, sanction, liberty, concession, consent, allowance, warrant **OPPOSITE:** refusal 3 = **departure**, parting, withdrawal, goodbye, farewell, retirement, leave-taking, adieu **OPPOSITE:** arrival

lecture NOUN 1 = **talk**, address, speech, lesson, instruction, presentation, discourse, sermon, webinar 2 = **telling-off** (*informal*), rebuke, reprimand, talking-to (*informal*), scolding, dressing-down (*informal*), reproof
▷ VERB 3 = **talk**, speak, teach, address, discourse, spout, expound, hold forth 4 = **tell off** (*informal*), berate, scold, reprimand, censure, castigate, admonish, reprove

lees = **sediment**, grounds, deposit, dregs

left 1 = **left-hand**, port, larboard (*nautical*) 2 (*of politics*) = **socialist**, radical, left-wing, leftist

left-wing = **socialist**, communist, red (*informal*), radical, revolutionary, militant, Bolshevik, Leninist

leg 1 = **limb**, member, shank, lower limb, pin (*informal*), stump (*informal*) 2 = **support**, prop, brace, upright 3 = **stage**, part, section, stretch, lap, segment, portion
▷ PHRASES: pull someone's leg (*informal*) = **tease**, trick, fool, kid (*informal*), wind up (*Brit slang*), hoax, make fun of, lead up the garden path

legacy = **bequest**, inheritance, gift, estate, heirloom

legal 1 = **judicial**, judiciary, forensic, juridical, jurisdictive 2 = **lawful**, allowed, sanctioned, constitutional, valid, legitimate, authorized, permissible

legend 1 = **myth**, story, tale, fiction, saga, fable, folk tale, folk story 2 = **celebrity**, star, phenomenon, genius, prodigy, luminary, megastar (*informal*) 3 = **inscription**, title, caption, device, motto, rubric

legendary 1 = **famous**, celebrated, well-known, acclaimed, renowned, famed, immortal, illustrious OPPOSITE: unknown 2 = **mythical**, fabled, traditional, romantic, fabulous, fictitious, storybook, apocryphal OPPOSITE: factual

legion 1 = **army**, company, force, division, troop, brigade 2 = **multitude**, host, mass, drove, number, horde, myriad, throng

legislation 1 = **law**, act, ruling, rule, bill, measure, regulation, charter 2 = **lawmaking**, regulation, prescription, enactment

legislative = **law-making**, judicial, law-giving

legislator = **lawmaker**, lawgiver

legislature = **parliament**, congress, senate, assembly, chamber

legitimate ADJECTIVE 1 = **lawful**, legal, genuine, authentic, authorized, rightful, kosher (*informal*), dinkum (*Austral & NZ informal*), licit **OPPOSITE:** unlawful **2** = **reasonable**, correct, sensible, valid, warranted, logical, justifiable, well-founded **OPPOSITE:** unreasonable ▷ **VERB 3** = **legitimize**, allow, permit, sanction, authorize, legalize, pronounce lawful

leisure = **spare time**, free time, rest, ease, relaxation, recreation **OPPOSITE:** work

lekker (*S African slang*) = **delicious**, tasty, luscious, palatable, delectable, mouthwatering, scrumptious (*informal*), appetizing, yummo (*Austral slang*)

lemon
• *See panel* **SHADES OF YELLOW**

lend 1 = **loan**, advance, sub (*Brit informal*) **2** = **give**, provide, add, supply, grant, confer, bestow, impart
▷ **PHRASES:** lend itself to something = be appropriate for, suit, be suitable for, be appropriate to, be serviceable for

length 1 = **distance**, reach, measure, extent, span, longitude **2** = **duration**, term, period, space, stretch, span, expanse **3** = **piece**, measure, section, segment, portion
▷ **PHRASES:** at length **1** = at last, finally, eventually, in time, in the end, at long last **2** = for a long time, completely, fully, thoroughly, for hours, in detail, for ages, in depth

lengthen 1 = **extend**, continue, increase, stretch, expand, elongate **OPPOSITE:** shorten **2** = **protract**, extend, prolong, draw out, spin out, make longer **OPPOSITE:** cut down

lengthy 1 = **protracted**, long, prolonged, tedious, drawn-out, interminable, long-winded, long-drawn-out **2** = **very long**, rambling, interminable, long-winded, wordy, discursive, extended **OPPOSITE:** brief

lesbian = **homosexual**, gay, sapphic

less ADJECTIVE 1 = **smaller**, shorter, not so much
▷ **PREPOSITION 2** = **minus**, without, lacking, excepting, subtracting

> **USAGE NOTE**
> *Less* should not be confused with *fewer*. *Less* refers strictly only to quantity and not to number: *there is less water than before*. *Fewer* means smaller in number: *there are fewer people than before*.

lessen 1 = **reduce**, lower, diminish, decrease, ease, narrow, minimize **OPPOSITE:** increase **2** = **grow less**, diminish, decrease, contract, ease, shrink

lesser = **lower**, secondary, subsidiary, inferior, less important **OPPOSITE:** greater

lesson 1 = **class**, schooling, period, teaching, coaching, session, instruction, lecture 2 = **example**, warning, message, moral, deterrent 3 = **Bible reading**, reading, text, Bible passage, Scripture passage

let 1 = **allow**, permit, authorize, give the go-ahead, give permission 2 = **lease**, hire, rent, rent out, hire out, sublease ▷ **PHRASES: let on** (*informal*) = **reveal**, disclose, say, tell, admit, give away, divulge, let slip ▶ **let someone down** = **disappoint**, fail, abandon, desert, disillusion, fall short, leave stranded, leave in the lurch ▶ **let someone off** (*informal*) = **excuse**, release, discharge, pardon, spare, forgive, exempt, exonerate ▶ **let something down** = **deflate**, empty, exhaust, flatten, puncture ▶ **let something off** 1 = **fire**, explode, set off, discharge, detonate 2 = **emit**, release, leak, exude, give off ▶ **let something out** 1 = **release**, discharge 2 = **emit**, make, produce, give vent to ▶ **let something** *or* **someone in** = **admit**, include, receive, welcome, greet, take in, incorporate, give access to ▶ **let up** = **stop**, diminish, decrease, subside, relax, ease (up), moderate, lessen

lethal = **deadly**, terminal, fatal, dangerous, devastating, destructive, mortal, murderous **OPPOSITE:** harmless

letter 1 = **message**, line, note, communication, dispatch, missive, epistle, email *or* e-mail 2 = **character**, mark, sign, symbol, glyph (*computing*)

level NOUN 1 = **position**, standard, degree, grade, standing, stage, rank, status ▷ **ADJECTIVE** 2 = **equal**, balanced, at the same height 3 = **horizontal**, even, flat, smooth, uniform **OPPOSITE:** slanted 4 = **even**, tied, equal, drawn, neck and neck, all square, level pegging ▷ **VERB** 5 = **equalize**, balance, even up 6 = **destroy**, devastate, demolish, flatten, knock down, pull down, tear down, bulldoze, kennet (*Austral slang*), jeff (*Austral slang*) **OPPOSITE:** build 7 = **direct**, point, turn, train, aim, focus 8 = **flatten**, plane, smooth, even off *or* out ▷ **PHRASES: on the level** (*informal*) = **honest**, genuine, straight, fair, square, dinkum (*Austral & NZ informal*), above board

lever NOUN 1 = **handle**, bar ▷ **VERB** 2 = **prise**, force

leverage 1 = **influence**, authority, pull (*informal*), weight, clout (*informal*) 2 = **force**, hold, pull, strength, grip, grasp

levy NOUN 1 = **tax**, fee, toll, tariff, duty, excise, exaction

▷ **VERB 2** = **impose**, charge, collect, demand, exact

liability 1 = **disadvantage**, burden, drawback, inconvenience, handicap, nuisance, hindrance, millstone **2** = **responsibility**, accountability, culpability, answerability

liable 1 = **likely**, tending, inclined, disposed, prone, apt **2** = **vulnerable**, subject, exposed, prone, susceptible, open, at risk of **3** = **responsible**, accountable, answerable, obligated

> **USAGE NOTE**
> In the past, it was considered incorrect to use *liable* to mean 'probable' or 'likely', as in *it's liable to happen soon*. However, this usage is now generally considered acceptable.

liaison 1 = **contact**, communication, connection, interchange **2** = **intermediary**, contact, hook-up **3** = **affair**, romance, intrigue, fling, love affair, amour, entanglement

liar = **falsifier**, perjurer, fibber, fabricator

libel NOUN 1 = **defamation**, misrepresentation, denigration, smear, calumny, aspersion
▷ **VERB 2** = **defame**, smear, slur, blacken, malign, denigrate, revile, vilify

liberal 1 = **tolerant**, open-minded, permissive, indulgent, easy-going, broad-minded **OPPOSITE:** intolerant **2** = **progressive**, radical, reformist, libertarian, forward-looking, free-thinking **OPPOSITE:** conservative **3** = **abundant**, generous, handsome, lavish, ample, rich, plentiful, copious **OPPOSITE:** limited **4** = **generous**, kind, charitable, extravagant, open-hearted, bountiful, magnanimous, open-handed **OPPOSITE:** stingy

liberate = **free**, release, rescue, save, deliver, let out, set free, let loose **OPPOSITE:** imprison

liberty = **independence**, sovereignty, liberation, autonomy, immunity, self-determination, emancipation, self-government **OPPOSITE:** restraint
▷ **PHRASES:** at liberty **1** = **free**, escaped, unlimited, at large, not confined, untied, on the loose, unchained **2** = **able**, free, allowed, permitted, entitled, authorized ▶ **take liberties or a liberty** = **not show enough respect**, show disrespect, act presumptuously, behave too familiarly, behave impertinently

licence 1 = **certificate**, document, permit, charter, warrant **2** = **permission**, the right, authority, leave, sanction, liberty, immunity, entitlement **OPPOSITE:** denial

3 = **freedom**, creativity, latitude, independence, liberty, deviation, leeway, free rein **OPPOSITE:** restraint **4** = **laxity**, excess, indulgence, irresponsibility, licentiousness, immoderation **OPPOSITE:** moderation

license = **permit**, sanction, allow, warrant, authorize, empower, certify, accredit **OPPOSITE:** forbid

lick VERB 1 = **taste**, lap, tongue **2** (*informal*) = **beat**, defeat, overcome, rout, outstrip, outdo, trounce, vanquish **3** (*of flames*) = **flicker**, touch, flick, dart, ripple, play over
▷ **NOUN 4** = **dab**, touch, stroke **5** (*informal*) = **pace**, rate, speed, clip (*informal*)

lie¹ NOUN 1 = **falsehood**, deceit, fabrication, fib, fiction, invention, deception, untruth
▷ **VERB 2** = **fib**, fabricate, falsify, prevaricate, not tell the truth, equivocate, dissimulate, tell untruths
▷ **PHRASES: give the lie to something** = **disprove**, expose, discredit, contradict, refute, negate, invalidate, rebut

lie² 1 = **recline**, rest, lounge, sprawl, stretch out, loll, repose **2** = **be placed**, be, rest, exist, be situated **3** = **be situated**, sit, be located, be positioned **4** = **be buried**, remain, rest, be entombed

life 1 = **being**, existence, vitality, sentience **2** = **existence**, being, lifetime, time, days, span **3** = **way of life**, situation, conduct, behaviour, life style **4** = **liveliness**, energy, spirit, vitality, animation, vigour, verve, zest **5** = **biography**, story, history, profile, confessions, autobiography, memoirs, life story

> **RELATED WORDS**
> *adjectives*: animate, vital

lifelong = **long-lasting**, enduring, lasting, persistent, long-standing, perennial

lifetime = **existence**, time, day(s), span

lift VERB 1 = **raise**, pick up, hoist, draw up, elevate, uplift, heave up, upraise **OPPOSITE:** lower **2** = **revoke**, end, remove, withdraw, stop, cancel, terminate, rescind **OPPOSITE:** impose **3** = **disappear**, clear, vanish, disperse, dissipate, rise, be dispelled
▷ **NOUN 4** = **boost**, encouragement, stimulus, pick-me-up, fillip, shot in the arm (*informal*), gee-up **OPPOSITE:** blow **5** = **elevator** (*chiefly US*), hoist, paternoster **6** = **ride**, run, drive, hitch (*informal*)
▷ **PHRASES: lift off** = **take off**, be launched, blast off, take to the air

light¹ NOUN 1 = **brightness**, illumination, luminosity,

shining, glow, glare, gleam, brilliance **OPPOSITE**: dark
2 = lamp, torch, candle, flare, beacon, lantern, taper
3 = match, spark, flame, lighter
4 = aspect, context, angle, point of view, interpretation, viewpoint, slant, standpoint
▷ **ADJECTIVE 5 = bright**, brilliant, shining, illuminated, luminous, well-lit, lustrous, well-illuminated **OPPOSITE**: dark
6 = pale, fair, faded, blonde, blond, bleached, pastel, light-coloured **OPPOSITE**: dark
▷ **VERB 7 = illuminate**, light up, brighten **OPPOSITE**: darken
8 = ignite, inflame, kindle, touch off, set alight **OPPOSITE**: put out
▷ **PHRASES: light up 1 = cheer**, shine, blaze, sparkle, animate, brighten, lighten, irradiate
2 = shine, flash, beam, blaze, sparkle, flare, glare, gleam
light² 1 = insubstantial, thin, slight, portable, buoyant, airy, flimsy, underweight **OPPOSITE**: heavy **2 = weak**, soft, gentle, moderate, slight, mild, faint, indistinct **OPPOSITE**: strong
3 = digestible, modest, frugal **OPPOSITE**: substantial
4 = insignificant, small, slight, petty, trivial, trifling, inconsequential, inconsiderable **OPPOSITE**: serious **5 = light-hearted**, funny, entertaining, amusing, witty, humorous, frivolous, unserious **OPPOSITE**:

serious **6 = nimble**, graceful, deft, agile, sprightly, lithe, limber, lissom **OPPOSITE**: clumsy
▷ **PHRASES: light on or upon something 1 = settle**, land, perch, alight **2 = come across**, find, discover, encounter, stumble on, hit upon, happen upon
lighten¹ = brighten, illuminate, light up, irradiate, become light
lighten² 1 = ease, relieve, alleviate, allay, reduce, lessen, mitigate, assuage **OPPOSITE**: intensify **2 = cheer**, lift, revive, brighten, perk up, buoy up **OPPOSITE**: depress
lightly 1 = moderately, thinly, slightly, sparsely, sparingly **OPPOSITE**: heavily
2 = gently, softly, slightly, faintly, delicately **OPPOSITE**: forcefully **3 = carelessly**, breezily, thoughtlessly, flippantly, frivolously, heedlessly **OPPOSITE**: seriously **4 = easily**, simply, readily, effortlessly, unthinkingly, without thought, flippantly, heedlessly **OPPOSITE**: with difficulty
lightweight 1 = thin, fine, delicate, sheer, flimsy, gossamer, diaphanous, filmy
2 = unimportant, shallow, trivial, insignificant, slight, petty, worthless, trifling **OPPOSITE**: significant
like¹ = similar to, same as, equivalent to, parallel to,

identical to, alike, corresponding to, comparable to **OPPOSITE:** different

> **USAGE NOTE**
> The use of *like* to mean 'such as' was in the past considered undesirable in formal writing, but has now become acceptable, for example in *I enjoy team sports like football and rugby*. However, the common use of *look like* and *seem like* to mean 'look or seem as if' is thought by many people to be incorrect or nonstandard. You might say *it looks as if* (or *as though*) *he's coming*, but it is still wise to avoid *it looks like he's coming*, particularly in formal or written contexts.

like² 1 = **enjoy**, love, delight in, go for, relish, savour, revel in, be fond of **OPPOSITE:** dislike 2 = **admire**, approve of, appreciate, prize, take to, esteem, cherish, hold dear **OPPOSITE:** dislike 3 = **wish**, want, choose, prefer, desire, fancy, care, feel inclined

likelihood = **probability**, chance, possibility, prospect

likely 1 = **inclined**, disposed, prone, liable, tending, apt 2 = **probable**, expected, anticipated, odds-on, on the cards, to be expected 3 = **plausible**, possible, reasonable, credible, feasible, believable

liken = **compare**, match, relate, parallel, equate, set beside

likewise = **similarly**, the same, in the same way, in similar fashion, in like manner

liking = **fondness**, love, taste, weakness, preference, affection, inclination, penchant **OPPOSITE:** dislike

limb 1 = **part**, member, arm, leg, wing, extremity, appendage 2 = **branch**, spur, projection, offshoot, bough

limelight = **publicity**, recognition, fame, the spotlight, attention, prominence, stardom, public eye

limit NOUN 1 = **end**, ultimate, deadline, breaking point, extremity 2 = **boundary**, edge, border, frontier, perimeter ▷ **VERB** 3 = **restrict**, control, check, bound, confine, curb, restrain, ration

limitation 1 = **restriction**, control, check, curb, restraint, constraint 2 = **weakness**, failing, qualification, reservation, defect, flaw, shortcoming, imperfection

limited = **restricted**, controlled, checked, bounded, confined, curbed, constrained, finite **OPPOSITE:** unlimited

limp¹ VERB 1 = **hobble**, stagger, stumble, shuffle, hop, falter, shamble, totter ▷ **NOUN** 2 = **lameness**, hobble

limp² = **floppy**, soft, slack, drooping, flabby, pliable, flaccid
OPPOSITE: stiff

line NOUN 1 = **stroke**, mark, score, band, scratch, slash, streak, stripe **2** = **wrinkle**, mark, crease, furrow, crow's foot **3** = **row**, queue, rank, file, column, convoy, procession **4** = **string**, cable, wire, rope, thread, cord **5** = **trajectory**, way, course, track, channel, direction, route, path **6** = **boundary**, limit, edge, border, frontier, partition, borderline **7** = **occupation**, work, calling, business, job, area, trade, field
▷ **VERB 8** = **border**, edge, bound, fringe **9** = **mark**, crease, furrow, rule, score
▷ **PHRASES: in line for** = **due for**, shortlisted for, in the running for

lined 1 = **wrinkled**, worn, furrowed, wizened **2** = **ruled**, feint

line-up = **arrangement**, team, row, selection, array

linger = **stay**, remain, stop, wait, delay, hang around, idle, dally

link NOUN 1 = **connection**, relationship, association, tie-up, affinity **2** = **relationship**, association, bond, connection, attachment, affinity **3** = **component**, part, piece, element, constituent
▷ **VERB 4** = **associate**, relate, identify, connect, bracket

5 = **connect**, join, unite, couple, tie, bind, attach, fasten
OPPOSITE: separate

lip 1 = **edge**, rim, brim, margin, brink **2** (slang) = **impudence**, insolence, impertinence, cheek (informal), effrontery, backchat (informal), brass neck (informal)

liquid NOUN 1 = **fluid**, solution, juice, sap
▷ **ADJECTIVE 2** = **fluid**, running, flowing, melted, watery, molten, runny, aqueous **3** (of assets) = **convertible**, disposable, negotiable, realizable

liquor 1 = **alcohol**, drink, spirits, booze (informal), hard stuff (informal), strong drink **2** = **juice**, stock, liquid, extract, broth

list¹ NOUN 1 = **inventory**, record, series, roll, index, register, catalogue, directory
▷ **VERB 2** = **itemize**, record, enter, register, catalogue, enumerate, note down, tabulate

list² VERB 1 = **lean**, tip, incline, tilt, heel over, careen
▷ **NOUN 2** = **tilt**, leaning, slant, cant

listen 1 = **hear**, attend, pay attention, lend an ear, prick up your ears **2** = **pay attention**, observe, obey, mind, heed, take notice, take note of, take heed of

literacy = **education**, learning, knowledge

literal 1 = **exact**, close, strict, accurate, faithful, verbatim, word for word 2 = **actual**, real, true, simple, plain, genuine, bona fide, unvarnished

literally = **exactly**, really, closely, actually, truly, precisely, strictly, faithfully

literary = **well-read**, learned, formal, intellectual, scholarly, erudite, bookish

literate = **educated**, informed, knowledgeable

literature = **writings**, letters, compositions, lore, creative writing (*informal*)
• *See panel* **SHAKESPEARE**

litigation = **lawsuit**, case, action, prosecution

litter NOUN 1 = **rubbish**, refuse, waste, junk, debris, garbage (*chiefly US*), trash, muck
2 = **brood**, young, offspring, progeny
▷ VERB 3 = **clutter**, mess up, clutter up, be scattered about, disorder, disarrange, derange, muss (*US & Canad*) 4 = **scatter**, spread, shower, strew

little ADJECTIVE 1 = **small**, minute, short, tiny, wee, compact, miniature, diminutive OPPOSITE: big 2 = **young**, small, junior, infant, immature, undeveloped, babyish
▷ ADVERB 3 = **hardly**, barely, scarcely OPPOSITE: much
4 = **rarely**, seldom, scarcely, not often, infrequently, hardly ever

OPPOSITE: always
▷ NOUN 5 = **bit**, touch, spot, trace, hint, particle, fragment, speck OPPOSITE: lot
▷ PHRASES: a little = **to a small extent**, slightly, to some extent, to a certain extent, to a small degree

live[1] 1 = **dwell**, board, settle, lodge, occupy, abide, inhabit, reside 2 = **exist**, last, prevail, be, have being, breathe, persist, be alive 3 = **survive**, get along, make a living, make ends meet, subsist, eke out a living, support yourself, maintain yourself
4 = **thrive**, flourish, prosper, have fun, enjoy yourself, live life to the full

live[2] 1 = **living**, alive, breathing, animate 2 = **active**, unexploded 3 = **topical**, important, pressing, current, hot, burning, controversial, prevalent

livelihood = **occupation**, work, employment, living, job, bread and butter (*informal*)

lively 1 = **animated**, spirited, quick, keen, active, alert, dynamic, vigorous OPPOSITE: dull 2 = **vivid**, strong, striking, bright, exciting, stimulating, bold, colourful OPPOSITE: dull
3 = **enthusiastic**, strong, keen, stimulating, eager, formidable, vigorous, animated

living NOUN 1 = **lifestyle**, ways, situation, conduct, behaviour, customs, way of life

▷ **ADJECTIVE 2 = alive**, existing, moving, active, breathing, animate **OPPOSITE:** dead
3 = current, present, active, contemporary, in use, extant **OPPOSITE:** obsolete

lizard
• See panel **REPTILES**

load VERB 1 = fill, stuff, pack, pile, stack, heap, cram, freight
2 = make ready, charge, prime
▷ **NOUN 3 = cargo**, delivery, haul, shipment, batch, freight, consignment **4 = oppression**, charge, worry, trouble, weight, responsibility, burden, onus
▷ **PHRASES: load someone down = burden**, worry, oppress, weigh down, saddle with, encumber, snow under

loaded 1 = tricky, charged, sensitive, delicate, manipulative, emotive, insidious, artful **2 = biased**, weighted, rigged, distorted **3** (slang) **= rich**, wealthy, affluent, well off, flush (informal), well-heeled (informal), well-to-do, moneyed, minted (Brit slang)

loaf¹ 1 = lump, block, cake, cube, slab **2** (slang) **= head**, mind, sense, common sense, nous (Brit slang), gumption (Brit informal)

loaf² = idle, hang around, take it easy, lie around, loiter, laze, lounge around

loan NOUN 1 = advance, credit, overdraft
▷ **VERB 2 = lend**, advance, let out

loathe = hate, dislike, despise, detest, abhor, abominate

loathing = hatred, hate, disgust, aversion, revulsion, antipathy, repulsion, abhorrence

lobby VERB 1 = campaign, press, pressure, push, influence, promote, urge, persuade
▷ **NOUN 2 = pressure group**, group, camp, faction, lobbyists, interest group, special-interest group, ginger group, public-interest group (US & Canad)
3 = corridor, passage, entrance, porch, hallway, foyer, entrance hall, vestibule

lobola (S African) **= dowry**, portion, marriage settlement, dot (archaic)

local ADJECTIVE 1 = community, regional **2 = confined**, limited, restricted
▷ **NOUN 3 = resident**, native, inhabitant

locate 1 = find, discover, detect, come across, track down, pinpoint, unearth, pin down
2 = place, put, set, position, seat, site, establish, settle

location = place, point, setting, position, situation, spot, venue, locale

lock¹ VERB 1 = fasten, close, secure, shut, bar, seal, bolt
2 = unite, join, link, engage, clench, entangle, interlock, entwine **3 = embrace**, press, grasp, clutch, hug, enclose, clasp, encircle

▷ **NOUN 4 = fastening**, catch, bolt, clasp, padlock

▷ **PHRASES:** lock someone up **= imprison**, jail, confine, cage, detain, shut up, incarcerate, send down (*informal*)

lock²= strand, curl, tuft, tress, ringlet

lodge NOUN 1 = cabin, shelter, cottage, hut, chalet, gatehouse **2 = society**, group, club, section, wing, chapter, branch ▷ **VERB 3 = register**, enter, file, submit, put on record **4 = stay**, room, board, reside **5 = stick**, remain, implant, come to rest, imbed

lodging *often plural* **= accommodation**, rooms, apartments, quarters, digs (*Brit informal*), shelter, residence, abode, bachelor apartment (*Canad*)

lofty 1 = noble, grand, distinguished, renowned, elevated, dignified, illustrious, exalted **OPPOSITE:** humble **2 = high**, raised, towering, soaring, elevated **OPPOSITE:** low **3 = haughty**, proud, arrogant, patronizing, condescending, disdainful, supercilious **OPPOSITE:** modest

log NOUN 1 = stump, block, branch, chunk, trunk **2 = record**, account, register, journal, diary, logbook, blog (*informal*) ▷ **VERB 3 = record**, enter, note,

register, chart, put down, set down

logic = reason, reasoning, sense, good sense

logical 1 = rational, clear, reasoned, sound, consistent, valid, coherent, well-organized **OPPOSITE:** illogical **2 = reasonable**, sensible, natural, wise, plausible **OPPOSITE:** unlikely

lone = solitary, single, one, only, sole, unaccompanied

loneliness = solitude, isolation, desolation, seclusion

lonely 1 = solitary, alone, isolated, abandoned, lone, withdrawn, single, forsaken, lonesome (*chiefly US & Canad*) **OPPOSITE:** accompanied **2 = desolate**, deserted, remote, isolated, out-of-the-way, secluded, uninhabited, godforsaken **OPPOSITE:** crowded

lonesome (*chiefly US & Canad*) **= lonely**, gloomy, dreary, desolate, forlorn, friendless, companionless

long¹ 1 = elongated, extended, stretched, expanded, extensive, lengthy, far-reaching, spread out **OPPOSITE:** short **2 = prolonged**, sustained, lengthy, lingering, protracted, interminable, spun out, long-drawn-out **OPPOSITE:** brief

long² = desire, want, wish, burn, pine, lust, crave, yearn

longing = **desire**, hope, wish, burning, urge, ambition, hunger, yen (*informal*) **OPPOSITE**: indifference

long-standing = **established**, fixed, enduring, abiding, long-lasting, long-established, time-honoured

look VERB 1 = **see**, view, consider, watch, eye, study, survey, examine 2 = **search**, seek, hunt, forage, fossick (*Austral & NZ*) 3 = **consider**, contemplate 4 = **face**, overlook 5 = **hope**, expect, await, anticipate, reckon on 6 = **seem**, appear, look like, strike you as ▷ NOUN 7 = **glimpse**, view, glance, observation, sight, examination, gaze, inspection 8 = **appearance**, bearing, air, style, aspect, manner, expression, impression ▷ PHRASES: **look after something** *or* **someone** = **take care of**, mind, protect, tend, guard, nurse, care for, supervise ▶ **look down on** *or* **upon someone** = **disdain**, despise, scorn, sneer at, spurn, contemn (*formal*) ▶ **look forward to something** = **anticipate**, expect, look for, wait for, await, hope for, long for ▶ **look out for something** = **be careful of**, beware, watch out for, pay attention to, be wary of, keep an eye out for ▶ **look someone up** = **visit**, call on, drop in on

(*informal*), look in on ▶ **look something up** = **research**, find, search for, hunt for, track down, seek out ▶ **look up** = **improve**, develop, advance, pick up, progress, get better, shape up (*informal*), perk up ▶ **look up to someone** = **respect**, honour, admire, esteem, revere, defer to, think highly of

lookout 1 = **watchman**, guard, sentry, sentinel 2 = **watch**, guard, vigil 3 = **watchtower**, post, observatory, observation post 4 (*informal*) = **concern**, business, worry

loom = **appear**, emerge, hover, take shape, threaten, bulk, menace, come into view

loop NOUN 1 = **curve**, ring, circle, twist, curl, spiral, coil, twirl ▷ VERB 2 = **twist**, turn, roll, knot, curl, spiral, coil, wind round

loophole = **let-out**, escape, excuse

loose ADJECTIVE 1 = **free**, detached, insecure, unfettered, unrestricted, untied, unattached, unfastened 2 = **slack**, easy, relaxed, sloppy, loose-fitting **OPPOSITE**: tight 3 (*Old-fashioned*) = **promiscuous**, fast, abandoned, immoral, dissipated, profligate, debauched, dissolute **OPPOSITE**: chaste 4 = **vague**, random, inaccurate, rambling, imprecise, ill-defined, indistinct, inexact **OPPOSITE**: precise

▷ **VERB 5 = free**, release, liberate, detach, unleash, disconnect, set free, untie **OPPOSITE:** fasten

loosen = untie, undo, release, separate, detach, unloose

▷ **PHRASES: loosen up = relax**, chill (*slang*), soften, unwind, go easy (*informal*), hang loose, outspan (*S African*), ease up *or* off

loot VERB 1 = plunder, rob, raid, sack, rifle, ravage, ransack, pillage

▷ **NOUN 2 = plunder**, goods, prize, haul, spoils, booty, swag (*slang*)

lord 1 = peer, nobleman, count, duke, gentleman, earl, noble, baron **2 = ruler**, leader, chief, master, governor, commander, superior, liege

▷ **PHRASES: lord it over someone = boss around** *or* **about** (*informal*), order around, threaten, bully, menace, intimidate, hector, bluster ▶ **the Lord** *or* **Our Lord = Jesus Christ**, God, Christ, Messiah, Jehovah, the Almighty

lose 1 = be defeated, be beaten, lose out, come to grief **2 = mislay**, drop, forget, be deprived of, lose track of, misplace **3 = forfeit**, miss, yield, be deprived of, pass up (*informal*)

loser = failure, flop (*informal*), also-ran, no-hoper (*Austral slang*), dud (*informal*), non-achiever, luser (*computing slang*)

loss 1 = losing, waste, squandering, forfeiture **OPPOSITE:** gain **2** *sometimes plural* **= deficit**, debt, deficiency, debit, depletion **OPPOSITE:** gain **3 = damage**, cost, injury, hurt, harm **OPPOSITE:** advantage

▷ **PHRASES: at a loss = confused**, puzzled, baffled, bewildered, helpless, stumped, perplexed, mystified

lost = missing, disappeared, vanished, wayward, misplaced, mislaid

lot 1 = bunch (*informal*), group, crowd, crew, set, band, quantity, assortment **2 = destiny**, situation, circumstances, fortune, chance, accident, fate, doom

▷ **PHRASES: a lot** *or* **lots 1 = plenty**, scores, masses (*informal*), load(s) (*informal*), wealth, piles (*informal*), a great deal, stack(s) **2 = often**, regularly, a great deal, frequently, a good deal

lotion = cream, solution, balm, salve, liniment, embrocation

lottery 1 = raffle, draw, lotto (*Brit, NZ & S African*), sweepstake **2 = gamble**, chance, risk, hazard, toss-up (*informal*)

loud 1 = noisy, booming, roaring, thundering, forte (*music*), resounding, deafening, thunderous **OPPOSITE:** quiet **2 = garish**, bold, glaring, flamboyant, brash, flashy, lurid, gaudy **OPPOSITE:** sombre

loudly = **noisily**, vigorously, vehemently, vociferously, uproariously, lustily, shrilly, fortissimo (*music*)

lounge VERB 1 = **relax**, loaf, sprawl, lie about, take it easy, loiter, loll, laze, outspan (*S African*)
▷ **NOUN** 2 = **sitting room**, living room, parlour, drawing room, front room, reception room, television room

love VERB 1 = **adore**, care for, treasure, cherish, prize, worship, be devoted to, dote on **OPPOSITE:** hate 2 = **enjoy**, like, appreciate, relish, delight in, savour, take pleasure in, have a soft spot for **OPPOSITE:** dislike
▷ **NOUN** 3 = **passion**, affection, warmth, attachment, intimacy, devotion, tenderness, adoration, aroha (*NZ*)
OPPOSITE: hatred 4 = **liking**, taste, bent for, weakness for, relish for, enjoyment, devotion to, penchant for 5 = **beloved**, dear, dearest, lover, darling, honey, sweetheart, truelove
OPPOSITE: enemy
6 = **sympathy**, understanding, pity, humanity, warmth, mercy, sorrow, kindness, aroha (*NZ*)
▷ **PHRASES: make love** = **have sexual intercourse**, have sex, go to bed, sleep together, do it

(*informal*), mate, have sexual relations, have it off (*slang*)

love affair = **romance**, relationship, affair, intrigue, liaison, amour

lovely 1 = **beautiful**, appealing, attractive, charming, pretty, handsome, good-looking, exquisite, fit (*Brit informal*)
OPPOSITE: ugly 2 = **wonderful**, pleasing, nice, pleasant, engaging, marvellous, delightful, enjoyable **OPPOSITE:** horrible

lover = **sweetheart**, beloved, loved one, flame (*informal*), mistress, admirer, suitor, woman friend

loving 1 = **affectionate**, dear, devoted, tender, fond, doting, amorous, warm-hearted
OPPOSITE: cruel 2 = **tender**, kind, caring, warm, gentle, sympathetic, considerate

low 1 = **small**, little, short, stunted, squat **OPPOSITE:** tall 2 = **inferior**, bad, poor, inadequate, unsatisfactory, deficient, second-rate, shoddy, half-pie (*NZ informal*), bodger or bodgie (*Austral slang*) 3 = **quiet**, soft, gentle, whispered, muted, subdued, hushed, muffled
OPPOSITE: loud 4 = **dejected**, depressed, miserable, fed up, moody, gloomy, glum, despondent **OPPOSITE:** happy
5 = **coarse**, common, rough, crude, rude, vulgar, undignified,

disreputable **6 = ill**, weak, frail, stricken, debilitated **OPPOSITE:** strong

lower ADJECTIVE
1 = **subordinate**, under, smaller, junior, minor, secondary, lesser, inferior 2 = **reduced**, cut, diminished, decreased, lessened, curtailed **OPPOSITE:** increased
▷ **VERB** 3 = **drop**, sink, depress, let down, submerge, take down, let fall **OPPOSITE:** raise 4 = **lessen**, cut, reduce, diminish, slash, decrease, prune, minimize **OPPOSITE:** increase

low-key = **subdued**, quiet, restrained, muted, understated, toned down

loyal = **faithful**, true, devoted, dependable, constant, staunch, trustworthy, trusty **OPPOSITE:** disloyal

loyalty = **faithfulness**, commitment, devotion, allegiance, fidelity, homage, obedience, constancy

luck 1 = **good fortune**, success, advantage, prosperity, blessing, windfall, godsend, serendipity 2 = **fortune**, lot, stars, chance, accident, fate, destiny, twist of fate

luckily = **fortunately**, happily, opportunely

lucky = **fortunate**, successful, favoured, charmed, blessed, jammy (*Brit slang*), serendipitous **OPPOSITE:** unlucky

lucrative = **profitable**, rewarding, productive, fruitful, well-paid, advantageous, remunerative

ludicrous = **ridiculous**, crazy, absurd, preposterous, silly, laughable, farcical, outlandish **OPPOSITE:** sensible

luggage = **baggage**, things, cases, bags, gear, suitcases, paraphernalia, impedimenta

lull NOUN 1 = **respite**, pause, quiet, silence, calm, hush, let-up (*informal*)
▷ **VERB** 2 = **calm**, soothe, subdue, quell, allay, pacify, tranquillize

lumber¹ VERB 1(*Brit informal*) = **burden**, land, load, saddle, encumber
▷ **NOUN** 2(*Brit*) = **junk**, refuse, rubbish, trash, clutter, jumble

lumber² = **plod**, shuffle, shamble, trudge, stump, waddle, trundle

lumbering = **awkward**, heavy, hulking, ponderous, ungainly

lump NOUN 1 = **piece**, ball, block, mass, chunk, hunk, nugget 2 = **swelling**, growth, bump, tumour, bulge, hump, protrusion
▷ **VERB** 3 = **group**, throw, mass, combine, collect, pool, consolidate, conglomerate

lunatic NOUN 1 = **madman**, maniac, psychopath, nutcase (*slang*), crazy (*informal*)
▷ **ADJECTIVE** 2 = **mad**, crazy,

insane, irrational, daft, deranged, crackpot (*informal*), crackbrained, off the air (*Austral slang*)

lunge VERB 1 = **pounce**, charge, dive, leap, plunge, thrust
▷ NOUN 2 = **thrust**, charge, pounce, spring, swing, jab

lurch 1 = **tilt**, roll, pitch, list, rock, lean, heel 2 = **stagger**, reel, stumble, weave, sway, totter

lure VERB 1 = **tempt**, draw, attract, invite, trick, seduce, entice, allure
▷ NOUN 2 = **temptation**, attraction, incentive, bait, carrot (*informal*), inducement, enticement, allurement

lurk = **hide**, sneak, prowl, lie in wait, slink, skulk, conceal yourself

lush 1 = **abundant**, green, flourishing, dense, rank, verdant 2 = **luxurious**, grand, elaborate, lavish, extravagant, sumptuous, plush (*informal*), ornate

lust 1 = **lechery**, sensuality, lewdness, lasciviousness
2 = **desire**, longing, passion, appetite, craving, greed, thirst
▷ PHRASES: lust for *or* after someone *or* something
= **desire**, want, crave, yearn for, covet, hunger for *or* after

luxurious = **sumptuous**, expensive, comfortable, magnificent, splendid, lavish, plush (*informal*), opulent
OPPOSITE: austere

USAGE NOTE
Luxurious is sometimes wrongly used where *luxuriant* is meant: *he had a luxuriant (not luxurious) moustache; the walls were covered with a luxuriant growth of wisteria.*

luxury 1 = **opulence**, splendour, richness, extravagance, affluence, hedonism, a bed of roses, the life of Riley OPPOSITE: poverty 2 = **extravagance**, treat, extra, indulgence, frill OPPOSITE: necessity

lyrical = **enthusiastic**, inspired, poetic, impassioned, effusive, rhapsodic

Mm

machine 1 = **appliance**,
device, apparatus, engine,
tool, instrument, mechanism,
gadget 2 = **system**, structure,
organization, machinery, setup
(*informal*)

machinery = **equipment**,
gear, instruments, apparatus,
technology, tackle, tools,
gadgetry

macho = **manly**, masculine,
chauvinist, virile

mad 1 = **insane**, crazy (*informal*),
nuts (*slang*), raving, unstable,
psychotic, demented, deranged,
off the air (*Austral slang*)
OPPOSITE: sane 2 = **foolish**,
absurd, wild, stupid, daft
(*informal*), irrational, senseless,
preposterous **OPPOSITE:**
sensible 3 (*informal*) = **angry**,
furious, incensed, enraged,
livid (*informal*), berserk, berko
(*Austral slang*), tooshie (*Austral
slang*), off the air (*Austral slang*)
OPPOSITE: calm 4 *usually
with* **about** = **enthusiastic**,
wild, crazy (*informal*), ardent,
fanatical, avid, impassioned,

infatuated **OPPOSITE:**
nonchalant 5 = **frenzied**, wild,
excited, frenetic, uncontrolled,
unrestrained

madden = **infuriate**, irritate,
incense, enrage, upset, annoy,
inflame, drive you crazy
OPPOSITE: calm

madly 1 (*informal*)
= **passionately**, wildly,
desperately, intensely,
to distraction, devotedly
2 = **foolishly**, wildly, absurdly,
ludicrously, irrationally,
senselessly 3 = **energetically**,
wildly, furiously, excitedly,
recklessly, speedily, like mad
(*informal*) 4 = **insanely**,
frantically, hysterically, crazily,
deliriously, distractedly,
frenziedly

madness 1 = **insanity**,
derangement, delusion,
mania, dementia, distraction,
aberration, psychosis
2 = **foolishness**, nonsense,
folly, absurdity, idiocy,
wildness, daftness (*informal*),
foolhardiness

magazine = **journal**,
publication, supplement,
rag (*informal*), issue, glossy
(*informal*), pamphlet, periodical,
ezine *or* e-zine

magic NOUN 1 = **sorcery**,
wizardry, witchcraft,
enchantment, black art,
necromancy 2 = **conjuring**,
illusion, trickery, sleight of hand,

m

legerdemain, prestidigitation
3 = charm, power, glamour, fascination, magnetism, enchantment, allurement, mojo (*slang*)
▷ ADJECTIVE **4 = miraculous**, entrancing, charming, fascinating, marvellous, magical, enchanting, bewitching

magician 1 = conjuror, illusionist, prestidigitator
2 = sorcerer, witch, wizard, illusionist, warlock, necromancer, enchanter *or* enchantress

magistrate = judge, justice, justice of the peace, J.P.

magnetic = attractive, irresistible, seductive, captivating, charming, fascinating, charismatic, hypnotic **OPPOSITE**: repulsive

magnificent 1 = splendid, impressive, imposing, glorious, gorgeous, majestic, regal, sublime **OPPOSITE**: ordinary
2 = brilliant, fine, excellent, outstanding, superb, splendid

magnify 1 = enlarge, increase, boost, expand, intensify, blow up (*informal*), heighten, amplify **OPPOSITE**: reduce **2 = make worse**, exaggerate, intensify, worsen, exacerbate, increase, inflame **3 = exaggerate**, overstate, inflate, overplay, overemphasize **OPPOSITE**: understate

magnitude 1 = importance, consequence, significance, moment, note, weight, greatness **OPPOSITE**: unimportance **2 = immensity**, size, extent, enormity, volume, vastness **OPPOSITE**: smallness **3 = intensity**, amplitude

maid 1 = servant, chambermaid, housemaid, menial, maidservant, female servant, domestic (*archaic*), parlourmaid **2** (*archaic literary*) **= girl**, maiden, lass, damsel, lassie (*informal*), wench

maiden NOUN **1** (*archaic literary*) **= girl**, maid, lass, damsel, virgin, lassie (*informal*), wench
▷ MODIFIER **2 = first**, initial, inaugural, introductory
3 = unmarried, unwed

mail NOUN **1 = letters**, post, correspondence
▷ VERB **2 = post**, send, forward, dispatch **3 = email** *or* **e-mail**, send, forward

main ADJECTIVE **1 = chief**, leading, head, central, essential, primary, principal, foremost **OPPOSITE**: minor
▷ PLURAL NOUN **2 = pipeline**, channel, pipe, conduit, duct **3 = cable**, line, electricity supply, mains supply
▷ PHRASES: **in the main = on the whole**, generally, mainly, mostly, in general, for the most part

mainly = **chiefly**, mostly, largely, principally, primarily, on the whole, predominantly, in the main

mainstream = **conventional**, general, established, received, accepted, current, prevailing, orthodox, lamestream (*informal*) **OPPOSITE:** unconventional

maintain 1 = **continue**, retain, preserve, sustain, carry on, keep up, prolong, perpetuate **OPPOSITE:** end 2 = **assert**, state, claim, insist, declare, contend, profess, avow **OPPOSITE:** disavow 3 = **look after**, care for, take care of, conserve, keep in good condition

maintenance 1 = **upkeep**, keeping, care, repairs, conservation, nurture, preservation 2 = **allowance**, support, keep, alimony 3 = **continuation**, carrying-on, perpetuation, prolongation

majestic = **grand**, magnificent, impressive, superb, splendid, regal, stately, monumental **OPPOSITE:** modest

majesty = **grandeur**, glory, splendour, magnificence, nobility **OPPOSITE:** triviality

major 1 = **important**, critical, significant, great, serious, crucial, outstanding, notable 2 = **main**, higher, greater, bigger, leading, chief, senior, supreme **OPPOSITE:** minor

majority 1 = **most**, mass, bulk, best part, better part, lion's share, preponderance, greater number 2 = **adulthood**, maturity, age of consent, seniority, manhood *or* womanhood

▎**USAGE NOTE**
▎*The majority of* should always
▎refer to a countable number
▎of things or people. If you
▎are talking about an amount
▎or quantity, rather than a
▎countable number, use *most*
▎*of*, as in *most of the harvest was*
▎*saved* (not *the majority of the*
▎*harvest was saved*).

make VERB 1 = **produce**, cause, create, effect, lead to, generate, bring about, give rise to 2 = **perform**, do, effect, carry out, execute 3 = **force**, cause, compel, drive, require, oblige, induce, constrain 4 = **create**, build, produce, manufacture, form, fashion, construct, assemble 5 = **earn**, get, gain, net, win, clear, obtain, bring in 6 = **amount to**, total, constitute, add up to, count as, tot up to (*informal*)
▷ NOUN 7 = **brand**, sort, style, model, kind, type, variety, marque
▷ PHRASES: **make for something** = **head for**, aim for, head towards, be bound for
▶ **make it** (*informal*) = **succeed**, prosper, arrive (*informal*),

m

get on, crack it (*informal*)
▶ **make off = flee**, clear out (*informal*), bolt, take to your heels, run away *or* off ▶ **make something up = invent**, create, construct, compose, frame, coin, devise, originate ▶ **make up = settle your differences**, bury the hatchet, call it quits, declare a truce, be friends again ▶ **make up for something = compensate for**, make amends for, atone for, balance out, offset, make recompense for ▶ **make up something 1 = form**, account for, constitute, compose, comprise **2 = complete**, supply, fill, round off

maker = manufacturer, producer, builder, constructor

makeshift = temporary, provisional, substitute, expedient, stopgap

make-up 1 = cosmetics, paint (*informal*), powder, face (*informal*), greasepaint (*theatre*) **2 = nature**, character, constitution, temperament, disposition **3 = structure**, organization, arrangement, construction, assembly, constitution, format, composition

making NOUN 1 = creation, production, manufacture, construction, assembly, composition, fabrication
▷ **PLURAL NOUN**

2 = beginnings, potential, capacity, ingredients

male = masculine, manly, macho, virile **OPPOSITE:** female

malfunction VERB 1 = break down, fail, go wrong, stop working, be defective, conk out (*informal*), crash (*of a computer*)
▷ **NOUN 2 = fault**, failure, breakdown, defect, flaw, glitch

malicious = spiteful, malevolent, resentful, vengeful, rancorous, ill-disposed, ill-natured **OPPOSITE:** benevolent

mammal
• *See panels* **BATS, CARNIVORES, MARSUPIALS, MONKEYS, APES AND OTHER PRIMATES, RODENTS, EXTINCT MAMMALS, SEA MAMMALS, WHALES AND DOLPHINS**

mammoth = colossal, huge, giant, massive, enormous, immense, gigantic, monumental, supersize **OPPOSITE:** tiny

man NOUN 1 = male, guy (*informal*), fellow (*informal*), gentleman, bloke (*Brit informal*), chap (*Brit informal*), dude (*US informal*), geezer (*informal*) **2 = human**, human being, person, individual, soul **3 = mankind**, humanity, people, human race, humankind, Homo sapiens
▷ **VERB 4 = staff**, people, crew, occupy, garrison

EXTINCT MAMMALS

apeman
aurochs
australopithecine
baluchitherium
chalicothere
creodont
dinoceras or uintathere
dinothere
dryopithecine
eohippus
glyptodont

Irish elk
labyrinthodont
mammoth
mastodon
megathere
nototherium
quagga
sabre-toothed tiger or cat
tarpan
titanothere

mana (*NZ*) = **authority**, influence, power, might, standing, status, importance, eminence

manage 1 = **be in charge of**, run, handle, direct, conduct, command, administer, supervise 2 = **organize**, use, handle, regulate 3 = **cope**, survive, succeed, carry on, make do, get by (*informal*), muddle through 4 = **perform**, do, achieve, carry out, undertake, cope with, accomplish, contrive 5 = **control**, handle, manipulate

management 1 = **administration**, control, running, operation, handling, direction, command, supervision 2 = **directors**, board, executive(s), administration, employers

manager = **supervisor**, head, director, executive, boss (*informal*), governor, administrator, organizer, baas (*S African*), sherang (*Austral & NZ*)

mandate = **command**, order, commission, instruction, decree, directive, edict

mandatory = **compulsory**, required, binding, obligatory, requisite **OPPOSITE:** optional

manhood = **manliness**, masculinity, virility

manifest ADJECTIVE 1 = **obvious**, apparent, patent, evident, clear, glaring, noticeable, blatant **OPPOSITE:** concealed
▷ VERB 2 = **display**, show, reveal, express, demonstrate, expose, exhibit **OPPOSITE:** conceal

manifestation 1 = **sign**, symptom, indication, mark, example, evidence, proof, testimony 2 = **display**,

m

show, exhibition, expression, demonstration

manipulate 1 = **influence**, control, direct, negotiate, exploit, manoeuvre 2 = **work**, use, operate, handle

mankind = **people**, man, humanity, human race, humankind, Homo sapiens

> **USAGE NOTE**
> Some people object to the use of *mankind* to refer to all human beings on the grounds that it is sexist. A preferable term is *humankind*, which refers to both men and women.

manly = **virile**, masculine, strong, brave, bold, strapping, vigorous, courageous **OPPOSITE:** effeminate

man-made = **artificial**, manufactured, mock, synthetic, ersatz

manner NOUN 1 = **style**, way, fashion, method, custom, mode 2 = **behaviour**, air, bearing, conduct, aspect, demeanour 3 = **type**, form, sort, kind, variety, brand, category
▷ PLURAL NOUN 4 = **conduct**, behaviour, demeanour 5 = **politeness**, courtesy, etiquette, refinement, decorum, p's and q's 6 = **protocol**, customs, social graces

mannered = **affected**, artificial, pretentious, stilted, arty-farty (*informal*) **OPPOSITE:** natural

manoeuvre VERB 1 = **scheme**, wangle (*informal*), machinate 2 = **manipulate**, arrange, organize, set up, engineer, fix, orchestrate, contrive
▷ NOUN 3 = **stratagem**, scheme, trick, tactic, intrigue, dodge, ploy, ruse 4 *often plural* = **movement**, operation, exercise, war game

mansion = **residence**, manor, hall, villa, seat

mantle 1 = **covering**, screen, curtain, blanket, veil, shroud, canopy, pall 2 (*archaic*) = **cloak**, wrap, cape, hood, shawl

manual ADJECTIVE 1 = **physical**, human 2 = **hand-operated**, hand, non-automatic
▷ NOUN 3 = **handbook**, guide, instructions, bible

manufacture VERB 1 = **make**, build, produce, construct, create, turn out, assemble, put together 2 = **concoct**, make up, invent, devise, fabricate, think up, cook up (*informal*), trump up
▷ NOUN 3 = **making**, production, construction, assembly, creation

manufacturer = **maker**, producer, builder, creator, industrialist, constructor

many ADJECTIVE 1 = **numerous**, various, countless, abundant, myriad, innumerable, manifold, umpteen (*informal*)
▷ PRONOUN 2 = **a lot**, lots (*informal*), plenty, scores, heaps (*informal*)

mar 1 = **harm**, damage, hurt, spoil, stain, taint, tarnish 2 = **ruin**, spoil, scar, flaw, impair, detract from, deform, blemish
OPPOSITE: improve

march VERB 1 = **parade**, walk, file, pace, stride, swagger 2 = **walk**, strut, storm, sweep, stride, flounce
▷ NOUN 3 = **walk**, trek, slog, yomp (*Brit informal*), routemarch 4 = **progress**, development, advance, evolution, progression

margin = **edge**, side, border, boundary, verge, brink, rim, perimeter

marginal 1 = **insignificant**, small, minor, slight, minimal, negligible 2 = **borderline**, bordering, on the edge, peripheral

marijuana = **cannabis**, pot (*slang*), dope (*slang*), grass (*slang*), hemp, dagga (*S African*)

marine = **nautical**, maritime, naval, seafaring, seagoing

mariner = **sailor**, seaman, sea dog, seafarer, salt

marital = **matrimonial**, nuptial, conjugal, connubial

maritime 1 = **nautical**, marine, naval, oceanic, seafaring 2 = **coastal**, seaside, littoral

mark NOUN 1 = **spot**, stain, streak, smudge, line, scratch, scar, blot 2 = **characteristic**, feature, standard, quality, measure, stamp, attribute, criterion 3 = **indication**, sign, symbol, token 4 = **brand**, impression, label, device, flag, symbol, token, emblem 5 = **target**, goal, aim, purpose, object, objective
▷ VERB 6 = **scar**, scratch, stain, streak, blot, smudge, blemish 7 = **label**, identify, brand, flag, stamp, characterize 8 = **grade**, correct, assess, evaluate, appraise 9 = **distinguish**, show, illustrate, exemplify, denote 10 = **observe**, mind, note, notice, attend to, pay attention to, pay heed to

marked = **noticeable**, clear, decided, striking, obvious, prominent, patent, distinct
OPPOSITE: imperceptible

markedly = **noticeably**, clearly, obviously, considerably, distinctly, decidedly, strikingly, conspicuously

market NOUN 1 = **fair**, mart, bazaar, souk (*Arabic*)
▷ VERB 2 = **sell**, promote, retail, peddle, vend

maroon = **abandon**, leave, desert, strand, leave high and dry (*informal*)

marriage = **wedding**, match, nuptials, wedlock, matrimony

marry 1 = **tie the knot** (*informal*), wed, get hitched (*slang*) 2 = **unite**, join, link, bond, ally, merge, knit, unify

marsh = **swamp**, bog, slough, fen, quagmire, morass, muskeg (*Canad*)

marshal 1 = conduct, take, lead, guide, steer, escort, shepherd, usher **2 = arrange**, group, order, line up, organize, deploy, array, draw up

marsupial
• See panel **MARSUPIALS**

martial = military, belligerent, warlike, bellicose

marvel VERB **1 = be amazed**, wonder, gape, be awed
▷ NOUN **2 = wonder**, phenomenon, miracle, portent **3 = genius**, prodigy

marvellous = excellent, great (informal), wonderful, brilliant, amazing, extraordinary, superb, spectacular, booshit (Austral slang), exo (Austral slang), sik (Austral slang), rad (informal), phat (slang), schmick (Austral informal) OPPOSITE: terrible

masculine = male, manly, mannish, manlike, virile

mask NOUN **1 = façade**, disguise, front, cover, screen, veil, guise, camouflage
▷ VERB **2 = disguise**, hide, conceal, obscure, cover (up), screen, blanket, veil

mass NOUN **1 = lot**, collection, load, pile, quantity, bunch, stack, heap **2 = piece**, block, lump, chunk, hunk **3 = size**, matter, weight, extent, bulk, magnitude, greatness
▷ ADJECTIVE **4 = large-scale**, general, widespread, extensive, universal, wholesale, indiscriminate
▷ VERB **5 = gather**, assemble, accumulate, collect, rally, swarm, throng, congregate

massacre NOUN **1 = slaughter**, murder, holocaust, carnage, extermination, annihilation, butchery, blood bath
▷ VERB **2 = slaughter**, kill, murder, butcher, wipe out, exterminate, mow down, cut to pieces

massage NOUN **1 = rub-down**, manipulation
▷ VERB **2 = rub down**, manipulate, knead **3 = manipulate**, alter, distort, doctor, cook (informal), fix (informal), rig, fiddle (informal)

massive = huge, big, enormous, immense, hefty, gigantic, monumental, mammoth, supersize OPPOSITE: tiny

master NOUN **1 = lord**, ruler, commander, chief, director, manager, boss (informal), head, baas (S African) OPPOSITE: servant **2 = expert**, maestro, ace (informal), genius, wizard, virtuoso, doyen, past master, fundi (S African) OPPOSITE: amateur **3 = teacher**, tutor, instructor OPPOSITE: student
▷ ADJECTIVE **4 = main**, principal, chief, prime, foremost, predominant OPPOSITE: lesser
▷ VERB **5 = learn**, understand,

m

MARSUPIALS

agile wallaby, river wallaby, sandy wallaby, or jungle kangaroo

antechinus

antelope kangaroo or antilopine wallaby

bandicoot

barred bandicoot or marl

Bennett's tree kangaroo or tcharibeena

bettong

bilby, rabbit(-eared) bandicoot, long-eared bandicoot, dalgyte, or dalgite

bobuck or mountain (brushtail) possum

boodie (rat), burrowing rat-kangaroo, Lesueur's rat-kangaroo, tungoo, or tungo

boongary or Lumholtz's tree kangaroo

bridled nail-tail wallaby or merrin

brindled bandicoot or northern brown bandicoot

brush-tail(ed) possum

burramys or (mountain) pygmy possum

crest-tailed marsupial mouse, Cannings' little dog, or mulgara

crescent nail-tail wallaby or wurrung

cuscus

dasyurid, dasyure, native cat, marsupial cat, or wild cat

desert bandicoot

desert-rat kangaroo

dibbler

diprotodon

dunnart

eastern grey kangaroo, great grey kangaroo, forest kangaroo, or (grey) forester

fluffy glider or yellow-bellied glider

flying phalanger, flying squirrel, glider, or pongo

green ringtail possum or toolah

hairy-nosed wombat

hare-wallaby

honey mouse, honey possum, noolbenger, or tait

jerboa, jerboa pouched mouse, jerboa kangaroo, or kultarr

kangaroo or (Austral informal) roo

koala (bear) or (Austral) native bear

kowari

larapinta or Darling Downs dunnart

Leadbeater's possum or fairy possum

lemuroid ringtail possum

long-nosed bandicoot

mardo or yellow-footed antechinus

marlu

marsupial mole

marsupial mouse

mongan or Herbert River ringtail possum

munning

musky rat-kangaroo

naked-nose wombat

ningaui

m

MARSUPIALS *continued*

northern nail-tail wallaby *or* karrabul

northern native cat *or* satanellus

numbat *or* banded anteater

opossum *or* possum

pademelon *or* paddymelon

parma wallaby

phalanger

pig-footed bandicoot

pitchi-pitchi *or* wuhl-wuhl

platypus, duck-billed platypus, *or* duckbill

potoroo

pretty-face wallaby *or* whiptail wallaby

pygmy glider, feather glider, *or* flying mouse

quenda *or* (southern) brown bandicoot

quokka

quoll

rat kangaroo

red kangaroo *or* plains kangaroo

red(-necked) wallaby, Bennett's wallaby, eastern brush wallaby, rufous wallaby, *or* brush kangaroo

ringtail *or* ringtail(ed) possum

rock wallaby *or* brush-tailed wallaby

rufous rat-kangaroo

scrub wallaby

short-eared bandicoot

short-nosed bandicoot

short-nosed rat kangaroo *or* squeaker

squirrel glider

striped possum

sugar glider

swamp wallaby, black wallaby, *or* black-tailed wallaby

tammar, damar, *or* dama

Tasmanian barred bandicoot *or* Gunn's bandicoot

Tasmanian devil *or* ursine dasyure

thylacine, Tasmanian wolf, *or* Tasmanian tiger

tiger cat *or* spotted native cat

toolache *or* Grey's brush wallaby

tree kangaroo

tuan, phascogale, *or* wambenger

wallaby

wallaroo, uroo, *or* biggada

warabi

western grey kangaroo, black-faced kangaroo, sooty kangaroo, *or* mallee kangaroo

wintarro *or* golden bandicoot

wogoit *or* rock possum

wombat *or* (*Austral*) badger

woylie *or* brush-tailed bettong

yapok

yallara

yellow-footed rock wallaby *or* ring-tailed rock wallaby

pick up, grasp, get the hang of (*informal*), know inside out, know backwards **6 = overcome**, defeat, conquer, tame, triumph over, vanquish **OPPOSITE:** give in to

masterly = **skilful**, expert, crack
(*informal*), supreme, world-
class, consummate, first-rate,
masterful

mastermind VERB 1 = **plan**,
manage, direct, organize,
devise, conceive
▷ NOUN 2 = **organizer**, director,
manager, engineer, brain(s)
(*informal*), architect, planner

masterpiece = **classic**, tour
de force (*French*), pièce de
résistance (*French*), magnum
opus, jewel

mastery 1 = **understanding**,
skill, know-how, expertise,
prowess, finesse, proficiency,
virtuosity 2 = **control**,
command, domination,
superiority, supremacy, upper
hand, ascendancy, mana (*NZ*),
whip hand

match NOUN 1 = **game**, test,
competition, trial, tie, contest,
fixture, bout 2 = **marriage**,
pairing, alliance, partnership
3 = **equal**, rival, peer,
counterpart
▷ VERB 4 = **correspond with**, go
with, fit with, harmonize with
5 = **correspond**, agree, accord,
square, coincide, tally, conform,
match up 6 = **rival**, equal,
compete with, compare with,
emulate, measure up to

matching = **identical**,
like, twin, equivalent,
corresponding, coordinating
OPPOSITE: different

mate NOUN 1 (*informal*) = **friend**,
pal (*informal*), companion, buddy
(*informal*), comrade, chum
(*informal*), mucker (*Brit informal*),
crony, cobber (*Austral & NZ
old-fashioned informal*), E hoa (*NZ*)
2 = **partner**, lover, companion,
spouse, consort, helpmeet,
husband *or* wife 3 = **assistant**,
subordinate, apprentice, helper,
accomplice, sidekick (*informal*)
4 = **colleague**, associate,
companion
▷ VERB 5 = **pair**, couple, breed

material NOUN 1 = **substance**,
matter, stuff 2 = **cloth**, fabric,
textile 3 = **information**,
details, facts, notes, evidence,
particulars, data, info (*informal*)
▷ ADJECTIVE 4 = **physical**, solid,
substantial, concrete, bodily,
tangible, palpable, corporeal
5 = **relevant**, important,
significant, essential, vital,
serious, meaningful, applicable

materially = **significantly**,
much, greatly, essentially,
seriously, gravely, substantially
OPPOSITE: insignificantly

maternal = **motherly**,
protective, nurturing,
maternalistic

maternity = **motherhood**,
parenthood, motherliness

matted = **tangled**, knotted,
unkempt, knotty, tousled, ratty,
uncombed

matter NOUN 1 = **situation**,
concern, business, question,

m

event, subject, affair, incident

2 = substance, material, body, stuff

▷ **VERB 3 = be important**, make a difference, count, be relevant, make any difference, carry weight, cut any ice (*informal*), be of account

matter-of-fact
= **unsentimental**, plain, sober, down-to-earth, mundane, prosaic, deadpan, unimaginative

mature **VERB 1 = develop**, grow up, bloom, blossom, come of age, age

▷ **ADJECTIVE 2 = matured**, seasoned, ripe, mellow

3 = grown-up, adult, of age, fully fledged, full-grown **OPPOSITE:** immature

maturity 1 = adulthood, puberty, coming of age, pubescence, manhood *or* womanhood **OPPOSITE:** immaturity **2 = ripeness**

maul 1 = mangle, claw, lacerate, tear, mangulate (*Austral slang*)

2 = ill-treat, abuse, batter, molest, manhandle

maverick **NOUN 1 = rebel**, radical, dissenter, individualist, protester, eccentric, heretic, nonconformist **OPPOSITE:** traditionalist

▷ **ADJECTIVE 2 = rebel**, radical, dissenting, individualistic, eccentric, heretical, iconoclastic, nonconformist

maximum **ADJECTIVE**

1 = greatest, highest, supreme, paramount, utmost, most, topmost **OPPOSITE:** minimal

▷ **NOUN 2 = top**, peak, ceiling, utmost, upper limit **OPPOSITE:** minimum

maybe = **perhaps**, possibly, perchance (*archaic*)

mayhem = **chaos**, trouble, violence, disorder, destruction, confusion, havoc, fracas

maze = **web**, confusion, tangle, labyrinth, imbroglio, complex network

meadow = **field**, pasture, grassland, lea (*poetic*)

mean¹ 1 = signify, indicate, represent, express, stand for, convey, spell out, symbolize

2 = imply, suggest, intend, hint at, insinuate **3 = intend**, want, plan, expect, design, aim, wish, think

▎**USAGE NOTE**
In standard British English, *mean* should not be followed by *for* when expressing intention. *I didn't mean this to happen* is acceptable, but not *I didn't mean for this to happen*.

mean² 1 = miserly, stingy, parsimonious, niggardly, mercenary, penny-pinching, ungenerous, tight-fisted, snoep (*S African informal*) **OPPOSITE:** generous **2 = dishonourable**, petty, shameful, shabby, vile, callous, sordid, despicable, scungy (*Austral & NZ*) **OPPOSITE:** honourable

mean³ NOUN 1 = **average**, middle, balance, norm, midpoint
▷ ADJECTIVE 2 = **average**, middle, standard

meaning 1 = **significance**, message, substance, drift, connotation, gist 2 = **definition**, sense

meaningful = **significant**, important, material, useful, relevant, valid, worthwhile, purposeful **OPPOSITE:** trivial

meaningless = **nonsensical**, senseless, inconsequential, inane **OPPOSITE:** worthwhile

means 1 = **method**, way, process, medium, agency, instrument, mode 2 = **money**, funds, capital, income, resources, fortune, wealth, affluence
▷ PHRASES: by all means = **certainly**, surely, of course, definitely, doubtlessly ▸ by no means = **in no way**, definitely not, not in the least, on no account

meantime *or* **meanwhile** = **at the same time**, simultaneously, concurrently

meanwhile *or* **meantime** = **for now**, in the interim

measure VERB 1 = **quantify**, determine, assess, weigh, calculate, evaluate, compute, gauge

▷ NOUN 2 = **quantity**, share, amount, allowance, portion, quota, ration, allotment
3 = **action**, act, step, procedure, means, control, initiative, manoeuvre 4 = **gauge**, rule, scale, metre, ruler, yardstick
5 = **law**, act, bill, legislation, resolution, statute

measured 1 = **steady**, even, slow, regular, dignified, stately, solemn, leisurely
2 = **considered**, reasoned, studied, calculated, deliberate, sober, well-thought-out

measurement = **calculation**, assessment, evaluation, valuation, computation, calibration, mensuration

meat = **food**, flesh, kai (*NZ informal*)

mechanical 1 = **automatic**, automated, mechanized, power-driven, motor-driven **OPPOSITE:** manual
2 = **unthinking**, routine, automatic, instinctive, involuntary, impersonal, cursory, perfunctory **OPPOSITE:** conscious

mechanism 1 = **process**, way, means, system, operation, agency, method, technique
2 = **machine**, device, tool, instrument, appliance, apparatus, contrivance

mediate = **intervene**, step in (*informal*), intercede, referee, umpire, reconcile, arbitrate, conciliate

mediation = **arbitration**, intervention, reconciliation, conciliation, intercession

mediator = **negotiator**, arbitrator, referee, umpire, intermediary, middleman, arbiter, peacemaker

medicine = **remedy**, drug, cure, prescription, medication, nostrum, medicament

mediocre = **second-rate**, average, ordinary, indifferent, middling, pedestrian, inferior, so-so (*informal*), half-pie (*NZ informal*) **OPPOSITE:** excellent

meditation = **reflection**, thought, study, musing, pondering, contemplation, rumination, cogitation

medium ADJECTIVE
1 = **average**, mean, middle, middling, fair, intermediate, midway, mediocre **OPPOSITE:** extraordinary
▷ NOUN 2 = **spiritualist**, seer, clairvoyant, fortune teller, channeller 3 = **middle**, mean, centre, average, compromise, midpoint

meet 1 = **encounter**, come across, run into, happen on, find, contact, confront, bump into (*informal*) **OPPOSITE:** avoid
2 = **gather**, collect, assemble, get together, come together, muster, convene, congregate **OPPOSITE:** disperse 3 = **fulfil**,

match (up to), answer, satisfy, discharge, comply with, come up to, conform to **OPPOSITE:** fall short of 4 = **experience**, face, suffer, bear, go through, encounter, endure, undergo
5 = **converge**, join, cross, touch, connect, come together, link up, intersect **OPPOSITE:** diverge

meeting 1 = **conference**, gathering, assembly, congress, session, convention, get-together (*informal*), reunion, hui (*NZ*) 2 = **encounter**, introduction, confrontation, engagement, rendezvous, tryst, assignation

melancholy ADJECTIVE 1 = **sad**, depressed, miserable, gloomy, glum, mournful, despondent, dispirited **OPPOSITE:** happy
▷ NOUN 2 = **sadness**, depression, misery, gloom, sorrow, unhappiness, despondency, dejection **OPPOSITE:** happiness

mellow ADJECTIVE 1 = **full-flavoured**, rich, sweet, delicate 2 = **ripe**, mature, ripened **OPPOSITE:** unripe
▷ VERB 3 = **relax**, improve, settle, calm, mature, soften, sweeten 4 = **season**, develop, improve, ripen

melody 1 = **tune**, song, theme, air, music, strain 2 = **tunefulness**, harmony, musicality, euphony, melodiousness

melt 1 = **dissolve**, run, soften, fuse, thaw, defrost, liquefy, unfreeze 2 *often with* **away** = **disappear**, fade, vanish, dissolve, disperse, evaporate, evanesce 3 = **soften**, relax, disarm, mollify

member = **representative**, associate, supporter, fellow, subscriber, comrade, disciple

membership 1 = **participation**, belonging, fellowship, enrolment 2 = **members**, body, associates, fellows

memoir = **account**, life, record, journal, essay, biography, narrative, monograph

memoirs = **autobiography**, diary, life story, experiences, memories, journals, recollections, reminiscences

memorable = **noteworthy**, celebrated, historic, striking, famous, significant, remarkable, notable **OPPOSITE:** forgettable

memorandum = **note**, minute, message, communication, reminder, memo, jotting, e-mail

memorial NOUN
1 = **monument**, shrine, plaque, cenotaph
▷ ADJECTIVE
2 = **commemorative**, remembrance, monumental

memory 1 = **recall**, mind, retention, ability to remember, powers of recall, powers of retention 2 = **recollection**, reminder, reminiscence, impression, echo, remembrance 3 = **commemoration**, respect, honour, recognition, tribute, remembrance, observance

menace NOUN 1 (*informal*) = **nuisance**, plague, pest, annoyance, troublemaker 2 = **threat**, warning, intimidation, ill-omen, ominousness
▷ VERB 3 = **bully**, threaten, intimidate, terrorize, frighten, scare

menacing = **threatening**, frightening, forbidding, looming, intimidating, ominous, louring *or* lowering **OPPOSITE:** encouraging

mend 1 = **repair**, fix, restore, renew, patch up, renovate, refit, retouch 2 = **darn**, repair, patch, stitch, sew 3 = **heal**, improve, recover, get better, be all right, be cured, recuperate, pull through 4 = **improve**, reform, correct, revise, amend, rectify, ameliorate, emend
▷ PHRASES: on the mend = **convalescent**, improving, recovering, getting better, recuperating

mental 1 = **intellectual**, rational, theoretical, cognitive, brain, conceptual, cerebral 2 (*slang*) = **insane**, mad, disturbed, unstable, demented, psychotic, unbalanced, deranged

mentality = **attitude**, character, personality, psychology, make-up, outlook, disposition, cast of mind

mentally = **psychologically**, intellectually, inwardly

mention VERB 1 = **refer to**, point out, bring up, state, reveal, declare, disclose, intimate ▷ NOUN 2 *often with* **of** = **reference**, observation, indication, remark, allusion 3 = **acknowledgment**, recognition, tribute, citation, honourable mention

mentor = **guide**, teacher, coach, adviser, tutor, instructor, counsellor, guru

menu = **bill of fare**, tariff (*chiefly Brit*), set menu, table d'hôte, carte du jour (*French*)

merchandise = **goods**, produce, stock, products, commodities, wares

merchant = **tradesman**, dealer, trader, broker, retailer, supplier, seller, salesman

mercy 1 = **compassion**, pity, forgiveness, grace, kindness, clemency, leniency, forbearance **OPPOSITE:** cruelty 2 = **blessing**, boon, godsend

mere 1 = **simple**, nothing more than, common, plain, pure 2 = **bare**, slender, trifling, meagre, just, only, basic, no more than

merge 1 = **combine**, blend, fuse, amalgamate, unite, join, mix, mingle **OPPOSITE:** separate 2 = **join**, unite, combine, fuse **OPPOSITE:** separate 3 = **melt**, blend, mingle

merger = **union**, fusion, consolidation, amalgamation, combination, coalition, incorporation

merit NOUN 1 = **advantage**, value, quality, worth, strength, asset, virtue, strong point ▷ VERB 2 = **deserve**, warrant, be entitled to, earn, have a right to, be worthy of

merry 1 = **cheerful**, happy, carefree, jolly, festive, joyous, convivial, blithe **OPPOSITE:** gloomy 2 (*Brit informal*) = **tipsy**, happy, mellow, tiddly (*slang, chiefly Brit*), squiffy (*Brit informal*)

mesh NOUN 1 = **net**, netting, network, web, tracery ▷ VERB 2 = **engage**, combine, connect, knit, coordinate, interlock, dovetail, harmonize

mess 1 = **untidiness**, disorder, confusion, chaos, litter, clutter, disarray, jumble 2 = **shambles** 3 = **difficulty**, dilemma, plight, hole (*informal*), fix (*informal*), jam (*informal*), muddle, pickle (*informal*), uphill (*S African*) ▷ PHRASES: **mess about** *or* **around** = **potter about**, dabble, amuse yourself, fool about *or* around, muck about *or* around (*informal*), play about *or* around ▶ **mess something up** 1 = **botch**, muck something up

m

(Brit slang), muddle something up 2 = **dirty**, pollute, clutter, disarrange, dishevel ▶ **mess with something** or **someone** = **interfere with**, play with, fiddle with (informal), tamper with, tinker with, meddle with

message NOUN

1 = **communication**, note, bulletin, word, letter, dispatch, memorandum, communiqué, email or e-mail, text or text message, SMS, IMS, tweet (on the Twitter website), mention or @mention (on the Twitter website) 2 = **point**, meaning, idea, moral, theme, import, purport ▷ VERB 3 (S.M.S., computing) = **text**, send, communicate, email or e-mail, SMS, IM or instant message, DM or direct message, poke (on the Facebook website), tweet (on the Twitter website), chat (computing)

messenger = **courier**, runner, carrier, herald, envoy, go-between, emissary, delivery boy

messy 1 = **disorganized**, sloppy (informal), untidy 2 = **dirty** 3 = **untidy**, disordered, chaotic, muddled, cluttered, shambolic, disorganized, daggy (Austral & NZ informal) OPPOSITE: tidy 4 = **dishevelled**, ruffled, untidy, rumpled, bedraggled, tousled, uncombed, daggy (Austral & NZ informal) 5 = **confusing**, difficult, complex, confused, tangled, chaotic, tortuous

metaphor = **figure of speech**, image, symbol, analogy, conceit (literary), allegory, trope, figurative expression

method 1 = **manner**, process, approach, technique, way, system, style, procedure 2 = **orderliness**, planning, order, system, purpose, pattern, organization, regularity

midday = **noon**, twelve o'clock, noonday

middle NOUN 1 = **centre**, heart, midst, halfway point, midpoint, midsection ▷ ADJECTIVE 2 = **central**, medium, mid, intervening, halfway, intermediate, median 3 = **intermediate**, intervening

middle-class = **bourgeois**, traditional, conventional

middling 1 = **mediocre**, all right, indifferent, so-so (informal), unremarkable, tolerable, run-of-the-mill, passable, half-pie (NZ informal) 2 = **moderate**, medium, average, fair, ordinary, modest, adequate

midnight = **twelve o'clock**, middle of the night, dead of night, the witching hour

midst ▷ PHRASES: **in the midst of** 1 = **during**, in the middle of, amidst 2 = **among**, in the middle of, surrounded by, amidst, in the thick of

midway = **halfway**, in the middle of, part-way, equidistant, at the midpoint, betwixt and between

might = **power**, force, energy, strength, vigour

mighty = **powerful**, strong, strapping, robust, vigorous, sturdy, forceful, lusty **OPPOSITE:** weak

migrant NOUN 1 = **wanderer**, immigrant, traveller, rover, nomad, emigrant, itinerant, drifter·
▷ ADJECTIVE 2 = **itinerant**, wandering, drifting, roving, travelling, shifting, immigrant, transient

migrate = **move**, travel, journey, wander, trek, voyage, roam, emigrate

migration = **wandering**, journey, voyage, travel, movement, trek, emigration, roving

mild 1 = **gentle**, calm, easy-going, meek, placid, docile, peaceable, equable, chilled (*informal*) **OPPOSITE:** harsh
2 = **temperate**, warm, calm, moderate, tranquil, balmy **OPPOSITE:** cold 3 = **bland**, thin, smooth, tasteless, insipid, flavourless

militant = **aggressive**, active, vigorous, assertive, combative **OPPOSITE:** peaceful

military = **warlike**, armed, soldierly, martial
▷ PHRASES: **the military** = **the armed forces**, the forces, the services, the army

milk = **exploit**, pump, take advantage of

mill NOUN 1 = **grinder**, crusher, quern 2 = **factory**, works, plant, workshop, foundry
▷ VERB 3 = **grind**, pound, crush, powder, grate
▷ PHRASES: **mill about** or **around** = **swarm**, crowd, stream, surge, throng

mimic VERB 1 = **imitate**, do (*informal*), take off (*informal*), ape, parody, caricature, impersonate
▷ NOUN 2 = **imitator**, impressionist, copycat (*informal*), impersonator, caricaturist

mince 1 = **cut**, grind, crumble, dice, hash, chop up 2 = **tone down**, spare, moderate, weaken, soften

mincing = **affected**, camp (*informal*), precious, pretentious, dainty, sissy, effeminate, foppish

mind NOUN 1 = **memory**, recollection, remembrance, powers of recollection
2 = **intelligence**, reason, reasoning, understanding, sense, brain(s) (*informal*), wits, intellect 3 = **intention**, wish, desire, urge, fancy, leaning, notion, inclination 4 = **sanity**, reason, senses, judgment, wits, marbles (*informal*), rationality, mental balance
▷ VERB 5 = **take offence at**, dislike, care about, object to,

resent, disapprove of, be bothered by, be affronted by
6 = be careful, watch, take care, be wary, be cautious, be on your guard **7 = look after**, watch, protect, tend, guard, take care of, attend to, keep an eye on
8 = pay attention to, mark, note, listen to, observe, obey, heed, take heed of

mine NOUN **1 = pit**, deposit, shaft, colliery, excavation
2 = source, store, fund, stock, supply, reserve, treasury, wealth
▷ VERB **3 = dig up**, extract, quarry, unearth, excavate, hew, dig for

miner = **coalminer**, pitman (*Brit*), collier (*Brit*)

mingle 1 = mix, combine, blend, merge, unite, join, interweave, intermingle **OPPOSITE**: separate **2 = associate**, consort, socialize, rub shoulders (*informal*), hobnob, fraternize, hang about *or* around **OPPOSITE**: dissociate

miniature = **small**, little, minute, tiny, toy, scaled-down, diminutive, minuscule **OPPOSITE**: giant

minimal = **minimum**, smallest, least, slightest, token, nominal, negligible, least possible

minimize 1 = reduce, decrease, shrink, diminish, prune, curtail, miniaturize **OPPOSITE**: increase
2 = play down, discount, belittle, disparage, decry, underrate, deprecate, make light *or* little of **OPPOSITE**: praise

minimum ADJECTIVE
1 = lowest, smallest, least, slightest, minimal, least possible **OPPOSITE**: maximum
▷ NOUN **2 = lowest**, least, lowest level, nadir

minister = **clergyman**, priest, vicar, parson, preacher, pastor, cleric, rector
▷ PHRASES: **minister to**
= **attend to**, serve, tend to, take care of, cater to, pander to, administer to

ministry 1 = department, office, bureau, government department
2 = administration, council
3 = the priesthood, the church, the cloth, holy orders

minor = **small**, lesser, slight, petty, trivial, insignificant, unimportant, inconsequential **OPPOSITE**: major

mint = **make**, produce, strike, cast, stamp, punch, coin

minute¹ = **moment**, second, bit, flash, instant, tick (*Brit informal*), sec (*informal*), short time

minute² 1 = small, little, tiny, miniature, microscopic, diminutive, minuscule, infinitesimal **OPPOSITE**: huge
2 = precise, close, detailed, critical, exact, meticulous, exhaustive, painstaking **OPPOSITE**: imprecise

m

minutes = **record**, notes, proceedings, transactions, transcript, memorandum

miracle = **wonder**, phenomenon, sensation, marvel, amazing achievement, astonishing feat

miraculous = **wonderful**, amazing, extraordinary, incredible, astonishing, unbelievable, phenomenal, astounding **OPPOSITE:** ordinary

mirror NOUN 1 = **looking-glass**, glass (*Brit*), reflector
▷ VERB 2 = **reflect**, follow, copy, echo, emulate

miscarriage = **failure**, error, breakdown, mishap, perversion

misconduct = **immorality**, wrongdoing, mismanagement, malpractice, impropriety

miserable 1 NOUN = **sad**, depressed, gloomy, forlorn, dejected, despondent, sorrowful, wretched **OPPOSITE:** happy 2 = **pathetic**, sorry, shameful, despicable, deplorable, lamentable **OPPOSITE:** respectable

misery 1 = **unhappiness**, distress, despair, grief, suffering, depression, gloom, torment **OPPOSITE:** happiness 2 (*Brit informal*) = **moaner**, pessimist, killjoy, spoilsport, prophet of doom, wet blanket (*informal*), sourpuss (*informal*), wowser (*Austral & NZ slang*)

misfortune 1 *often plural* = **bad luck**, adversity, hard luck, ill luck, infelicity, bad trot (*Austral slang*) 2 = **mishap**, trouble, disaster, reverse, tragedy, setback, calamity, affliction **OPPOSITE:** good luck

misguided = **unwise**, mistaken, misplaced, deluded, ill-advised, imprudent, injudicious

mislead = **deceive**, fool, delude, take someone in (*informal*), misdirect, misinform, hoodwink, misguide

misleading = **confusing**, false, ambiguous, deceptive, evasive, disingenuous **OPPOSITE:** straightforward

misogynist ADJECTIVE 1 = **chauvinist**, sexist, patriarchal
▷ NOUN 2 = **woman-hater**, male chauvinist, anti-feminist, MCP (*informal*), male chauvinist pig (*informal*), male supremacist

miss VERB 1 = **fail to notice**, overlook, pass over 2 = **long for**, yearn for, pine for, long to see, ache for, feel the loss of, regret the absence of 3 = **not go to**, skip, cut, omit, be absent from, fail to attend, skive off (*informal*), play truant from, bludge (*Austral & NZ informal*) 4 = **avoid**, beat, escape, skirt, duck, cheat, bypass, dodge
▷ NOUN 5 = **mistake**, failure, error, blunder, omission, oversight

missile = **projectile**, weapon, shell, rocket

missing = **lost**, misplaced, not present, astray, unaccounted for, mislaid

mission = **task**, job, commission, duty, undertaking, quest, assignment, vocation

missionary = **evangelist**, preacher, apostle

mist = **fog**, cloud, steam, spray, film, haze, vapour, smog

mistake NOUN 1 = **error**, blunder, oversight, slip, gaffe (*informal*), miscalculation, faux pas, barry *or* Barry Crocker (*Austral slang*) 2 = **oversight**, error, slip, fault, howler (*informal*), erratum, barry *or* Barry Crocker (*Austral slang*)

▷ VERB 3 = **misunderstand**, misinterpret, misjudge, misread, misconstrue, misapprehend

▷ PHRASES: mistake something *or* someone for something *or* someone = **confuse with**, take for, mix up with

mistaken 1 = **wrong**, incorrect, misguided, wide of the mark OPPOSITE: correct 2 = **inaccurate**, false, faulty, erroneous, unsound OPPOSITE: accurate

mistress = **lover**, girlfriend, concubine, kept woman, paramour

misunderstand
1 = **misinterpret**, misread,

mistake, misjudge, misconstrue, misapprehend, be at cross-purposes with 2 = **miss the point**, get the wrong end of the stick

misunderstanding = **mistake**, error, mix-up, misconception, misinterpretation, misjudgment

misuse NOUN 1 = **waste**, squandering 2 = **abuse** 3 = **misapplication**, abuse, illegal use, wrong use 4 = **perversion**, desecration 5 = **misapplication**

▷ VERB 6 = **abuse**, misapply, prostitute 7 = **waste**, squander, embezzle, misappropriate

mix VERB 1 = **combine**, blend, merge, join, cross, fuse, mingle, jumble 2 = **socialize**, associate, hang out (*informal*), mingle, circulate, consort, hobnob, fraternize 3 *often with* **up** = **combine**, marry, blend, integrate, amalgamate, coalesce, meld

▷ NOUN 4 = **mixture**, combination, blend, fusion, compound, assortment, alloy, medley

▷ PHRASES: mix something up 1 = **confuse**, scramble, muddle, confound 2 = **blend**, beat, mix, stir, fold

mixed 1 = **varied**, diverse, different, differing, cosmopolitan, assorted, jumbled, disparate OPPOSITE:

m

homogeneous 2 = **combined**, blended, united, compound, composite, mingled, amalgamated **OPPOSITE:** pure

mixed-up = **confused**, disturbed, puzzled, bewildered, at sea, upset, distraught, muddled

mixture 1 = **blend**, mix, variety, fusion, assortment, brew, jumble, medley
2 = **composite**, compound
3 = **cross**, combination, blend
4 = **concoction**, compound, blend, brew, amalgam

mix-up = **confusion**, mistake, misunderstanding, mess, tangle, muddle

moan VERB 1 = **groan**, sigh, sob, whine, lament 2 (*informal*) = **grumble**, complain, groan, whine, carp, grouse, whinge (*informal*), bleat
▷ NOUN 3 = **groan**, sigh, sob, lament, wail, grunt, whine
4 (*informal*) = **complaint**, protest, grumble, whine, grouse, gripe (*informal*), grouch (*informal*)

mob NOUN 1 = **crowd**, pack, mass, host, drove, flock, swarm, horde 2 = **gang**, group, set, lot, crew (*informal*)
▷ VERB 3 = **surround**, besiege, jostle, fall on, set upon, crowd around, swarm around

mobile = **movable**, moving, travelling, wandering, portable, itinerant, peripatetic

mobilize 1 = **rally**, organize, stimulate, excite, prompt, marshal, activate, awaken
2 = **deploy**, prepare, ready, rally, assemble, call up, marshal, muster

mock VERB 1 = **laugh at**, tease, ridicule, taunt, scorn, sneer, scoff, deride **OPPOSITE:** respect
▷ ADJECTIVE 2 = **imitation**, pretended, artificial, fake, false, dummy, sham, feigned **OPPOSITE:** genuine

mocking = **scornful**, scoffing, satirical, contemptuous, sarcastic, sardonic, disrespectful, disdainful

mode 1 = **method**, way, system, form, process, style, technique, manner 2 = **fashion**, style, trend, rage, vogue, look, craze

model NOUN
1 = **representation**, image, copy, miniature, dummy, replica, imitation, duplicate
2 = **pattern**, example, standard, original, ideal, prototype, paradigm, archetype 3 = **sitter**, subject, poser
▷ VERB 4 = **show off** (*informal*), wear, display, sport 5 = **shape**, form, design, fashion, carve, mould, sculpt

moderate ADJECTIVE 1 = **mild**, reasonable, controlled, limited, steady, modest, restrained, middle-of-the-road **OPPOSITE:** extreme 2 = **average**, middling, fair, ordinary, indifferent,

mediocre, so-so (*informal*), passable, half-pie (*NZ informal*)
▷ **VERB 3** = **soften**, control, temper, regulate, curb, restrain, subdue, lessen **4** = **lessen**, ease
OPPOSITE: intensify

modern 1 = **current**, contemporary, recent, present-day, latter-day **2** = **up-to-date**, fresh, new, novel, newfangled
OPPOSITE: old-fashioned

modest 1 = **moderate**, small, limited, fair, ordinary, middling, meagre, frugal **2** = **unpretentious**, reserved, retiring, shy, coy, reticent, self-effacing, demure

modesty = **reserve**, humility, shyness, reticence, timidity, diffidence, coyness, bashfulness
OPPOSITE: conceit

modification = **change**, variation, qualification, adjustment, revision, alteration, refinement

modify 1 = **change**, reform, convert, alter, adjust, adapt, revise, remodel **2** = **tone down**, lower, qualify, ease, moderate, temper, soften, restrain

mogul = **tycoon**, baron, magnate, big shot (*informal*), big noise (*informal*), big hitter (*informal*), heavy hitter (*informal*), V.I.P.

moist = **damp**, wet, soggy, humid, clammy, dewy

moisture = **damp**, water, liquid, dew, wetness

molecule = **particle**, jot, speck

mom (*US & Canad*) = **mum**, mother, ma

moment 1 = **instant**, second, flash, twinkling, split second, jiffy (*informal*), trice **2** = **time**, point, stage, juncture

momentous = **significant**, important, vital, critical, crucial, historic, pivotal, fateful
OPPOSITE: unimportant

momentum = **impetus**, force, power, drive, push, energy, strength, thrust

monarch = **ruler**, king *or* queen, sovereign, tsar, potentate, emperor *or* empress, prince *or* princess

monarchy 1 = **sovereignty**, autocracy, kingship, royalism, monocracy **2** = **kingdom**, empire, realm, principality

monastery = **abbey**, convent, priory, cloister, nunnery, friary

monetary = **financial**, money, economic, capital, cash, fiscal, budgetary, pecuniary

money = **cash**, capital, currency, hard cash, readies (*informal*), riches, silver, coin, kembla (*Austral slang*)

monitor VERB 1 = **check**, follow, watch, survey, observe, keep an eye on, keep track of, keep tabs on
▷ **NOUN 2** = **guide**, observer, supervisor, invigilator
3 = **prefect** (*Brit*), head girl, head boy, senior boy, senior girl

m

monk = friar, brother
> **RELATED WORD**
> *adjective:* monastic

monkey 1 = simian, ape, primate 2 = rascal, horror, devil, rogue, imp, tyke, scallywag, scamp, nointer (*Austral slang*)
> **RELATED WORD**
> *adjective:* simian

• See panel **MONKEYS, APES AND OTHER PRIMATES**

monster 1 = giant, mammoth, titan, colossus, monstrosity 2 = brute, devil, beast, demon, villain, fiend

monstrous 1 = outrageous, shocking, foul, intolerable, disgraceful, scandalous, inhuman, diabolical **OPPOSITE:** decent 2 = huge, massive, enormous, tremendous, immense, mammoth, colossal, prodigious **OPPOSITE:** tiny

MONKEYS, APES AND OTHER PRIMATES

aye-aye	loris
baboon	macaco
Barbary ape	macaque
bonnet monkey	mandrill
bushbaby *or* galago	mangabey
capuchin	marmoset
chacma	mona
chimpanzee *or* chimp	monkey *or* (*archaic*) jackanapes
colobus	orang-outang, orang-utan,
douc	*or* orang
douroucouli	proboscis monkey
drill	rhesus monkey
flying lemur *or* colugo	saki
gelada	siamang
gibbon	sifaka
gorilla	spider monkey
green monkey	squirrel monkey
grivet	talapoin
guenon	tamarin
guereza	tana
howler monkey	tarsier
indris *or* indri	titi
langur	vervet
lemur	wanderoo

3 = **unnatural**, horrible, hideous, grotesque, gruesome, frightful, freakish, fiendish **OPPOSITE:** normal

monument = **memorial**, cairn, marker, shrine, tombstone, mausoleum, commemoration, headstone

monumental 1 = **important**, significant, enormous, historic, memorable, awesome, majestic, unforgettable **OPPOSITE:** unimportant 2 (*informal*) = **immense**, great, massive, staggering, colossal **OPPOSITE:** tiny

mood = **state of mind**, spirit, humour, temper, disposition, frame of mind

moody 1 = **changeable**, volatile, unpredictable, erratic, fickle, temperamental, impulsive, mercurial **OPPOSITE:** stable 2 = **sulky**, irritable, temperamental, touchy, ill-tempered, tooshie (*Austral slang*) **OPPOSITE:** cheerful 3 = **gloomy**, sad, sullen, glum, morose **OPPOSITE:** cheerful 4 = **sad**, gloomy, melancholy, sombre

moon NOUN 1 = **satellite** ▷ VERB 2 = **idle**, drift, loaf, languish, waste time, daydream, mope

 RELATED WORD
 adjective: lunar

moor¹ = **moorland**, fell (*Brit*), heath

moor² = **tie up**, secure, anchor, dock, lash, berth, make fast

mop NOUN 1 = **squeegee**, sponge, swab 2 = **mane**, shock, mass, tangle, mat, thatch ▷ VERB 3 = **clean**, wash, wipe, sponge, swab (*Military*)

moral ADJECTIVE 1 = **good**, just, right, principled, decent, noble, ethical, honourable **OPPOSITE:** immoral ▷ NOUN 2 = **lesson**, meaning, point, message, teaching, import, significance, precept ▷ PLURAL NOUN 3 = **morality**, standards, conduct, principles, behaviour, manners, habits, ethics

morale = **confidence**, heart, spirit, self-esteem, team spirit, esprit de corps

morality 1 = **virtue**, justice, morals, honour, integrity, goodness, honesty, decency 2 = **ethics**, conduct, principles, morals, manners, philosophy, mores 3 = **rights and wrongs**, ethics

moratorium = **postponement**, freeze, halt, suspension, standstill

more DETERMINER 1 = **extra**, additional, new, other, added, further, new-found, supplementary ▷ ADVERB 2 = **to a greater extent**, longer, better, further, some more 3 = **moreover**, also, in addition, besides,

m

furthermore, what's more, on top of that, to boot

moreover = **furthermore**, also, further, in addition, too, as well, besides, additionally

morning 1 = **before noon**, forenoon, morn (*poetic*), a.m. 2 = **dawn**, sunrise, first light, daybreak, break of day

mortal ADJECTIVE 1 = **human**, worldly, passing, fleshly, temporal, transient, ephemeral, perishable 2 = **fatal**, killing, terminal, deadly, destructive, lethal, murderous, death-dealing
▷ NOUN 3 = **human being**, being, man, woman, person, human, individual, earthling

mortality 1 = **humanity**, transience, impermanence, corporeality, impermanency 2 = **death**, dying, fatality

mostly 1 = **mainly**, largely, chiefly, principally, primarily, on the whole, predominantly 2 = **generally**, usually, on the whole, as a rule

moth

> **RELATED WORDS**
> *young*: caterpillar
> *enthusiast*: lepidopterist
> • See panel **BUTTERFLIES AND MOTHS**

mother NOUN 1 = **female parent**, mum (*Brit informal*), ma (*informal*), mater, dam, mummy (*Brit informal*), foster mother, biological mother
▷ VERB 2 = **nurture**, raise, protect, tend, nurse, rear, care for, cherish
▷ MODIFIER 3 = **native**, natural, innate, inborn

> **RELATED WORD**
> *adjective*: maternal

motherly = **maternal**, loving, caring, comforting, sheltering, protective, affectionate

motif 1 = **design**, shape, decoration, ornament 2 = **theme**, idea, subject, concept, leitmotif

motion NOUN 1 = **movement**, mobility, travel, progress, flow, locomotion 2 = **proposal**, suggestion, recommendation, proposition, submission
▷ VERB 3 = **gesture**, direct, wave, signal, nod, beckon, gesticulate

motivate 1 = **inspire**, drive, stimulate, move, cause, prompt, stir, induce 2 = **stimulate**, drive, inspire, stir, arouse, galvanize, incentivize

motivation = **incentive**, inspiration, motive, stimulus, reason, spur, inducement, incitement

motive = **reason**, ground(s), purpose, object, incentive, inspiration, stimulus, rationale

motto = **saying**, slogan, maxim, rule, adage, proverb, dictum, precept

mould¹ NOUN 1 = **cast**, shape, pattern 2 = **design**, style,

fashion, build, form, kind, shape, pattern **3 = nature**, character, sort, kind, quality, type, stamp, calibre
▷ VERB **4 = shape**, make, work, form, create, model, fashion, construct **5 = influence**, make, form, control, direct, affect, shape

mould² = **fungus**, blight, mildew

mound 1 = heap, pile, drift, stack, rick **2 = hill**, bank, rise, dune, embankment, knoll, hillock, kopje *or* koppie (*S African*)

mount VERB **1 = increase**, build, grow, swell, intensify, escalate, multiply OPPOSITE: decrease **2 = accumulate**, increase, collect, gather, build up, pile up, amass **3 = ascend**, scale, climb (up), go up, clamber up OPPOSITE: descend **4 = get (up) on**, jump on, straddle, climb onto, hop on to, bestride, get on the back of OPPOSITE: get off **5 = display**, present, prepare, put on, organize, put on display
▷ NOUN **6 = horse**, steed (*literary*) **7 = backing**, setting, support, stand, base, frame

mountain 1 = peak, mount, horn, ridge, fell (*Brit*), berg (*S African*), alp, pinnacle **2 = heap**, mass, masses, pile, a great deal, ton, stack, abundance

mourn 1 *often with* **for = grieve for**, lament, weep for, wail for **2 = bemoan**, rue, deplore, bewail

mourning 1 = grieving, grief, bereavement, weeping, woe, lamentation **2 = black**, sackcloth and ashes, widow's weeds

mouth 1 = lips, jaws, gob (*slang, esp. Brit*), maw, cakehole (*Brit slang*) **2 = entrance**, opening, gateway, door, aperture, orifice **3 = opening 4 = inlet**, outlet, estuary, firth, outfall, debouchment

move VERB **1 = transfer**, change, switch, shift, transpose **2 = go**, advance, progress, shift, proceed, stir, budge, make a move **3 = relocate**, leave, remove, quit, migrate, emigrate, decamp, up sticks (*Brit informal*) **4 = drive**, cause, influence, persuade, shift, inspire, prompt, induce OPPOSITE: discourage **5 = touch**, affect, excite, impress, stir, disquiet **6 = propose**, suggest, urge, recommend, request, advocate, submit, put forward
▷ NOUN **7 = action**, step, manoeuvre **8 = ploy**, action, measure, step, initiative, stroke, tactic, manoeuvre **9 = transfer**, posting, shift, removal, relocation **10 = turn**, go, play, chance, shot (*informal*), opportunity

movement 1 = group, party, organization, grouping, front, faction **2 = campaign**, drive, push, crusade **3 = move**,

action, motion, manoeuvre
4 = **activity**, moving,
stirring, bustle **5** = **advance**,
progress, flow **6** = **transfer**,
transportation, displacement
7 = **development**, change,
variation, fluctuation
8 = **progression**, progress
9 (*Music*) = **section**, part,
division, passage
movie = **film**, picture, feature,
flick (*slang*), MP4, MPEG
moving 1 = **emotional**,
touching, affecting, inspiring,
stirring, poignant **OPPOSITE:**
unemotional **2** = **mobile**,
running, active, going,
operational, in motion, driving,
kinetic **OPPOSITE:** stationary
mow = **cut**, crop, trim, shear,
scythe
▷ **PHRASES:** mow something
or someone down = **massacre**,
butcher, slaughter, cut down,
shoot down, cut to pieces
much ADVERB 1 = **greatly**, a
lot, considerably, decidedly,
exceedingly, appreciably
OPPOSITE: hardly **2** = **often**, a
lot, routinely, a great deal, many
times, habitually, on many
occasions, customarily
▷ **ADJECTIVE 3** = **great**, a lot
of, plenty of, considerable,
substantial, piles of (*informal*),
ample, abundant, shedful (*slang*)
OPPOSITE: little
▷ **PRONOUN 4** = **a lot**, plenty,
a great deal, lots (*informal*),

masses (*informal*), loads
(*informal*), tons (*informal*), heaps
(*informal*) **OPPOSITE:** little
muck 1 = **dirt**, mud, filth, ooze,
sludge, mire, slime, gunge
(*informal*), kak (*S African informal*)
2 = **manure**, dung, ordure
mud = **dirt**, clay, ooze, silt,
sludge, mire, slime
muddle NOUN 1 = **confusion**,
mess, disorder, chaos, tangle,
mix-up, disarray, predicament
▷ **VERB 2** = **jumble**, disorder,
scramble, tangle, mix up
3 = **confuse**, bewilder, daze,
confound, perplex, disorient,
stupefy, befuddle
muddy 1 = **boggy**, swampy,
marshy, quaggy **2** = **dirty**,
soiled, grimy, mucky, mud-
caked, bespattered
mug¹ = **cup**, pot, beaker, tankard
mug² NOUN 1 (*slang*) = **face**,
features, countenance, visage
2 (*Brit slang*) = **fool**, sucker
(*slang*), chump (*informal*),
simpleton, easy *or* soft touch
(*slang*), dorba *or* dorb (*Austral
slang*), bogan (*Austral slang*)
▷ **VERB 3** (*informal*) = **attack**,
assault, beat up, rob, set about
or upon
▷ **PHRASES:** mug up (on)
something = **study**, cram
(*informal*), bone up on (*informal*),
swot up on (*Brit informal*)
multiple = **many**, several,
various, numerous, sundry,
manifold, multitudinous

multiply 1 = **increase**, extend, expand, spread, build up, proliferate **OPPOSITE:** decrease 2 = **reproduce**, breed, propagate

multitude 1 = **great number**, host, army, mass, horde, myriad 2 = **crowd**, host, mass, mob, swarm, horde, throng

mundane 1 = **ordinary**, routine, commonplace, banal, everyday, day-to-day, prosaic, humdrum **OPPOSITE:** extraordinary 2 = **earthly**, worldly, secular, mortal, terrestrial, temporal **OPPOSITE:** spiritual

municipal = **civic**, public, local, council, district, urban, metropolitan

murder NOUN 1 = **killing**, homicide, massacre, assassination, slaying, bloodshed, carnage, butchery ▷ VERB 2 = **kill**, massacre, slaughter, assassinate, eliminate (*slang*), butcher, slay, bump off (*slang*)

murderer = **killer**, assassin, slayer, butcher, slaughterer, cut-throat, hit man (*slang*)

murderous = **deadly**, savage, brutal, cruel, lethal, ferocious, cut-throat, bloodthirsty

murky 1 = **dark**, gloomy, grey, dull, dim, cloudy, misty, overcast **OPPOSITE:** bright 2 = **dark**, cloudy

murmur VERB 1 = **mumble**, whisper, mutter ▷ NOUN 2 = **whisper**, drone, purr

muscle 1 = **tendon**, sinew 2 = **strength**, might, power, weight, stamina, brawn ▷ PHRASES: **muscle in** (*informal*) = **impose yourself**, encroach, butt in, force your way in

muscular = **strong**, powerful, athletic, strapping, robust, vigorous, sturdy, sinewy

muse = **ponder**, consider, reflect, contemplate, deliberate, brood, meditate, mull over

musical = **melodious**, lyrical, harmonious, melodic, tuneful, dulcet, sweet-sounding, euphonious **OPPOSITE:** discordant

muskeg (*Canad*) = **swamp**, bog, marsh, quagmire, slough, fen, mire, morass, pakihi (*NZ*)

muss (*US & Canad*) = **mess (up)**, disarrange, dishevel, ruffle, rumple, make untidy, tumble

must = **necessity**, essential, requirement, fundamental, imperative, requisite, prerequisite, sine qua non (*Latin*)

muster VERB 1 = **summon up**, marshal 2 = **rally**, gather, assemble, marshal, mobilize, call together 3 = **assemble**, convene ▷ NOUN 4 = **assembly**, meeting, collection, gathering, rally, convention, congregation, roundup, hui (*NZ*), runanga (*NZ*)

mutation 1 = **anomaly**, variation, deviant, freak of nature 2 = **change**, variation,

evolution, transformation,
modification, alteration,
metamorphosis, transfiguration

mute 1 = **close-mouthed**, silent
2 = **silent**, dumb, unspoken,
tacit, wordless, voiceless,
unvoiced 3 = **dumb**, speechless,
voiceless

mutter = **grumble**, complain,
murmur, rumble, whine,
mumble, grouse, bleat

mutual = **shared**, common,
joint, returned, reciprocal,
interchangeable, requited

> **USAGE NOTE**
> *Mutual* is sometimes used,
> as in *a mutual friend*, to mean
> 'common to or shared by two
> or more people'. This use has
> sometimes been frowned on
> in the past because it does
> not reflect the two-way
> relationship contained in
> the origins of the word,
> which comes from Latin
> *mutuus* meaning 'reciprocal'.
> However, this usage is very
> common and is now generally
> regarded as acceptable.

myriad NOUN 1 = **multitude**,
host, army, swarm, horde
▷ ADJECTIVE 2 = **innumerable**,
countless, untold, incalculable,
immeasurable, multitudinous

mysterious 1 = **strange**,
puzzling, secret, weird,
perplexing, uncanny, mystifying,
arcane **OPPOSITE:** clear
2 = **secretive**, enigmatic,

evasive, discreet, covert,
reticent, furtive, inscrutable

mystery = **puzzle**, problem,
question, secret, riddle, enigma,
conundrum, teaser

mystical *or* **mystic**
= **supernatural**, mysterious,
transcendental, occult,
metaphysical, paranormal,
inscrutable, otherworldly

myth 1 = **legend**, story, fiction,
saga, fable, allegory, fairy story,
folk tale 2 = **illusion**, story,
fancy, fantasy, imagination,
invention, delusion, superstition

mythology = **legend**, folklore,
tradition, lore

m

Nn

nab = **catch**, arrest, apprehend, seize, grab, capture, collar (*informal*), snatch

nag¹ VERB 1 = **scold**, harass, badger, pester, worry, plague, hassle (*informal*), upbraid
▷ NOUN 2 = **scold**, complainer, grumbler, virago, shrew, tartar, moaner, harpy

nag² *often derog.* = **horse** (*US*), hack

nagging 1 = **continuous**, persistent, continual, niggling, repeated, constant, endless, perpetual 2 = **scolding**, shrewish

nail NOUN 1 = **tack**, spike, rivet, hobnail, brad (*technical*)
2 = **fingernail**, toenail, talon, thumbnail, claw
▷ VERB 3 = **fasten**, fix, secure, attach, pin, hammer, tack
4 (*informal*) = **catch**, arrest, capture, apprehend, trap, snare, ensnare, entrap

naive *or* **naïve** = **gullible**, trusting, credulous, unsuspicious, green, simple, innocent, callow OPPOSITE: worldly

naked = **nude**, stripped, exposed, bare, undressed, starkers (*informal*), stark-naked, unclothed OPPOSITE: dressed

name NOUN 1 = **title**, nickname, designation, term, handle (*slang*), epithet, sobriquet, moniker *or* monicker (*slang*)
▷ VERB 2 = **call**, christen, baptize, dub, term, style, label, entitle 3 = **nominate**, choose, select, appoint, specify, designate

namely = **specifically**, to wit, viz.

nap¹ VERB 1 = **sleep**, rest, drop off (*informal*), doze, kip (*Brit slang*), snooze (*informal*), nod off (*informal*), catnap
▷ NOUN 2 = **sleep**, rest, kip (*Brit slang*), siesta, catnap, forty winks (*informal*)

nap² = **pile**, down, fibre, weave, grain

napkin = **serviette**, cloth

narcotic NOUN 1 = **drug**, anaesthetic, painkiller, sedative, opiate, tranquillizer, anodyne, analgesic
▷ ADJECTIVE 2 = **sedative**, calming, hypnotic, analgesic, soporific, painkilling

narrative = **story**, report, history, account, statement, tale, chronicle

narrator = **storyteller**, writer, author, reporter, commentator, chronicler

narrow ADJECTIVE 1 = **thin**, fine, slim, slender, tapering,

n

attenuated **OPPOSITE:** broad
2 = **limited**, restricted, confined,
tight, close, meagre, constricted
OPPOSITE: wide **3** = **insular**,
prejudiced, partial, dogmatic,
intolerant, narrow-minded,
small-minded, illiberal
OPPOSITE: broad-minded
▷ **VERB 4** *often with* **down**
= **restrict**, limit, reduce,
constrict **5** = **get narrower**,
taper, shrink, tighten, constrict
narrowly = **just**, barely, only
just, scarcely, by the skin of
your teeth
nasty 1 = **unpleasant**, ugly,
disagreeable **OPPOSITE:**
pleasant **2** = **spiteful**,
mean, offensive, vicious,
unpleasant, vile, malicious,
despicable **OPPOSITE:** pleasant
3 = **disgusting**, unpleasant,
offensive, vile, distasteful,
obnoxious, objectionable,
disagreeable, festy (*Austral
slang*), yucko (*Austral slang*)
4 = **serious**, bad, dangerous,
critical, severe, painful
nation 1 = **country**, state, realm,
micronation **2** = **public**, people,
society
national ADJECTIVE
1 = **nationwide**, public,
widespread, countrywide
▷ **NOUN 2** = **citizen**, subject,
resident, native, inhabitant
nationalism = **patriotism**,
loyalty to your country,
chauvinism, jingoism, allegiance

nationality 1 = **citizenship**,
birth **2** = **race**, nation
nationwide = **national**,
general, widespread,
countrywide
native ADJECTIVE 1 = **mother**,
indigenous, vernacular
▷ **NOUN 2** *usually with* **of**
= **inhabitant**, national, resident,
citizen, countryman, aborigine
(*often offensive*), dweller
natural 1 = **logical**, valid,
legitimate **2** = **normal**,
common, regular, usual,
ordinary, typical, everyday
OPPOSITE: abnormal **3** = **innate**,
native, characteristic,
inherent, instinctive,
intuitive, inborn, essential
4 = **unaffected**, open, genuine,
spontaneous, unpretentious,
unsophisticated, dinkum
(*Austral & NZ informal*),
ingenuous, real **OPPOSITE:**
affected **5** = **pure**, plain,
organic, whole, unrefined
OPPOSITE: processed
naturally 1 = **of course**,
certainly **2** = **typically**, simply,
normally, spontaneously
nature 1 = **creation**, world,
earth, environment, universe,
cosmos, natural world
2 = **quality**, character, make-
up, constitution, essence,
complexion **3** = **temperament**,
character, personality,
disposition, outlook, mood,
humour, temper **4** = **kind**, sort,

style, type, variety, species, category, description

naughty 1 = **disobedient**, bad, mischievous, badly behaved, wayward, wicked, impish, refractory **OPPOSITE:** good 2 = **obscene**, vulgar, improper, lewd, risqué, smutty, ribald **OPPOSITE:** clean

nausea = **sickness**, vomiting, retching, squeamishness, queasiness, biliousness

naval = **nautical**, marine, maritime

navigation = **sailing**, voyaging, seamanship, helmsmanship

navy = **fleet**, flotilla, armada

near 1 = **close**, neighbouring, nearby, adjacent, adjoining **OPPOSITE:** far 2 = **imminent**, forthcoming, approaching, looming, impending, upcoming, nigh, in the offing **OPPOSITE:** far-off

nearby = **neighbouring**, adjacent, adjoining

nearly 1 = **practically**, almost, virtually, just about, as good as, well-nigh 2 = **almost**, approaching, roughly, just about, approximately

neat 1 = **tidy**, trim, orderly, spruce, shipshape, spick-and-span **OPPOSITE:** untidy 2 = **methodical**, tidy, systematic, fastidious **OPPOSITE:** disorganized 3 = **smart**, trim, tidy, spruce, dapper, natty (*informal*),

well-groomed, well-turned out 4 = **graceful**, elegant, adept, nimble, adroit, efficient **OPPOSITE:** clumsy 5 = **clever**, efficient, handy, apt, well-judged **OPPOSITE:** inefficient 6 (*chiefly US & Canad slang*) = **cool**, great (*informal*), excellent, brilliant, superb, fantastic (*informal*), tremendous, fabulous (*informal*), booshit (*Austral slang*), exo (*Austral slang*), sik (*Austral slang*), rad (*informal*), phat (*slang*), schmick (*Austral informal*) **OPPOSITE:** terrible 7 (*of alcoholic drinks*) = **undiluted**, straight, pure, unmixed

neatly 1 = **tidily**, smartly, systematically, methodically, fastidiously 2 = **smartly**, elegantly, tidily, nattily 3 = **gracefully**, expertly, efficiently, adeptly, skilfully, nimbly, adroitly, dexterously 4 = **cleverly**, efficiently

necessarily 1 = **automatically**, naturally, definitely, undoubtedly, certainly 2 = **inevitably**, of necessity, unavoidably, incontrovertibly, nolens volens (*Latin*)

necessary 1 = **needed**, required, essential, vital, compulsory, mandatory, imperative, indispensable **OPPOSITE:** unnecessary 2 = **inevitable**, certain, unavoidable, inescapable **OPPOSITE:** avoidable

n

necessity 1 = **essential**, need, requirement, fundamental, requisite, prerequisite, sine qua non (*Latin*), desideratum, must-have 2 = **inevitability**, certainty 3 = **essential**, need, requirement, fundamental

need VERB 1 = **want**, miss, require, lack, have to have, demand 2 = **require**, want, demand, call for, entail, necessitate 3 = **have to**, be obliged to
▷ NOUN 4 = **requirement**, demand, essential, necessity, requisite, desideratum, must-have 5 = **necessity**, call, demand, obligation 6 = **emergency**, want, necessity, urgency, exigency 7 = **poverty**, deprivation, destitution, penury

needed = **necessary**, wanted, required, lacked, called for, desired

needle = **irritate**, provoke, annoy, harass, taunt, nag, goad, rile

needless = **unnecessary**, pointless, gratuitous, useless, unwanted, redundant, superfluous, groundless
OPPOSITE: essential

needy = **poor**, deprived, disadvantaged, impoverished, penniless, destitute, poverty-stricken, underprivileged
OPPOSITE: wealthy

negative ADJECTIVE
1 = **pessimistic**, cynical, unwilling, gloomy, jaundiced, uncooperative OPPOSITE: optimistic 2 = **dissenting**, contradictory, refusing, denying, rejecting, opposing, resisting, contrary OPPOSITE: assenting
▷ NOUN 3 = **denial**, no, refusal, rejection, contradiction

neglect VERB 1 = **disregard**, ignore, fail to look after
OPPOSITE: look after 2 = **shirk**, forget, overlook, omit, evade, pass over, skimp, be remiss in or about 3 = **fail**, forget, omit
▷ NOUN 4 = **negligence**, inattention OPPOSITE: care
5 = **shirking**, failure, oversight, carelessness, dereliction, slackness, laxity

neglected 1 = **uncared-for**, abandoned, underestimated, disregarded, undervalued, unappreciated 2 = **run down**, derelict, overgrown, uncared-for

negligence = **carelessness**, neglect, disregard, dereliction, slackness, inattention, laxity, thoughtlessness

negotiate 1 = **bargain**, deal, discuss, debate, mediate, hold talks, cut a deal, conciliate
2 = **arrange**, work out, bring about, transact 3 = **get round**, clear, pass, cross, get over, get past, surmount

negotiation 1 = **bargaining**, debate, discussion, transaction, dialogue, mediation, arbitration,

wheeling and dealing (*informal*)
2 = arrangement, working out,
transaction, bringing about
negotiator = mediator,
ambassador, diplomat,
delegate, intermediary,
moderator, honest broker
neighbourhood or (*US*)
neighborhood 1 = district,
community, quarter, region,
locality, locale **2 = vicinity**,
environs
neighbouring or (*US*)
neighboring = nearby, next,
near, bordering, surrounding,
connecting, adjacent, adjoining
OPPOSITE: remote
neighbourly or (*US*)
neighborly = helpful, kind,
friendly, obliging, harmonious,
considerate, sociable,
hospitable
nerd (*slang*) **= bore**, obsessive,
anorak (*informal*), geek
(*informal*), trainspotter
(*informal*), dork (*slang*), wonk
(*informal*), techie (*informal*),
alpha geek
nerve NOUN **1 = bravery**,
courage, bottle (*Brit slang*),
resolution, daring, guts
(*informal*), pluck, grit **2** (*informal*)
= impudence, cheek (*informal*),
audacity, boldness, temerity,
insolence, impertinence,
brazenness
▷ PLURAL NOUN **3** (*informal*)
= tension, stress, strain, anxiety,
butterflies (in your stomach)

(*informal*), nervousness, cold feet
(*informal*), worry
▷ PHRASES: **nerve yourself**
= brace yourself, prepare
yourself, steel yourself, fortify
yourself, gear yourself up, gee
yourself up
nervous *often with* **of**
= apprehensive, anxious,
uneasy, edgy, worried, tense,
fearful, uptight (*informal*), toey
(*Austral slang*), adrenalized
OPPOSITE: calm
nest = refuge, retreat, haunt,
den, hideaway
nestle *often with* **up** or **down**
= snuggle, cuddle, huddle, curl
up, nuzzle
nestling = chick, fledgling,
baby bird
net¹ NOUN **1 = mesh**, netting,
network, web, lattice,
openwork
▷ VERB **2 = catch**, bag, capture,
trap, entangle, ensnare, enmesh
net² or **nett** ADJECTIVE **1 = after**
taxes, final, clear, take-home
▷ VERB **2 = earn**, make,
clear, gain, realize, bring in,
accumulate, reap
network 1 = web, system,
arrangement, grid, lattice
2 = maze, warren, labyrinth
neurotic = unstable, nervous,
disturbed, abnormal, obsessive,
compulsive, manic, unhealthy
OPPOSITE: rational
neutral 1 = unbiased,
impartial, disinterested,

n

even-handed, uninvolved, nonpartisan, unprejudiced, nonaligned **OPPOSITE:** biased **2 = expressionless**, dull **3 = uncontroversial** or **noncontroversial**, inoffensive **4 = colourless**

never 1 = at no time, not once, not ever **OPPOSITE:** always **2 = under no circumstances**, not at all, on no account, not ever

> **USAGE NOTE**
> *Never* is sometimes used in informal speech and writing as an emphatic form of *not*, with simple past tenses of certain verbs: *I never said that* - and in very informal speech as a denial in place of *did not*: *he says I hit him, but I never*. These uses of *never* should be avoided in careful writing.

nevertheless = even so, still, however, yet, regardless, nonetheless, notwithstanding, in spite of that

new 1 = modern, recent, contemporary, up-to-date, latest, current, original, fresh **OPPOSITE:** old-fashioned **2 = brand new 3 = extra**, more, added, new-found, supplementary **4 = unfamiliar**, strange **5 = renewed**, changed, improved, restored, altered, revitalized

newcomer 1 = new arrival, stranger **2 = beginner**, novice, new arrival, parvenu, Johnny-come-lately (*informal*), noob (*derogatory slang*)

news = information, latest (*informal*), report, story, exposé, intelligence, rumour, revelation, goss (*informal*)

next ADJECTIVE 1 = following, later, succeeding, subsequent **2 = adjacent**, closest, nearest, neighbouring, adjoining ▷ **ADVERB 3 = afterwards**, then, later, following, subsequently, thereafter

nice 1 = pleasant, delightful, agreeable, good, attractive, charming, pleasurable, enjoyable **OPPOSITE:** unpleasant **2 = kind**, helpful, obliging, considerate **OPPOSITE:** unkind **3 = likable** or **likeable**, friendly, engaging, charming, pleasant, agreeable **4 = polite**, courteous, well-mannered **OPPOSITE:** vulgar **5 = precise**, fine, careful, strict, subtle, delicate, meticulous, fastidious **OPPOSITE:** vague

nicely 1 = pleasantly, well, delightfully, attractively, charmingly, agreeably, acceptably, pleasurably **OPPOSITE:** unpleasantly **2 = kindly**, politely, thoughtfully, amiably, courteously

niche 1 = recess, opening, corner, hollow, nook, alcove **2 = position**, calling, place, slot (*informal*), vocation, pigeonhole (*informal*)

nick NOUN 1 = **cut**, mark, scratch, chip, scar, notch, dent
▷ VERB 2 (*slang*, *chiefly Brit*) = **steal**, pinch (*informal*), swipe (*slang*), pilfer 3 = **cut**, mark, score, chip, scratch, scar, notch, dent

nickname = **pet name**, label, diminutive, epithet, sobriquet, moniker *or* monicker (*slang*)

night = **darkness**, dark, night-time

RELATED WORD
adjective: nocturnal

nightly ADJECTIVE
1 = **nocturnal**, night-time
▷ ADVERB 2 = **every night**, nights (*informal*), each night, night after night

nightmare 1 = **bad dream**, hallucination 2 = **ordeal**, trial, hell, horror, torture, torment, tribulation, purgatory

nil 1 = **nothing**, love, zero
2 = **zero**, nothing, none, naught

nip¹ 1 *with* **along**, **up**, **out** (*Brit informal*) = **pop**, go, run, rush, dash 2 = **bite** 3 = **pinch**, squeeze, tweak
▷ PHRASES: **nip something in the bud** = **thwart**, check, frustrate

nip² = **dram**, shot (*informal*), drop, sip, draught, mouthful, snifter (*informal*)

nirvana (*Buddhism*, *Hinduism*) = **paradise**, peace, joy, bliss, serenity, tranquillity

no SENTENCE SUBSTITUTE 1 = **not at all**, certainly not, of course not, absolutely not, never, no way, nay OPPOSITE: yes
▷ NOUN 2 = **refusal**, rejection, denial, negation OPPOSITE: consent

noble ADJECTIVE 1 = **worthy**, generous, upright, honourable, virtuous, magnanimous OPPOSITE: despicable
2 = **dignified**, great, imposing, impressive, distinguished, splendid, stately OPPOSITE: lowly 3 = **aristocratic**, lordly, titled, patrician, blue-blooded, highborn OPPOSITE: humble
▷ NOUN 4 = **lord**, peer, aristocrat, nobleman OPPOSITE: commoner

nobody PRONOUN 1 = **no-one**
▷ NOUN 2 = **nonentity**, lightweight (*informal*), zero, no-mark (*Brit slang*), cipher OPPOSITE: celebrity

nod VERB 1 = **incline**, bow 2 = **signal**, indicate, motion, gesture 3 = **salute**, acknowledge
▷ NOUN 4 = **signal**, sign, motion, gesture, indication 5 = **salute**, greeting, acknowledgment

noise = **sound**, row, racket, clamour, din, uproar, commotion, hubbub OPPOSITE: silence

noisy 1 = **rowdy**, strident, boisterous, vociferous, uproarious, clamorous OPPOSITE: quiet 2 = **loud**, piercing, deafening,

n

tumultuous, ear-splitting, cacophonous, clamorous **OPPOSITE:** quiet

nominal 1 = **titular**, formal, purported, in name only, supposed, so-called, theoretical, professed 2 = **token**, small, symbolic, minimal, trivial, trifling, insignificant, inconsiderable

nominate 1 = **propose**, suggest, recommend, put forward 2 = **appoint**, name, choose, select, elect, assign, designate

nomination 1 = **proposal**, suggestion, recommendation 2 = **appointment**, election, selection, designation, choice

nominee = **candidate**, applicant, entrant, contestant, aspirant, runner

none 1 = **not any**, nothing, zero, not one, nil 2 = **no-one**, nobody, not one

nonetheless = **nevertheless**, however, yet, even so, despite that, in spite of that

nonexistent = **imaginary**, fictional, mythical, unreal, hypothetical, illusory **OPPOSITE:** real

nonsense 1 = **rubbish**, hot air (*informal*), twaddle, drivel, tripe (*informal*), gibberish, claptrap (*informal*), double Dutch (*Brit informal*), bizzo (*Austral slang*), bull's wool (*Austral & NZ slang*) **OPPOSITE:** sense 2 = **idiocy**, stupidity

nonstop ADJECTIVE 1 = **continuous**, constant, relentless, uninterrupted, endless, unbroken, interminable, incessant **OPPOSITE:** occasional ▷ ADVERB 2 = **continuously**, constantly, endlessly, relentlessly, perpetually, incessantly, ceaselessly, interminably

noon = **midday**, high noon, noonday, twelve noon, noontide

norm = **standard**, rule, pattern, average, par, criterion, benchmark, yardstick

normal 1 = **usual**, common, standard, average, natural, regular, ordinary, typical **OPPOSITE:** unusual 2 = **sane**, reasonable, rational, well-adjusted, compos mentis (*Latin*), in your right mind, mentally sound

normally 1 = **usually**, generally, commonly, regularly, typically, ordinarily, as a rule, habitually 2 = **as usual**, naturally, properly, conventionally, in the usual way

north ADJECTIVE 1 = **northern**, polar, arctic, boreal, northerly ▷ ADVERB 2 = **northward(s)**, in a northerly direction

nose NOUN 1 = **snout**, bill, beak, hooter (*slang*), proboscis ▷ VERB 2 = **ease forward**, push, edge, shove, nudge

nostalgia = **reminiscence**, longing, pining, yearning, remembrance, homesickness, wistfulness

nostalgic = **sentimental**, longing, emotional, homesick, wistful, maudlin, regretful

notable ADJECTIVE
1 = **remarkable**, striking, unusual, extraordinary, outstanding, memorable, uncommon, conspicuous
OPPOSITE: imperceptible
2 = **prominent**, famous
OPPOSITE: unknown
▷ NOUN 3 = **celebrity**, big name, dignitary, luminary, personage, V.I.P.

notably = **remarkably**, unusually, extraordinarily, noticeably, strikingly, singularly, outstandingly, uncommonly

notch NOUN 1 (*informal*) = **level**, step, degree, grade 2 = **cut**, nick, incision, indentation, mark, score, cleft
▷ VERB 3 = **cut**, mark, score, nick, scratch, indent

note NOUN 1 = **message**, letter, communication, memo, memorandum, epistle, e-mail, text 2 = **record**, reminder, memo, memorandum, jotting, minute 3 = **annotation**, comment, remark
4 = **document**, form, record, certificate 5 = **symbol**, mark, sign, indication, token 6 = **tone**, touch, trace, hint, sound
▷ VERB 7 = **notice**, see, observe, perceive 8 = **bear in mind**,

be aware, take into account
9 = **mention**, record, mark, indicate, register, remark
10 = **write down**, record, scribble, set down, jot down

notebook = **notepad**, exercise book, journal, diary

noted = **famous**, celebrated, distinguished, well-known, prominent, acclaimed, notable, renowned **OPPOSITE:** unknown

nothing PRONOUN 1 = **nought**, zero, nil, not a thing, zilch (*slang*)
2 = **a trifle** 3 = **void**, emptiness, nothingness, nullity
▷ NOUN 4 (*informal*) = **nobody**, cipher, nonentity

notice NOUN 1 = **notification**, warning, advice, intimation, news, communication, announcement, instruction, heads up (*US & Canad*)
2 = **attention**, interest, note, regard, consideration, observation, scrutiny, heed
OPPOSITE: oversight 3 (*chiefly Brit*) = **the sack** (*informal*), dismissal, the boot (*slang*), the push (*slang*), marching orders (*informal*)
▷ VERB 4 = **observe**, see, note, spot, distinguish, perceive, detect, discern **OPPOSITE:** overlook

noticeable = **obvious**, clear, striking, plain, evident, manifest, conspicuous, perceptible

notify = **inform**, tell, advise, alert to, announce, warn

notion 1 = **idea**, view, opinion, belief, concept, impression, sentiment, inkling 2 = **whim**, wish, desire, fancy, impulse, inclination, caprice

notorious = **infamous**, disreputable, opprobrious

notoriously = **infamously**, disreputably

notwithstanding = **despite**, in spite of, regardless of

nought (*archaic literary*) or **naught** = **zero**, nothing, nil

nourish 1 = **feed**, supply, sustain, nurture 2 = **encourage**, support, maintain, promote, sustain, foster

nourishing = **nutritious**, beneficial, wholesome, nutritive

novel[1] = **story**, tale, fiction, romance, narrative

novel[2] = **new**, different, original, fresh, unusual, innovative, uncommon **OPPOSITE:** ordinary

novelty 1 = **newness**, originality, freshness, innovation, surprise, uniqueness, strangeness, unfamiliarity 2 = **curiosity**, rarity, oddity, wonder 3 = **trinket**, souvenir, memento, bauble, trifle, knick-knack

novice = **beginner**, pupil, amateur, newcomer, trainee, apprentice, learner, probationer **OPPOSITE:** expert

now 1 = **nowadays**, at the moment 2 = **immediately**, promptly, instantly, at once, straightaway
▷ **PHRASES: now and then** *or* **again** = **occasionally**, sometimes, from time to time, on and off, intermittently, infrequently, sporadically

nowadays = **now**, today, at the moment, in this day and age

nucleus = **centre**, heart, focus, basis, core, pivot, kernel, nub

nude = **naked**, stripped, bare, undressed, stark-naked, disrobed, unclothed, unclad **OPPOSITE:** dressed

nudge VERB 1 = **push**, touch, dig, jog, prod, elbow, shove, poke 2 = **prompt**, influence, persuade, spur, prod, coax
▷ NOUN 3 = **push**, touch, dig, elbow, bump, shove, poke, jog 4 = **prompting**, push, encouragement, prod

nuisance = **trouble**, problem, trial, drag (*informal*), bother, pest, irritation, hassle (*informal*) **OPPOSITE:** benefit

numb ADJECTIVE 1 = **unfeeling**, dead, frozen, paralysed, insensitive, deadened, immobilized, torpid **OPPOSITE:** sensitive 2 = **stupefied**, deadened, unfeeling
▷ VERB 3 = **stun**, knock out, paralyse, daze 4 = **deaden**, freeze, dull, paralyse, immobilize, benumb

number NOUN 1 = **numeral**, figure, character, digit, integer 2 = **amount**, quantity,

collection, aggregate **OPPOSITE:**
shortage 3 = **crowd**, horde,
multitude, throng 4 = **group**,
set, band, crowd, gang
5 = **issue**, copy, edition, imprint,
printing
▷ VERB 6 = **amount to**, come to,
total, add up to 7 = **calculate**,
account, reckon, compute,
enumerate **OPPOSITE:** guess
8 = **include**, count

numerous = **many**, several,
countless, lots, abundant,
plentiful, innumerable, copious
OPPOSITE: few

nurse 1 = **look after**, treat, tend,
care for, take care of, minister
to 2 = **harbour**, have, maintain,
preserve, entertain, cherish
3 = **breast-feed**, feed, nurture,
nourish, suckle, wet-nurse

nursery = **crèche**, kindergarten,
playgroup, play-centre (NZ)

nurture NOUN 1 = **upbringing**,
training, education, instruction,
rearing, development
▷ VERB 2 = **bring up**, raise, look
after, rear, care for, develop
OPPOSITE: neglect

nut 1 (slang) = **madman**, psycho
(slang), crank (informal), lunatic,
maniac, nutcase (slang), crazy
(informal) 2 (slang) = **head**, skull

nutrition = **food**, nourishment,
sustenance, nutriment

oath 1 = **promise**, bond,
pledge, vow, word, affirmation,
avowal 2 = **swear word**, curse,
obscenity, blasphemy, expletive,
four-letter word, profanity

obedience = **compliance**,
respect, reverence, observance,
subservience, submissiveness,
docility **OPPOSITE:** disobedience

obey 1 = **submit to**, surrender
(to), give way to, bow to, give in
to, yield to, do what you are told
by **OPPOSITE:** disobey 2 = **carry
out**, follow, implement, act
upon, carry through **OPPOSITE:**
disregard 3 = **abide by**, keep,
follow, comply with, observe,
heed, conform to, keep to

object[1] 1 = **thing**, article, body,
item, entity 2 = **purpose**, aim,
end, point, plan, idea, goal,
design 3 = **target**, victim, focus,
recipient

object[2] 1 often with **to** = **protest
against**, oppose, argue against,
draw the line at, take exception
to, cry out against, complain
against, expostulate against
OPPOSITE: accept 2 = **disagree**,

o

demur, remonstrate, express disapproval **OPPOSITE:** agree

objection = **protest**, opposition, complaint, doubt, dissent, outcry, protestation, scruple **OPPOSITE:** agreement

objective ADJECTIVE 1 = **factual**, real 2 = **unbiased**, detached, fair, open-minded, impartial, impersonal, disinterested, even-handed **OPPOSITE:** subjective ▷ NOUN 3 = **purpose**, aim, goal, end, plan, hope, idea, target

objectively = **impartially**, neutrally, fairly, justly, without prejudice, dispassionately, with an open mind, equitably

obligation 1 = **duty**, compulsion 2 = **task**, job, duty, work, charge, role, function, mission 3 = **responsibility**, duty, liability, accountability, answerability

oblige 1 = **compel**, make, force, require, bind, constrain, necessitate, impel 2 = **help**, assist, benefit, please, humour, accommodate, indulge, gratify **OPPOSITE:** bother

obliged 1 = **forced**, required, bound, compelled, duty-bound 2 = **grateful**, in (someone's) debt, thankful, indebted, appreciative, beholden

obliging = **accommodating**, kind, helpful, willing, polite, cooperative, agreeable, considerate **OPPOSITE:** unhelpful

obscene 1 = **indecent**, dirty, offensive, filthy, improper, immoral, pornographic, lewd **OPPOSITE:** decent 2 = **offensive**, shocking, evil, disgusting, outrageous, revolting, sickening, vile

obscure ADJECTIVE 1 = **unknown**, little-known, humble, unfamiliar, out-of-the-way, lowly, unheard-of, undistinguished **OPPOSITE:** famous 2 = **abstruse**, complex, confusing, mysterious, vague, unclear, ambiguous, enigmatic **OPPOSITE:** straightforward 3 = **unclear**, uncertain, confused, mysterious, doubtful, indeterminate **OPPOSITE:** well-known 4 = **indistinct**, vague, blurred, dark, faint, dim, gloomy, murky **OPPOSITE:** clear ▷ VERB 5 = **obstruct**, hinder 6 = **hide**, screen, mask, disguise, conceal, veil, cloak, camouflage **OPPOSITE:** expose

observation 1 = **watching**, study, survey, review, investigation, monitoring, examination, inspection 2 = **comment**, thought, note, statement, opinion, remark, explanation, reflection 3 = **remark**, comment, statement, reflection, utterance 4 with of = **observance of**, compliance with, honouring of, fulfilment of, carrying out of

observe 1 = **watch**, study, view, look at, check, survey, monitor, keep an eye on (*informal*) 2 = **notice**, see, note, discover, spot, regard, witness, distinguish 3 = **remark**, say, comment, state, note, reflect, mention, opine 4 = **comply with**, keep, follow, respect, carry out, honour, discharge, obey **OPPOSITE:** disregard

observer 1 = **witness**, viewer, spectator, looker-on, watcher, onlooker, eyewitness, bystander 2 = **commentator**, reporter, special correspondent 3 = **monitor**, watchdog, supervisor, scrutineer

obsessed = **absorbed**, dominated, gripped, haunted, distracted, hung up (*slang*), preoccupied **OPPOSITE:** indifferent

obsession = **preoccupation**, thing (*informal*), complex, hang-up (*informal*), mania, phobia, fetish, fixation

obsessive = **compulsive**, gripping, consuming, haunting, irresistible, neurotic, besetting, uncontrollable

obsolete = **outdated**, old, passé, old-fashioned, discarded, extinct, out of date, archaic **OPPOSITE:** up-to-date

obstacle 1 = **obstruction**, block, barrier, hurdle, snag, impediment, blockage, hindrance 2 = **hindrance**, bar, difficulty, barrier, handicap, hurdle, hitch, drawback, uphill (*S African*) **OPPOSITE:** help

obstruct 1 = **block**, close, bar, plug, barricade, stop up, bung up (*informal*) 2 = **hold up**, stop, check, block, restrict, slow down, hamper, hinder 3 = **impede**, hamper, hold back, thwart, hinder **OPPOSITE:** help 4 = **obscure**, screen, cover

obtain 1 = **get**, gain, acquire, land, net, pick up, secure, procure **OPPOSITE:** lose 2 = **achieve**, get, gain, accomplish, attain 3 (*formal*) = **prevail**, hold, exist, be the case, abound, predominate, be in force, be current

obvious = **clear**, plain, apparent, evident, distinct, manifest, noticeable, conspicuous **OPPOSITE:** unclear

obviously 1 = **clearly**, of course, without doubt, assuredly 2 = **plainly**, patently, undoubtedly, evidently, manifestly, markedly, without doubt, unquestionably

occasion NOUN 1 = **time**, moment, point, stage, instance, juncture 2 = **function**, event, affair, do (*informal*), happening, experience, gathering, celebration 3 = **opportunity**, chance, time, opening, window 4 = **reason**, cause, call, ground(s), excuse, incentive, motive, justification

o

▷ **VERB 5** (*formal*) = **cause**, produce, lead to, inspire, result in, generate, prompt, provoke

occasional = **infrequent**, odd, rare, irregular, sporadic, intermittent, few and far between, periodic **OPPOSITE:** constant

occasionally = **sometimes**, at times, from time to time, now and then, irregularly, now and again, periodically, once in a while **OPPOSITE:** constantly

occult = **supernatural**, magical, mysterious, psychic, mystical, unearthly, esoteric, uncanny
▷ **PHRASES: the occult** = **magic**, witchcraft, sorcery, wizardry, enchantment, black art, necromancy

occupant = **occupier**, resident, tenant, inmate, inhabitant, incumbent, dweller, lessee

occupation 1 = **job**, calling, business, line (of work), trade, career, employment, profession **2** = **hobby**, pastime, diversion, relaxation, leisure pursuit, (leisure) activity **3** = **invasion**, seizure, conquest, incursion, subjugation **4** = **occupancy**, residence, holding, control, possession, tenure, tenancy

occupied 1 = **in use**, taken, full, engaged, unavailable **2** = **inhabited**, peopled, lived-in, settled, tenanted **OPPOSITE:** uninhabited **3** = **busy**, engaged, employed, working,

active, hard at work, rushed off your feet

occupy 1 = **inhabit**, own, live in, dwell in, reside in, abide in **OPPOSITE:** vacate **2** = **invade**, take over, capture, seize, conquer, overrun, annex, colonize, cybersquat (*computing*) **OPPOSITE:** withdraw **3** = **hold**, control, dominate, possess **4** = **take up**, consume, tie up, use up, monopolize **5** *often passive* = **engage**, involve, employ, divert, preoccupy, engross **6** = **fill**, take up, cover, fill up, pervade, permeate, extend over

occur 1 = **happen**, take place, come about, turn up (*informal*), crop up (*informal*), transpire (*informal*), befall **2** = **exist**, appear, be found, develop, turn up, be present, manifest itself, present itself
▷ **PHRASES: occur to someone** = **come to mind**, strike someone, dawn on someone, spring to mind, cross someone's mind, enter someone's head, suggest itself to someone

| **USAGE NOTE**
It is usually regarded as incorrect to talk of pre-arranged events *occurring* or *happening*. For this meaning a synonym such as *take place* would be more appropriate: *the wedding took place* (not *occurred* or *happened*) *in the afternoon*.

occurrence 1 = **incident**, happening, event, fact, matter, affair, circumstance, episode 2 = **existence**, instance, appearance, manifestation, materialization

odd 1 = **peculiar**, strange, unusual, extraordinary, bizarre, offbeat, freakish, daggy (*Austral & NZ informal*) 2 = **unusual**, strange, rare, extraordinary, remarkable, bizarre, peculiar, irregular **OPPOSITE:** normal 3 = **occasional**, various, random, casual, irregular, periodic, sundry, incidental **OPPOSITE:** regular 4 = **spare**, remaining, extra, surplus, solitary, leftover, unmatched, unpaired **OPPOSITE:** matched

odds = **probability**, chances, likelihood
▷ **PHRASES: at odds** 1 = **in conflict**, arguing, quarrelling, at loggerheads, at daggers drawn 2 = **at variance**, conflicting, contrary to, at odds, out of line, out of step, at sixes and sevens (*informal*)
▶ **odds and ends** = **scraps**, bits, remains, fragments, debris, remnants, bits and pieces, bric-a-brac

odour *or* (*US*) **odor** = **smell**, scent, perfume, fragrance, stink, bouquet, aroma, stench

Odyssey *often not cap.* = **journey**, tour, trip, quest, trek, expedition, voyage, crusade

off ADVERB 1 = **away**, out, apart, elsewhere, aside, hence, from here 2 = **absent**, gone, unavailable
▷ ADJECTIVE 3 = **cancelled**, abandoned, postponed, shelved 4 = **bad**, rotten, rancid, mouldy, turned, spoiled, sour, decayed

offence *or* (*US*) **offense** 1 = **crime**, sin, fault, violation, wrongdoing, trespass, felony, misdemeanour 2 = **outrage**, shock, anger, trouble, bother, resentment, irritation, hassle (*informal*) 3 = **insult**, slight, hurt, outrage, injustice, snub, affront, indignity

offend 1 = **distress**, upset, outrage, wound, slight, insult, annoy, snub **OPPOSITE:** please 2 = **break the law**, sin, err, do wrong, fall, go astray

offended = **upset**, hurt, bothered, disturbed, distressed, outraged, stung, put out (*informal*), tooshie (*Austral slang*)

offender = **criminal**, convict, crook, villain, culprit, sinner, delinquent, felon, perp (*US & Canad informal*)

offensive ADJECTIVE 1 = **insulting**, rude, abusive, degrading, contemptuous, disparaging, objectionable, disrespectful **OPPOSITE:** respectful 2 = **disgusting**, gross, foul, unpleasant, revolting, vile, repellent, obnoxious, festy (*Austral slang*), yucko (*Austral slang*)

OPPOSITE: pleasant
3 = **attacking**, threatening, aggressive, striking, hostile, invading, combative **OPPOSITE**: defensive
▷ **NOUN 4** = **attack**, charge, campaign, strike, push (*informal*), assault, raid, drive

offer VERB **1** = **provide**, present, furnish, afford **OPPOSITE**: withhold **2** = **volunteer**, come forward, offer your services **3** = **propose**, suggest, advance, submit **4** = **give**, show, bring, provide, render, impart **5** = **put up for sale**, sell **6** = **bid**, submit, propose, tender, proffer
▷ **NOUN 7** = **proposal**, suggestion, proposition, submission **8** = **bid**, tender, bidding price

offering 1 = **contribution**, gift, donation, present, subscription, hand-out **2** = **sacrifice**, tribute, libation, burnt offering

office 1 = **place of work**, workplace, base, workroom, place of business **2** = **branch**, department, division, section, wing, subdivision, subsection **3** = **post**, place, role, situation, responsibility, function, occupation

officer 1 = **official**, executive, agent, representative, appointee, functionary, office-holder, office bearer **2** = **police officer**, detective, PC, police

constable, police man, police woman

official ADJECTIVE
1 = **authorized**, formal, sanctioned, licensed, proper, legitimate, authentic, certified **OPPOSITE**: unofficial **2** = **formal**, bureaucratic, ceremonial, solemn, ritualistic
▷ **NOUN 3** = **officer**, executive, agent, representative, bureaucrat, appointee, functionary, office-holder

offset = **cancel out**, balance, set off, make up for, compensate for, counteract, neutralize, counterbalance

offspring 1 = **child**, baby, kid (*informal*), youngster, infant, successor, babe, toddler, littlie (*Austral informal*), ankle-biter (*Austral slang*), tacker (*Austral slang*) **OPPOSITE**: parent **2** = **children**, young, family, issue, stock, heirs, descendants, brood

often = **frequently**, generally, commonly, repeatedly, time and again, habitually, not infrequently **OPPOSITE**: never

oil NOUN **1** = **lubricant**, grease, lubrication, fuel oil **2** = **lotion**, cream, balm, salve, liniment, embrocation, solution
▷ VERB **3** = **lubricate**, grease

oily = **greasy**, slimy, fatty, slippery, oleaginous

O.K. *or* **okay** SENTENCE SUBSTITUTE **1** = **all right**, right,

yes, agreed, very good, roger, very well, ya (S African), righto (Brit informal), yebo (S African informal)
▷ ADJECTIVE **2** (informal) = **all right**, fine, fitting, in order, permitted, suitable, acceptable, allowable **OPPOSITE:** unacceptable
3 = **fine**, good, average, fair, all right, acceptable, adequate, satisfactory **OPPOSITE:** unsatisfactory **4** = **well**, all right, safe, sound, healthy, unharmed, uninjured
▷ VERB **5** = **approve**, allow, agree to, permit, sanction, endorse, authorize, rubber-stamp (informal)
▷ NOUN **6** = **authorization**, agreement, sanction, approval, go-ahead (informal), blessing, permission, consent
old 1 = **aged**, elderly, ancient, mature, venerable, antiquated, senile, decrepit **OPPOSITE:** young **2** = **former**, earlier, past, previous, prior, one-time, erstwhile **3** = **long-standing**, established, fixed, enduring, abiding, long-lasting, long-established, time-honoured **4** = **stale**, worn-out, banal, threadbare, trite, overused, timeworn
old-fashioned 1 = **out of date**, dated, outdated, unfashionable, outmoded, passé, old hat, behind the times **OPPOSITE:**
up-to-date **2** = **oldfangled**, square (informal), outdated, unfashionable, obsolescent
ominous = **threatening**, sinister, grim, fateful, foreboding, unpromising, portentous, inauspicious **OPPOSITE:** promising
omission 1 = **exclusion**, removal, elimination, deletion, excision **OPPOSITE:** inclusion **2** = **gap**, space, exclusion, lacuna
omit 1 = **leave out**, drop, exclude, eliminate, skip **OPPOSITE:** include **2** = **forget**, overlook, neglect, pass over, lose sight of
once ADVERB **1** = **on one occasion**, one time, one single time **2** = **at one time**, previously, formerly, long ago, once upon a time
▷ CONJUNCTION **3** = **as soon as**, when, after, the moment, immediately, the instant
▷ PHRASES: **at once 1** = **immediately**, now, straight away, directly, promptly, instantly, right away, forthwith **2** = **simultaneously**, together, at the same time, concurrently
one-sided 1 = **unequal**, unfair, uneven, unjust, unbalanced, lopsided, ill-matched **OPPOSITE:** equal **2** = **biased**, prejudiced, weighted, unfair, partial, distorted, partisan, slanted **OPPOSITE:** unbiased

o

ongoing = **in progress**,
developing, progressing,
evolving, unfolding, unfinished

onlooker = **spectator**, witness,
observer, viewer, looker-on,
watcher, eyewitness, bystander

only ADJECTIVE 1 = **sole**, one,
single, individual, exclusive,
unique, lone, solitary
▷ ADVERB 2 = **just**, simply,
purely, merely 3 = **hardly**, just,
barely, only just, scarcely, at
a push

onset = **beginning**, start,
birth, outbreak, inception,
commencement **OPPOSITE:** end

onslaught = **attack**, charge,
campaign, strike, assault, raid,
invasion, offensive **OPPOSITE:**
retreat

onwards or **onward** = **forward**,
on, forwards, ahead, beyond, in
front, forth

ooze¹ 1 = **seep**, well, escape,
leak, drain, filter, drip, trickle
2 = **emit**, release, leak, drip,
dribble, give off, pour forth
3 = **exude**, emit

ooze² = **mud**, clay, dirt, silt,
sludge, mire, slime, alluvium

open ADJECTIVE 1 = **unclosed**,
unlocked, ajar, unfastened,
yawning **OPPOSITE:** closed
2 = **unsealed**, unstoppered
OPPOSITE: unopened
3 = **extended**, unfolded,
stretched out, unfurled,
straightened out, unrolled
OPPOSITE: shut 4 = **frank**,

direct, straightforward,
sincere, transparent, honest,
candid, truthful **OPPOSITE:** sly
5 = **receptive**, sympathetic,
responsive, amenable
6 = **unresolved**, unsettled,
undecided, debatable,
moot, arguable 7 = **clear**,
passable, unhindered,
unimpeded, navigable,
unobstructed **OPPOSITE:**
obstructed 8 = **available**, to
hand, accessible, handy, at
your disposal 9 = **general**,
public, free, universal, blanket,
across-the-board, unrestricted,
overarching **OPPOSITE:**
restricted 10 = **vacant**, free,
available, empty, unoccupied,
unfilled
▷ VERB 11 = **unfasten**, unlock,
unzip (~a computer file)
OPPOSITE: close 12 = **unwrap**,
uncover, undo, unravel, untie
OPPOSITE: wrap 13 = **uncork**
14 = **unfold**, spread (out),
expand, unfurl, unroll
OPPOSITE: fold 15 = **clear**,
unblock **OPPOSITE:** block
16 = **undo**, unbutton, unfasten
OPPOSITE: fasten 17 = **begin**
business 18 = **start**, begin,
launch, trigger, kick off
(informal), initiate, commence,
get going **OPPOSITE:** end
19 = **begin**, start, commence
OPPOSITE: end

open-air = **outdoor**, outside,
out-of-door(s), alfresco

opening ADJECTIVE 1 = **first**, earliest, beginning, premier, primary, initial, maiden, inaugural
▷ NOUN 2 = **beginning**, start, launch, dawn, outset, initiation, inception, commencement OPPOSITE: ending 3 = **hole**, space, tear, crack, gap, slot, puncture, aperture OPPOSITE: blockage 4 = **opportunity**, chance, time, moment, occasion, look-in (*informal*) 5 = **job**, position, post, situation, opportunity, vacancy

openly = **frankly**, plainly, honestly, overtly, candidly, unreservedly, unhesitatingly, forthrightly OPPOSITE: privately

open-minded = **unprejudiced**, liberal, balanced, objective, reasonable, tolerant, impartial, receptive OPPOSITE: narrow-minded

operate 1 = **manage**, run, direct, handle, supervise, be in charge of 2 = **function**, work, act 3 = **run**, work, use, control, manoeuvre 4 = **work**, go, run, perform, function OPPOSITE: break down

operation = **performance**, action, movement, motion

operational = **working**, going, running, ready, functioning, operative, viable, functional OPPOSITE: inoperative

operative ADJECTIVE 1 = **in force**, effective, functioning, active, in effect, operational, in operation OPPOSITE: inoperative
▷ NOUN 2 = **worker**, employee, labourer, workman, artisan 3 (*US & Canad*) = **spy**, undercover agent, mole, nark (*Brit, Austral & NZ slang*)

operator = **worker**, driver, mechanic, operative, conductor, technician, handler

opinion 1 = **belief**, feeling, view, idea, theory, conviction, point of view, sentiment 2 = **estimation**, view, impression, assessment, judgment, appraisal, considered opinion

opponent 1 = **adversary**, rival, enemy, competitor, challenger, foe, contestant, antagonist OPPOSITE: ally 2 = **opposer**, dissident, objector OPPOSITE: supporter

opportunity = **chance**, opening, time, turn, moment, possibility, occasion, slot

oppose = **be against**, fight (against), block, take on, counter, contest, resist, combat OPPOSITE: support

opposed 1 *with* to = **against**, hostile, adverse, in opposition, averse, antagonistic, (dead) set against 2 = **contrary**, conflicting, clashing, counter, adverse, contradictory, dissentient

opposing 1 = **conflicting**, different, contrasting,

opposite, differing, contrary, contradictory, incompatible
2 = rival, conflicting, competing, enemy, opposite, hostile
opposite ADJECTIVE 1 = facing, other, opposing **2 = different**, conflicting, contrasted, contrasting, unlike, contrary, dissimilar, divergent **OPPOSITE:** alike **3 = rival**, conflicting, opposing, competing
▷ **PREPOSITION 4** *often with* **to = facing**, face to face with, across from, eyeball to eyeball with (*informal*)
▷ **NOUN 5 = reverse**, contrary, converse, antithesis, contradiction, inverse, obverse
opposition 1 = hostility, resistance, resentment, disapproval, obstruction, animosity, antagonism, antipathy **OPPOSITE:** support **2 = opponent(s)**, competition, rival(s), enemy, competitor(s), other side, challenger(s), foe
oppress 1 = subjugate, abuse, suppress, wrong, master, overcome, subdue, persecute **OPPOSITE:** liberate **2 = depress**, burden, discourage, torment, harass, afflict, sadden, vex
oppression = persecution, control, abuse, injury, injustice, cruelty, domination, repression **OPPOSITE:** justice
oppressive 1 = tyrannical, severe, harsh, cruel, brutal, authoritarian, unjust, repressive

OPPOSITE: merciful **2 = stifling**, close, sticky, stuffy, humid, sultry, airless, muggy
opt = choose, decide, prefer, select, elect **OPPOSITE:** reject
▷ **PHRASES: opt for something** *or* **someone = choose**, pick, select, adopt, go for, designate, decide on, plump for
optimistic 1 = hopeful, positive, confident, encouraged, cheerful, rosy, buoyant, sanguine **OPPOSITE:** pessimistic **2 = encouraging**, promising, bright, good, reassuring, rosy, heartening, auspicious **OPPOSITE:** discouraging
optimum = ideal, best, highest, finest, perfect, supreme, peak, outstanding **OPPOSITE:** worst
option = choice, alternative, selection, preference, freedom of choice, power to choose
optional = voluntary, open, discretionary, possible, extra, elective **OPPOSITE:** compulsory
opus = work, piece, production, creation, composition, work of art, brainchild, oeuvre (*French*)
oral = spoken, vocal, verbal, unwritten
orbit NOUN 1 = path, course, cycle, circle, revolution, rotation, trajectory, sweep **2 = sphere of influence**, reach, range, influence, province, scope, domain, compass
▷ **VERB 3 = circle**, ring,

go round, revolve around, encircle, circumscribe, circumnavigate

orchestrate 1 = **organize**, plan, run, set up, arrange, put together, marshal, coordinate 2 = **score**, set, arrange, adapt

ordain 1 = **appoint**, name, commission, select, invest, nominate, anoint, consecrate 2 (*formal*) = **order**, will, rule, demand, require, direct, command, dictate

ordeal = **hardship**, trial, difficulty, test, suffering, nightmare, torture, agony **OPPOSITE:** pleasure

order VERB 1 = **command**, instruct, direct, charge, demand, require, bid, compel **OPPOSITE:** forbid 2 = **decree**, rule, demand, prescribe, pronounce, ordain **OPPOSITE:** ban 3 = **request**, ask (for), book, seek, reserve, apply for, solicit, send away for 4 = **arrange**, group, sort, position, line up, organize, catalogue, sort out **OPPOSITE:** disarrange ▷ NOUN 5 = **instruction**, ruling, demand, direction, command, dictate, decree, mandate 6 = **request**, booking, demand, commission, application, reservation, requisition 7 = **sequence**, grouping, series, structure, chain, arrangement, line-up, array 8 = **organization**, system, method, pattern, symmetry, regularity, neatness,

tidiness **OPPOSITE:** chaos 9 = **peace**, control, law, quiet, calm, discipline, law and order, tranquillity 10 = **society**, company, group, club, community, association, institute, organization 11 = **class**, set, rank, grade, caste 12 (*Biology*) = **kind**, group, class, family, sort, type, variety, category

orderly 1 = **well-behaved**, controlled, disciplined, quiet, restrained, law-abiding, peaceable **OPPOSITE:** disorderly 2 = **well-organized**, regular, in order, organized, precise, neat, tidy, systematic **OPPOSITE:** disorganized

ordinary 1 = **usual**, standard, normal, common, regular, typical, conventional, routine 2 = **commonplace**, plain, modest, humble, mundane, banal, unremarkable, run-of-the-mill

organ 1 = **body part**, part of the body, element, biological structure 2 = **newspaper**, medium, voice, vehicle, gazette, mouthpiece

organic 1 = **natural**, biological, living, live, animate 2 = **systematic**, ordered, structured, organized, integrated, orderly, methodical

organism = **creature**, being, thing, body, animal, structure, beast, entity

o

organization *or*
  organisation 1 = **group**,
  company, party, body,
  association, band, institution,
  corporation 2 = **management**,
  running, planning, control,
  operation, handling,
  structuring, administration
  3 = **structure**, form, pattern,
  make-up, arrangement,
  construction, format, formation
organize 1 = **arrange**, run, plan,
  prepare, set up, devise, put
  together, take care of, jack up
  (*NZ informal*) **OPPOSITE:** disrupt
  2 = **put in order**, arrange, group,
  list, file, index, classify, inventory
  OPPOSITE: muddle
orient *or* **orientate** = **adjust**,
  adapt, alter, accustom, align,
  familiarize, acclimatize
  ▷ **PHRASES:** orient yourself
  = **get your bearings**, establish
  your location
orientation 1 = **inclination**,
  tendency, disposition,
  predisposition, predilection,
  proclivity, partiality
  2 = **induction**, introduction,
  adjustment, settling in,
  adaptation, assimilation,
  familiarization, acclimatization
  3 = **position**, situation,
  location, bearings, direction,
  arrangement, whereabouts
origin 1 = **beginning**, start,
  birth, launch, foundation,
  creation, emergence, onset
  OPPOSITE: end 2 = **root**, source,

basis, base, seed, foundation,
nucleus, derivation
original **ADJECTIVE** 1 = **first**,
earliest, initial 2 = **initial**, first,
starting, opening, primary,
introductory **OPPOSITE:** final
3 = **new**, fresh, novel, unusual,
unprecedented, innovative,
unfamiliar, seminal **OPPOSITE:**
unoriginal 4 = **creative**,
inspired, imaginative, artistic,
fertile, ingenious, visionary,
inventive
▷ **NOUN** 5 = **prototype**, master,
pattern **OPPOSITE:** copy
originally = **initially**, first, firstly,
at first, primarily, to begin with,
in the beginning
originate 1 = **begin**, start,
emerge, come, happen, rise,
appear, spring **OPPOSITE:** end
2 = **invent**, create, design,
launch, introduce, institute,
generate, pioneer
ornament **NOUN**
1 = **decoration**, trimming,
accessory, festoon, trinket,
bauble, knick-knack
2 = **embellishment**, decoration,
embroidery, elaboration,
adornment, ornamentation
▷ **VERB** 3 = **decorate**, adorn,
array, do up (*informal*), embellish,
festoon, beautify, prettify
orthodox 1 = **established**,
official, accepted, received,
common, traditional, normal,
usual **OPPOSITE:** unorthodox
2 = **conformist**, conservative,

traditional, strict, devout, observant **OPPOSITE:** nonconformist

orthodoxy 1 = **doctrine**, teaching, opinion, principle, belief, convention, creed, dogma 2 = **conformity**, received wisdom, traditionalism, conventionality **OPPOSITE:** nonconformity

other 1 = **additional**, more, further, new, added, extra, fresh, spare 2 = **different**, alternative, contrasting, distinct, diverse, dissimilar, separate, alternative

otherwise SENTENCE CONNECTOR 1 = **or else**, or, if not, or then
▷ ADVERB 2 = **apart from that**, in other ways, in (all) other respects 3 = **differently**, any other way, contrarily

ounce = **shred**, bit, drop, trace, scrap, grain, fragment, atom

oust = **expel**, turn out, dismiss, exclude, exile, throw out, displace, topple

out ADJECTIVE 1 = **not in**, away, elsewhere, outside, gone, abroad, from home, absent 2 = **extinguished**, ended, finished, dead, exhausted, expired, used up, at an end **OPPOSITE:** alight 3 = **in bloom**, opening, open, flowering, blooming, in flower, in full bloom 4 = **available**, on sale, in the shops, to be had, purchasable

5 = **revealed**, exposed, common knowledge, public knowledge, (out) in the open **OPPOSITE:** kept secret
▷ VERB 6 = **expose**

outbreak 1 = **eruption**, burst, explosion, epidemic, rash, outburst, flare-up, upsurge 2 = **onset**, beginning, outset, opening, dawn, commencement

outburst 1 = **explosion**, surge, outbreak, eruption, flare-up 2 = **fit**, flare-up, eruption, spasm, outpouring

outcome = **result**, end, consequence, conclusion, payoff (*informal*), upshot

outcry = **protest**, complaint, objection, dissent, outburst, clamour, uproar, commotion

outdated = **old-fashioned**, dated, obsolete, out of date, passé, archaic, unfashionable, antiquated **OPPOSITE:** modern

outdoor = **open-air**, outside, out-of-door(s), alfresco **OPPOSITE:** indoor

outer 1 = **external**, outside, outward, exterior, exposed, outermost **OPPOSITE:** inner 2 = **surface** 3 = **outlying**, distant, provincial, out-of-the-way, peripheral, far-flung **OPPOSITE:** central

outfit 1 = **costume**, dress, clothes, clothing, suit, get-up (*informal*), kit, ensemble 2 (*informal*) = **group**, company,

o

team, party, unit, crowd, squad, organization

outgoing 1 = **leaving**, former, previous, retiring, withdrawing, prior, departing, erstwhile **OPPOSITE:** incoming 2 = **sociable**, open, social, warm, friendly, expansive, affable, extrovert **OPPOSITE:** reserved

outgoings = **expenses**, costs, payments, expenditure, overheads, outlay

outing = **journey**, run, trip, tour, expedition, excursion, spin (*informal*), jaunt

outlaw NOUN 1 = **bandit**, criminal, thief, robber, fugitive, outcast, felon, highwayman ▷ VERB 2 = **ban**, bar, veto, forbid, exclude, prohibit, disallow, proscribe **OPPOSITE:** legalise 3 = **banish**, put a price on (someone's) head

outlet 1 = **shop**, store, supermarket, market, boutique, emporium, hypermarket 2 = **channel**, release, medium, avenue, vent, conduit 3 = **pipe**, opening, channel, exit, duct

outline NOUN 1 = **summary**, review, résumé, rundown, synopsis, précis, thumbnail sketch, recapitulation 2 = **shape**, lines, form, figure, profile, silhouette, configuration, contour(s) ▷ VERB 3 = **summarize**, draft,

plan, trace, sketch (in), sum up, encapsulate, delineate 4 = **silhouette**, etch

outlook 1 = **attitude**, opinion, position, approach, mood, perspective, point of view, stance 2 = **prospect(s)**, future, expectations, forecast, prediction, probability, prognosis

out of date 1 = **old-fashioned**, dated, outdated, obsolete, démodé (*French*), antiquated, outmoded, passé **OPPOSITE:** modern 2 = **invalid**, expired, lapsed, void, null and void, dead (~*data*)

output = **production**, manufacture, manufacturing, yield, productivity

outrage NOUN 1 = **indignation**, shock, anger, rage, fury, hurt, resentment, scorn ▷ VERB 2 = **offend**, shock, upset, wound, insult, infuriate, incense, madden

outrageous 1 = **atrocious**, shocking, terrible, offensive, appalling, cruel, savage, horrifying **OPPOSITE:** mild 2 = **unreasonable**, unfair, steep (*informal*), shocking, extravagant, scandalous, preposterous, unwarranted **OPPOSITE:** reasonable

outright ADJECTIVE 1 = **absolute**, complete, total, perfect, sheer, thorough, unconditional, unqualified

2 = **definite**, clear, certain, flat, absolute, black-and-white, straightforward, unequivocal ▷ ADVERB **3** = **openly**, frankly, plainly, overtly, candidly, unreservedly, unhesitatingly, forthrightly **4** = **absolutely**, completely, totally, fully, entirely, thoroughly, wholly, utterly

outset = **beginning**, start, opening, onset, inauguration, inception, commencement, kickoff (*informal*) **OPPOSITE:** finish

outside ADJECTIVE **1** = **external**, outer, exterior, outward, extraneous **OPPOSITE:** inner **2** = **remote**, small, unlikely, slight, slim, distant, faint, marginal ▷ ADVERB **3** = **outdoors**, out of the house, out-of-doors ▷ NOUN **4** = **exterior**, face, front, covering, skin, surface, shell, coating

> **USAGE NOTE**
> The use of *outside of* and *inside of*, although fairly common, is generally thought to be incorrect or nonstandard: *She waits outside* (not *outside of*) *the school*.

outsider = **stranger**, incomer, visitor, newcomer, intruder, interloper, odd one out

outskirts = **edge**, boundary, suburbs, fringe, perimeter, periphery, suburbia, environs

outspan (*S African*) = **relax**, chill out (*slang, chiefly US*), take it easy, loosen up, put your feet up

outspoken = **forthright**, open, frank, straightforward, blunt, explicit, upfront (*informal*), unequivocal **OPPOSITE:** reserved

outstanding 1 = **excellent**, good, great, important, special, fine, brilliant, impressive, booshit (*Austral slang*), exo (*Austral slang*), sik (*Austral slang*), rad (*informal*), phat (*slang*), schmick (*Austral informal*) **OPPOSITE:** mediocre **2** = **unpaid**, remaining, due, pending, payable, unsettled, uncollected **3** = **undone**, left, omitted, unfinished, unfulfilled, unperformed

outward = **apparent**, seeming, surface, ostensible **OPPOSITE:** inward

outwardly = **apparently**, externally, seemingly, it seems that, on the surface, it appears that, ostensibly, on the face of it

outweigh = **override**, cancel (out), eclipse, offset, compensate for, supersede, neutralize, counterbalance

oval = **elliptical**, egg-shaped, ovoid

ovation = **applause**, hand, cheers, praise, tribute, acclaim, clapping, accolade **OPPOSITE:** derision

over PREPOSITION **1** = **above**, on top of **2** = **on top of**, on,

o

across, upon **3 = across**, (looking) onto **4 = more than**, above, exceeding, in excess of, upwards of **5 = about**, regarding, relating to, concerning, apropos of
▷ **ADVERB 6 = above**, overhead, in the sky, on high, aloft, up above **7 = extra**, more, further, beyond, additional, in addition, surplus, in excess
▷ **ADJECTIVE 8 = finished**, done (with), through, ended, closed, past, completed, complete

overall ADJECTIVE 1 = total, full, whole, general, complete, entire, global, comprehensive
▷ **ADVERB 2 = in general**, generally, mostly, all things considered, on average, on the whole, predominantly, in the main

overcome 1 = defeat, beat, conquer, master, overwhelm, subdue, rout, overpower **2 = conquer**, beat, master, subdue, triumph over, vanquish

overdue 1 = delayed, belated, late, behind schedule, tardy, unpunctual, behindhand **OPPOSITE:** early **2 = unpaid**, owing

overflow VERB 1 = spill over, well over, run over, pour over, bubble over, brim over
▷ **NOUN 2 = flood**, spilling over **3 = surplus**, extra, excess, overspill, overabundance, additional people *or* things

overhaul VERB 1 = check, service, maintain, examine, restore, tune (up), repair, go over **2 = overtake**, pass, leave behind, catch up with, get past, outstrip, get ahead of, outdistance
▷ **NOUN 3 = check**, service, examination, going-over (*informal*), inspection, once-over (*informal*), checkup, reconditioning

overhead ADJECTIVE 1 = raised, suspended, elevated, aerial, overhanging
▷ **ADVERB 2 = above**, in the sky, on high, aloft, up above **OPPOSITE:** underneath

overheads = running costs, expenses, outgoings, operating costs

overlook 1 = look over *or* **out on**, have a view of **2 = miss**, forget, neglect, omit, disregard, pass over **OPPOSITE:** notice **3 = ignore**, excuse, forgive, pardon, disregard, condone, turn a blind eye to, wink at

overpower 1 = overcome, master, overwhelm, overthrow, subdue, quell, subjugate, prevail over **2 = defeat**, crush, triumph over, vanquish **3 = overwhelm**, overcome, bowl over (*informal*), stagger

override 1 = outweigh, eclipse, supersede, take precedence over, prevail over **2 = overrule**, cancel, overturn, repeal, rescind,

annul, nullify, countermand
3 = ignore, reject, discount, overlook, disregard, pass over, take no notice of

overrun 1 = overwhelm, attack, assault, occupy, raid, invade, penetrate, rout **2 = spread over**, overwhelm, choke, swamp, infest, inundate, permeate, swarm over **3 = exceed**, go beyond, surpass, overshoot, run over *or* on

overshadow 1 = spoil, ruin, mar, wreck, blight, crool *or* cruel (*Austral slang*), mess up, put a damper on **2 = outshine**, eclipse, surpass, dwarf, tower above. leave *or* put in the shade

overt = open, obvious, plain, public, manifest, blatant, observable, undisguised **OPPOSITE:** hidden

overtake 1 = pass, leave behind, overhaul, catch up with, get past, outdistance, go by *or* past **2 = outdo**, top, exceed, eclipse, surpass, outstrip, get the better of, outclass **3 = befall**, hit, happen to, catch off guard, catch unawares **4 = engulf**, overwhelm, hit, strike, swamp, envelop, swallow up

overthrow VERB **1 = defeat**, overcome, conquer, bring down, oust, topple, rout, overpower **OPPOSITE:** uphold ▷ NOUN **2 = downfall**, fall, defeat, collapse, destruction,

ousting, undoing, unseating **OPPOSITE:** preservation

overturn 1 = tip over, topple, upturn, capsize, upend, keel over, overbalance **2 = knock over** *or* **down**, upturn, tip over, upend **3 = reverse**, change, cancel, abolish, overthrow, set aside, repeal, quash **4 = overthrow**, defeat, destroy, overcome, bring down, oust, topple, depose

overweight = fat, heavy, stout, hefty, plump, bulky, chunky, chubby **OPPOSITE:** underweight

overwhelm 1 = overcome, devastate, stagger, bowl over (*informal*), knock (someone) for six (*informal*), sweep (someone) off his *or* her feet, take (someone's) breath away **2 = destroy**, defeat, overcome, crush, massacre, conquer, wipe out, overthrow

overwhelming 1 = overpowering, strong, powerful, towering, stunning, crushing, devastating, shattering **OPPOSITE:** negligible **2 = vast**, huge, massive, enormous, tremendous, immense, very large **OPPOSITE:** insignificant

owe = be in debt (to), be in arrears (to), be overdrawn (by), be obligated *or* indebted (to)

owing
▷ PHRASES: owing to = because of, thanks to, as a result of, on account of, by reason of

own DETERMINER 1 = **personal**,
special, private, individual,
particular, exclusive
▷ VERB 2 = **possess**, have,
keep, hold, enjoy, retain, be
in possession of, have to your
name
owner = **possessor**, holder,
proprietor, titleholder, landlord
or landlady
ownership = **possession**,
occupation, tenure, dominion

pace NOUN 1 = **speed**, rate,
tempo, velocity 2 = **step**, walk,
stride, tread, gait 3 = **footstep**,
step, stride
▷ VERB 4 = **stride**, walk, pound,
patrol, march up and down
pack VERB 1 = **package**, load,
store, bundle, stow 2 = **cram**,
crowd, press, fill, stuff, jam, ram,
compress
▷ NOUN 3 = **packet**, box,
package, carton 4 = **bundle**,
parcel, load, burden, rucksack,
knapsack, back pack, kitbag
5 = **group**, crowd, company,
band, troop, gang, bunch, mob
▷ PHRASES: **pack someone
off** = **send away**, dismiss,
send packing (*informal*) ▶ **pack
something in** 1 = **resign from**,
leave, give up, quit (*informal*),
chuck (*informal*), jack in (*informal*)
2 = **stop**, give up, kick (*informal*),
cease, chuck (*Brit & NZ informal*)
package NOUN 1 = **parcel**,
box, container, packet, carton
2 = **collection**, lot, unit,
combination, compilation
▷ VERB 3 = **pack**, box, parcel (up)

packet 1 = **container**, box, package, carton 2 = **package**, parcel 3 (*slang*) = **a fortune**, a bomb (*Brit slang*), a pile (*informal*), a small fortune, a tidy sum (*informal*), a king's ransom (*informal*), top whack (*informal*)

pact = **agreement**, alliance, treaty, deal, understanding, bargain, covenant

pad¹ NOUN 1 = **wad**, dressing, pack, padding, compress, wadding 2 = **cushion**, filling, stuffing, pillow, bolster, upholstery 3 = **notepad**, block, notebook, jotter, writing pad 4 (*slang*) = **home**, flat, apartment, place, bachelor apartment (*Canad*) 5 = **paw**, foot, sole
▷ VERB 6 = **pack**, fill, protect, stuff, cushion

pad² = **sneak**, creep, steal, go barefoot

padding 1 = **filling**, stuffing, packing, wadding 2 = **waffle** (*informal, chiefly Brit*), hot air (*informal*), verbiage, wordiness, verbosity

paddle¹ NOUN 1 = **oar**, scull
▷ VERB 2 = **row**, pull, scull

paddle² = **wade**, splash (about), slop

pagan NOUN 1 = **heathen**, infidel, polytheist, idolater
▷ ADJECTIVE 2 = **heathen**, infidel, polytheistic, idolatrous

page¹ = **folio**, side, leaf, sheet

page² NOUN 1 = **attendant**, pageboy 2 = **servant**, attendant, squire, pageboy
▷ VERB 3 = **call**, summon, send for

pain NOUN 1 = **suffering**, discomfort, hurt, irritation, tenderness, soreness 2 = **ache**, stinging, aching, throb, throbbing, pang, twinge 3 = **sorrow**, suffering, torture, distress, despair, misery, agony, sadness
▷ PLURAL NOUN 4 = **trouble**, effort, care, bother, diligence
▷ VERB 5 = **distress**, hurt, torture, grieve, torment, sadden, agonize, cut to the quick 6 = **hurt**

painful 1 = **sore**, smarting, aching, tender OPPOSITE: painless 2 = **distressing**, unpleasant, grievous, distasteful, agonizing, disagreeable OPPOSITE: pleasant 3 = **difficult**, arduous, trying, hard, troublesome, laborious OPPOSITE: easy

painfully = **distressingly**, clearly, sadly, unfortunately, dreadfully

paint NOUN 1 = **colouring**, colour, stain, dye, tint, pigment, emulsion
▷ VERB 2 = **colour**, cover, coat, stain, whitewash, daub, distemper, apply paint to 3 = **depict**, draw, portray, picture, represent, sketch

pair NOUN 1 = **set** 2 = **couple**, brace, duo
▷ VERB 3 *often with* **off** = **team**, match (up), join, couple, twin, bracket

> **USAGE NOTE**
> Like other collective nouns, *pair* takes a singular or a plural verb according to whether it is seen as a unit or as a collection of two things: *the pair are said to dislike each other; a pair of good shoes is essential.*

pal (*informal*) = **friend**, companion, mate (*informal*), buddy (*informal*), comrade, chum (*informal*), crony, cobber (*Austral & NZ old-fashioned informal*), E hoa (*NZ*)

pale ADJECTIVE 1 = **light**, soft, faded, subtle, muted, bleached, pastel, light-coloured 2 = **dim**, weak, faint, feeble, thin, wan, watery 3 = **white**, pasty, bleached, wan, colourless, pallid, ashen OPPOSITE: rosy-cheeked
▷ VERB 4 = **become pale**, blanch, whiten, go white, lose colour

pamper = **spoil**, indulge, pet, cosset, coddle, mollycoddle

pamphlet = **booklet**, leaflet, brochure, circular, tract

pan¹ NOUN 1 = **pot**, container, saucepan
▷ VERB 2 (*informal*) = **criticize**, knock, slam (*slang*), censure,

tear into (*informal*) 3 = **sift out**, look for, search for

pan² = **move along** *or* **across**, follow, track, sweep

panic NOUN 1 = **fear**, alarm, terror, anxiety, hysteria, fright, trepidation, a flap (*informal*)
▷ VERB 2 = **go to pieces**, become hysterical, lose your nerve 3 = **alarm**, scare, unnerve

panorama 1 = **view**, prospect, vista 2 = **survey**, perspective, overview, overall picture

pant = **puff**, blow, breathe, gasp, wheeze, heave

pants 1 (*Brit*) = **underpants**, briefs, drawers, knickers, panties, boxer shorts, broekies (*S African*), underdaks (*Austral slang*) 2 (*US*) = **trousers**, slacks

paper NOUN 1 = **newspaper**, daily, journal, gazette 2 = **essay**, article, treatise, dissertation 3 = **examination**, test, exam 4 = **report**
▷ PLURAL NOUN 5 = **letters**, records, documents, file, diaries, archive, paperwork, dossier 6 = **documents**, records, certificates, identification, deeds, identity papers, I.D. (*informal*)
▷ VERB 7 = **wallpaper**, hang

parade NOUN 1 = **procession**, march, pageant, cavalcade 2 = **show**, display, spectacle
▷ VERB 3 = **march**, process, promenade 4 = **flaunt**, display,

exhibit, show off (*informal*)
5 = **strut**, show off (*informal*),
swagger, swank

paradigm = **model**, example,
pattern, ideal

paradise 1 = **heaven**, Promised
Land, Happy Valley (*Islam*),
Elysian fields 2 = **bliss**, delight,
heaven, felicity, utopia

paradox = **contradiction**,
puzzle, anomaly, enigma,
oddity

paragraph = **section**, part,
item, passage, clause,
subdivision

parallel NOUN 1 = **equivalent**,
counterpart, match, equal,
twin, analogue **OPPOSITE:**
opposite 2 = **similarity**,
comparison, analogy,
resemblance, likeness
OPPOSITE: difference
▷ ADJECTIVE 3 = **matching**,
corresponding, like, similar,
resembling, analogous
OPPOSITE: different
4 = **equidistant**, alongside,
side by side **OPPOSITE:**
divergent

paralyse 1 = **disable**, cripple,
lame, incapacitate 2 = **freeze**,
stun, numb, petrify, halt,
immobilize 3 = **immobilize**,
freeze, halt, disable, cripple,
incapacitate, bring to a
standstill

paralysis 1 = **immobility**, palsy
2 = **standstill**, breakdown,
stoppage, halt

parameter (*informal usually
plural*) = **limit**, restriction,
framework, limitation,
specification

paramount = **principal**, prime,
first, chief, main, primary,
supreme, cardinal **OPPOSITE:**
secondary

paranoid 1 (*informal*)
= **suspicious**, worried, nervous,
fearful, antsy (*informal*)
2 = **obsessive**, disturbed, manic,
neurotic, psychotic, deluded,
paranoiac

parasite = **sponger** (*informal*),
leech, hanger-on, scrounger
(*informal*), bloodsucker
(*informal*), quandong (*Austral
slang*)

parcel NOUN 1 = **package**, case,
box, pack, bundle
▷ VERB 2 *often with* **up** = **wrap**,
pack, package, tie up, do up,
gift-wrap, box up, fasten
together

pardon VERB 1 = **acquit**, let off
(*informal*), exonerate, absolve
OPPOSITE: punish
▷ NOUN 2 = **forgiveness**,
absolution **OPPOSITE:**
condemnation 3 = **acquittal**,
amnesty, exoneration
OPPOSITE: punishment
▷ PHRASES: pardon me = **forgive
me**, excuse me

parent = **father** *or* **mother**,
sire, progenitor, procreator,
old (*Austral & NZ informal*), oldie
(*Austral informal*), patriarch

parish 1 = **district**, community 2 = **community**, flock, church, congregation

park 1 = **recreation ground**, garden, playground, pleasure garden, playpark, domain (NZ), forest park (NZ) 2 = **parkland**, grounds, estate, lawns, woodland, grassland 3 = **field**, pitch, playing field

parliament 1 = **assembly**, council, congress, senate, convention, legislature 2 = **sitting**

parliamentary = **governmental**, legislative, law-making

parlour or (US) **parlor** 1 (old-fashioned) = **sitting room**, lounge, living room, drawing room, front room 2 = **establishment**, shop, store, salon

parody NOUN 1 = **takeoff** (informal), satire, caricature, send-up (Brit informal), spoof (informal), skit, burlesque, piss-take (informal)
▷ VERB 2 = **take off** (informal), caricature, send up (Brit informal), burlesque, satirize, do a takeoff of (informal)

parrot = **repeat**, echo, imitate, copy, mimic

parry 1 = **evade**, avoid, dodge, sidestep 2 = **ward off**, block, deflect, repel, rebuff, repulse

parson = **clergyman**, minister, priest, vicar, preacher, pastor, cleric, churchman

part NOUN 1 = **piece**, share, proportion, percentage, bit, section, scrap, portion OPPOSITE: entirety 2 often plural = **region**, area, district, neighbourhood, quarter, vicinity 3 = **component**, bit, unit, constituent 4 = **branch**, division, office, section, wing, subdivision, subsection 5 = **organ**, member, limb 6 (Theatre) = **role**, representation, persona, portrayal, depiction, character part 7 (Theatre) = **lines**, words, script, dialogue 8 = **side**, behalf
▷ VERB 9 = **divide**, separate, break, tear, split, rend, detach, sever OPPOSITE: join 10 = **part company**, separate, split up OPPOSITE: meet
▷ PHRASES: in good part = **good-naturedly**, well, cheerfully, without offence

partial 1 = **incomplete**, unfinished, imperfect, uncompleted OPPOSITE: complete 2 = **biased**, prejudiced, discriminatory, partisan, unfair, one-sided, unjust OPPOSITE: unbiased

partially = **partly**, somewhat, in part, not wholly, fractionally, incompletely

participant = **participator**, member, player, contributor, stakeholder

participate = **take part**, be involved, perform, join, partake OPPOSITE: refrain from

p

participation = taking part, contribution, involvement, sharing in, joining in, partaking

particle = bit, piece, scrap, grain, shred, mite, jot, speck

particular ADJECTIVE
1 = specific, special, exact, precise, distinct, peculiar OPPOSITE: general 2 = special, exceptional, notable, uncommon, marked, unusual, remarkable, singular 3 = fussy, demanding, fastidious, choosy (informal), picky (informal), finicky, pernickety (informal), nit-picky (informal) OPPOSITE: indiscriminate
▷ NOUN 4 usually plural = detail, fact, feature, item, circumstance, specification

particularly 1 = specifically, expressly, explicitly, especially, in particular, distinctly
2 = especially, notably, unusually, exceptionally, singularly, uncommonly

parting 1 = farewell, goodbye 2 = division, breaking, split, separation, rift, rupture

partisan ADJECTIVE
1 = prejudiced, one-sided, biased, partial, sectarian OPPOSITE: unbiased
▷ NOUN 2 = supporter, devotee, adherent, upholder OPPOSITE: opponent
3 = underground fighter, guerrilla, freedom fighter, resistance fighter

partition NOUN 1 = screen, wall, barrier 2 = division, separation, segregation
▷ VERB 3 = separate, screen, divide

partly = partially, somewhat, slightly OPPOSITE: completely
USAGE NOTE
Partly and partially are to some extent interchangeable, but partly should be used when referring to a part or parts of something: the building is partly (not partially) made of stone, while partially is preferred for the meaning to some extent: his mother is partially (not partly) sighted.

partner 1 = spouse, consort, significant other (US informal), mate, husband or wife, plus-one (informal) 2 = companion, ally, colleague, associate, mate, comrade 3 = associate, colleague, collaborator

partnership 1 = cooperation, alliance, sharing, union, connection, participation, copartnership 2 = company, firm, house, interest, society, cooperative

party 1 = faction, set, side, league, camp, clique, coterie 2 = get-together (informal), celebration, do (informal), gathering, function, reception, festivity, social gathering
3 = group, team, band,

p

company, unit, squad, crew, gang

pass VERB 1 = **go by** or **past**, overtake, drive past, lap, leave behind, pull ahead of **OPPOSITE:** stop 2 = **go**, move, travel, progress, flow, proceed 3 = **run**, move, stroke 4 = **give**, hand, send, transfer, deliver, convey 5 = **be left**, come, be bequeathed, be inherited by 6 = **kick**, hit, loft, head, lob 7 = **elapse**, progress, go by, lapse, wear on, go past, tick by 8 = **end**, go, cease, blow over 9 = **spend**, fill, occupy, while away 10 = **exceed**, beat, overtake, go beyond, surpass, outstrip, outdo 11 = **be successful in**, qualify (in), succeed (in), graduate (in), get through, do, gain a pass (in) **OPPOSITE:** fail 12 = **approve**, accept, decree, enact, ratify, ordain, legislate (for) **OPPOSITE:** ban ▷ NOUN 13 = **licence**, ticket, permit, passport, warrant, authorization 14 = **gap**, route, canyon, gorge, ravine ▷ PHRASES: **pass away** or **on** (euphemistic) = **die**, pass on, expire, pass over, snuff it (informal), kick the bucket (slang), shuffle off this mortal coil, cark it (Austral & NZ informal) ▶ **pass out** (informal) = **faint**, black out (informal), lose consciousness, become unconscious ▶ **pass something over** = **disregard**, ignore, not dwell on ▶ **pass something up** (informal) = **miss**, let slip, decline, neglect, forgo, abstain from, give (something) a miss (informal)

| **USAGE NOTE**
The past participle of *pass* is sometimes wrongly spelt *past*: *the time for recriminations has passed* (not *past*).

passage 1 = **corridor**, hall, lobby, vestibule 2 = **alley**, way, close (*Brit*), course, road, channel, route, path 3 = **extract**, reading, piece, section, text, excerpt, quotation 4 = **journey**, crossing, trip, trek, voyage 5 = **safe-conduct**, right to travel, freedom to travel, permission to travel

passenger = **traveller**, rider, fare, commuter, fare payer

passer-by = **bystander**, witness, observer, viewer, spectator, looker-on, watcher, onlooker

passing 1 = **momentary**, fleeting, short-lived, transient, ephemeral, brief, temporary, transitory 2 = **superficial**, short, quick, glancing, casual, summary, cursory, perfunctory

passion 1 = **love**, desire, lust, infatuation, ardour 2 = **emotion**, feeling, fire, heat, excitement, intensity, warmth, zeal **OPPOSITE:** indifference

3 = mania, enthusiasm, obsession, bug (*informal*), craving, fascination, craze
4 = rage, fit, storm, anger, fury, outburst, frenzy, paroxysm
passionate 1 = emotional, eager, strong, intense, fierce, ardent, fervent, heartfelt **OPPOSITE:** unemotional
2 = loving, erotic, hot, ardent, amorous, lustful **OPPOSITE:** cold
passive 1 = submissive, compliant, receptive, docile, quiescent **OPPOSITE:** spirited
2 = inactive, uninvolved **OPPOSITE:** active
past NOUN 1 = former times, long ago, days gone by, the olden days **OPPOSITE:** future
2 = background, life, history, past life, life story, career to date
▷ **ADJECTIVE 3 = former**, early, previous, ancient, bygone, olden **OPPOSITE:** future **4 = previous**, former, one-time, ex- **5 = last**, previous **6 = over**, done, ended, finished, gone
▷ **PREPOSITION 7 = after**, beyond, later than **8 = by**, across, in front of
▷ **ADVERB 9 = on**, by, along

> **USAGE NOTE**
> The past participle of *pass* is sometimes wrongly spelt *past*: *the time for recrimination has passed* (not *past*).

paste NOUN 1 = adhesive, glue, cement, gum **2 = purée**, pâté, spread

▷ **VERB 3 = stick**, glue, cement, gum
pastel = pale, light, soft, delicate, muted **OPPOSITE:** bright
pastime = activity, game, entertainment, hobby, recreation, amusement, diversion
pastor = clergyman, minister, priest, vicar, parson, rector, curate, churchman
pastoral 1 = ecclesiastical, priestly, ministerial, clerical
2 = rustic, country, rural, bucolic
pasture = grassland, grass, meadow, grazing
pat VERB 1 = stroke, touch, tap, pet, caress, fondle
▷ **NOUN 2 = tap**, stroke, clap
patch NOUN 1 = spot, bit, scrap, shred, small piece **2 = plot**, area, ground, land, tract
3 = reinforcement, piece of fabric, piece of cloth, piece of material, piece sewn on
▷ **VERB 4** *often with* **up = sew (up)**, mend, repair, reinforce, stitch (up) **5** *often with* **up = mend**, cover, reinforce
patent NOUN 1 = copyright, licence, franchise, registered trademark
▷ **ADJECTIVE 2 = obvious**, apparent, evident, clear, glaring, manifest
path 1 = way, road, walk, track, trail, avenue, footpath, berm (*NZ*) **2 = route**, way, course,

direction 3 = **course**, way, road, route

pathetic = **sad**, moving, touching, affecting, distressing, tender, poignant, plaintive **OPPOSITE:** funny

patience 1 = **forbearance**, tolerance, serenity, restraint, calmness, sufferance **OPPOSITE:** impatience 2 = **endurance**, resignation, submission, fortitude, long-suffering, perseverance, stoicism, constancy

patient NOUN 1 = **sick person**, case, sufferer, invalid
▷ ADJECTIVE 2 = **forbearing**, understanding, forgiving, mild, tolerant, indulgent, lenient, even-tempered **OPPOSITE:** impatient 3 = **long-suffering**, resigned, calm, enduring, philosophical, persevering, stoical, submissive

patriot = **nationalist**, loyalist, chauvinist

patriotic = **nationalistic**, loyal, chauvinistic, jingoistic

patriotism = **nationalism**, jingoism

patrol VERB 1 = **police**, guard, keep watch (on), inspect, safeguard, keep guard (on)
▷ NOUN 2 = **guard**, watch, watchman, sentinel, patrolman

patron 1 = **supporter**, friend, champion, sponsor, backer, helper, benefactor, philanthropist 2 = **customer**, client, buyer, frequenter, shopper, habitué

patronage = **support**, promotion, sponsorship, backing, help, aid, assistance

pattern 1 = **order**, plan, system, method, sequence 2 = **design**, arrangement, motif, figure, device, decoration 3 = **plan**, design, original, guide, diagram, stencil, template

pause VERB 1 = **stop briefly**, delay, break, wait, rest, halt, cease, interrupt **OPPOSITE:** continue
▷ NOUN 2 = **stop**, break, interval, rest, gap, halt, respite, lull **OPPOSITE:** continuance

pave = **cover**, floor, surface, concrete, tile

paw (*informal*) = **manhandle**, grab, maul, molest, handle roughly

pay VERB 1 = **reward**, compensate, reimburse, recompense, requite, remunerate, front up 2 = **spend**, give, fork out (*informal*), remit, shell out (*informal*) 3 = **settle** 4 = **bring in**, earn, return, net, yield 5 = **be profitable**, make money, make a return 6 = **benefit**, repay, be worthwhile 7 = **give**, extend, present with, grant, hand out, bestow
▷ NOUN 8 = **wages**, income, payment, earnings, fee, reward, salary, allowance

▷ **PHRASES: pay off = succeed**, work, be effective ▶ **pay something off = settle**, clear, square, discharge, pay in full (*informal*)

payable = due, outstanding, owed, owing

payment 1 = **remittance**, advance, deposit, premium, instalment, e-payment 2 = **settlement**, paying, discharge, remittance 3 = **wages**, fee, reward, hire, remuneration

peace 1 = **truce**, ceasefire, treaty, armistice **OPPOSITE:** war 2 = **stillness**, rest, quiet, silence, calm, hush, tranquillity, seclusion 3 = **serenity**, calm, composure, contentment, repose, equanimity, peacefulness, harmoniousness 4 = **harmony**, accord, agreement, concord

peaceful 1 = **at peace**, friendly, harmonious, amicable, nonviolent **OPPOSITE:** hostile 2 = **peace-loving**, conciliatory, peaceable, unwarlike **OPPOSITE:** belligerent 3 = **calm**, still, quiet, tranquil, restful, chilled (*informal*) **OPPOSITE:** agitated 4 = **serene**, placid, undisturbed

peak NOUN 1 = **high point**, crown, climax, culmination, zenith, acme 2 = **point**, top, tip, summit, brow, crest, pinnacle, apex

▷ **VERB** 3 = **culminate**, climax, come to a head

peasant = rustic, countryman

peck VERB 1 = **pick**, hit, strike, tap, poke, jab, prick 2 = **kiss**, plant a kiss, give someone a smacker, give someone a peck *or* kiss

▷ **NOUN** 3 = **kiss**, smacker, osculation (*rare*)

peculiar 1 = **odd**, strange, unusual, bizarre, funny, extraordinary, curious, weird **OPPOSITE:** ordinary 2 = **special**, particular, unique, characteristic **OPPOSITE:** common

peddle = sell, trade, push (*informal*), market, hawk, flog (*slang*)

pedestrian NOUN 1 = **walker**, foot-traveller **OPPOSITE:** driver ▷ **ADJECTIVE** 2 = **dull**, ordinary, boring, commonplace, mundane, mediocre, banal, prosaic, half-pie (*NZ informal*) **OPPOSITE:** exciting

pedigree MODIFIER 1 = **purebred**, thoroughbred, full-blooded ▷ **NOUN** 2 = **lineage**, family, line, race, stock, blood, breed, descent

peel NOUN 1 = **rind**, skin, peeling ▷ **VERB** 2 = **skin**, scale, strip, pare, shuck, flake off, take the skin *or* rind off

peep VERB 1 = **peek**, look, eyeball (*slang*), sneak a look, steal a look

P

▷ **NOUN** 2 = **look**, glimpse, peek, look-see (slang)

peer¹ 1 = **noble**, lord, aristocrat, nobleman 2 = **equal**, like, fellow, contemporary, compeer

peer² = **squint**, look, spy, gaze, scan, inspect, peep, peek

peg NOUN 1 = **pin**, spike, rivet, skewer, dowel, spigot
▷ **VERB** 2 = **fasten**, join, fix, secure, attach

pen¹ = **write (down)**, draft, compose, pencil, draw up, scribble, take down, inscribe

pen² NOUN 1 = **enclosure**, pound, fold, cage, coop, hutch, sty
▷ **VERB** 2 = **enclose**, confine, cage, fence in, coop up, hedge in, shut up or in

penalty = **punishment**, price, fine, handicap, forfeit

pending ADJECTIVE
1 = **undecided**, unsettled, in the balance, undetermined
2 = **forthcoming**, imminent, prospective, impending, in the wind
▷ **PREPOSITION** 3 = **awaiting**, until, waiting for, till

penetrate 1 = **pierce**, enter, go through, bore, stab, prick
2 = **grasp**, work out, figure out (informal), comprehend, fathom, decipher, suss (out) (slang), get to the bottom of

penetrating 1 = **sharp**, harsh, piercing, carrying, piping, loud, strident, shrill **OPPOSITE:**

sweet 2 = **pungent** 3 = **piercing**
4 = **intelligent**, quick, sharp, keen, acute, shrewd, astute, perceptive **OPPOSITE:** dull
5 = **perceptive**, sharp, keen **OPPOSITE:** unperceptive

penetration 1 = **piercing**, entry, entrance, puncturing, incision 2 = **entry**, entrance

pension = **allowance**, benefit, welfare, annuity, superannuation

pensioner = **senior citizen**, retired person, retiree (US), old-age pensioner, O.A.P.

people PLURAL NOUN
1 = **persons**, individuals, folk (informal), men and women, humanity, mankind, mortals, the human race 2 = **nation**, public, community, subjects, population, residents, citizens, folk 3 = **race**, tribe 4 = **family**, parents, relations, relatives, folk, folks (informal), clan, kin, rellies (Austral slang)
▷ **VERB** 5 = **inhabit**, occupy, settle, populate, colonize

pepper NOUN 1 = **seasoning**, flavour, spice
▷ **VERB** 2 = **pelt**, hit, shower, blitz, rake, bombard, assail, strafe 3 = **sprinkle**, spot, scatter, dot, fleck, intersperse, speck, spatter

perceive 1 = **see**, notice, note, identify, discover, spot, observe, recognize 2 = **understand**, gather, see, learn, realize, grasp,

comprehend, suss (out) (*slang*)
3 = consider, believe, judge, suppose, rate, deem, adjudge
perception 1 = awareness, understanding, sense, impression, feeling, idea, notion, consciousness
2 = understanding, intelligence, observation, discrimination, insight, sharpness, cleverness, keenness
perch VERB **1 = sit**, rest, balance, settle **2 = place**, put, rest, balance **3 = land**, alight, roost
▷ NOUN **4 = resting place**, post, branch, pole
perennial = continual, lasting, constant, enduring, persistent, abiding, recurrent, incessant
perfect ADJECTIVE **1 = faultless**, correct, pure, impeccable, exemplary, flawless, foolproof OPPOSITE: deficient **2 = excellent**, ideal, supreme, superb, splendid, sublime, superlative **3 = immaculate**, impeccable, flawless, spotless, unblemished OPPOSITE: flawed **4 = complete**, absolute, sheer, utter, consummate, unmitigated OPPOSITE: partial **5 = exact**, true, accurate, precise, correct, faithful, unerring
▷ VERB **6 = improve**, develop, polish, refine OPPOSITE: mar

USAGE NOTE
For most of its meanings, the adjective *perfect* describes an absolute state, so that something either is or is not *perfect*, and cannot be referred to in terms of degree - thus, one thing should not be described as *more perfect* or *less perfect* than another thing. However, when *perfect* is used in the sense of 'excellent in all respects', *more* and *most* are acceptable, for example *the next day the weather was even more perfect*.

perfection = excellence, integrity, superiority, purity, wholeness, sublimity, exquisiteness, faultlessness
perfectly 1 = completely, totally, absolutely, quite, fully, altogether, thoroughly, wholly OPPOSITE: partially **2 = flawlessly**, ideally, wonderfully, superbly, supremely, impeccably, faultlessly OPPOSITE: badly
perform 1 = do, achieve, carry out, complete, fulfil, accomplish, execute, pull off **2 = fulfil**, carry out, execute, discharge **3 = present**, act (out), stage, play, produce, represent, put on, enact **4 = appear on stage**, act
performance 1 = presentation, playing, acting (out), staging, production, exhibition, rendering, portrayal **2 = show**, appearance, concert, gig (*informal*), recital **3 = work**,

acts, conduct, exploits, feats
4 = carrying out, practice,
achievement, execution,
completion, accomplishment,
fulfilment
performer = artiste, player,
Thespian, trouper, actor *or*
actress
perfume 1 = fragrance, scent
2 = scent, smell, fragrance,
bouquet, aroma, odour
perhaps = maybe, possibly,
it may be, it is possible (that),
conceivably, perchance (*archaic*),
feasibly, happen (*Northern
English dialect*)
peril 1 = danger, risk, threat,
hazard, menace, jeopardy,
perilousness **2** *often plural*
= pitfall, problem, risk, hazard
OPPOSITE: safety
perimeter = boundary, edge,
border, bounds, limit, margin,
confines, periphery **OPPOSITE:**
centre
period = time, term, season,
space, run, stretch, spell, phase
periodic = recurrent, regular,
repeated, occasional, cyclical,
sporadic, intermittent
peripheral 1 = secondary,
minor, marginal, irrelevant,
unimportant, incidental,
inessential **2 = outermost**,
outside, external, outer, exterior
perish 1 = die, be killed, expire,
pass away, lose your life, cark
it (*Austral & NZ slang*) **2 = be
destroyed**, fall, decline,

collapse, disappear, vanish
3 = rot, waste away, decay,
disintegrate, decompose,
moulder
perk (*Brit informal*) **= bonus**,
benefit, extra, plus, fringe
benefit, perquisite
permanent 1 = lasting,
constant, enduring, persistent,
eternal, abiding, perpetual,
everlasting **OPPOSITE:**
temporary **2 = long-term**,
established, secure, stable,
steady **OPPOSITE:** temporary
permission = authorization,
sanction, licence, approval,
leave, go-ahead (*informal*),
liberty, consent **OPPOSITE:**
prohibition
permit VERB **1 = allow**, grant,
sanction, let, entitle, license,
authorize, consent to **OPPOSITE:**
forbid **2 = enable**, let, allow,
cause
▷ NOUN **3 = licence**, pass,
document, certificate, passport,
visa, warrant, authorization
OPPOSITE: prohibition
perpetual 1 = everlasting,
permanent, endless, eternal,
lasting, perennial, infinite, never-
ending **OPPOSITE:** temporary
2 = continual, repeated,
constant, endless, continuous,
persistent, recurrent, never-
ending **OPPOSITE:** brief
perpetuate = maintain,
preserve, keep going,
immortalize **OPPOSITE:** end

persecute 1 = victimize, torture, torment, oppress, pick on, ill-treat, maltreat **OPPOSITE:** mollycoddle 2 = harass, bother, annoy, tease, hassle (*informal*), badger, pester **OPPOSITE:** leave alone

persist 1 = continue, last, remain, carry on, keep up, linger 2 = persevere, continue, go on, carry on, keep on, keep going, press on, not give up, crack on (*informal*)

persistence = determination, resolution, grit, endurance, tenacity, perseverance, doggedness, pertinacity

persistent 1 = continuous, constant, repeated, endless, perpetual, continual, never-ending, incessant **OPPOSITE:** occasional 2 = determined, dogged, steady, stubborn, persevering, tireless, tenacious, steadfast **OPPOSITE:** irresolute

person = individual, being, body, human, soul, creature, mortal, man *or* woman
▷ **PHRASES:** in person 1 = personally, yourself 2 = in the flesh, actually, physically, bodily

personal 1 = own, special, private, individual, particular, peculiar 2 = individual, special, particular, exclusive 3 = private 4 = offensive, nasty, insulting, disparaging, derogatory

personality 1 = nature, character, make-up, identity, temperament, disposition, individuality 2 = character, charm, attraction, charisma, magnetism 3 = celebrity, star, notable, household name, famous name, personage, megastar (*informal*)

personally 1 = in your opinion, in your book, for your part, from your own viewpoint, in your own view 2 = by yourself, alone, independently, solely, on your own 3 = individually, specially, subjectively, individualistically 4 = privately, in private, off the record

personnel = employees, people, staff, workers, workforce, human resources, helpers

perspective 1 = outlook, attitude, context, angle, frame of reference 2 = objectivity, proportion, relation, relativity, relative importance

persuade 1 = talk (someone) into, urge, influence, win (someone) over, induce, sway, entice, coax **OPPOSITE:** dissuade 2 = cause, lead, move, influence, motivate, induce, incline, dispose 3 = convince, satisfy, assure, cause to believe

persuasion 1 = urging, inducement, wheedling, enticement, cajolery 2 = belief, views, opinion, party, school, side, camp, faith

p

persuasive = **convincing**, telling, effective, sound, compelling, influential, valid, credible **OPPOSITE:** unconvincing

pervasive = **widespread**, general, common, extensive, universal, prevalent, ubiquitous, rife

perverse 1 = **stubborn**, contrary, dogged, troublesome, rebellious, wayward, intractable, wilful **OPPOSITE:** cooperative 2 = **ill-natured**, cross, surly, fractious, churlish, ill-tempered, stroppy (*Brit slang*), peevish **OPPOSITE:** good-natured 3 = **abnormal**, unhealthy, improper, deviant

pervert VERB 1 = **distort**, abuse, twist, misuse, warp, misrepresent, falsify 2 = **corrupt**, degrade, deprave, debase, debauch, lead astray ▷ NOUN 3 = **deviant**, degenerate, sicko (*informal*), weirdo *or* weirdie (*informal*)

pessimistic = **gloomy**, dark, despairing, bleak, depressed, cynical, hopeless, glum **OPPOSITE:** optimistic

pest 1 = **infection**, bug, insect, plague, epidemic, blight, scourge, pestilence, gogga (*S African informal*) 2 = **nuisance**, trial, pain (*informal*), drag (*informal*), bother, irritation, annoyance, bane

pet ADJECTIVE 1 = **favourite**, favoured, dearest, cherished,

fave (*informal*), dear to your heart ▷ NOUN 2 = **favourite**, treasure, darling, jewel, idol ▷ VERB 3 = **fondle**, pat, stroke, caress 4 = **pamper**, spoil, indulge, cosset, baby, dote on, coddle, mollycoddle 5 (*informal*) = **cuddle**, kiss, snog (*Brit slang*), smooch (*informal*), neck (*informal*), canoodle (*slang*)

petition NOUN 1 = **appeal**, round robin, list of signatures 2 = **entreaty**, appeal, suit, application, request, prayer, plea, solicitation ▷ VERB 3 = **appeal**, plead, ask, pray, beg, solicit, beseech, entreat

petty 1 = **trivial**, insignificant, little, small, slight, trifling, negligible, unimportant **OPPOSITE:** important 2 = **small-minded**, mean, shabby, spiteful, ungenerous, mean-minded **OPPOSITE:** broad-minded

phantom = **spectre**, ghost, spirit, shade (*literary*), spook (*informal*), apparition, wraith, phantasm

phase = **stage**, time, point, position, step, development, period, chapter ▷ PHRASES: **phase something in** = **introduce**, incorporate, ease in, start ▶ **phase something out** = **eliminate**, close, remove, withdraw, pull out, wind up, run down, terminate

p

phenomenal = extraordinary, outstanding, remarkable, fantastic, unusual, marvellous, exceptional, miraculous **OPPOSITE:** unremarkable

phenomenon 1 = **occurrence**, happening, fact, event, incident, circumstance, episode 2 = **wonder**, sensation, exception, miracle, marvel, prodigy, rarity

> **USAGE NOTE**
> Although *phenomena* is often treated as a singular, this is not grammatically correct. *Phenomenon* is the singular form of this word, and *phenomena* the plural; so *several new phenomena were recorded in his notes* is correct, but *that is an interesting phenomena* is not.

philosopher = thinker, theorist, sage, wise man, logician, metaphysician

philosophical or **philosophic** 1 = **theoretical**, abstract, wise, rational, logical, thoughtful, sagacious **OPPOSITE:** practical 2 = **stoical**, calm, composed, cool, collected, serene, tranquil, unruffled **OPPOSITE:** emotional

philosophy 1 = **thought**, knowledge, thinking, reasoning, wisdom, logic, metaphysics 2 = **outlook**, values, principles, convictions, thinking, beliefs, doctrine, ideology

phlegm = mucus, catarrh, sputum, mucous secretion

phone NOUN 1 = **telephone**, blower (*informal*), smartphone, mobile (phone), landline, iPhone®, cellphone *or* cellular phone (*US & Canad*), camera phone, handset, Blackberry, picture phone 2 = **call**, ring (*informal, chiefly Brit*), tinkle (*Brit informal*)
▷ VERB 3 = **call**, telephone, ring (up) (*informal, chiefly Brit*), give someone a call, give someone a ring (*informal, chiefly Brit*), make a call, conference call, Skype®, video call, get on the blower (*informal*), give someone a tinkle (*Brit informal*), video phone

photograph NOUN 1 = **picture**, photo (*informal*), shot, print, snap (*informal*), snapshot, selfie (*informal*), transparency, JPEG, thumbnail, avatar
▷ VERB 2 = **take a picture of**, record, film, shoot, snap (*informal*), take (someone's) picture

photographic 1 = **pictorial**, visual, graphic, cinematic, filmic 2 = **accurate**, exact, precise, faithful, retentive

phrase NOUN 1 = **expression**, saying, remark, construction, quotation, maxim, idiom, adage
▷ VERB 2 = **express**, say, word, put, voice, communicate, convey, put into words

physical 1 = **corporal**, fleshly, bodily, corporeal 2 = **earthly**, fleshly, mortal, incarnate 3 = **material**, real, substantial, natural, solid, tangible, palpable

physician = **doctor**, doc (*informal*), medic (*informal*), general practitioner, medical practitioner, doctor of medicine, G.P., M.D.

pick VERB 1 = **select**, choose, identify, elect, nominate, specify, opt for, single out, flag up OPPOSITE: reject 2 = **gather**, pull, collect, take in, harvest, pluck, garner 3 = **provoke**, start, cause, stir up, incite, instigate 4 = **open**, force, crack (*informal*), break into, break open
▷ NOUN 5 = **choice**, decision, option, selection, preference 6 = **best**, prime, finest, elect, elite, cream, jewel in the crown, the crème de la crème
▷ PHRASES: **pick on someone** 1 = **torment**, bully, bait, tease, get at (*informal*), badger, persecute, hector 2 = **choose**, select, prefer, elect, single out, fix on, settle upon ▶ **pick something or someone out** = **identify**, recognize, distinguish, perceive, discriminate, make someone or something out, tell someone or something apart ▶ **pick something up** 1 = **learn**, master, acquire, get the hang of (*informal*), become proficient in 2 = **obtain**, get, find, buy, discover, purchase, acquire, locate ▶ **pick something or someone up** 1 = **lift**, raise, gather, take up, grasp, uplift 2 = **collect**, get, call for ▶ **pick up** 1 = **improve**, recover, rally, get better, bounce back, make progress, perk up, turn the corner 2 = **recover**, improve, rally, get better, mend, turn the corner, be on the mend, take a turn for the better

picket VERB 1 = **blockade**, boycott, demonstrate outside
▷ NOUN 2 = **demonstration**, strike, blockade 3 = **protester**, demonstrator, picketer 4 = **lookout**, watch, guard, patrol, sentry, sentinel 5 = **stake**, post, pale, paling, upright, stanchion

pickle VERB 1 = **preserve**, marinade, steep
▷ NOUN 2 = **chutney**, relish, piccalilli 3 (*informal*) = **predicament**, fix (*informal*), difficulty, bind (*informal*), jam (*informal*), dilemma, scrape (*informal*), hot water (*informal*), uphill (*S African*)

pick-up = **improvement**, recovery, rise, rally, strengthening, revival, upturn, change for the better

picnic = **excursion**, barbecue, barbie (*informal*), cookout (*US & Canad*), alfresco meal, clambake (*US & Canad*), outdoor meal, outing

picture NOUN 1 = **representation**, drawing, painting, portrait, image, print, illustration, sketch, avatar 2 = **photograph**, photo, still, shot, selfie (*informal*), image, print, frame, slide, JPEG, thumbnail 3 = **film**, movie (*US informal*), flick (*slang*), feature film, motion picture 4 = **idea**, vision, concept, impression, notion, visualization, mental picture, mental image 5 = **description**, impression, explanation, report, account, image, sketch, depiction 6 = **personification**, embodiment, essence, epitome, avatar

▷ VERB 7 = **imagine**, see, envision, visualize, conceive of, fantasize about, conjure up an image of 8 = **represent**, show, draw, paint, illustrate, sketch, depict 9 = **show**, photograph, capture on film

picturesque 1 = **interesting**, pretty, beautiful, attractive, charming, scenic, quaint OPPOSITE: unattractive 2 = **vivid**, striking, graphic, colourful, memorable OPPOSITE: dull

piece 1 = **bit**, slice, part, block, quantity, segment, portion, fragment 2 = **component**, part, section, bit, unit, segment, constituent, module 3 = **item**, report, story, study, review, article 4 = **composition**, work, production, opus 5 = **work of art**, work, creation 6 = **share**, cut (*informal*), slice, percentage, quantity, portion, quota, fraction

pier 1 = **jetty**, wharf, quay, promenade, landing place 2 = **pillar**, support, post, column, pile, upright, buttress

pierce = **penetrate**, stab, spike, enter, bore, drill, puncture, prick

piercing 1 = **penetrating**, sharp, loud, shrill, high-pitched, ear-splitting OPPOSITE: low 2 = **perceptive**, sharp, keen, alert, penetrating, shrewd, perspicacious, quick-witted OPPOSITE: unperceptive 3 = **sharp**, acute, severe, intense, painful, stabbing, excruciating, agonizing 4 = **cold**, biting, freezing, bitter, arctic, wintry, nippy

pig 1 = **hog**, sow, boar, swine, porker 2 (*informal*) = **slob**, glutton 3 (*informal*) = **brute**, monster, scoundrel, rogue, swine, rotter, boor

pigment = **colour**, colouring, paint, stain, dye, tint, tincture

pile¹ NOUN 1 = **heap**, collection, mountain, mass, stack, mound, accumulation, hoard 2 (*informal often plural*) = **lot(s)**, mountain(s), load(s) (*informal*), oceans, wealth, great deal, stack(s), abundance

P

3 = mansion, building, residence, manor, country house, seat, big house, stately home
▷ VERB **4 = load**, stuff, pack, stack, charge, heap, cram, lade **5 = crowd**, pack, rush, climb, flood, stream, crush, squeeze
▷ PHRASES: **pile up = accumulate**, collect, gather (up), build up, amass

pile² = foundation, support, post, column, beam, upright, pillar

pile³ = nap, fibre, down, hair, fur, plush

pile-up (*informal*) **= collision**, crash, accident, smash, smash-up (*informal*), multiple collision

pilgrim = traveller, wanderer, devotee, wayfarer

pilgrimage = journey, tour, trip, mission, expedition, excursion

pill = tablet, capsule, pellet

pillar 1 = support, post, column, prop, shaft, upright, pier, stanchion **2 = supporter**, leader, mainstay, leading light (*informal*), upholder

pilot NOUN **1 = airman**, flyer, aviator, aeronaut **2 = helmsman**, navigator, steersman
▷ VERB **3 = fly**, operate, be at the controls of **4 = navigate**, drive, direct, guide, handle, conduct, steer **5 = direct**, conduct, steer
▷ MODIFIER **6 = trial**, test, model, sample, experimental

pin NOUN **1 = tack**, nail, needle, safety pin **2 = peg**, rod, brace, bolt
▷ VERB **3 = fasten**, stick, attach, join, fix, secure, nail, clip **4 = hold fast**, hold down, constrain, immobilize, pinion
▷ PHRASES: **pin someone down = force**, pressure, compel, put pressure on, pressurize, nail someone down, make someone commit themselves ▶ **pin something down = determine**, identify, locate, name, specify, pinpoint

pinch VERB **1 = nip**, press, squeeze, grasp, compress **2 = hurt**, crush, squeeze, pain, cramp **3** (*Brit informal*) **= steal**, lift (*informal*), nick (*slang, chiefly Brit*), swipe (*slang*), knock off (*slang*), pilfer, purloin, filch
▷ NOUN **4 = nip**, squeeze **5 = dash**, bit, mite, jot, speck, soupçon (*French*) **6 = emergency**, crisis, difficulty, plight, scrape (*informal*), strait, uphill (*S African*), predicament

pine = waste, decline, sicken, fade, languish
▷ PHRASES: **pine for something** *or* **someone 1 = long**, ache, crave, yearn, eat your heart out over **2 = hanker after**, crave, wish for, yearn for, thirst for, hunger for

pink = rosy, rose, salmon, flushed, reddish, roseate
• *See panel* **SHADES OF RED**

P

pinnacle 1 = **summit**, top, height, peak 2 = **height**, top, crown, crest, zenith, apex, vertex

pinpoint 1 = **identify**, discover, define, distinguish, put your finger on 2 = **locate**, find, identify, zero in on

pioneer NOUN 1 = **founder**, leader, developer, innovator, trailblazer 2 = **settler**, explorer, colonist
▷ VERB 3 = **develop**, create, establish, start, discover, institute, invent, initiate

pipe NOUN 1 = **tube**, drain, canal, pipeline, line, main, passage, cylinder
▷ VERB 2 = **convey**, channel, conduct
▷ PHRASES: pipe down (*informal*) = **be quiet**, shut up (*informal*), hush, stop talking, quieten down, shush, shut your mouth, hold your tongue

pipeline = **tube**, passage, pipe, conduit, duct

pirate NOUN 1 = **buccaneer**, raider, marauder, corsair, freebooter
▷ VERB 2 = **copy**, steal, reproduce, bootleg, appropriate, poach, crib (*informal*), plagiarize

pit NOUN 1 = **coal mine**, mine, shaft, colliery, mine shaft 2 = **hole**, depression, hollow, crater, trough, cavity, abyss, chasm
▷ VERB 3 = **scar**, mark, dent, indent, pockmark

pitch NOUN 1 = **sports field**, ground, stadium, arena, park, field of play 2 = **tone**, sound, key, frequency, timbre, modulation 3 = **level**, point, degree, summit, extent, height, intensity, high point 4 = **talk**, patter, spiel (*informal*)
▷ VERB 5 = **throw**, cast, toss, hurl, fling, chuck (*informal*), sling, lob (*informal*) 6 = **fall**, drop, plunge, dive, tumble, topple, plummet, fall headlong 7 = **set up**, raise, settle, put up, erect 8 = **toss (about)**, roll, plunge, lurch
▷ PHRASES: pitch in = **help**, contribute, participate, join in, cooperate, chip in (*informal*), get stuck in (*Brit informal*), lend a hand

pitfall *usually plural* = **danger**, difficulty, peril, catch, trap, hazard, drawback, snag, uphill (*S African*)

pity NOUN 1 = **compassion**, charity, sympathy, kindness, fellow feeling OPPOSITE: mercilessness 2 = **shame**, sin (*informal*), misfortune, bummer (*slang*), crying shame 3 = **mercy**, kindness, clemency, forbearance
▷ VERB 4 = **feel sorry for**, feel for, sympathize with, grieve for, weep for, bleed for, have compassion for

pivotal = **crucial**, central, vital, critical, decisive

p

place NOUN 1 = **spot**, point, position, site, area, location, venue, whereabouts
2 = **region**, quarter, district, neighbourhood, vicinity, locality, locale, dorp (*S African*)
3 = **position**, point, spot, location 4 = **space**, position, seat, chair 5 = **job**, position, post, situation, office, employment, appointment
6 = **home**, house, room, property, accommodation, pad (*slang*), residence, dwelling, bachelor apartment (*Canad*) 7 = **duty**, right, job, charge, concern, role, affair, responsibility
▷ VERB 8 = **lay (down)**, put (down), set (down), stand, position, rest, station, stick (*informal*) 9 = **put**, lay, set, invest, pin 10 = **classify**, class, group, put, order, sort, rank, arrange 11 = **entrust to**, give to, assign to, appoint to, allocate to, find a home for 12 = **identify**, remember, recognize, pin someone down, put your finger on, put a name to
▷ PHRASES: **in your/his/ her/their place** = **situation**, position, circumstances, shoes (*informal*) ▸ **know one's place** = **know one's rank**, know one's standing, know one's position, know one's footing, know one's station, know one's status, know one's grade, know one's

niche ▸ **take place** = **happen**, occur, go on, go down (*US & Canad*), arise, come about, crop up, transpire (*informal*)

plague NOUN 1 = **disease**, infection, epidemic, pestilence
2 = **infestation**, invasion, epidemic, influx, host, swarm, multitude
▷ VERB 3 = **torment**, trouble, torture 4 = **pester**, trouble, bother, annoy, tease, harry, harass, hassle

plain ADJECTIVE 1 = **unadorned**, simple, basic, severe, bare, stark, austere, spartan, bare-bones OPPOSITE: ornate 2 = **clear**, obvious, patent, evident, visible, distinct, understandable, manifest OPPOSITE: hidden
3 = **straightforward**, open, direct, frank, blunt, outspoken, honest, downright OPPOSITE: roundabout
4 = **ugly**, unattractive, homely (*US & Canad*), unlovely, unprepossessing, not beautiful, no oil painting (*informal*), ill-favoured OPPOSITE: attractive
5 = **ordinary**, common, simple, everyday, commonplace, unaffected, unpretentious OPPOSITE: sophisticated
▷ NOUN 6 = **flatland**, plateau, prairie, grassland, steppe, veld

plan NOUN 1 = **scheme**, system, design, programme, proposal, strategy, method, suggestion
2 = **diagram**, map, drawing,

chart, representation, sketch, blueprint, layout
▷ VERB 3 = **devise**, arrange, scheme, plot, draft, organize, outline, formulate 4 = **intend**, aim, mean, propose, purpose 5 = **design**, outline, draw up a plan of

plane NOUN 1 = **aeroplane**, aircraft, jet, airliner, jumbo jet 2 = **flat surface**, the flat, horizontal, level surface 3 = **level**, position, stage, condition, standard, degree, rung, echelon
▷ ADJECTIVE 4 = **level**, even, flat, regular, smooth, horizontal
▷ VERB 5 = **skim**, sail, skate, glide

plant¹ NOUN 1 = **flower**, bush, vegetable, herb, weed, shrub
▷ VERB 2 = **sow**, scatter, transplant, implant, put in the ground 3 = **seed**, sow, implant 4 = **place**, put, set, fix 5 = **hide**, put, place, conceal 6 = **place**, put, establish, found, fix, insert

plant² 1 = **factory**, works, shop, yard, mill, foundry 2 = **machinery**, equipment, gear, apparatus

plaster NOUN 1 = **mortar**, stucco, gypsum, plaster of Paris 2 = **bandage**, dressing, sticking plaster, Elastoplast®, adhesive plaster
▷ VERB 3 = **cover**, spread, coat, smear, overlay, daub

plastic = **pliant**, soft, flexible, supple, pliable, ductile, mouldable **OPPOSITE:** rigid

plate NOUN 1 = **platter**, dish, dinner plate, salver, trencher (*archaic*) 2 = **helping**, course, serving, dish, portion, platter, plateful 3 = **layer**, panel, sheet, slab 4 = **illustration**, picture, photograph, print, engraving, lithograph
▷ VERB 5 = **coat**, gild, laminate, cover, overlay

plateau 1 = **upland**, table, highland, tableland 2 = **levelling off**, level, stage, stability

platform 1 = **stage**, stand, podium, rostrum, dais, soapbox 2 = **policy**, programme, principle, objective(s), manifesto, party line

plausible 1 = **believable**, possible, likely, reasonable, credible, probable, persuasive, conceivable **OPPOSITE:** unbelievable 2 = **glib**, smooth, specious, smooth-talking, smooth-tongued

play VERB 1 = **amuse yourself**, have fun, sport, fool, romp, revel, trifle, entertain yourself 2 = **take part in**, be involved in, engage in, participate in, compete in 3 = **compete against**, challenge, take on, oppose, contend against 4 = **perform**, carry out 5 = **act**, portray, represent, perform, act the part of 6 = **perform on**,

strum, make music on
▷ NOUN 7 = **amusement**,
pleasure, leisure, games, sport,
fun, entertainment, relaxation,
me-time 8 = **drama**, show,
piece, comedy, tragedy, farce,
soapie or soapy (Austral slang),
pantomime
▷ PHRASES: play on or upon
something = **take advantage
of**, abuse, exploit, impose
on, trade on, capitalize on
▶ play something down
= **minimize**, make light
of, gloss over, talk down,
underrate, underplay, pooh-
pooh (informal), soft-pedal
(informal) ▶ play something
up = **emphasize**, highlight,
underline, stress, accentuate
▶ play up 1 = **hurt**, be painful,
bother you, trouble you, be
sore, pain you 2 = **malfunction**,
not work properly, be on the
blink (slang) 3 = **be awkward**,
misbehave, give trouble, be
disobedient, be stroppy (Brit
slang)
playboy = **womanizer**,
philanderer, rake, lady-killer
(informal), roué, ladies' man
player 1 = **sportsman** or
sportswoman, competitor,
participant, contestant
2 = **musician**, artist, performer,
virtuoso, instrumentalist
3 = **performer**, entertainer,
Thespian, trouper, actor
or actress

plea 1 = **appeal**, request, suit,
prayer, petition, entreaty,
intercession, supplication
2 = **excuse**, defence,
explanation, justification
plead = **appeal**, ask, request,
beg, petition, implore, beseech,
entreat
pleasant 1 = **pleasing**, nice,
fine, lovely, amusing, delightful,
enjoyable, agreeable, lekker (S
African slang) OPPOSITE: horrible
2 = **friendly**, nice, agreeable,
likable or likeable, engaging,
charming, amiable, genial
OPPOSITE: disagreeable
please = **delight**, entertain,
humour, amuse, suit, satisfy,
indulge, gratify OPPOSITE: annoy
pleased = **happy**, delighted,
contented, satisfied, thrilled,
glad, gratified, over the moon
(informal)
pleasing 1 = **enjoyable**,
satisfying, charming, delightful,
gratifying, agreeable,
pleasurable OPPOSITE:
unpleasant 2 = **likable** or
likeable, engaging, charming,
delightful, agreeable OPPOSITE:
disagreeable
pleasure 1 = **happiness**, delight,
satisfaction, enjoyment,
bliss, gratification, gladness,
delectation OPPOSITE:
displeasure 2 = **amusement**, joy
OPPOSITE: duty
pledge NOUN 1 = **promise**, vow,
assurance, word, undertaking,

warrant, oath, covenant
2 = **guarantee**, security, deposit,
bail, collateral, pawn, surety
▷ VERB 3 = **promise**, vow, swear,
contract, engage, give your
word, give your oath
plentiful = **abundant**, liberal,
generous, lavish, ample,
overflowing, copious, bountiful
OPPOSITE: scarce
plenty 1 = **abundance**, wealth,
prosperity, fertility, profusion,
affluence, plenitude, fruitfulness
2 *usually with* **of** = **lots of**
(*informal*), enough, a great deal
of, masses of, piles of (*informal*),
stacks of, heaps of (*informal*), an
abundance of
plight = **difficulty**, condition,
state, situation, trouble,
predicament
plot¹ NOUN 1 = **plan**, scheme,
intrigue, conspiracy, cabal,
stratagem, machination
2 = **story**, action, subject,
theme, outline, scenario,
narrative, story line
▷ VERB 3 = **plan**, scheme,
conspire, intrigue, manoeuvre,
contrive, collude, machinate
4 = **devise**, design, lay, conceive,
hatch, contrive, concoct, cook
up (*informal*) 5 = **chart**, mark,
map, locate, calculate, outline
plot² = **patch**, lot, area, ground,
parcel, tract, allotment
plough *or* **plow** (*US*) = **turn over**,
dig, till, cultivate
▷ PHRASES: **plough through**

something = **forge**, cut, drive,
press, push, plunge, wade
ploy = **tactic**, move, trick, device,
scheme, manoeuvre, dodge,
ruse
pluck VERB 1 = **pull out** *or* **off**,
pick, draw, collect, gather,
harvest 2 = **tug**, catch, snatch,
clutch, jerk, yank, tweak, pull at
3 = **strum**, pick, finger, twang
▷ NOUN 4 = **courage**, nerve,
bottle (*Brit slang*), guts (*informal*),
grit, bravery, backbone,
boldness
plug NOUN 1 = **stopper**, cork,
bung, spigot 2 (*informal*)
= **mention**, advertisement,
advert (*Brit informal*), push,
publicity, hype
▷ VERB 3 = **seal**, close, stop,
fill, block, stuff, pack, cork
4 (*informal*) = **mention**, push,
promote, publicize, advertise,
build up, hype (*slang*)
▷ PHRASES: **plug away** (*informal*)
= **slog away**, labour, toil away,
grind away (*informal*), peg away,
plod away
plum = **choice**, prize, first-class
plumb VERB 1 = **delve into**,
explore, probe, go into,
penetrate, gauge, unravel,
fathom
▷ ADVERB 2 = **exactly**, precisely,
bang, slap, spot-on (*Brit
informal*)
plummet 1 = **drop**, fall, crash,
nosedive, descend rapidly
2 = **plunge**, fall, drop, crash,

P

tumble, nosedive, descend
rapidly

plump = **chubby**, fat, stout,
round, tubby, dumpy, roly-poly,
rotund **OPPOSITE:** scrawny

plunder VERB 1 = **loot**, strip,
sack, rob, raid, rifle, ransack,
pillage 2 = **steal**, rob, take,
nick (*informal*), pinch (*informal*),
embezzle, pilfer, thieve
▷ NOUN 3 = **pillage** 4 = **loot**,
spoils, booty, swag (*slang*), ill-
gotten gains

plunge VERB 1 = **descend**, fall,
drop, crash, pitch, sink, dive,
tumble 2 = **hurtle**, charge,
career, jump, tear, rush, dive,
dash 3 = **submerge**, dip
4 = **throw**, cast, pitch, propel
5 = **fall steeply**, drop, crash
(*informal*), slump, plummet, take
a nosedive (*informal*)
▷ NOUN 6 = **fall**, crash (*informal*),
slump, drop, tumble 7 = **dive**,
jump, duck, descent

plus PREPOSITION 1 = **and**, with,
added to, coupled with
▷ NOUN 2(*informal*)
= **advantage**, benefit, asset,
gain, extra, bonus, good point
▷ ADJECTIVE 3 = **additional**,
added, extra, supplementary,
add-on

> **USAGE NOTE**
> When you have a sentence
> with more than one subject
> linked by *and*, this makes the
> subject plural and means
> it should take a plural verb:
> *the doctor and all the nurses
> were* (not *was*) *waiting for
> the patient*. However, where
> the subjects are linked by
> *plus*, *together with*, or *along
> with*, the number of the verb
> remains just as it would have
> been if the extra subjects
> had not been mentioned.
> Therefore you would say *the
> doctor, together with all the
> nurses, was* (not *were*) *waiting
> for the patient*.

plush = **luxurious**, luxury, lavish,
rich, sumptuous, opulent, de
luxe **OPPOSITE:** cheap

ply = **work at**, follow, exercise,
pursue, carry on, practise

pocket NOUN 1 = **pouch**, bag,
sack, compartment, receptacle
▷ MODIFIER 2 = **small**, compact,
miniature, portable, little
▷ VERB 3 = **steal**, take, lift
(*informal*), appropriate, pilfer,
purloin, filch

pod = **shell**, case, hull, husk,
shuck

podcast (*Computing*) NOUN
1 = **broadcast**, webcast,
vodcast, mobcast, Godcast,
webisode, webinar
▷ VERB 2 = **upload**, broadcast,
webcast, vodcast, mobcast,
Godcast, update

podium = **platform**, stand,
stage, rostrum, dais

poem = **verse**, song, lyric,
rhyme, sonnet, ode, verse
composition

poet = **bard**, rhymer, lyricist, lyric poet, versifier, elegist

poetic 1 = **figurative**, creative, lyric, symbolic, lyrical **2** = **lyrical**, lyric, elegiac, metrical

poetry = **verse**, poems, rhyme, rhyming, verse composition

pogey (*Canad*) = **benefits**, the dole (*Brit & Austral*), welfare, social security, unemployment benefit, state benefit, allowance

poignant = **moving**, touching, sad, bitter, intense, painful, distressing, pathetic

point NOUN **1** = **essence**, meaning, subject, question, heart, import, drift, thrust **2** = **purpose**, aim, object, end, reason, goal, intention, objective **3** = **aspect**, detail, feature, quality, particular, respect, item, characteristic **4** = **place**, area, position, site, spot, location, locality, locale **5** = **moment**, time, stage, period, phase, instant, juncture, moment in time **6** = **stage**, level, position, condition, degree, pitch, circumstance, extent **7** = **end**, tip, sharp end, top, spur, spike, apex, prong **8** = **score**, tally, mark **9** = **pinpoint**, mark, spot, dot, fleck ▷ VERB **10** *usually followed by* **at** *or* **to** = **aim**, level, train, direct **11** = **face**, look, direct ▷ PHRASES: **point at** *or* **to something** *or* **someone**

= **indicate**, show, signal, point to, point out, specify, designate, gesture towards

pointed 1 = **sharp**, edged, acute, barbed **2** = **cutting**, telling, biting, sharp, keen, acute, penetrating, pertinent

pointer 1 = **hint**, tip, suggestion, recommendation, caution, piece of information, piece of advice **2** = **indicator**, hand, guide, needle, arrow

pointless = **senseless**, meaningless, futile, fruitless, stupid, silly, useless, absurd OPPOSITE: worthwhile

poised 1 = **ready**, waiting, prepared, standing by, all set **2** = **composed**, calm, together (*informal*), collected, dignified, self-confident, self-possessed OPPOSITE: agitated

poison NOUN **1** = **toxin**, venom, bane (*archaic*) ▷ VERB **2** = **murder**, kill, give someone poison, administer poison to **3** = **contaminate**, foul, infect, spoil, pollute, blight, taint, befoul **4** = **corrupt**, colour, undermine, bias, sour, pervert, warp, taint

poisonous 1 = **toxic**, fatal, deadly, lethal, mortal, virulent, noxious, venomous **2** = **evil**, malicious, corrupting, pernicious, baleful

poke VERB **1** = **jab**, push, stick, dig, stab, thrust, shove, nudge **2** = **protrude**, stick, thrust, jut

P

▷ **NOUN** 3 = **jab**, dig, thrust, nudge, prod

pole = **rod**, post, support, staff, bar, stick, stake, paling

police **NOUN** 1 = **the law** (*informal*), police force, constabulary, the fuzz (*slang*), boys in blue (*informal*), the Old Bill (*slang*), the rozzers (*slang*)
▷ **VERB** 2 = **control**, patrol, guard, watch, protect, regulate

policy 1 = **procedure**, plan, action, practice, scheme, code, custom 2 = **line**, rules, approach

polish **NOUN** 1 = **varnish**, wax, glaze, lacquer, japan 2 = **sheen**, finish, glaze, gloss, brightness, lustre 3 = **style**, class (*informal*), finish, breeding, grace, elegance, refinement, finesse
▷ **VERB** 4 = **shine**, wax, smooth, rub, buff, brighten, burnish 5 *often with* **up** = **perfect**, improve, enhance, refine, finish, brush up, touch up

polished 1 = **elegant**, sophisticated, refined, polite, cultivated, suave, well-bred **OPPOSITE:** unsophisticated 2 = **accomplished**, professional, masterly, fine, expert, skilful, adept, superlative **OPPOSITE:** amateurish 3 = **shining**, bright, smooth, gleaming, glossy, burnished **OPPOSITE:** dull

polite 1 = **mannerly**, civil, courteous, gracious, respectful, well-behaved, complaisant, well-mannered **OPPOSITE:** rude

2 = **refined**, cultured, civilized, polished, sophisticated, elegant, genteel, well-bred **OPPOSITE:** uncultured

politic = **wise**, diplomatic, sensible, prudent, advisable, expedient, judicious

political = **governmental**, government, state, parliamentary, constitutional, administrative, legislative, ministerial

politician = **statesman** *or* **stateswoman**, representative, senator (*US*), congressman (*US*), Member of Parliament, legislator, public servant, congresswoman (*US*)

politics 1 = **affairs of state**, government, public affairs, civics 2 = **political beliefs**, party politics, political allegiances, political leanings, political sympathies 3 = **political science**, statesmanship, civics, statecraft

poll **NOUN** 1 = **survey**, figures, count, sampling, returns, ballot, tally, census 2 = **election**, vote, voting, referendum, ballot, plebiscite
▷ **VERB** 3 = **question**, interview, survey, sample, ballot, canvass 4 = **gain**, return, record, register, tally

pollute 1 = **contaminate**, dirty, poison, soil, foul, infect, spoil, stain **OPPOSITE:** decontaminate 2 = **defile**, corrupt, sully, deprave, debase, profane, desecrate, dishonour **OPPOSITE:** honour

pollution 1 = **contamination**, dirtying, corruption, taint, foulness, defilement, uncleanness 2 = **waste**, poisons, dirt, impurities

pond = **pool**, tarn, small lake, fish pond, duck pond, millpond

ponder = **think about**, consider, reflect on, contemplate, deliberate about, muse on, brood on, meditate on

pool¹ 1 = **swimming pool**, lido, swimming bath(s) (*Brit*), bathing pool (*archaic*) 2 = **pond**, lake, mere, tarn 3 = **puddle**, drop, patch

pool² NOUN 1 = **supply**, reserve, fall-back 2 = **kitty**, bank, fund, stock, store, pot, jackpot, stockpile
▷ VERB 3 = **combine**, share, merge, put together, amalgamate, lump together, join forces on

poor 1 = **impoverished**, broke (*informal*), hard up (*informal*), short, needy, penniless, destitute, poverty-stricken **OPPOSITE:** rich 2 = **unfortunate**, unlucky, hapless, pitiful, luckless, wretched, ill-starred, pitiable **OPPOSITE:** fortunate 3 = **inferior**, unsatisfactory, mediocre, second-rate, rotten (*informal*), low-grade, below par, substandard, half-pie (*NZ*

informal), bodger or bodgie (*Austral slang*) **OPPOSITE:** excellent 4 = **meagre**, inadequate, insufficient, lacking, incomplete, scant, deficient, skimpy **OPPOSITE:** ample

poorly ADVERB 1 = **badly**, incompetently, inadequately, unsuccessfully, insufficiently, unsatisfactorily, inexpertly **OPPOSITE:** well
▷ ADJECTIVE 2 (*informal*) = **ill**, sick, unwell, crook (*Austral & NZ informal*), seedy (*informal*), below par, off colour, under the weather (*informal*), feeling rotten (*informal*) **OPPOSITE:** healthy

pop NOUN 1 = **bang**, report, crack, noise, burst, explosion
▷ VERB 2 = **burst**, crack, snap, bang, explode, go off (with a bang) 3 = **put**, insert, push, stick, slip, thrust, tuck, shove

pope = **Holy Father**, pontiff, His Holiness, Bishop of Rome, Vicar of Christ

popular 1 = **well-liked**, liked, in, accepted, favourite, approved, in favour, fashionable, trending **OPPOSITE:** unpopular 2 = **common**, general, prevailing, current, conventional, universal, prevalent **OPPOSITE:** rare

popularity 1 = **favour**, esteem, acclaim, regard, approval, vogue 2 = **currency**, acceptance, circulation, vogue, prevalence

populate 1 = **inhabit**, people,
live in, occupy, reside in, dwell
in (*formal*) 2 = **settle**, occupy,
pioneer, colonize

population = **inhabitants**,
people, community, society,
residents, natives, folk,
occupants

pore = **opening**, hole, outlet,
orifice

pornography = **obscenity**,
porn (*informal*), dirt, filth,
indecency, smut

port = **harbour**, haven,
anchorage, seaport

portable = **light**, compact,
convenient, handy, manageable,
movable, easily carried

porter¹ = **baggage attendant**,
carrier, bearer, baggage-carrier

porter² (*chiefly Brit*) = **doorman**,
caretaker, janitor, concierge,
gatekeeper

portion 1 = **part**, bit, piece,
section, scrap, segment,
fragment, chunk 2 = **helping**,
serving, piece, plateful
3 = **share**, allowance, lot,
measure, quantity, quota,
ration, allocation

portrait 1 = **picture**,
painting, image, photograph,
representation, likeness
2 = **description**, profile,
portrayal, depiction,
characterization, thumbnail
sketch

portray 1 = **play**, take the
role of, act the part of,
represent, personate (*rare*)
2 = **describe**, present, depict,
evoke, delineate, put in words
3 = **represent**, draw, paint,
illustrate, sketch, figure, picture,
depict 4 = **characterize**,
represent, depict

portrayal 1 = **performance**,
interpretation, characterization
2 = **depiction**, picture,
representation, sketch,
rendering 3 = **description**,
account, representation
4 = **characterization**,
representation, depiction

pose VERB 1 = **position yourself**,
sit, model, arrange yourself
2 = **put on airs**, posture, show
off (*informal*)
▷ NOUN 3 = **posture**,
position, bearing, attitude,
stance 4 = **act**, façade, air,
front, posturing, pretence,
mannerism, affectation
▷ PHRASES: pose as something
or someone = **impersonate**,
pretend to be, profess to be,
masquerade as, pass yourself
off as

posh (*informal*, *chiefly Brit*)
1 = **smart**, grand, stylish,
luxurious, classy (*slang*), swish
(*informal*, *chiefly Brit*), up-market,
swanky (*informal*), schmick
(*Austral informal*) 2 = **upper-
class**, high-class

position NOUN 1 = **location**,
place, point, area, post,
situation, station, spot

2 = **posture**, attitude, arrangement, pose, stance
3 = **status**, place, standing, footing, station, rank, reputation, importance
4 = **job**, place, post, opening, office, role, situation, duty
5 = **place**, standing, rank, status
6 = **attitude**, view, perspective, point of view, opinion, belief, stance, outlook
▷ VERB 7 = **place**, put, set, stand, arrange, locate, lay out

positive 1 = **beneficial**, useful, practical, helpful, progressive, productive, worthwhile, constructive **OPPOSITE:** harmful
2 = **certain**, sure, convinced, confident, satisfied, assured, free from doubt **OPPOSITE:** uncertain 3 = **definite**, real, clear, firm, certain, express, absolute, decisive, nailed-on (*slang*) **OPPOSITE:** inconclusive 4 (*informal*) = **absolute**, complete, perfect, right (*Brit informal*), real, total, sheer, utter

positively 1 = **definitely**, surely, firmly, certainly, absolutely, emphatically, unquestionably, categorically
2 = **really**, completely, simply, plain (*informal*), absolutely, thoroughly, utterly, downright

possess 1 = **own**, have, hold, be in possession of, be the owner of, have in your possession 2 = **be endowed with**, have, enjoy, benefit from, be possessed of,

be gifted with 3 = **seize**, hold, control, dominate, occupy, take someone over, have power over, have mastery over

possession NOUN
1 = **ownership**, control, custody, hold, hands, tenure
▷ PLURAL NOUN 2 = **property**, things, effects, estate, assets, belongings, chattels

possibility 1 = **feasibility**, likelihood, potentiality, practicability, workableness
2 = **likelihood**, chance, risk, odds, prospect, liability, probability 3 *often plural*
= **potential**, promise, prospects, talent, capabilities, potentiality

possible 1 = **feasible**, viable, workable, achievable, practicable, attainable, doable, realizable **OPPOSITE:** unfeasible 2 = **likely**, potential, anticipated, probable, odds-on, on the cards **OPPOSITE:** improbable 3 = **conceivable**, likely, credible, plausible, hypothetical, imaginable, believable, thinkable **OPPOSITE:** inconceivable 4 = **aspiring**, would-be, promising, hopeful, prospective, wannabe (*informal*)

│ USAGE NOTE
Although it is very common to talk about something's being *very possible* or *more possible*, many people object to such uses, claiming that *possible* describes an absolute state,

P

and therefore something can only be either *possible* or *not possible*. If you want to refer to different degrees of probability, a word such as *likely* or *easy* may be more appropriate than *possible*, for example *it is very likely that he will resign* (not *very possible*).

possibly = **perhaps**, maybe, perchance (*archaic*)

post¹ NOUN 1 = **support**, stake, pole, column, shaft, upright, pillar, picket
▷ VERB 2 = **put up**, display, affix, pin something up

post² NOUN 1 = **job**, place, office, position, situation, employment, appointment, assignment 2 = **position**, place, base, beat, station
▷ VERB 3 = **station**, assign, put, place, position, situate, put on duty

post³ NOUN 1 = **mail**, collection, delivery, postal service, snail mail (*informal*) 2 = **correspondence**, letters, cards, mail
▷ VERB 3 = **send (off)**, forward, mail, get off, transmit, dispatch, consign
▷ PHRASES: keep someone posted = **notify**, brief, advise, inform, report to, keep someone informed, keep someone up to date, apprise

poster = **notice**, bill, announcement, advertisement, sticker, placard, public notice

postpone = **put off**, delay, suspend, adjourn, shelve, defer, put back, put on the back burner (*informal*) OPPOSITE: go ahead with

posture NOUN 1 = **bearing**, set, attitude, stance, carriage, disposition
▷ VERB 2 = **show off** (*informal*), pose, affect, put on airs

pot = **container**, bowl, pan, vessel, basin, cauldron, skillet

potent 1 = **powerful**, commanding, dynamic, dominant, influential, authoritative 2 = **strong**, powerful, mighty, vigorous, forceful OPPOSITE: weak

potential ADJECTIVE 1 = **possible**, future, likely, promising, probable 2 = **hidden**, possible, inherent, dormant, latent
▷ NOUN 3 = **ability**, possibilities, capacity, capability, aptitude, wherewithal, potentiality

potter *usually with* **around** *or* **about** = **mess about**, tinker, dabble, footle (*informal*)

pottery = **ceramics**, terracotta, crockery, earthenware, stoneware

pounce *often followed by* **on** *or* **upon** = **attack**, strike, jump, leap, swoop

pound¹ 1 *sometimes with* **on** = **beat**, strike, hammer, batter, thrash, thump, clobber (*slang*), pummel 2 = **crush**, powder, pulverize 3 = **pulsate**, beat, pulse, throb, palpitate 4 = **stomp**, tramp, march, thunder (*informal*)

pound² = **enclosure**, yard, pen, compound, kennels

pour 1 = **let flow**, spill, splash, dribble, drizzle, slop (*informal*), slosh (*informal*), decant 2 = **flow**, stream, run, course, rush, emit, cascade, gush 3 = **rain**, pelt (down), teem, bucket down (*informal*) 4 = **stream**, crowd, flood, swarm, gush, throng, teem

> **USAGE NOTE**
> The spelling of *pour* (as in *she poured cream on her strudel*) should be carefully distinguished from that of *pore over* or *through* (as in *she pored over the manuscript*).

pout VERB 1 = **sulk**, glower, look petulant, pull a long face
▷ NOUN 2 = **sullen look**, glower, long face

poverty 1 = **pennilessness**, want, need, hardship, insolvency, privation, penury, destitution OPPOSITE: wealth 2 = **scarcity**, lack, absence, want, deficit, shortage, deficiency, inadequacy OPPOSITE: abundance

powder NOUN 1 = **dust**, talc, fine grains, loose particles
▷ VERB 2 = **dust**, cover, scatter, sprinkle, strew, dredge

power 1 = **control**, authority, influence, command, dominance, domination, mastery, dominion, mana (*NZ*) 2 = **ability**, capacity, faculty, property, potential, capability, competence, competency OPPOSITE: inability 3 = **authority**, right, licence, privilege, warrant, prerogative, authorization 4 = **strength**, might, energy, muscle, vigour, potency, brawn, hard power OPPOSITE: weakness 5 = **forcefulness**, force, strength, punch (*informal*), intensity, potency, eloquence, persuasiveness

powerful 1 = **influential**, dominant, controlling, commanding, prevailing, authoritative, skookum (*Canad*) OPPOSITE: powerless 2 = **strong**, strapping, mighty, vigorous, potent, energetic, sturdy OPPOSITE: weak 3 = **persuasive**, convincing, telling, moving, striking, storming, dramatic, impressive

powerless 1 = **defenceless**, vulnerable, dependent, subject, tied, ineffective, unarmed 2 = **weak**, disabled, helpless, incapable, frail, feeble, debilitated, impotent OPPOSITE: strong

practical 1 = **functional**, realistic, pragmatic OPPOSITE: impractical 2 = **empirical**, real, applied, actual, hands-on, in the field, experimental,

factual **OPPOSITE:** theoretical
3 = **sensible**, ordinary, realistic,
down-to-earth, matter-of-
fact, businesslike, hard-
headed, grounded **OPPOSITE:**
impractical 4 = **feasible**,
possible, viable, workable,
practicable, doable **OPPOSITE:**
impractical 5 = **useful**,
ordinary, appropriate, sensible,
everyday, functional, utilitarian,
serviceable 6 = **skilled**,
experienced, efficient,
accomplished, proficient
OPPOSITE: inexperienced

> **USAGE NOTE**
> A distinction is usually
> made between *practical* and
> *practicable*. *Practical* refers to
> a person, idea, project, etc. as
> being more concerned with
> or relevant to practice than
> theory: *he is a very practical
> person; the idea had no practical
> application*. *Practicable* refers
> to a project or idea as being
> capable of being done or
> put into effect: *the plan was
> expensive, yet practicable*.

practically 1 = **almost**, nearly,
essentially, virtually, basically,
fundamentally, all but, just
about 2 = **sensibly**, reasonably,
matter-of-factly, realistically,
rationally, pragmatically
practice 1 = **custom**, way,
system, rule, method, tradition,
habit, routine, tikanga (*NZ*)
2 = **training**, study, exercise,
preparation, drill, rehearsal,
repetition 3 = **profession**, work,
business, career, occupation,
pursuit, vocation 4 = **business**,
company, office, firm,
enterprise, partnership, outfit
(*informal*) 5 = **use**, experience,
action, operation, application,
enactment
practise 1 = **rehearse**, study,
prepare, perfect, repeat, go
through, go over, refine 2 = **do**,
train, exercise, drill 3 = **carry
out**, follow, apply, perform,
observe, engage in 4 = **work at**,
pursue, carry on
practised = **skilled**, trained,
experienced, seasoned, able,
expert, accomplished, proficient
OPPOSITE: inexperienced
pragmatic = **practical**, sensible,
realistic, down-to-earth,
utilitarian, businesslike, hard-
headed **OPPOSITE:** idealistic
praise VERB 1 = **acclaim**,
approve of, honour, cheer,
admire, applaud, compliment,
congratulate **OPPOSITE:** criticize
2 = **give thanks to**, bless,
worship, adore, glorify, exalt
▷ NOUN 3 = **approval**,
acclaim, tribute, compliment,
congratulations, eulogy,
commendation, approbation
OPPOSITE: criticism 4 = **thanks**,
glory, worship, homage,
adoration
pray 1 = **say your prayers**, offer a
prayer, recite the rosary 2 = **beg**,

ask, plead, petition, request, solicit, implore, beseech

prayer 1 = **supplication**, devotion 2 = **orison**, litany, invocation, intercession 3 = **plea**, appeal, request, petition, entreaty, supplication

preach 1 *often with* **to** = **deliver a sermon**, address, evangelize, preach a sermon 2 = **urge**, teach, champion, recommend, advise, counsel, advocate, exhort

preacher = **clergyman**, minister, parson, missionary, evangelist

precarious 1 = **insecure**, dangerous, tricky, risky, dodgy (*Brit, Austral & NZ informal*), unsure, hazardous, shaky, shonky (*Austral & NZ informal*) **OPPOSITE:** secure 2 = **dangerous**, shaky, insecure, unsafe, unreliable **OPPOSITE:** stable

precaution = **safeguard**, insurance, protection, provision, safety measure

precede 1 = **go before**, antedate 2 = **go ahead of**, lead, head, go before 3 = **preface**, introduce, go before

precedent = **instance**, example, standard, model, pattern, prototype, paradigm, antecedent

precinct = **area**, quarter, section, sector, district, zone

precious 1 = **valuable**, expensive, fine, prized, dear, costly, invaluable, priceless **OPPOSITE:** worthless 2 = **loved**, prized, dear, treasured, darling, beloved, adored, cherished 3 = **affected**, artificial, twee (*Brit informal*), overrefined, overnice

precipitate VERB 1 = **quicken**, trigger, accelerate, advance, hurry, speed up, bring on, hasten 2 = **throw**, launch, cast, hurl, fling, let fly ▷ ADJECTIVE 3 = **hasty**, rash, reckless, impulsive, precipitous, impetuous, heedless 4 = **sudden**, quick, brief, rushing, rapid, unexpected, swift, abrupt

precise 1 = **exact**, specific, particular, express, correct, absolute, accurate, explicit **OPPOSITE:** vague 2 = **strict**, particular, exact, formal, careful, stiff, rigid, meticulous **OPPOSITE:** inexact

precisely 1 = **exactly**, squarely, correctly, absolutely, strictly, accurately, plumb (*informal*), square on 2 = **just so**, yes, absolutely, exactly, quite so, you bet (*informal*), without a doubt, indubitably 3 = **just**, entirely, absolutely, altogether, exactly, in all respects 4 = **word for word**, literally, exactly, to the letter

precision = **exactness**, care, accuracy, particularity, meticulousness, preciseness

P

predecessor 1 = **previous job holder**, precursor, forerunner, antecedent 2 = **ancestor**, forebear, antecedent, forefather, tupuna or tipuna (NZ)

predicament = **fix** (informal), situation, spot (informal), hole (slang), mess, jam (informal), dilemma, pinch

predict = **foretell**, forecast, divine, prophesy, augur, portend

predictable = **likely**, expected, sure, certain, anticipated, reliable, foreseeable **OPPOSITE:** unpredictable

prediction = **prophecy**, forecast, prognosis, divination, prognostication, augury

predominantly = **mainly**, largely, chiefly, mostly, generally, principally, primarily, for the most part

prefer 1 = **like better**, favour, go for, pick, fancy, opt for, incline towards, be partial to 2 = **choose**, opt for, pick, desire, would rather, would sooner, incline towards

> **USAGE NOTE**
> Normally, to (not than) is used after prefer and preferable. Therefore, you would say I prefer skating to skiing, and a small income is preferable to no income at all. However, when expressing a preference between two activities stated as infinitive verbs, for example

to skate and to ski, use than, as in I prefer to skate than to ski.

preferable = **better**, best, chosen, preferred, recommended, favoured, superior, more suitable **OPPOSITE:** undesirable

preferably = **ideally**, if possible, rather, sooner, by choice, in or for preference

preference 1 = **liking**, wish, taste, desire, leaning, bent, bias, inclination 2 = **first choice**, choice, favourite, pick, option, selection 3 = **priority**, first place, precedence, favouritism, favoured treatment

pregnant 1 = **expectant**, expecting (informal), with child, in the club (Brit slang), big or heavy with child 2 = **meaningful**, pointed, charged, significant, telling, loaded, expressive, eloquent

prejudice NOUN
1 = **discrimination**, injustice, intolerance, bigotry, unfairness, chauvinism, narrow-mindedness, faith hate 2 = **bias**, preconception, partiality, preconceived notion, prejudgment
▷ VERB 3 = **bias**, influence, colour, poison, distort, slant, predispose 4 = **harm**, damage, hurt, injure, mar, undermine, spoil, impair, crool or cruel (Austral slang)

prejudiced = **biased**, influenced, unfair, one-sided, bigoted, intolerant, opinionated, narrow-minded **OPPOSITE:** unbiased

preliminary ADJECTIVE
1 = **first**, opening, trial, initial, test, pilot, prior, introductory
2 = **qualifying**, eliminating
▷ NOUN 3 = **introduction**, opening, beginning, start, prelude, preface, overture, preamble

prelude 1 = **introduction**, beginning, start 2 = **overture**, opening, introduction, introductory movement

premature 1 = **early**, untimely, before time, unseasonable
2 = **hasty**, rash, too soon, untimely, ill-timed, overhasty

premier NOUN 1 = **head of government**, prime minister, chancellor, chief minister, P.M.
▷ ADJECTIVE 2 = **chief**, leading, first, highest, head, main, prime, primary

premiere = **first night**, opening, debut

premise = **assumption**, proposition, argument, hypothesis, assertion, supposition, presupposition, postulation

premises = **building(s)**, place, office, property, site, establishment

premium 1 = **fee**, charge, payment, instalment

2 = **surcharge**, extra charge, additional fee or charge
3 = **bonus**, reward, prize, perk (*Brit informal*), bounty, perquisite
▷ PHRASES: at a premium = in **great demand**, rare, scarce, in short supply, hard to come by

preoccupation 1 = **obsession**, fixation, bee in your bonnet
2 = **absorption**, abstraction, daydreaming, immersion, reverie, absent-mindedness, engrossment, woolgathering

preoccupied 1 = **absorbed**, lost, wrapped up, immersed, engrossed, rapt 2 = **lost in thought**, distracted, oblivious, absent-minded

preparation 1 = **groundwork**, preparing, getting ready
2 *usually plural* = **arrangement**, plan, measure, provision
3 = **mixture**, medicine, compound, concoction

prepare 1 = **make** or **get ready**, arrange, jack up (*NZ informal*)
2 = **train**, guide, prime, direct, brief, discipline, put someone in the picture 3 = **make**, cook, put together, get, produce, assemble, muster, concoct
4 = **get ready** 5 = **practise**, get ready, train, exercise, warm up, get into shape

prepared 1 = **willing**, inclined, disposed 2 = **ready**, set 3 = **fit**, primed, in order, arranged, in readiness

P

prescribe 1 = **specify**, order, direct, stipulate, write a prescription for 2 = **ordain**, set, order, rule, recommend, dictate, lay down, decree

prescription 1 = **instruction**, direction, formula, script (*informal*), recipe 2 = **medicine**, drug, treatment, preparation, cure, mixture, dose, remedy

presence 1 = **being**, existence, residence, attendance, showing up, occupancy, inhabitance 2 = **personality**, bearing, appearance, aspect, air, carriage, aura, poise
▷ **PHRASES: presence of mind** = **level-headedness**, assurance, composure, poise, cool (*slang*), wits, countenance, coolness

present¹ 1 = **current**, existing, immediate, contemporary, present-day, existent 2 = **here**, there, near, ready, nearby, at hand **OPPOSITE:** absent 3 = **in existence**, existing, existent, extant
▷ **PHRASES: the present** = **now**, today, the time being, here and now, the present moment

present² NOUN 1 = **gift**, offering, grant, donation, hand-out, endowment, boon, gratuity, bonsela (*S African*), koha (*NZ*)
▷ **VERB** 2 = **give**, award, hand over, grant, hand out, confer, bestow 3 = **put on**, stage, perform, give, show, render 4 = **launch**, display, parade,

exhibit, unveil 5 = **introduce**, make known, acquaint someone with

presentation 1 = **giving**, award, offering, donation, bestowal, conferral 2 = **appearance**, look, display, packaging, arrangement, layout 3 = **performance**, production, show

presently 1 = **at present**, currently, now, today, these days, nowadays, at the present time, in this day and age 2 = **soon**, shortly, directly, before long, momentarily (*US & Canad*), by and by, in a jiffy (*informal*)

preservation 1 = **upholding**, support, maintenance 2 = **protection**, safety, maintenance, conservation, salvation, safeguarding, safekeeping

preserve VERB 1 = **maintain**, keep, continue, sustain, keep up, prolong, uphold, conserve **OPPOSITE:** end 2 = **protect**, keep, save, maintain, defend, shelter, shield, care for **OPPOSITE:** attack
▷ **NOUN** 3 = **area**, department, field, territory, province, arena, sphere

preside = **officiate**, chair, moderate, be chairperson

press 1 = **push (down)**, depress, lean on, press down, force down 2 = **push**, squeeze, jam, thrust, ram, wedge, shove 3 = **hug**, squeeze, embrace, clasp, crush, hold close, fold in your arms 4 = **urge**, beg, petition, exhort, implore, pressurize, entreat 5 = **plead**, present, lodge, submit, tender, advance insistently 6 = **steam**, iron, smooth, flatten 7 = **compress**, grind, reduce, mill, crush, pound, squeeze, tread 8 = **crowd**, push, gather, surge, flock, herd, swarm, seethe

pressing = **urgent**, serious, vital, crucial, imperative, important, high-priority, importunate **OPPOSITE:** unimportant

pressure 1 = **force**, crushing, squeezing, compressing, weight, compression 2 = **power**, influence, force, constraint, sway, compulsion, coercion 3 = **stress**, demands, strain, heat, load, burden, urgency, hassle (*informal*), uphill (*S African*)

prestige = **status**, standing, credit, reputation, honour, importance, fame, distinction, mana (*NZ*)

prestigious = **celebrated**, respected, prominent, great, important, esteemed, notable, renowned **OPPOSITE:** unknown

presumably = **it would seem**, probably, apparently, seemingly, on the face of it, in all probability, in all likelihood

presume 1 = **believe**, think, suppose, assume, guess (*informal, chiefly US & Canad*), take for granted, infer, conjecture 2 = **dare**, venture, go so far as, take the liberty, make so bold as

pretend 1 = **feign**, affect, assume, allege, fake, simulate, profess, sham 2 = **make believe**, suppose, imagine, act, make up

pretty ADJECTIVE 1 = **attractive**, beautiful, lovely, charming, fair, good-looking, bonny, comely, fit (*Brit informal*) **OPPOSITE:** plain ▷ ADVERB 2 (*informal*) = **fairly**, rather, quite, kind of (*informal*), somewhat, moderately, reasonably

prevail 1 = **win**, succeed, triumph, overcome, overrule, be victorious 2 = **be widespread**, abound, predominate, be current, be prevalent, exist generally

prevailing 1 = **widespread**, general, established, popular, common, current, usual, ordinary 2 = **predominating**, ruling, main, existing, principal

prevalent = **common**, established, popular, general, current, usual, widespread, universal **OPPOSITE:** rare

prevent = **stop**, avoid, frustrate, hamper, foil, inhibit, avert, thwart **OPPOSITE:** help

prevention = **elimination**, safeguard, precaution, thwarting, avoidance, deterrence

P

preview = sample, sneak preview, trailer, taster, foretaste, advance showing

previous 1 = earlier, former, past, prior, preceding, erstwhile **OPPOSITE:** later **2** = preceding, past, prior, foregoing

previously = before, earlier, once, in the past, formerly, hitherto, beforehand

prey 1 = quarry, game, kill **2** = victim, target, mug (Brit slang), dupe, fall guy (informal)
• See panel **BIRDS OF PREY**

BIRDS OF PREY

accipiter
Australian goshawk or chicken hawk
bald eagle
barn owl
bateleur eagle
boobook
brown owl
buzzard
caracara
condor
Cooper's hawk
duck hawk
eagle
eagle-hawk or wedge-tailed eagle
falcon or (NZ) bush-hawk or karearea
falconet
golden eagle
goshawk
gyrfalcon or gerfalcon
harrier
hawk
hawk owl
hobby
honey buzzard
hoot owl

horned owl
kestrel
kite
lammergeier, lammergeyer, bearded vulture, or (archaic) ossifrage
lanner
little owl
long-eared owl
merlin
Montagu's harrier
mopoke or (NZ) ruru
osprey, fish eagle, or (archaic) ossifrage
owl
peregrine falcon
red kite or (archaic) gled(e)
rough-legged buzzard
saker
screech owl
sea eagle, erne, or ern
secretary bird
snowy owl
sparrowhawk
tawny owl
turkey buzzard or vulture
vulture

price NOUN 1 = **cost**, value, rate, charge, figure, worth, damage (*informal*), amount 2 = **consequences**, penalty, cost, result, toll, forfeit ▷ VERB 3 = **evaluate**, value, estimate, rate, cost, assess

priceless = **valuable**, expensive, precious, invaluable, dear, costly **OPPOSITE:** worthless

prick VERB 1 = **pierce**, stab, puncture, punch, lance, jab, perforate ▷ NOUN 2 = **puncture**, hole, wound, perforation, pinhole

prickly 1 = **spiny**, barbed, thorny, bristly 2 = **itchy**, sharp, smarting, stinging, crawling, tingling, scratchy

pride 1 = **satisfaction**, achievement, fulfilment, delight, content, pleasure, joy, gratification 2 = **self-respect**, honour, ego, dignity, self-esteem, self-image, self-worth 3 = **conceit**, vanity, arrogance, pretension, hubris, self-importance, egotism, self-love **OPPOSITE:** humility

priest = **clergyman**, minister, father, divine, vicar, pastor, cleric, curate

primarily 1 = **chiefly**, largely, generally, mainly, essentially, mostly, principally, fundamentally 2 = **at first**, originally, initially, in the first place, in the beginning, first and foremost, at *or* from the start

primary = **chief**, main, first, highest, greatest, prime, principal, cardinal **OPPOSITE:** subordinate

prime ADJECTIVE 1 = **main**, leading, chief, central, major, key, primary, supreme 2 = **best**, top, select, highest, quality, choice, excellent, first-class ▷ NOUN 3 = **peak**, flower, bloom, height, heyday, zenith ▷ VERB 4 = **inform**, tell, train, coach, brief, fill in (*informal*), notify, clue in (*informal*) 5 = **prepare**, set up, load, equip, get ready, make ready

primitive 1 = **early**, first, earliest, original, primary, elementary, primordial, primeval **OPPOSITE:** modern 2 = **crude**, simple, rough, rudimentary, unrefined **OPPOSITE:** elaborate

prince = **ruler**, lord, monarch, sovereign, crown prince, liege, prince regent, crowned head

princely 1 = **substantial**, considerable, large, huge, massive, enormous, sizable *or* sizeable 2 = **regal**, royal, imperial, noble, sovereign, majestic

princess = **ruler**, lady, monarch, sovereign, liege, crowned head, crowned princess, dynast

principal ADJECTIVE 1 = **main**, leading, chief, prime, first, key, essential, primary **OPPOSITE:** minor

P

▷ NOUN 2 = **headmaster** or **headmistress**, head (informal), dean, head teacher, rector, master or mistress 3 = **star**, lead, leader, prima ballerina, leading man or lady, coryphée 4 = **capital**, money, assets, working capital

principally = **mainly**, largely, chiefly, especially, mostly, primarily, predominantly

principle 1 = **morals**, standards, ideals, honour, virtue, ethics, integrity, conscience, kaupapa (NZ) 2 = **rule**, law, truth, precept ▷ PHRASES: **in principle** 1 = **in general** 2 = **in theory**, ideally, on paper, theoretically, in an ideal world, en principe (French)

> **USAGE NOTE**
> *Principle* and *principal* are often confused: *the principal* (not *principle*) *reason for his departure; the plan was approved in principle* (not *principal*).

print VERB 1 = **run off**, publish, copy, reproduce, issue, engrave 2 = **publish**, release, circulate, issue, disseminate 3 = **mark**, impress, stamp, imprint ▷ NOUN 4 = **photograph**, photo, snap 5 = **picture**, plate, etching, engraving, lithograph, woodcut, linocut 6 = **copy**, photo (informal), picture, reproduction, replica

prior = **earlier**, previous, former, preceding, foregoing, pre-existing, pre-existent ▷ PHRASES: **prior to** = **before**, preceding, earlier than, in advance of, previous to

priority 1 = **prime concern** 2 = **precedence**, preference, primacy, predominance 3 = **supremacy**, rank, precedence, seniority, right of way, pre-eminence

prison = **jail**, confinement, nick (Brit slang), cooler (slang), jug (slang), dungeon, clink (slang), gaol, boob (Austral slang)

prisoner 1 = **convict**, con (slang), lag (slang), jailbird 2 = **captive**, hostage, detainee, internee

privacy = **seclusion**, isolation, solitude, retirement, retreat

private 1 = **exclusive**, individual, privately owned, own, special, reserved OPPOSITE: public 2 = **secret**, confidential, covert, unofficial, clandestine, off the record, hush-hush (informal) OPPOSITE: public 3 = **personal**, individual, secret, intimate, undisclosed, unspoken, innermost, unvoiced 4 = **secluded**, secret, separate, isolated, sequestered OPPOSITE: busy 5 = **solitary**, reserved, retiring, withdrawn, discreet, secretive, self-contained, reclusive OPPOSITE: sociable

privilege = **right**, due, advantage, claim, freedom, liberty, concession, entitlement

privileged = **special**, advantaged, favoured, honoured, entitled, elite

prize¹ NOUN 1 = **reward**, cup, award, honour, medal, trophy, accolade 2 = **winnings**, haul, jackpot, stakes, purse
▷ MODIFIER 3 = **champion**, best, winning, top, outstanding, award-winning, first-rate

prize² = **value**, treasure, esteem, cherish, hold dear

probability 1 = **likelihood**, prospect, chance, odds, expectation, liability, likeliness 2 = **chance**, odds, possibility, likelihood

probable = **likely**, possible, apparent, reasonable to think, credible, plausible, feasible, presumable OPPOSITE: unlikely

probably = **likely**, perhaps, maybe, possibly, presumably, most likely, doubtless, perchance (archaic)

probation = **trial period**, trial, apprenticeship

probe VERB 1 often with **into** = **examine**, go into, investigate, explore, search, look into, analyze, dissect 2 = **explore**, examine, poke, prod, feel around
▷ NOUN 3 = **investigation**, study, inquiry, analysis, examination, exploration, scrutiny, scrutinization

problem 1 = **difficulty**, trouble, dispute, plight, obstacle, dilemma, headache (informal),

complication 2 = **puzzle**, question, riddle, enigma, conundrum, poser

problematic = **tricky**, puzzling, doubtful, dubious, debatable, problematical OPPOSITE: clear

procedure = **method**, policy, process, course, system, action, practice, strategy

proceed 1 = **begin**, go ahead 2 = **continue**, go on, progress, carry on, go ahead, press on, crack on (informal) OPPOSITE: discontinue 3 = **go on**, continue, progress, carry on, go ahead, move on, move forward, press on, crack on (informal) OPPOSITE: stop 4 = **arise**, come, issue, result, spring, flow, stem, derive

proceeding = **action**, process, procedure, move, act, step, measure, deed

proceeds = **income**, profit, revenue, returns, products, gain, earnings, yield

process NOUN 1 = **procedure**, means, course, system, action, performance, operation, measure 2 = **development**, growth, progress, movement, advance, evolution, progression 3 = **method**, system, practice, technique, procedure
▷ VERB 4 = **handle**, manage, action, deal with, fulfil

procession = **parade**, train, march, file, cavalcade, cortege

P

proclaim 1 = **announce**, declare, advertise, publish, indicate, herald, circulate, profess **OPPOSITE:** keep secret 2 = **pronounce**, announce, declare

prod VERB 1 = **poke**, push, dig, shove, nudge, jab 2 = **prompt**, move, urge, motivate, spur, stimulate, rouse, incite ▷ NOUN 3 = **poke**, push, dig, shove, nudge, jab 4 = **prompt**, signal, cue, reminder, stimulus

prodigy = **genius**, talent, wizard, mastermind, whizz (informal), up-and-comer (informal)

produce VERB 1 = **cause**, effect, generate, bring about, give rise to 2 = **make**, create, develop, manufacture, construct, invent, fabricate 3 = **create**, develop, write, turn out, compose, originate, churn out (informal) 4 = **yield**, provide, grow, bear, give, supply, afford, render 5 = **bring forth**, bear, deliver, breed, give birth to, beget, bring into the world 6 = **show**, provide, present, advance, demonstrate, offer, come up with, exhibit 7 = **display**, show, present, proffer 8 = **present**, stage, direct, put on, do, show, mount, exhibit ▷ NOUN 9 = **fruit and vegetables**, goods, food, products, crops, yield, harvest, greengrocery (Brit)

producer 1 = **director**, promoter, impresario 2 = **maker**, manufacturer, builder, creator, fabricator 3 = **grower**, farmer

product 1 = **goods**, produce, creation, commodity, invention, merchandise, artefact 2 = **result**, consequence, effect, outcome, upshot

production 1 = **producing**, making, manufacture, manufacturing, construction, formation, fabrication 2 = **creation**, development, fashioning, composition, origination 3 = **management**, administration, direction 4 = **presentation**, staging, mounting

productive 1 = **fertile**, rich, prolific, plentiful, fruitful, fecund **OPPOSITE:** barren 2 = **creative**, inventive 3 = **useful**, rewarding, valuable, profitable, effective, worthwhile, beneficial, constructive **OPPOSITE:** useless

productivity = **output**, production, capacity, yield, efficiency, work rate

profess 1 = **claim**, allege, pretend, fake, make out, purport, feign 2 = **state**, admit, announce, declare, confess, assert, proclaim, affirm

professed 1 = **supposed**, would-be, alleged, so-called, pretended, purported, self-styled, ostensible 2 = **declared**,

confirmed, confessed,
proclaimed, self-confessed,
avowed, self-acknowledged

profession = occupation,
calling, business, career,
employment, office, position,
sphere

professional ADJECTIVE
1 = **qualified**, trained, skilled,
white-collar 2 = **expert**,
experienced, skilled, masterly,
efficient, competent,
adept, proficient **OPPOSITE:**
amateurish
▷ NOUN 3 = **expert**, master,
pro (*informal*), specialist, guru,
adept, maestro, virtuoso, fundi
(*S African*)

professor = don (*Brit*), fellow
(*Brit*), prof (*informal*)

profile 1 = **outline**, lines, form,
figure, silhouette, contour, side
view 2 = **biography**, sketch,
vignette, characterization,
thumbnail sketch

profit NOUN 1 *often plural*
= **earnings**, return, revenue,
gain, yield, proceeds, receipts,
takings **OPPOSITE:** loss
2 = **benefit**, good, use, value,
gain, advantage, advancement
OPPOSITE: disadvantage
▷ VERB 3 = **make money**,
gain, earn 4 = **benefit**, help,
serve, gain, promote, be of
advantage to

profitable 1 = **money-
making**, lucrative, paying,
commercial, worthwhile,
cost-effective, fruitful,
remunerative 2 = **beneficial**,
useful, rewarding, valuable,
productive, worthwhile, fruitful,
advantageous **OPPOSITE:**
useless

profound 1 = **sincere**,
acute, intense, great, keen,
extreme, heartfelt, deeply felt
OPPOSITE: insincere 2 = **wise**,
learned, deep, penetrating,
philosophical, sage, abstruse,
sagacious **OPPOSITE:**
uninformed

programme 1 = **schedule**,
plan, agenda, timetable,
listing, list, line-up, calendar
2 = **course**, curriculum, syllabus
3 = **show**, performance,
production, broadcast, episode,
presentation, transmission,
telecast, podcast

progress NOUN
1 = **development**, growth,
advance, gain, improvement,
breakthrough, headway
OPPOSITE: regression
2 = **movement forward**,
passage, advancement, course,
advance, headway **OPPOSITE:**
movement backward
▷ VERB 3 = **move on**, continue,
travel, advance, proceed, go
forward, make headway, crack
on (*informal*) **OPPOSITE:** move
back 4 = **develop**, improve,
advance, grow, gain **OPPOSITE:**
get behind
▷ PHRASES: **in progress** = going

P

on, happening, continuing, being done, occurring, taking place, proceeding, under way

progression 1 = **progress**, advance, advancement, gain, headway, furtherance, movement forward 2 = **sequence**, course, series, chain, cycle, string, succession

progressive 1 = **enlightened**, liberal, modern, advanced, radical, revolutionary, avant-garde, reformist 2 = **growing**, continuing, increasing, developing, advancing, ongoing

prohibit 1 = **forbid**, ban, veto, outlaw, disallow, proscribe, debar **OPPOSITE:** permit 2 = **prevent**, restrict, stop, hamper, hinder, impede **OPPOSITE:** allow

prohibition = **ban**, boycott, embargo, bar, veto, prevention, exclusion, injunction, restraining order (US law)

project NOUN 1 = **scheme**, plan, job, idea, campaign, operation, activity, venture 2 = **assignment**, task, homework, piece of research ▷ VERB 3 = **forecast**, expect, estimate, predict, reckon, calculate, gauge, extrapolate 4 = **stick out**, extend, stand out, bulge, protrude, overhang, jut

projection = **forecast**, estimate, reckoning, calculation, estimation, computation, extrapolation

proliferation = **multiplication**, increase, spread, expansion

prolific 1 = **productive**, creative, fertile, inventive, copious 2 = **fruitful**, fertile, abundant, luxuriant, profuse, fecund **OPPOSITE:** unproductive

prolong = **lengthen**, continue, perpetuate, draw out, extend, delay, stretch out, spin out **OPPOSITE:** shorten

prominence 1 = **fame**, name, reputation, importance, celebrity, distinction, prestige, eminence 2 = **conspicuousness**, markedness

prominent 1 = **famous**, leading, top, important, main, distinguished, well-known, notable **OPPOSITE:** unknown 2 = **noticeable**, obvious, outstanding, pronounced, conspicuous, eye-catching, obtrusive **OPPOSITE:** inconspicuous

promise VERB 1 = **guarantee**, pledge, vow, swear, contract, assure, undertake, warrant 2 = **seem likely**, look like, show signs of, augur, betoken ▷ NOUN 3 = **guarantee**, word, bond, vow, commitment, pledge, undertaking, assurance 4 = **potential**, ability, talent, capacity, capability, aptitude

promising 1 = **encouraging**, likely, bright, reassuring, hopeful, favourable, rosy, auspicious **OPPOSITE:**

unpromising 2 = **talented**, able, gifted, rising

promote 1 = **help**, back, support, aid, forward, encourage, advance, boost **OPPOSITE:** impede 2 = **advertise**, sell, hype, publicize, push, plug (*informal*) 3 = **raise**, upgrade, elevate, exalt **OPPOSITE:** demote

promotion 1 = **rise**, upgrading, move up, advancement, elevation, exaltation, preferment 2 = **publicity**, advertising, plugging (*informal*) 3 = **encouragement**, support, boosting, advancement, furtherance

prompt VERB 1 = **cause**, occasion, provoke, give rise to, elicit **OPPOSITE:** discourage 2 = **remind**, assist, cue, help out ▷ ADJECTIVE 3 = **immediate**, quick, rapid, instant, timely, early, swift, speedy **OPPOSITE:** slow ▷ ADVERB 4 (*informal*) = **exactly**, sharp, promptly, on the dot, punctually

promptly 1 = **immediately**, swiftly, directly, quickly, at once, speedily 2 = **punctually**, on time, spot on (*informal*), bang on (*informal*), on the dot, on the button (*US*), on the nail

prone 1 = **liable**, given, subject, inclined, tending, bent, disposed, susceptible **OPPOSITE:** disinclined 2 = **face down**, flat, horizontal, prostrate, recumbent **OPPOSITE:** face up

pronounce 1 = **say**, speak, sound, articulate, enunciate 2 = **declare**, announce, deliver, proclaim, decree, affirm

pronounced = **noticeable**, decided, marked, striking, obvious, evident, distinct, definite **OPPOSITE:** imperceptible

proof NOUN 1 = **evidence**, demonstration, testimony, confirmation, verification, corroboration, authentication, substantiation ▷ ADJECTIVE 2 = **impervious**, strong, resistant, impenetrable, repellent

prop VERB 1 = **lean**, place, set, stand, position, rest, lay, balance 2 *often with* **up** = **support**, sustain, hold up, brace, uphold, bolster, buttress ▷ NOUN 3 = **support**, stay, brace, mainstay, buttress, stanchion 4 = **mainstay**, support, sustainer, anchor, backbone, cornerstone, upholder

propaganda = **information**, advertising, promotion, publicity, hype, disinformation

propel 1 = **drive**, launch, force, send, shoot, push, thrust, shove **OPPOSITE:** stop 2 = **impel**, drive, push, prompt, spur, motivate **OPPOSITE:** hold back

proper 1 = **real**, actual, genuine, true, bona fide, dinkum (*Austral*

& *NZ informal*) **2 = correct**, accepted, established, appropriate, right, formal, conventional, precise **OPPOSITE:** improper **3 = polite**, right, becoming, seemly, fitting, fit, mannerly, suitable **OPPOSITE:** unseemly

properly 1 = correctly, rightly, fittingly, appropriately, accurately, suitably, aptly **OPPOSITE:** incorrectly **2 = politely**, decently, respectably **OPPOSITE:** badly

property 1 = possessions, goods, effects, holdings, capital, riches, estate, assets **2 = land**, holding, estate, real estate, freehold **3 = quality**, feature, characteristic, attribute, trait, hallmark

prophecy 1 = prediction, forecast, prognostication, augury **2 = second sight**, divination, augury, telling the future, soothsaying

prophet *or* **prophetess** **= soothsayer**, forecaster, diviner, oracle, seer, sibyl, prophesier

proportion NOUN 1 = part, share, amount, division, percentage, segment, quota, fraction **2 = relative amount**, relationship, ratio **3 = balance**, harmony, correspondence, symmetry, concord, congruity ▷ **PLURAL NOUN 4 = dimensions**, size, volume, capacity, extent, expanse

proportional *or* **proportionate** **= correspondent**, corresponding, even, balanced, consistent, compatible, equitable, in proportion **OPPOSITE:** disproportionate

proposal = suggestion, plan, programme, scheme, offer, project, bid, recommendation

propose 1 = put forward, present, suggest, advance, submit **2 = intend**, mean, plan, aim, design, scheme, have in mind **3 = nominate**, name, present, recommend **4 = offer marriage**, pop the question (*informal*), ask for someone's hand (in marriage)

proposition NOUN 1 = task, problem, activity, job, affair, venture, undertaking **2 = theory**, idea, argument, concept, thesis, hypothesis, theorem, premise **3 = proposal**, plan, suggestion, scheme, bid, recommendation **4 = advance**, pass (*informal*), proposal, overture, improper suggestion, come-on (*informal*) ▷ **VERB 5 = make a pass at**, solicit, accost, make an improper suggestion to

proprietor *or* **proprietress** **= owner**, titleholder, landlord *or* landlady

prosecute (*Law*) **= take someone to court**, try, sue, indict, arraign, put someone on trial, litigate, bring someone to trial

prospect NOUN 1 = **likelihood**, chance, possibility, hope, promise, odds, expectation, probability 2 = **idea**, outlook 3 = **view**, landscape, scene, sight, outlook, spectacle, vista

▷ PLURAL NOUN

4 = **possibilities**, chances, future, potential, expectations, outlook, scope

▷ VERB 5 = **look**, search, seek, dowse

prospective 1 = **potential**, possible 2 = **expected**, coming, future, likely, intended, anticipated, forthcoming, imminent

prospectus = **catalogue**, list, programme, outline, syllabus, synopsis

prosper = **succeed**, advance, progress, thrive, get on, do well, flourish

prosperity = **success**, riches, plenty, fortune, wealth, luxury, good fortune, affluence OPPOSITE: poverty

prosperous 1 = **wealthy**, rich, affluent, well-off, well-heeled (*informal*), well-to-do, moneyed, minted (*Brit slang*) OPPOSITE: poor 2 = **successful**, booming, thriving, flourishing, doing well OPPOSITE: unsuccessful

prostitute NOUN 1 = **whore**, hooker (*US slang*), pro (*slang*), tart (*informal*), call girl, harlot, streetwalker, loose woman

▷ VERB 2 = **cheapen**, sell out, pervert, degrade, devalue, squander, demean, debase

protagonist 1 = **supporter**, champion, advocate, exponent 2 = **leading character**, principal, central character, hero *or* heroine

protect = **keep someone safe**, defend, support, save, guard, preserve, look after, shelter OPPOSITE: endanger

protection 1 = **safety**, care, defence, protecting, security, custody, safeguard, aegis 2 = **safeguard**, cover, guard, shelter, screen, barrier, shield, buffer 3 = **armour**, cover, screen, barrier, shelter, shield

protective 1 = **protecting** 2 = **caring**, defensive, motherly, fatherly, maternal, vigilant, watchful, paternal

protector 1 = **defender**, champion, guard, guardian, patron, bodyguard 2 = **guard**, screen, protection, shield, pad, cushion, buffer

protest VERB 1 = **object**, demonstrate, oppose, complain, disagree, cry out, disapprove, demur 2 = **assert**, insist, maintain, declare, affirm, profess, attest, avow

▷ NOUN 3 = **demonstration**, march, rally, sit-in, demo (*informal*), hikoi (*NZ*)

4 = **objection**, complaint,

dissent, outcry, protestation, remonstrance

protocol = **code of behaviour**, manners, conventions, customs, etiquette, propriety, decorum

prototype = **original**, model, first, example, standard

protracted = **extended**, prolonged, drawn-out, spun out, dragged out, long-drawn-out

proud 1 = **satisfied**, pleased, content, thrilled, glad, gratified, joyful, well-pleased **OPPOSITE:** dissatisfied 2 = **conceited**, arrogant, lordly, imperious, overbearing, haughty, snobbish, self-satisfied **OPPOSITE:** humble

prove 1 = **turn out**, come out, end up 2 = **verify**, establish, determine, show, confirm, demonstrate, justify, substantiate **OPPOSITE:** disprove

proven = **established**, proved, confirmed, tested, reliable, definite, verified, attested

provide 1 = **supply**, give, distribute, outfit, equip, donate, furnish, dispense **OPPOSITE:** withhold 2 = **give**, bring, add, produce, present, serve, afford, yield
▷ **PHRASES: provide for someone** = **support**, care for, keep, maintain, sustain, take care of, fend for ▶ **provide for** *or* **against something** = **take**

precautions against, plan for, prepare for, anticipate, plan ahead for, forearm for

provider 1 = **supplier**, giver, source, donor 2 = **breadwinner**, supporter, earner, wage earner

providing *or* **provided** *often with* **that** = **on condition that**, if, given that, as long as

province 1 = **region**, section, district, zone, patch, colony, domain

provincial 1 = **regional**, state, local, county, district, territorial, parochial 2 = **rural**, country, local, rustic, homespun, hick (*informal, chiefly US & Canad*), backwoods **OPPOSITE:** urban 3 = **parochial**, insular, narrow-minded, unsophisticated, limited, narrow, small-town (*chiefly US*), inward-looking **OPPOSITE:** cosmopolitan

provision NOUN 1 = **supplying**, giving, providing, supply, delivery, distribution, catering, presentation 2 = **condition**, term, requirement, demand, rider, restriction, qualification, clause
▷ **PLURAL NOUN** 3 = **food**, supplies, stores, fare, rations, foodstuff, kai (*NZ informal*), victuals, edibles

provisional 1 = **temporary**, interim **OPPOSITE:** permanent 2 = **conditional**, limited, qualified, contingent, tentative **OPPOSITE:** definite

provocation 1 = **cause**, reason, grounds, motivation, stimulus, incitement 2 = **offence**, challenge, insult, taunt, injury, dare, grievance, annoyance

provocative = **offensive**, provoking, insulting, stimulating, annoying, galling, goading

provoke 1 = **anger**, annoy, irritate, infuriate, hassle (*informal*), aggravate (*informal*), incense, enrage **OPPOSITE:** pacify 2 = **rouse**, cause, produce, promote, occasion, prompt, stir, induce **OPPOSITE:** curb

prowess 1 = **skill**, ability, talent, expertise, genius, excellence, accomplishment, mastery **OPPOSITE:** inability 2 = **bravery**, daring, courage, heroism, mettle, valour, fearlessness, valiance **OPPOSITE:** cowardice

proximity = **nearness**, closeness

proxy = **representative**, agent, deputy, substitute, factor, delegate

prudent 1 = **cautious**, careful, wary, discreet, vigilant **OPPOSITE:** careless 2 = **wise**, politic, sensible, shrewd, discerning, judicious **OPPOSITE:** unwise 3 = **thrifty**, economical, sparing, careful, canny, provident, frugal, far-sighted **OPPOSITE:** extravagant

prune 1 = **cut**, trim, clip, dock, shape, shorten, snip 2 = **reduce**, cut, cut back, trim, cut down, pare down, make reductions in

psyche = **soul**, mind, self, spirit, personality, individuality, anima, wairua (*NZ*)

psychiatrist = **psychotherapist**, analyst, therapist, psychologist, shrink (*slang*), psychoanalyst, headshrinker (*slang*)

psychic ADJECTIVE 1 = **supernatural**, mystic, occult 2 = **mystical**, spiritual, magical, other-worldly, paranormal, preternatural 3 = **psychological**, emotional, mental, spiritual, inner, psychiatric, cognitive ▷ NOUN 4 = **clairvoyant**, fortune teller

psychological 1 = **mental**, emotional, intellectual, inner, cognitive, cerebral 2 = **imaginary**, psychosomatic, irrational, unreal, all in the mind

psychology 1 = **behaviourism**, study of personality, science of mind 2 (*informal*) = **way of thinking**, attitude, behaviour, temperament, mentality, thought processes, mental processes, what makes you tick

pub *or* **public house** = **tavern**, bar, inn, saloon, beer parlour (*Canad*), beverage room (*Canad*)

public NOUN 1 = **people**, society, community, nation, everyone,

citizens, electorate, populace
▷ **ADJECTIVE 2 = civic**, government, state, national, local, official, community, social **3 = general**, popular, national, shared, common, widespread, universal, collective **4 = open**, accessible, communal, unrestricted **OPPOSITE:** private **5 = well-known**, leading, important, respected, famous, celebrated, recognized, distinguished **6 = known**, open, obvious, acknowledged, plain, patent, overt **OPPOSITE:** secret

publication 1 = pamphlet, newspaper, magazine, issue, title, leaflet, brochure, periodical, blog (*informal*) **2 = announcement**, publishing, broadcasting, reporting, declaration, disclosure, proclamation, notification

publicity 1 = advertising, press, promotion, hype, boost, plug (*informal*) **2 = attention**, exposure, fame, celebrity, fuss, public interest, limelight, notoriety

publish 1 = put out, issue, produce, print **2 = announce**, reveal, spread, advertise, broadcast, disclose, proclaim, circulate

pudding = dessert, afters (*Brit informal*), sweet, pud (*informal*)

puff VERB 1 = smoke, draw, drag (*slang*), suck, inhale, pull

at *or* on **2 = breathe heavily**, pant, exhale, blow, gasp, gulp, wheeze, fight for breath
▷ **NOUN 3 = drag**, pull (*slang*), smoke **4 = blast**, breath, whiff, draught, gust

pull VERB 1 = draw, haul, drag, trail, tow, tug, jerk, yank **OPPOSITE:** push **2 = extract**, pick, remove, gather, take out, pluck, uproot, draw out **OPPOSITE:** insert **3** (*informal*) **= attract**, draw, bring in, tempt, lure, interest, entice, pull in **OPPOSITE:** repel **4 = strain**, tear, stretch, rip, wrench, dislocate, sprain
▷ **NOUN 5 = tug**, jerk, yank, twitch, heave **OPPOSITE:** shove **6 = puff**, drag (*slang*), inhalation **7** (*informal*) **= influence**, power, weight, muscle, clout (*informal*), kai (*NZ informal*)
▷ **PHRASES: pull out (of) 1 = withdraw**, quit **2 = leave**, abandon, get out, quit, retreat from, depart, evacuate ▶ **pull someone up = reprimand**, rebuke, admonish, read the riot act to, tell someone off (*informal*), reprove, bawl someone out (*informal*), tear someone off a strip (*Brit informal*) ▶ **pull something off = succeed in**, manage, carry out, accomplish ▶ **pull something out = produce**, draw, bring out, draw out ▶ **pull up = stop**, halt, brake (*informal*)

pulp NOUN 1 = **paste**, mash, mush 2 = **flesh**, meat, soft part
▷ MODIFIER 3 = **cheap**, lurid, trashy, rubbishy
▷ VERB 4 = **crush**, squash, mash, pulverize

pulse NOUN 1 = **beat**, rhythm, vibration, beating, throb, throbbing, pulsation
▷ VERB 2 = **beat**, throb, vibrate, pulsate

pump 1 = **supply**, send, pour, inject 2 = **interrogate**, probe, quiz, cross-examine

punch¹ VERB 1 = **hit**, strike, box, smash, belt (*informal*), sock (*slang*), swipe (*informal*), bop (*informal*)
▷ NOUN 2 = **blow**, hit, sock (*slang*), jab, swipe (*informal*), bop (*informal*), wallop (*informal*) 3 (*informal*) = **effectiveness**, bite, impact, drive, vigour, verve, forcefulness

punch² = **pierce**, cut, bore, drill, stamp, puncture, prick, perforate

punctuate = **interrupt**, break, pepper, sprinkle, intersperse

puncture NOUN 1 = **flat tyre**, flat, flattie (*NZ*) 2 = **hole**, opening, break, cut, nick, leak, slit
▷ VERB 3 = **pierce**, cut, nick, penetrate, prick, rupture, perforate, bore a hole (in)

punish = **discipline**, correct, castigate, chastise, sentence, chasten, penalize

punishing = **hard**, taxing, wearing, tiring, exhausting, gruelling, strenuous, arduous
OPPOSITE: easy

punishment 1 = **penalizing**, discipline, correction, retribution, chastening, chastisement 2 = **penalty**, penance

punitive = **retaliatory**, in reprisal, retaliative

punt VERB 1 = **bet**, back, stake, gamble, lay, wager
▷ NOUN 2 = **bet**, stake, gamble, wager

punter 1 = **gambler**, better, backer 2 (*informal*) = **person**, man in the street

pupil 1 = **student**, schoolboy *or* schoolgirl, schoolchild
OPPOSITE: teacher 2 = **learner**, novice, beginner, disciple
OPPOSITE: instructor

puppet 1 = **marionette**, doll, glove puppet, sock puppet, finger puppet 2 = **pawn**, tool, instrument, mouthpiece, stooge, cat's-paw

purchase VERB 1 = **buy**, pay for, obtain, get, score (*slang*), gain, pick up, acquire
OPPOSITE: sell
▷ NOUN 2 = **acquisition**, buy, investment, property, gain, asset, possession 3 = **grip**, hold, support, leverage, foothold

pure 1 = **unmixed**, real, simple, natural, straight, genuine, neat, authentic OPPOSITE:

P

adulterated 2 = **clean**, wholesome, sanitary, spotless, sterilized, squeaky-clean, untainted, uncontaminated **OPPOSITE:** contaminated 3 = **complete**, total, perfect, absolute, sheer, patent, utter, outright **OPPOSITE:** qualified 4 = **innocent**, modest, good, moral, impeccable, righteous, virtuous, squeaky-clean **OPPOSITE:** corrupt

purely = **absolutely**, just, only, completely, simply, entirely, exclusively, merely

purge VERB 1 = **rid**, clear, cleanse, strip, empty, void 2 = **get rid of**, remove, expel, wipe out, eradicate, do away with, exterminate ▷ NOUN 3 = **removal**, elimination, expulsion, eradication, ejection

purity 1 = **cleanness**, cleanliness, wholesomeness, pureness, faultlessness, immaculateness **OPPOSITE:** impurity 2 = **innocence**, virtue, integrity, honesty, decency, virginity, chastity, chasteness **OPPOSITE:** immorality

purple
• See panel **SHADES OF PURPLE**

purport = **claim**, allege, assert, profess

purpose 1 = **reason**, point, idea, aim, object, intention 2 = **aim**, end, plan, hope, goal, wish, desire, object 3 = **determination**, resolve, will, resolution, ambition, persistence, tenacity, firmness ▷ PHRASES: on purpose = **deliberately**, purposely, intentionally, knowingly, designedly

p

SHADES OF PURPLE

amethyst	magenta
aubergine	mauve
burgundy	mulberry
carmine	pansy
claret	peach-blow
dubonnet	periwinkle
gentian	plum
gentian blue	puce
heather	royal purple
heliotrope	Tyrian purple
indigo	violet
lavender	wine
lilac	

USAGE NOTE
The two concepts *purposeful* and *on purpose* should be carefully distinguished. *On purpose* and *purposely* have roughly the same meaning, and imply that a person's action is deliberate, rather than accidental. However, *purposeful* and its related adverb *purposefully* refer to the way that someone acts as being full of purpose or determination.

purposely = **deliberately**, expressly, consciously, intentionally, knowingly, with intent, on purpose **OPPOSITE:** accidentally

purse NOUN 1 = **pouch**, wallet, money-bag, e-wallet *or* eWallet 2 (*US*) = **handbag**, bag, shoulder bag, pocket book, clutch bag 3 = **funds**, means, money, resources, treasury, wealth, exchequer
▷ VERB 4 = **pucker**, contract, tighten, pout, press together

pursue 1 = **engage in**, perform, conduct, carry on, practise 2 = **try for**, seek, desire, search for, aim for, work towards, strive for 3 = **continue**, maintain, carry on, keep on, persist in, proceed in, persevere in 4 = **follow**, track, hunt, chase, dog, shadow, tail (*informal*), hound **OPPOSITE:** flee

pursuit 1 = **quest**, seeking, search, aim, aspiration, striving towards 2 = **pursuing**, seeking, search, hunt, chase, trailing 3 = **occupation**, activity, interest, line, pleasure, hobby, pastime

push VERB 1 = **shove**, force, press, thrust, drive, knock, sweep, plunge **OPPOSITE:** pull 2 = **press**, operate, depress, squeeze, activate, hold down 3 = **make** *or* **force your way**, move, shoulder, inch, squeeze, thrust, elbow, shove 4 = **urge**, encourage, persuade, spur, press, incite, impel **OPPOSITE:** discourage
▷ NOUN 5 = **shove**, thrust, butt, elbow, nudge **OPPOSITE:** pull 6 (*informal*) = **drive**, go (*informal*), energy, initiative, enterprise, ambition, vitality, vigour
▷ PHRASES: **the push** (*informal*, *chiefly Brit*) = **dismissal**, the sack (*informal*), discharge, the boot (*slang*), your cards (*informal*)

put 1 = **place**, leave, set, position, rest, park (*informal*), plant, lay 2 = **express**, state, word, phrase, utter
▷ PHRASES: **put someone off** 1 = **discourage**, intimidate, deter, daunt, dissuade, demoralize, scare off, dishearten 2 = **disconcert**, confuse, unsettle, throw (*informal*), dismay, perturb, faze, discomfit ▶ **put someone**

P

up 1 = **accommodate**, house, board, lodge, quarter, take someone in, billet 2 = **nominate**, put forward, offer, present, propose, recommend, submit ▶ **put something across** or **over** = **communicate**, explain, convey, make clear, get across, make yourself understood ▶ **put something off** = **postpone**, delay, defer, adjourn, hold over, put on the back burner (*informal*), take a rain check on (*US & Canad informal*) ▶ **put something up** 1 = **build**, raise, set up, construct, erect, fabricate 2 = **offer**, present, mount, put forward (*informal*)

puzzle VERB 1 = **perplex**, confuse, baffle, stump, bewilder, confound, mystify, faze ▷ NOUN 2 = **problem**, riddle, question, conundrum, poser 3 = **mystery**, problem, paradox, enigma, conundrum

puzzling = **perplexing**, baffling, bewildering, involved, enigmatic, incomprehensible, mystifying, abstruse **OPPOSITE:** simple

q

Qq

quake = **shake**, tremble, quiver, move, rock, shiver, shudder, vibrate

qualification 1 = **eligibility**, quality, ability, skill, fitness, attribute, capability, aptitude 2 = **condition**, proviso, requirement, rider, reservation, limitation, modification, caveat

qualified 1 = **capable**, trained, experienced, seasoned, able, fit, expert, chartered **OPPOSITE:** untrained 2 = **restricted**, limited, provisional, conditional, reserved, bounded, adjusted, moderated **OPPOSITE:** unconditional

qualify 1 = **certify**, equip, empower, train, prepare, fit, ready, permit **OPPOSITE:** disqualify 2 = **restrict**, limit, reduce, ease, moderate, regulate, diminish, temper

quality 1 = **standard**, standing, class, condition, rank, grade, merit, classification 2 = **excellence**, status, merit, position, value, worth, distinction, virtue

3 = **characteristic**, feature, attribute, point, side, mark, property, aspect 4 = **nature**, character, make, sort, kind

quantity 1 = **amount**, lot, total, sum, part, number 2 = **size**, measure, mass, volume, length, capacity, extent, bulk

> **USAGE NOTE**
> The use of a plural noun after *quantity of*, as in *a large quantity of bananas*, used to be considered incorrect, the objection being that the word *quantity* should only be used to refer to an uncountable amount, which was grammatically regarded as a singular concept. Nowadays, however, most people consider the use of *quantity* with a plural noun to be acceptable.

quarrel NOUN
1 = **disagreement**, fight, row, argument, dispute, controversy, breach, contention, biffo (*Austral slang*) **OPPOSITE:** accord
▷ VERB 2 = **disagree**, fight, argue, row, clash, dispute, differ, fall out (*informal*) **OPPOSITE:** get on *or* along (with)

quarry = **prey**, victim, game, goal, aim, prize, objective

quarter NOUN 1 = **district**, region, neighbourhood, place, part, side, area, zone 2 = **mercy**, pity, compassion, charity, sympathy, tolerance, kindness, forgiveness

▷ VERB 3 = **accommodate**, house, lodge, place, board, post, station, billet

quarters = **lodgings**, rooms, chambers, residence, dwelling, barracks, abode, habitation

quash 1 = **annul**, overturn, reverse, cancel, overthrow, revoke, overrule, rescind
2 = **suppress**, crush, put down, beat, overthrow, squash, subdue, repress

queen 1 = **sovereign**, ruler, monarch, leader, Crown, princess, majesty, head of state
2 = **leading light**, star, favourite, celebrity, darling, mistress, big name

queer 1 = **strange**, odd, funny, unusual, extraordinary, curious, weird, peculiar **OPPOSITE:** normal 2 = **faint**, dizzy, giddy, queasy, light-headed

query NOUN 1 = **question**, inquiry, enquiry, problem
2 = **doubt**, suspicion, objection
▷ VERB 3 = **question**, challenge, doubt, suspect, dispute, object to, distrust, mistrust 4 = **ask**, inquire *or* enquire, question

quest 1 = **search**, hunt, mission, enterprise, crusade
2 = **expedition**, journey, adventure

question NOUN 1 = **inquiry**, enquiry, query, investigation, examination, interrogation
OPPOSITE: answer 2 = **difficulty**, problem, doubt, argument,

q

dispute, controversy, query, contention **3 = issue**, point, matter, subject, problem, debate, proposal, theme
▷ VERB **4 = interrogate**, cross-examine, interview, examine, probe, quiz, ask questions
5 = dispute, challenge, doubt, suspect, oppose, query, mistrust, disbelieve **OPPOSITE:** accept
▷ PHRASES: **out of the question = impossible**, unthinkable, inconceivable, not on (*informal*), hopeless, unimaginable, unworkable, unattainable

questionable = dubious, suspect, doubtful, controversial, suspicious, dodgy (*Brit, Austral & NZ informal*), debatable, moot, shonky (*Austral & NZ informal*) **OPPOSITE:** indisputable

questionnaire = set of questions, form, survey form, question sheet

queue = line, row, file, train, series, chain, string, column

quick 1 = fast, swift, speedy, express, cracking (*Brit informal*), smart, rapid, fleet **OPPOSITE:** slow **2 = brief**, passing, hurried, flying, fleeting, summary, lightning, short-lived **OPPOSITE:** long **3 = immediate**, instant, prompt, sudden, abrupt, instantaneous **4 = excitable**, passionate, irritable, touchy, irascible, testy **OPPOSITE:** calm **5 = intelligent**, bright (*informal*),

alert, sharp, acute, smart, clever, shrewd **OPPOSITE:** stupid

quicken 1 = speed up, hurry, accelerate, hasten, gee up (*informal*) **2 = stimulate**, inspire, arouse, excite, revive, incite, energize, invigorate

quickly 1 = swiftly, rapidly, hurriedly, fast, hastily, briskly, apace **OPPOSITE:** slowly
2 = soon, speedily, as soon as possible, momentarily (*US*), instantaneously, pronto (*informal*), a.s.a.p. (*informal*)
3 = immediately, at once, directly, promptly, abruptly, without delay

quiet ADJECTIVE **1 = soft**, low, muted, lowered, whispered, faint, suppressed, stifled **OPPOSITE:** loud **2 = peaceful**, silent, hushed, soundless, noiseless **OPPOSITE:** noisy **3 = calm**, peaceful, tranquil, mild, serene, placid, restful, chilled (*informal*) **OPPOSITE:** exciting **4 = still**, calm, peaceful, tranquil **OPPOSITE:** troubled **5 = undisturbed**, isolated, secluded, private, sequestered, unfrequented **OPPOSITE:** crowded **6 = silent** **7 = reserved**, retiring, shy, gentle, mild, sedate, meek **OPPOSITE:** excitable
▷ NOUN **8 = peace**, rest, tranquillity, ease, silence, solitude, serenity, stillness **OPPOSITE:** noise

q

quietly 1 = **noiselessly**, silently
2 = **softly**, inaudibly, in an
undertone, under your breath
3 = **calmly**, serenely, placidly,
patiently, mildly 4 = **silently**,
mutely

quilt = **bedspread**, duvet,
coverlet, eiderdown,
counterpane, doona (*Austral*),
continental quilt

quip = **joke**, sally, jest, riposte,
wisecrack (*informal*), retort,
pleasantry, gibe

quirky = **odd**, unusual, eccentric,
idiosyncratic, peculiar, offbeat

quit 1 = **resign (from)**, leave,
retire (from), pull out (of), step
down (from) (*informal*), abdicate
2 = **stop**, give up, cease, end,
drop, abandon, halt, discontinue
OPPOSITE: continue 3 = **leave**,
depart from, go out of, go away
from, pull out from

quite 1 = **somewhat**, rather,
fairly, reasonably, relatively,
moderately 2 = **absolutely**,
perfectly, completely, totally,
fully, entirely, wholly

quiz NOUN 1 = **examination**,
questioning, interrogation,
interview, investigation, grilling
(*informal*), cross-examination,
cross-questioning
▷ VERB 2 = **question**, ask,
interrogate, examine,
investigate

quota = **share**, allowance,
ration, part, limit, slice,
quantity, portion

quotation 1 = **passage**, quote
(*informal*), excerpt, reference,
extract, citation 2 (*Commerce*)
= **estimate**, price, tender, rate,
cost, charge, figure, quote
(*informal*)

quote 1 = **repeat**, recite, recall
2 = **refer to**, cite, give, name,
detail, relate, mention, instance

q

Rr

race¹ NOUN 1 = competition, contest, chase, dash, pursuit **2 = contest**, competition, rivalry
▷ **VERB 3 = compete against**, run against **4 = compete**, run, contend, take part in a race **5 = run**, fly, career, speed, tear, dash, hurry, dart

race² = people, nation, blood, stock, type, folk, tribe

racial = ethnic, ethnological, national, folk, genetic, tribal, genealogical

rack NOUN 1 = frame, stand, structure, framework
▷ **VERB 2 = torture**, torment, afflict, oppress, harrow, crucify, agonize, pain

> **USAGE NOTE**
> The use of the spelling *wrack* rather than *rack* in sentences such as *she was wracked by grief* or *the country was wracked by civil war* is very common, but is thought by many people to be incorrect.

racket 1 = noise, row, fuss, disturbance, outcry, clamour, din, pandemonium **2 = fraud**, scheme

radiate 1 = emit, spread, send out, pour, shed, scatter **2 = shine**, be diffused **3 = show**, display, demonstrate, exhibit, emanate, give off *or* out **4 = spread out**, diverge, branch out

radical ADJECTIVE 1 = extreme, complete, entire, sweeping, severe, thorough, drastic **2 = revolutionary**, extremist, fanatical **3 = fundamental**, natural, basic, profound, innate, deep-seated **OPPOSITE:** superficial
▷ **NOUN 4 = extremist**, revolutionary, militant, fanatic **OPPOSITE:** conservative

rage NOUN 1 = fury, temper, frenzy, rampage, tantrum, foulie (*Austral slang*), hissy fit (*informal*), strop (*Brit informal*) **OPPOSITE:** calmness **2 = anger**, passion, madness, wrath, ire **3 = craze**, fashion, enthusiasm, vogue, fad (*informal*), latest thing
▷ **VERB 4 = be furious**, blow up (*informal*), fume, lose it (*informal*), seethe, lose the plot (*informal*), go ballistic (*slang, chiefly US*), lose your temper **OPPOSITE:** stay calm

ragged 1 = tatty, worn, torn, rundown, shabby, seedy, scruffy, in tatters **OPPOSITE:** smart **2 = rough**, rugged, unfinished, uneven, jagged, serrated

raid VERB 1 = **steal from**, plunder, pillage, sack 2 = **attack**, invade, assault 3 = **make a search of**, search, bust (*informal*), make a raid on, make a swoop on
▷ NOUN 4 = **attack**, invasion, foray, sortie, incursion, sally, inroad 5 = **bust** (*informal*), swoop

raider = **attacker**, thief, robber, plunderer, invader, marauder

railing = **fence**, rails, barrier, paling, balustrade

rain NOUN 1 = **rainfall**, fall, showers, deluge, drizzle, downpour, raindrops, cloudburst
▷ VERB 2 = **pour**, pelt (down), teem, bucket down (*informal*), drizzle, come down in buckets (*informal*) 3 = **fall**, shower, be dropped, sprinkle, be deposited

rainy = **wet**, damp, drizzly, showery OPPOSITE: dry

raise 1 = **lift**, elevate, uplift, heave 2 = **set upright**, lift, elevate 3 = **increase**, intensify, heighten, advance, boost, strengthen, enhance, enlarge OPPOSITE: reduce 4 = **make louder**, heighten, amplify, louden 5 = **collect**, gather, obtain 6 = **cause**, start, produce, create, occasion, provoke, originate, engender 7 = **put forward**, suggest, introduce, advance, broach, moot 8 = **bring up**, develop,

rear, nurture 9 = **build**, construct, put up, erect OPPOSITE: demolish

rake¹ 1 = **gather**, collect, remove 2 *with* **through** = **search**, comb, scour, scrutinize, fossick (*Austral & NZ*)

rake² = **libertine**, playboy, swinger (*slang*), lecher, roué, debauchee OPPOSITE: puritan

rally NOUN 1 = **gathering**, convention, meeting, congress, assembly, hui (*NZ*) 2 = **recovery**, improvement, revival, recuperation OPPOSITE: relapse
▷ VERB 3 = **gather together**, unite, regroup, reorganize, reassemble 4 = **recover**, improve, revive, get better, recuperate OPPOSITE: get worse

ram 1 = **hit**, force, drive into, crash, impact, smash, dash, butt 2 = **cram**, force, stuff, jam, thrust

ramble NOUN 1 = **walk**, tour, stroll, hike, roaming, roving, saunter
▷ VERB 2 = **walk**, range, wander, stroll, stray, roam, rove, saunter, go walkabout (*Austral*) 3 *often with* **on** = **babble**, rabbit (on) (*Brit informal*), waffle (*informal, chiefly Brit*), witter on (*informal*)

ramp = **slope**, incline, gradient, rise

rampage = **go berserk**, storm, rage, run riot, run amok
▷ PHRASES: **on the rampage** = **berserk**, wild, violent, raging,

out of control, amok, riotous, berko (*Austral slang*)

rampant 1 = **widespread**, prevalent, rife, uncontrolled, unchecked, unrestrained, profuse, spreading like wildfire 2 (*Heraldry*) = **upright**, standing, rearing, erect

random 1 = **chance**, casual, accidental, incidental, haphazard, fortuitous, hit or miss, adventitious **OPPOSITE:** planned 2 = **casual**
▷ **PHRASES: at random** = **haphazardly**, randomly, arbitrarily, by chance, willy-nilly, unsystematically

randy (*informal*) = **lustful**, hot, turned-on (*slang*), aroused, horny (*slang*), amorous, lascivious

range NOUN 1 = **series**, variety, selection, assortment, lot, collection, gamut 2 = **limits**, reach 3 = **scope**, area, bounds, province, orbit, radius
▷ **VERB** 4 = **vary**, run, reach, extend, stretch 5 = **roam**, wander, rove, ramble, traverse

rank¹ NOUN 1 = **status**, level, position, grade, order, sort, type, division 2 = **class**, caste 3 = **row**, line, file, column, group, range, series, tier
▷ **VERB** 4 = **order**, dispose 5 = **arrange**, sort, line up, array, align

rank² 1 = **absolute**, complete, total, gross, sheer, utter, thorough, blatant 2 = **foul**, bad, offensive, disgusting, revolting, stinking, noxious, rancid, festy (*Austral slang*) 3 = **abundant**, lush, luxuriant, dense, profuse

ransom = **payment**, money, price, payoff

rant = **shout**, roar, yell, rave, cry, declaim

rap VERB 1 = **hit**, strike, knock, crack, tap
▷ NOUN 2 = **blow**, knock, crack, tap, clout (*informal*) 3 (*slang*) = **rebuke**, blame, responsibility, punishment

rape VERB 1 = **sexually assault**, violate, abuse, ravish, force, outrage
▷ NOUN 2 = **sexual assault**, violation, ravishment, outrage

rapid 1 = **sudden**, prompt, speedy, express, swift **OPPOSITE:** gradual 2 = **quick**, fast, hurried, swift, brisk, hasty **OPPOSITE:** slow

rapidly = **quickly**, fast, swiftly, briskly, promptly, hastily, hurriedly, speedily

rare 1 = **uncommon**, unusual, few, strange, scarce, singular, sparse, infrequent **OPPOSITE:** common 2 = **superb**, great, fine, excellent, superlative, choice, peerless

rarely = **seldom**, hardly, hardly ever, infrequently **OPPOSITE:** often

| **USAGE NOTE**
Since the meaning of *rarely* is

'hardly ever', the combination *rarely ever* is repetitive and should be avoided in careful writing, even though you may sometimes hear this phrase used in informal speech.

raring
▷ **PHRASES: raring to = eager to**, impatient to, longing to, ready to, keen to, desperate to, enthusiastic to

rarity 1 = **curio**, find, treasure, gem, collector's item
2 = **uncommonness**, scarcity, infrequency, unusualness, shortage, strangeness, sparseness

rash¹ = **reckless**, hasty, impulsive, imprudent, careless, ill-advised, foolhardy, impetuous **OPPOSITE:** cautious

rash² 1 = **outbreak of spots**, (skin) eruption 2 = **spate**, series, wave, flood, plague, outbreak

rate NOUN 1 = **speed**, pace, tempo, velocity, frequency
2 = **degree**, standard, scale, proportion, ratio 3 = **charge**, price, cost, fee, figure
▷ VERB 4 = **evaluate**, consider, rank, reckon, value, measure, estimate, count 5 = **deserve**, merit, be entitled to, be worthy of
▷ **PHRASES: at any rate = in any case**, anyway, anyhow, at all events

rather 1 = **preferably**, sooner, more readily, more willingly
2 = **to some extent**, quite, a little, fairly, relatively, somewhat, moderately, to some degree

▷ **USAGE NOTE**
It is acceptable to use either *would rather* or *had rather* in sentences such as *I would rather* (or *had rather*) *see a film than a play.* *Had rather*, however, is less common than *would rather*, and sounds a little old-fashioned nowadays.

ratify = **approve**, establish, confirm, sanction, endorse, uphold, authorize, affirm **OPPOSITE:** annul

rating = **position**, placing, rate, order, class, degree, rank, status

ratio = **proportion**, rate, relation, percentage, fraction

ration NOUN 1 = **allowance**, quota, allotment, helping, part, share, measure, portion
▷ VERB 2 = **limit**, control, restrict, budget

rational = **sensible**, sound, wise, reasonable, intelligent, realistic, logical, sane, grounded

rationale = **reason**, grounds, theory, principle, philosophy, logic, motivation, raison d'être (*French*)

rattle 1 = **clatter**, bang, jangle
2 = **shake**, jolt, vibrate, bounce, jar 3 (*informal*) = **fluster**, shake, upset, disturb, disconcert, perturb, faze

r

ravage VERB 1 = **destroy**, ruin, devastate, spoil, demolish, ransack, lay waste, despoil
▷ NOUN 2 *often plural* = **damage**, destruction, devastation, ruin, havoc, ruination, spoliation

rave 1 = **rant**, rage, roar, go mad (*informal*), babble, be delirious 2 (*informal*) = **enthuse**, praise, gush, be mad about (*informal*), be wild about (*informal*)

raving = **mad**, wild, crazy, hysterical, insane, irrational, crazed, delirious, berko (*Austral slang*), off the air (*Austral slang*)

raw 1 = **unrefined**, natural, crude, unprocessed, basic, rough, coarse, unfinished **OPPOSITE:** refined
2 = **uncooked**, natural, fresh **OPPOSITE:** cooked
3 = **inexperienced**, new, green, immature, callow **OPPOSITE:** experienced 4 = **chilly**, biting, cold, freezing, bitter, piercing, parky (*Brit informal*)

ray = **beam**, bar, flash, shaft, gleam

re = **concerning**, about, regarding, with regard to, with reference to, apropos
USAGE NOTE
In contexts such as *re your letter, your remarks have been noted* or *he spoke to me re your complaint*, *re* is common in business or official correspondence. In spoken and in general written English

with reference to is preferable in the former case and *about* or *concerning* in the latter. Even in business correspondence, the use of *re* is often restricted to the letter heading.

reach VERB 1 = **arrive at**, get to, make, attain 2 = **attain**, get to 3 = **touch**, grasp, extend to, stretch to, contact 4 = **contact**, get in touch with, get through to, communicate with, get hold of
▷ NOUN 5 = **grasp**, range, distance, stretch, capacity, extent, extension, scope
6 = **jurisdiction**, power, influence

react = **respond**, act, proceed, behave

reaction 1 = **response**, answer, reply 2 = **counteraction**, backlash, recoil
3 = **conservatism**, the right
USAGE NOTE
Some people say that *reaction* should always refer to an instant response to something (as in *his reaction was one of amazement*), and that this word should not be used to refer to a considered response given in the form of a statement (as in *the Minister gave his reaction to the court's decision*). Use *response* instead.

reactionary ADJECTIVE
1 = **conservative**, right-wing **OPPOSITE:** radical

▷ **NOUN** 2 = **conservative**, die-hard, right-winger **OPPOSITE:** radical

read 1 = **scan**, study, look at, pore over, peruse, follow (~*a blog or microblog*) 2 = **understand**, interpret, comprehend, construe, decipher, see, discover 3 = **register**, show, record, display, indicate

readily 1 = **willingly**, freely, quickly, gladly, eagerly **OPPOSITE:** reluctantly 2 = **promptly**, quickly, easily, smoothly, effortlessly, speedily, unhesitatingly **OPPOSITE:** with difficulty

readiness 1 = **willingness**, eagerness, keenness 2 = **promptness**, facility, ease, dexterity, adroitness

reading 1 = **perusal**, study, examination, inspection, scrutiny 2 = **learning**, education, knowledge, scholarship, erudition 3 = **recital**, performance, lesson, sermon 4 = **interpretation**, version, impression, grasp

ready 1 = **prepared**, set, primed, organized **OPPOSITE:** unprepared 2 = **completed**, arranged 3 = **mature**, ripe, mellow, ripened, seasoned 4 = **willing**, happy, glad, disposed, keen, eager, inclined, prone **OPPOSITE:** reluctant 5 = **prompt**, smart, quick, bright, sharp, keen, alert, clever

OPPOSITE: slow 6 = **available**, handy, present, near, accessible, convenient **OPPOSITE:** unavailable

real 1 = **true**, genuine, sincere, factual, dinkum (*Austral & NZ informal*), unfeigned 2 = **genuine**, authentic, dinkum (*Austral & NZ informal*) **OPPOSITE:** fake 3 = **proper**, true, valid 4 = **true**, actual 5 = **typical**, true, genuine, sincere, dinkum (*Austral & NZ informal*), unfeigned 6 = **complete**, total, perfect, utter, thorough

realistic 1 = **practical**, real, sensible, common-sense, down-to-earth, matter-of-fact, level-headed, grounded **OPPOSITE:** impractical 2 = **attainable**, sensible 3 = **lifelike**, true to life, authentic, true, natural, genuine, faithful

reality 1 = **fact**, truth, realism, validity, verity, actuality 2 = **truth**, fact, actuality

realization 1 = **awareness**, understanding, recognition, perception, grasp, conception, comprehension, cognizance 2 = **achievement**, accomplishment, fulfilment

realize 1 = **become aware of**, understand, take in, grasp, comprehend, get the message 2 = **fulfil**, achieve, accomplish, make real 3 = **achieve**, do, effect, complete, perform, fulfil, accomplish, carry out *or* through

r

really 1 = **certainly**, genuinely, positively, surely 2 = **truly**, actually, in fact, indeed, in actuality

realm 1 = **field**, world, area, province, sphere, department, branch, territory 2 = **kingdom**, country, empire, land, domain, dominion

reap 1 = **get**, gain, obtain, acquire, derive 2 = **collect**, gather, bring in, harvest, garner, cut

rear¹ NOUN 1 = **back part**, back OPPOSITE: front 2 = **back**, end, tail, rearguard, tail end
▷ MODIFIER 3 = **back**, hind, last, following OPPOSITE: front

rear² 1 = **bring up**, raise, educate, train, foster, nurture 2 = **breed**, keep 3 *often with* **up** *or* **over** = **rise**, tower, soar, loom

reason NOUN 1 = **cause**, grounds, purpose, motive, goal, aim, object, intention 2 = **sense**, mind, understanding, judgment, logic, intellect, sanity, rationality OPPOSITE: emotion
▷ VERB 3 = **deduce**, conclude, work out, make out, infer, think
▷ PHRASES: **reason with someone** = **persuade**, bring round, urge, win over, prevail upon (*informal*), talk into *or* out of

> **USAGE NOTE**
> Many people object to the expression *the reason is because*, on the grounds that it is repetitive. It is therefore advisable to use either *this is because* or *the reason is that*.

reasonable 1 = **sensible**, sound, practical, wise, logical, sober, plausible, sane, grounded OPPOSITE: irrational 2 = **fair**, just, right, moderate, equitable, tenable OPPOSITE: unfair 3 = **within reason**, fit, proper OPPOSITE: impossible 4 = **low**, cheap, competitive, moderate, modest, inexpensive 5 = **average**, fair, moderate, modest, O.K. *or* okay (*informal*)

reassure = **encourage**, comfort, hearten, gee up, restore confidence to, put *or* set your mind at rest

rebate = **refund**, discount, reduction, bonus, allowance, deduction

rebel NOUN 1 = **revolutionary**, insurgent, secessionist, revolutionist
2 = **nonconformist**, dissenter, heretic, apostate, schismatic
▷ VERB 3 = **revolt**, resist, rise up, mutiny 4 = **defy**, dissent, disobey
▷ MODIFIER 5 = **rebellious**, revolutionary, insurgent, insurrectionary

rebellion 1 = **resistance**, rising, revolution, revolt, uprising, mutiny 2 = **nonconformity**, defiance, heresy, schism

rebellious 1 = **defiant**, difficult, resistant, unmanageable, refractory **OPPOSITE:** obedient 2 = **revolutionary**, rebel, disorderly, unruly, insurgent, disloyal, seditious, mutinous **OPPOSITE:** obedient

rebound 1 = **bounce**, ricochet, recoil 2 = **misfire**, backfire, recoil, boomerang

rebuff VERB 1 = **reject**, refuse, turn down, cut, slight, snub, spurn, knock back (*slang*) **OPPOSITE:** encourage ▷ NOUN 2 = **rejection**, snub, knock-back, slight, refusal, repulse, cold shoulder, slap in the face (*informal*) **OPPOSITE:** encouragement

rebuke VERB 1 = **scold**, censure, reprimand, castigate, chide, dress down (*informal*), admonish, tell off (*informal*) **OPPOSITE:** praise ▷ NOUN 2 = **scolding**, censure, reprimand, row, dressing-down (*informal*), telling-off (*informal*), admonition **OPPOSITE:** praise

recall VERB 1 = **recollect**, remember, evoke, call to mind 2 = **call back** 3 = **annul**, withdraw, cancel, repeal, revoke, retract, countermand ▷ NOUN 4 = **recollection**, memory, remembrance 5 = **annulment**, withdrawal, repeal, cancellation, retraction, rescindment

recede = **fall back**, withdraw, retreat, return, retire, regress

receipt 1 = **sales slip**, proof of purchase, counterfoil 2 = **receiving**, delivery, reception, acceptance

receive 1 = **get**, accept, be given, pick up, collect, obtain, acquire, take 2 = **experience**, suffer, bear, encounter, sustain, undergo 3 = **greet**, meet, admit, welcome, entertain, accommodate

recent = **new**, modern, up-to-date, late, current, fresh, novel, present-day **OPPOSITE:** old

recently = **not long ago**, newly, lately, currently, freshly, of late, latterly

reception 1 = **party**, gathering, get-together, social gathering, function, celebration, festivity, soirée 2 = **response**, reaction, acknowledgment, treatment, welcome, greeting

recess 1 = **break**, rest, holiday, interval, vacation, respite, intermission, schoolie (*Austral*) 2 = **alcove**, corner, bay, hollow, niche, nook

recession = **depression**, drop, decline, credit crunch, slump **OPPOSITE:** boom

recipe = **directions**, instructions, ingredients

recital 1 = **performance**, rendering, rehearsal, reading 2 = **account**, telling,

statement, relation, narrative
3 = **recitation**
recite = **perform**, deliver, repeat,
declaim
reckless = **careless**, wild, rash,
precipitate, hasty, mindless,
headlong, thoughtless
OPPOSITE: cautious
reckon 1 (*informal*) = **think**,
believe, suppose, imagine,
assume, guess (*informal*, *chiefly
US & Canad*) 2 = **consider**, rate,
account, judge, regard, count,
esteem, deem 3 = **count**, figure,
total, calculate, compute, add
up, tally, number *used in negative
constructions*
reckoning = **count**, estimate,
calculation, addition
reclaim 1 = **retrieve**, regain
2 = **regain**, salvage, recapture
recognition 1 = **identification**,
recollection, discovery,
remembrance 2 = **acceptance**,
admission, allowance,
confession
recognize 1 = **identify**,
know, place, remember,
spot, notice, recall, recollect
2 = **acknowledge**, allow,
accept, admit, grant,
concede **OPPOSITE:** ignore
3 = **appreciate**, respect, notice
recollection = **memory**, recall,
impression, remembrance,
reminiscence
recommend 1 = **advocate**,
suggest, propose, approve,
endorse, commend **OPPOSITE:**

disapprove of 2 = **put forward**,
approve, endorse, commend,
praise 3 = **advise**, suggest,
advance, propose, counsel,
advocate, prescribe, put
forward
recommendation 1 = **advice**,
proposal, suggestion, counsel
2 = **commendation**, reference,
praise, sanction, approval,
endorsement, advocacy,
testimonial
reconcile 1 = **resolve**, settle,
square, adjust, compose,
rectify, put to rights 2 = **reunite**,
bring back together, conciliate
3 = **make peace between**,
reunite, propitiate
reconciliation = **reunion**,
conciliation, pacification,
reconcilement **OPPOSITE:**
separation
reconsider = **rethink**, review,
revise, think again, reassess
reconstruct 1 = **rebuild**,
restore, recreate, remake,
renovate, remodel, regenerate
2 = **build up a picture of**, build
up, piece together, deduce
record NOUN 1 = **document**,
file, register, log, report,
account, entry, journal, blog
(*informal*) 2 = **evidence**, trace,
documentation, testimony,
witness 3 = **disc**, single, album,
LP, vinyl 4 = **background**,
history, performance, career
▷ VERB 5 = **set down**, minute,
note, enter, document, register,

log, chronicle **6** = **make a recording of**, video, tape, video-tape, tape-record
7 = **register**, show, indicate, give evidence of

recorder = **chronicler**, archivist, historian, clerk, scribe, diarist

recording = **record**, video, tape, disc

recount = **tell**, report, describe, relate, repeat, depict, recite, narrate

recover **1** = **get better**, improve, get well, recuperate, heal, revive, mend, convalesce **OPPOSITE**: relapse **2** = **rally 3** = **save**, rescue, retrieve, salvage, reclaim **OPPOSITE**: abandon **4** = **recoup**, restore, get back, regain, retrieve, reclaim, redeem, recapture **OPPOSITE**: lose

recovery **1** = **improvement**, healing, revival, mending, recuperation, convalescence **2** = **retrieval**, repossession, reclamation, restoration

recreation = **leisure**, play, sport, fun, entertainment, relaxation, enjoyment, amusement, me-time

recruit VERB **1** = **gather**, obtain, engage, procure **2** = **assemble**, raise, levy, muster, mobilize **3** = **enlist**, draft, enrol **OPPOSITE**: dismiss
▷ NOUN **4** = **beginner**, trainee, apprentice, novice, convert, initiate, helper, learner

recur = **happen again**, return, repeat, persist, revert, reappear, come again

recycle = **reprocess**, reuse, salvage, reclaim, save

red NOUN **1** = **crimson**, scarlet, ruby, vermilion, cherry, coral, carmine
▷ ADJECTIVE **2** = **crimson**, scarlet, ruby, vermilion, cherry, coral, carmine **3** = **flushed**, embarrassed, blushing, florid, shamefaced **4** (of hair) = **chestnut**, reddish, flame-coloured, sandy, Titian, carroty, ginger
▷ PHRASES: in the red (informal) = **in debt**, insolvent, in arrears, overdrawn ▶ see red (informal) = **lose your temper**, lose it (informal), go mad (informal), crack up (informal), lose the plot (informal), go ballistic (slang, chiefly US), fly off the handle (informal), blow your top
• See panel **SHADES OF RED**

redeem **1** = **reinstate**, absolve, restore to favour **2** = **make up for**, compensate for, atone for, make amends for **3** = **buy back**, recover, regain, retrieve, reclaim, repurchase **4** = **save**, free, deliver, liberate, ransom, emancipate

redemption
1 = **compensation**, amends, reparation, atonement
2 = **salvation**, release, rescue,

r

SHADES OF RED

auburn	maroon
baby pink	mulberry
bay	old rose
burgundy	oxblood
burnt sienna	oyster pink
cardinal red	peach
carmine	peach-blow
carnation	pink
carroty	plum
cerise	poppy
cherry	puce
chestnut	raspberry
cinnabar	rose
claret	roseate
copper *or* coppery	rosy
coral	ruby
crimson	russet
cyclamen	rust
damask	salmon pink
dubonnet	sandy
flame	scarlet
flesh	shell pink
foxy	strawberry
fuchsia	tea rose
ginger	terracotta
grenadine	Titian
gules (*Heraldry*)	Turkey red
henna	vermeil
liver	vermilion
magenta	wine

liberation, emancipation, deliverance

redress VERB 1 = **make amends for**, make up for, compensate for 2 = **put right**, balance, correct, adjust, regulate, rectify, even up

▷ NOUN 3 = **amends**, payment, compensation, reparation, atonement, recompense

reduce 1 = **lessen**, cut, lower, moderate, dial down, weaken, diminish, decrease, cut down, kennet (*Austral slang*), jeff (*Austral slang*) **OPPOSITE:** increase 2 = **degrade**, downgrade, break, humble, bring low **OPPOSITE:** promote

redundancy 1 = **layoff**, sacking, dismissal 2 = **unemployment**, the sack (*informal*), the axe (*informal*), joblessness

redundant = **superfluous**, extra, surplus, unnecessary, unwanted, inessential, supernumerary **OPPOSITE:** essential

reel 1 = **stagger**, rock, roll, pitch, sway, lurch 2 = **whirl**, spin, revolve, swirl

refer = **direct**, point, send, guide
▷ **PHRASES: refer to something** *or* **someone** 1 = **allude to**, mention, cite, speak of, bring up 2 = **relate to**, concern, apply to, pertain to, be relevant to 3 = **consult**, go, apply, turn to, look up

USAGE NOTE
It is usually unnecessary to add *back* to the verb *refer*, since the sense of *back* is already contained in the *re-* part of this word. For example, you might say *This refers to* (not *refers back to*) *what has already been said*. *Refer back* is only considered acceptable when used to

mean 'return a document or question to the person it came from for further consideration', as in *he referred the matter back to me*.

referee NOUN 1 = **umpire**, umpie (*Austral slang*), judge, ref (*informal*), arbiter, arbitrator, adjudicator
▷ VERB 2 = **umpire**, judge, mediate, adjudicate, arbitrate

reference 1 = **allusion**, note, mention, quotation 2 = **citation** 3 = **testimonial**, recommendation, credentials, endorsement, character reference

referendum = **public vote**, popular vote, plebiscite

refine 1 = **purify**, process, filter, cleanse, clarify, distil 2 = **improve**, perfect, polish, hone

refined 1 = **purified**, processed, pure, filtered, clean, clarified, distilled **OPPOSITE:** unrefined 2 = **cultured**, polished, elegant, polite, cultivated, civilized, well-bred **OPPOSITE:** coarse 3 = **discerning**, fine, sensitive, delicate, precise, discriminating, fastidious

reflect 1 = **show**, reveal, display, indicate, demonstrate, manifest 2 = **throw back**, return, mirror, echo, reproduce 3 *usually followed by* **on** = **consider**, think, muse, ponder, meditate, ruminate, cogitate, wonder

r

reflection 1 = **image**, echo, mirror image 2 = **consideration**, thinking, thought, idea, opinion, observation, musing, meditation

reflective = **thoughtful**, contemplative, meditative, pensive

reform NOUN 1 = **improvement**, amendment, rehabilitation, betterment
▷ VERB 2 = **improve**, correct, restore, amend, mend, rectify
3 = **mend your ways**, go straight (*informal*), shape up (*informal*), turn over a new leaf, clean up your act (*informal*), pull your socks up (*Brit informal*)

refrain¹ = **stop**, avoid, cease, renounce, abstain, leave off, desist, forbear

refrain² = **chorus**, tune, melody

refresh 1 = **revive**, freshen, revitalize, stimulate, brace, enliven, invigorate
2 = **stimulate**, prompt, renew, jog

refreshing 1 = **new**, original, novel 2 = **stimulating**, fresh, bracing, invigorating OPPOSITE: tiring

refreshment *plural* = **food and drink**, drinks, snacks, titbits, kai (*NZ informal*)

refrigerator = **fridge**, chiller, cooler, ice-box (*US & Canad*)

refuge 1 = **protection**, shelter, asylum 2 = **haven**, retreat, sanctuary, hide-out

refugee = **exile**, émigré, displaced person, escapee

refund NOUN 1 = **repayment**, reimbursement, return
▷ VERB 2 = **repay**, return, restore, pay back, reimburse

refurbish = **renovate**, restore, repair, clean up, overhaul, revamp, mend, do up (*informal*)

refusal = **rejection**, denial, rebuff, knock-back (*slang*)

refuse¹ 1 = **decline**, reject, turn down, say no to 2 = **deny**, decline, withhold OPPOSITE: allow

refuse² = **rubbish**, waste, junk (*informal*), litter, garbage (*chiefly US*), trash

regain 1 = **recover**, get back, retrieve, recapture, win back, take back, recoup 2 = **get back to**, return to, reach again

regal = **royal**, majestic, kingly *or* queenly, noble, princely, magnificent

regard VERB 1 = **consider**, see, rate, view, judge, think of, esteem, deem 2 = **look at**, view, eye, watch, observe, clock (*Brit slang*), check out (*informal*), gaze at
▷ NOUN 3 = **respect**, esteem, thought, concern, care, consideration 4 = **look**, gaze, scrutiny, stare, glance 5 *plural* = **good wishes**, respects, greetings, compliments, best wishes
▷ PHRASES: **as regards**

= **concerning**, regarding, relating to, pertaining to

regarding = **concerning**, about, on the subject of, re, respecting, as regards, with reference to, in or with regard to

regardless ADVERB 1 = **in spite of everything**, anyway, nevertheless, in any case
▷ ADJECTIVE 2 *with* **of** = **irrespective of**, heedless of, unmindful of

regime 1 = **government**, rule, management, leadership, reign 2 = **plan**, course, system, policy, programme, scheme, regimen

region = **area**, place, part, quarter, section, sector, district, territory

regional = **local**, district, provincial, parochial, zonal

register NOUN 1 = **list**, record, roll, file, diary, catalogue, log, archives
▷ VERB 2 = **enrol**, enlist, list, note, enter 3 = **record**, catalogue, chronicle
4 = **indicate**, show 5 = **show**, mark, indicate, manifest
6 = **express**, show, reveal, display, exhibit

regret VERB 1 = **be** or **feel sorry about**, rue, deplore, bemoan, repent (of), bewail **OPPOSITE:** be satisfied with 2 = **mourn**, miss, grieve for or over
▷ NOUN 3 = **remorse**, compunction, bitterness, repentance, contrition, penitence 4 = **sorrow**
OPPOSITE: satisfaction

regular 1 = **frequent**
2 = **normal**, common, usual, ordinary, typical, routine, customary, habitual **OPPOSITE:** infrequent 3 = **steady**, consistent 4 = **even**, level, balanced, straight, flat, fixed, smooth, uniform **OPPOSITE:** uneven

regulate 1 = **control**, run, rule, manage, direct, guide, handle, govern 2 = **moderate**, control, modulate, fit, tune, adjust

regulation 1 = **rule**, order, law, dictate, decree, statute, edict, precept 2 = **control**, government, management, direction, supervision

rehearsal = **practice**, rehearsing, run-through, preparation, drill

rehearse = **practise**, prepare, run through, go over, train, repeat, drill, recite

reign VERB 1 = **be supreme**, prevail, predominate, hold sway 2 = **rule**, govern, be in power, influence, command
▷ NOUN 3 = **rule**, power,

control, command, monarchy, dominion

> **USAGE NOTE**
> The words *rein* and *reign* should not be confused; note the correct spellings in *he gave full rein to his feelings* (not *reign*); and *it will be necessary to rein in public spending* (not *reign in*).

rein = **control**, harness, bridle, hold, check, brake, curb, restraint

reincarnation = rebirth

reinforce 1 = **support**, strengthen, fortify, toughen, stress, prop, supplement, emphasize 2 = **increase**, extend, add to, strengthen, supplement

reinforcement
1 = **strengthening**, increase, fortification, augmentation
2 = **support**, stay, prop, brace, buttress 3 *plural* = **reserves**, support, auxiliaries, additional *or* fresh troops

reinstate = **restore**, recall, re-establish, return

reiterate (*formal*) = **repeat**, restate, say again, do again

reject VERB 1 = **rebuff**, jilt, turn down, spurn, refuse, say no to, repulse, defriend (*computing*), unfollow (*computing*) **OPPOSITE:** accept 2 = **deny**, exclude, veto, relinquish, renounce, disallow, forsake, disown **OPPOSITE:** approve 3 = **discard**, decline, eliminate, scrap, jettison, throw

away *or* out **OPPOSITE:** accept
▷ NOUN 4 = **castoff**, second, discard **OPPOSITE:** treasure
5 = **failure**, loser, flop

rejection 1 = **denial**, veto, dismissal, exclusion, disowning, thumbs down, renunciation, repudiation **OPPOSITE:** approval 2 = **rebuff**, refusal, knock-back (*slang*), kick in the teeth (*slang*), brushoff (*slang*) **OPPOSITE:** acceptance

rejoice = **be glad**, celebrate, be happy, glory, be overjoyed, exult **OPPOSITE:** lament

rejoin = **reply**, answer, respond, retort, riposte

relate = **tell**, recount, report, detail, describe, recite, narrate
▷ PHRASES: relate to something *or* someone 1 = **concern**, refer to, apply to, have to do with, pertain to, be relevant to 2 = **connect with**, associate with, link with, couple with, join with, correlate to

related 1 = **associated**, linked, joint, connected, affiliated, akin, interconnected **OPPOSITE:** unconnected 2 = **akin**, kindred **OPPOSITE:** unrelated

relation NOUN 1 = **similarity**, link, bearing, bond, comparison, correlation, connection 2 = **relative**, kin, kinsman *or* kinswoman, rellie (*Austral slang*)
▷ PLURAL NOUN 3 = **dealings**, relationship, affairs, contact, connections, interaction,

intercourse 4 = **family**, relatives, tribe, clan, kin, kindred, kinsmen, kinsfolk, ainga (*NZ*), rellies (*Austral slang*)

relationship 1 = **association**, bond, connection, affinity, rapport, kinship 2 = **affair**, romance, liaison, amour, intrigue 3 = **connection**, link, parallel, similarity, tie-up, correlation, read-across

relative NOUN 1 = **relation**, kinsman *or* kinswoman, member of your *or* the family, cuzzie *or* cuzzie-bro (*NZ*), rellie (*Austral slang*)

▷ ADJECTIVE 2 = **comparative** 3 = **corresponding** 4 *with* to = **in proportion to**, proportionate to

relatively = **comparatively**, rather, somewhat

relax 1 = **be** *or* **feel at ease**, chill out (*slang, chiefly US*), take it easy, lighten up (*slang*), outspan (*S African*) OPPOSITE: be alarmed 2 = **calm down**, calm, unwind 3 = **make less tense**, rest 4 = **lessen**, reduce, ease, relieve, weaken, loosen, let up, slacken OPPOSITE: tighten 5 = **moderate**, ease, relieve, weaken, slacken OPPOSITE: tighten up

relaxation = **leisure**, rest, fun, pleasure, recreation, enjoyment, me-time

relay = **broadcast**, carry, spread, communicate, transmit, send out, stream

release VERB 1 = **set free**, free, discharge, liberate, drop, loose, undo, extricate OPPOSITE: imprison 2 = **acquit**, let go, let off, exonerate, absolve 3 = **issue**, publish, make public, make known, launch, distribute, put out, circulate OPPOSITE: withhold

▷ NOUN 4 = **liberation**, freedom, liberty, discharge, emancipation, deliverance OPPOSITE: imprisonment 5 = **acquittal**, exemption, absolution, exoneration 6 = **issue**, publication, proclamation

relegate = **demote**, degrade, downgrade

relentless 1 = **merciless**, fierce, cruel, ruthless, unrelenting, implacable, remorseless, pitiless OPPOSITE: merciful 2 = **unremitting**, persistent, unrelenting, incessant, nonstop, unrelieved

relevant = **significant**, appropriate, related, fitting, to the point, apt, pertinent, apposite OPPOSITE: irrelevant

reliable 1 = **dependable**, trustworthy, sure, sound, true, faithful, staunch OPPOSITE: unreliable 2 = **safe**, dependable 3 = **definitive**, sound, dependable, trustworthy

reliance 1 = **dependency**, dependence 2 = **trust**, confidence, belief, faith

r

relic = remnant, vestige, memento, trace, fragment, souvenir, keepsake

relief 1 = ease, release, comfort, cure, remedy, solace, deliverance, mitigation
2 = rest, respite, relaxation, break, breather (*informal*)
3 = aid, help, support, assistance, succour

relieve 1 = ease, soothe, alleviate, relax, comfort, calm, cure, soften **OPPOSITE**: intensify
2 = help, support, aid, sustain, assist, succour

religion = belief, faith, theology, creed
• See panel **RELIGION**

religious 1 = spiritual, holy, sacred, devotional
2 = conscientious, faithful, rigid, meticulous, scrupulous, punctilious

relinquish (*formal*) = give up, leave, drop, abandon, surrender, let go, renounce, forsake

relish VERB 1 = enjoy, like, savour, revel in **OPPOSITE**: dislike
2 = look forward to, fancy, delight in
▷ NOUN 3 = enjoyment, liking, love, taste, fancy, penchant, fondness, gusto **OPPOSITE**: distaste 4 = condiment, seasoning, sauce

reluctance = unwillingness, dislike, loathing, distaste, aversion, disinclination, repugnance

reluctant = unwilling, hesitant, loath, disinclined, unenthusiastic **OPPOSITE**: willing

> **USAGE NOTE**
> *Reticent* is quite commonly used nowadays as a synonym of *reluctant* and followed by *to* and a verb. In careful writing it is advisable to avoid this use, since many people would regard it as mistaken.

rely on 1 = depend on, lean on
2 = be confident of, bank on, trust, count on, bet on

remain 1 = stay, continue, go on, stand, dwell 2 = stay behind, wait, delay **OPPOSITE**: go 3 = continue, be left, linger

remainder = rest, remains, balance, excess, surplus, remnant, residue, leavings

remains 1 = remnants, leftovers, rest, debris, residue, dregs, leavings 2 = relics
3 = corpse, body, carcass, cadaver

remark VERB 1 = comment, say, state, reflect, mention, declare, observe, pass comment
2 = notice, note, observe, perceive, see, mark, make out, espy
▷ NOUN 3 = comment, observation, reflection, statement, utterance

remarkable = extraordinary, striking, outstanding,

RELIGION
Religions

animism
Babi *or* Babism
Baha'ism
Buddhism
Christianity
Confucianism
druidism
heliolatry
Hinduism *or* Hindooism
Islam
Jainism
Judaism
Macumba
Manichaeism *or* Manicheism
Mithraism *or* Mithraicism
Orphism

paganism
Rastafarianism
Ryobu Shinto
Santeria
Satanism
Scientology®
shamanism
Shango
Shembe
Shinto
Sikhism
Taoism
voodoo *or* voodooism
Yezidis
Zoroastrianism *or* Zoroastrism

Religious Festivals

Advent
Al Hijrah
Ascension Day
Ash Wednesday
Baisakhi
Bodhi Day
Candlemas
Chanukah *or* Hanukkah
Ching Ming
Christmas
Corpus Christi
Day of Atonement
Dhammacakka
Diwali
Dragon Boat Festival
Dussehra
Easter

Eid ul-Adha *or* Id-ul-Adha
Eid ul-Fitr *or* Id-ul-Fitr
Epiphany
Feast of Tabernacles
Good Friday
Guru Nanak's Birthday
Hirja
Hola Mohalla
Holi
Janamashtami
Lailat ul-Barah
Lailat ul-Isra Wal Mi'raj
Lailat ul-Qadr
Lent
Mahashivaratri
Maundy Thursday
Michaelmas

r

Religious Festivals *continued*

Moon Festival	Rosh Hashanah
Palm Sunday	Septuagesima
Passion Sunday	Sexagesima
Passover	Shavuot
Pentecost	Shrove Tuesday
Pesach	Sukkoth *or* Succoth
Purim	Trinity
Quadragesima	Wesak
Quinquagesima	Whitsun
Raksha Bandhan	Winter Festival
Ramadan	Yom Kippur
Rama Naumi	Yuan Tan
Rogation	

wonderful, rare, unusual, surprising, notable **OPPOSITE:** ordinary

remedy NOUN 1 = **cure**, treatment, medicine, nostrum
▷ VERB 2 = **put right**, rectify, fix, correct, set to rights

remember 1 = **recall**, think back to, recollect, reminisce about, call to mind **OPPOSITE:** forget 2 = **bear in mind**, keep in mind 3 = **look back (on)**, commemorate

remembrance
1 = **commemoration**, memorial 2 = **souvenir**, token, reminder, monument, memento, keepsake 3 = **memory**, recollection, thought, recall, reminiscence

remind = **jog your memory**, prompt, make you remember

reminiscent = **suggestive**, evocative, similar

remnant = **remainder**, remains, trace, fragment, end, rest, residue, leftovers

remorse = **regret**, shame, guilt, grief, sorrow, anguish, repentance, contrition

remote 1 = **distant**, far, isolated, out-of-the-way, secluded, inaccessible, in the middle of nowhere **OPPOSITE:** nearby 2 = **far**, distant 3 = **slight**, small, outside, unlikely, slim, faint, doubtful, dubious **OPPOSITE:** strong 4 = **aloof**, cold, reserved, withdrawn, distant, abstracted, detached, uncommunicative **OPPOSITE:** outgoing

removal 1 = **extraction**, withdrawal, uprooting,

eradication, dislodgment, taking away *or* off *or* out
2 = dismissal, expulsion, elimination, ejection **3 = move**, transfer, departure, relocation, flitting (*Scot & Northern English dialect*)
remove 1 = take out, withdraw, extract **OPPOSITE:** insert
2 = take off OPPOSITE: put on
3 = erase, eliminate, take out
4 = dismiss, eliminate, get rid of, discharge, abolish, expel, throw out, oust **OPPOSITE:** appoint
5 = get rid of, erase, eradicate, expunge **6 = take away**, detach, displace **OPPOSITE:** put back **7 = delete**, get rid of, erase, excise **8 = move**, depart, relocate, flit (*Scot & Northern English dialect*)
renaissance *or* **renascence** **= rebirth**, revival, restoration, renewal, resurgence, reappearance, reawakening
rend (*literary*) **= tear**, rip, separate, wrench, rupture
render 1 = make, cause to become, leave **2 = provide**, give, pay, present, supply, submit, tender, hand out **3 = represent**, portray, depict, do, give, play, act, perform
renew 1 = recommence, continue, extend, repeat, resume, reopen, recreate, reaffirm **2 = reaffirm**, resume, recommence **3 = replace**, refresh, replenish, restock

4 = restore, repair, overhaul, mend, refurbish, renovate, refit, modernize
renounce 1 = disown, quit, forsake, recant, forswear, abjure **2 = disclaim**, deny, give up, relinquish, waive, abjure **OPPOSITE:** assert
renovate = restore, repair, refurbish, do up (*informal*), renew, overhaul, refit, modernize
renowned = famous, noted, celebrated, well-known, distinguished, esteemed, notable, eminent **OPPOSITE:** unknown
rent¹ VERB 1 = hire, lease **2 = let**, lease
▷ **NOUN 3 = hire**, rental, lease, fee, payment
rent² 1 = tear, split, rip, slash, slit, gash, hole **2 = opening**, hole
repair VERB 1 = mend, fix, restore, heal, patch, renovate, patch up **OPPOSITE:** damage
2 = put right, make up for, compensate for, rectify, redress
▷ **NOUN 3 = mend**, restoration, overhaul **4 = darn**, mend, patch
5 = condition, state, form, shape (*informal*)
repay = pay back, refund, settle up, return, square, compensate, reimburse, recompense
repeal VERB 1 = abolish, reverse, revoke, annul, recall, cancel, invalidate, nullify **OPPOSITE:** pass

r

▷ **NOUN 2 = abolition**,
cancellation, annulment,
invalidation, rescindment
OPPOSITE: passing
repeat VERB **1 = reiterate**,
restate **2 = retell**, echo, replay,
reproduce, rerun, reshow
▷ **NOUN 3 = repetition**, echo,
reiteration **4 = rerun**, replay,
reshowing

> **USAGE NOTE**
> Since the sense of *again* is
> already contained within the
> *re-* part of the word *repeat*,
> it is unnecessary to say that
> something is *repeated again*.

repeatedly = over and over,
often, frequently, many times
repel 1 = drive off, fight, resist,
parry, hold off, rebuff, ward
off, repulse **OPPOSITE:** submit
to **2 = disgust**, offend, revolt,
sicken, nauseate, gross you out
(*US slang*) **OPPOSITE:** delight
repertoire = range, list, stock,
supply, store, collection,
repertory
repetition 1 = recurrence,
repeating, echo **2 = repeating**,
replication, restatement,
reiteration, tautology
replace 1 = take the place of,
follow, succeed, oust, take
over from, supersede, supplant
2 = substitute, change,
exchange, switch, swap **3 = put
back**, restore
replacement 1 = replacing
2 = successor, double,

substitute, stand-in, proxy,
surrogate, understudy
replica 1 = reproduction, model,
copy, imitation, facsimile,
carbon copy **OPPOSITE:** original
2 = duplicate, copy, carbon copy
replicate = copy, reproduce,
recreate, mimic, duplicate,
reduplicate
reply VERB **1 = answer**, respond,
retort, counter, rejoin, retaliate,
reciprocate
▷ **NOUN 2 = answer**, response,
reaction, counter, retort,
retaliation, counterattack,
rejoinder
report VERB **1 = inform of**,
communicate, recount **2** *often
with* **on = communicate**, tell,
state, detail, describe, relate,
broadcast, post, tweet, pass
on **3 = present yourself**, come,
appear, arrive, turn up
▷ **NOUN 4 = article**, story, piece,
write-up **5 = account**, record,
statement, communication,
description, narrative **6** *often
plural* **= news**, word **7 = bang**,
sound, crack, noise, blast,
boom, explosion, discharge
8 = rumour, talk, buzz, gossip,
goss (*informal*), hearsay
reporter = journalist,
writer, correspondent, hack
(*derogatory*), pressman, journo
(*slang*)
represent 1 = act for, speak
for **2 = stand for**, serve as
3 = express, correspond to,

symbolize, mean **4 = exemplify**, embody, symbolize, typify, personify, epitomize **5 = depict**, show, describe, picture, illustrate, outline, portray, denote

representation 1 = picture, model, image, portrait, illustration, likeness **2 = portrayal**, depiction, account, description

representative NOUN **1 = delegate**, member, agent, deputy, proxy, spokesman or spokeswoman **2 = agent**, salesman, rep, commercial traveller
▷ ADJECTIVE **3 = typical**, characteristic, archetypal, exemplary **OPPOSITE:** uncharacteristic **4 = symbolic**

repress 1 = control, suppress, hold back, bottle up, check, curb, restrain, inhibit **OPPOSITE:** release **2 = hold back**, suppress, stifle **3 = subdue**, abuse, wrong, persecute, quell, subjugate, maltreat **OPPOSITE:** liberate

repression 1 = subjugation, control, constraint, domination, tyranny, despotism **2 = suppression**, crushing, quashing **3 = inhibition**, control, restraint, bottling up

reprieve VERB **1 = grant a stay of execution to**, pardon, let off the hook (slang)
▷ NOUN **2 = stay of execution**, amnesty, pardon, remission,

deferment, postponement of punishment

reproduce 1 = copy, recreate, replicate, duplicate, match, mirror, echo, imitate **2 = print**, copy **3** (Biology) **= breed**, procreate, multiply, spawn, propagate

reproduction 1 = copy, picture, print, replica, imitation, duplicate, facsimile **OPPOSITE:** original **2** (Biology) **= breeding**, increase, generation, multiplication

reptile
• See panel **REPTILES**

Republican ADJECTIVE **1 = right-wing**, Conservative, red (US)
▷ NOUN **2 = right-winger**, Conservative

reputation = name, standing, character, esteem, stature, renown, repute

request VERB **1 = ask for**, appeal for, put in for, demand, desire **2 = invite**, entreat **3 = seek**, ask (for), solicit
▷ NOUN **4 = appeal**, call, demand, plea, desire, entreaty, suit **5 = asking**, plea

require 1 = need, crave, want, miss, lack, wish, desire **2 = order**, demand, command, compel, exact, oblige, call upon, insist upon **3 = ask**

USAGE NOTE
The use of require to as in I require to see the manager

REPTILES

adder
agama
agamid
alligator
amphisbaena
anaconda or (Caribbean) camoodi
anole
asp
bandy-bandy
black snake or red-bellied black snake
blind snake
blue racer
blue tongue
boa
boa constrictor
boomslang
box turtle
brown snake or (Austral) mallee snake
bull snake or gopher snake
bushmaster
carpet snake or python
cayman or caiman
cerastes
chameleon
chuckwalla
cobra
cobra de capello
constrictor
copperhead
coral snake
crocodile
death adder or deaf adder
diamondback, diamondback terrapin, or diamondback turtle

diamond snake or diamond python
dugite or dukite
elapid
fer-de-lance
flying lizard or flying dragon
freshwater crocodile or (Austral informal) freshy
frill-necked lizard, frilled lizard, bicycle lizard, cycling lizard, or (Austral informal) frillie
gaboon viper
galliwasp
garter snake
gavial, gharial, or garial
gecko
giant tortoise
Gila monster
glass snake
goanna, bungarra (Austral), or go (Austral informal)
grass snake
green turtle
habu
harlequin snake
hawksbill or hawksbill turtle
hognose snake or puff adder
hoop snake
horned toad or lizard
horned viper
iguana
indigo snake
jew lizard, bearded lizard, or bearded dragon
kabaragoya or Malayan monitor
king cobra or hamadryad
king snake

Komodo dragon or Komodo lizard

krait

leatherback or (Brit) leathery turtle

leguan

lizard

loggerhead or loggerhead turtle

mamba

massasauga

milk snake

moloch, thorny devil, thorn lizard, or mountain devil

monitor

mud turtle

ngarara (NZ)

perentie or perenty

pit viper

puff adder

python

racer

rat snake

rattlesnake or (US & Canad informal) rattler

ringhals

rock snake, rock python, amethystine python, or Schneider python

saltwater crocodile or (Austral informal) saltie

sand lizard

sand viper

sea snake

sidewinder

skink

slowworm or blindworm

smooth snake

snake

snapping turtle

soft-shelled turtle

swift

taipan

terrapin

tiger snake

tokay

tortoise

tree snake

tuatara or (technical) sphenodon (NZ)

turtle

viper

wall lizard

water moccasin, moccasin, or cottonmouth

water snake

whip snake

worm lizard

r

or *you require to complete a special form* is thought by many people to be incorrect. Useful alternatives are: *I need to see the manager* and *you are required to complete a special form*.

requirement = necessity, demand, stipulation, want, need, must, essential, prerequisite

rescue VERB 1 = **save**, get out, release, deliver, recover, liberate
OPPOSITE: desert 2 = **salvage**,

deliver, redeem
▷ **NOUN 3 = saving**, salvage, deliverance, release, recovery, liberation, salvation, redemption

research NOUN
1 = **investigation**, study, analysis, examination, probe, exploration
▷ **VERB 2 = investigate**, study, examine, explore, probe, analyse

resemblance = **similarity**, correspondence, parallel, likeness, kinship, sameness, similitude **OPPOSITE:** dissimilarity

resemble = **be like**, look like, mirror, parallel, be similar to, bear a resemblance to

resent = **be bitter about**, object to, grudge, begrudge, take exception to, take offence at **OPPOSITE:** be content with

resentment = **bitterness**, indignation, ill feeling, ill will, grudge, animosity, pique, rancour

reservation 1 *often plural* = **doubt**, scruples, hesitancy 2 = **reserve**, territory, preserve, sanctuary

reserve VERB 1 = **book**, prearrange, engage 2 = **put by**, secure 3 = **keep**, hold, save, store, retain, set aside, stockpile, hoard
▷ **NOUN 4 = store**, fund, savings, stock, supply, reservoir, hoard, cache 5 = **park**, reservation,

preserve, sanctuary, tract, forest park (*NZ*) 6 = **shyness**, silence, restraint, constraint, reticence, secretiveness, taciturnity
7 = **reservation**, doubt, delay, uncertainty, indecision, hesitancy, vacillation, irresolution 8 = **substitute**, extra, spare, fall-back, auxiliary

reserved
1 = **uncommunicative**, retiring, silent, shy, restrained, secretive, reticent, taciturn **OPPOSITE:** uninhibited 2 = **set aside**, taken, kept, held, booked, retained, engaged, restricted

reservoir 1 = **lake**, pond, basin 2 = **store**, stock, source, supply, reserves, pool

reside (*formal*) = **live**, lodge, dwell, stay, abide **OPPOSITE:** visit

residence = **home**, house, dwelling, place, flat, lodging, abode, habitation

resident 1 = **inhabitant**, citizen, local **OPPOSITE:** nonresident
2 = **tenant**, occupant, lodger
3 = **guest**, lodger

residue = **remainder**, remains, remnant, leftovers, rest, extra, excess, surplus

resign 1 = **quit**, leave, step down (*informal*), vacate, abdicate, give *or* hand in your notice 2 = **give up**, abandon, yield, surrender, relinquish, renounce, forsake, forgo
▷ **PHRASES: resign yourself to something** = **accept**, succumb

to, submit to, give in to, yield to,
acquiesce to

resignation 1 = **leaving**,
departure, abandonment,
abdication 2 = **acceptance**,
patience, submission,
compliance, endurance,
passivity, acquiescence,
sufferance **OPPOSITE:** resistance

resigned = **stoical**, patient,
subdued, long-suffering,
compliant, unresisting

resist 1 = **oppose**, battle
against, combat, defy, stand
up to, hinder **OPPOSITE:** accept
2 = **refrain from**, avoid, keep
from, forgo, abstain from,
forbear **OPPOSITE:** indulge in
3 = **withstand**, be proof against

resistance 1 = **opposition**,
hostility, aversion 2 = **fighting**,
fight, battle, struggle, defiance,
obstruction, impediment,
hindrance

resistant 1 = **opposed**,
hostile, unwilling, intractable,
antagonistic, intransigent
2 = **impervious**, hard, strong,
tough, unaffected

resolution 1 = **declaration**
2 = **decision**, resolve, intention,
aim, purpose, determination,
intent 3 = **determination**,
purpose, resolve, tenacity,
perseverance, willpower,
firmness, steadfastness

resolve VERB 1 = **work out**,
answer, clear up, crack, fathom
2 = **decide**, determine, agree,

purpose, intend, fix, conclude
▷ NOUN 3 = **determination**,
resolution, willpower, firmness,
steadfastness, resoluteness
OPPOSITE: indecision
4 = **decision**, resolution,
objective, purpose, intention

resort 1 = **holiday centre**, spot,
retreat, haunt, tourist centre
2 (with **to**) = **recourse to**,
reference to

resound 1 = **echo**, resonate,
reverberate, re-echo 2 = **ring**

resounding = **echoing**, full,
ringing, powerful, booming,
reverberating, resonant,
sonorous

resource NOUN 1 = **facility**
2 = **means**, course, resort,
device, expedient
▷ PLURAL NOUN 3 = **funds**,
holdings, money, capital, riches,
assets, wealth 4 = **reserves**,
supplies, stocks

respect VERB 1 = **think highly
of**, value, honour, admire,
esteem, look up to, defer to,
have a good or high opinion of
2 = **show consideration for**,
honour, observe, heed 3 = **abide
by**, follow, observe, comply
with, obey, heed, keep to,
adhere to **OPPOSITE:** disregard
▷ NOUN 4 = **regard**, honour,
recognition, esteem,
admiration, estimation
OPPOSITE: contempt
5 = **consideration**, kindness,
deference, tact, thoughtfulness,

r

considerateness 6 = **particular**, way, point, matter, sense, detail, feature, aspect

respectable 1 = **honourable**, good, decent, worthy, upright, honest, reputable, estimable **OPPOSITE:** disreputable 2 = **decent**, neat, spruce 3 = **reasonable**, considerable, substantial, fair, ample, appreciable, sizable *or* sizeable **OPPOSITE:** small

respective = **specific**, own, individual, particular, relevant

respite = **pause**, break, rest, relief, halt, interval, recess, lull

respond 1 = **answer**, return, reply, counter, retort, rejoin **OPPOSITE:** remain silent 2 *often with* **to** = **reply to**, answer 3 = **react**, retaliate, reciprocate

response = **answer**, return, reply, reaction, feedback, retort, counterattack, rejoinder

responsibility 1 = **duty**, business, job, role, task, accountability, answerability 2 = **fault**, blame, liability, guilt, culpability 3 = **obligation**, duty, liability, charge, care 4 = **authority**, power, importance, mana (*NZ*) 5 = **job**, task, function, role 6 = **level-headedness**, rationality, dependability, trustworthiness, conscientiousness, sensibleness

responsible 1 = **to blame**, guilty, at fault, culpable 2 = **in charge**, in control, in

authority 3 = **accountable**, liable, answerable **OPPOSITE:** unaccountable 4 = **sensible**, reliable, rational, dependable, trustworthy, level-headed **OPPOSITE:** unreliable

responsive = **sensitive**, open, alive, susceptible, receptive, reactive, impressionable **OPPOSITE:** unresponsive

rest¹ VERB 1 = **relax**, take it easy, sit down, be at ease, put your feet up, outspan (*S African*) **OPPOSITE:** work 2 = **stop**, have a break, break off, take a breather (*informal*), halt, cease **OPPOSITE:** keep going 3 = **place**, repose, sit, lean, prop 4 = **be placed**, sit, lie, be supported, recline ▷ NOUN 5 = **relaxation**, repose, leisure, me-time **OPPOSITE:** work 6 = **pause**, break, stop, halt, interval, respite, lull, interlude 7 = **refreshment**, release, relief, ease, comfort, cure, remedy, solace 8 = **inactivity** 9 = **support**, stand, base, holder, prop 10 = **calm**, tranquillity, stillness

rest² = **remainder**, remains, excess, remnants, others, balance, surplus, residue

restaurant = **café**, diner (*chiefly US & Canad*), bistro, cafeteria, tearoom, eatery *or* eaterie

restless 1 = **unsettled**, nervous, edgy, fidgeting, on edge, restive, jumpy, fidgety **OPPOSITE:** relaxed 2 = **moving**, wandering,

r

unsettled, unstable, roving, transient, nomadic **OPPOSITE:** settled

restoration 1 = **reinstatement**, return, revival, restitution, re-establishment, replacement **OPPOSITE:** abolition 2 = **repair**, reconstruction, renewal, renovation, revitalization **OPPOSITE:** demolition

restore 1 = **reinstate**, re-establish, reintroduce **OPPOSITE:** abolish 2 = **revive**, build up, strengthen, refresh, revitalize **OPPOSITE:** make worse 3 = **re-establish**, replace, reinstate, give back 4 = **repair**, refurbish, renovate, reconstruct, fix (up), renew, rebuild, mend **OPPOSITE:** demolish 5 = **return**, replace, recover, bring back, send back, hand back

restrain 1 = **hold back**, control, check, contain, restrict, curb, hamper, hinder **OPPOSITE:** encourage 2 = **control**, inhibit

restrained 1 = **controlled**, moderate, self-controlled, calm, mild, undemonstrative **OPPOSITE:** hot-headed 2 = **unobtrusive**, discreet, subdued, tasteful, quiet **OPPOSITE:** garish

restraint 1 = **limitation**, limit, check, ban, embargo, curb, rein, interdict, restraining order (*US law*) **OPPOSITE:** freedom 2 = **self-control**, self-discipline, self-restraint, self-possession

OPPOSITE: self-indulgence 3 = **constraint**, limitation, inhibition, control, restriction

restrict 1 = **limit**, regulate, curb, ration **OPPOSITE:** widen 2 = **hamper**, handicap, restrain, inhibit

restriction 1 = **control**, rule, regulation, curb, restraint, confinement 2 = **limitation**, handicap, inhibition

result NOUN 1 = **consequence**, effect, outcome, end result, product, sequel, upshot **OPPOSITE:** cause 2 = **outcome**, end ▷ VERB 3 *often followed by* **from** = **arise**, follow, issue, happen, appear, develop, spring, derive

resume = **begin again**, continue, go on with, proceed with, carry on, reopen, restart **OPPOSITE:** discontinue

résumé = **summary**, synopsis, précis, rundown, recapitulation

resumption = **continuation**, carrying on, reopening, renewal, restart, resurgence, re-establishment

resurgence = **revival**, return, renaissance, resurrection, resumption, rebirth, re-emergence

resurrect 1 = **revive**, renew, bring back, reintroduce 2 = **restore to life**, raise from the dead

resurrection 1 = **revival**, restoration, renewal,

r

resurgence, return, renaissance, rebirth, reappearance **OPPOSITE**: killing off 2 = **raising** or **rising from the dead**, return from the dead **OPPOSITE**: demise

retain 1 = **maintain**, reserve, preserve, keep up, continue to have 2 = **keep**, save **OPPOSITE**: let go

retaliate = **pay someone back**, hit back, strike back, reciprocate, take revenge, get even with (informal), get your own back (informal) **OPPOSITE**: turn the other cheek

retaliation = **revenge**, repayment, vengeance, reprisal, an eye for an eye, reciprocation, requital, counterblow

retard = **slow down**, check, arrest, delay, handicap, hinder, impede, set back **OPPOSITE**: speed up

retire 1 = **stop working**, give up work 2 = **withdraw**, leave, exit, go away, depart 3 = **go to bed**, turn in (informal), hit the sack (slang), hit the hay (slang)

retirement = **withdrawal**, retreat, privacy, solitude, seclusion

retiring = **shy**, reserved, quiet, timid, unassuming, self-effacing, bashful, unassertive **OPPOSITE**: outgoing

retort VERB 1 = **reply**, return, answer, respond, counter, come back with, riposte
▷ NOUN 2 = **reply**, answer,

response, comeback, riposte, rejoinder

retreat VERB 1 = **withdraw**, back off, draw back, leave, go back, depart, fall back, pull back **OPPOSITE**: advance
▷ NOUN 2 = **flight**, retirement, departure, withdrawal, evacuation **OPPOSITE**: advance
3 = **refuge**, haven, shelter, sanctuary, hideaway, seclusion

retrieve 1 = **get back**, regain, recover, restore, recapture
2 = **redeem**, save, win back, recoup

retrospect = **hindsight**, review, re-examination **OPPOSITE**: foresight

return VERB 1 = **come back**, go back, retreat, turn back, revert, reappear **OPPOSITE**: depart
2 = **put back**, replace, restore, reinstate **OPPOSITE**: keep
3 = **give back**, repay, refund, pay back, reimburse, recompense **OPPOSITE**: keep 4 = **recur**, repeat, persist, revert, happen again, reappear, come again
5 = **elect**, choose, vote in
▷ NOUN 6 = **reappearance** **OPPOSITE**: departure
7 = **restoration**, reinstatement, re-establishment **OPPOSITE**: removal 8 = **recurrence**, repetition, reappearance, reversion, persistence
9 = **profit**, interest, gain, income, revenue, yield, proceeds, takings

r

10 = **statement**, report, form, list, account, summary

revamp = **renovate**, restore, overhaul, refurbish, do up (*informal*), recondition

reveal 1 = **make known**, disclose, give away, make public, tell, announce, proclaim, let out **OPPOSITE:** keep secret 2 = **show**, display, exhibit, unveil, uncover, manifest, unearth, unmask **OPPOSITE:** hide

revel VERB 1 = **celebrate**, carouse, live it up (*informal*), make merry
▷ NOUN 2 *often plural* = **merrymaking**, party, celebration, spree, festivity, carousal

revelation 1 = **disclosure**, news, announcement, publication, leak, confession, divulgence 2 = **exhibition**, publication, exposure, unveiling, uncovering, unearthing, proclamation

revenge NOUN 1 = **retaliation**, vengeance, reprisal, retribution, an eye for an eye
▷ VERB 2 = **avenge**, repay, take revenge for, get your own back for (*informal*)

revenue = **income**, returns, profits, gain, yield, proceeds, receipts, takings **OPPOSITE:** expenditure

revere = **be in awe of**, respect, honour, worship, reverence,

exalt, look up to, venerate **OPPOSITE:** despise

reverse VERB 1 (*Law*) = **change**, cancel, overturn, overthrow, undo, repeal, quash, revoke **OPPOSITE:** implement 2 = **turn round**, turn over, turn upside down, upend 3 = **transpose**, change, move, exchange, transfer, switch, shift, alter 4 = **go backwards**, retreat, back up, turn back, move backwards, back **OPPOSITE:** go forward
▷ NOUN 5 = **opposite**, contrary, converse, inverse 6 = **misfortune**, blow, failure, disappointment, setback, hardship, reversal, adversity 7 = **back**, rear, other side, wrong side, underside **OPPOSITE:** front
▷ ADJECTIVE 8 = **opposite**, contrary, converse

revert 1 = **go back**, return, come back, resume 2 = **return**

> **USAGE NOTE**
> Since the concept *back* is already contained in the *re-* part of the word *revert*, it is unnecessary to say that someone *reverts back* to a particular type of behaviour.

review NOUN 1 = **survey**, study, analysis, examination, scrutiny 2 = **critique**, commentary, evaluation, notice, criticism, judgment 3 = **inspection**, parade, march past 4 = **magazine**, journal, periodical, zine (*informal*)

▷ **VERB 5 = reconsider**,
revise, rethink, reassess,
re-examine, re-evaluate, think
over **6 = assess**, study, judge,
evaluate, criticize **7 = inspect**,
check, survey, examine, vet
8 = look back on, remember,
recall, reflect on, recollect
reviewer = critic, judge,
commentator
revise 1 = change, review
2 = edit, correct, alter, update,
amend, rework, redo, emend
3 = study, go over, run through,
cram (*informal*), swot up on (*Brit
informal*)
revision 1 = emendation,
updating, correction
2 = change, amendment
3 = studying, cramming
(*informal*), swotting (*Brit
informal*), homework
revival 1 = resurgence
OPPOSITE: decline
2 = reawakening, renaissance,
renewal, resurrection, rebirth,
revitalization
revive 1 = revitalize, restore,
renew, rekindle, invigorate,
reanimate **2 = bring round**,
awaken **3 = come round**,
recover **4 = refresh OPPOSITE:**
exhaust
revolt NOUN 1 = uprising, rising,
revolution, rebellion, mutiny,
insurrection, insurgency
▷ **VERB 2 = rebel**, rise up, resist,
mutiny **3 = disgust**, sicken,
repel, repulse, nauseate,

gross out (*US slang*), turn your
stomach, make your flesh creep
revolting = disgusting, foul,
horrible, sickening, horrid,
repellent, repulsive, nauseating,
yucko (*Austral slang*) **OPPOSITE:**
delightful
revolution 1 = revolt,
rising, coup, rebellion,
uprising, mutiny, insurgency
2 = transformation, shift,
innovation, upheaval,
reformation, sea change
3 = rotation, turn, cycle, circle,
spin, lap, circuit, orbit
revolutionary ADJECTIVE
1 = rebel, radical, extremist,
subversive, insurgent **OPPOSITE:**
reactionary **2 = innovative**,
new, different, novel,
radical, progressive, drastic,
ground-breaking **OPPOSITE:**
conventional
▷ **NOUN 3 = rebel**, insurgent,
revolutionist **OPPOSITE:**
reactionary
revolve 1 = go round, circle,
orbit **2 = rotate**, turn, wheel,
spin, twist, whirl
reward NOUN 1 = punishment,
retribution, comeuppance
(*slang*), just deserts
2 = payment, return, prize,
wages, compensation, bonus,
premium, repayment **OPPOSITE:**
penalty
▷ **VERB 3 = compensate**, pay,
repay, recompense, remunerate
OPPOSITE: penalize

rewarding = **satisfying**, fulfilling, valuable, profitable, productive, worthwhile, beneficial, enriching **OPPOSITE:** unrewarding

rhetoric 1 = **hyperbole**, bombast, wordiness, verbosity, grandiloquence, magniloquence 2 = **oratory**, eloquence, public speaking, speech-making, elocution, declamation, grandiloquence, whaikorero (*NZ*)

rhetorical = **high-flown**, bombastic, verbose, oratorical, grandiloquent, declamatory, arty-farty (*informal*), magniloquent

rhyme = **poem**, song, verse, ode

rhythm 1 = **beat**, swing, accent, pulse, tempo, cadence, lilt 2 = **metre**, time

rich 1 = **wealthy**, affluent, well-off, loaded (*slang*), prosperous, well-heeled (*informal*), well-to-do, moneyed, minted (*Brit slang*) **OPPOSITE:** poor 2 = **well-stocked**, full, productive, ample, abundant, plentiful, copious, well-supplied **OPPOSITE:** scarce 3 = **full-bodied**, sweet, fatty, tasty, creamy, luscious, succulent **OPPOSITE:** bland 4 = **fruitful**, productive, fertile, prolific **OPPOSITE:** barren 5 = **abounding**, luxurious, lush, abundant

riches 1 = **wealth**, assets, plenty, fortune, substance, treasure, affluence, top whack (*informal*) **OPPOSITE:** poverty 2 = **resources**, treasures

richly 1 = **elaborately**, lavishly, elegantly, splendidly, exquisitely, expensively, luxuriously, gorgeously 2 = **fully**, well, thoroughly, amply, appropriately, properly, suitably

rid = **free**, clear, deliver, relieve, purge, unburden, make free, disencumber
▷ **PHRASES: get rid of something** *or* **someone** = **dispose of**, throw away *or* out, dump, remove, eliminate, expel, eject

riddle¹ 1 = **puzzle**, problem, conundrum, poser 2 = **enigma**, question, secret, mystery, puzzle, conundrum, teaser, problem

riddle² 1 = **pierce**, pepper, puncture, perforate, honeycomb 2 = **pervade**, fill, spread through, spoil, pervade, infest, permeate

ride VERB 1 = **control**, handle, manage 2 = **travel**, be carried, go, move
▷ **NOUN** 3 = **journey**, drive, trip, lift, outing, jaunt

ridicule VERB 1 = **laugh at**, mock, make fun of, sneer at, jeer at, deride, poke fun at, chaff
▷ **NOUN** 2 = **mockery**, scorn, derision, laughter, jeer, chaff, gibe, raillery

r

ridiculous = **laughable**, stupid, silly, absurd, ludicrous, farcical, comical, risible **OPPOSITE:** sensible

rife = **widespread**, rampant, general, common, universal, frequent, prevalent, ubiquitous

rifle = **ransack**, rob, burgle, loot, strip, sack, plunder, pillage

rift 1 = **breach**, division, split, separation, falling out (*informal*), disagreement, quarrel 2 = **split**, opening, crack, gap, break, fault, flaw, cleft

rig 1 = **fix**, engineer (*informal*), arrange, manipulate, tamper with, gerrymander 2 (*Nautical*) = **equip**, fit out, kit out, outfit, supply, furnish

▷ **PHRASES: rig something up** = **set up**, build, construct, put up, arrange, assemble, put together, erect

right ADJECTIVE 1 = **correct**, true, genuine, accurate, exact, precise, valid, factual, dinkum (*Austral & NZ informal*) **OPPOSITE:** wrong 2 = **proper**, done, becoming, seemly, fitting, fit, appropriate, suitable **OPPOSITE:** inappropriate 3 = **just**, good, fair, moral, proper, ethical, honest, equitable **OPPOSITE:** unfair

▷ ADVERB 4 = **correctly**, truly, precisely, exactly, genuinely, accurately **OPPOSITE:** wrongly 5 = **suitably**, fittingly, appropriately, properly, aptly **OPPOSITE:** improperly 6 = **exactly**, squarely, precisely 7 = **directly**, straight, precisely, exactly, unswervingly, without deviation, by the shortest route, in a beeline 8 = **straight**, directly, quickly, promptly, straightaway **OPPOSITE:** indirectly

▷ NOUN 9 = **prerogative**, business, power, claim, authority, due, freedom, licence 10 = **justice**, truth, fairness, legality, righteousness, lawfulness **OPPOSITE:** injustice

▷ VERB 11 = **rectify**, settle, fix, correct, sort out, straighten, redress, put right

right away = **immediately**, now, directly, instantly, at once, straightaway, forthwith, pronto (*informal*)

righteous = **virtuous**, good, just, fair, moral, pure, ethical, upright **OPPOSITE:** wicked

rigid 1 = **strict**, set, fixed, exact, rigorous, stringent **OPPOSITE:** flexible 2 = **inflexible**, uncompromising, unbending 3 = **stiff**, inflexible, inelastic **OPPOSITE:** pliable

rigorous = **strict**, hard, demanding, tough, severe, exacting, harsh, stern **OPPOSITE:** soft

rim 1 = **edge**, lip, brim 2 = **border**, edge, trim 3 = **margin**, border, verge, brink

ring[1] NOUN 1 = **circle**, round, band, circuit, loop, hoop, halo 2 = **arena**, enclosure, circus, rink 3 = **gang**, group, association, band, circle, mob, syndicate, cartel
▷ VERB 4 = **encircle**, surround, enclose, girdle, gird

ring[2] VERB 1 = **phone**, call, telephone, buzz (*informal*, *chiefly Brit*) 2 = **chime**, sound, toll, reverberate, clang, peal 3 = **reverberate**
▷ NOUN 4 = **call**, phone call, buzz (*informal*, *chiefly Brit*) 5 = **chime**, knell, peal

> **USAGE NOTE**
> *Rang* is the past tense of the verb *ring*, as in *he rang the bell*. *Rung* is the past participle, as in *he has already rung the bell*, and care should be taken not to use it as if it were a variant form of the past tense.

rinse VERB 1 = **wash**, clean, dip, splash, cleanse, bathe
▷ NOUN 2 = **wash**, dip, splash, bath

riot NOUN 1 = **disturbance**, disorder, confusion, turmoil, upheaval, strife, turbulence, lawlessness 2 = **display**, show, splash, extravaganza, profusion 3 = **laugh**, joke, scream (*informal*), hoot (*informal*), lark
▷ VERB 4 = **rampage**, run riot, go on the rampage
▷ PHRASES: **run riot** 1 = **rampage**, go wild, be out

of control 2 = **grow profusely**, spread like wildfire

rip VERB 1 = **tear**, cut, split, burst, rend, slash, claw, slit 2 = **be torn**, tear, split, burst
▷ NOUN 3 = **tear**, cut, hole, split, rent, slash, slit, gash
▷ PHRASES: **rip someone off** (*slang*) = **cheat**, rob, con (*informal*), skin (*slang*), fleece, defraud, swindle, scam (*slang*)

ripe 1 = **ripened**, seasoned, ready, mature, mellow **OPPOSITE:** unripe 2 = **right**, suitable 3 = **mature** 4 = **suitable**, timely, ideal, favourable, auspicious, opportune **OPPOSITE:** unsuitable

rip-off *or* **ripoff** (*slang*) = **cheat**, con (*informal*), scam (*slang*), con trick (*informal*), fraud, theft, swindle

rise VERB 1 = **get up**, stand up, get to your feet 2 = **arise** 3 = **go up**, climb, ascend **OPPOSITE:** descend 4 = **loom**, tower 5 = **get steeper**, ascend, go uphill, slope upwards **OPPOSITE:** drop 6 = **increase**, mount **OPPOSITE:** decrease 7 = **grow**, go up, intensify 8 = **rebel**, revolt, mutiny 9 = **advance**, progress, get on, prosper
▷ NOUN 10 = **upward slope**, incline, elevation, ascent, kopje *or* koppie (*S African*) 11 = **increase**, upturn, upswing, upsurge, bounce

r

OPPOSITE: decrease 12 = **pay increase**, raise (*US*), increment 13 = **advancement**, progress, climb, promotion

▷ **PHRASES: give rise to something** = **cause**, produce, effect, result in, bring about

risk NOUN 1 = **danger**, chance, possibility, hazard 2 = **gamble**, chance, speculation, leap in the dark 3 = **peril**, jeopardy

▷ VERB 4 = **stand a chance of** 5 = **dare**, endanger, jeopardize, imperil, venture, gamble, hazard

risky = **dangerous**, hazardous, unsafe, perilous, uncertain, dodgy (*Brit, Austral & NZ informal*), dicey (*informal, chiefly Brit*), chancy (*informal*), shonky (*Austral & NZ informal*) **OPPOSITE:** safe

rite = **ceremony**, custom, ritual, practice, procedure, observance

ritual NOUN 1 = **ceremony**, rite, observance 2 = **custom**, tradition, routine, convention, practice, procedure, habit, protocol, tikanga (*NZ*), lockstep (*US & Canad*)

▷ ADJECTIVE 3 = **ceremonial**, conventional, routine, customary, habitual

rival NOUN 1 = **opponent**, competitor, contender, contestant, adversary

OPPOSITE: supporter

▷ VERB 2 = **compete with**, match, equal, compare with, come up to, be a match for

▷ MODIFIER 3 = **competing**, conflicting, opposing

rivalry = **competition**, opposition, conflict, contest, contention

river 1 = **stream**, brook, creek, waterway, tributary, burn (*Scot*) 2 = **flow**, rush, flood, spate, torrent

riveting = **enthralling**, gripping, fascinating, absorbing, captivating, hypnotic, engrossing, spellbinding

road 1 = **roadway**, highway, motorway, track, route, path, lane, pathway 2 = **way**, path

roam = **wander**, walk, range, travel, stray, ramble, prowl, rove

roar VERB 1 = **thunder** 2 = **guffaw**, laugh heartily, hoot, split your sides (*informal*) 3 = **cry**, shout, yell, howl, bellow, bawl, bay

▷ NOUN 4 = **guffaw**, hoot 5 = **cry**, shout, yell, howl, outcry, bellow

rob 1 = **steal from**, hold up, mug (*informal*) 2 = **raid**, hold up, loot, plunder, burgle, pillage 3 = **dispossess**, con (*informal*), cheat, defraud 4 = **deprive**, do out of (*informal*)

robber = **thief**, raider, burglar, looter, fraud, cheat, bandit, plunderer, rogue trader

robbery 1 = **burglary**, raid, hold-up, rip-off (*slang*), stick-up (*slang, chiefly US*), home invasion (*Austral & NZ*) 2 = **theft**, stealing, mugging (*informal*), plunder, swindle, pillage, larceny

robe = **gown**, costume, habit

robot = **machine**, automaton, android, mechanical man

robust = **strong**, tough, powerful, fit, healthy, strapping, hardy, vigorous **OPPOSITE:** weak

rock¹ = **stone**, boulder

rock² 1 = **sway**, pitch, swing, reel, toss, lurch, roll 2 = **shock**, surprise, shake, stun, astonish, stagger, astound

rocky¹ = **rough**, rugged, stony, craggy

rocky² = **unstable**, shaky, wobbly, rickety, unsteady

rod 1 = **stick**, bar, pole, shaft, cane 2 = **staff**, baton, wand

rodent
• See panel **RODENTS**

rogue 1 = **scoundrel**, crook (*informal*), villain, fraud, blackguard, skelm (*S African*), rorter (*Austral slang*), wrong 'un (*slang*) 2 = **scamp**, rascal, scally (*Northwest English dialect*), nointer (*Austral slang*)

role 1 = **job**, part, position, post, task, duty, function, capacity 2 = **part**, character, representation, portrayal

roll VERB 1 = **turn**, wheel, spin, go round, revolve, rotate, whirl, swivel 2 = **trundle**, go, move 3 = **flow**, run, course 4 *often with* **up** = **wind**, bind, wrap, swathe, envelop, furl, enfold 5 *often with* **out** = **level**, even, press, smooth,

flatten 6 = **toss**, rock, lurch, reel, tumble, sway
▷ NOUN 7 = **rumble**, boom, roar, thunder, reverberation 8 = **register**, record, list, index, census 9 = **turn**, spin, rotation, cycle, wheel, revolution, reel, whirl

romance 1 = **love affair**, relationship, affair, attachment, liaison, amour 2 = **excitement**, colour, charm, mystery, glamour, fascination 3 = **story**, tale, fantasy, legend, fairy tale, love story, melodrama

romantic ADJECTIVE 1 = **loving**, tender, passionate, fond, sentimental, amorous, icky (*informal*) **OPPOSITE:** unromantic 2 = **idealistic**, unrealistic, impractical, dreamy, starry-eyed **OPPOSITE:** realistic 3 = **exciting**, fascinating, mysterious, colourful, glamorous **OPPOSITE:** unexciting
▷ NOUN 4 = **idealist**, dreamer, sentimentalist

romp VERB 1 = **frolic**, sport, have fun, caper, cavort, frisk, gambol
▷ NOUN 2 = **frolic**, lark (*informal*), caper

room 1 = **chamber**, office, apartment 2 = **space**, area, capacity, extent, expanse 3 = **opportunity**, scope, leeway, chance, range, occasion, margin

root¹ NOUN 1 = **stem**, tuber, rhizome 2 = **source**, cause, heart, bottom, base, seat, seed,

r

RODENTS

acouchi *or* acouchy	jumping mouse
agouti	kangaroo rat
beaver	kiore (*NZ*)
black rat	lemming
brown rat *or* Norway rat	Māori rat *or* (*NZ*) kiore
cane rat	mara
capybara	marmot
cavy	mole rat
chinchilla	mouse
chipmunk	muskrat *or* musquash
coypu *or* nutria	paca
deer mouse	pack rat
desert rat	pocket mouse
dormouse	porcupine
fieldmouse	rat
flying squirrel	red squirrel *or* chickaree
fox squirrel	spinifex hopping mouse *or*
gerbil, gerbille, *or* jerbil	(*Austral*) dargawarra
gopher *or* pocket gopher	springhaas
gopher *or* ground squirrel	squirrel
grey squirrel	suslik *or* souslik
groundhog *or* woodchuck	taguan
ground squirrel *or* gopher	tucotuco
guinea pig *or* cavy	viscacha *or* vizcacha
hamster	vole
harvest mouse	water rat
hedgehog	water vole *or* water rat
hopping mouse *or* jerboa rat	white-footed mouse
house mouse	white rat
jerboa	

foundation
▷ **PLURAL NOUN 3 = sense of belonging**, origins, heritage, birthplace, home, family, cradle
▷ **PHRASES: root something** *or* **someone out = get rid of**, remove, eliminate, abolish, eradicate, do away with, weed out, exterminate

root² = **dig**, burrow, ferret

rope = **cord**, line, cable, strand, hawser

▷ **PHRASES: know the ropes** = **be experienced**, be knowledgeable, be an old hand

▶ **rope someone in** or **into something** (*Brit*) = **persuade**, involve, engage, enlist, talk into, inveigle

rosy 1 = **glowing**, blooming, radiant, ruddy, healthy-looking **OPPOSITE:** pale 2 = **promising**, encouraging, bright, optimistic, hopeful, cheerful, favourable, auspicious **OPPOSITE:** gloomy 3 = **pink**, red

• *See panel* **SHADES OF RED**

rot VERB 1 = **decay**, spoil, deteriorate, perish, decompose, moulder, go bad, putrefy 2 = **crumble** 3 = **deteriorate**, decline, waste away

▷ NOUN 4 = **decay**, decomposition, corruption, mould, blight, canker, putrefaction 5 (*informal*) = **nonsense**, rubbish, drivel, twaddle, garbage (*chiefly US*), trash, tripe (*informal*), claptrap (*informal*), bizzo (*Austral slang*), bull's wool (*Austral & NZ slang*)

▌ **RELATED WORD** *adjective:* putrid

rotate 1 = **revolve**, turn, wheel, spin, reel, go round, swivel, pivot 2 = **follow in sequence**, switch, alternate, take turns

rotation 1 = **revolution**, turning, turn, wheel, spin, spinning, reel, orbit 2 = **sequence**, switching, cycle, succession, alternation

rotten 1 = **decaying**, bad, rank, corrupt, sour, stinking, perished, festering, festy (*Austral slang*) **OPPOSITE:** fresh 2 = **crumbling**, perished 3 (*informal*) = **despicable**, mean, base, dirty, nasty, contemptible 4 (*informal*) = **inferior**, poor, inadequate, duff (*Brit informal*), unsatisfactory, lousy (*slang*), substandard, crummy (*slang*), bodger or bodgie (*Austral slang*) 5 = **corrupt**, immoral, crooked (*informal*), dishonest, dishonourable, perfidious **OPPOSITE:** honourable

rough ADJECTIVE 1 = **uneven**, broken, rocky, irregular, jagged, bumpy, stony, craggy **OPPOSITE:** even 2 = **boisterous**, hard, tough, arduous 3 = **ungracious**, blunt, rude, coarse, brusque, uncouth, impolite, uncivil **OPPOSITE:** refined 4 = **unpleasant**, hard, difficult, tough, uncomfortable **OPPOSITE:** easy 5 = **approximate**, estimated **OPPOSITE:** exact 6 = **vague**, general, sketchy, imprecise, inexact 7 = **basic**, crude, unfinished, incomplete, imperfect, rudimentary, sketchy, unrefined **OPPOSITE:** complete 8 = **stormy**, wild, turbulent, choppy, squally **OPPOSITE:** calm

r

9 = **harsh**, tough, nasty, cruel, unfeeling **OPPOSITE:** gentle
▷ **NOUN 10** = **outline**, draft, mock-up, preliminary sketch (*informal*)
▷ **PHRASES:** **rough and ready 1** = **makeshift**, crude, provisional, improvised, sketchy, stopgap **2** = **unrefined**, shabby, untidy, unkempt, unpolished, ill-groomed, daggy (*Austral & NZ informal*) ▶ **rough something out** = **outline**, plan, draft, sketch

round NOUN **1** = **series**, session, cycle, sequence, succession **2** = **stage**, turn, level, period, division, session, lap **3** = **sphere**, ball, band, ring, circle, disc, globe, orb **4** = **course**, tour, circuit, beat, series, schedule, routine
▷ **ADJECTIVE 5** = **spherical**, rounded, curved, circular, cylindrical, rotund, globular **6** = **plump**, full, ample, fleshy, rotund, full-fleshed
▷ **VERB 7** = **go round**, circle, skirt, flank, bypass, encircle, turn
▷ **PHRASES:** **round something** *or* **someone up** = **gather**, muster, group, drive, collect, rally, herd, marshal

roundabout 1 = **indirect**, devious, tortuous, circuitous, evasive, discursive **OPPOSITE:** direct **2** = **oblique**, implied, indirect, circuitous

roundup = **muster**, collection, rally, assembly, herding

rouse 1 = **wake up**, call, wake, awaken **2** = **excite**, move, stir, provoke, anger, animate, agitate, inflame **3** = **stimulate**, provoke, incite

rousing = **lively**, moving, spirited, exciting, inspiring, stirring, stimulating **OPPOSITE:** dull

rout VERB **1** = **defeat**, beat, overthrow, thrash, destroy, crush, conquer, wipe the floor with (*informal*)
▷ **NOUN 2** = **defeat**, beating, overthrow, thrashing, pasting (*slang*), debacle, drubbing

route 1 = **way**, course, road, direction, path, journey, itinerary **2** = **beat**, circuit

routine NOUN **1** = **procedure**, programme, order, practice, method, pattern, custom
▷ **ADJECTIVE 2** = **usual**, standard, normal, customary, ordinary, typical, everyday, habitual **OPPOSITE:** unusual **3** = **boring**, dull, predictable, tedious, tiresome, humdrum

row¹ = **line**, bank, range, series, file, string, column
▷ **PHRASES:** **in a row** = **consecutively**, running, in turn, one after the other, successively, in sequence

row² NOUN **1** = **quarrel**, dispute, argument, squabble, tiff, trouble, brawl **2** = **disturbance**,

r

noise, racket, uproar, commotion, rumpus, tumult
▷ VERB 3 = **quarrel**, fight, argue, dispute, squabble, wrangle

royal 1 = **regal**, kingly or queenly, princely, imperial, sovereign 2 = **splendid**, grand, impressive, magnificent, majestic, stately

rub VERB 1 = **stroke**, massage, caress 2 = **polish**, clean, shine, wipe, scour 3 = **chafe**, scrape, grate, abrade
▷ NOUN 4 = **massage**, caress, kneading 5 = **polish**, stroke, shine, wipe
▷ PHRASES: **rub something out** = **erase**, remove, cancel, wipe out, delete, obliterate, efface

rubbish 1 = **waste**, refuse, scrap, junk (informal), litter, garbage (chiefly US), trash, lumber 2 = **nonsense**, garbage (chiefly US), twaddle, rot, trash, hot air (informal), tripe (informal), claptrap (informal), bizzo (Austral slang), bull's wool (Austral & NZ slang)

rude 1 = **impolite**, insulting, cheeky, abusive, disrespectful, impertinent, insolent, impudent OPPOSITE: polite 2 = **uncivilized**, rough, coarse, brutish, boorish, uncouth, loutish, graceless 3 = **vulgar** OPPOSITE: refined 4 = **unpleasant**, sharp, sudden, harsh, startling, abrupt 5 = **roughly-made**, simple, rough, raw, crude, primitive, makeshift, artless OPPOSITE: well-made

rue (literary) = **regret**, mourn, lament, repent, be sorry for, kick yourself for

ruffle 1 = **disarrange**, disorder, mess up, rumple, tousle, dishevel, muss (US & Canad) 2 = **annoy**, upset, irritate, agitate, nettle, fluster, peeve (informal) OPPOSITE: calm

rugged 1 = **rocky**, broken, rough, craggy, difficult, ragged, irregular, uneven OPPOSITE: even 2 = **strong-featured**, rough-hewn, weather-beaten OPPOSITE: delicate 3 = **well-built**, strong, tough, robust, sturdy 4 (chiefly US & Canad) = **tough**, strong, robust, muscular, sturdy, burly, husky (informal), brawny OPPOSITE: delicate

ruin VERB 1 = **destroy**, devastate, wreck, defeat, smash, crush, demolish, lay waste, kennet (Austral slang), jeff (Austral slang) OPPOSITE: create 2 = **bankrupt**, break, impoverish, beggar, pauperize 3 = **spoil**, damage, mess up, blow (slang), screw up (informal), botch, make a mess of, crool or cruel (Austral slang) OPPOSITE: improve
▷ NOUN 4 = **bankruptcy**, insolvency, destitution 5 = **disrepair**, decay, disintegration, ruination,

r

wreckage 6 = **destruction**, fall, breakdown, defeat, collapse, wreck, undoing, downfall **OPPOSITE:** preservation

rule NOUN 1 = **regulation**, law, direction, guideline, decree 2 = **precept**, principle, canon, maxim, tenet, axiom 3 = **custom**, procedure, practice, routine, tradition, habit, convention 4 = **government**, power, control, authority, command, regime, reign, jurisdiction, mana (*NZ*)

▷ VERB 5 = **govern**, control, direct, have power over, command over, have charge of 6 = **reign**, govern, be in power, be in authority 7 = **decree**, decide, judge, settle, pronounce 8 = **be prevalent**, prevail, predominate, be customary, preponderate

▷ PHRASES: as a rule = **usually**, generally, mainly, normally, on the whole, ordinarily ▶ **rule someone out** = **exclude**, eliminate, disqualify, ban, reject, dismiss, prohibit, leave out ▶ **rule something out** = **reject**, exclude, eliminate

ruler 1 = **governor**, leader, lord, commander, controller, monarch, sovereign, head of state 2 = **measure**, rule, yardstick

ruling ADJECTIVE 1 = **governing**, reigning, controlling, commanding 2 = **predominant**, dominant, prevailing, preponderant, chief, main, principal, pre-eminent **OPPOSITE:** minor

▷ NOUN 3 = **decision**, verdict, judgment, decree, adjudication, pronouncement

rumour = **story**, news, report, talk, word, whisper, buzz, gossip, goss (*informal*)

run VERB 1 = **race**, rush, dash, hurry, sprint, bolt, gallop, hare (*Brit informal*) **OPPOSITE:** dawdle 2 = **flee**, escape, take off (*informal*), bolt, beat it (*slang*), leg it (*informal*), take flight, do a runner (*slang*) **OPPOSITE:** stay 3 = **take part**, compete 4 = **continue**, go, stretch, reach, extend, proceed **OPPOSITE:** stop 5 (*chiefly US & Canad*) = **compete**, stand, contend, be a candidate, put yourself up for, take part 6 = **manage**, lead, direct, be in charge of, head, control, operate, handle 7 = **go**, work, operate, perform, function 8 = **perform**, carry out 9 = **work**, go, operate, function 10 = **pass**, go, move, roll, glide, skim 11 = **flow**, pour, stream, go, leak, spill, discharge, gush 12 = **publish**, feature, display, print 13 = **melt**, dissolve, liquefy, go soft 14 = **smuggle**, traffic in, bootleg

▷ NOUN 15 = **race**, rush, dash, sprint, gallop, jog, spurt

16 = **ride**, drive, trip, spin
(*informal*), outing, excursion,
jaunt 17 = **sequence**, period,
stretch, spell, course, season,
series, string 18 = **enclosure**,
pen, coop
▷ **PHRASES: run away = flee**,
escape, bolt, abscond, do a
runner (*slang*), make a run
for it, scram (*informal*), fly the
coop (*US & Canad informal*),
do a Skase (*Austral informal*)
▶ **run into someone = meet**,
encounter, bump into, run
across, come across *or* upon
▶ **run into something 1 = be
beset by**, encounter, come
across *or* upon, face, experience
2 = **collide with**, hit, strike ▶ **run
out 1 = be used up**, dry up, give
out, fail, finish, be exhausted
2 = **expire**, end, terminate ▶ **run
over something 1 = exceed**,
overstep, go over the top of,
go over the limit of 2 = **review**,
check, go through, go over, run
through, rehearse ▶ **run over
something** *or* **someone = knock
down**, hit, run down, knock over
▶ **run something** *or* **someone
down 1 = criticize**, denigrate,
belittle, knock (*informal*), rubbish
(*informal*), slag (off) (*slang*),
disparage, decry 2 = **downsize**,
cut, reduce, trim, decrease, cut
back, curtail, kennet (*Austral
slang*), jeff (*Austral slang*)
3 = **knock down**, hit, run into,
run over, knock over

rundown *or* **run-down**
1 = **exhausted**, weak, drained,
weary, unhealthy, worn-
out, debilitated, below par
OPPOSITE: fit 2 = **dilapidated**,
broken-down, shabby, worn-
out, seedy, ramshackle, decrepit
runner 1 = **athlete**, sprinter,
jogger 2 = **messenger**, courier,
errand boy, dispatch bearer
running NOUN
1 = **management**, control,
administration, direction,
leadership, organization,
supervision 2 = **working**,
performance, operation,
functioning, maintenance
▷ **ADJECTIVE** 3 = **continuous**,
constant, perpetual,
uninterrupted, incessant
4 = **in succession**, unbroken
5 = **flowing**, moving, streaming,
coursing
rupture NOUN 1 = **break**, tear,
split, crack, rent, burst, breach,
fissure
▷ **VERB** 2 = **break**, separate, tear,
split, crack, burst, sever
rural 1 = **agricultural**, country
2 = **rustic**, country, pastoral,
sylvan **OPPOSITE:** urban
rush VERB 1 = **hurry**, run, race,
shoot, fly, career, speed, tear
OPPOSITE: dawdle 2 = **push**,
hurry, press, hustle 3 = **attack**,
storm, charge at
▷ NOUN 4 = **dash**, charge, race,
scramble, stampede 5 = **hurry**,
haste, hustle 6 = **surge**, flow,

r

gush 7 = **attack**, charge,
assault, onslaught
▷ ADJECTIVE 8 = **hasty**, fast,
quick, hurried, rapid, urgent,
swift **OPPOSITE:** leisurely
rust NOUN 1 = **corrosion**,
oxidation 2 = **mildew**, must,
mould, rot, blight
▷ VERB 3 = **corrode**, oxidize
rusty 1 = **corroded**, rusted,
oxidized, rust-covered 2 = **out
of practice**, weak, stale,
unpractised 3 = **reddish-brown**,
chestnut, reddish, russet,
coppery, rust-coloured
• See panel **SHADES OF RED**
ruthless = **merciless**, harsh,
cruel, brutal, relentless,
callous, heartless, remorseless
OPPOSITE: merciful

Ss

sabotage VERB 1 = **damage**,
destroy, wreck, disable,
disrupt, subvert, incapacitate,
vandalize
▷ NOUN 2 = **damage**,
destruction, wrecking
sack¹ NOUN 1 = **bag**, pocket, sac,
pouch, receptacle
▷ VERB 2 (*informal*) = **dismiss**,
fire (*informal*), axe (*informal*),
discharge, kiss off (*slang, chiefly
US & Canad*), give (someone) the
push (*informal*), kennet (*Austral
slang*), jeff (*Austral slang*)
▷ PHRASES: **the sack** (*informal*)
= **dismissal**, discharge, the boot
(*slang*), the axe (*informal*), the
push (*slang*)
sack² VERB 1 = **plunder**, loot,
pillage, strip, rob, raid, ruin
▷ NOUN 2 = **plundering**, looting,
pillage
sacred 1 = **holy**, hallowed,
blessed, divine, revered,
sanctified **OPPOSITE:**
secular 2 = **religious**, holy,
ecclesiastical, hallowed
OPPOSITE: unconsecrated
3 = **inviolable**, protected,

sacrosanct, hallowed, inalienable, unalterable

sacrifice VERB 1 = **offer**, offer up, immolate 2 = **give up**, abandon, relinquish, lose, surrender, let go, do without, renounce

▷ NOUN 3 = **offering**, oblation 4 = **surrender**, loss, giving up, rejection, abdication, renunciation, repudiation, forswearing

sad 1 = **unhappy**, down, low, blue, depressed, melancholy, mournful, dejected OPPOSITE: happy 2 = **tragic**, moving, upsetting, depressing, dismal, pathetic, poignant, harrowing 3 = **deplorable**, bad, sorry, terrible, unfortunate, regrettable, lamentable, wretched OPPOSITE: good

sadden = **upset**, depress, distress, grieve, make sad, deject

saddle = **burden**, load, lumber (*Brit informal*), encumber

sadness = **unhappiness**, sorrow, grief, depression, the blues, misery, melancholy, poignancy OPPOSITE: happiness

safe ADJECTIVE 1 = **protected**, secure, impregnable, out of danger, safe and sound, in safe hands, out of harm's way OPPOSITE: endangered 2 = **all right**, intact, unscathed, unhurt, unharmed, undamaged, O.K. *or* okay (*informal*) 3 = **risk-free**, sound, secure, certain, impregnable

▷ NOUN 4 = **strongbox**, vault, coffer, repository, deposit box, safe-deposit box

safeguard VERB 1 = **protect**, guard, defend, save, preserve, look after, keep safe

▷ NOUN 2 = **protection**, security, defence, guard

safely = **in safety**, with impunity, without risk, safe and sound

safety 1 = **security**, protection, safeguards, precautions, safety measures, impregnability OPPOSITE: risk 2 = **shelter**, haven, protection, cover, retreat, asylum, refuge, sanctuary

sag 1 = **sink**, bag, droop, fall, slump, dip, give way, hang loosely 2 = **drop**, sink, slump, flop, droop, loll 3 = **decline**, tire, flag, weaken, wilt, wane, droop

saga 1 = **carry-on** (*informal*), performance (*informal*), pantomime (*informal*) 2 = **epic**, story, tale, narrative, yarn

sage NOUN 1 = **wise man**, philosopher, guru, master, elder, tohunga (*NZ*)

▷ ADJECTIVE 2 = **wise**, sensible, judicious, sagacious, sapient

sail NOUN 1 = **sheet**, canvas

▷ VERB 2 = **go by water**, cruise, voyage, ride the waves, go by sea 3 = **set sail**, embark, get under way, put to sea, put off, leave port, hoist sail, cast *or* weigh anchor 4 = **pilot**, steer

S

5 = glide, sweep, float, fly, wing, soar, drift, skim

sailor = mariner, marine, seaman, sea dog, seafarer

sake = purpose, interest, reason, end, aim, objective, motive
▷ **PHRASES: for someone's sake = in someone's interests**, to someone's advantage, on someone's account, for the benefit of, for the good of, for the welfare of, out of respect for, out of consideration for

salary = pay, income, wage, fee, payment, wages, earnings, allowance

sale 1 = selling, marketing, dealing, transaction, disposal **2 = auction**, fair, mart, bazaar

salt NOUN 1 = seasoning
▷ **ADJECTIVE 2 = salty**, saline, brackish, briny

salute VERB 1 = greet, welcome, acknowledge, address, hail, mihi (NZ) **2 = honour**, acknowledge, recognize, pay tribute or homage to
▷ **NOUN 3 = greeting**, recognition, salutation, address

salvage = save, recover, rescue, get back, retrieve, redeem

salvation = saving, rescue, recovery, salvage, redemption, deliverance **OPPOSITE:** ruin

same 1 = identical, similar, alike, equal, twin, corresponding, duplicate **OPPOSITE:** different **2 = the very same**, one and the same, selfsame

3 = aforementioned, aforesaid
4 = unchanged, consistent, constant, unaltered, invariable, unvarying, changeless
OPPOSITE: altered

USAGE NOTE
The use of *same* as in *If you send us your order for the materials, we will deliver same tomorrow* is common in business and official English. In general English, however, this use of the word is best avoided, as it may sound rather stilted: *May I borrow your book? I will return it* (not *same*) *tomorrow.*

sample NOUN 1 = specimen, example, model, pattern, instance **2 = cross section**
▷ **VERB 3 = test**, try, experience, taste, inspect

sanction VERB 1 = permit, allow, approve, endorse, authorize **OPPOSITE:** forbid
▷ **NOUN 2** *often plural* **= ban**, boycott, embargo, exclusion, penalty, coercive measures **OPPOSITE:** permission **3 = permission**, backing, authority, approval, authorization, O.K. or okay (*informal*), stamp or seal of approval **OPPOSITE:** ban

sanctuary 1 = protection, shelter, refuge, haven, retreat, asylum **2 = reserve**, park, preserve, reservation, national park, tract, nature reserve, conservation area

sane 1 = **rational**, all there (*informal*), of sound mind, compos mentis (*Latin*), in your right mind, mentally sound **OPPOSITE:** insane 2 = **sensible**, sound, reasonable, balanced, judicious, level-headed, grounded **OPPOSITE:** foolish

sap¹ 1 = **juice**, essence, vital fluid, lifeblood 2 (*slang*) = **fool**, jerk (*slang, chiefly US & Canad*), idiot, wally (*slang*), twit (*informal*), simpleton, ninny, dorba or dorb (*Austral slang*), bogan (*Austral slang*)

sap² = **weaken**, drain, undermine, exhaust, deplete

satanic = **evil**, demonic, hellish, black, wicked, devilish, infernal, fiendish **OPPOSITE:** godly

satire 1 = **mockery**, irony, ridicule 2 = **parody**, mockery, caricature, lampoon, burlesque

satisfaction 1 = **fulfilment**, pleasure, achievement, relish, gratification, pride **OPPOSITE:** dissatisfaction 2 = **contentment**, content, comfort, pleasure, happiness, enjoyment, satiety, repletion **OPPOSITE:** discontent

satisfactory = **adequate**, acceptable, good enough, average, fair, all right, sufficient, passable **OPPOSITE:** unsatisfactory

satisfy 1 = **content**, please, indulge, gratify, pander to, assuage, pacify, quench **OPPOSITE:** dissatisfy 2 = **convince**, persuade, assure, reassure **OPPOSITE:** dissuade 3 = **comply with**, meet, fulfil, answer, serve, fill, observe, obey **OPPOSITE:** fail to meet

saturate 1 = **flood**, overwhelm, swamp, overrun 2 = **soak**, steep, drench, imbue, suffuse, wet through, waterlog, souse

saturated = **soaked**, soaking (wet), drenched, sodden, dripping, waterlogged, sopping (wet), wet through

sauce = **dressing**, dip, relish, condiment

sausage = **banger**

savage ADJECTIVE 1 = **cruel**, brutal, vicious, fierce, harsh, ruthless, ferocious, sadistic **OPPOSITE:** gentle 2 = **wild**, fierce, ferocious, unbroken, feral, untamed, undomesticated **OPPOSITE:** tame 3 = **primitive**, undeveloped, uncultivated, uncivilized 4 = **uncultivated**, rugged, unspoilt, uninhabited, rough, uncivilized **OPPOSITE:** cultivated
▷ NOUN 5 = **lout**, yob (*Brit slang*), barbarian, yahoo, hoon (*Austral & NZ*), boor, cougan (*Austral slang*), scozza (*Austral slang*), bogan (*Austral slang*)
▷ VERB 6 = **maul**, tear, claw, attack, mangle, lacerate, mangulate (*Austral slang*)

save 1 = **rescue**, free, release, deliver, recover, get out, liberate, salvage **OPPOSITE:** endanger **2 = keep**, reserve, set aside, store, collect, gather, hold, hoard **OPPOSITE:** spend **3 = protect**, keep, guard, preserve, look after, safeguard, salvage, conserve **4 = put aside**, keep, reserve, collect, retain, set aside, put by

saving NOUN **1 = economy**, discount, reduction, bargain
▷ PLURAL NOUN **2 = nest egg**, fund, store, reserves, resources

Saviour = Christ, Jesus, the Messiah, the Redeemer

saviour = rescuer, deliverer, defender, protector, liberator, redeemer, preserver

savour VERB **1 = relish**, delight in, revel in, luxuriate in **2 = enjoy**, appreciate, relish, delight in, revel in, luxuriate in
▷ NOUN **3 = flavour**, taste, smell, relish, smack, tang, piquancy

say VERB **1 = state**, declare, remark, announce, maintain, mention, assert, affirm **2 = speak**, utter, voice, express, pronounce **3 = suggest**, express, imply, communicate, disclose, give away, convey, divulge **4 = suppose**, supposing, imagine, assume, presume **5 = estimate**, suppose, guess, conjecture, surmise
▷ NOUN **6 = influence**, power, control, authority, weight, clout

(*informal*), mana (*NZ*) **7 = chance to speak**, vote, voice

saying = proverb, maxim, adage, dictum, axiom, aphorism

scale¹ = flake, plate, layer, lamina

scale² NOUN **1 = degree**, size, range, extent, dimensions, scope, magnitude, breadth **2 = system of measurement**, measuring system **3 = ranking**, ladder, hierarchy, series, sequence, progression **4 = ratio**, proportion
▷ VERB **5 = climb up**, mount, ascend, surmount, clamber up, escalade

scan 1 = glance over, skim, look over, eye, check, examine, check out (*informal*), run over, surf (*computing*) **2 = survey**, search, investigate, sweep, scour, scrutinize

scandal 1 = disgrace, crime, offence, sin, embarrassment, wrongdoing, dishonourable behaviour, discreditable behaviour **2 = gossip**, goss (*informal*), talk, rumours, dirt, slander, tattle, aspersion **3 = shame**, disgrace, stigma, infamy, opprobrium **4 = outrage**, shame, insult, disgrace, injustice, crying shame

scant = inadequate, meagre, sparse, little, minimal, barely sufficient **OPPOSITE:** adequate

scapegoat = fall guy, whipping boy

scar NOUN 1 = **mark**, injury, wound, blemish 2 = **trauma**, suffering, pain, torture, anguish
▷ VERB 3 = **mark**, disfigure, damage, mar, mutilate, blemish, deface

scarce 1 = **in short supply**, insufficient OPPOSITE: plentiful 2 = **rare**, few, uncommon, few and far between, infrequent OPPOSITE: common

scarcely 1 = **hardly**, barely 2 (*often used ironically*) = **by no means**, hardly, definitely not

> **USAGE NOTE**
> Since *scarcely*, *hardly*, and *barely* already have negative force, it is unnecessary to use another negative word with them. Therefore, say *he had hardly had time to think* (not *he hadn't hardly had time to think*); and *there was scarcely any bread left* (not *there was scarcely no bread left*). When *scarcely*, *hardly*, and *barely* are used at the beginning of a sentence, as in *scarcely had I arrived*, the following clause should start with *when*: *scarcely had I arrived when I was asked to chair a meeting*. The word *before* can be used in place of *when* in this context, but the word *than* used in the same way is considered incorrect by many people, though this use is becoming increasingly common.

scare VERB 1 = **frighten**, alarm, terrify, panic, shock, startle, intimidate, dismay
▷ NOUN 2 = **fright**, shock, start 3 = **panic**, hysteria 4 = **alert**, warning, alarm

scared = **afraid**, alarmed, frightened, terrified, shaken, startled, fearful, petrified

scary (*informal*) = **frightening**, alarming, terrifying, chilling, horrifying, spooky (*informal*), creepy (*informal*), spine-chilling

scatter 1 = **throw about**, spread, sprinkle, strew, shower, fling, diffuse, disseminate OPPOSITE: gather 2 = **disperse**, dispel, disband, dissipate OPPOSITE: assemble

scenario 1 = **situation** 2 = **story line**, résumé, outline, summary, synopsis

scene 1 = **act**, part, division, episode 2 = **setting**, set, background, location, backdrop 3 = **site**, place, setting, area, position, spot, locality 4 (*informal*) = **world**, business, environment, arena 5 = **view**, prospect, panorama, vista, landscape, outlook 6 = **fuss**, to-do, row, performance, exhibition, carry-on (*informal*, *chiefly Brit*), tantrum, commotion, hissy fit (*informal*)

scenery 1 = **landscape**, view, surroundings, terrain, vista 2 (*Theatre*) = **set**, setting, backdrop, flats, stage set

S

scenic = **picturesque**, beautiful, spectacular, striking, panoramic

scent NOUN 1 = **fragrance**, smell, perfume, bouquet, aroma, odour 2 = **trail**, track, spoor
▷ VERB 3 = **smell**, sense, detect, sniff, discern, nose out

scented = **fragrant**, perfumed, aromatic, sweet-smelling, odoriferous

sceptic 1 = **doubter**, cynic, disbeliever 2 = **agnostic**, doubter, unbeliever, doubting Thomas

sceptical = **doubtful**, cynical, dubious, unconvinced, disbelieving, incredulous, mistrustful **OPPOSITE:** convinced

scepticism = **doubt**, suspicion, disbelief, cynicism, incredulity

schedule NOUN 1 = **plan**, programme, agenda, calendar, timetable
▷ VERB 2 = **plan**, set up, book, programme, arrange, organize

scheme NOUN 1 = **plan**, programme, strategy, system, project, proposal, tactics 2 = **plot**, ploy, ruse, intrigue, conspiracy, manoeuvre, subterfuge, stratagem
▷ VERB 3 = **plot**, plan, intrigue, manoeuvre, conspire, contrive, collude, machinate

scheming = **calculating**, cunning, sly, tricky, wily, artful, conniving, underhand **OPPOSITE:** straightforward

scholar 1 = **intellectual**, academic, savant, acca (*Austral slang*) 2 = **student**, pupil, learner, schoolboy or schoolgirl

scholarly = **learned**, academic, intellectual, lettered, erudite, scholastic, bookish **OPPOSITE:** uneducated

scholarship 1 = **grant**, award, payment, endowment, fellowship, bursary 2 = **learning**, education, knowledge, erudition, book-learning

school NOUN 1 = **academy**, college, institution, institute, seminary 2 = **group**, set, circle, faction, followers, disciples, devotees, denomination
▷ VERB 3 = **train**, coach, discipline, educate, drill, tutor, instruct

science = **discipline**, body of knowledge, branch of knowledge

scientific = **systematic**, accurate, exact, precise, controlled, mathematical

scientist = **researcher**, inventor, boffin (*informal*), technophile

scoff[1] = **scorn**, mock, laugh at, ridicule, knock (*informal*), despise, sneer, jeer

scoff[2] = **gobble (up)**, wolf, devour, bolt, guzzle, gulp down, gorge yourself on

scoop VERB 1 = **win**, get, land, gain, achieve, earn, secure, obtain
▷ NOUN 2 = **ladle**, spoon, dipper 3 = **exclusive**, exposé, revelation, sensation
▷ PHRASES: scoop something out 1 = **take out**, empty, spoon out, bail or bale out 2 = **dig**, shovel, excavate, gouge, hollow out ▸ scoop something or someone up = **gather up**, lift, pick up, take up, sweep up or away

scope 1 = **opportunity**, room, freedom, space, liberty, latitude 2 = **range**, capacity, reach, area, outlook, orbit, span, sphere

scorch = **burn**, sear, roast, wither, shrivel, parch, singe

scorching = **burning**, boiling, baking, flaming, roasting, searing, fiery, red-hot

score VERB 1 = **gain**, win, achieve, make, get, attain, notch up (*informal*), chalk up (*informal*) 2 (*Music*) = **arrange**, set, orchestrate, adapt 3 = **cut**, scratch, mark, slash, scrape, graze, gouge, deface
▷ NOUN 4 = **rating**, mark, grade, percentage 5 = **points**, result, total, outcome 6 = **composition**, soundtrack, arrangement, orchestration 7 = **grievance**, wrong, injury, injustice, grudge
▷ PLURAL NOUN 8 = **lots**, loads, many, millions, hundreds, masses, swarms, multitudes
▷ PHRASES: score something out or through = **cross out**, delete, strike out, cancel, obliterate

scorn NOUN 1 = **contempt**, disdain, mockery, derision, sarcasm, disparagement OPPOSITE: respect
▷ VERB 2 = **despise**, reject, disdain, slight, be above, spurn, deride, flout OPPOSITE: respect

scour¹ = **scrub**, clean, polish, rub, buff, abrade

scour² = **search**, hunt, comb, ransack

scout NOUN 1 = **vanguard**, lookout, precursor, outrider, reconnoitrer, advance guard
▷ VERB 2 = **reconnoitre**, investigate, watch, survey, observe, spy, probe, recce (*slang*)

scramble VERB 1 = **struggle**, climb, crawl, swarm, scrabble 2 = **strive**, rush, contend, vie, run, push, jostle 3 = **jumble**, mix up, muddle, shuffle
▷ NOUN 4 = **clamber**, ascent 5 = **race**, competition, struggle, rush, confusion, commotion, melee or mêlée

scrap¹ NOUN 1 = **piece**, fragment, bit, grain, particle, portion, part, crumb 2 = **waste**, junk, off cuts
▷ PLURAL NOUN 3 = **leftovers**, remains, bits, leavings
▷ VERB 4 = **get rid of**, drop, abandon, ditch (*slang*), discard,

write off, jettison, throw away *or* out **OPPOSITE:** bring back

scrap² (*informal*) **NOUN 1 = fight**, battle, row, argument, dispute, disagreement, quarrel, squabble, biffo (*Austral slang*) ▷ **VERB 2 = fight**, argue, row, squabble, wrangle

scrape VERB 1 = rake, sweep, drag, brush **2 = grate**, grind, scratch, squeak, rasp **3 = graze**, skin, scratch, bark, scuff, rub **4 = clean**, remove, scour ▷ **NOUN 5** (*informal*) **= predicament**, difficulty, fix (*informal*), mess, dilemma, plight, tight spot, awkward situation

scratch VERB 1 = rub, scrape, claw at **2 = mark**, cut, score, damage, grate, graze, etch, lacerate ▷ **NOUN 3 = mark**, scrape, graze, blemish, gash, laceration, claw mark ▷ **PHRASES: not up to scratch** (*informal*) **= inadequate**, unacceptable, unsatisfactory, insufficient, not up to standard

scream VERB 1 = cry, yell, shriek, screech, bawl, howl ▷ **NOUN 2 = cry**, yell, howl, shriek, screech, yelp

screen NOUN 1 = cover, guard, shade, shelter, shield, partition, cloak, canopy ▷ **VERB 2 = broadcast**, show, put on, present, air, cable, beam, transmit, stream **3 = cover**, hide, conceal, shade, mask, veil, cloak **4 = investigate**, test, check, examine, scan **5 = process**, sort, examine, filter, scan, evaluate, gauge, sift **6 = protect**, guard, shield, defend, shelter

screw NOUN 1 = nail, pin, tack, rivet, fastener, spike ▷ **VERB 2 = fasten**, fix, attach, bolt, clamp, rivet **3 = turn**, twist, tighten **4** (*informal*) **= cheat**, do (*slang*), rip (someone) off (*slang*), skin (*slang*), trick, con, sting (*informal*), fleece **5** (*informal*) *often with* **out of = squeeze**, wring, extract, wrest ▷ **PHRASES: screw something up 1 = contort**, wrinkle, distort, pucker **2 = bungle**, botch, mess up, spoil, mishandle, make a mess of (*slang*), make a hash of (*informal*), crool *or* cruel (*Austral slang*)

scribble = scrawl, write, jot, dash off

script NOUN 1 = text, lines, words, book, copy, dialogue, libretto **2 = handwriting**, writing, calligraphy, penmanship ▷ **VERB 3 = write**, draft

scripture = The Bible, The Gospels, The Scriptures, The Good Book, Holy Scripture, Holy Writ, Holy Bible

scrub 1 = scour, clean, polish, rub, wash, cleanse, buff, exfoliate **2** (*informal*) **= cancel**, drop, give up, abolish, forget about, call off, delete

scrutiny = examination, study, investigation, search, analysis, inspection, exploration, perusal

sculpture NOUN 1 = statue, figure, model, bust, effigy, figurine, statuette
▷ VERB 2 = carve, form, model, fashion, shape, mould, sculpt, chisel

sea 1 = ocean, the deep, the waves, main 2 = mass, army, host, crowd, mob, abundance, swarm, horde
▷ PHRASES: at sea = bewildered, lost, confused, puzzled, baffled, perplexed, mystified, flummoxed

sea bird
• See panel SEA BIRDS

seal VERB 1 = settle, clinch, conclude, consummate, finalize
▷ NOUN 2 = sealant, sealer, adhesive 3 = authentication, stamp, confirmation, ratification, insignia, imprimatur

seam 1 = joint, closure 2 = layer, vein, stratum, lode

sea mammal
• See panel SEA MAMMALS

sear = wither, burn, scorch, sizzle

search VERB 1 = examine, investigate, explore, inspect, comb, scour, ransack, scrutinize, fossick (*Austral & NZ*)
▷ NOUN 2 = hunt, look, investigation, examination, pursuit, quest, inspection, exploration, Google (*computing*), googlewhack (*computing informal*)
▷ PHRASES: search for something *or* someone = look for, hunt for, pursue

searching = keen, sharp, probing, close, intent, piercing, penetrating, quizzical
OPPOSITE: superficial

searing 1 = acute, intense, shooting, severe, painful, stabbing, piercing, gut-wrenching 2 = cutting, biting, bitter, harsh, barbed, hurtful, caustic

season NOUN 1 = period, time, term, spell
▷ VERB 2 = flavour, salt, spice, enliven, pep up

seasoned = experienced, veteran, practised, hardened, time-served OPPOSITE: inexperienced

seasoning = flavouring, spice, salt and pepper, condiment

seat NOUN 1 = chair, bench, stall, stool, pew, settle
2 = membership, place, constituency, chair, incumbency
3 = centre, place, site, heart, capital, situation, source, hub
4 = mansion, house, residence, abode, ancestral hall
▷ VERB 5 = sit, place, settle, set, fix, locate, install 6 = hold, take, accommodate, sit, contain, cater for

S

SEA BIRDS

albatross or (informal) gooney bird
auk
auklet
black-backed gull
black guillemot
black shag or kawau (NZ)
blue penguin, korora or little blue penguin (NZ)
blue shag (NZ)
booby (Austral)
caspian tern or taranui (NZ)
coot
cormorant
fairy penguin, little penguin, or (NZ) korora
fish hawk
fulmar
gannet
glaucous gull
guillemot
gull or (archaic or dialect) cob(b)
herring gull
ivory gull
kittiwake
man-of-war bird or frigate bird

murrelet
old squaw or oldwife
oystercatcher
petrel
prion
razorbill or razor-billed auk
scoter
sea duck
sea eagle, erne, or ern
seagull
shearwater
short-tailed shearwater, (Tasmanian) mutton bird, or (NZ) titi
skua
storm petrel, stormy petrel, or Mother Carey's chicken
surf scoter or surf duck
takapu (NZ)
velvet scoter
wandering albatross
white-fronted tern, black cap, kahawai bird, sea swallow or tara (NZ)
Wilson's petrel

SEA MAMMALS

dugong
eared seal
earless seal
elephant seal
harp seal
hooded seal

manatee
sea cow
seal
sea lion
walrus or (archaic) sea horse

second¹ ADJECTIVE 1 = **next**, following, succeeding, subsequent, sophomore (*US & Canad*) 2 = **additional**, other, further, extra, alternative 3 = **inferior**, secondary, subordinate, lower, lesser ▷ NOUN 4 = **supporter**, assistant, aide, colleague, backer, helper, right-hand man ▷ VERB 5 = **support**, back, endorse, approve, go along with

second² = **moment**, minute, instant, flash, sec (*informal*), jiffy (*informal*), trice

secondary 1 = **subordinate**, minor, lesser, lower, inferior, unimportant OPPOSITE: main 2 = **resultant**, contingent, derived, indirect OPPOSITE: original

second-hand = **used**, old, hand-me-down (*informal*), nearly new, preloved (*Austral slang*)

secondly = **next**, second, moreover, furthermore, also, in the second place

secrecy 1 = **mystery**, stealth, concealment, furtiveness, secretiveness, clandestineness, covertness 2 = **confidentiality**, privacy 3 = **privacy**, silence, seclusion

secret ADJECTIVE 1 = **undisclosed**, unknown, confidential, underground, undercover, unrevealed 2 = **concealed**, hidden, disguised OPPOSITE: unconcealed

3 = **undercover**, furtive OPPOSITE: open 4 = **secretive**, reserved, close OPPOSITE: frank 5 = **mysterious**, cryptic, abstruse, occult, clandestine, arcane OPPOSITE: straightforward ▷ NOUN 6 = **private affair** ▷ PHRASES: in secret = **secretly**, surreptitiously, slyly

secretive = **reticent**, reserved, close, deep, uncommunicative, tight-lipped OPPOSITE: open

secretly = **in secret**, privately, surreptitiously, quietly, covertly, furtively, stealthily, clandestinely

sect = **group**, division, faction, party, camp, denomination, schism

section 1 = **part**, piece, portion, division, slice, passage, segment, fraction 2 = **district**, area, region, sector, zone

sector 1 = **part**, division 2 = **area**, part, region, district, zone, quarter

secular = **worldly**, lay, earthly, civil, temporal, nonspiritual OPPOSITE: religious

secure VERB 1 = **obtain**, get, acquire, score (*slang*), gain, procure OPPOSITE: lose 2 = **attach**, stick, fix, bind, fasten OPPOSITE: detach ▷ ADJECTIVE 3 = **safe**, protected, immune, unassailable OPPOSITE: unprotected 4 = **fast**, firm, fixed, stable, steady,

S

fastened, immovable **OPPOSITE:** insecure **5** = **confident**, sure, easy, certain, assured, reassured **OPPOSITE:** uneasy

security 1 = **precautions**, defence, safeguards, protection, safety measures **2** = **assurance**, confidence, conviction, certainty, reliance, sureness, positiveness **OPPOSITE:** insecurity **3** = **pledge**, insurance, guarantee, hostage, collateral, pawn, gage, surety **4** = **protection**, safety, custody, refuge, sanctuary, safekeeping **OPPOSITE:** vulnerability

sediment = **dregs**, grounds, residue, lees, deposit

seduce 1 = **tempt**, lure, entice, mislead, deceive, beguile, lead astray, inveigle **2** = **corrupt**, deprave, dishonour, debauch, deflower

seductive = **tempting**, inviting, attractive, enticing, provocative, alluring, bewitching, hot (*informal*)

see 1 = **perceive**, spot, notice, sight, witness, observe, distinguish, glimpse **2** = **understand**, get, follow, realize, appreciate, grasp, comprehend, fathom **3** = **find out**, learn, discover, determine, verify, ascertain **4** = **consider**, decide, reflect, deliberate, think over **5** = **make sure**, ensure, guarantee, make certain, see

to it **6** = **accompany**, show, escort, lead, walk, usher **7** = **speak to**, receive, interview, consult, confer with **8** = **meet**, come across, happen on, bump into, run across, chance on **9** = **go out with**, court, date (*informal, chiefly US*), go steady with (*informal*), step out with (*informal*)

▷ **PHRASES: seeing as** = **since**, as, in view of the fact that, inasmuch as

> **USAGE NOTE**
> It is common to hear *seeing as how*, as in *Seeing as how the bus is always late, I don't need to hurry*. However, the use of *how* here is considered incorrect or nonstandard, and should be avoided.

seed 1 = **grain**, pip, germ, kernel, egg, embryo, spore, ovum **2** = **beginning**, start, germ **3** = **origin**, source, nucleus **4** (*chiefly Bible*) = **offspring**, children, descendants, issue, progeny

▷ **PHRASES: go** *or* **run to seed** = **decline**, deteriorate, degenerate, decay, go downhill (*informal*), let yourself go, go to pot

seek 1 = **look for**, pursue, search for, be after, hunt **2** = **try**, attempt, aim, strive, endeavour, essay, aspire to

seem = **appear**, give the impression of being, look

seep = ooze, well, leak, soak, trickle, exude, permeate

seethe 1 = be furious, rage, fume, simmer, see red (informal), be livid, go ballistic (slang, chiefly US) 2 = boil, bubble, foam, fizz, froth

segment = section, part, piece, division, slice, portion, wedge

segregate = set apart, divide, separate, isolate, discriminate against, dissociate OPPOSITE: unite

segregation = separation, discrimination, apartheid, isolation

seize 1 = grab, grip, grasp, take, snatch, clutch, snap up, pluck OPPOSITE: let go 2 = take by storm, take over, acquire, occupy, conquer 3 = capture, catch, arrest, apprehend, take captive OPPOSITE: release

seizure 1 = attack, fit, spasm, convulsion, paroxysm 2 = taking, grabbing, annexation, confiscation, commandeering 3 = capture, arrest, apprehension

seldom = rarely, not often, infrequently, hardly ever OPPOSITE: often

select VERB 1 = choose, take, pick, opt for, decide on, adopt, settle upon OPPOSITE: reject ▷ ADJECTIVE 2 = choice, special, excellent, superior, first-class, hand-picked, top-notch (informal) OPPOSITE:

ordinary 3 = exclusive, elite, privileged, cliquish OPPOSITE: indiscriminate

selection 1 = choice, choosing, pick, option, preference 2 = anthology, collection, medley, choice

selective = particular, discriminating, careful, discerning, tasteful, fastidious OPPOSITE: indiscriminate

selfish = self-centred, self-interested, greedy, ungenerous, egoistic or egoistical, egotistic or egotistical OPPOSITE: unselfish

sell 1 = trade, exchange, barter OPPOSITE: buy 2 = deal in, market, trade in, stock, handle, retail, peddle, traffic in OPPOSITE: buy ▷ PHRASES: sell out of something = run out of, be out of stock of

seller = dealer, merchant, vendor, agent, retailer, supplier, purveyor, salesman or saleswoman

send 1 = dispatch, forward, direct, convey, remit 2 = propel, hurl, fling, shoot, fire, cast, let fly (old-fashioned slang) ▷ PHRASES: send something or someone up (Brit informal) = mock, mimic, parody, spoof (informal), imitate, take off (informal), make fun of, lampoon

sendoff = farewell, departure, leave-taking, valediction

S

senior 1 = **higher ranking**,
superior **OPPOSITE:** subordinate
2 = **the elder**, major (*Brit*)
OPPOSITE: junior

sensation 1 = **feeling**, sense,
impression, perception,
awareness, consciousness
2 = **excitement**, thrill, stir,
furore, commotion

sensational 1 = **amazing**,
dramatic, thrilling, astounding
OPPOSITE: dull 2 = **shocking**,
exciting, melodramatic, shock-
horror (*facetious*) **OPPOSITE:**
unexciting 3 (*informal*)
= **excellent**, superb, mean
(*slang*), impressive, smashing
(*informal*), fabulous (*informal*),
marvellous, out of this world
(*informal*), booshit (*Austral
slang*), exo (*Austral slang*), sik
(*Austral slang*), rad (*informal*),
phat (*slang*), schmick (*Austral
informal*), funky **OPPOSITE:**
ordinary

sense NOUN 1 = **faculty**
2 = **feeling**, impression,
perception, awareness,
consciousness, atmosphere,
aura 3 = **understanding**,
awareness 4 *sometimes
plural* = **intelligence**, reason,
understanding, brains (*informal*),
judgment, wisdom, wit(s),
common sense **OPPOSITE:**
foolishness 5 = **meaning**,
significance, import,
implication, drift, gist
▷ VERB 6 = **perceive**, feel,

understand, pick up, realize,
be aware of, discern, get the
impression **OPPOSITE:** be
unaware of

sensibility *often plural*
= **feelings**, emotions,
sentiments, susceptibilities,
moral sense

sensible 1 = **wise**,
practical, prudent, shrewd,
judicious **OPPOSITE:** foolish
2 = **intelligent**, practical,
rational, sound, realistic,
sage, shrewd, down-to-earth,
grounded **OPPOSITE:** senseless

sensitive 1 = **thoughtful**,
kindly, concerned, patient,
attentive, tactful, unselfish
2 = **delicate**, tender
3 = **susceptible**, responsive,
easily affected 4 = **touchy**,
oversensitive, easily upset,
easily offended, easily
hurt **OPPOSITE:** insensitive
5 = **precise**, fine, acute, keen,
responsive **OPPOSITE:** imprecise

sensitivity 1 = **susceptibility**,
responsiveness,
receptiveness, sensitiveness
2 = **consideration**,
patience, thoughtfulness
3 = **touchiness**, oversensitivity
4 = **responsiveness**, precision,
keenness, acuteness

sensual 1 = **sexual**, erotic,
raunchy (*slang*), lewd, lascivious,
lustful, lecherous 2 = **physical**,
bodily, voluptuous, animal,
luxurious, fleshly, carnal

sentence NOUN

  1 = **punishment**, condemnation
  2 = **verdict**, order, ruling,
  decision, judgment, decree
  ▷ VERB 3 = **condemn**, doom
  4 = **convict**, condemn, penalize

sentiment 1 = **feeling**, idea,
  view, opinion, attitude, belief,
  judgment 2 = **sentimentality**,
  emotion, tenderness,
  romanticism, sensibility,
  emotionalism, mawkishness

sentimental = **romantic**,
  touching, emotional,
  nostalgic, maudlin, weepy
  (*informal*), slushy (*informal*),
  schmaltzy (*slang*) **OPPOSITE:**
  unsentimental

separate ADJECTIVE

  1 = **unconnected**, individual,
  particular, divided, divorced,
  isolated, detached,
  disconnected **OPPOSITE:**
  connected 2 = **individual**,
  independent, apart, distinct
  OPPOSITE: joined
  ▷ VERB 3 = **divide**, detach,
  disconnect, disjoin **OPPOSITE:**
  combine 4 = **come apart**, split,
  come away **OPPOSITE:** connect
  5 = **sever**, break apart, split in
  two, divide in two **OPPOSITE:**
  join 6 = **split up**, part, divorce,
  break up, part company,
  get divorced, be estranged
  7 = **distinguish**, mark, single
  out, set apart **OPPOSITE:** link

separated 1 = **estranged**,
  parted, separate, apart,

disunited 2 = **disconnected**,
  parted, divided, separate,
  disassociated, disunited,
  sundered

separately 1 = **alone**, apart, not
  together, severally **OPPOSITE:**
  together 2 = **individually**, singly

separation 1 = **division**, break,
  dissociation, disconnection,
  disunion 2 = **split-up**, parting,
  split, divorce, break-up, rift

sequel 1 = **follow-up**,
  continuation, development
  2 = **consequence**, result,
  outcome, conclusion, end,
  upshot

sequence = **succession**, course,
  series, order, chain, cycle,
  arrangement, progression

series 1 = **sequence**, course,
  chain, succession, run, set,
  order, train 2 = **drama**,
  serial, soap (*informal*), sitcom
  (*informal*), soap opera, soapie *or*
  soapy (*Austral slang*), situation
  comedy

serious 1 = **grave**, bad, critical,
  dangerous, acute, severe
  2 = **important**, crucial, urgent,
  pressing, worrying, significant,
  grim, momentous **OPPOSITE:**
  unimportant 3 = **thoughtful**,
  detailed, careful, deep,
  profound, in-depth 4 = **deep**,
  sophisticated 5 = **solemn**,
  earnest, grave, sober, staid,
  humourless, unsmiling
  OPPOSITE: light-hearted
  6 = **sincere**, earnest, genuine,

S

honest, in earnest **OPPOSITE:** insincere

seriously 1 = **truly**, in earnest, all joking aside 2 = **badly**, severely, gravely, critically, acutely, dangerously

seriousness 1 = **importance**, gravity, urgency, significance 2 = **solemnity**, gravity, earnestness, gravitas

sermon = **homily**, address

servant = **attendant**, domestic, slave, maid, help, retainer, skivvy (*chiefly Brit*)

serve 1 = **work for**, help, aid, assist, be in the service of 2 = **perform**, do, complete, fulfil, discharge 3 = **be adequate**, do, suffice, suit, satisfy, be acceptable, answer the purpose 4 = **present**, provide, supply, deliver, set out, dish up

service NOUN 1 = **facility**, system, resource, utility, amenity 2 = **ceremony**, worship, rite, observance 3 = **work**, labour, employment, business, office, duty 4 = **check**, maintenance check
▷ VERB 5 = **overhaul**, check, maintain, tune (up), go over, fine tune

session = **meeting**, hearing, sitting, period, conference, congress, discussion, assembly

set¹ VERB 1 = **put**, place, lay, position, rest, plant, station, stick 2 = **arrange**, decide (upon), settle, establish,

determine, fix, schedule, appoint 3 = **assign**, give, allot, prescribe 4 = **harden**, stiffen, solidify, cake, thicken, crystallize, congeal 5 = **go down**, sink, dip, decline, disappear, vanish, subside 6 = **prepare**, lay, spread, arrange, make ready
▷ ADJECTIVE 7 = **established**, planned, decided, agreed, arranged, rigid, definite, inflexible 8 = **strict**, rigid, stubborn, inflexible **OPPOSITE:** flexible 9 = **conventional**, traditional, stereotyped, unspontaneous
▷ NOUN 10 = **scenery**, setting, scene, stage set 11 = **position**, bearing, attitude, carriage, posture
▷ PHRASES: **set on** *or* **upon something** = **determined to**, intent on, bent on, resolute about ▶ **set something up** 1 = **arrange**, organize, prepare, prearrange 2 = **establish**, begin, found, institute, initiate 3 = **build**, raise, construct, put up, assemble, put together, erect 4 = **assemble**, put up

set² 1 = **series**, collection, assortment, batch, compendium, ensemble 2 = **group**, company, crowd, circle, band, gang, faction, clique

setback = **hold-up**, check, defeat, blow, reverse,

disappointment, hitch, misfortune

setting = **surroundings**, site, location, set, scene, background, context, backdrop

settle 1 = **resolve**, work out, put an end to, straighten out 2 = **pay**, clear, square (up), discharge 3 = **move to**, take up residence in, live in, dwell in, inhabit, reside in, set up home in, put down roots in 4 = **colonize**, populate, people, pioneer 5 = **land**, alight, descend, light, come to rest 6 = **calm**, quiet, relax, relieve, reassure, soothe, lull, quell **OPPOSITE:** disturb

settlement 1 = **agreement**, arrangement, working out, conclusion, establishment, confirmation 2 = **payment**, clearing, discharge 3 = **colony**, community, outpost, encampment, kainga or kaika (NZ)

settler = **colonist**, immigrant, pioneer, frontiersman

setup (informal) = **arrangement**, system, structure, organization, conditions, regime

sever 1 = **cut**, separate, split, part, divide, detach, disconnect, cut in two **OPPOSITE:** join 2 = **discontinue**, terminate, break off, put an end to, dissociate **OPPOSITE:** continue

several = **various**, different, diverse, sundry

severe 1 = **serious**, critical, terrible, desperate, extreme, awful, drastic, catastrophic 2 = **acute**, intense, violent, piercing, harrowing, unbearable, agonizing, insufferable 3 = **strict**, hard, harsh, cruel, rigid, drastic, oppressive, austere **OPPOSITE:** lenient 4 = **grim**, serious, grave, forbidding, stern, unsmiling, tight-lipped **OPPOSITE:** genial 5 = **plain**, simple, austere, classic, restrained, Spartan, unadorned, unfussy, bare-bones **OPPOSITE:** fancy

severely 1 = **seriously**, badly, extremely, gravely, acutely 2 = **strictly**, harshly, sternly, sharply

severity = **strictness**, harshness, toughness, hardness, sternness, severeness

sew = **stitch**, tack, seam, hem

sex 1 = **gender** 2 (informal) = **lovemaking**, sexual relations, copulation, fornication, coitus, coition, cybersex

sexual 1 = **carnal**, erotic, intimate 2 = **sexy**, erotic, sensual, arousing, naughty, provocative, seductive, sensuous

sexuality = **desire**, lust, eroticism, sensuality, sexiness (informal), carnality

sexy = **erotic**, sensual, seductive, arousing, naughty, provocative,

S

sensuous, suggestive, hot (*informal*)

shabby 1 = **tatty**, worn, ragged, scruffy, tattered, threadbare **OPPOSITE:** smart 2 = **rundown**, seedy, mean, dilapidated 3 = **mean**, low, rotten (*informal*), cheap, dirty, despicable, contemptible, scurvy **OPPOSITE:** fair

shack = **hut**, cabin, shanty, whare (*NZ*)

shade NOUN 1 = **hue**, tone, colour, tint 2 = **shadow** 3 = **dash**, trace, hint, suggestion 4 = **nuance**, difference, degree 5 = **screen**, covering, cover, blind, curtain, shield, veil, canopy 6 (*literary*) = **ghost**, spirit, phantom, spectre, apparition, kehua (*NZ*) ▷ VERB 7 = **darken**, shadow, cloud, dim 8 = **cover**, protect, screen, hide, shield, conceal, obscure, veil

shadow NOUN 1 = **silhouette**, shape, outline, profile 2 = **shade**, dimness, darkness, gloom, cover, dusk ▷ VERB 3 = **shade**, screen, shield, darken, overhang 4 = **follow**, tail (*informal*), trail, stalk

shady 1 = **shaded**, cool, dim **OPPOSITE:** sunny 2 (*informal*) = **crooked**, dodgy (*Brit, Austral & NZ informal*), unethical, suspect, suspicious, dubious, questionable, shifty, shonky (*Austral & NZ informal*) **OPPOSITE:** honest

shaft 1 = **tunnel**, hole, passage, burrow, passageway, channel 2 = **handle**, staff, pole, rod, stem, baton, shank 3 = **ray**, beam, gleam

shake VERB 1 = **jiggle**, agitate 2 = **tremble**, shiver, quake, quiver 3 = **rock**, totter 4 = **wave**, wield, flourish, brandish 5 = **upset**, shock, frighten, disturb, distress, rattle (*informal*), unnerve, traumatize ▷ NOUN 6 = **vibration**, trembling, quaking, jerk, shiver, shudder, jolt, tremor

Shakespeare
• *See panel* **SHAKESPEARE**

shaky 1 = **unstable**, weak, precarious, rickety **OPPOSITE:** stable 2 = **unsteady**, faint, trembling, faltering, quivery 3 = **uncertain**, suspect, dubious, questionable, iffy (*informal*) **OPPOSITE:** reliable

shallow = **superficial**, surface, empty, slight, foolish, trivial, meaningless, frivolous **OPPOSITE:** deep

sham NOUN 1 = **fraud**, imitation, hoax, pretence, forgery, counterfeit, humbug, impostor **OPPOSITE:** the real thing ▷ ADJECTIVE 2 = **false**, artificial, bogus, pretended, mock, imitation, simulated, counterfeit **OPPOSITE:** real

SHAKESPEARE

Characters in Shakespeare	Play
Sir Andrew Aguecheek	Twelfth Night
Antonio	The Merchant of Venice
Antony	Antony and Cleopatra, Julius Caesar
Ariel	The Tempest
Aufidius	Coriolanus
Autolycus	The Winter's Tale
Banquo	Macbeth
Bassanio	The Merchant of Venice
Beatrice	Much Ado About Nothing
Sir Toby Belch	Twelfth Night
Benedick	Much Ado About Nothing
Bolingbroke	Richard II
Bottom	A Midsummer Night's Dream
Brutus	Julius Caesar
Caliban	The Tempest
Casca	Julius Caesar
Cassio	Othello
Cassius	Julius Caesar
Claudio	Much Ado About Nothing, Measure for Measure
Claudius	Hamlet
Cleopatra	Antony and Cleopatra
Cordelia	King Lear
Coriolanus	Coriolanus
Cressida	Troilus and Cressida
Demetrius	A Midsummer Night's Dream
Desdemona	Othello
Dogberry	Much Ado About Nothing
Edmund	King Lear
Enobarbus	Antony and Cleopatra
Falstaff	Henry IV Parts I and II, The Merry Wives of Windsor
Ferdinand	The Tempest
Feste	Twelfth Night
Fluellen	Henry V

S

Characters in Shakespeare	Play
Fool	King Lear
Gertrude	Hamlet
Gloucester	King Lear
Goneril	King Lear
Guildenstern	Hamlet
Hamlet	Hamlet
Helena	All's Well that Ends Well, A Midsummer Night's Dream
Hermia	A Midsummer Night's Dream
Hero	Much Ado About Nothing
Hotspur	Henry IV Part I
Iago	Othello
Jaques	As You Like It
John of Gaunt	Richard II
Juliet	Romeo and Juliet
Julius Caesar	Julius Caesar
Katharina or Kate	The Taming of the Shrew
Kent	King Lear
Laertes	Hamlet
Lear	King Lear
Lysander	A Midsummer Night's Dream
Macbeth	Macbeth
Lady Macbeth	Macbeth
Macduff	Macbeth
Malcolm	Macbeth
Malvolio	Twelfth Night
Mercutio	Romeo and Juliet
Miranda	The Tempest
Oberon	A Midsummer Night's Dream
Octavius	Antony and Cleopatra
Olivia	Twelfth Night
Ophelia	Hamlet
Orlando	As You Like It
Orsino	Twelfth Night
Othello	Othello
Pandarus	Troilus and Cressida
Perdita	The Winter's Tale

Characters in Shakespeare	Play
Petruchio	The Taming of the Shrew
Pistol	Henry IV Part II, Henry V, The Merry Wives of Windsor
Polonius	Hamlet
Portia	The Merchant of Venice
Prospero	The Tempest
Puck	A Midsummer Night's Dream
Mistress Quickly	The Merry Wives of Windsor
Regan	King Lear
Romeo	Romeo and Juliet
Rosalind	As You Like It
Rosencrantz	Hamlet
Sebastian	The Tempest, Twelfth Night
Shylock	The Merchant of Venice
Thersites	Troilus and Cressida
Timon	Timon of Athens
Titania	A Midsummer Night's Dream
Touchstone	As You Like It
Troilus	Troilus and Cressida
Tybalt	Romeo and Juliet
Viola	Twelfth Night

Plays of Shakespeare

All's Well that Ends Well	Henry VIII
Antony and Cleopatra	Julius Caesar
As You Like It	King John
The Comedy of Errors	King Lear
Coriolanus	Love's Labour's Lost
Cymbeline	Macbeth
Hamlet	Measure for Measure
Henry IV Part I	The Merchant of Venice
Henry IV Part II	The Merry Wives of Windsor
Henry V	A Midsummer Night's Dream
Henry VI Part I	Much Ado About Nothing
Henry VI Part II	Othello
Henry VI Part III	Pericles, Prince of Tyre

S

shambles 1 = **chaos**, mess, disorder, confusion, muddle, havoc, disarray, madhouse 2 = **mess**, jumble, untidiness

shame NOUN 1 = **embarrassment**, humiliation, ignominy, mortification, abashment OPPOSITE: shamelessness 2 = **disgrace**, scandal, discredit, smear, disrepute, reproach, dishonour, infamy OPPOSITE: honour ▷ VERB 3 = **embarrass**, disgrace, humiliate, humble, mortify, abash OPPOSITE: make proud 4 = **dishonour**, degrade, stain, smear, blot, debase, defile OPPOSITE: honour

shameful = **disgraceful**, outrageous, scandalous, mean, low, base, wicked, dishonourable OPPOSITE: admirable

shape NOUN 1 = **appearance**, form, aspect, guise, likeness, semblance 2 = **form**, profile, outline, lines, build, figure, silhouette, configuration

3 = **pattern**, model, frame, mould 4 = **condition**, state, health, trim, fettle ▷ VERB 5 = **form**, make, produce, create, model, fashion, mould 6 = **mould**, form, make, fashion, model, frame

share NOUN 1 = **part**, portion, quota, ration, lot, due, contribution, allowance ▷ VERB 2 = **divide**, split, distribute, assign 3 = **go halves on**, go fifty-fifty on (*informal*)

shark
• *See panel* SHARKS

sharp ADJECTIVE 1 = **keen**, jagged, serrated OPPOSITE: blunt 2 = **quick-witted**, clever, astute, knowing, quick, bright, alert, penetrating OPPOSITE: dim 3 = **cutting**, biting, bitter, harsh, barbed, hurtful, caustic OPPOSITE: gentle 4 = **sudden**, marked, abrupt, extreme, distinct OPPOSITE: gradual 5 = **clear**, distinct, well-defined, crisp OPPOSITE: indistinct 6 = **sour**, tart, pungent, hot, acid, acrid, piquant OPPOSITE:

SHARKS

angel shark, angelfish, *or* monkfish
basking shark, sailfish *or* (NZ) reremai
blue pointer *or* (NZ) blue shark *or* blue whaler
bronze whaler (*Austral*)
carpet shark *or* (*Austral*) wobbegong
cow shark *or* six-gilled shark
dogfish *or* (*Austral*) dog shark
great white (shark)
grey nurse shark
gummy (shark)
hammerhead

mako
nursehound
nurse shark
porbeagle *or* mackerel shark
requiem shark
school shark (*Austral*)
seven-gill shark (*Austral*)
shovelhead
soupfin *or* soupfin shark
thrasher *or* thresher shark
tiger shark
tope
whale shark
whaler shark

bland **7 = acute**, severe, intense, painful, shooting, stabbing, piercing, gut-wrenching
▷ ADVERB **8 = promptly**, precisely, exactly, on time, on the dot, punctually OPPOSITE: approximately
sharpen = make sharp, hone, whet, grind, edge
shatter 1 = smash, break, burst, crack, crush, pulverize **2 = destroy**, ruin, wreck, demolish, torpedo
shattered 1 = devastated, crushed, gutted (*slang*) **2** (*informal*) **= exhausted**, drained, worn out, done in (*informal*), all in (*slang*), knackered (*slang*), tired out, ready to drop

shave 1 = trim, crop **2 = scrape**, trim, shear, pare
shed¹ = hut, shack, outhouse, whare (*NZ*)
shed² 1 = drop, spill, scatter **2 = cast off**, discard, moult, slough off **3 = give out**, cast, emit, give, radiate
sheen = shine, gleam, gloss, polish, brightness, lustre
sheer 1 = total, complete, absolute, utter, pure, downright, out-and-out, unmitigated OPPOSITE: moderate **2 = steep**, abrupt, precipitous OPPOSITE: gradual **3 = fine**, thin, transparent, see-through, gossamer, diaphanous, gauzy OPPOSITE: thick
sheet 1 = page, leaf, folio, piece of paper **2 = plate**, piece,

S

panel, slab 3 = **coat**, film, layer, surface, stratum, veneer, overlay, lamina 4 = **expanse**, area, stretch, sweep, covering, blanket

shell NOUN 1 = **husk**, case, pod 2 = **carapace** 3 = **frame**, structure, hull, framework, chassis
▷ VERB 4 = **bomb**, bombard, attack, blitz, strafe
▷ PHRASES: **shell something out** (*informal*) = **pay out**, fork out (*slang*), give, hand over

shelter NOUN 1 = **cover**, screen 2 = **protection**, safety, refuge, cover 3 = **refuge**, haven, sanctuary, retreat, asylum
▷ VERB 4 = **take shelter**, hide, seek refuge, take cover 5 = **protect**, shield, harbour, safeguard, cover, hide, guard, defend OPPOSITE: endanger

sheltered 1 = **screened**, covered, protected, shielded, secluded OPPOSITE: exposed 2 = **protected**, screened, shielded, quiet, isolated, secluded, cloistered

shelve = **postpone**, defer, freeze, suspend, put aside, put on ice, put on the back burner (*informal*), take a rain check on (*US & Canad informal*)

shepherd NOUN 1 = **drover**, stockman, herdsman, grazier
▷ VERB 2 = **guide**, conduct, steer, herd, usher

sherang (*Austral & NZ*) = **boss**, manager, head, leader, director, chief, master, employer, supervisor, baas (*S African*)

shield NOUN 1 = **protection**, cover, defence, screen, guard, shelter, safeguard
▷ VERB 2 = **protect**, cover, screen, guard, defend, shelter, safeguard

shift VERB 1 = **move**, move around, budge 2 = **remove**, move, displace, relocate, rearrange, reposition
▷ NOUN 3 = **change**, shifting, displacement 4 = **move**, rearrangement

shimmer VERB 1 = **gleam**, twinkle, glisten, scintillate
▷ NOUN 2 = **gleam**, iridescence

shine VERB 1 = **gleam**, flash, beam, glow, sparkle, glitter, glare, radiate 2 = **polish**, buff, burnish, brush 3 = **be outstanding**, stand out, excel, be conspicuous
▷ NOUN 4 = **polish**, gloss, sheen, lustre 5 = **brightness**, light, sparkle, radiance

shining = **bright**, brilliant, gleaming, beaming, sparkling, shimmering, radiant, luminous

shiny = **bright**, gleaming, glossy, glistening, polished, lustrous

ship = **vessel**, boat, craft

shiver VERB 1 = **shudder**, shake, tremble, quake, quiver
▷ NOUN 2 = **tremble**, shudder, quiver, trembling, flutter, tremor

shock NOUN 1 = **upset**, blow, trauma, bombshell, turn (*informal*), distress, disturbance 2 = **impact**, blow, clash, collision 3 = **start**, scare, fright, turn, jolt ▷ VERB 4 = **shake**, stun, stagger, jolt, stupefy 5 = **horrify**, appal, disgust, revolt, sicken, nauseate, scandalize

shocking 1 (*informal*) = **terrible**, appalling, dreadful, bad, horrendous, ghastly, deplorable, abysmal 2 = **appalling**, outrageous, disgraceful, disgusting, dreadful, horrifying, revolting, sickening **OPPOSITE:** wonderful

shoot VERB 1 = **open fire on**, blast (*slang*), hit, kill, plug (*slang*), bring down 2 = **fire**, launch, discharge, project, hurl, fling, propel, emit 3 = **speed**, race, rush, charge, fly, tear, dash, barrel (along) (*informal, chiefly US & Canad*) ▷ NOUN 4 = **sprout**, branch, bud, sprig, offshoot

shop = **store**, supermarket, boutique, emporium, hypermarket, dairy (*NZ*)

shore = **beach**, coast, sands, strand (*poetic*), seashore

short ADJECTIVE 1 = **brief**, fleeting, momentary **OPPOSITE:** long 2 = **concise**, brief, succinct, summary, compressed, terse, laconic, pithy **OPPOSITE:** lengthy 3 = **small**, little, squat, diminutive, petite, dumpy

OPPOSITE: tall 4 = **abrupt**, sharp, terse, curt, brusque, impolite, discourteous, uncivil **OPPOSITE:** polite 5 = **scarce**, wanting, low, limited, lacking, scant, deficient **OPPOSITE:** plentiful ▷ ADVERB 6 = **abruptly**, suddenly, without warning **OPPOSITE:** gradually

shortage = **deficiency**, want, lack, scarcity, dearth, paucity, insufficiency **OPPOSITE:** abundance

shortcoming = **failing**, fault, weakness, defect, flaw, imperfection

shorten 1 = **cut**, reduce, decrease, diminish, lessen, curtail, abbreviate, abridge **OPPOSITE:** increase 2 = **turn up**

shortly = **soon**, presently, before long, in a little while

shot 1 = **discharge**, gunfire, crack, blast, explosion, bang 2 = **ammunition**, bullet, slug, pellet, projectile, lead, ball 3 = **marksman**, shooter, markswoman 4 = **strike**, throw, lob 5 (*informal*) = **attempt**, go (*informal*), try, turn, effort, stab (*informal*), endeavour

shoulder 1 = **bear**, carry, take on, accept, assume, be responsible for 2 = **push**, elbow, shove, jostle, press

shout VERB 1 = **cry (out)**, call (out), yell, scream, roar, bellow, bawl, holler (*informal*)

S

▷ NOUN 2 = **cry**, call, yell, scream, roar, bellow
▷ PHRASES: **shout someone down** = **drown out**, overwhelm, drown, silence

shove VERB 1 = **push**, thrust, elbow, drive, press, propel, jostle, impel
▷ NOUN 2 = **push**, knock, thrust, elbow, bump, nudge, jostle
▷ PHRASES: **shove off** (*informal*) = **go away**, leave, clear off (*informal*), depart, push off (*informal*), scram (*informal*), rack off (*Austral & NZ slang*)

shovel 1 = **move**, scoop, dredge, load, heap 2 = **stuff**, ladle

show VERB 1 = **indicate**, demonstrate, prove, reveal, display, point out, manifest, testify to, flag up OPPOSITE: disprove 2 = **display**, exhibit 3 = **guide**, lead, conduct, accompany, direct, escort 4 = **demonstrate**, describe, explain, teach, illustrate, instruct 5 = **be visible**, be seen OPPOSITE: be invisible 6 = **express**, display, reveal, indicate, register, demonstrate, manifest OPPOSITE: hide 7 (*informal*) = **turn up**, appear, attend 8 = **broadcast**, transmit, air, beam, relay, televise, put on the air, podcast
▷ NOUN 9 = **display**, sight, spectacle, array 10 = **exhibition**, fair, display, parade, pageant 11 = **appearance**, display, pose, parade 12 = **pretence**, appearance, illusion, affectation 13 = **programme**, broadcast, presentation, production 14 = **entertainment**, production, presentation
▷ PHRASES: **show off** (*informal*) = **boast**, brag, blow your own trumpet, swagger ▶ **show someone up** (*informal*) = **embarrass**, let down, mortify, put to shame ▶ **show something off** = **exhibit**, display, parade, demonstrate, flaunt ▶ **show something up** = **reveal**, expose, highlight, lay bare (*informal*)

showdown (*informal*) = **confrontation**, clash, face-off (*slang*)

shower NOUN 1 = **deluge**
▷ VERB 2 = **cover**, dust, spray, sprinkle 3 = **inundate**, heap, lavish, pour, deluge

show-off (*informal*) = **exhibitionist**, boaster, poseur, braggart, figjam (*Austral slang*)

shred 1 = **strip**, bit, piece, scrap, fragment, sliver, tatter 2 = **particle**, trace, scrap, grain, atom, jot, iota

shrewd = **astute**, clever, sharp, keen, smart, calculating, intelligent, cunning OPPOSITE: naive

shriek VERB 1 = **scream**, cry, yell, screech, squeal
▷ NOUN 2 = **scream**, cry, yell, screech, squeal

shrink = **decrease**, dwindle, lessen, grow or get smaller, contract, narrow, diminish, shorten **OPPOSITE:** grow

shroud NOUN 1 = **winding sheet**, grave clothes
2 = **covering**, veil, mantle, screen, pall
▷ VERB 3 = **conceal**, cover, screen, hide, blanket, veil, cloak, envelop

shudder VERB 1 = **shiver**, shake, tremble, quake, quiver, convulse
▷ NOUN 2 = **shiver**, tremor, quiver, spasm

shuffle 1 = **shamble**, stagger, stumble, dodder 2 = **scuffle**, drag, scrape 3 = **rearrange**, jumble, mix, disorder, disarrange

shun = **avoid**, steer clear of, keep away from

shut VERB 1 = **close**, secure, fasten, seal, slam **OPPOSITE:** open
▷ ADJECTIVE 2 = **closed**, fastened, sealed, locked **OPPOSITE:** open
▷ PHRASES: **shut down** = **stop work**, halt work, close down (informal)

shuttle = **go back and forth**, commute, go to and fro, alternate

shy ADJECTIVE 1 = **timid**, self-conscious, bashful, retiring, shrinking, coy, self-effacing, diffident **OPPOSITE:** confident
2 = **cautious**, wary, hesitant, suspicious, distrustful, chary

OPPOSITE: reckless
▷ VERB 3 sometimes with **off** or **away** = **recoil**, flinch, draw back, start, balk

sick 1 = **unwell**, ill, poorly (informal), diseased, crook (Austral & NZ informal), ailing, under the weather (informal), indisposed **OPPOSITE:** well
2 = **nauseous**, ill, queasy, nauseated 3 (informal) = **tired**, bored, fed up, weary, jaded
4 (informal) = **morbid**, sadistic, black, macabre, ghoulish

sicken 1 = **disgust**, revolt, nauseate, repel, gross out (US slang), turn your stomach
2 = **fall ill**, take sick, ail

sickening = **disgusting**, revolting, offensive, foul, distasteful, repulsive, nauseating, loathsome, yucko (Austral slang) **OPPOSITE:** delightful

sickness 1 = **illness**, disorder, ailment, disease, complaint, bug (informal), affliction, malady 2 = **nausea**, queasiness
3 = **vomiting**

side NOUN 1 = **border**, margin, boundary, verge, flank, rim, perimeter, edge **OPPOSITE:** middle 2 = **face**, surface, facet
3 = **party**, camp, faction, cause
4 = **point of view**, viewpoint, position, opinion, angle, slant, standpoint 5 = **team**, squad, line-up 6 = **aspect**, feature, angle, facet

S

▷ **ADJECTIVE 7 = subordinate**, minor, secondary, subsidiary, lesser, marginal, incidental, ancillary **OPPOSITE:** main
▷ **PHRASES: side with someone = support**, agree with, stand up for, favour, go along with, take the part of, ally yourself with

sidewalk (US & Canad) **= pavement**, footpath (Austral & NZ)

sideways ADVERB
1 **= indirectly**, obliquely 2 **= to the side**, laterally
▷ **ADJECTIVE 3 = sidelong**, oblique

siege = blockade, encirclement, besiegement

sift 1 **= part**, filter, strain, separate, sieve 2 **= examine**, investigate, go through, research, analyse, work over, scrutinize

sight NOUN 1 **= vision**, eyes, eyesight, seeing, eye 2 **= spectacle**, show, scene, display, exhibition, vista, pageant 3 **= view**, range of vision, visibility 4 (informal) **= eyesore**, mess, monstrosity
▷ **VERB 5 = spot**, see, observe, distinguish, perceive, make out, discern, behold

▌ **RELATED WORDS**
adjectives: optical, visual

sign NOUN 1 **= symbol**, mark, device, logo, badge, emblem 2 **= figure** 3 **= notice**, board, warning, placard

4 **= indication**, evidence, mark, signal, symptom, hint, proof, gesture 5 **= omen**, warning, portent, foreboding, augury, auspice
▷ **VERB 6 = gesture**, indicate, signal, beckon, gesticulate
7 **= autograph**, initial, inscribe

signal NOUN 1 **= flare**, beam, beacon 2 **= cue**, sign, prompting, reminder 3 **= sign**, gesture, indication, mark, note, expression, token
▷ **VERB 4 = gesture**, sign, wave, indicate, motion, beckon, gesticulate

significance = importance, consequence, moment, weight

significant 1 **= important**, serious, material, vital, critical, momentous, weighty, noteworthy **OPPOSITE:** insignificant 2 **= meaningful**, expressive, eloquent, indicative, suggestive **OPPOSITE:** meaningless

signify = indicate, mean, suggest, imply, intimate, be a sign of, denote, connote, flag up

silence NOUN 1 **= quiet**, peace, calm, hush, lull, stillness **OPPOSITE:** noise 2 **= reticence**, dumbness, taciturnity, muteness **OPPOSITE:** speech
▷ **VERB 3 = quieten**, still, quiet, cut off, stifle, cut short, muffle, deaden **OPPOSITE:** make louder

silent 1 **= mute**, dumb, speechless, wordless,

voiceless **OPPOSITE:** noisy
2 = **uncommunicative**, quiet,
taciturn 3 = **quiet**, still, hushed,
soundless, noiseless, muted
OPPOSITE: loud

silently 1 = **quietly**, in silence,
soundlessly, noiselessly,
inaudibly, without a sound
2 = **mutely**, in silence,
wordlessly

silhouette NOUN 1 = **outline**,
form, shape, profile
▷ **VERB** 2 = **outline**, etch

silly 1 = **stupid**, ridiculous,
absurd, daft, inane, senseless,
idiotic, fatuous **OPPOSITE:** clever
2 = **foolish**, stupid, unwise,
rash, irresponsible, thoughtless,
imprudent **OPPOSITE:** sensible

similar 1 = **alike**, resembling,
comparable **OPPOSITE:** different
2 *with* **to** = **like**, comparable to,
analogous to, close to

> **USAGE NOTE**
>
> *As* should not be used after
> *similar* - so *Wilson held a similar*
> *position to Jones* is correct,
> but not *Wilson held a similar*
> *position as Jones*; and *The*
> *system is similar to the one in*
> *France* is correct, but not *The*
> *system is similar as in France*.

similarity = **resemblance**,
likeness, sameness, agreement,
correspondence, analogy,
affinity, closeness **OPPOSITE:**
difference

simmer 1 = **bubble**, boil gently,
seethe 2 = **fume**, seethe,

smoulder, rage, be angry
▷ **PHRASES:** simmer down
(*informal*) = **calm down**, control
yourself, cool off *or* down

simple 1 = **uncomplicated**,
clear, plain, understandable,
lucid, recognizable,
comprehensible, intelligible
OPPOSITE: complicated
2 = **easy**, straightforward, not
difficult, effortless, painless,
uncomplicated, undemanding
3 = **plain**, natural, classic,
unfussy, unembellished, bare-
bones **OPPOSITE:** elaborate
4 = **pure**, mere, sheer, unalloyed
5 = **artless**, innocent, naive,
natural, sincere, unaffected,
childlike, unsophisticated
OPPOSITE: sophisticated
6 = **unpretentious**, modest,
humble, homely, unfussy,
unembellished **OPPOSITE:** fancy

simplicity
1 = **straightforwardness**, ease,
clarity, clearness **OPPOSITE:**
complexity 2 = **plainness**,
restraint, purity, lack of
adornment **OPPOSITE:**
elaborateness

simplify = **make simpler**,
streamline, disentangle, dumb
down, reduce to essentials,
declutter

simply 1 = **just**, only, merely,
purely, solely 2 = **totally**,
really, completely, absolutely,
wholly, utterly 3 = **clearly**,
straightforwardly, directly,

S

plainly, intelligibly **4** = **plainly**, naturally, modestly, unpretentiously **5** = **without doubt**, surely, certainly, definitely, beyond question

simulate = **pretend**, act, feign, affect, put on, sham

simultaneous = **coinciding**, concurrent, contemporaneous, coincident, synchronous, happening at the same time

simultaneously = **at the same time**, together, concurrently

sin NOUN **1** = **wickedness**, evil, crime, error, transgression, iniquity **2** = **crime**, offence, error, wrongdoing, misdeed, transgression, act of evil, guilt ▷ VERB **3** = **transgress**, offend, lapse, err, go astray, do wrong

sincere = **honest**, genuine, real, true, serious, earnest, frank, candid, dinkum (*Austral & NZ informal*) **OPPOSITE:** false

sincerely = **honestly**, truly, genuinely, seriously, earnestly, wholeheartedly, in earnest

sincerity = **honesty**, truth, candour, frankness, seriousness, genuineness

sing 1 = **croon**, carol, chant, warble, yodel, pipe **2** = **trill**, chirp, warble

> **USAGE NOTE**
> *Sang* is the past tense of the verb *sing*, as in *she sang sweetly*. *Sung* is the past participle, as in *we have sung our song*, and care should be taken not to use it as if it were a variant form of the past tense.

singer = **vocalist**, divo, diva *fem.*, crooner, minstrel, soloist, chorister, balladeer

single 1 = **one**, sole, lone, solitary, only, only one **2** = **individual**, separate, distinct **3** = **unmarried**, free, unattached, unwed **4** = **separate**, individual, exclusive, undivided, unshared **5** = **simple**, unmixed, unblended (*formal*) ▷ **PHRASES: single something** *or* **someone out** = **pick**, choose, select, separate, distinguish, fix on, set apart, pick on *or* out, flag up

singly = **one by one**, individually, one at a time, separately

singular 1 = **single**, individual **2** = **remarkable**, outstanding, exceptional, notable, eminent, noteworthy **OPPOSITE:** ordinary **3** = **unusual**, odd, strange, extraordinary, curious, peculiar, eccentric, queer, daggy (*Austral & NZ informal*) **OPPOSITE:** conventional

sinister = **threatening**, evil, menacing, dire, ominous, malign, disquieting **OPPOSITE:** reassuring

sink 1 = **go down**, founder, go under, submerge, capsize **2** = **slump**, drop **3** = **fall**, drop, slip, plunge, subside, abate

4 = **drop**, fall **5** = **stoop**, be reduced to, lower yourself
6 = **decline**, fade, fail, flag, weaken, diminish, decrease, deteriorate **OPPOSITE:** improve
7 = **dig**, bore, drill, drive, excavate

sip VERB **1** = **drink**, taste, sample, sup
▷ NOUN **2** = **swallow**, drop, taste, thimbleful

sit **1** = **take a seat**, perch, settle down **2** = **place**, set, put, position, rest, lay, settle, deposit
3 = **be a member of**, serve on, have a seat on, preside on
4 = **convene**, meet, assemble, officiate

site NOUN **1** = **area**, plot
2 = **location**, place, setting, point, position, situation, spot
▷ VERB **3** = **locate**, put, place, set, position, establish, install, situate

situation **1** = **position**, state, case, condition, circumstances, equation, plight, state of affairs
2 = **scenario**, state of affairs
3 = **location**, place, setting, position, site, spot

> **USAGE NOTE**
> It is common to hear the word *situation* used in sentences such as *the company is in a crisis situation*. This use of *situation* is considered bad style and the word should be left out, since it adds nothing to the sentence's meaning.

size = **dimensions**, extent, range, amount, mass, volume, proportions, bulk
▷ **PHRASES: size something** or **someone up** (*informal*) = **assess**, evaluate, appraise, take stock of

sizeable or **sizable** = **large**, considerable, substantial, goodly, decent, respectable, largish

sizzle = **hiss**, spit, crackle, fry, frizzle

skeleton = **bones**, bare bones

sketch NOUN **1** = **drawing**, design, draft, delineation
▷ VERB **2** = **draw**, outline, represent, draft, depict, delineate, rough out

skilful = **expert**, skilled, masterly, able, professional, clever, practised, competent **OPPOSITE:** clumsy

skill = **expertise**, ability, proficiency, art, technique, facility, talent, craft **OPPOSITE:** clumsiness

skilled = **expert**, professional, able, masterly, skilful, proficient **OPPOSITE:** unskilled

skim **1** = **remove**, separate, cream **2** = **glide**, fly, coast, sail, float **3** *usually with* **over** or **through** = **scan**, glance, run your eye over

skin NOUN **1** = **hide**, pelt, fell
2 = **peel**, rind, husk, casing, outside, crust **3** = **film**, coating
▷ VERB **4** = **peel** **5** = **scrape**, flay

S

skinny = thin, lean, scrawny, emaciated, undernourished **OPPOSITE:** fat

skip 1 = hop, dance, bob, trip, bounce, caper, prance, frisk 2 = miss out, omit, leave out, overlook, pass over, eschew, give (something) a miss

skirt 1 = border, edge, flank 2 *often with* **around** *or* **round** = go round, circumvent 3 *often with* **around** *or* **round** = avoid, evade, steer clear of, circumvent

skookum (*Canad*) = powerful, influential, big, dominant, controlling, commanding, supreme, prevailing, authoritative

sky = heavens, firmament, rangi (*NZ*)

slab = piece, slice, lump, chunk, wedge, portion

slack ADJECTIVE 1 = limp, relaxed, loose, lax 2 = loose, baggy **OPPOSITE:** taut 3 = slow, quiet, inactive, dull, sluggish, slow-moving **OPPOSITE:** busy 4 = negligent, lazy, lax, idle, inactive, slapdash, neglectful, slipshod **OPPOSITE:** strict ▷ NOUN 5 = surplus, excess, glut, surfeit, superabundance, superfluity 6 = room, excess, leeway, give (*informal*) ▷ VERB 7 = shirk, idle, dodge, skive (*Brit slang*), bludge (*Austral & NZ informal*)

slam 1 = bang, crash, smash 2 = throw, dash, hurl, fling

slant VERB 1 = slope, incline, tilt, list, bend, lean, heel, cant 2 = bias, colour, twist, angle, distort ▷ NOUN 3 = slope, incline, tilt, gradient, camber 4 = bias, emphasis, prejudice, angle, point of view, one-sidedness

slanting = sloping, angled, inclined, tilted, tilting, bent, diagonal, oblique

slap VERB 1 = smack, beat, clap, cuff, swipe, spank, clobber (*slang*), wallop (*informal*) ▷ NOUN 2 = smack, blow, cuff, swipe, spank

slash VERB 1 = cut, slit, gash, lacerate, score, rend, rip, hack 2 = reduce, cut, decrease, drop, lower, moderate, diminish, cut down ▷ NOUN 3 = cut, slit, gash, rent, rip, incision, laceration

slate (*informal, chiefly Brit*) = criticize, censure, rebuke, scold, tear into (*informal*)

slaughter VERB 1 = kill, murder, massacre, destroy, execute, assassinate 2 = butcher, kill, slay, massacre ▷ NOUN 3 = slaying, killing, murder, massacre, bloodshed, carnage, butchery

slave NOUN 1 = servant, serf, vassal 2 = drudge, skivvy (*chiefly Brit*) ▷ VERB 3 = toil, drudge, slog

slavery = enslavement, servitude, subjugation,

captivity, bondage **OPPOSITE:**
freedom

slay 1 (*archaic literary*) = **kill**,
slaughter, massacre, butcher
2 = **murder**, kill, massacre,
slaughter, mow down

sleaze (*informal*) = **corruption**,
fraud, dishonesty, bribery,
extortion, venality,
unscrupulousness

sleek = **glossy**, shiny, lustrous,
smooth **OPPOSITE:** shaggy

sleep NOUN 1 = **slumber(s)**,
nap, doze, snooze (*informal*),
hibernation, siesta, forty winks
(*informal*), zizz (*Brit informal*)
▷ VERB 2 = **slumber**, doze,
snooze (*informal*), hibernate,
take a nap, catnap, drowse

sleepy = **drowsy**, sluggish,
lethargic, heavy, dull, inactive
OPPOSITE: wide-awake

slender 1 = **slim**, narrow,
slight, lean, willowy **OPPOSITE:**
chubby 2 = **faint**, slight,
remote, slim, thin, tenuous
OPPOSITE: strong 3 = **meagre**,
little, small, scant, scanty
OPPOSITE: large

slice NOUN 1 = **piece**, segment,
portion, wedge, sliver, helping,
share, cut
▷ VERB 2 = **cut**, divide, carve,
sever, dissect, bisect

slick ADJECTIVE 1 = **skilful**, deft,
adroit, dexterous, professional,
polished **OPPOSITE:** clumsy
2 = **glib**, smooth, plausible,
polished, specious

▷ VERB 3 = **smooth**, sleek,
plaster down

slide = **slip**, slither, glide, skim,
coast

slight ADJECTIVE 1 = **small**,
minor, insignificant, trivial,
feeble, trifling, meagre,
unimportant **OPPOSITE:** large
2 = **slim**, small, delicate, spare,
fragile, lightly-built **OPPOSITE:**
sturdy
▷ VERB 3 = **snub**, insult,
ignore, affront, scorn, disdain
OPPOSITE: compliment
▷ NOUN 4 = **insult**, snub,
affront, rebuff, slap in the face
(*informal*), (the) cold shoulder
OPPOSITE: compliment

slightly = **a little**, a bit,
somewhat

slim ADJECTIVE 1 = **slender**,
slight, trim, thin, narrow, lean,
svelte, willowy **OPPOSITE:**
chubby 2 = **slight**, remote, faint,
slender **OPPOSITE:** strong
▷ VERB 3 = **lose weight**, diet
OPPOSITE: put on weight

sling 1 (*informal*) = **throw**, cast,
toss, hurl, fling, chuck (*informal*),
lob (*informal*), heave 2 = **hang**,
suspend

slip VERB 1 = **fall**, skid 2 = **slide**,
slither 3 = **sneak**, creep, steal
▷ NOUN 4 = **mistake**, failure,
error, blunder, lapse, omission,
oversight, barry or Barry Crocker
(*Austral slang*)
▷ PHRASES: **give someone
the slip** = **escape from**, get

S

away from, evade, elude, lose
(someone), flee, dodge ▸ **slip up**
= **make a mistake**, blunder, err,
miscalculate

slippery 1 = **smooth**, icy, greasy,
glassy, slippy (*informal dialect*),
unsafe 2 = **untrustworthy**,
tricky, cunning, dishonest,
devious, crafty, evasive, shifty

slit VERB 1 = **cut (open)**, rip,
slash, knife, pierce, lance, gash
▷ NOUN 2 = **cut**, gash, incision,
tear, rent 3 = **opening**, split

slogan = **catch phrase**, motto,
tag-line, catchword, catchcry
(*Austral*)

slope NOUN 1 = **inclination**,
rise, incline, tilt, slant, ramp,
gradient
▷ VERB 2 = **slant**, incline, drop
away, fall, rise, lean, tilt
▷ PHRASES: **slope off** = **slink
away**, slip away, creep away

sloping = **slanting**, leaning,
inclined, oblique

sloppy 1 (*informal*) = **careless**,
slovenly, slipshod, messy, untidy
2 (*informal*) = **sentimental**,
soppy (*Brit informal*), slushy
(*informal*), gushing, mawkish,
icky (*informal*)

slot NOUN 1 = **opening**, hole,
groove, vent, slit, aperture
2 (*informal*) = **place**, time, space,
opening, position, vacancy
▷ VERB 2 = **fit**, insert

slow ADJECTIVE 1 = **unhurried**,
sluggish, leisurely, lazy,
ponderous, dawdling, laggard,

lackadaisical OPPOSITE: quick
2 = **prolonged**, protracted,
long-drawn-out, lingering,
gradual 3 = **late**, behind, tardy
4 = **stupid**, dim, dense, thick,
dozy (*Brit informal*), obtuse,
braindead (*informal*) OPPOSITE:
bright
▷ VERB 5 *often with* **down**
= **decelerate**, brake 6 *often
with* **down** = **delay**, hold up,
handicap, retard OPPOSITE:
speed up

> **USAGE NOTE**
> While not as unkind as *thick*
> and *stupid*, words like *slow*
> and *backward*, when used to
> talk about a person's mental
> abilities, are both unhelpful
> and likely to cause offence.
> It is preferable to say that a
> person has *special educational
> needs* or *learning difficulties*.

slowly = **gradually**, unhurriedly
OPPOSITE: quickly

slug
• *See panel* **SNAILS, SLUGS AND
OTHER GASTROPODS**

sluggish = **inactive**, slow,
lethargic, heavy, dull, inert,
indolent, torpid OPPOSITE:
energetic

slum = **hovel**, ghetto, shanty

slump VERB 1 = **fall**, sink,
plunge, crash, collapse, slip
OPPOSITE: increase 2 = **sag**,
hunch, droop, slouch, loll
▷ NOUN 3 = **fall**, drop, decline,
crash, collapse, reverse,

SNAILS, SLUGS AND OTHER GASTROPODS

abalone *or* ear shell
conch
cowrie *or* cowry
limpet
murex
nudibranch *or* sea slug
ormer *or* sea-ear
periwinkle *or* winkle
ramshorn snail

Roman snail
sea hare
slug
snail
top-shell
triton
wentletrap
whelk

---

downturn, trough **OPPOSITE:**
increase **4 = recession**,
depression, stagnation,
inactivity, hard *or* bad times
slur = insult, stain, smear,
affront, innuendo, calumny,
insinuation, aspersion
sly 1 = roguish, knowing,
arch, mischievous, impish
2 = cunning, scheming, devious,
secret, clever, subtle, wily, crafty
OPPOSITE: open
▷ **PHRASES: on the sly**
= secretly, privately, covertly,
surreptitiously, on the quiet
smack VERB 1 = slap, hit,
strike, clap, cuff, swipe, spank
2 = drive, hit, strike
▷ **NOUN 3 = slap**, blow, cuff,
swipe, spank
▷ **ADVERB 4** (*informal*) **= directly**,
right, straight, squarely,
precisely, exactly, slap (*informal*)
small 1 = little, minute, tiny,
mini, miniature, minuscule,
diminutive, petite **OPPOSITE:**

big **2 = young**, little, junior, wee,
juvenile, youthful, immature
3 = unimportant, minor, trivial,
insignificant, little, petty,
trifling, negligible **OPPOSITE:**
important **4 = modest**, humble,
unpretentious **OPPOSITE:** grand
smart ADJECTIVE 1 = chic, trim,
neat, stylish, elegant, spruce,
snappy, natty (*informal*), schmick
(*Austral informal*) **OPPOSITE:**
scruffy **2 = clever**, bright,
intelligent, quick, sharp, keen,
acute, shrewd **OPPOSITE:** stupid
3 = brisk, quick, lively, vigorous
▷ **VERB 4 = sting**, burn, hurt
smash VERB 1 = break, crush,
shatter, crack, demolish,
pulverize **2 = shatter**, break,
disintegrate, crack, splinter
3 = collide, crash, meet head-
on, clash, come into collision
4 = destroy, ruin, wreck, trash
(*slang*), lay waste
▷ **NOUN 5 = collision**, crash,
accident

S

smashing (*informal, chiefly Brit*) = **excellent**, mean (*slang*), great (*informal*), wonderful, brilliant (*informal*), cracking (*Brit informal*), superb, fantastic (*informal*), booshit (*Austral slang*), exo (*Austral slang*), sik (*Austral slang*), rad (*informal*), phat (*slang*), schmick (*Austral informal*)
OPPOSITE: awful

smear VERB 1 = **spread over**, daub, rub on, cover, coat, bedaub 2 = **slander**, malign, blacken, besmirch 3 = **smudge**, soil, dirty, stain, sully
▷ NOUN 4 = **smudge**, daub, streak, blot, blotch, splotch 5 = **slander**, libel, defamation, calumny

smell NOUN 1 = **odour**, scent, fragrance, perfume, bouquet, aroma 2 = **stink**, stench, pong (*Brit informal*), fetor
▷ VERB 3 = **stink**, reek, pong (*Brit informal*) 4 = **sniff**, scent

smile VERB 1 = **grin**, beam, smirk, twinkle, grin from ear to ear
▷ NOUN 2 = **grin**, beam, smirk

smoke VERB 1 = **smoulder**, fume 2 = **puff on**, draw on, inhale, vape

smooth ADJECTIVE 1 = **even**, level, flat, plane, flush, horizontal **OPPOSITE:** uneven 2 = **sleek**, polished, shiny, glossy, silky, velvety **OPPOSITE:** rough 3 = **mellow**, pleasant, mild, agreeable 4 = **flowing**, steady, regular, uniform, rhythmic 5 = **easy**, effortless, well-ordered 6 = **suave**, slick, persuasive, urbane, glib, facile, unctuous, smarmy (*Brit informal*)
▷ VERB 7 = **flatten**, level, press, plane, iron 8 = **ease**, facilitate **OPPOSITE:** hinder

smother 1 = **extinguish**, put out, stifle, snuff 2 = **suffocate**, choke, strangle, stifle 3 = **suppress**, stifle, repress, hide, conceal, muffle

smug = **self-satisfied**, superior, complacent, conceited

snack = **light meal**, bite, refreshment(s)

snag NOUN 1 = **difficulty**, hitch, problem, obstacle, catch, disadvantage, complication, drawback
▷ VERB 2 = **catch**, tear, rip

snail
• *See panel* **SNAILS, SLUGS AND OTHER GASTROPODS**

snake = serpent
• *See panel* **REPTILES**

snap VERB 1 = **break**, crack, separate 2 = **pop**, click, crackle 3 = **speak sharply**, bark, lash out at, jump down (someone's) throat (*informal*) 4 = **bite at**, bite, nip
▷ MODIFIER 5 = **instant**, immediate, sudden, spur-of-the-moment
▷ PHRASES: snap something up = **grab**, seize, take advantage of, pounce upon

snare NOUN 1 = **trap**, net, wire, gin, noose

▷ VERB 2 = **trap**, catch, net, wire, seize, entrap

snatch VERB 1 = **grab**, grip, grasp, clutch 2 = **steal**, take, nick (*slang, chiefly Brit*), pinch (*informal*), lift (*informal*), pilfer, filch, thieve 3 = **win** 4 = **save**, recover, get out, salvage
▷ NOUN 5 = **bit**, part, fragment, piece, snippet

sneak VERB 1 = **slink**, slip, steal, pad, skulk 2 = **slip**, smuggle, spirit
▷ NOUN 3 = **informer**, betrayer, telltale, Judas, accuser, stool pigeon, nark (*Brit, Austral & NZ slang*), fizgig (*Austral slang*)

sneaking 1 = **nagging**, worrying, persistent, uncomfortable 2 = **secret**, private, hidden, unexpressed, unvoiced, undivulged

sneer VERB 1 = **scorn**, mock, ridicule, laugh, jeer, disdain, deride 2 = **say contemptuously**, snigger
▷ NOUN 3 = **scorn**, ridicule, mockery, derision, jeer, gibe

sniff 1 = **breathe in**, inhale 2 = **smell**, scent 3 = **inhale**, breathe in, suck in, draw in

snub VERB 1 = **insult**, slight, put down, humiliate, cut (*informal*), rebuff, cold-shoulder
▷ NOUN 2 = **insult**, put-down, affront, slap in the face (*informal*)

so = **therefore**, thus, hence, consequently, then, as a result, accordingly, thence

soak 1 = **steep** 2 = **wet**, damp, saturate, drench, moisten, suffuse, wet through, waterlog 3 = **penetrate**, permeate, seep
▷ PHRASES: **soak something up** = **absorb**, suck up, assimilate

soaking = **soaked**, dripping, saturated, drenched, sodden, streaming, sopping, wet through

soar 1 = **rise**, increase, grow, mount, climb, go up, rocket, escalate 2 = **fly**, wing, climb, ascend OPPOSITE: plunge 3 = **tower**, climb, go up

sob VERB 1 = **cry**, weep, howl, shed tears
▷ NOUN 2 = **cry**, whimper, howl

sober 1 = **abstinent**, temperate, abstemious, moderate OPPOSITE: drunk 2 = **serious**, cool, grave, reasonable, steady, composed, rational, solemn, grounded OPPOSITE: frivolous 3 = **plain**, dark, sombre, quiet, subdued, drab OPPOSITE: bright

so-called = **alleged**, supposed, professed, pretended, self-styled

social ADJECTIVE 1 = **communal**, community, collective, group, public, general, common 2 = **organized**, gregarious
▷ NOUN 3 = **get-together** (*informal*), party, gathering, function, reception, social gathering
• *See panel* SOCIAL NETWORKING

society 1 = **the community**, people, the public, humanity,

S

SOCIAL NETWORKING
Social Networking and Social Bookmarking Sites

Ask.fm	LiveMocha®
Blogger	Meetup
Classmates®	Mixi
Delicious	Mumsnet
Digg	MySpace®
Facebook	Newsvine
Fark®	Pinterest
Flickr®	Reddit
Freecycle®	Renren Network
Friends Reunited	StumbleUpon
Friendster	Tumblr®
Google Plus+®	Twitter®
Hi5	VampireFreaks
Instagram	Vine®
Last.fm	VK
LinkedIn®	

Social Networking Terms

add	news feed
app	panic button
avatar	phishing
block	plugin
blog	poke
chat	post
comment	profile
defriend	retweet or RT
follow	status
friend	tag
friend request	trend
group	tweet
hashtag	unfollow
inbox	unfriend
instant message or IM	update
like	wall
mention or @mention	
microblog	

S

civilization, mankind
2 = **culture**, community,
population 3 = **organization**,
group, club, union, league,
association, institute, circle
4 = **upper classes**, gentry,
elite, high society, beau
monde 5 (*old-fashioned*)
= **companionship**, company,
fellowship, friendship
sofa = **couch**, settee, divan,
chaise longue
soft 1 = **velvety**, smooth,
silky, feathery, downy, fleecy
OPPOSITE: rough 2 = **yielding**,
elastic **OPPOSITE:** hard
3 = **soggy**, swampy, marshy,
boggy 4 = **squashy**, sloppy,
mushy, spongy, gelatinous,
pulpy 5 = **pliable**, flexible,
supple, malleable, plastic,
elastic, bendable, mouldable
6 = **quiet**, gentle, murmured,
muted, dulcet, soft-toned
OPPOSITE: loud 7 = **lenient**,
easy-going, lax, indulgent,
permissive, spineless,
overindulgent **OPPOSITE:** harsh
8 = **kind**, tender, sentimental,
compassionate, sensitive,
gentle, tenderhearted,
touchy-feely (*informal*)
9 (*informal*) = **easy**, comfortable,
undemanding, cushy (*informal*)
10 = **pale**, light, subdued, pastel,
bland, mellow **OPPOSITE:**
bright 11 = **dim**, faint, dimmed
OPPOSITE: bright 12 = **mild**,
temperate, balmy

soften 1 = **melt**, tenderize
2 = **lessen**, moderate, temper,
ease, cushion, subdue, allay,
mitigate
software = **computer program**,
operating system, application,
system, product, app, program,
platform, network
• *See panel* **SOFTWARE AND
OPERATING SYSTEMS**
soil¹ 1 = **earth**, ground, clay, dust,
dirt 2 = **territory**, country, land
soil² = **dirty**, foul, stain, pollute,
tarnish, sully, defile, besmirch
OPPOSITE: clean
soldier = **fighter**, serviceman,
trooper, warrior, man-at-arms,
squaddie *or* squaddy (*Brit slang*)
sole = **only**, one, single,
individual, alone, exclusive,
solitary
solely = **only**, completely,
entirely, exclusively, alone,
merely
solemn 1 = **serious**, earnest,
grave, sober, sedate, staid
OPPOSITE: cheerful 2 = **formal**,
grand, grave, dignified,
ceremonial, stately, momentous
OPPOSITE: informal
solid 1 = **firm**, hard, compact,
dense, concrete **OPPOSITE:**
unsubstantial 2 = **strong**,
stable, sturdy, substantial,
unshakable **OPPOSITE:** unstable
3 = **reliable**, dependable,
upstanding, worthy, upright,
trusty **OPPOSITE:** unreliable
4 = **sound**, real, reliable, good,

S

SOFTWARE AND OPERATING SYSTEMS

abandonware
adware
Android®
antivirus
browser or internet browser
Chrome OS®
CP/M
disk operating system or
  DOS
Firefox®
firmware
freeware
groupware
Internet Explorer®

iOS or iPhone Operating
  System®
Mac OS X®
malware
middleware
MP/M
MS-DOS®
open system
Safari®
shareware
spyware
trialware
UNIX®
warez

---

genuine, dinkum (*Austral & NZ
  informal*) **OPPOSITE:** unsound
solidarity = **unity**, unification,
  accord, cohesion, team spirit,
  unanimity, concordance, like-
  mindedness, kotahitanga (*NZ*)
solitary 1 = **unsociable**,
  reclusive, unsocial, isolated,
  lonely, cloistered, lonesome,
  friendless **OPPOSITE:** sociable
  2 = **lone**, alone **3** = **isolated**,
  remote, out-of-the-way,
  hidden, unfrequented
  OPPOSITE: busy
solution 1 = **answer**, key,
  result, explanation **2** (*Chemistry*)
  = **mixture**, mix, compound,
  blend, solvent
solve = **answer**, work out,
  resolve, crack, clear up, unravel,
  decipher, suss (out) (*slang*)

sombre 1 = **gloomy**, sad,
  sober, grave, dismal, mournful,
  lugubrious, joyless **OPPOSITE:**
  cheerful **2** = **dark**, dull, gloomy,
  sober, drab **OPPOSITE:** bright
somebody = **celebrity**, name,
  star, notable, household name,
  dignitary, luminary, personage
  OPPOSITE: nobody
somehow = **one way or
  another**, come what may, come
  hell or high water (*informal*),
  by fair means or foul, by hook
  or (by) crook, by some means
  or other
sometimes = **occasionally**, at
  times, now and then **OPPOSITE:**
  always
song = **ballad**, air, tune, carol,
  chant, chorus, anthem, number,
  waiata (*NZ*)

soon = **before long**, shortly, in the near future

soothe 1 = **calm**, still, quiet, hush, appease, lull, pacify, mollify **OPPOSITE:** upset
2 = **relieve**, ease, alleviate, assuage **OPPOSITE:** irritate

soothing 1 = **calming**, relaxing, peaceful, quiet, calm, restful
2 = **emollient**, palliative

sophisticated 1 = **complex**, advanced, complicated, subtle, delicate, elaborate, refined, intricate **OPPOSITE:** simple
2 = **cultured**, refined, cultivated, worldly, cosmopolitan, urbane **OPPOSITE:** unsophisticated

sophistication = **poise**, worldliness, savoir-faire, urbanity, finesse, worldly wisdom

sore 1 = **painful**, smarting, raw, tender, burning, angry, sensitive, irritated 2 = **annoyed**, cross, angry, pained, hurt, upset, stung, irritated, tooshie (*Austral slang*), hoha (*NZ*) 3 = **annoying**, troublesome 4 = **urgent**, desperate, extreme, dire, pressing, critical, acute

sorrow NOUN 1 = **grief**, sadness, woe, regret, distress, misery, mourning, anguish **OPPOSITE:** joy 2 = **hardship**, trial, tribulation, affliction, trouble, woe, misfortune **OPPOSITE:** good fortune
▷ VERB 3 = **grieve**, mourn, lament, be sad, bemoan, agonize, bewail **OPPOSITE:** rejoice

sorry 1 = **regretful**, apologetic, contrite, repentant, remorseful, penitent, shamefaced, conscience-stricken **OPPOSITE:** unapologetic 2 = **sympathetic**, moved, full of pity, compassionate, commiserative **OPPOSITE:** unsympathetic
3 = **wretched**, miserable, pathetic, mean, poor, sad, pitiful, deplorable

sort NOUN 1 = **kind**, type, class, make, order, style, quality, nature
▷ VERB 2 = **arrange**, group, order, rank, divide, grade, classify, categorize

> **USAGE NOTE**
> It is common in informal speech to combine singular and plural in sentences like *These sort of distinctions are becoming blurred*. This is not acceptable in careful writing, where the plural must be used consistently: *These sorts of distinctions are becoming blurred*.

soul 1 = **spirit**, essence, life, vital force, wairua (*NZ*)
2 = **embodiment**, essence, epitome, personification, quintessence, type 3 = **person**, being, individual, body, creature, man *or* woman

sound¹ NOUN 1 = **noise**, din, report, tone, reverberation

S

2 = **idea**, impression, drift

3 = **cry**, noise, peep, squeak

4 = **tone**, music, note

▷ VERB 5 = **toll**, set off

6 = **resound**, echo, go off, toll, set off, chime, reverberate, clang 7 = **seem**, seem to be, appear to be

RELATED WORDS
adjectives: sonic, acoustic

sound² 1 = **fit**, healthy, perfect, intact, unhurt, uninjured, unimpaired **OPPOSITE**: frail

2 = **sturdy**, strong, solid, stable

3 = **sensible**, wise, reasonable, right, correct, proper, valid, rational, grounded **OPPOSITE**: irresponsible 4 = **deep**, unbroken, undisturbed, untroubled **OPPOSITE**: troubled

sour 1 = **sharp**, acid, tart, bitter, pungent, acetic **OPPOSITE**: sweet 2 = **rancid**, turned, gone off, curdled, gone bad, off **OPPOSITE**: fresh 3 = **bitter**, tart, acrimonious, embittered, disagreeable, ill-tempered, waspish, ungenerous **OPPOSITE**: good-natured

source 1 = **cause**, origin, derivation, beginning, author

2 = **informant**, authority

3 = **origin**, fount

souvenir = **keepsake**, reminder, memento

sovereign ADJECTIVE

1 = **supreme**, ruling, absolute, royal, principal, imperial, kingly *or* queenly 2 = **excellent**,

efficient, effectual

▷ NOUN 3 = **monarch**, ruler, king *or* queen, chief, potentate, emperor *or* empress, prince *or* princess

sovereignty = **supreme power**, domination, supremacy, primacy, kingship, rangatiratanga (*NZ*)

sow = **scatter**, plant, seed, implant

space 1 = **room**, capacity, extent, margin, scope, play, expanse, leeway 2 = **period**, interval, time, while, span, duration, time frame, timeline

3 = **outer space**, the universe, the galaxy, the solar system, the cosmos 4 = **blank**, gap, interval

spacious = **roomy**, large, huge, broad, extensive, ample, expansive, capacious **OPPOSITE**: cramped

span NOUN 1 = **period**, term, duration, spell 2 = **extent**, reach, spread, length, distance, stretch

▷ VERB 3 = **extend across**, cross, bridge, cover, link, traverse

spar = **argue**, row, squabble, scrap (*informal*), wrangle, bicker

spare ADJECTIVE 1 = **back-up**, reserve, second, extra, additional, auxiliary 2 = **extra**, surplus, leftover, over, free, odd, unwanted, unused **OPPOSITE**: necessary 3 = **free**, leisure, unoccupied 4 = **thin**, lean,

meagre, gaunt, wiry **OPPOSITE:** plump
▷ VERB 5 = **afford**, give, grant, do without, part with, manage without, let someone have
6 = **have mercy on**, pardon, leave, let off (*informal*), go easy on (*informal*), save (from harm) **OPPOSITE:** show no mercy to
sparing = **economical**, frugal, thrifty, saving, careful, prudent **OPPOSITE:** lavish
spark NOUN 1 = **flicker**, flash, gleam, glint, flare 2 = **trace**, hint, scrap, atom, jot, vestige
▷ VERB 3 *often with* **off** = **start**, stimulate, provoke, inspire, trigger (off), set off, precipitate
sparkle VERB 1 = **glitter**, flash, shine, gleam, shimmer, twinkle, dance, glint
▷ NOUN 2 = **glitter**, flash, gleam, flicker, brilliance, twinkle, glint
3 = **vivacity**, life, spirit, dash, vitality, élan, liveliness
spate 1 = **flood**, flow, torrent, rush, deluge, outpouring
2 = **series**, sequence, course, chain, succession, run, train
speak 1 = **talk**, say something
2 = **articulate**, say, pronounce, utter, tell, state, talk, express
3 = **converse**, talk, chat, discourse, confer, commune, exchange views, korero (*NZ*)
4 = **lecture**, address an audience
speaker = **orator**, public speaker, lecturer, spokesperson, spokesman *or* spokeswoman

spearhead = **lead**, head, pioneer, launch, set off, initiate, set in motion
special 1 = **exceptional**, important, significant, particular, unique, unusual, extraordinary, memorable **OPPOSITE:** ordinary 2 = **specific**, particular, distinctive, individual, appropriate, precise **OPPOSITE:** general
specialist = **expert**, authority, professional, master, consultant, guru, buff (*informal*), connoisseur, fundi (*S African*)
speciality = **forte**, métier, specialty, bag (*slang*), pièce de résistance (*French*)
species = **kind**, sort, type, group, class, variety, breed, category
specific 1 = **particular**, special, characteristic, distinguishing **OPPOSITE:** general 2 = **precise**, exact, explicit, definite, express, clear-cut, unequivocal **OPPOSITE:** vague 3 = **peculiar**, appropriate, individual, particular, unique
specification = **requirement**, detail, particular, stipulation, condition, qualification
specify = **state**, designate, stipulate, name, detail, mention, indicate, define
specimen 1 = **sample**, example, model, type, pattern, instance, representative, exemplification 2 = **example**, model, type

S

spectacle 1 = **show**, display, exhibition, event, performance, extravaganza, pageant
2 = **sight**, wonder, scene, phenomenon, curiosity, marvel

spectacular ADJECTIVE
1 = **impressive**, striking, dramatic, stunning (*informal*), grand, magnificent, splendid, dazzling OPPOSITE: unimpressive
▷ NOUN 2 = **show**, display, spectacle

spectator = **onlooker**, observer, viewer, looker-on, watcher, bystander OPPOSITE: participant

spectre = **ghost**, spirit, phantom, vision, apparition, wraith, kehua (*NZ*)

speculate 1 = **conjecture**, consider, wonder, guess, surmise, theorize, hypothesize
2 = **gamble**, risk, venture, hazard

speculation 1 = **theory**, opinion, hypothesis, conjecture, guess, surmise, guesswork, supposition 2 = **gamble**, risk, hazard

speculative = **hypothetical**, academic, theoretical, notional, conjectural, suppositional

speech 1 = **communication**, talk, conversation, discussion, dialogue 2 = **diction**, pronunciation, articulation, delivery, fluency, inflection, intonation, elocution

3 = **language**, tongue, jargon, dialect, idiom, parlance, articulation, diction 4 = **talk**, address, lecture, discourse, homily, oration, spiel (*informal*), whaikorero (*NZ*)

speed NOUN 1 = **rate**, pace
2 = **swiftness**, rush, hurry, haste, rapidity, quickness OPPOSITE: slowness
▷ VERB 3 = **race**, rush, hurry, zoom, career, tear, barrel (along) (*informal, chiefly US & Canad*), gallop OPPOSITE: crawl
4 = **help**, advance, aid, boost, assist, facilitate, expedite OPPOSITE: hinder

> **USAGE NOTE**
> The past tense of *speed up* is *speeded up* (not *sped up*), for example *I speeded up to overtake the lorry*. The past participle is also *speeded up*, for example *I had already speeded up when I spotted the police car*.

speedy = **quick**, fast, rapid, swift, express, immediate, prompt, hurried OPPOSITE: slow

spell¹ = **indicate**, mean, signify, point to, imply, augur, portend

spell² 1 = **incantation**, charm, makutu (*NZ*) 2 = **enchantment**, magic, fascination, glamour, allure, bewitchment

spell³ = **period**, time, term, stretch, course, season, interval, bout

spend 1 = **pay out**, fork out (*slang*), expend, disburse **OPPOSITE:** save 2 = **pass**, fill, occupy, while away 3 = **use up**, waste, squander, empty, drain, exhaust, consume, run through **OPPOSITE:** save

sphere 1 = **ball**, globe, orb, globule, circle 2 = **field**, department, function, territory, capacity, province, patch, scope

spice 1 = **seasoning** 2 = **excitement**, zest, colour, pep, zing (*informal*), piquancy

spicy 1 = **hot**, seasoned, aromatic, savoury, piquant 2 (*informal*) = **risqué**, racy, ribald, hot (*informal*), suggestive, titillating, indelicate

spider *phobia*: arachnophobia

• *See panel* **SPIDERS AND OTHER ARACHNIDS**

spike NOUN 1 = **point**, stake, spine, barb, prong ▷ VERB 2 = **impale**, spit, spear, stick

spill 1 = **tip over**, overturn, capsize, knock over 2 = **shed**, discharge, disgorge 3 = **slop**, flow, pour, run, overflow

spin VERB 1 = **revolve**, turn, rotate, reel, whirl, twirl, gyrate, pirouette 2 = **reel**, swim, whirl ▷ NOUN 3 (*informal*) = **drive**, ride, joy ride (*informal*) 4 = **revolution**, roll, whirl, gyration ▷ PHRASES: **spin something out** = **prolong**, extend, lengthen, draw out, drag out, delay, amplify

SPIDERS AND OTHER ARACHNIDS

bird spider	jumping spider
black widow	katipo (*NZ*)
book scorpion	mite
cardinal spider	money spider
cheese mite	red-back (spider) (*Austral*)
chigger, chigoe, or (*US & Canad*) redbug	spider
	spider mite
false scorpion	tarantula
funnel-web	tick
harvestman or (*US & Canad*) daddy-longlegs	trap-door spider
	vinegarroon
house spider	water spider
itch mite	whip scorpion
jigger, or sand flea	wolf spider or hunting spider
jockey spider	

spine 1 = **backbone**, vertebrae, spinal column, vertebral column 2 = **barb**, spur, needle, spike, ray, quill

spiral ADJECTIVE 1 = **coiled**, winding, whorled, helical ▷ NOUN 2 = **coil**, helix, corkscrew, whorl

spirit 1 = **soul**, life 2 = **life force**, vital spark, mauri (*NZ*) 3 = **ghost**, phantom, spectre, apparition, atua (*NZ*), kehua (*NZ*) 4 = **courage**, guts (*informal*), grit, backbone, spunk (*informal*), gameness 5 = **liveliness**, energy, vigour, life, force, fire, enthusiasm, animation 6 = **attitude**, character, temper, outlook, temperament, disposition 7 = **heart**, sense, nature, soul, core, substance, essence, quintessence 8 = **intention**, meaning, purpose, purport, gist 9 = **feeling**, atmosphere, character, tone, mood, tenor, ambience 10 *plural* = **mood**, feelings, morale, temper, disposition, state of mind, frame of mind

spirited = **lively**, energetic, animated, active, feisty (*informal, chiefly US & Canad*), vivacious, mettlesome, (as) game as Ned Kelly (*Austral slang*) OPPOSITE: lifeless

spiritual 1 = **nonmaterial**, immaterial, incorporeal OPPOSITE: material 2 = **sacred**, religious, holy, divine, devotional

spit VERB 1 = **expectorate** 2 = **eject**, throw out ▷ NOUN 3 = **saliva**, dribble, spittle, drool, slaver

spite NOUN 1 = **malice**, malevolence, ill will, hatred, animosity, venom, spleen, spitefulness OPPOSITE: kindness ▷ VERB 2 = **annoy**, hurt, injure, harm, vex OPPOSITE: benefit ▷ PHRASES: **in spite of** = **despite**, regardless of, notwithstanding, (even) though

splash VERB 1 = **paddle**, plunge, bathe, dabble, wade, wallow 2 = **scatter**, shower, spray, sprinkle, wet, spatter, slop 3 = **spatter**, mark, stain, speck, speckle ▷ NOUN 4 = **dash**, touch, spattering 5 = **spot**, burst, patch, spurt 6 = **blob**, spot, smudge, stain, smear, fleck, speck

splendid 1 = **excellent**, wonderful, marvellous, great (*informal*), cracking (*Brit informal*), fantastic (*informal*), first-class, glorious, booshit (*Austral slang*), exo (*Austral slang*), sik (*Austral slang*), rad (*informal*), phat (*slang*), schmick (*Austral informal*) OPPOSITE: poor 2 = **magnificent**, grand, impressive, rich, superb, costly, gorgeous, lavish OPPOSITE: squalid

splendour = magnificence, grandeur, show, display, spectacle, richness, nobility, pomp **OPPOSITE:** squalor

splinter NOUN 1 = sliver, fragment, chip, flake
▷ VERB 2 = shatter, split, fracture, disintegrate

split VERB 1 = break, crack, burst, open, give way, come apart, come undone 2 = cut, break, crack, snap, chop 3 = divide, separate, disunite, disband, cleave 4 = diverge, separate, branch, fork, part 5 = tear, rend, rip 6 = share out, divide, distribute, halve, allocate, partition, allot, apportion
▷ NOUN 7 = division, breach, rift, rupture, discord, schism, estrangement, dissension 8 = separation, break-up, split-up 9 = crack, tear, rip, gap, rent, breach, slit, fissure
▷ ADJECTIVE 10 = divided 11 = broken, cracked, fractured, ruptured, cleft

spoil 1 = ruin, destroy, wreck, damage, injure, harm, mar, trash (slang), crool or cruel (Austral slang) **OPPOSITE:** improve 2 = overindulge, indulge, pamper, cosset, coddle, mollycoddle **OPPOSITE:** deprive 3 = indulge, pamper, satisfy, gratify, pander to 4 = go bad, turn, go off (Brit informal), rot, decay, decompose, curdle, addle

spoils = booty, loot, plunder, prey, swag (slang)

spoken = verbal, voiced, expressed, uttered, oral, said, told, unwritten

spokesperson = speaker, official, spokesman or spokeswoman, voice, spin doctor (informal), mouthpiece

sponsor VERB 1 = back, fund, finance, promote, subsidize, patronize
▷ NOUN 2 = backer, patron, promoter

spontaneous = unplanned, impromptu, unprompted, willing, natural, voluntary, instinctive, impulsive **OPPOSITE:** planned

sport NOUN 1 = game, exercise, recreation, play, amusement, diversion, pastime 2 = fun, joking, teasing, banter, jest, badinage
▷ VERB 3 (informal) = wear, display, flaunt, exhibit, flourish, show off, vaunt

sporting = fair, sportsmanlike, game (informal) **OPPOSITE:** unfair

sporty = athletic, outdoor, energetic

spot NOUN 1 = mark, stain, speck, scar, blot, smudge, blemish, speckle 2 = pimple, pustule, zit (slang) 3 = place, site, point, position, scene, location 4 (informal) = predicament, trouble,

S

difficulty, mess, plight, hot water (*informal*), quandary, tight spot
▷ **VERB** 5 = **see**, observe, catch sight of, recognize, detect, make out, discern 6 = **mark**, stain, soil, dirty, fleck, spatter, speckle, splodge

spotlight NOUN 1 = **attention**, limelight, public eye, fame
▷ **VERB** 2 = **highlight**, draw attention to, accentuate

spotted = **speckled**, dotted, flecked, mottled, dappled

spouse = **partner**, mate, husband *or* wife, consort, significant other (*US informal*)

sprawl = **loll**, slump, lounge, flop, slouch

spray¹ NOUN 1 = **droplets**, fine mist, drizzle 2 = **aerosol**, sprinkler, atomizer
▷ **VERB** 3 = **scatter**, shower, sprinkle, diffuse

spray² = **sprig**, floral arrangement, branch, corsage

spread VERB 1 = **open (out)**, extend, stretch, unfold, sprawl, unroll 2 = **extend**, open, stretch 3 = **grow**, increase, expand, widen, escalate, proliferate, multiply, broaden 4 = **circulate**, broadcast, propagate, disseminate, make known
OPPOSITE: suppress 5 = **diffuse**, cast, shed, radiate
▷ **NOUN** 6 = **increase**, development, advance, expansion, proliferation,

dissemination, dispersal
7 = **extent**, span, stretch, sweep

spree = **fling**, binge (*informal*), orgy

spring NOUN 1 = **flexibility**, bounce, resilience, elasticity, buoyancy
▷ **VERB** 2 = **jump**, bound, leap, bounce, vault 3 *usually followed by from* = **originate**, come, derive, start, issue, proceed, arise, stem

sprinkle = **scatter**, dust, strew, pepper, shower, spray, powder, dredge

sprinkling = **scattering**, dusting, few, dash, handful, sprinkle

sprint = **run**, race, shoot, tear, dash, dart, hare (*Brit informal*)

sprout 1 = **germinate**, bud, shoot, spring 2 = **grow**, develop, ripen

spur VERB 1 = **incite**, drive, prompt, urge, stimulate, animate, prod, prick
▷ **NOUN** 2 = **stimulus**, incentive, impetus, motive, impulse, inducement, incitement
▷ **PHRASES:** on the spur of the moment = **on impulse**, impulsively, on the spot, impromptu, without planning

spurn = **reject**, slight, scorn, rebuff, snub, despise, disdain, repulse **OPPOSITE:** accept

spy NOUN 1 = **undercover agent**, mole, nark (*Brit, Austral & NZ slang*)

S

▷ VERB 2 = **catch sight of**, spot, notice, observe, glimpse, espy

squabble VERB 1 = **quarrel**, fight, argue, row, dispute, wrangle, bicker
▷ NOUN 2 = **quarrel**, fight, row, argument, dispute, disagreement, tiff

squad = **team**, group, band, company, force, troop, crew, gang

squander = **waste**, spend, fritter away, blow (*slang*), misuse, expend, misspend
OPPOSITE: save

square ADJECTIVE 1 = **fair**, straight, genuine, ethical, honest, on the level (*informal*), kosher (*informal*), dinkum (*Austral & NZ informal*), above board
▷ VERB 2 *often followed by with* = **agree**, match, fit, correspond, tally, reconcile

squash 1 = **crush**, press, flatten, mash, smash, distort, pulp, compress 2 = **suppress**, quell, silence, crush, annihilate 3 = **embarrass**, put down, shame, degrade, mortify

squeeze VERB 1 = **press**, crush, squash, pinch 2 = **clutch**, press, grip, crush, pinch, squash, compress, wring 3 = **cram**, press, crowd, force, stuff, pack, jam, ram 4 = **hug**, embrace, cuddle, clasp, enfold
▷ NOUN 5 = **press**, grip, clasp, crush, pinch, squash, wring

6 = **crush**, jam, squash, press, crowd, congestion 7 = **hug**, embrace, clasp

stab VERB 1 = **pierce**, stick, wound, knife, thrust, spear, jab, transfix
▷ NOUN 2 (*informal*) = **attempt**, go (*informal*), try, endeavour 3 = **twinge**, prick, pang, ache

stability = **firmness**, strength, soundness, solidity, steadiness
OPPOSITE: instability

stable 1 = **secure**, lasting, strong, sound, fast, sure, established, permanent
OPPOSITE: insecure 2 = **well-balanced**, balanced, sensible, reasonable, rational 3 = **solid**, firm, fixed, substantial, durable, well-made, well-built, immovable **OPPOSITE:** unstable

stack NOUN 1 = **pile**, heap, mountain, mass, load, mound 2 = **lot**, mass, load (*informal*), ton (*informal*), heap (*informal*), great amount
▷ VERB 3 = **pile**, heap up, load, assemble, accumulate, amass

staff 1 = **workers**, employees, personnel, workforce, team 2 = **stick**, pole, rod, crook, cane, stave, wand, sceptre

stage = **step**, leg, phase, point, level, period, division, lap

stagger 1 = **totter**, reel, sway, lurch, wobble 2 = **astound**, amaze, stun, shock, shake, overwhelm, astonish, confound

S

stain NOUN 1 = **mark**, spot, blot, blemish, discoloration, smirch 2 = **stigma**, shame, disgrace, slur, dishonour 3 = **dye**, colour, tint
▷ VERB 4 = **mark**, soil, discolour, dirty, tinge, spot, blot, blemish 5 = **dye**, colour, tint

stake¹ = **pole**, post, stick, pale, paling, picket, palisade

stake² NOUN 1 = **bet**, ante, wager 2 = **interest**, share, involvement, concern, investment
▷ VERB 3 = **bet**, gamble, wager, chance, risk, venture, hazard

stale 1 = **old**, hard, dry, decayed OPPOSITE: fresh 2 = **musty**, fusty 3 = **tasteless**, flat, sour 4 = **unoriginal**, banal, trite, stereotyped, worn-out, threadbare, hackneyed, overused OPPOSITE: original

stalk = **pursue**, follow, track, hunt, shadow, haunt

stall¹ VERB 1 = **stop dead**, jam, seize up, catch, stick, stop short
▷ NOUN 2 = **stand**, table, counter, booth, kiosk

stall² = **play for time**, delay, hedge, temporize

stalwart 1 = **loyal**, faithful, firm, true, dependable, steadfast 2 = **strong**, strapping, sturdy, stout OPPOSITE: puny

stamina = **staying power**, endurance, resilience, force, power, energy, strength

stammer = **stutter**, falter, pause, hesitate, stumble over your words

stamp NOUN 1 = **imprint**, mark, brand, signature, earmark, hallmark
▷ VERB 2 = **print**, mark, impress 3 = **trample**, step, tread, crush 4 = **identify**, mark, brand, label, reveal, show to be, categorize
▷ PHRASES: stamp something out = **eliminate**, destroy, eradicate, crush, suppress, put down, scotch, quell

stance 1 = **attitude**, stand, position, viewpoint, standpoint 2 = **posture**, carriage, bearing, deportment

stand VERB 1 = **be upright**, be erect, be vertical 2 = **get to your feet**, rise, stand up, straighten up 3 = **be located**, be, sit, be positioned, be situated or located 4 = **be valid**, continue, exist, prevail, remain valid 5 = **put**, place, position, set, mount 6 = **sit**, mellow 7 = **resist**, endure, tolerate, stand up to 8 = **tolerate**, bear, abide, stomach, endure, brook 9 = **take**, bear, handle, endure, put up with (*informal*), countenance
▷ NOUN 10 = **position**, attitude, stance, opinion, determination 11 = **stall**, booth, kiosk, table
▷ PHRASES: stand by = **be prepared**, wait ▶ stand for

something = **represent**, mean, signify, denote, indicate, symbolize, betoken **2** = **tolerate**, bear, endure, put up with, brook ▶ **stand in for someone** = **be a substitute for**, represent, cover for, take the place of, deputize for ▶ **stand up for something** or **someone** = **support**, champion, defend, uphold, stick up for (*informal*)

standard NOUN **1** = **level**, grade **2** = **criterion**, measure, guideline, example, model, average, norm, gauge **3** *often plural* = **principles**, ideals, morals, ethics **4** = **flag**, banner, ensign
▷ ADJECTIVE **5** = **usual**, normal, customary, average, basic, regular, typical, orthodox **OPPOSITE:** unusual **6** = **accepted**, official, established, approved, recognized, definitive, authoritative **OPPOSITE:** unofficial

stand-in = **substitute**, deputy, replacement, reserve, surrogate, understudy, locum, stopgap

standing NOUN **1** = **status**, position, footing, rank, reputation, eminence, repute **2** = **duration**, existence, continuance
▷ ADJECTIVE **3** = **permanent**, lasting, fixed, regular **4** = **upright**, erect, vertical

staple = **principal**, chief, main, key, basic, fundamental, predominant

star NOUN **1** = **heavenly body**, celestial body **2** = **celebrity**, big name, megastar (*informal*), name, luminary, leading man *or* lady, hero *or* heroine, principal, main attraction
▷ VERB **3** = **play the lead**, appear, feature, perform

stare = **gaze**, look, goggle, watch, gape, eyeball (*slang*), gawp (*Brit slang*), gawk

stark ADJECTIVE **1** = **plain**, harsh, basic, grim, straightforward, blunt **2** = **sharp**, clear, striking, distinct, clear-cut **3** = **austere**, severe, plain, bare, harsh, bare-bones **4** = **bleak**, grim, barren, hard **5** = **absolute**, pure, sheer, utter, downright, out-and-out, unmitigated
▷ ADVERB **6** = **absolutely**, quite, completely, entirely, altogether, wholly, utterly

start VERB **1** = **set about**, begin, proceed, embark upon, take the first step, make a beginning **OPPOSITE:** stop **2** = **begin**, arise, originate, issue, appear, commence **OPPOSITE:** end **3** = **set in motion**, initiate, instigate, open, trigger, originate, get going, kick-start **OPPOSITE:** stop **4** = **establish**, begin, found, create, launch, set up, institute, pioneer **OPPOSITE:** terminate **5** = **start up**,

S

activate, get something going **OPPOSITE:** turn off **6 = jump**, shy, jerk, flinch, recoil ▷ **NOUN 7 = beginning**, outset, opening, birth, foundation, dawn, onset, initiation **OPPOSITE:** end **8 = jump**, spasm, convulsion

startle = surprise, shock, frighten, scare, make (someone) jump

starving = hungry, starved, ravenous, famished

state NOUN 1 = country, nation, land, republic, territory, federation, commonwealth, kingdom **2 = government**, ministry, administration, executive, regime, powers-that-be **3 = condition**, shape **4 = frame of mind**, condition, spirits, attitude, mood, humour **5 = ceremony**, glory, grandeur, splendour, majesty, pomp **6 = circumstances**, situation, position, predicament ▷ **VERB 7 = say**, declare, present, voice, express, assert, utter

stately = grand, majestic, dignified, royal, august, noble, regal, lofty **OPPOSITE:** lowly

statement 1 = announcement, declaration, communication, communiqué, proclamation **2 = account**, report

station NOUN 1 = railway station, stop, stage, halt, terminal, train station, terminus **2 = headquarters**, base, depot

3 = position, rank, status, standing, post, situation **4 = post**, place, location, position, situation ▷ **VERB 5 = assign**, post, locate, set, establish, install

stature 1 = height, build, size **2 = importance**, standing, prestige, rank, prominence, eminence

status 1 = position, rank, grade **2 = prestige**, standing, authority, influence, weight, honour, importance, fame, mana (NZ) **3 = state of play**, development, progress, condition, evolution

staunch = loyal, faithful, stalwart, firm, sound, true, trusty, steadfast

stay VERB 1 = remain, continue to be, linger, stop, wait, halt, pause, abide **OPPOSITE:** go **2** often with **at = lodge**, visit, sojourn (literary), put up at, be accommodated at **3 = continue**, remain, go on, survive, endure ▷ **NOUN 4 = visit**, stop, holiday, stopover, sojourn (literary) **5 = postponement**, delay, suspension, stopping, halt, deferment

steady 1 = continuous, regular, constant, consistent, persistent, unbroken, uninterrupted, incessant **OPPOSITE:** irregular **2 = stable**, fixed, secure, firm, safe **OPPOSITE:** unstable

S

3 = **regular**, established
4 = **dependable**, sensible, reliable, secure, calm, supportive, sober, level-headed **OPPOSITE:** undependable

steal 1 = **take**, nick (*slang, chiefly Brit*), pinch (*informal*), lift (*informal*), embezzle, pilfer, misappropriate, purloin
2 = **copy**, take, appropriate, pinch (*informal*), rip (*computing*)
3 = **sneak**, slip, creep, tiptoe, slink

stealth = **secrecy**, furtiveness, slyness, sneakiness, unobtrusiveness, stealthiness, surreptitiousness

steep¹ 1 = **sheer**, precipitous, abrupt, vertical **OPPOSITE:** gradual 2 = **sharp**, sudden, abrupt, marked, extreme, distinct 3 (*informal*) = **high**, exorbitant, extreme, unreasonable, overpriced, extortionate **OPPOSITE:** reasonable

steep² = **soak**, immerse, marinate (*cookery*), submerge, drench, moisten, souse

steeped = **saturated**, pervaded, permeated, filled, infused, imbued, suffused

steer 1 = **drive**, control, direct, handle, pilot 2 = **direct**, lead, guide, conduct, escort

stem¹ = **stalk**, branch, trunk, shoot, axis
▷ **PHRASES: stem from something** = **originate from**,

be caused by, derive from, arise from

stem² = **stop**, hold back, staunch, check, dam, curb

step NOUN 1 = **pace**, stride, footstep 2 = **footfall** 3 = **move**, measure, action, means, act, deed, expedient 4 = **stage**, point, phase 5 = **level**, rank, degree
▷ **VERB** 6 = **walk**, pace, tread, move
▷ **PHRASES: step in** (*informal*) = **intervene**, take action, become involved ▶ **step something up** = **increase**, intensify, raise

stereotype NOUN 1 = **formula**, pattern
▷ **VERB** 2 = **categorize**, typecast, pigeonhole, standardize

sterile 1 = **germ-free**, sterilized, disinfected, aseptic **OPPOSITE:** unhygienic 2 = **barren**, infertile, unproductive, childless **OPPOSITE:** fertile

sterling = **excellent**, sound, fine, superlative

stern 1 = **strict**, harsh, hard, grim, rigid, austere, inflexible **OPPOSITE:** lenient 2 = **severe**, serious, forbidding **OPPOSITE:** friendly

stick¹ 1 = **twig**, branch 2 = **cane**, staff, pole, rod, crook, baton 3 (*slang*) = **abuse**, criticism, flak (*informal*), fault-finding

stick² 1 (*informal*) = **put**, place, set, lay, deposit 2 = **poke**, dig,

S

stab, thrust, pierce, penetrate, spear, prod **3 = fasten**, fix, bind, hold, bond, attach, glue, paste **4 = adhere**, cling, become joined, become welded **5 = stay**, remain, linger, persist **6** (*slang*) **= tolerate**, take, stand, stomach, abide

▷ **PHRASES: stick out = protrude**, stand out, jut out, show, project, bulge, obtrude

▶ **stick up for someone** (*informal*) **= defend**, support, champion, stand up for (*informal*)

sticky 1 = adhesive, gummed, adherent, grippy **2 = gooey**, tacky (*informal*), viscous, glutinous, gummy, icky (*informal*), gluey, clinging **3** (*informal*) **= difficult**, awkward, tricky, embarrassing, nasty, delicate, unpleasant, barro (*Austral slang*) **4 = humid**, close, sultry, oppressive, sweltering, clammy, muggy

stiff 1 = inflexible, rigid, unyielding, hard, firm, tight, solid, tense **OPPOSITE:** flexible **2 = formal**, constrained, forced, unnatural, stilted, unrelaxed **OPPOSITE:** informal **3 = vigorous**, great, strong **4 = severe**, strict, harsh, hard, heavy, extreme, drastic **5 = difficult**, hard, tough, exacting, arduous

stifle 1 = suppress, repress, stop, check, silence, restrain, hush,

smother **2 = restrain**, suppress, repress, smother

stigma = disgrace, shame, dishonour, stain, slur, smirch

still ADJECTIVE 1 = motionless, stationary, calm, peaceful, serene, tranquil, undisturbed, restful **OPPOSITE:** moving **2 = silent**, quiet, hushed **OPPOSITE:** noisy

▷ **VERB 3 = quieten**, calm, settle, quiet, silence, soothe, hush, lull **OPPOSITE:** get louder

▷ **SENTENCE CONNECTOR 4 = however**, but, yet, nevertheless, notwithstanding

stimulate = encourage, inspire, prompt, fire, spur, provoke, arouse, rouse

stimulating = exciting, inspiring, stirring, rousing, provocative, exhilarating **OPPOSITE:** boring

stimulus = incentive, spur, encouragement, impetus, inducement, goad, incitement, fillip

sting 1 = hurt, burn, wound **2 = smart**, burn, pain, hurt, tingle

stink VERB 1 = reek, pong (*Brit informal*)

▷ **NOUN 2 = stench**, pong (*Brit informal*), foul smell, fetor

stint NOUN 1 = term, time, turn, period, share, shift, stretch, spell

▷ **VERB 2 = be mean**, hold back, be sparing, skimp on, be frugal

stipulate = specify, agree,
require, contract, settle,
covenant, insist upon

stir VERB 1 = **mix**, beat,
agitate 2 = **stimulate**, move,
excite, spur, provoke, arouse,
awaken, rouse OPPOSITE:
inhibit 3 = **spur**, drive, prompt,
stimulate, prod, urge, animate,
prick
▷ NOUN 4 = **commotion**,
excitement, activity, disorder,
fuss, disturbance, bustle, flurry

stock NOUN 1 = **shares**,
holdings, securities,
investments, bonds, equities
2 = **property**, capital, assets,
funds 3 = **goods**, merchandise,
wares, range, choice, variety,
selection, commodities
4 = **supply**, store, reserve, fund,
stockpile, hoard 5 = **livestock**,
cattle, beasts, domestic animals
▷ VERB 6 = **sell**, supply, handle,
keep, trade in, deal in 7 = **fill**,
supply, provide with, equip,
furnish, fit out
▷ ADJECTIVE 8 = **hackneyed**,
routine, banal, trite, overused
9 = **regular**, usual, ordinary,
conventional, customary

stomach NOUN 1 = **belly**, gut
(informal), abdomen, tummy
(informal), puku (NZ) 2 = **tummy**,
pot, spare tyre (informal)
3 = **inclination**, taste, desire,
appetite, relish
▷ VERB 4 = **bear**, take, tolerate,
endure, swallow, abide

RELATED WORD
adjective: gastric

stone 1 = **masonry**, rock
2 = **rock**, pebble 3 = **pip**, seed,
pit, kernel

stoop VERB 1 = **hunch** 2 = **bend**,
lean, bow, duck, crouch
▷ NOUN 3 = **slouch**, bad posture,
round-shoulderedness

stop VERB 1 = **quit**, cease,
refrain, put an end to,
discontinue, desist OPPOSITE:
start 2 = **prevent**, cut short,
arrest, restrain, hold back,
hinder, repress, impede
OPPOSITE: facilitate 3 = **end**,
conclude, finish, terminate
OPPOSITE: continue 4 = **cease**,
shut down, discontinue,
desist OPPOSITE: continue
5 = **halt**, pause OPPOSITE: keep
going 6 = **pause**, wait, rest,
take a break, have a breather
(informal), stop briefly 7 = **stay**,
rest, lodge
▷ NOUN 8 = **halt**, standstill
9 = **station**, stage, depot,
terminus 10 = **stay**, break, rest

store NOUN 1 = **shop**, outlet,
market, mart 2 = **supply**,
stock, reserve, fund, quantity,
accumulation, stockpile, hoard
3 = **repository**, warehouse,
depository, storeroom
▷ VERB 4 often with **away**
or **up** = **put by**, save, hoard,
keep, reserve, deposit, garner,
stockpile 5 = **put away**, put in
storage, put in store 6 = **keep**,

S

hold, preserve, maintain, retain, conserve

storm NOUN 1 = **tempest**, hurricane, gale, blizzard, squall 2 = **outburst**, row, outcry, furore, outbreak, turmoil, disturbance, strife
▷ VERB 3 = **rush**, stamp, flounce, fly 4 = **rage**, rant, thunder, rave, bluster 5 = **attack**, charge, rush, assault, assail

stormy 1 = **wild**, rough, raging, turbulent, windy, blustery, inclement, squally 2 = **rough**, wild, turbulent, raging 3 = **angry**, heated, fierce, passionate, fiery, impassioned

story 1 = **tale**, romance, narrative, history, legend, yarn 2 = **anecdote**, account, tale, report 3 = **report**, news, article, feature, scoop, news item

stout 1 = **fat**, big, heavy, overweight, plump, bulky, burly, fleshy **OPPOSITE:** slim 2 = **strong**, strapping, muscular, robust, sturdy, stalwart, brawny, able-bodied **OPPOSITE:** puny 3 = **brave**, bold, courageous, fearless, resolute, gallant, intrepid, valiant **OPPOSITE:** timid

straight ADJECTIVE 1 = **direct**, unswerving **OPPOSITE:** indirect 2 = **level**, even, right, square, true, smooth, aligned, horizontal **OPPOSITE:** crooked 3 = **frank**, plain, straightforward, blunt,

outright, honest, candid, forthright **OPPOSITE:** evasive 4 = **successive**, consecutive, continuous, running, solid, nonstop **OPPOSITE:** discontinuous 5 (slang) = **conventional**, conservative, bourgeois **OPPOSITE:** fashionable 6 = **honest**, just, fair, reliable, respectable, upright, honourable, law-abiding **OPPOSITE:** dishonest 7 = **undiluted**, pure, neat, unadulterated, unmixed 8 = **in order**, organized, arranged, neat, tidy, orderly, shipshape **OPPOSITE:** untidy
▷ ADVERB 9 = **directly**, precisely, exactly, unswervingly, by the shortest route, in a beeline 10 = **immediately**, directly, promptly, instantly, at once, straightaway, without delay, forthwith

straightaway = **immediately**, now, at once, directly, instantly, right away

straighten = **neaten**, arrange, tidy (up), order, put in order

straightforward 1 (chiefly Brit) = **simple**, easy, uncomplicated, routine, elementary, easy-peasy (slang) **OPPOSITE:** complicated 2 = **honest**, open, direct, genuine, sincere, candid, truthful, forthright, dinkum (Austral & NZ informal) **OPPOSITE:** devious

strain¹ NOUN 1 = **pressure**, stress, demands, burden

2 = **stress**, anxiety 3 = **worry**,
effort, struggle **OPPOSITE:** ease
4 = **burden**, tension 5 = **injury**,
wrench, sprain, pull
▷ VERB 6 = **stretch**, tax, overtax
7 = **strive**, struggle, endeavour,
labour, go for it (*informal*), bend
over backwards (*informal*), give it
your best shot (*informal*), knock
yourself out (*informal*) **OPPOSITE:**
relax 8 = **sieve**, filter, sift, purify

strain² 1 = **trace**, suggestion,
tendency, streak 2 = **breed**,
family, race, blood, descent,
extraction, ancestry, lineage

strained 1 = **tense**, difficult,
awkward, embarrassed, stiff,
uneasy **OPPOSITE:** relaxed
2 = **forced**, put on, false,
artificial, unnatural **OPPOSITE:**
natural

strait NOUN 1 *often plural*
= **channel**, sound, narrows
▷ PLURAL NOUN 2 = **difficulty**,
dilemma, plight, hardship,
uphill (*S African*), predicament,
extremity

strand = **filament**, fibre, thread,
string

stranded 1 = **beached**,
grounded, marooned, ashore,
shipwrecked, aground
2 = **helpless**, abandoned, high
and dry

strange 1 = **odd**, curious, weird,
wonderful, extraordinary,
bizarre, peculiar, abnormal,
daggy (*Austral & NZ informal*)
OPPOSITE: ordinary

2 = **unfamiliar**, new, unknown,
foreign, novel, alien, exotic,
untried **OPPOSITE:** familiar

stranger 1 = **unknown person**
2 = **newcomer**, incomer,
foreigner, guest, visitor, alien,
outlander

strangle 1 = **throttle**, choke,
asphyxiate, strangulate
2 = **suppress**, inhibit, subdue,
stifle, repress, overpower,
quash, quell

strap NOUN 1 = **tie**, thong, belt
▷ VERB 2 = **fasten**, tie, secure,
bind, lash, buckle

strapping = **well-built**, big,
powerful, robust, sturdy, husky
(*informal*), brawny

strategic 1 = **tactical**,
calculated, deliberate, planned,
politic, diplomatic 2 = **crucial**,
important, key, vital, critical,
decisive, cardinal

strategy 1 = **policy**, procedure,
approach, scheme 2 = **plan**,
approach, scheme

stray VERB 1 = **wander**,
go astray, drift 2 = **drift**,
wander, roam, meander, rove
3 = **digress**, diverge, deviate, get
off the point
▷ MODIFIER 4 = **lost**,
abandoned, homeless, roaming,
vagrant
▷ ADJECTIVE 5 = **random**,
chance, accidental

streak NOUN 1 = **band**, line,
strip, stroke, layer, slash, vein,
stripe 2 = **trace**, touch, element,

S

strain, dash, vein
▷ VERB 3 = **speed**, fly, tear, flash, sprint, dart, zoom, whizz (informal)
stream NOUN 1 = **river**, brook, burn (Scot), beck, tributary, bayou, rivulet 2 = **flow**, current, rush, run, course, drift, surge, tide
▷ VERB 3 = **flow**, run, pour, issue, flood, spill, cascade, gush 4 = **rush**, fly, speed, tear, flood, pour
streamlined = **efficient**, organized, rationalized, slick, smooth-running
street = **road**, lane, avenue, terrace, row, roadway
strength 1 = **might**, muscle, brawn OPPOSITE: weakness 2 = **will**, resolution, courage, character, nerve, determination, pluck, stamina 3 = **health**, fitness, vigour 4 = **mainstay** 5 = **toughness**, soundness, robustness, sturdiness 6 = **force**, power, intensity OPPOSITE: weakness 7 = **potency**, effectiveness, efficacy 8 = **strong point**, skill, asset, advantage, talent, forte, speciality OPPOSITE: failing
strengthen 1 = **fortify**, harden, toughen, consolidate, stiffen, gee up, brace up OPPOSITE: weaken 2 = **reinforce**, support, intensify, bolster, buttress 3 = **bolster**, harden, reinforce 4 = **heighten**, intensify

5 = **make stronger**, build up, invigorate, restore, give strength to 6 = **support**, brace, reinforce, consolidate, harden, bolster, augment, buttress 7 = **become stronger**, intensify, gain strength
stress VERB 1 = **emphasize**, underline, dwell on 2 = **place the emphasis on**, emphasize, give emphasis to, lay emphasis upon
▷ NOUN 3 = **emphasis**, significance, force, weight 4 = **strain**, pressure, worry, tension, burden, anxiety, trauma 5 = **accent**, beat, emphasis, accentuation
stretch VERB 1 = **extend**, cover, spread, reach, put forth, unroll 2 = **last**, continue, go on, carry on, reach 3 = **expand** 4 = **pull**, distend, strain, tighten, draw out, elongate
▷ NOUN 5 = **expanse**, area, tract, spread, distance, extent 6 = **period**, time, spell, stint, term, space
strict 1 = **severe**, harsh, stern, firm, stringent OPPOSITE: easy-going 2 = **stern**, firm, severe, harsh, authoritarian 3 = **exact**, accurate, precise, close, true, faithful, meticulous, scrupulous 4 = **absolute**, total, utter
strife = **conflict**, battle, clash, quarrel, friction, discord, dissension

strike NOUN 1 = **walkout**, industrial action, mutiny, revolt, stop-work or stop-work meeting (*Austral*)
▷ VERB 2 = **walk out**, down tools, revolt, mutiny 3 = **hit**, smack, thump, beat, knock, punch, hammer, slap 4 = **drive**, hit, smack, wallop (*informal*) 5 = **collide with**, hit, run into, bump into 6 = **knock**, smack, thump, beat 7 = **affect**, touch, devastate, overwhelm, leave a mark on 8 = **attack**, assault someone, set upon someone, lay into someone (*informal*) 9 = **occur to**, hit, come to, register (*informal*), dawn on or upon 10 = **seem to**, appear to, look to, give the impression to 11 = **move**, touch, hit, affect, overcome, stir, disturb, perturb

striking = **impressive**, dramatic, outstanding, noticeable, conspicuous, jaw-dropping OPPOSITE: unimpressive

string 1 = **cord**, twine, fibre 2 = **series**, line, row, file, sequence, succession, procession 3 = **sequence**, run, series, chain, succession

stringent = **strict**, tough, rigorous, tight, severe, rigid, inflexible OPPOSITE: lax

strip¹ 1 = **undress**, disrobe, unclothe 2 = **plunder**, rob, loot, empty, sack, ransack, pillage, divest

strip² 1 = **piece**, shred, band, belt 2 = **stretch**, area, tract, expanse, extent

strive = **try**, labour, struggle, attempt, toil, go all out (*informal*), bend over backwards (*informal*), do your best

stroke VERB 1 = **caress**, rub, fondle, pet
▷ NOUN 2 = **apoplexy**, fit, seizure, attack, collapse 3 = **blow**, hit, knock, pat, rap, thump, swipe

stroll VERB 1 = **walk**, ramble, amble, promenade, saunter
▷ NOUN 2 = **walk**, promenade, constitutional, ramble, breath of air

strong 1 = **powerful**, muscular, tough, athletic, strapping, hardy, sturdy, burly OPPOSITE: weak 2 = **fit**, robust, lusty 3 = **durable**, substantial, sturdy, heavy-duty, well-built, hard-wearing OPPOSITE: flimsy 4 = **extreme**, radical, drastic, strict, harsh, rigid, forceful, uncompromising 5 = **decisive**, firm, forceful, decided, determined, resolute, incisive 6 = **persuasive**, convincing, compelling, telling, sound, effective, potent, weighty 7 = **keen**, deep, acute, fervent, zealous, vehement 8 = **intense**, deep, passionate, ardent, fierce, fervent, vehement, fervid 9 = **staunch**, firm, fierce, ardent, enthusiastic, passionate,

S

fervent **10** = **distinct**, marked, clear, unmistakable **OPPOSITE:** slight **11** = **bright**, brilliant, dazzling, bold **OPPOSITE:** dull

stronghold 1 = **bastion**, fortress, bulwark **2** = **refuge**, haven, retreat, sanctuary, hide-out

structure NOUN
1 = **arrangement**, form, make-up, design, organization, construction, formation, configuration **2** = **building**, construction, erection, edifice ▷ VERB **3** = **arrange**, organize, design, shape, build up, assemble

struggle VERB **1** = **strive**, labour, toil, work, strain, go all out (*informal*), give it your best shot (*informal*), exert yourself **2** = **fight**, battle, wrestle, grapple, compete, contend ▷ NOUN **3** = **effort**, labour, toil, work, pains, scramble, exertion **4** = **fight**, battle, conflict, clash, contest, brush, combat, tussle, biffo (*Austral slang*)

strut = **swagger**, parade, peacock, prance

stubborn = **obstinate**, dogged, inflexible, persistent, intractable, tenacious, recalcitrant, unyielding **OPPOSITE:** compliant

stuck 1 = **fastened**, fast, fixed, joined, glued, cemented **2** (*informal*) = **baffled**, stumped, beaten

student 1 = **undergraduate**, scholar **2** = **pupil**, scholar, schoolchild, schoolboy *or* schoolgirl **3** = **learner**, trainee, apprentice, disciple

studied = **planned**, deliberate, conscious, intentional, premeditated **OPPOSITE:** unplanned

studio = **workshop**, workroom, atelier

study VERB **1** = **learn**, cram (*informal*), swot (up) (*Brit informal*), read up, mug up (*Brit slang*) **2** = **examine**, survey, look at, scrutinize **3** = **contemplate**, read, examine, consider, go into, pore over ▷ NOUN **4** = **examination**, investigation, analysis, consideration, inspection, scrutiny, contemplation **5** = **piece of research**, survey, report, review, inquiry, investigation **6** = **learning**, lessons, school work, reading, research, swotting (*Brit informal*)

stuff NOUN **1** = **things**, gear, possessions, effects, equipment, objects, tackle, kit **2** = **substance**, material, essence, matter ▷ VERB **3** = **shove**, force, push, squeeze, jam, ram **4** = **cram**, fill, pack, crowd

stuffing = **wadding**, filling, packing

stumble 1 = **trip**, fall, slip, reel, stagger, falter, lurch **2** = **totter**,

reel, lurch, wobble
▷ **PHRASES: stumble across**
or **on** *or* **upon something** *or*
someone = discover, find, come
across, chance upon
stump NOUN 1 = **tail end**, end,
remnant, remainder
▷ **VERB** 2 = **baffle**, confuse,
puzzle, bewilder, perplex,
mystify, flummox, nonplus
stun 1 = **overcome**, shock,
confuse, astonish, stagger,
bewilder, astound, overpower
2 = **daze**, knock out, stupefy,
numb, benumb
stunning (*informal*) = **wonderful**,
beautiful, impressive,
striking, lovely, spectacular,
marvellous, splendid **OPPOSITE:**
unimpressive
stunt = **feat**, act, trick, exploit,
deed
stunted = **undersized**, little,
small, tiny, diminutive
stupid 1 = **unintelligent**, thick,
simple, slow, dim, dense,
simple-minded, moronic
OPPOSITE: intelligent 2 = **silly**,
foolish, daft (*informal*), rash,
pointless, senseless, idiotic,
fatuous **OPPOSITE:** sensible
3 = **senseless**, dazed, groggy,
insensate, semiconscious
sturdy 1 = **robust**, hardy,
powerful, athletic, muscular,
lusty, brawny **OPPOSITE:** puny
2 = **substantial**, solid, durable,
well-made, well-built **OPPOSITE:**
flimsy

style NOUN 1 = **manner**, way,
method, approach, technique,
mode 2 = **elegance**, taste, chic,
flair, polish, sophistication,
panache, élan 3 = **design**, form,
cut 4 = **type**, sort, kind, variety,
category, genre 5 = **fashion**,
trend, mode, vogue, rage
6 = **luxury**, ease, comfort,
elegance, grandeur, affluence
▷ **VERB** 7 = **design**, cut, tailor,
fashion, shape, arrange, adapt
8 = **call**, name, term, label,
entitle, dub, designate
stylish = **smart**, chic,
fashionable, trendy (*Brit
informal*), modish, dressy
(*informal*), voguish, schmick
(*Austral informal*), funky
OPPOSITE: scruffy
subdue 1 = **overcome**, defeat,
master, break, control, crush,
conquer, tame 2 = **moderate**,
suppress, soften, mellow, tone
down, quieten down **OPPOSITE:**
arouse
subdued 1 = **quiet**, serious, sad,
chastened, dejected, downcast,
crestfallen, down in the mouth
OPPOSITE: lively 2 = **hushed**,
soft, quiet, muted **OPPOSITE:**
loud
subject NOUN 1 = **topic**,
question, issue, matter,
point, business, affair,
object 2 = **citizen**, resident,
native, inhabitant, national
3 = **dependant**, subordinate
▷ **ADJECTIVE** 4 = **subordinate**,

S

dependent, satellite, inferior, obedient
▷ **VERB** 5 = **put through**, expose, submit, lay open
▷ **PHRASES: subject to**
1 = **liable to**, open to, exposed to, vulnerable to, prone to, susceptible to 2 = **bound by**
3 = **dependent on**, contingent on, controlled by, conditional on

subjective = **personal**, prejudiced, biased, nonobjective **OPPOSITE:** objective

sublime = **noble**, glorious, high, great, grand, elevated, lofty, exalted **OPPOSITE:** lowly

submerge 1 = **flood**, swamp, engulf, overflow, inundate, deluge 2 = **immerse**, plunge, duck 3 = **sink**, plunge, go under water 4 = **overwhelm**, swamp, engulf, deluge

submission 1 = **surrender**, yielding, giving in, cave-in (*informal*), capitulation
2 = **presentation**, handing in, entry, tendering
3 = **compliance**, obedience, meekness, resignation, deference, passivity, docility

submit 1 = **surrender**, yield, give in, agree, endure, tolerate, comply, succumb 2 = **present**, hand in, tender, put forward, table, proffer

subordinate NOUN 1 = **inferior**, junior, assistant, aide, second, attendant **OPPOSITE:** superior
▷ **ADJECTIVE** 2 = **inferior**,

lesser, lower, junior, subject, minor, secondary, dependent **OPPOSITE:** superior

subscribe to 1 = **support**, advocate, endorse
2 = **contribute to**, give to, donate to

subscription (*chiefly Brit*) = **membership fee**, dues, annual payment

subsequent = **following**, later, succeeding, after, successive, ensuing **OPPOSITE:** previous

subsequently = **later**, afterwards

subside 1 = **decrease**, diminish, lessen, ease, wane, ebb, abate, slacken **OPPOSITE:** increase
2 = **collapse**, sink, cave in, drop, lower, settle

subsidiary NOUN 1 = **branch**, division, section, office, department, wing, subdivision, subsection
▷ **ADJECTIVE** 2 = **secondary**, lesser, subordinate, minor, supplementary, auxiliary, ancillary **OPPOSITE:** main

subsidy = **aid**, help, support, grant, assistance, allowance

substance 1 = **material**, body, stuff, fabric 2 = **importance**, significance, concreteness
3 = **meaning**, main point, gist, import, significance, essence
4 = **wealth**, means, property, assets, resources, estate

substantial = **big**, significant, considerable, large, important,

S

ample, sizable *or* sizeable
OPPOSITE: small
substitute VERB 1 = **replace**,
exchange, swap, change,
switch, interchange
▷ NOUN 2 = **replacement**,
reserve, surrogate, deputy, sub,
proxy, locum

> **USAGE NOTE**
> Although *substitute* and
> *replace* have the same
> meaning, the structures
> they are used in are different.
> You replace A *with* B, while
> you substitute B *for* A.
> Accordingly, *he replaced the
> worn tyre with a new one*, and
> *he substituted a new tyre for the
> worn one* are both correct ways
> of saying the same thing.

subtle 1 = **faint**, slight,
implied, delicate, understated
OPPOSITE: obvious 2 = **crafty**,
cunning, sly, shrewd,
ingenious, devious, wily, artful
OPPOSITE: straightforward
3 = **muted**, soft, subdued,
low-key, toned down 4 = **fine**,
minute, narrow, tenuous, hairsplitting
subtlety 1 = **fine point**,
refinement, sophistication,
delicacy 2 = **skill**, ingenuity,
cleverness, deviousness,
craftiness, artfulness, slyness,
wiliness
subversive ADJECTIVE
1 = **seditious**, riotous,
treasonous

▷ NOUN 2 = **dissident**, terrorist,
saboteur, fifth columnist
succeed 1 = **triumph**, win,
prevail 2 = **work out**, work,
be successful 3 = **make it**
(*informal*), do well, be successful,
triumph, thrive, flourish, make
good, prosper **OPPOSITE:** fail
4 = **take over from**, assume the
office of 5 *with* **to** = **take over**,
assume, attain, come into,
inherit, accede to, come into
possession of 6 = **follow**, come
after, follow after **OPPOSITE:**
precede
success 1 = **victory**,
triumph **OPPOSITE:** failure
2 = **prosperity**, fortune, luck,
fame 3 = **hit** (*informal*), winner,
smash (*informal*), triumph,
sensation **OPPOSITE:** flop
(*informal*) 4 = **big name**, star, hit
(*informal*), celebrity, sensation,
megastar (*informal*) **OPPOSITE:**
nobody
successful 1 = **triumphant**,
victorious, lucky, fortunate
2 = **thriving**, profitable,
rewarding, booming,
flourishing, fruitful **OPPOSITE:**
unprofitable 3 = **top**,
prosperous, wealthy
successfully = **well**, favourably,
with flying colours, victoriously
succession 1 = **series**, run,
sequence, course, order, train,
chain, cycle 2 = **taking over**,
assumption, inheritance,
accession

successive = consecutive, following, in succession

succumb 1 *often with* **to** = **surrender (to)**, yield (to), submit (to), give in (to), cave in (to) (*informal*), capitulate (to) **OPPOSITE:** beat 2 *with* **to** (~*an illness*) = **catch**, fall ill with

suck 1 = **drink**, sip, draw 2 = **take**, draw, pull, extract

sudden = **quick**, rapid, unexpected, swift, hurried, abrupt, hasty **OPPOSITE:** gradual

suddenly = **abruptly**, all of a sudden, unexpectedly

sue (*Law*) = **take (someone) to court**, prosecute, charge, summon, indict

suffer 1 = **be in pain**, hurt, ache 2 = **be affected**, have trouble with, be afflicted, be troubled with 3 = **undergo**, experience, sustain, bear, go through, endure 4 = **tolerate**, stand, put up with (*informal*), bear, endure

suffering = **pain**, distress, agony, misery, ordeal, discomfort, torment, hardship

suffice = **be enough**, do, be sufficient, be adequate, serve, meet requirements, tick all the boxes

sufficient = **adequate**, enough, ample, satisfactory **OPPOSITE:** insufficient

suggest 1 = **recommend**, propose, advise, advocate, prescribe 2 = **indicate** 3 = **hint at**, imply, intimate 4 = **bring to mind**, evoke

suggestion 1 = **recommendation**, proposal, proposition, plan, motion 2 = **hint**, insinuation, intimation 3 = **trace**, touch, hint, breath, indication, whisper, intimation

suit NOUN 1 = **outfit**, costume, ensemble, dress, clothing, habit 2 = **lawsuit**, case, trial, proceeding, cause, action, prosecution ▷ VERB 3 = **be acceptable to**, please, satisfy, do, gratify 4 = **agree with**, become, match, go with, harmonize with

suitable 1 = **appropriate**, right, fitting, fit, becoming, satisfactory, apt, befitting **OPPOSITE:** inappropriate 2 = **seemly**, fitting, becoming, proper, correct **OPPOSITE:** unseemly 3 = **suited**, appropriate, in keeping with **OPPOSITE:** out of keeping 4 = **pertinent**, relevant, applicable, fitting, appropriate, to the point, apt **OPPOSITE:** irrelevant 5 = **convenient**, timely, appropriate, well-timed, opportune **OPPOSITE:** inopportune

suite = **rooms**, apartment

sum 1 = **amount**, quantity, volume 2 = **calculation**, figures, arithmetic, mathematics, maths (*Brit informal*), tally, math (*US informal*), arithmetical

problem **3** = **total**, aggregate
4 = **totality**, whole

summarize = **sum up**,
condense, encapsulate,
epitomize, abridge, précis

summary = **synopsis**, résumé,
précis, review, outline,
rundown, abridgment

summit 1 = **peak**, top, tip,
pinnacle, apex, head **OPPOSITE:**
base **2** = **height**, pinnacle, peak,
zenith, acme **OPPOSITE:** depths

summon 1 = **send for**, call, bid,
invite **2** *often with* **up** = **gather**,
muster, draw on

sumptuous = **luxurious**, grand,
superb, splendid, gorgeous,
lavish, opulent **OPPOSITE:** plain

sunny 1 = **bright**, clear, fine,
radiant, sunlit, summery,
unclouded **OPPOSITE:** dull
2 = **cheerful**, happy, cheery,
buoyant, joyful, light-hearted
OPPOSITE: gloomy

sunset = **nightfall**, dusk,
eventide, close of (the) day

superb 1 = **splendid**,
excellent, magnificent, fine,
grand, superior, marvellous,
world-class, booshit (*Austral
slang*), exo (*Austral slang*), sik
(*Austral slang*), rad (*informal*),
phat (*slang*), schmick (*Austral
informal*) **OPPOSITE:** inferior
2 = **magnificent**, superior,
marvellous, exquisite,
superlative **OPPOSITE:** terrible

superficial 1 = **shallow**,
frivolous, empty-headed,

silly, trivial **OPPOSITE:** serious
2 = **hasty**, cursory, perfunctory,
hurried, casual, sketchy,
desultory, slapdash **OPPOSITE:**
thorough **3** = **slight**, surface,
external, on the surface, exterior
OPPOSITE: profound

superintendent = **supervisor**,
director, manager, chief,
governor, inspector, controller,
overseer

superior ADJECTIVE **1** = **better**,
higher, greater, grander,
surpassing, unrivalled **OPPOSITE:**
inferior **2** = **first-class**, excellent,
first-rate, choice, exclusive,
exceptional, de luxe, booshit
(*Austral slang*), exo (*Austral
slang*), sik (*Austral slang*), rad
(*informal*), phat (*slang*), schmick
(*Austral informal*) **OPPOSITE:**
average **3** = **supercilious**,
patronizing, condescending,
haughty, disdainful, lordly, lofty,
pretentious
▷ NOUN **4** = **boss**, senior,
director, manager, chief
(*informal*), principal, supervisor,
baas (*S African*), sherang (*Austral
& NZ*) **OPPOSITE:** subordinate

USAGE NOTE

Superior should not be used
with *than*: *He is a better* (not *a
superior*) *poet than his brother*;
His poetry is superior to (not
than) *his brother's.*

superiority = **supremacy**,
lead, advantage, excellence,
ascendancy, predominance

supernatural = **paranormal**, unearthly, uncanny, ghostly, psychic, mystic, miraculous, occult

supervise 1 = **observe**, guide, monitor, oversee, keep an eye on 2 = **oversee**, run, manage, control, direct, handle, look after, superintend

supervision = **superintendence**, direction, control, charge, care, management, guidance

supervisor = **boss** (*informal*), manager, chief, inspector, administrator, foreman, overseer, baas (*S African*)

supplement VERB 1 = **add to**, reinforce, augment, extend ▷ NOUN 2 = **pull-out**, insert 3 = **appendix**, add-on, postscript 4 = **addition**, extra

supply VERB 1 = **provide**, give, furnish, produce, stock, grant, contribute, yield 2 = **furnish**, provide, equip, endow ▷ NOUN 3 = **store**, fund, stock, source, reserve, quantity, hoard, cache ▷ PLURAL NOUN 4 = **provisions**, necessities, stores, food, materials, equipment, rations

support VERB 1 = **help**, back, champion, second, aid, defend, assist, side with OPPOSITE: oppose 2 = **provide for**, maintain, look after, keep, fund, finance, sustain OPPOSITE: live off 3 = **bear out**, confirm, verify, substantiate, corroborate OPPOSITE: refute 4 = **bear**, carry, sustain, prop (up), reinforce, hold, brace, buttress ▷ NOUN 5 = **furtherance**, backing, promotion, assistance, encouragement 6 = **help**, loyalty OPPOSITE: opposition 7 = **aid**, help, benefits, relief, assistance 8 = **prop**, post, foundation, brace, pillar 9 = **supporter**, prop, mainstay, tower of strength, second, backer OPPOSITE: antagonist 10 = **upkeep**, maintenance, keep, subsistence, sustenance

supporter = **follower**, fan, advocate, friend, champion, sponsor, patron, helper OPPOSITE: opponent

supportive = **helpful**, encouraging, understanding, sympathetic

suppose 1 = **imagine**, consider, conjecture, postulate, hypothesize 2 = **think**, imagine, expect, assume, guess (*informal, chiefly US & Canad*), presume, conjecture

supposed 1 *usually with* to = **meant**, expected, required, obliged 2 = **presumed**, alleged, professed, accepted, assumed

supposedly = **presumably**, allegedly, ostensibly, theoretically, hypothetically OPPOSITE: actually

suppress 1 = **stamp out**, stop, check, crush, conquer, subdue,

put an end to, overpower
OPPOSITE: encourage 2 = **check**,
inhibit, subdue, stop, quell
3 = **restrain**, stifle, contain,
silence, conceal, curb, repress,
smother
suppression 1 = **elimination**,
crushing, check, quashing
2 = **inhibition**, blocking,
restraint, smothering
supremacy = **domination**,
sovereignty, sway, mastery,
primacy, predominance,
supreme power
supreme 1 = **paramount**,
surpassing **OPPOSITE:** least
2 = **chief**, leading, principal,
highest, head, top, prime,
foremost **OPPOSITE:** lowest
3 = **ultimate**, highest, greatest
supremo (*Brit informal*) = **head**,
leader, boss (*informal*), director,
master, governor, commander,
principal, baas (*S African*)
sure 1 = **certain**, positive, decided,
convinced, confident, assured,
definite **OPPOSITE:** uncertain
2 = **inevitable**, guaranteed,
bound, assured, inescapable,
nailed-on (*slang*) **OPPOSITE:**
unsure 3 = **reliable**, accurate,
dependable, undoubted,
undeniable, foolproof, infallible,
unerring **OPPOSITE:** unreliable
surely 1 = **it must be the
case that** 2 = **undoubtedly**,
certainly, definitely, without
doubt, unquestionably,
indubitably, doubtlessly

surface NOUN 1 = **covering**,
face, exterior, side, top, veneer
2 = **façade**
▷ VERB 3 = **emerge**, come up,
come to the surface 4 = **appear**,
emerge, arise, come to light,
crop up (*informal*), transpire,
materialize
surge NOUN 1 = **rush**, flood
2 = **flow**, wave, rush, roller,
gush, outpouring 3 = **tide**, swell,
billowing 4 = **rush**, wave, storm,
torrent, eruption
▷ VERB 5 = **rush**, pour, rise, gush
6 = **roll**, rush, heave 7 = **sweep**,
rush, storm
surpass = **outdo**, beat, exceed,
eclipse, excel, transcend,
outstrip, outshine
surpassing = **supreme**,
extraordinary, outstanding,
exceptional, unrivalled,
incomparable, matchless
surplus NOUN 1 = **excess**, surfeit
OPPOSITE: shortage
▷ ADJECTIVE 2 = **extra**,
spare, excess, remaining,
odd, superfluous **OPPOSITE:**
insufficient
surprise NOUN 1 = **shock**,
revelation, jolt, bombshell,
eye-opener (*informal*)
2 = **amazement**,
astonishment, wonder,
incredulity
▷ VERB 3 = **amaze**, astonish,
stun, startle, stagger, take
aback 4 = **catch unawares** or
off-guard, spring upon

S

surprised = amazed, astonished, speechless, thunderstruck

surprising = amazing, remarkable, incredible, astonishing, unusual, extraordinary, unexpected, staggering

surrender VERB 1 = give in, yield, submit, give way, succumb, cave in (*informal*), capitulate OPPOSITE: resist 2 = give up, abandon, relinquish, yield, concede, part with, renounce, waive ▷ NOUN 3 = submission, cave-in (*informal*), capitulation, resignation, renunciation, relinquishment

surround = enclose, ring, encircle, encompass, envelop, hem in

surrounding = nearby, neighbouring

surroundings = environment, setting, background, location, milieu

surveillance = observation, watch, scrutiny, supervision, inspection

survey NOUN 1 = poll, study, research, review, inquiry, investigation 2 = examination, inspection, scrutiny 3 = valuation, estimate, assessment, appraisal ▷ VERB 4 = interview, question, poll, research, investigate 5 = look over, view, examine,

observe, contemplate, inspect, eyeball (*slang*), scrutinize 6 = measure, estimate, assess, appraise

survive 1 = remain alive, last, live on, endure 2 = continue, last, live on 3 = live longer than, outlive, outlast

susceptible 1 = responsive, sensitive, receptive, impressionable, suggestible OPPOSITE: unresponsive 2 *usually with* to = liable, inclined, prone, given, subject, vulnerable, disposed OPPOSITE: resistant

suspect VERB 1 = believe, feel, guess, consider, suppose, speculate OPPOSITE: know 2 = distrust, doubt, mistrust OPPOSITE: trust ▷ ADJECTIVE 3 = dubious, doubtful, questionable, iffy (*informal*), shonky (*Austral & NZ informal*) OPPOSITE: innocent

suspend 1 = postpone, put off, cease, interrupt, shelve, defer, cut short, discontinue OPPOSITE: continue 2 = hang, attach, dangle

suspension = postponement, break, breaking off, interruption, abeyance, deferment, discontinuation

suspicion 1 = distrust, scepticism, mistrust, doubt, misgiving, qualm, wariness, dubiety 2 = idea, notion, hunch, guess, impression 3 = trace, touch, hint, suggestion, shade, streak, tinge, soupçon (*French*)

suspicious 1 = **distrustful**, sceptical, doubtful, unbelieving, wary **OPPOSITE:** trusting
2 = **suspect**, dubious, questionable, doubtful, dodgy (*Brit, Austral & NZ informal*), fishy (*informal*), shonky (*Austral & NZ informal*) **OPPOSITE:** beyond suspicion

sustain 1 = **maintain**, continue, keep up, prolong, protract
2 = **suffer**, experience, undergo, feel, bear, endure, withstand
3 = **help**, aid, assist 4 = **keep alive**, nourish, provide for
5 = **support**, bear, uphold

sustained = **continuous**, constant, steady, prolonged, perpetual, unremitting, nonstop **OPPOSITE:** periodic

swallow 1 = **eat**, consume, devour, swig (*informal*) 2 = **gulp**, drink

swamp NOUN 1 = **bog**, marsh, quagmire, slough, fen, mire, morass, pakihi (*NZ*), muskeg (*Canad*)
▷ VERB 2 = **flood**, engulf, submerge, inundate
3 = **overload**, overwhelm, inundate

swap *or* **swop** = **exchange**, trade, switch, interchange, barter

swarm NOUN 1 = **multitude**, crowd, mass, army, host, flock, herd, horde

▷ VERB 2 = **crowd**, flock, throng, mass, stream 3 = **teem**, crawl, abound, bristle

swath *or* **swathe** = **area**, section, tract

swathe = **wrap**, drape, envelop, cloak, shroud, bundle up

sway VERB 1 = **move from side to side**, rock, roll, swing, bend, lean 2 = **influence**, affect, guide, persuade, induce
▷ NOUN 3 = **power**, control, influence, authority, clout (*informal*)

swear 1 = **curse**, blaspheme, be foul-mouthed 2 = **vow**, promise, testify, attest 3 = **declare**, assert, affirm

swearing = **bad language**, cursing, profanity, blasphemy, foul language

sweat NOUN 1 = **perspiration**
2 (*informal*) = **panic**, anxiety, worry, distress, agitation
▷ VERB 3 = **perspire**, glow
4 (*informal*) = **worry**, fret, agonize, torture yourself

sweep VERB 1 = **brush**, clean
2 = **clear**, remove, brush, clean
3 = **sail**, pass, fly, tear, zoom, glide, skim
▷ NOUN 4 = **movement**, move, swing, stroke 5 = **extent**, range, stretch, scope

sweeping 1 = **indiscriminate**, blanket, wholesale, exaggerated, overstated, unqualified 2 = **wide-ranging**, global, comprehensive, wide,

S

broad, extensive, all-inclusive, all-embracing **OPPOSITE:** limited

sweet ADJECTIVE 1 = **sugary**, cloying, saccharine, icky (*informal*) **OPPOSITE:** sour 2 = **fragrant**, aromatic **OPPOSITE:** stinking 3 = **fresh**, clean, pure 4 = **melodious**, musical, harmonious, mellow, dulcet **OPPOSITE:** harsh 5 = **charming**, kind, agreeable **OPPOSITE:** nasty 6 = **delightful**, appealing, cute, winning, engaging, lovable, likable *or* likeable **OPPOSITE:** unpleasant ▷ NOUN 7 (*Brit usually plural*) = **confectionery**, candy (*US*), lolly (*Austral & NZ*), bonbon 8 (*Brit*) = **dessert**, pudding

sweetheart 1 = **dearest**, beloved, sweet, angel, treasure, honey, dear, sweetie (*informal*) 2 = **love**, boyfriend *or* girlfriend, beloved, lover, darling

swell VERB 1 = **increase**, rise, grow, mount, expand, accelerate, escalate, multiply **OPPOSITE:** decrease 2 = **expand**, increase, grow, rise, balloon, enlarge, bulge, dilate **OPPOSITE:** shrink ▷ NOUN 3 = **wave**, surge, billow

swelling = **enlargement**, lump, bump, bulge, inflammation, protuberance, distension

swift 1 = **quick**, prompt, rapid 2 = **fast**, quick, rapid, hurried, speedy **OPPOSITE:** slow

swiftly 1 = **quickly**, rapidly, speedily 2 = **fast**, promptly, hurriedly

swing VERB 1 = **brandish**, wave, shake, flourish, wield, dangle 2 = **sway**, rock, wave, veer, oscillate 3 *usually with* **round** = **turn**, swivel, curve, rotate, pivot 4 = **hit out**, strike, swipe, lash out at, slap 5 = **hang**, dangle, suspend ▷ NOUN 6 = **swaying**, sway 7 = **fluctuation**, change, shift, switch, variation

swirl = **whirl**, churn, spin, twist, eddy

switch NOUN 1 = **control**, button, lever, on/off device 2 = **change**, shift, reversal ▷ VERB 3 = **change**, shift, divert, deviate 4 = **exchange**, swap, substitute

swollen = **enlarged**, bloated, inflamed, puffed up, distended

swoop 1 = **pounce**, attack, charge, rush, descend 2 = **drop**, plunge, dive, sweep, descend, pounce, stoop

symbol 1 = **metaphor**, image, sign, representation, token 2 = **representation**, sign, figure, mark, image, token, logo, badge, glyph (*computing*)

symbolic 1 = **representative**, emblematic, allegorical 2 = **figurative**, representative

sympathetic 1 = **caring**, kind, understanding, concerned, interested, warm, pitying,

supportive **OPPOSITE:** uncaring
2 = **like-minded**, compatible,
agreeable, friendly, congenial,
companionable **OPPOSITE:**
uncongenial
sympathy 1 = **compassion**,
understanding, pity,
commiseration, aroha
(*NZ*) **OPPOSITE:** indifference
2 = **affinity**, agreement,
rapport, fellow feeling
OPPOSITE: opposition
symptom 1 = **sign**, mark,
indication, warning
2 = **manifestation**, sign,
indication, mark, evidence,
expression, proof, token
synthetic = **artificial**, fake,
man-made **OPPOSITE:** real
system 1 = **arrangement**,
structure, organization,
scheme, classification
2 = **method**, practice,
technique, procedure, routine
systematic = **methodical**,
organized, efficient, orderly
OPPOSITE: unmethodical

table NOUN 1 = **counter**,
bench, stand, board, surface,
work surface 2 = **list**, chart,
tabulation, record, roll, register,
diagram, itemization
▷ VERB 3 (*Brit*) = **submit**,
propose, put forward, move,
suggest, enter, file, lodge
taboo *or* **tabu** ADJECTIVE
1 = **forbidden**, banned,
prohibited, unacceptable,
outlawed, anathema,
proscribed, unmentionable
OPPOSITE: permitted
▷ NOUN 2 = **prohibition**, ban,
restriction, anathema, interdict,
proscription, tapu (*NZ*)
tack NOUN 1 = **nail**, pin, drawing
pin
▷ VERB 2 = **fasten**, fix, attach,
pin, nail, affix 3 (*Brit*) = **stitch**,
sew, hem, bind, baste
▷ PHRASES: **tack something on
to something** = **append**, add,
attach, tag
tackle NOUN 1 (*Sport*) = **block**,
challenge 2 = **rig**, apparatus
▷ VERB 3 = **deal with**, set about,
get stuck into (*informal*), come *or*

t

get to grips with **4** = **undertake**, attempt, embark upon, get stuck into (*informal*), have a go or stab at (*informal*) **5** (*Sport*) = **intercept**, stop, challenge

tactic = **policy**, approach, move, scheme, plans, method, manoeuvre, ploy

tactical = **strategic**, shrewd, smart, diplomatic, cunning **OPPOSITE:** impolitic

tactics = **strategy**, campaigning, manoeuvres, generalship

tag NOUN **1** = **label**, tab, note, ticket, slip, identification, marker, flap
▷ VERB **2** = **label**, mark

tail NOUN **1** = **extremity**, appendage, brush, rear end, hindquarters, hind part **2** (*Astronomy*) = **train**, end, trail, tailpiece
▷ VERB **3** (*informal*) = **follow**, track, shadow, trail, stalk
▷ PHRASES: turn tail = **run away**, flee, run off, retreat, cut and run, take to your heels

tailor NOUN **1** = **outfitter**, couturier, dressmaker, seamstress, clothier, costumier
▷ VERB **2** = **adapt**, adjust, modify, style, fashion, shape, alter, mould

taint = **spoil**, ruin, contaminate, damage, stain, corrupt, pollute, tarnish **OPPOSITE:** purify

take VERB **1** = **grip**, grab, seize, catch, grasp, clasp,

take hold of **2** = **carry**, bring, bear, transport, ferry, haul, convey, fetch **OPPOSITE:** send **3** = **accompany**, lead, bring, guide, conduct, escort, convoy, usher **4** = **remove**, draw, pull, fish, withdraw, extract **5** = **steal**, appropriate, pocket, pinch (*informal*), misappropriate, purloin **OPPOSITE:** return **6** = **capture**, seize, take into custody, lay hold of **OPPOSITE:** release **7** = **tolerate**, stand, bear, stomach, endure, abide, put up with (*informal*), withstand **OPPOSITE:** avoid **8** = **require**, need, involve, demand, call for, entail, necessitate **9** = **understand**, follow, comprehend, get, see, grasp, apprehend **10** = **have room for**, hold, contain, accommodate, accept
▷ PHRASES: take off **1** = **lift off**, take to the air **2** = **depart**, go, leave, disappear, abscond, decamp, slope off ▶ take someone for something (*informal*) = **regard as**, believe to be, consider to be, perceive to be, presume to be ▶ take someone off (*informal*) = **parody**, imitate, mimic, mock, caricature, send up (*Brit informal*), lampoon, satirize ▶ take something in **1** = **understand**, absorb, grasp, digest, comprehend, assimilate, get the hang of

(*informal*) ▶ **take something up 1 = start**, begin, engage in, adopt, become involved in **2 = occupy**, absorb, consume, use up, cover, fill, waste, squander (*informal*)

takeover = merger, coup, incorporation

tale = story, narrative, anecdote, account, legend, saga, yarn (*informal*), fable

talent = ability, gift, aptitude, capacity, genius, flair, knack

talented = gifted, able, expert, master, masterly, brilliant, ace (*informal*), consummate

talk VERB **1 = speak**, chat, chatter, converse, communicate, natter, earbash (*Austral & NZ slang*) **2 = discuss**, confer, negotiate, parley, confabulate, korero (*NZ*) **3 = inform**, grass (*Brit slang*), tell all, give the game away, blab, let the cat out of the bag
▷ NOUN **4 = speech**, lecture, presentation, report, address, discourse, sermon, symposium, whaikorero (*NZ*)

talking-to (*informal*) **= reprimand**, lecture, rebuke, scolding, criticism, reproach, ticking-off (*informal*), dressing-down (*informal*) **OPPOSITE:** praise

tall 1 = lofty, big, giant, long-legged, lanky, leggy **2 = high**, towering, soaring, steep, elevated, lofty **OPPOSITE:** short

tally VERB **1 = agree**, match, accord, fit, square, coincide, correspond, conform **OPPOSITE:** disagree
▷ NOUN **2 = record**, score, total, count, reckoning, running total

tame ADJECTIVE
1 = domesticated, docile, broken, gentle, obedient, amenable, tractable **OPPOSITE:** wild **2 = submissive**, meek, compliant, subdued, manageable, obedient, docile, unresisting **OPPOSITE:** stubborn **3 = unexciting**, boring, dull, bland, uninspiring, humdrum, uninteresting, insipid **OPPOSITE:** exciting
▷ VERB **4 = domesticate**, train, break in, house-train **OPPOSITE:** make fiercer **5 = subdue**, suppress, master, discipline, humble, conquer, subjugate **OPPOSITE:** arouse

tangible = definite, real, positive, material, actual, concrete, palpable, perceptible **OPPOSITE:** intangible

tangle NOUN **1 = knot**, twist, web, jungle, coil, entanglement **2 = mess**, jam, fix (*informal*), confusion, complication, mix-up, shambles, entanglement
▷ VERB **3 = twist**, knot, mat, coil, mesh, entangle, interweave, ravel **OPPOSITE:** disentangle
▷ PHRASES: tangle with someone **= come into conflict with**, come up against, cross

t

swords with, dispute with, contend with, contest with, lock horns with

tantrum = **outburst**, temper, hysterics, fit, flare-up, foulie (*Austral slang*), hissy fit (*informal*), strop (*Brit informal*)

tap¹ VERB 1 = **knock**, strike, pat, rap, beat, touch, drum
▷ NOUN 2 = **knock**, pat, rap, touch, drumming

tap² NOUN 1 = **valve**, faucet (*US & Canad*), stopcock
▷ VERB 2 = **listen in on**, monitor, bug (*informal*), spy on, eavesdrop on, wiretap
▷ PHRASES: **on tap 1** = (*informal*) **available**, ready, standing by, to hand, on hand, at hand. in reserve **2** = **on draught**, cask-conditioned, from barrels, not bottled *or* canned

tape NOUN 1 = **binding**, strip, band, string, ribbon
▷ VERB 2 = **record**, video, tape-record, make a recording of **3** *sometimes with* **up** = **bind**, secure, stick, seal, wrap

target 1 = **mark**, goal 2 = **goal**, aim, objective, end, mark, object, intention, ambition **3** = **victim**, butt, prey, scapegoat

tariff 1 = **tax**, duty, toll, levy, excise **2** = **price list**, schedule

tarnish VERB 1 = **stain**, discolour, darken, blot, blemish **OPPOSITE**: brighten **2** = **damage**, taint, blacken, sully, smirch **OPPOSITE**: enhance

▷ NOUN 3 = **stain**, taint, discoloration, spot, blot, blemish

tart¹ = **pie**, pastry, pasty, tartlet, patty

tart² = **sharp**, acid, sour, bitter, pungent, tangy, piquant, vinegary **OPPOSITE**: sweet

tart³ (*informal*) = **slut**, prostitute, whore, call girl, trollop, floozy (*slang*), hornbag (*Austral slang*)

task = **job**, duty, assignment, exercise, mission, enterprise, undertaking, chore
▷ PHRASES: **take someone to task** = **criticize**, blame, censure, rebuke, reprimand, reproach, scold, tell off (*informal*)

taste NOUN 1 = **flavour**, savour, relish, smack, tang **OPPOSITE**: blandness **2** = **bit**, bite, mouthful, sample, dash, spoonful, morsel, titbit **3** = **liking**, preference, penchant, fondness, partiality, fancy, appetite, inclination **OPPOSITE**: dislike **4** = **refinement**, style, judgment, discrimination, appreciation, elegance, sophistication, discernment **OPPOSITE**: lack of judgment
▷ VERB 5 *often with* **of** = **have a flavour of**, smack of, savour of **6** = **sample**, try, test, sip, savour **7** = **distinguish**, perceive, discern, differentiate **8** = **experience**, know, undergo, partake of, encounter, meet with **OPPOSITE**: miss

tasty = **delicious**, luscious, palatable, delectable, savoury, full-flavoured, scrumptious (*informal*), appetizing, lekker (*S African slang*), yummo (*Austral slang*) **OPPOSITE:** bland

tattletale (*chiefly US & Canad*) = **gossip**, busybody, chatterbox (*informal*), chatterer, bigmouth (*slang*), scandalmonger, gossipmonger

taunt VERB 1 = **jeer**, mock, tease, ridicule, provoke, insult, torment, deride
▷ NOUN 2 = **jeer**, dig, insult, ridicule, teasing, provocation, derision, sarcasm

tavern = **inn**, bar, pub (*informal, chiefly Brit*), public house, beer parlour (*Canad*), beverage room (*Canad*), hostelry, alehouse (*archaic*)

tax NOUN 1 = **charge**, duty, toll, levy, tariff, excise, tithe
▷ VERB 2 = **charge**, rate, assess 3 = **strain**, stretch, try, test, load, burden, exhaust, weaken

teach 1 = **instruct**, train, coach, inform, educate, drill, tutor, enlighten 2 *often with* **how** = **show**, train

teacher = **instructor**, coach, tutor, guide, trainer, lecturer, mentor, educator

team = **side**, squad 2 = **group**, company, set, body, band, gang, line-up, bunch
▷ PHRASES: **team up** = **join**, unite, work together, cooperate, couple, link up, get together, band together

tear VERB 1 = **rip**, split, rend, shred, rupture 2 = **run** 3 = **scratch**, cut (open), gash, lacerate, injure, mangle, cut to pieces, cut to ribbons, mangulate (*Austral slang*) 4 = **pull apart**, claw, lacerate, mutilate, mangle, mangulate (*Austral slang*) 5 = **rush**, run, charge, race, fly, speed, dash, hurry
▷ NOUN 6 = **hole**, split, rip, rent, snag, rupture

tears = **crying**, weeping, sobbing, wailing, blubbering
▷ PHRASES: **in tears** = **weeping**, crying, sobbing, blubbering

tease 1 = **mock**, provoke, torment, taunt, goad, pull someone's leg (*informal*), make fun of 2 = **tantalize**, lead on, flirt with, titillate

technical = **scientific**, technological, skilled, specialist, specialized, hi-tech *or* high-tech

technique 1 = **method**, way, system, approach, means, style, manner, procedure 2 = **skill**, performance, craft, touch, execution, artistry, craftsmanship, proficiency

tedious = **boring**, dull, dreary, monotonous, drab, tiresome, laborious, humdrum **OPPOSITE:** exciting

teenager = **youth**, minor, adolescent, juvenile, girl, boy

t

telephone NOUN 1 = **phone**, mobile, mobile phone *or* (*informal*) moby, cellphone *or* cellular phone (*US*), handset, landline, dog and bone (*slang*), iPhone®, smartphone, Blackberry, camera phone, picture phone
▷ VERB 2 = **call**, phone, ring (*chiefly Brit*), dial

telescope NOUN 1 = **glass**, scope (*informal*), spyglass
▷ VERB 2 = **shorten**, contract, compress, shrink, condense, abbreviate, abridge OPPOSITE: lengthen

television = **TV**, telly (*Brit informal*), small screen (*informal*), the box (*Brit informal*), the tube (*slang*)

tell 1 = **inform**, notify, state to, reveal to, express to, disclose to, proclaim to, divulge, flag up 2 = **describe**, relate, recount, report, portray, depict, chronicle, narrate 3 = **instruct**, order, command, direct, bid 4 = **distinguish**, discriminate, discern, differentiate, identify 5 = **have** *or* **take effect**, register, weigh, count, take its toll, carry weight, make its presence felt
▷ PHRASES: **tell someone off** = **reprimand**, rebuke, scold, lecture, censure, reproach, berate, chide

telling = **effective**, significant, considerable, marked, striking, powerful, impressive, influential OPPOSITE: unimportant

temper NOUN 1 = **irritability**, irascibility, passion, resentment, petulance, surliness, hot-headedness OPPOSITE: good humour 2 = **frame of mind**, nature, mind, mood, constitution, humour, temperament, disposition 3 = **rage**, fury, bad mood, passion, tantrum, foulie (*Austral slang*), hissy fit (*informal*), strop (*Brit informal*) 4 = **self-control**, composure, cool (*slang*), calmness, equanimity OPPOSITE: anger
▷ VERB 5 = **moderate**, restrain, tone down, soften, soothe, lessen, mitigate, assuage OPPOSITE: intensify 6 = **strengthen**, harden, toughen, anneal OPPOSITE: soften

temperament = **nature**, character, personality, make-up, constitution, bent, humour, temper

temple = **shrine**, church, sanctuary, house of God

temporarily = **briefly**, for the time being, momentarily, fleetingly, pro tem

temporary 1 = **impermanent**, transitory, brief, fleeting, interim, short-lived, momentary, ephemeral OPPOSITE: permanent 2 = **short-term**, acting, interim, supply, stand-in, fill-in, caretaker, provisional, pop-up

tempt 1 = **attract**, allure 2 = **entice**, lure, lead on, invite, seduce, coax **OPPOSITE:** discourage

temptation 1 = **enticement**, lure, inducement, pull, seduction, allurement, tantalization 2 = **appeal**, attraction

tempting = **inviting**, enticing, seductive, alluring, attractive, mouthwatering, appetizing **OPPOSITE:** uninviting

tenant = **leaseholder**, resident, renter, occupant, inhabitant, occupier, lodger, boarder

tend¹ = **be inclined**, be liable, have a tendency, be apt, be prone, lean, incline, gravitate

tend² 1 = **take care of**, look after, keep, attend, nurture, watch over **OPPOSITE:** neglect 2 = **maintain**, take care of, nurture, cultivate, manage **OPPOSITE:** neglect

tendency = **inclination**, leaning, liability, disposition, propensity, susceptibility, proclivity, proneness

tender¹ 1 = **gentle**, loving, kind, caring, sympathetic, affectionate, compassionate, considerate **OPPOSITE:** harsh 2 = **vulnerable**, young, sensitive, raw, youthful, inexperienced, immature, impressionable **OPPOSITE:** experienced

3 = **sensitive**, painful, sore, raw, bruised, inflamed

tender² VERB 1 = **offer**, present, submit, give, propose, volunteer, hand in, put forward ▷ NOUN 2 = **offer**, bid, estimate, proposal, submission

tense ADJECTIVE 1 = **strained**, uneasy, stressful, fraught, charged, difficult, worrying, exciting 2 = **nervous**, edgy, strained, anxious, apprehensive, uptight (*informal*), on edge, jumpy, adrenalized **OPPOSITE:** calm 3 = **rigid**, strained, taut, stretched, tight **OPPOSITE:** relaxed ▷ VERB 4 = **tighten**, strain, brace, stretch, flex, stiffen **OPPOSITE:** relax

tension 1 = **strain**, stress, nervousness, pressure, anxiety, unease, apprehension, suspense **OPPOSITE:** calmness 2 = **friction**, hostility, unease, antagonism, antipathy, enmity 3 = **rigidity**, tightness, stiffness, pressure, stress, stretching, tautness

tentative 1 = **unconfirmed**, provisional, indefinite, test, trial, pilot, preliminary, experimental **OPPOSITE:** confirmed 2 = **hesitant**, cautious, uncertain, doubtful, faltering, unsure, timid, undecided **OPPOSITE:** confident

term NOUN 1 = **word**, name, expression, title, label,

t

phrase 2 = **period**, time, spell, while, season, interval, span, duration

▷ VERB 3 = **call**, name, label, style, entitle, tag, dub, designate

terminal ADJECTIVE 1 = **fatal**, deadly, lethal, killing, mortal, incurable, inoperable, untreatable 2 = **final**, last, closing, finishing, concluding, ultimate, terminating **OPPOSITE:** initial

▷ NOUN 3 = **terminus**, station, depot, end of the line

terminate 1 = **end**, stop, conclude, finish, complete, discontinue **OPPOSITE:** begin 2 = **cease**, end, close, finish 3 = **abort**, end

terrain = **ground**, country, land, landscape, topography, going

terrestrial = **earthly**, worldly, global

terrible 1 = **awful**, shocking, terrifying, horrible, dreadful, horrifying, fearful, horrendous 2 (*informal*) = **bad**, awful, dreadful, dire, abysmal, poor, rotten (*informal*) **OPPOSITE:** wonderful 3 = **serious**, desperate, severe, extreme, dangerous, insufferable **OPPOSITE:** mild

terribly 1 = **very much**, very, dreadfully, seriously, extremely, desperately, thoroughly, decidedly 2 = **extremely**, very, dreadfully, seriously,

desperately, thoroughly, decidedly, awfully (*informal*)

terrific 1 (*informal*) = **excellent**, wonderful, brilliant, amazing, outstanding, superb, fantastic (*informal*), magnificent, booshit (*Austral slang*), exo (*Austral slang*), sik (*Austral slang*), ka pai (*NZ*), rad (*informal*), phat (*slang*), schmick (*Austral informal*) **OPPOSITE:** awful 2 = **intense**, great, huge, enormous, tremendous, fearful, gigantic

terrified = **frightened**, scared, petrified, alarmed, panic-stricken, horror-struck

terrify = **frighten**, scare, alarm, terrorize

territory = **district**, area, land, region, country, zone, province, patch

terror 1 = **fear**, alarm, dread, fright, panic, anxiety 2 = **nightmare**, monster, bogeyman, devil, fiend, bugbear

test VERB 1 = **check**, investigate, assess, research, analyse, experiment with, try out, put something to the test, run something up the flagpole 2 = **examine**, put someone to the test

▷ NOUN 3 = **trial**, research, check, investigation, analysis, assessment, examination, evaluation 4 = **examination**, paper, assessment, evaluation

testament 1 = proof, evidence, testimony, witness, demonstration, tribute 2 (*Law*) = **will**, last wishes

testify = **bear witness**, state, swear, certify, assert, affirm, attest, corroborate **OPPOSITE:** disprove

testimony 1 (*Law*) = **evidence**, statement, submission, affidavit, deposition 2 = **proof**, evidence, demonstration, indication, support, manifestation, verification, corroboration

testing = **difficult**, demanding, taxing, challenging, searching, tough, exacting, rigorous **OPPOSITE:** undemanding

text NOUN 1 = **contents**, words, content, wording, body, subject matter 2 = **words**, wording 3 = **transcript**, script 4 = **text message**, SMS, MMS, sext ▷ VERB 5 = **text message**, SMS, MMS, sext

texture = **feel**, consistency, structure, surface, tissue, grain

thank = **say thank you to**, show your appreciation to

thanks = **gratitude**, appreciation, credit, recognition, acknowledgment, gratefulness ▷ PHRASES: thanks to = **because of**, through, due to, as a result of, owing to

thaw = **melt**, dissolve, soften, defrost, warm, liquefy, unfreeze **OPPOSITE:** freeze

theatrical 1 = **dramatic**, stage, Thespian 2 = **exaggerated**, dramatic, melodramatic, histrionic, affected, mannered, showy, ostentatious **OPPOSITE:** natural

theft = **stealing**, robbery, thieving, fraud, embezzlement, pilfering, larceny, purloining

theme 1 = **motif**, leitmotif 2 = **subject**, idea, topic, essence, subject matter, keynote, gist

theological = **religious**, ecclesiastical, doctrinal

theoretical *or* **theoretic** 1 = **abstract**, speculative **OPPOSITE:** practical 2 = **hypothetical**, academic, notional, unproven, conjectural, postulatory

theory = **belief**, feeling, speculation, assumption, hunch, presumption, conjecture, surmise

therapeutic = **beneficial**, healing, restorative, good, corrective, remedial, salutary, curative **OPPOSITE:** harmful

therapist = **psychologist**, analyst, psychiatrist, shrink (*informal*), counsellor, healer, psychotherapist, psychoanalyst

therapy = **remedy**, treatment, cure, healing, method of healing

therefore = **consequently**, so, thus, as a result, hence, accordingly, thence, ergo

thesis 1 = **proposition**, theory, hypothesis, idea, view,

t

opinion, proposal, contention **2** = **dissertation**, paper, treatise, essay, monograph

thick 1 = **bulky**, broad, big, large, fat, solid, substantial, hefty **OPPOSITE:** thin **2** = **wide**, across, deep, broad, in extent *or* diameter **3** = **dense**, close, heavy, compact, impenetrable, lush **4** = **heavy**, heavyweight, dense, chunky, bulky, woolly **5** = **opaque**, heavy, dense, impenetrable **6** = **viscous**, concentrated, stiff, condensed, gelatinous, semi-solid, viscid **OPPOSITE:** runny **7** = **crowded**, full, covered, bursting, bristling, brimming **OPPOSITE:** empty **8** = **stupid**, slow, dense, dopey (*informal*), moronic, obtuse, brainless, dumb-ass (*informal*) **OPPOSITE:** clever **9** (*informal*) = **friendly**, close, intimate, familiar, pally (*informal*), devoted, inseparable **OPPOSITE:** unfriendly

thicken = **set**, condense, congeal, clot, jell, coagulate **OPPOSITE:** thin

thief = **robber**, burglar, stealer, plunderer, shoplifter, embezzler, pickpocket, pilferer

thin 1 = **narrow**, fine, attenuated **OPPOSITE:** thick **2** = **slim**, spare, lean, slight, slender, skinny, skeletal, bony **OPPOSITE:** fat **3** = **meagre**, sparse, scanty, poor, scattered, inadequate, insufficient, deficient **OPPOSITE:**

plentiful **4** = **fine**, delicate, flimsy, sheer, skimpy, gossamer, diaphanous, filmy **OPPOSITE:** thick **5** = **unconvincing**, inadequate, feeble, poor, weak, superficial, lame, flimsy **OPPOSITE:** convincing **6** = **wispy**, thinning, sparse, scarce, scanty

thing 1 = **substance**, stuff, being, body, material, fabric, entity **2** (*informal*) = **phobia**, fear, complex, horror, terror, hang-up (*informal*), aversion, neurosis **3** (*informal*) = **obsession**, liking, preoccupation, mania, fetish, fixation, soft spot, predilection **4** *often plural* = **possessions**, stuff, gear, belongings, effects, luggage, clobber (*Brit slang*), chattels **5** = **equipment**, gear, tool, stuff, tackle, implement, kit, apparatus **6** = **circumstances**, the situation, the state of affairs, matters, life, affairs

think 1 = **believe**, be of the opinion, be of the view **2** = **judge**, consider, estimate, reckon, deem, regard as **3** = **ponder**, reflect, contemplate, deliberate, meditate, ruminate, cogitate, be lost in thought (*informal*) ▷ **PHRASES: think something up** = **devise**, create, come up with, invent, contrive, visualize, concoct, dream up

thinker = philosopher, intellect (*informal*), wise man, sage, brain (*informal*), theorist, mastermind

thinking NOUN 1 = **reasoning**, idea, view, position, theory, opinion, judgment, conjecture ▷ ADJECTIVE 2 = **thoughtful**, intelligent, reasoning, rational, philosophical, reflective, contemplative, meditative

thirst 1 = **dryness**, thirstiness, drought 2 = **craving**, appetite, longing, desire, passion, yearning, hankering, keenness OPPOSITE: aversion

thorn = **prickle**, spike, spine, barb

thorough 1 = **comprehensive**, full, complete, sweeping, intensive, in-depth, exhaustive OPPOSITE: cursory 2 = **careful**, conscientious, painstaking, efficient, meticulous, exhaustive, assiduous OPPOSITE: careless 3 = **complete**, total, absolute, utter, perfect, outright, unqualified, out-and-out OPPOSITE: partial

thoroughly 1 = **carefully**, fully, efficiently, meticulously, painstakingly, scrupulously, assiduously, intensively OPPOSITE: carelessly 2 = **fully** 3 = **completely**, quite, totally, perfectly, absolutely, utterly, downright, to the hilt OPPOSITE: partly

though CONJUNCTION 1 = **although**, while, even if, even though, notwithstanding ▷ ADVERB 2 = **nevertheless**, still, however, yet, nonetheless, for all that, notwithstanding

thought 1 = **thinking**, consideration, reflection, deliberation, musing, meditation, rumination, cogitation 2 = **opinion**, view, idea, concept, notion, judgment 3 = **consideration**, study, attention, care, regard, scrutiny, heed 4 = **intention**, plan, idea, design, aim, purpose, object, notion 5 = **hope**, expectation, prospect, aspiration, anticipation

thoughtful 1 = **reflective**, pensive, contemplative, meditative, serious, studious, deliberative, ruminative OPPOSITE: shallow 2 = **considerate**, kind, caring, kindly, helpful, attentive, unselfish, solicitous OPPOSITE: inconsiderate

thrash 1 = **defeat**, beat, crush, slaughter (*informal*), rout, trounce, run rings around (*informal*), wipe the floor with (*informal*) 2 = **beat**, wallop, whip, belt (*informal*), cane, flog, scourge, spank 3 = **thresh**, flail, jerk, writhe, toss and turn ▷ PHRASES: **thrash something out** = **settle**, resolve, discuss,

t

debate, solve, argue out, have
out, talk over

thrashing 1 = **defeat**, beating,
hammering (*informal*), hiding
(*informal*), rout, trouncing,
drubbing 2 = **beating**, hiding
(*informal*), belting (*informal*),
whipping, flogging

thread NOUN 1 = **strand**, fibre,
yarn, filament, line, string,
twine 2 = **theme**, train of
thought, direction, plot, drift,
story line
▷ VERB 3 = **move**, pass, ease,
thrust, squeeze through, pick
your way

threat 1 = **danger**, risk, hazard,
menace, peril 2 = **threatening
remark**, menace 3 = **warning**,
foreshadowing, foreboding

threaten 1 = **intimidate**, bully,
menace, terrorize, lean on
(*slang*), pressurize, browbeat
OPPOSITE: defend 2 = **endanger**,
jeopardize, put at risk, imperil,
put in jeopardy, put on the
line **OPPOSITE:** protect 3 = **be
imminent**, impend

threshold 1 = **entrance**,
doorway, door, doorstep
2 = **start**, beginning, opening,
dawn, verge, brink, outset,
inception **OPPOSITE:** end
3 = **limit**, margin, starting point,
minimum

thrift = **economy**, prudence,
frugality, saving, parsimony,
carefulness, thriftiness
OPPOSITE: extravagance

thrill NOUN 1 = **pleasure**, kick
(*informal*), buzz (*slang*), high,
stimulation, tingle, titillation
OPPOSITE: tedium
▷ VERB 2 = **excite**, stimulate,
arouse, move, stir, electrify,
titillate, give someone a kick

thrilling = **exciting**, gripping,
stimulating, stirring,
sensational, rousing, riveting,
electrifying **OPPOSITE:** boring

thrive = **prosper**, do well,
flourish, increase, grow,
develop, succeed, get on
OPPOSITE: decline

thriving = **successful**,
flourishing, healthy, booming,
blooming, prosperous,
burgeoning **OPPOSITE:**
unsuccessful

throb VERB 1 = **pulsate**,
pound, beat, pulse, thump,
palpitate 2 = **vibrate**, pulsate,
reverberate, shake, judder
(*informal*)
▷ NOUN 3 = **pulse**, pounding,
beat, thump, thumping,
pulsating, palpitation
4 = **vibration**, throbbing,
reverberation, judder (*informal*),
pulsation

throng NOUN 1 = **crowd**, mob,
horde, host, pack, mass, crush,
swarm
▷ VERB 2 = **crowd**, flock,
congregate, converge, mill
around, swarm around
OPPOSITE: disperse 3 = **pack**,
crowd

throttle = **strangle**, choke, garrotte, strangulate

through PREPOSITION 1 = **via**, by way of, by, between, past, from one side to the other of 2 = **because of**, by way of, by means of 3 = **using**, via, by way of, by means of, by virtue of, with the assistance of 4 = **during**, throughout, for the duration of, in
▷ ADJECTIVE 5 = **completed**, done, finished, ended
▷ PHRASES: **through and through** = **completely**, totally, fully, thoroughly, entirely, altogether, wholly, utterly

throughout PREPOSITION 1 = **right through**, everywhere in, during the whole of, through the whole of 2 = **all over**, everywhere in, through the whole of
▷ ADVERB 3 = **from start to finish**, right through 4 = **all through**, right through

throw VERB 1 = **hurl**, toss, fling, send, launch, cast, pitch, chuck (informal) 2 = **toss**, fling, chuck (informal), cast, hurl, sling 3 (informal) = **confuse**, baffle, faze, astonish, confound, disconcert, dumbfound
▷ NOUN 4 = **toss**, pitch, fling, sling, lob (informal), heave

thrust VERB 1 = **push**, force, shove, drive, plunge, jam, ram, propel
▷ NOUN 2 = **stab**, pierce, lunge

3 = **push**, shove, poke, prod 4 = **momentum**, impetus, drive

thug = **ruffian**, hooligan, tough, heavy (slang), gangster, bully boy, bruiser (informal), tsotsi (S African)

thump NOUN 1 = **blow**, knock, punch, rap, smack, clout (informal), whack, swipe 2 = **thud**, crash, bang, clunk, thwack
▷ VERB 3 = **strike**, hit, punch, pound, beat, knock, smack, clout (informal)

thunder NOUN 1 = **rumble**, crash, boom, explosion
▷ VERB 2 = **rumble**, crash, boom, roar, resound, reverberate, peal 3 = **shout**, roar, yell, bark, bellow

thus 1 = **in this way**, so, like this, as follows 2 = **therefore**, so, hence, consequently, accordingly, for this reason, ergo, on that account

thwart = **frustrate**, foil, prevent, snooker, hinder, obstruct, outwit, stymie OPPOSITE: assist

tick NOUN 1 = **check mark**, mark, line, stroke, dash 2 = **click**, tapping, clicking, ticktock 3 (Brit informal) = **moment**, second, minute, flash, instant, twinkling, split second, trice
▷ VERB 4 = **mark**, indicate, check off 5 = **click**, tap, ticktock (informal, chiefly Brit & US)

ticket 1 = **voucher**, pass, coupon, card, slip, certificate, token, chit 2 = **label**, tag, marker, sticker, card, slip, tab, docket

tide 1 = **current**, flow, stream, ebb, undertow, tideway 2 = **course**, direction, trend, movement, tendency, drift

tidy ADJECTIVE 1 = **neat**, orderly, clean, spruce, well-kept, well-ordered, shipshape **OPPOSITE:** untidy 2 = **organized**, neat, methodical 3 (*informal*) = **considerable**, large, substantial, goodly, healthy, generous, handsome, ample **OPPOSITE:** small ▷ VERB 4 = **neaten**, straighten, order, clean, groom, spruce up **OPPOSITE:** disorder

tie VERB 1 = **fasten**, bind, join, link, connect, attach, knot **OPPOSITE:** unfasten 2 = **tether**, secure 3 = **restrict**, limit, confine, bind, restrain, hamper, hinder **OPPOSITE:** free 4 = **draw**, be level, match, equal ▷ NOUN 5 = **fastening**, binding, link, bond, knot, cord, fetter, ligature 6 = **bond**, relationship, connection, commitment, liaison, allegiance, affiliation 7 = **draw**, dead heat, deadlock, stalemate

tier = **row**, bank, layer, line, level, rank, storey, stratum

tight 1 = **close-fitting**, narrow, cramped, snug, constricted, close **OPPOSITE:** loose 2 = **secure**, firm, fast, fixed 3 = **taut**, stretched, rigid **OPPOSITE:** slack 4 = **close**, even, well-matched, hard-fought, evenly-balanced **OPPOSITE:** uneven 5 (*informal*) = **miserly**, mean, stingy, grasping, parsimonious, niggardly, tightfisted **OPPOSITE:** generous 6 (*informal*) = **drunk**, intoxicated, plastered (*slang*), under the influence (*informal*), tipsy, paralytic (*informal*), inebriated, out to it (*Austral & NZ slang*) **OPPOSITE:** sober

tighten = **close**, narrow, strengthen, squeeze, harden, constrict **OPPOSITE:** slacken

till¹ *See* UNTIL

till² = **cultivate**, dig, plough, work

till³ = **cash register**, cash box

tilt VERB 1 = **slant**, tip, slope, list, lean, heel, incline ▷ NOUN 2 = **slope**, angle, inclination, list, pitch, incline, slant, camber 3 (*Medieval history*) = **joust**, fight, tournament, lists, combat, duel

timber 1 = **beams**, boards, planks 2 = **wood**, logs

time NOUN 1 = **period**, term, space, stretch, spell, span, time frame, timeline 2 = **occasion**, point, moment, stage, instance, point in time, juncture 3 = **age**, duration 4 = **tempo**, beat, rhythm, measure ▷ VERB 5 = **schedule**, set, plan, book, programme, set up, fix, arrange

timeless = **eternal**, lasting, permanent, enduring, immortal, everlasting, ageless, changeless **OPPOSITE:** temporary

timely = **opportune**, appropriate, well-timed, suitable, convenient, judicious, propitious, seasonable **OPPOSITE:** untimely

timetable 1 = **schedule**, programme, agenda, list, diary, calendar 2 = **syllabus**, course, curriculum, programme, teaching programme

tinge NOUN 1 = **tint**, colour, shade 2 = **trace**, bit, drop, touch, suggestion, dash, sprinkling, smattering
▷ VERB 3 = **tint**, colour

tinker = **meddle**, play, potter, fiddle (*informal*), dabble, mess about

tint NOUN 1 = **shade**, colour, tone, hue 2 = **dye**, wash, rinse, tinge, tincture
▷ VERB 3 = **dye**, colour

tiny = **small**, little, minute, slight, miniature, negligible, microscopic, diminutive **OPPOSITE:** huge

tip¹ NOUN 1 = **end**, point, head, extremity, sharp end, nib, prong 2 = **peak**, top, summit, pinnacle, zenith, spire, acme, vertex
▷ VERB 3 = **cap**, top, crown, surmount, finish

tip² VERB 1 = **pour**, drop, empty, dump, drain, discharge, unload,

jettison 2 (*Brit*) = **dump**, empty, unload, pour out
▷ NOUN 3 (*Brit*) = **dump**, midden, rubbish heap, refuse heap

tip³ NOUN 1 = **gratuity**, gift, reward, present, sweetener (*informal*) 2 = **hint**, suggestion, piece of advice, pointer, heads up (*US & Canad*)
▷ VERB 3 = **reward**, remunerate, give a tip to, sweeten (*informal*) 4 = **predict**, back, recommend, think of

tire 1 = **exhaust**, drain, fatigue, weary, wear out **OPPOSITE:** refresh 2 = **flag**, become tired, fail

tired 1 = **exhausted**, fatigued, weary, flagging, drained, sleepy, worn out, drowsy, tuckered out (*Austral & NZ informal*) **OPPOSITE:** energetic 2 = **bored**, fed up, weary, sick, hoha (*NZ*) **OPPOSITE:** enthusiastic about 3 = **hackneyed**, stale, well-worn, old, corny (*slang*), threadbare, trite, clichéd **OPPOSITE:** original

tiring = **exhausting**, demanding, wearing, tough, exacting, strenuous, arduous, laborious

title 1 = **name**, designation, term, handle (*slang*), moniker or monicker (*slang*) 2 (*Sport*) = **championship**, trophy, bays, crown, honour 3 (*Law*) = **ownership**, right, claim, privilege, entitlement, tenure, prerogative, freehold

toast¹ 1 = **brown**, grill, crisp, roast 2 = **warm (up)**, heat (up), thaw, bring back to life

toast² NOUN 1 = **tribute**, compliment, salute, health, pledge, salutation 2 = **favourite**, celebrity, darling, talk, pet, focus of attention, hero or heroine, blue-eyed boy or girl (Brit informal)
▷ VERB 3 = **drink to**, honour, salute, drink (to) the health of

together ADVERB 1 = **collectively**, jointly, as one, with each other, in conjunction, side by side, mutually, in partnership OPPOSITE: separately 2 = **at the same time**, simultaneously, concurrently, contemporaneously, at one fell swoop
▷ ADJECTIVE 3 (informal) = **self-possessed**, composed, well-balanced, well-adjusted, grounded

toil NOUN 1 = **hard work**, effort, application, sweat, graft (informal), slog, exertion, drudgery OPPOSITE: idleness
▷ VERB 2 = **labour**, work, struggle, strive, sweat (informal), slave, graft (informal), slog 3 = **struggle**, trek, slog, trudge, fight your way, footslog

toilet 1 = **lavatory**, bathroom, loo (Brit informal), privy, cloakroom (Brit), urinal, latrine, washroom, dunny (Austral & NZ old-fashioned informal), bogger (Austral slang), brasco (Austral slang) 2 = **bathroom**, gents or ladies (Brit informal), privy, latrine, water closet, ladies' room, W.C.

token NOUN 1 = **symbol**, mark, sign, note, expression, indication, representation, badge
▷ ADJECTIVE 2 = **nominal**, symbolic, minimal, hollow, superficial, perfunctory

tolerance 1 = **broad-mindedness**, indulgence, forbearance, permissiveness, open-mindedness OPPOSITE: intolerance 2 = **endurance**, resistance, stamina, fortitude, resilience, toughness, staying power, hardiness 3 = **resistance**, immunity, resilience, non-susceptibility

tolerant = **broad-minded**, understanding, open-minded, catholic, long-suffering, permissive, forbearing, unprejudiced OPPOSITE: intolerant

tolerate 1 = **endure**, stand, take, stomach, put up with (informal) 2 = **allow**, accept, permit, take, brook, put up with (informal), condone OPPOSITE: forbid

toll¹ VERB 1 = **ring**, sound, strike, chime, knell, clang, peal
▷ NOUN 2 = **ringing**, chime, knell, clang, peal

toll² 1 = **charge**, tax, fee, duty, payment, levy, tariff 2 = **damage**, cost, loss, roll, penalty, sum, number, roster 3 = **adverse effects**, price, cost, suffering, damage, penalty, harm

tomb = **grave**, vault, crypt, mausoleum, sarcophagus, catacomb, sepulchre

tone NOUN 1 = **pitch**, inflection, intonation, timbre, modulation 2 = **volume**, timbre 3 = **character**, style, feel, air, spirit, attitude, manner, mood 4 = **colour**, shade, tint, tinge, hue ▷ VERB 5 = **harmonize**, match, blend, suit, go well with ▷ PHRASES: tone something down 1 = **moderate**, temper, soften, restrain, subdue, play down 2 = **reduce**, moderate

tongue = **language**, speech, dialect, parlance

tonic = **stimulant**, boost, pick-me-up (*informal*), fillip, shot in the arm (*informal*), restorative

too 1 = **also**, as well, further, in addition, moreover, besides, likewise, to boot 2 = **excessively**, very, extremely, overly, unduly, unreasonably, inordinately, immoderately

tool 1 = **implement**, device, appliance, machine, instrument, gadget, utensil, contraption 2 = **puppet**, creature, pawn, stooge (*slang*), minion, lackey, flunkey, hireling

top NOUN 1 = **peak**, summit, head, crown, height, ridge, brow, crest OPPOSITE: bottom 2 = **lid**, cover, cap, plug, stopper, bung 3 = **first place**, head, peak, lead, high point ▷ ADJECTIVE 4 = **highest**, loftiest, furthest up, uppermost 5 = **leading**, best, first, highest, head, finest, elite, foremost OPPOSITE: lowest 6 = **chief**, most important, principal, most powerful, highest, head, leading, main 7 = **prime**, best, select, first-class, quality, choice, excellent, premier ▷ VERB 8 = **lead**, head, be at the top of, be first in 9 = **cover**, garnish, finish, crown, cap 10 = **surpass**, better, beat, improve on, cap, exceed, eclipse, excel OPPOSITE: not be as good as

topic = **subject**, point, question, issue, matter, theme, subject matter

topical = **current**, popular, contemporary, up-to-date, up-to-the-minute, newsworthy

topple 1 = **fall over**, fall, collapse, tumble, overturn, totter, keel over, overbalance 2 = **knock over** 3 = **overthrow**, overturn, bring down, oust, unseat, bring low

torment VERB 1 = **torture**, distress, rack, crucify OPPOSITE: comfort 2 = **tease**, annoy, bother, irritate, harass,

t

hassle (*informal*), pester, vex
▷ NOUN 3 = **suffering**, distress,
misery, pain, hell, torture,
agony, anguish OPPOSITE: bliss

torn 1 = **cut**, split, rent,
ripped, ragged, slit, lacerated
2 = **undecided**, uncertain,
unsure, wavering, vacillating, in
two minds (*informal*), irresolute

tornado = **whirlwind**, storm,
hurricane, gale, cyclone,
typhoon, tempest, squall

torture VERB 1 = **torment**,
abuse, persecute, afflict,
scourge, molest, crucify,
mistreat OPPOSITE: comfort
2 = **distress**, torment, worry,
trouble, rack, afflict, harrow,
inflict anguish on
▷ NOUN 3 = **ill-treatment**,
abuse, torment, persecution,
maltreatment, harsh treatment
4 = **agony**, suffering, anguish,
distress, torment, heartbreak
OPPOSITE: bliss

toss VERB 1 = **throw**, pitch, hurl,
fling, launch, cast, flip, sling
2 = **shake** 3 = **thrash (about)**,
twitch, wriggle, squirm, writhe
▷ NOUN 4 = **throw**, pitch, lob
(*informal*)

tot 1 = **infant**, child, baby,
toddler, mite, littlie (*Austral
informal*), ankle-biter (*Austral
slang*), tacker (*Austral slang*)
2 = **measure**, shot (*informal*),
finger, nip, slug, dram, snifter
(*informal*)
▷ PHRASES: **tot something**

up = **add up**, calculate, total,
reckon, compute, tally,
enumerate, count up (*chiefly
Brit*)

total NOUN 1 = **sum**, entirety,
grand total, whole, aggregate,
totality, full amount, sum total
OPPOSITE: part
▷ ADJECTIVE 2 = **complete**,
absolute, utter, whole, entire,
undivided, overarching,
thoroughgoing OPPOSITE:
partial
▷ VERB 3 = **amount to**, make,
come to, reach, equal, run to,
number, add up to 4 = **add up**,
work out, compute, reckon, tot
up OPPOSITE: subtract

totally = **completely**,
entirely, absolutely, fully,
comprehensively, thoroughly,
wholly, utterly OPPOSITE: partly

touch VERB 1 = **feel**, handle,
finger, stroke, brush, make
contact with, caress, fondle
2 = **come into contact**, meet,
contact, border, graze, adjoin,
be in contact, abut 3 = **tap**
4 = **affect**, influence, inspire,
impress 5 = **consume**, take,
drink, eat, partake of 6 = **move**,
stir, disturb 7 = **match**, rival,
equal, compare with, parallel,
hold a candle to (*informal*)
▷ NOUN 8 = **contact**, push,
stroke, brush, press, tap, poke,
nudge 9 = **feeling**, handling,
physical contact 10 = **bit**, spot,
trace, drop, dash, small amount,

jot, smattering 11 = **style**, method, technique, way, manner, trademark

▷ **PHRASES: touch and go = risky**, close, near, critical, precarious, nerve-racking

▶ **touch on** *or* **upon something = refer to**, cover, raise, deal with, mention, bring in, speak of, hint at

touching = **moving**, affecting, sad, stirring, pathetic, poignant, emotive, pitiable

tough ADJECTIVE 1 = **strong**, determined OPPOSITE: weak 2 = **hardy**, strong, seasoned, strapping, vigorous, sturdy, stout 3 = **violent**, rough, ruthless, pugnacious, hard-bitten 4 = **strict**, severe, stern, hard, firm, resolute, merciless, unbending OPPOSITE: lenient 5 = **hard**, difficult, troublesome, uphill, strenuous, arduous, laborious 6 = **resilient**, hard, resistant, durable, strong, solid, rugged, sturdy OPPOSITE: fragile

▷ NOUN 7 = **ruffian**, bully, thug, hooligan, bruiser (*informal*), roughneck (*slang*), tsotsi (*S African*)

tour NOUN 1 = **journey**, expedition, excursion, trip, outing, jaunt, junket

▷ VERB 2 = **travel round**, travel through, journey round, trek round, go on a trip through 3 = **visit**, explore, go round,

inspect, walk round, drive round, sightsee

tourist = **traveller**, voyager, tripper, globetrotter, holiday-maker, sightseer, excursionist

tournament = **competition**, meeting, event, series, contest

tow = **drag**, draw, pull, haul, tug, yank, lug

towards 1 = **in the direction of**, to, for, on the way to, en route for 2 = **regarding**, about, concerning, respecting, in relation to, with regard to, with respect to, apropos

tower = **column**, pillar, turret, belfry, steeple, obelisk

toxic – **poisonous**, deadly, lethal, harmful, pernicious, noxious, septic, pestilential OPPOSITE: harmless

toy = **plaything**, game, doll

▷ **PHRASES: toy with something = play with**, consider, trifle with, dally with, entertain the possibility of, amuse yourself with, think idly of *usually with* **with**

trace NOUN 1 = **bit**, drop, touch, shadow, suggestion, hint, suspicion, tinge 2 = **remnant**, sign, record, mark, evidence, indication, vestige, footprint, electronic footprint 3 = **track**, trail, footstep, path, footprint, spoor, footmark, electronic footprint

▷ VERB 4 = **search for**, track, unearth, hunt down 5 = **find**, track (down), discover, detect, unearth, hunt down, ferret out, locate **6** = **outline**, sketch, draw **7** = **copy**, map, draft, outline, sketch, reproduce, draw over

track NOUN **1** = **path**, way, road, route, trail, pathway, footpath **2** = **course**, line, path, orbit, trajectory **3** = **line**, tramline ▷ VERB **4** = **follow**, pursue, chase, trace, tail (*informal*), shadow, trail, stalk
▷ PHRASES: **track something** or **someone down** = **find**, discover, trace, unearth, dig up, hunt down, sniff out, run to earth or ground

tract¹ = **area**, region, district, stretch, territory, extent, plot, expanse

tract² = **treatise**, essay, booklet, pamphlet, dissertation, monograph, homily

trade NOUN **1** = **commerce**, business, transactions, dealing, exchange, traffic, truck, barter **2** = **job**, employment, business, craft, profession, occupation, line of work, métier
▷ VERB **3** = **deal**, do business, traffic, truck, bargain, peddle, transact, cut a deal **4** = **exchange**, switch, swap, barter **5** = **operate**, run, deal, do business

trader = **dealer**, supplier, merchant, seller, purveyor

tradition 1 = **customs**, institution, ritual, folklore, lore,

tikanga (*NZ*) **2** = **established practice**, custom, convention, habit, ritual

traditional 1 = **old-fashioned**, old, established, conventional, usual, accustomed, customary, time-honoured **OPPOSITE:** revolutionary **2** = **folk**, old

traffic NOUN **1** = **transport**, vehicles, transportation, freight **2** = **trade**, commerce, business, exchange, truck, dealings, peddling
▷ VERB **3** *often with* **in** = **trade**, deal, exchange, bargain, do business, peddle, cut a deal, have dealings

tragedy = **disaster**, catastrophe, misfortune, adversity, calamity **OPPOSITE:** fortune

tragic *or* **tragical**
1 = **distressing**, sad, appalling, deadly, unfortunate, disastrous, dreadful, dire **OPPOSITE:** fortunate **2** = **sad**, miserable, pathetic, mournful **OPPOSITE:** happy

trail NOUN **1** = **path**, track, route, way, course, road, pathway, footpath **2** = **tracks**, path, marks, wake, trace, scent, footprints, spoor **3** = **wake**, stream, tail
▷ VERB **4** = **follow**, track, chase, pursue, dog, hunt, shadow, trace **5** = **drag**, draw, pull, sweep, haul, tow, dangle, droop **6** = **lag**, follow, drift, wander, linger, trudge, plod, meander

train 1 = **instruct**, school, prepare, coach, teach, guide, educate, drill 2 = **exercise**, prepare, work out, practise, do exercise, get into shape 3 = **aim**, point, level, position, direct, focus, sight, zero in 4 = **sequence**, series, chain, string, set, cycle, trail, succession

trainer = **coach**, manager, guide, adviser, tutor, instructor, counsellor, guru

trait = **characteristic**, feature, quality, attribute, quirk, peculiarity, mannerism, idiosyncrasy

traitor = **betrayer**, deserter, turncoat, renegade, defector, Judas, quisling, apostate, fizgig (*Austral slang*) **OPPOSITE:** loyalist

tramp VERB 1 = **trudge**, stump, toil, plod, traipse (*informal*) 2 = **hike**, walk, trek, roam, march, ramble, slog, rove ▷ NOUN 3 = **vagrant**, derelict, drifter, down-and-out, derro (*Austral slang*) 4 = **tread**, stamp, footstep, footfall 5 = **hike**, march, trek, ramble, slog

trample *often with* **on**, **upon**, *or* **over** = **stamp**, crush, squash, tread, flatten, run over, walk over

trance = **daze**, dream, abstraction, rapture, reverie, stupor, unconsciousness

transaction = **deal**, negotiation, business, enterprise, bargain, undertaking

transcend = **surpass**, exceed, go beyond, rise above, eclipse, excel, outstrip, outdo

transcript = **copy**, record, manuscript, reproduction, duplicate, transcription

transfer VERB 1 = **move**, transport, shift, relocate, transpose, change, download, upload ▷ NOUN 2 = **transference**, move, handover, change, shift, transmission, translation, relocation

transform 1 = **change**, convert, alter, transmute 2 = **make over**, remodel, revolutionize

transformation 1 = **change**, conversion, alteration, metamorphosis, transmutation 2 = **revolution**, sea change

transit = **movement**, transfer, transport, passage, crossing, transportation, carriage, conveyance

transition = **change**, passing, development, shift, conversion, alteration, progression, metamorphosis

transitional 1 = **changing**, passing, fluid, intermediate, unsettled, developmental 2 = **temporary**, working, acting, short-term, interim, fill-in, caretaker, provisional

translate = **render**, put, change, convert, interpret, decode, construe, paraphrase

t

translation = interpretation, version, rendering, rendition, decoding, paraphrase

transmission 1 = transfer, spread, spreading, passing on, circulation, dispatch, relaying, mediation 2 = broadcasting, showing, putting out, relaying, sending 3 = programme, broadcast, show, production, telecast, podcast

transmit 1 = broadcast, televise, relay, air, radio, send out, disseminate, beam out, stream, podcast 2 = pass on, carry, spread, send, bear, transfer, hand on, convey

transparent 1 = clear, sheer, see-through, lucid, translucent, crystalline, limpid, diaphanous OPPOSITE: opaque 2 = obvious, plain, patent, evident, explicit, manifest, recognizable, unambiguous OPPOSITE: uncertain

transplant 1 (Surgery) = implant, transfer, graft 2 = transfer, take, bring, carry, remove, transport, shift, convey

transport VERB 1 = convey, take, move, bring, send, carry, bear, transfer 2 = enrapture, move, delight, entrance, enchant, captivate, ravish 3 = exile, banish, deport ▷ NOUN 4 = vehicle, transportation, conveyance 5 = transference, carrying, delivery, distribution, transportation, shipment, freight, haulage 6 often plural = ecstasy, delight, heaven, bliss, euphoria, rapture, enchantment, ravishment OPPOSITE: despondency

trap NOUN 1 = snare, net, gin, pitfall, noose 2 = ambush, set-up (informal) 3 = trick, set-up (informal), deception, ploy, ruse, trickery, subterfuge, stratagem ▷ VERB 4 = catch, snare, ensnare, entrap, take, corner, bag, lay hold of 5 = trick, fool, cheat, lure, seduce, deceive, dupe, beguile 6 = capture, catch, arrest, seize, take, secure, collar (informal), apprehend

trash 1 = nonsense, rubbish, rot, drivel, twaddle, tripe (informal), moonshine, hogwash, kak (S African taboo slang), bizzo (Austral slang), bull's wool (Austral & NZ slang) OPPOSITE: sense 2 (chiefly US & Canad) = litter, refuse, waste, rubbish, junk (informal), garbage, dross

trauma 1 = shock, suffering, pain, torture, ordeal, anguish 2 (Pathology) = injury, damage, hurt, wound, agony

traumatic = shocking, upsetting, alarming, awful, disturbing, devastating, painful, distressing OPPOSITE: calming

travel VERB 1 = go, journey, move, tour, progress, wander, trek, voyage ▷ NOUN 2 usually plural

= **journey**, wandering, expedition, globetrotting, tour, trip, voyage, excursion

traveller = **voyager**, tourist, explorer, globetrotter, holiday-maker, wayfarer

tread VERB 1 = **step**, walk, march, pace, stamp, stride, hike ▷ NOUN 2 = **step**, walk, pace, stride, footstep, gait, footfall

treason = **disloyalty**, mutiny, treachery, duplicity, sedition, perfidy, lese-majesty, traitorousness **OPPOSITE:** loyalty

treasure NOUN 1 = **riches**, money, gold, fortune, wealth, valuables, jewels, cash 2 = **angel**, darling, jewel, gem, paragon, nonpareil ▷ VERB 3 = **prize**, value, esteem, adore, cherish, revere, hold dear, love

treasury = **storehouse**, bank, store, vault, hoard, cache, repository

treat VERB 1 = **behave towards**, deal with, handle, act towards, use, consider, serve, manage 2 = **take care of**, minister to, attend to, give medical treatment to, doctor (*informal*), nurse, care for, prescribe medicine for 3 *often with* **to** = **provide**, stand (*informal*), entertain, lay on, regale ▷ NOUN 4 = **entertainment**, party, surprise, gift, celebration, feast, outing, excursion

5 = **pleasure**, delight, joy, thrill, satisfaction, enjoyment, source of pleasure, fun

treatment 1 = **care**, medical care, nursing, medicine, surgery, therapy, healing, medication 2 = **cure**, remedy, medication, medicine 3 *often with* **of** = **handling**, dealings with, behaviour towards, conduct towards, management, manipulation, action towards

treaty = **agreement**, pact, contract, alliance, convention, compact, covenant, entente

trek NOUN 1 = **slog**, tramp 2 = **journey**, hike, expedition, safari, march, odyssey ▷ VERB 3 = **journey**, march, hike, tramp, rove, go walkabout (*Austral*) 4 = **trudge**, traipse (*informal*), footslog, slog

tremble VERB 1 = **shake**, shiver, quake, shudder, quiver, totter 2 = **vibrate**, shake, quake, wobble ▷ NOUN 3 = **shake**, shiver, quake, shudder, wobble, tremor, quiver, vibration

tremendous 1 = **huge**, great, enormous, terrific, formidable, immense, gigantic, colossal **OPPOSITE:** tiny 2 (*informal*) = **excellent**, great, wonderful, brilliant, amazing, extraordinary, fantastic (*informal*), marvellous, booshit (*Austral slang*), exo (*Austral slang*), sik (*Austral slang*), rad (*informal*),

phat (*slang*), schmick (*Austral informal*) **OPPOSITE:** terrible
trench = **ditch**, channel, drain, gutter, trough, furrow, excavation
trend 1 = **tendency**, swing, drift, inclination, current, direction, flow, leaning 2 = **fashion**, craze, fad (*informal*), mode, thing, style, rage, vogue
trendy (*Brit informal*) = **fashionable**, with it (*informal*), stylish, in fashion, in vogue, modish, voguish, schmick (*Austral informal*), funky
trial 1 (*Law*) = **hearing**, case, court case, inquiry, tribunal, lawsuit, appeal, litigation 2 = **test**, experiment, evaluation, audition, dry run (*informal*), assessment, probation, appraisal 3 = **hardship**, suffering, trouble, distress, ordeal, adversity, affliction, tribulation
tribe = **race**, people, family, clan, hapu (*NZ*), iwi (*NZ*)
tribunal = **hearing**, court, trial
tribute = **accolade**, testimonial, eulogy, recognition, compliment, commendation, panegyric **OPPOSITE:** criticism
trick NOUN 1 = **joke**, stunt, spoof (*informal*), prank, practical joke, antic, jape, leg-pull (*Brit informal*) 2 = **deception**, trap, fraud, manoeuvre, ploy, hoax, swindle, ruse, fastie (*Austral slang*) 3 = **sleight of hand**,

stunt, legerdemain 4 = **secret**, skill, knack, hang (*informal*), technique, know-how (*informal*) 5 = **mannerism**, habit, characteristic, trait, quirk, peculiarity, foible, idiosyncrasy ▷ **VERB** 6 = **deceive**, trap, take someone in (*informal*), fool, cheat, con (*informal*), kid (*informal*), mislead, scam (*slang*)
trickle VERB 1 = **dribble**, run, drop, stream, drip, ooze, seep, exude ▷ **NOUN** 2 = **dribble**, drip, seepage, thin stream
tricky 1 = **difficult**, sensitive, complicated, delicate, risky, hairy (*informal*), problematic, thorny **OPPOSITE:** simple 2 = **crafty**, scheming, cunning, slippery, sly, devious, wily, artful **OPPOSITE:** open
trifle = **knick-knack**, toy, plaything, bauble, bagatelle
trifling = **insignificant**, trivial, worthless, negligible, unimportant, paltry, measly **OPPOSITE:** significant
trigger = **bring about**, start, cause, produce, generate, prompt, provoke, set off **OPPOSITE:** prevent
trim ADJECTIVE 1 = **neat**, smart, tidy, spruce, dapper, natty (*informal*), well-groomed, shipshape **OPPOSITE:** untidy 2 = **slender**, fit, slim, sleek, streamlined, shapely, svelte, willowy

▷ **VERB** 3 = **cut**, crop, clip, shave, tidy, prune, pare, even up 4 = **decorate**, dress, array, adorn, ornament, embellish, deck out, beautify
▷ **NOUN** 5 = **decoration**, edging, border, piping, trimming, frill, embellishment, adornment 6 = **condition**, health, shape (*informal*), fitness, wellness, fettle 7 = **cut**, crop, clipping, shave, pruning, shearing, tidying up
trimming **NOUN** 1 = **decoration**, edging, border, piping, frill, embellishment, adornment, ornamentation
▷ **PLURAL NOUN** 2 = **extras**, accessories, ornaments, accompaniments, frills, trappings, paraphernalia
trinity = **threesome**, trio, triad, triumvirate
trio = **threesome**, trinity, trilogy, triad, triumvirate
trip **NOUN** 1 = **journey**, outing, excursion, day out, run, drive, tour, spin (*informal*) 2 = **stumble**, fall, slip, misstep
▷ **VERB** 3 *often with* **up** = **stumble**, fall, fall over, slip, tumble, topple, stagger, misstep 4 = **skip**, dance, hop, gambol
▷ **PHRASES: trip someone up** = **catch out**, trap, wrongfoot
triple **ADJECTIVE** 1 = **treble**, three times 2 = **three-way**, threefold, tripartite

▷ **VERB** 3 = **treble**, increase threefold
triumph **NOUN** 1 = **success**, victory, accomplishment, achievement, coup, feat, conquest, attainment **OPPOSITE:** failure 2 = **joy**, pride, happiness, rejoicing, elation, jubilation, exultation
▷ **VERB** 3 *often with* **over** = **succeed**, win, overcome, prevail, prosper, vanquish **OPPOSITE:** fail 4 = **rejoice**, celebrate, glory, revel, gloat, exult, crow
triumphant 1 = **victorious**, winning, successful, conquering **OPPOSITE:** defeated 2 = **celebratory**, jubilant, proud, elated, exultant, cock-a-hoop
trivial = **unimportant**, small, minor, petty, meaningless, worthless, trifling, insignificant **OPPOSITE:** important
troop **NOUN** 1 = **group**, company, team, body, unit, band, crowd, squad 2 *plural* = **soldiers**, men, armed forces, servicemen, army, soldiery
▷ **VERB** 3 = **flock**, march, stream, swarm, throng, traipse (*informal*)
trophy 1 = **prize**, cup, award, laurels 2 = **souvenir**, spoils, relic, memento, booty, keepsake
tropical = **hot**, stifling, steamy, torrid, sultry, sweltering **OPPOSITE:** cold

trot VERB 1 = **run**, jog, scamper, lope, canter
▷ NOUN 2 = **run**, jog, lope, canter

trouble NOUN 1 = **bother**, problems, concern, worry, stress, difficulty (*informal*), anxiety, distress 2 *often plural* = **distress**, problem, worry, pain, anxiety, grief, torment, sorrow OPPOSITE: pleasure 3 = **ailment**, disease, failure, complaint, illness, disorder, defect, malfunction 4 = **disorder**, fighting, conflict, bother, unrest, disturbance, to-do (*informal*), furore, biffo (*Austral slang*), boilover (*Austral*) OPPOSITE: peace 5 = **effort**, work, thought, care, labour, pains, hassle (*informal*), inconvenience OPPOSITE: convenience
▷ VERB 6 = **bother**, worry, upset, disturb, distress, plague, pain, sadden OPPOSITE: please 7 = **afflict**, hurt, bother, cause discomfort to, pain, grieve 8 = **inconvenience**, disturb, burden, put out, impose upon, incommode OPPOSITE: relieve 9 = **take pains**, take the time, make an effort, exert yourself OPPOSITE: avoid

troublesome 1 = **bothersome**, trying, taxing, demanding, difficult, worrying, annoying, tricky OPPOSITE: simple 2 = **disorderly**, violent, turbulent, rebellious, unruly, rowdy, undisciplined, uncooperative OPPOSITE: well-behaved

trough = **manger**, water trough

truce = **ceasefire**, peace, moratorium, respite, lull, cessation, let-up (*informal*), armistice

true 1 = **correct**, right, accurate, precise, factual, truthful, veracious OPPOSITE: false 2 = **actual**, real, genuine, proper, authentic, dinkum, dinky-di (*Austral & NZ informal*) 3 = **faithful**, loyal, devoted, dedicated, steady, reliable, staunch, trustworthy OPPOSITE: unfaithful 4 = **exact**, perfect, accurate, precise, spot-on (*Brit informal*), on target, unerring OPPOSITE: inaccurate

truly 1 = **genuinely**, correctly, truthfully, rightly, precisely, exactly, legitimately, authentically OPPOSITE: falsely 2 = **really**, very, greatly, indeed, extremely 3 = **faithfully**, steadily, sincerely, staunchly, dutifully, loyally, devotedly

trumpet NOUN 1 = **horn**, clarion, bugle
▷ VERB 2 = **proclaim**, advertise, tout (*informal*), announce, broadcast, shout from the rooftops OPPOSITE: keep secret

trunk 1 = **stem**, stalk, bole 2 = **chest**, case, box, crate, coffer, casket 3 = **body**, torso 4 = **snout**, nose, proboscis

trust NOUN 1 = **confidence**, credit, belief, faith, expectation, conviction, assurance, certainty **OPPOSITE:** distrust
▷ VERB 2 = **believe in**, have faith in, depend on, count on, bank on, rely upon **OPPOSITE:** distrust 3 = **entrust**, commit, assign, confide, consign, put into the hands of, allow to look after, hand over 4 = **expect**, hope, suppose, assume, presume, surmise

trustful or **trusting** = **unsuspecting**, naive, gullible, unwary, credulous, unsuspicious **OPPOSITE:** suspicious

truth 1 = **reality**, fact(s), real life **OPPOSITE:** unreality 2 = **truthfulness**, fact, accuracy, precision, validity, legitimacy, veracity, genuineness **OPPOSITE:** inaccuracy

try VERB 1 = **attempt**, seek, aim, strive, struggle, endeavour, have a go, make an effort 2 = **experiment with**, try out, put to the test, test, taste, examine, investigate, sample
▷ NOUN 3 = **attempt**, go (informal), shot (informal), effort, crack (informal), stab (informal), bash (informal), whack (informal)

trying = **annoying**, hard, taxing, difficult, tough, stressful, exasperating, tiresome **OPPOSITE:** straightforward

tuck VERB 1 = **push**, stick, stuff, slip, ease, insert, pop (informal)
▷ NOUN 2 (Brit informal) = **food**, grub (slang), kai (NZ informal), nosh (slang) 3 = **fold**, gather, pleat, pinch

tug VERB 1 = **pull**, pluck, jerk, yank, wrench 2 = **drag**, pull, haul, tow, lug, heave, draw
▷ NOUN 3 = **pull**, jerk, yank

tuition = **training**, schooling, education, teaching, lessons, instruction, tutoring, tutelage

tumble VERB 1 = **fall**, drop, topple, plummet, stumble, flop
▷ NOUN 2 = **fall**, drop, trip, plunge, spill, stumble

tumour = **growth**, cancer, swelling, lump, carcinoma (pathology), sarcoma (medical)

tune NOUN 1 = **melody**, air, song, theme, strain(s), jingle, ditty, choon (slang) 2 = **harmony**, pitch, euphony
▷ VERB 3 = **tune up**, adjust 4 = **regulate**, adapt, modulate, harmonize, attune, pitch

tunnel NOUN 1 = **passage**, underpass, passageway, subway, channel, hole, shaft
▷ VERB 2 = **dig**, burrow, mine, bore, drill, excavate

turbulent = **stormy**, rough, raging, tempestuous, furious, foaming, agitated, tumultuous **OPPOSITE:** calm

turf 1 = **grass**, sward 2 = **sod**
▷ PHRASES: **the turf** = **horse-racing**, the flat, racing

turmoil = **confusion**, disorder, chaos, upheaval, disarray,

t

uproar, agitation, commotion
OPPOSITE: peace
turn VERB **1** *sometimes with*
round = change course,
swing round, wheel round,
veer, move, switch, shift,
swerve **2 = rotate**, spin, go
round (and round), revolve,
roll, circle, twist, spiral **3** *with*
into = change, transform,
shape, convert, alter, mould,
remodel, mutate **4 = shape**,
form, fashion, cast, frame,
mould, make **5 = go bad**, go off
(*Brit informal*), curdle **6 = make
rancid**, spoil, sour, taint
▷ NOUN **7 = rotation**, cycle,
circle, revolution, spin, twist,
whirl, swivel **8 = change of
direction**, shift, departure,
deviation **9 = direction**,
course, tack, tendency, drift
10 = opportunity, go, time, try,
chance, crack (*informal*), stint
11 = deed, service, act, action,
favour, gesture
▷ PHRASES: **turn on someone
= attack**, assault, fall on, round
on, lash out at, assail, lay into
(*informal*), let fly at ▶ **turn
someone on** (*slang*) **= arouse**,
attract, excite, thrill, stimulate,
please, titillate ▶ **turn
something down 1 = refuse**,
decline, reject, spurn, rebuff,
repudiate **2 = lower**, soften,
mute, lessen, muffle, quieten
▶ **turn something in = hand in**,
return, deliver, give up, hand

over, submit, surrender, tender
▶ **turn something off = switch
off**, turn out, put out, stop, cut
out, shut down, unplug, flick off
▶ **turn something on = switch
on**, activate, start, start
up, ignite, kick-start ▶ **turn
something up 1 = find**, reveal,
discover, expose, disclose,
unearth, dig up **2 = increase**,
raise, boost, enhance, intensify,
amplify ▶ **turn up 1 = arrive**,
come, appear, show up
(*informal*), attend, put in an
appearance, show your face
2 = come to light, show up, pop
up, materialize
turning 1 = turn-off, turn,
junction, crossroads, side road,
exit **2 = bend**, turn, curve
turning point = crossroads,
change, crisis, crux, moment of
truth, tipping point
turnout = attendance, crowd,
audience, gate, assembly,
congregation, number, throng
turnover 1 = output, business,
productivity **2 = movement**,
coming and going, change
turtle
• *See panel* REPTILES
tutor NOUN **1 = teacher**, coach,
instructor, educator, guide,
guardian, lecturer, guru
▷ VERB **2 = teach**, educate,
school, train, coach, guide, drill,
instruct
twig = branch, stick, sprig,
shoot, spray

twilight 1 = **dusk**, evening, sunset, early evening, nightfall, sundown, gloaming (*Scot poetic*), close of day, evo (*Austral slang*) **OPPOSITE:** dawn 2 = **half-light**, gloom, dimness, semi-darkness

twin NOUN 1 = **double**, counterpart, mate, match, fellow, clone, duplicate, lookalike
▷ VERB 2 = **pair**, match, join, couple, link, yoke

twinkle VERB 1 = **sparkle**, flash, shine, glitter, gleam, blink, flicker, shimmer
▷ NOUN 2 = **sparkle**, flash, spark, gleam, flicker, shimmer, glimmer

twist VERB 1 = **coil**, curl, wind, wrap, screw, twirl 2 = **intertwine** 3 = **distort**, screw up, contort, mangle, mangulate (*Austral slang*) **OPPOSITE:** straighten
▷ NOUN 4 = **surprise**, change, turn, development, revelation 5 = **development**, emphasis, variation, slant 6 = **wind**, turn, spin, swivel, twirl 7 = **curve**, turn, bend, loop, arc, kink, zigzag, dog-leg

twitch VERB 1 = **jerk**, flutter, jump, squirm 2 = **pull (at)**, tug (at), pluck (at), yank (at)
▷ NOUN 3 = **jerk**, tic, spasm, jump, flutter

tycoon = **magnate**, capitalist, baron, industrialist, financier, fat cat (*slang, chiefly US*), mogul, plutocrat

type = **kind**, sort, class, variety, group, order, style, species

typical 1 = **archetypal**, standard, model, normal, stock, representative, usual, regular **OPPOSITE:** unusual 2 = **characteristic** 3 = **average**, normal, usual, routine, regular, orthodox, predictable, run-of-the-mill

tyranny = **oppression**, cruelty, dictatorship, authoritarianism, despotism, autocracy, absolutism, high-handedness **OPPOSITE:** liberality

t

Uu

ubiquitous = **ever-present**, pervasive, omnipresent, everywhere, universal

ugly 1 = **unattractive**, homely (*chiefly US*), plain, unsightly, unlovely, unprepossessing, ill-favoured **OPPOSITE:** beautiful 2 = **unpleasant**, shocking, terrible, nasty, distasteful, horrid, objectionable, disagreeable **OPPOSITE:** pleasant 3 = **bad-tempered**, dangerous, menacing, sinister, baleful **OPPOSITE:** good-natured

ulcer = **sore**, abscess, peptic ulcer, gumboil

ultimate 1 = **final**, last, end 2 = **supreme**, highest, greatest, paramount, superlative 3 = **worst**, greatest, utmost, extreme 4 = **best**, greatest, supreme, optimum, quintessential

ultimately 1 = **finally**, eventually, in the end, after all, at last, sooner or later, in due time 2 = **fundamentally**, essentially, basically, primarily, at heart, deep down

umpire NOUN 1 = **referee**, judge, arbiter, arbitrator, umpie (*Austral slang*)
▷ VERB 2 = **referee**, judge, adjudicate, arbitrate

unable *with* **to** = **incapable**, powerless, unfit, impotent, unqualified, ineffectual **OPPOSITE:** able

unanimous 1 = **agreed**, united, in agreement, harmonious, like-minded, of the same mind **OPPOSITE:** divided 2 = **united**, common, concerted, solid, consistent, harmonious, undivided, congruent **OPPOSITE:** split

unarmed = **defenceless**, helpless, unprotected **OPPOSITE:** armed

unaware = **ignorant**, unconscious, oblivious, uninformed, unknowing, not in the loop (*informal*) **OPPOSITE:** aware

unbearable = **intolerable**, insufferable, too much (*informal*), unacceptable **OPPOSITE:** tolerable

unborn = **expected**, awaited, embryonic

uncertain = **unsure**, undecided, vague, unclear, dubious, hazy, irresolute **OPPOSITE:** sure

uncertainty 1 = **unpredictability**, precariousness, ambiguity, unreliability, fickleness, chanciness, changeableness

OPPOSITE: predictability
2 = **doubt**, confusion **OPPOSITE:**
confidence 3 = **hesitancy**,
indecision

uncomfortable 1 = **uneasy**,
troubled, disturbed,
embarrassed, awkward,
discomfited **OPPOSITE:**
comfortable 2 = **painful**,
awkward, rough

uncommon 1 = **rare**, unusual,
odd, novel, strange, peculiar,
scarce, queer **OPPOSITE:**
common 2 = **extraordinary**,
remarkable, special,
outstanding, distinctive,
exceptional, notable **OPPOSITE:**
ordinary

uncompromising = **inflexible**,
strict, rigid, firm, tough,
inexorable, intransigent,
unbending

unconditional = **absolute**, full,
complete, total, positive, entire,
outright, unlimited **OPPOSITE:**
qualified

unconscious 1 = **senseless**,
knocked out, out cold
(*informal*), out, stunned,
dazed, in a coma, stupefied
OPPOSITE: awake 2 = **unaware**,
ignorant, oblivious,
unknowing **OPPOSITE:** aware
3 = **unintentional**, unwitting,
inadvertent, accidental
OPPOSITE: intentional

uncover 1 = **reveal**, expose,
disclose, divulge, make known
OPPOSITE: conceal 2 = **open**,

unveil, unwrap, show, strip,
expose, bare, lay bare

under PREPOSITION 1 = **below**,
beneath, underneath **OPPOSITE:**
over 2 = **subordinate to**, subject
to, governed by, secondary to
▷ ADVERB 3 = **below**, down,
beneath **OPPOSITE:** up

undercover = **secret**, covert,
private, hidden, concealed
OPPOSITE: open

underdog = **weaker party**, little
fellow (*informal*), outsider

underestimate
1 = **undervalue**, understate,
diminish, play down, minimize,
downgrade, miscalculate,
trivialize **OPPOSITE:**
overestimate 2 = **underrate**,
undervalue, belittle **OPPOSITE:**
overrate

> **USAGE NOTE**
> *Underestimate* is sometimes
> wrongly used where
> *overestimate* is meant: *The
> importance of his work cannot
> be overestimated* (not *cannot be
> underestimated*).

undergo = **experience**, go
through, stand, suffer, bear,
sustain, endure

underground
1 = **subterranean**, basement,
lower-level, sunken, covered,
buried, subterrestrial 2 = **secret**,
covert, hidden, guerrilla,
revolutionary, confidential,
dissident, closet
▷ PHRASES: **the underground**

u

1 = **the tube** (*Brit*), the subway, the metro 2 = **the Resistance**, partisans, freedom fighters

underline 1 = **emphasize**, stress, highlight, accentuate **OPPOSITE:** minimize
2 = **underscore**, mark

underlying = **fundamental**, basic, prime, primary, elementary, intrinsic

undermine = **weaken**, sabotage, subvert, compromise, disable **OPPOSITE:** reinforce

understand 1 = **comprehend**, get, take in, perceive, grasp, see, follow, realize 2 = **believe**, gather, think, see, suppose, notice, assume, fancy

understandable = **reasonable**, natural, justified, expected, inevitable, legitimate, predictable, accountable

understanding NOUN
1 = **perception**, knowledge, grasp, sense, know-how (*informal*), judgment, awareness, appreciation **OPPOSITE:** ignorance 2 = **agreement**, deal, promise, arrangement, accord, contract, bond, pledge **OPPOSITE:** disagreement
3 = **belief**, view, opinion, impression, interpretation, feeling, idea, notion
▷ ADJECTIVE 4 = **sympathetic**, kind, compassionate, considerate, patient, sensitive, tolerant **OPPOSITE:** unsympathetic

undertake = **agree**, promise, contract, guarantee, engage, pledge

undertaking 1 = **task**, business, operation, project, attempt, effort, affair, venture
2 = **promise**, commitment, pledge, word, vow, assurance

underwear = **underclothes**, lingerie, undies (*informal*), undergarments, underthings, broekies (*S African informal*), underdaks (*Austral slang*)

underworld 1 = **criminals**, gangsters, organized crime, gangland (*informal*) 2 = **nether world**, Hades, nether regions

underwrite = **finance**, back, fund, guarantee, sponsor, insure, ratify, subsidize

undesirable = **unwanted**, unwelcome, disagreeable, objectionable, unacceptable, unsuitable, unattractive, distasteful **OPPOSITE:** desirable

undo 1 = **open**, unfasten, loose, untie, unbutton, disentangle
2 = **reverse**, cancel, offset, neutralize, invalidate, annul
3 = **ruin**, defeat, destroy, wreck, shatter, upset, undermine, overturn

undone = **unfinished**, left, neglected, omitted, unfulfilled, unperformed **OPPOSITE:** finished

undoubtedly = **certainly**, definitely, surely, doubtless, without doubt, assuredly

u

unearth 1 = discover, find, reveal, expose, uncover **2 = dig up**, excavate, exhume, dredge up

unearthly = eerie, strange, supernatural, ghostly, weird, phantom, uncanny, spooky (*informal*)

uneasy 1 = anxious, worried, troubled, nervous, disturbed, uncomfortable, edgy, perturbed **OPPOSITE:** relaxed **2 = precarious**, strained, uncomfortable, tense, awkward, shaky, insecure

unemployed = out of work, redundant, laid off, jobless, idle **OPPOSITE:** working

unfair 1 = biased, prejudiced, unjust, one-sided, partial, partisan, bigoted **2 = unscrupulous**, dishonest, unethical, wrongful, unsporting **OPPOSITE:** ethical

unfit 1 = out of shape, feeble, unhealthy, flabby, in poor condition **OPPOSITE:** healthy **2 = incapable**, inadequate, incompetent, no good, useless, unqualified **OPPOSITE:** capable **3 = unsuitable**, inadequate, useless, unsuited **OPPOSITE:** suitable

unfold 1 = reveal, tell, present, show, disclose, uncover, divulge, make known **2 = open**, spread out, undo, expand, unfurl, unwrap, unroll

unfortunate 1 = disastrous, calamitous, adverse, ill-fated

OPPOSITE: opportune **2 = regrettable**, deplorable, lamentable, unsuitable, unbecoming **OPPOSITE:** becoming **3 = unlucky**, unhappy, doomed, cursed, unsuccessful, hapless, wretched **OPPOSITE:** fortunate

unhappy 1 = sad, depressed, miserable, blue, melancholy, mournful, dejected, despondent **OPPOSITE:** happy **2 = unlucky**, unfortunate, hapless, cursed, wretched, ill-fated **OPPOSITE:** fortunate

unhealthy 1 = harmful, detrimental, unwholesome, insanitary, insalubrious **OPPOSITE:** beneficial **2 = sick**, sickly, unwell, delicate, crook (*Austral & NZ informal*), ailing, frail, feeble, invalid **OPPOSITE:** well **3 = weak**, ailing **OPPOSITE:** strong

unification = union, uniting, alliance, coalition, federation, confederation, amalgamation, coalescence

uniform NOUN 1 = regalia, suit, livery, colours, habit **2 = outfit**, dress, costume, attire, gear (*informal*), get-up (*informal*), ensemble, garb
▷ **ADJECTIVE 3 = consistent**, unvarying, similar, even, same, matching, regular, constant **OPPOSITE:** varying **4 = alike**, similar, like, same, equal

unify = unite, join, combine, merge, consolidate,

u

confederate, amalgamate **OPPOSITE:** divide

union 1 = **joining**, uniting, unification, combination, coalition, merger, mixture, blend 2 = **alliance**, league, association, coalition, federation, confederacy

unique 1 = **distinct**, special, exclusive, peculiar, only, single, lone, solitary 2 = **unparalleled**, unmatched, unequalled, matchless, without equal

> **USAGE NOTE**
> *Unique* with the meaning 'being the only one' or 'having no equal' describes an absolute state: *a case unique in British law*. In this use it cannot therefore be qualified; something is either *unique* or *not unique*. However, *unique* is also very commonly used in the sense of 'remarkable' or 'exceptional', particularly in the language of advertising, and in this meaning it can be used with qualifying words such as *rather*, *quite*, etc. Since many people object to this use, it is best avoided in formal and serious writing.

unit 1 = **entity**, whole, item, feature 2 = **section**, company, group, force, detail, division, cell, squad 3 = **measure**, quantity, measurement 4 = **part**, section, segment,

class, element, component, constituent, tutorial

unite 1 = **join**, link, combine, couple, blend, merge, unify, fuse **OPPOSITE:** separate 2 = **cooperate**, ally, join forces, band, pool, collaborate **OPPOSITE:** split

unity 1 = **union**, unification, coalition, federation, integration, confederation, amalgamation 2 = **wholeness**, integrity, oneness, union, entity, singleness **OPPOSITE:** disunity 3 = **agreement**, accord, consensus, harmony, solidarity, unison, assent, concord **OPPOSITE:** disagreement

universal 1 = **widespread**, general, common, whole, total, unlimited, overarching 2 = **global**, worldwide, international, pandemic

universally = **without exception**, everywhere, always, invariably

universe = **cosmos**, space, creation, nature, heavens, macrocosm, all existence

unknown 1 = **strange**, new, undiscovered, uncharted, unexplored, virgin, remote, alien 2 = **unidentified**, mysterious, anonymous, unnamed, nameless, incognito 3 = **obscure**, humble, unfamiliar **OPPOSITE:** famous

unlike 1 = **different from**, dissimilar to, distinct from,

u

unequal to **OPPOSITE:** similar to
2 = **contrasted with**, not like,
in contradiction to, in contrast
with *or* to, as opposed to,
differently from, opposite to
unlikely 1 = **improbable**,
doubtful, remote, slight,
faint **OPPOSITE:** probable
2 = **unbelievable**, incredible,
implausible, questionable
OPPOSITE: believable
unload 1 = **empty**, clear, unpack,
dump, discharge 2 = **unburden**
unnatural 1 = **abnormal**, odd,
strange, unusual, extraordinary,
perverted, queer, irregular
OPPOSITE: normal 2 = **false**,
forced, artificial, affected,
stiff, feigned, stilted, insincere
OPPOSITE: genuine
unpleasant 1 = **nasty**, bad,
horrid, distasteful, displeasing,
objectionable, disagreeable
OPPOSITE: nice 2 = **obnoxious**,
rude **OPPOSITE:** likable *or*
likeable
unravel 1 = **solve**, explain, work
out, resolve, figure out (*informal*)
2 = **undo**, separate, disentangle,
free, unwind, untangle
unrest = **discontent**, rebellion,
protest, strife, agitation,
discord, sedition, dissension
OPPOSITE: peace
unsettled 1 = **unstable**, shaky,
insecure, disorderly, unsteady
2 = **restless**, tense, shaken,
confused, disturbed, anxious,
agitated, flustered, adrenalized

3 = **inconstant**, changing,
variable, uncertain
unstable 1 = **changeable**,
volatile, unpredictable,
variable, fluctuating, fitful,
inconstant **OPPOSITE:** constant
2 = **insecure**, shaky, precarious,
unsettled, wobbly, tottering,
unsteady 3 = **unpredictable**,
irrational, erratic, inconsistent,
temperamental, capricious,
changeable **OPPOSITE:** level-
headed
unthinkable
1 = **impossible**, out of the
question, inconceivable,
absurd, unreasonable
2 = **inconceivable**, incredible,
unimaginable
until PREPOSITION 1 = **till**, up
to, up till, up to the time, as late
as 2 = **before**, up to, prior to, in
advance of, previous to, pre-
▷ CONJUNCTION 3 = **till**, up to,
up till, up to the time, as late
as 4 = **before**, up to, prior to, in
advance of, previous to

> **USAGE NOTE**
> The use of *until such time as* (as
> in *Industrial action will continue
> until such time as our demands
> are met*) is unnecessary and
> should be avoided: *Industrial
> action will continue until our
> demands are met*. The use of *up*
> before *until* is also redundant
> and should be avoided: *the
> talks will continue until* (not *up
> until*) *23rd March*.

u

untold 1 = **indescribable**, unthinkable, unimaginable, undreamed of, unutterable, inexpressible **2** = **countless**, incalculable, innumerable, myriad, numberless, uncountable

untrue 1 = **false**, lying, wrong, mistaken, incorrect, inaccurate, dishonest, deceptive **OPPOSITE:** true **2** = **unfaithful**, disloyal, deceitful, treacherous, faithless, false, untrustworthy, inconstant **OPPOSITE:** faithful

unusual 1 = **rare**, odd, strange, extraordinary, different, curious, queer, uncommon **OPPOSITE:** common **2** = **extraordinary**, unique, remarkable, exceptional, uncommon, singular, unconventional **OPPOSITE:** average

upbeat (*informal*) = **cheerful**, positive, optimistic, encouraging, hopeful, cheery

upbringing = **education**, training, breeding, rearing, raising

update = **bring up to date**, improve, correct, renew, revise, upgrade, amend, overhaul, refresh (~*a webpage*)

upgrade 1 = **improve**, better, update, reform, add to, enhance, refurbish, renovate **2** = **promote**, raise, advance, boost, move up, elevate, kick upstairs (*informal*), give

promotion to **OPPOSITE:** demote

upheaval = **disturbance**, revolution, disorder, turmoil, disruption

uphill 1 = **ascending**, rising, upward, mounting, climbing **OPPOSITE:** descending **2** = **arduous**, hard, taxing, difficult, tough, exhausting, gruelling, strenuous

uphold 1 = **support**, back, defend, aid, champion, maintain, promote, sustain **2** = **confirm**, endorse

uplift VERB **1** = **improve**, better, raise, advance, inspire, refine, edify
▷ NOUN **2** = **improvement**, enlightenment, advancement, refinement, enhancement, enrichment, edification

upper 1 = **topmost**, top **OPPOSITE:** bottom **2** = **higher**, high **OPPOSITE:** lower **3** = **superior**, senior, higher-level, greater, top, important, chief, most important **OPPOSITE:** inferior

upper class = **aristocratic**, upper-class, noble, high-class, patrician, blue-blooded, highborn

upright 1 = **vertical**, straight, standing up, erect, perpendicular, bolt upright **OPPOSITE:** horizontal **2** = **honest**, good, principled, just, ethical, honourable,

righteous, conscientious
OPPOSITE: dishonourable

uprising = **rebellion**, rising, revolution, revolt, disturbance, mutiny, insurrection, insurgence

uproar 1 = **commotion**, noise, racket, riot, turmoil, mayhem, din, pandemonium 2 = **protest**, outrage, complaint, objection, fuss, stink (*informal*), outcry, furore

upset ADJECTIVE 1 = **distressed**, shaken, disturbed, worried, troubled, hurt, bothered, unhappy 2 = **sick**, queasy, bad, ill
▷ VERB 3 = **distress**, trouble, disturb, worry, alarm, bother, grieve, agitate 4 = **tip over**, overturn, capsize, knock over, spill 5 = **mess up**, spoil, disturb, change, confuse, disorder, unsettle, disorganize
▷ NOUN 6 = **distress**, worry, trouble, shock, bother, disturbance, agitation 7 = **reversal**, shake-up (*informal*), defeat 8 = **illness**, complaint, disorder, bug (*informal*), sickness, malady

upside down *or* **upside-down** ADVERB 1 = **wrong side up**
▷ ADJECTIVE 2 = **inverted**, overturned, upturned 3 (*informal*) = **confused**, disordered, chaotic, muddled, topsy-turvy, higgledy-piggledy (*informal*)

up-to-date = **modern**, fashionable, trendy (*Brit informal*), current, stylish, in vogue, up-to-the-minute
OPPOSITE: out-of-date

urban = **civic**, city, town, metropolitan, municipal, dorp (*S African*)

urge VERB 1 = **beg**, exhort, plead, implore, beseech, entreat 2 = **advocate**, recommend, advise, support, counsel
OPPOSITE: discourage
▷ NOUN 3 = **impulse**, longing, wish, desire, drive, yearning, itch (*informal*), thirst **OPPOSITE:** reluctance

urgency = **importance**, need, necessity, gravity, pressure, hurry, seriousness, extremity

urgent = **crucial**, desperate, pressing, great, important, crying, critical, immediate
OPPOSITE: unimportant

usage 1 = **use**, operation, employment, running, control, management, handling 2 = **practice**, method, procedure, habit, regime, custom, routine, convention

use VERB 1 = **employ**, utilize, work, apply, operate, exercise, practise, resort to, call into play 2 *sometimes with* **up** = **consume**, exhaust, spend, run through, expend 3 = **take advantage of**, exploit, manipulate
▷ NOUN 4 = **usage**, employment, operation,

u

application **5** = **purpose**, end, reason, object **6** = **good**, point, help, service, value, benefit, profit, advantage

used = **second-hand**, cast-off, nearly new, shopsoiled, preloved (*Austral slang*)
OPPOSITE: new

used to = **accustomed to**, familiar with

useful = **helpful**, effective, valuable, practical, profitable, worthwhile, beneficial, fruitful
OPPOSITE: useless

useless 1 = **worthless**, valueless, impractical, fruitless, unproductive, ineffectual, unsuitable **OPPOSITE:** useful **2** = **pointless**, futile, vain **OPPOSITE:** worthwhile **3** (*informal*) = **inept**, no good, hopeless, incompetent, ineffectual

usher VERB **1** = **escort**, lead, direct, guide, conduct
▷ NOUN **2** = **attendant**, guide, doorman, escort, doorkeeper

usual = **normal**, customary, regular, general, common, standard, ordinary, typical
OPPOSITE: unusual

usually = **normally**, generally, mainly, commonly, mostly, on the whole, as a rule, habitually

utility = **usefulness**, benefit, convenience, practicality, efficacy, serviceableness

utilize = **use**, employ, deploy, take advantage of, make use of, put to use, bring into play, avail yourself of

utmost ADJECTIVE **1** = **greatest**, highest, maximum, supreme, paramount, pre-eminent **2** = **farthest**, extreme, last, final
▷ NOUN **3** = **best**, greatest, maximum, highest, hardest

utter¹ = **say**, state, speak, voice, express, deliver, declare, mouth

utter² = **absolute**, complete, total, sheer, outright, thorough, downright, unmitigated

utterly = **totally**, completely, absolutely, perfectly, fully, entirely, extremely, thoroughly

u

Vv

vacancy 1 = **opening**, job, post, place, position, role, situation, opportunity 2 = **room**, space, available accommodation, unoccupied room

vacant 1 = **empty**, free, available, abandoned, deserted, for sale, on the market, void **OPPOSITE:** occupied 2 = **unfilled**, unoccupied **OPPOSITE:** taken 3 = **blank**, vague, dreamy, empty, abstracted, idle, vacuous, inane **OPPOSITE:** thoughtful

vacuum 1 = **gap**, lack, absence, space, deficiency, void 2 = **emptiness**, space, void, gap, nothingness, vacuity

vague 1 = **unclear**, indefinite, hazy, confused, loose, uncertain, unsure, superficial **OPPOSITE:** clear 2 = **imprecise**, unspecified, generalized, rough, loose, ambiguous, hazy, equivocal 3 = **absent-minded**, distracted, vacant, preoccupied, oblivious, inattentive 4 = **indistinct**, unclear, faint,

hazy, indeterminate, nebulous, ill-defined **OPPOSITE:** distinct

vain 1 = **futile**, useless, pointless, unsuccessful, idle, worthless, senseless, fruitless **OPPOSITE:** successful 2 = **conceited**, narcissistic, proud, arrogant, swaggering, egotistical, self-important **OPPOSITE:** modest ▷ **PHRASES:** in vain 1 = **useless**, to no avail, unsuccessful, fruitless, vain 2 = **uselessly**, to no avail, unsuccessfully, fruitlessly, vainly, ineffectually

valid 1 = **sound**, good, reasonable, telling, convincing, rational, logical, viable **OPPOSITE:** unfounded 2 = **legal**, official, legitimate, genuine, authentic, lawful, bona fide **OPPOSITE:** invalid

validity 1 = **soundness**, force, power, weight, strength, cogency 2 = **legality**, authority, legitimacy, right, lawfulness

valley = **hollow**, dale, glen, vale, depression, dell

valuable ADJECTIVE 1 = **useful**, important, profitable, worthwhile, beneficial, helpful **OPPOSITE:** useless 2 = **treasured**, prized, precious 3 = **precious**, expensive, costly, dear, high-priced, priceless, irreplaceable **OPPOSITE:** worthless ▷ **PLURAL NOUN** 4 = **treasures**, prized possessions, precious

V

items, heirlooms, personal
effects, costly articles
value NOUN 1 = **importance**,
benefit, worth, merit, point,
service, sense, profit **OPPOSITE:**
worthlessness 2 = **cost**, price,
worth, rate, market price, face
value, asking price, selling price
▷ PLURAL NOUN 3 = **principles**,
morals, ethics, mores, standards
of behaviour, (moral) standards
▷ VERB 4 = **appreciate**, rate,
prize, regard highly, respect,
admire, treasure, esteem
OPPOSITE: undervalue 5 *with*
at = **evaluate**, price, estimate,
rate, cost, assess, set at,
appraise
vanish 1 = **disappear**, dissolve,
evaporate, fade away, melt
away, evanesce **OPPOSITE:**
appear 2 = **die out**, disappear,
pass away, end, fade, dwindle,
cease to exist, become extinct
vanity = **pride**, arrogance,
conceit, narcissism, egotism,
conceitedness **OPPOSITE:**
modesty
variable = **changeable**,
unstable, fluctuating,
shifting, flexible, uneven,
temperamental, unsteady
OPPOSITE: constant
variant ADJECTIVE 1 = **different**,
alternative, modified, divergent
▷ NOUN 2 = **variation**, form,
version, development,
alternative, adaptation,
revision, modification

variation 1 = **alternative**,
variety, modification, departure,
innovation, variant 2 = **variety**,
change, deviation, difference,
diversity, diversion, novelty
OPPOSITE: uniformity
varied = **different**, mixed,
various, diverse, assorted,
miscellaneous, sundry, motley
OPPOSITE: unvarying
variety 1 = **diversity**,
change, variation, difference,
diversification, heterogeneity,
multifariousness **OPPOSITE:**
uniformity 2 = **range**, selection,
assortment, mix, collection,
line-up, mixture, array 3 = **type**,
sort, kind, class, brand, species,
breed, strain
various DETERMINER
1 = **different**, assorted,
miscellaneous, varied, distinct,
diverse, disparate, sundry
OPPOSITE: similar
▷ ADJECTIVE 2 = **many**,
numerous, countless, several,
abundant, innumerable, sundry,
profuse

> **USAGE NOTE**
> The use of *different* after
> *various*, which seems to be
> most common in speech, is
> unnecessary and should be
> avoided in serious writing:
> *The disease exists in various*
> *forms* (not *in various different*
> *forms*).

varnish NOUN 1 = **lacquer**,
polish, glaze, gloss

▷ VERB 2 = **lacquer**, polish, glaze, gloss

vary 1 = **differ**, be different, be dissimilar, disagree, diverge 2 = **change**, shift, swing, alter, fluctuate, oscillate, see-saw 3 = **alternate**

vast = **huge**, massive, enormous, great, wide, immense, gigantic, monumental **OPPOSITE:** tiny

vault[1] 1 = **strongroom**, repository, depository 2 = **crypt**, tomb, catacomb, cellar, mausoleum, charnel house, undercroft

vault[2] = **jump**, spring, leap, clear, bound, hurdle

veer = **change direction**, turn, swerve, shift, sheer, change course

vehicle 1 = **conveyance**, machine, motor vehicle 2 = **medium**, means, channel, mechanism, organ, apparatus

veil NOUN 1 = **mask**, cover, shroud, film, curtain, cloak 2 = **screen**, mask, disguise, blind 3 = **film**, cover, curtain, cloak, shroud
▷ VERB 4 = **cover**, screen, hide, mask, shield, disguise, conceal, obscure **OPPOSITE:** reveal

veiled = **disguised**, implied, hinted at, covert, masked, concealed, suppressed

vein 1 = **blood vessel** 2 = **mood**, style, note, tone, mode, temper, tenor 3 = **seam**, layer, stratum, course, current, bed, deposit, streak

velocity = **speed**, pace, rapidity, quickness, swiftness

vengeance = **revenge**, retaliation, reprisal, retribution, requital **OPPOSITE:** forgiveness

vent NOUN 1 = **outlet**, opening, aperture, duct, orifice
▷ VERB 2 = **express**, release, voice, air, discharge, utter, emit, pour out **OPPOSITE:** hold back

venture VERB 1 = **go**, travel, journey, set out, wander, stray, plunge into, rove 2 = **dare**, presume, have the courage to, be brave enough, hazard, go out on a limb (*informal*), take the liberty, go so far as 3 = **put forward**, volunteer
▷ NOUN 4 = **undertaking**, project, enterprise, campaign, risk, operation, activity, scheme

verbal = **spoken**, oral, word-of-mouth, unwritten

verdict = **decision**, finding, judgment, opinion, sentence, conclusion, conviction, adjudication

verge 1 = **brink**, point, edge, threshold 2 (*Brit*) = **border**, edge, margin, limit, boundary, threshold, brim
▷ PHRASES: verge on something = **come near to**, approach, border on, resemble, incline to, be similar to, touch on, be more or less

V

verify 1 = **check**, make sure, examine, monitor, inspect 2 = **confirm**, prove, substantiate, support, validate, bear out, corroborate, authenticate **OPPOSITE:** disprove

versatile 1 = **adaptable**, flexible, all-round, resourceful, multifaceted **OPPOSITE:** unadaptable 2 = **all-purpose**, variable, adjustable **OPPOSITE:** limited

versed with in = **knowledgeable**, experienced, seasoned, familiar, practised, acquainted, well-informed, proficient **OPPOSITE:** ignorant

version 1 = **form**, variety, variant, sort, class, design, style, model 2 = **adaptation**, edition, interpretation, form, copy, rendering, reproduction, portrayal 3 = **account**, report, description, record, reading, story, view, understanding

vertical = **upright**, sheer, perpendicular, straight (up and down), erect, plumb, on end, precipitous, vertiginous **OPPOSITE:** horizontal

very ADVERB 1 = **extremely**, highly, greatly, really, deeply, unusually, profoundly, decidedly ▷ ADJECTIVE 2 = **exact**, precise, selfsame 3 = **ideal**

vessel 1 = **ship**, boat, craft 2 = **container**, receptacle, can, bowl, tank, pot, drum, barrel

vest
▷ PHRASES: vest in something or someone usually passive = **place**, invest, entrust, settle, confer, endow, bestow, consign ▶ vest with something usually passive = **endow with**, entrust with

vet NOUN 1 = **veterinary surgeon**, veterinarian (US), animal doctor
▷ VERB 2 = **check**, examine, investigate, review, appraise, scrutinize

veteran NOUN 1 = **old hand**, past master, warhorse (informal), old stager **OPPOSITE:** novice
▷ MODIFIER 2 = **long-serving**, seasoned, experienced, old, established, qualified, mature, practised

veto NOUN 1 = **ban**, dismissal, rejection, vetoing, boycott, embargo, prohibiting, prohibition **OPPOSITE:** ratification
▷ VERB 2 = **ban**, block, reject, rule out, turn down, forbid, boycott, prohibit **OPPOSITE:** pass

viable = **workable**, practical, feasible, suitable, realistic, operational, applicable, usable **OPPOSITE:** unworkable

vibrant 1 = **energetic**, dynamic, sparkling, vivid, spirited, storming, alive, vigorous 2 = **vivid**, bright, brilliant, intense, clear, rich, glowing

v

vice 1 = **fault**, failing, weakness, limitation, defect, deficiency, flaw, shortcoming **OPPOSITE**: good point 2 = **wickedness**, evil, corruption, sin, depravity, immorality, iniquity, turpitude **OPPOSITE**: virtue

vice versa = **the other way round**, conversely, in reverse, contrariwise

vicious 1 = **savage**, brutal, violent, cruel, ferocious, barbarous **OPPOSITE**: gentle 2 = **malicious**, vindictive, spiteful, mean, cruel, venomous **OPPOSITE**: complimentary

victim 1 = **casualty**, sufferer, fatality **OPPOSITE**: survivor 2 = **scapegoat**, sacrifice, martyr

victor = **winner**, champion, conqueror, vanquisher, prizewinner **OPPOSITE**: loser

victorious = **winning**, successful, triumphant, first, champion, conquering, vanquishing, prizewinning **OPPOSITE**: losing

victory = **win**, success, triumph, conquest, walkover (*informal*) **OPPOSITE**: defeat

vie with **with** or **for** = **compete**, struggle, contend, strive

view NOUN 1*sometimes plural* = **opinion**, belief, feeling, attitude, impression, conviction, point of view, sentiment 2 = **scene**, picture, sight, prospect, perspective, landscape, outlook, spectacle 3 = **vision**, sight, visibility, perspective, eyeshot ▷ VERB 4 = **regard**, see, consider, perceive, treat, estimate, reckon, deem

viewer = **watcher**, observer, spectator, onlooker

vigorous 1 = **strenuous**, energetic, arduous, hard, taxing, active, rigorous 2 = **spirited**, lively, energetic, active, dynamic, animated, forceful, feisty (*informal*) **OPPOSITE**: lethargic 3 = **strong**, powerful, lively, lusty **OPPOSITE**: weak

vigorously 1 = **energetically**, hard, forcefully, strongly, strenuously, lustily 2 = **forcefully**, strongly, vehemently, strenuously

vigour or (US) **vigor** = **energy**, vitality, power, spirit, strength, animation, verve, gusto **OPPOSITE**: weakness

vile 1 = **wicked**, evil, corrupt, perverted, degenerate, depraved, nefarious **OPPOSITE**: honourable 2 = **disgusting**, foul, revolting, offensive, nasty, sickening, horrid, repulsive, yucko (*Austral slang*) **OPPOSITE**: pleasant

villain 1 = **evildoer**, criminal, rogue, scoundrel, wretch, reprobate, miscreant, blackguard, wrong 'un (*Austral slang*) 2 = **baddy** (*informal*), antihero **OPPOSITE**: hero

V

vindicate 1 = **clear**, acquit, exonerate, absolve, let off the hook, exculpate **OPPOSITE:** condemn 2 = **support**, defend, excuse, justify

vintage NOUN 1 (of wine) = **harvest**
▷ ADJECTIVE 2 (of wines) = **high-quality**, best, prime, quality, choice, select, superior 3 = **classic**, old, veteran, historic, heritage, enduring, antique, timeless

violate 1 = **break**, infringe, disobey, transgress, ignore, defy, disregard, flout **OPPOSITE:** obey 2 = **invade**, infringe on, disturb, upset, shatter, disrupt, impinge on, encroach on 3 = **desecrate**, profane, defile, abuse, pollute, deface, dishonour, vandalize **OPPOSITE:** honour 4 = **rape**, molest, sexually assault, ravish, abuse, assault, interfere with, sexually abuse

violation 1 = **breach**, abuse, infringement, contravention, trespass, transgression, infraction 2 = **invasion**, intrusion, trespass, breach, disturbance, disruption, interruption, encroachment 3 = **desecration**, sacrilege, defilement, profanation, spoliation 4 = **rape**, sexual assault, molesting, ravishing (old-fashioned), abuse, sexual abuse, indecent assault, molestation

violence 1 = **brutality**, bloodshed, savagery, fighting, terrorism 2 = **force**, power, strength, might, ferocity, forcefulness, powerfulness 3 = **intensity**, force, cruelty, severity, fervour, vehemence

violent 1 = **brutal**, aggressive, savage, wild, fierce, bullying, cruel, vicious **OPPOSITE:** gentle 2 = **sharp** 3 = **passionate**, uncontrollable, unrestrained 4 = **fiery**, fierce, passionate

VIP = **celebrity**, big name, star, somebody, luminary, big hitter (informal), heavy hitter (informal)

virgin NOUN 1 = **maiden**, girl (archaic)
▷ ADJECTIVE 2 = **pure**, chaste, immaculate, virginal, vestal, uncorrupted, undefiled **OPPOSITE:** corrupted

virtual = **practical**, essential, in all but name

virtually = **practically**, almost, nearly, in effect, in essence, as good as, in all but name

virtue 1 = **goodness**, integrity, worth, morality, righteousness, probity, rectitude, incorruptibility **OPPOSITE:** vice 2 = **merit**, strength, asset, plus (informal), attribute, good point, strong point **OPPOSITE:** failing 3 = **advantage**, benefit, merit, credit, usefulness, efficacy

visible = **perceptible**, observable, clear, apparent,

evident, manifest, in view, discernible **OPPOSITE:** invisible

vision 1 = **image**, idea, dream, plans, hopes, prospect, ideal, concept 2 = **hallucination**, illusion, apparition, revelation, delusion, mirage, chimera 3 = **sight**, seeing, eyesight, view, perception 4 = **foresight**, imagination, perception, insight, awareness, inspiration, innovation, creativity

visionary ADJECTIVE 1 = **idealistic**, romantic, unrealistic, utopian, speculative, impractical, unworkable, quixotic **OPPOSITE:** realistic 2 = **prophetic**, mystical, predictive, oracular, sibylline
▷ NOUN 3 = **idealist**, romantic, dreamer, daydreamer **OPPOSITE:** realist 4 = **prophet**, diviner, mystic, seer, soothsayer, sibyl, scryer, spaewife (Scot)

visit VERB 1 = **call on**, drop in on (informal), stop by, look up, go see (US), swing by (informal) 2 = **stay at**, stay with, spend time with 3 = **stay in**, stop by
▷ NOUN 4 = **call**, social call 5 = **trip**, stop, stay, break, tour, holiday, vacation (informal), stopover

visitor = **guest**, caller, company, manu(w)hiri (NZ)

vista = **view**, scene, prospect, landscape, panorama, perspective

visual 1 = **optical**, optic, ocular 2 = **observable**, visible, perceptible, discernible **OPPOSITE:** imperceptible

vital 1 = **essential**, important, necessary, key, basic, significant, critical, crucial **OPPOSITE:** unnecessary 2 = **lively**, vigorous, energetic, spirited, dynamic, animated, vibrant, vivacious **OPPOSITE:** lethargic

vitality = **energy**, vivacity, life, strength, animation, vigour, exuberance, liveliness **OPPOSITE:** lethargy

vivid 1 = **clear**, detailed, realistic, telling, moving, affecting, arresting, powerful **OPPOSITE:** vague 2 = **bright**, brilliant, intense, clear, rich, glowing, colourful **OPPOSITE:** dull

vocabulary 1 = **language**, words, lexicon 2 = **wordbook**, dictionary, glossary, lexicon

vocal 1 = **outspoken**, frank, forthright, strident, vociferous, articulate, expressive, eloquent **OPPOSITE:** quiet 2 = **spoken**, voiced, uttered, oral, said

vocation = **profession**, calling, job, trade, career, mission, pursuit

vogue = **fashion**, trend, craze, style, mode, passing fancy, dernier cri (French)

voice NOUN 1 = **tone**, sound, articulation 2 = **utterance** 3 = **opinion**, will, feeling, wish,

V

desire 4 = **say**, view, vote, comment, input

▷ VERB 5 = **express**, declare, air, raise, reveal, mention, mouth, pronounce

| **RELATED WORD**
adjective: vocal

void ADJECTIVE 1 = **invalid**, null and void, inoperative, useless, ineffective, worthless

▷ NOUN 2 = **gap**, space, lack, hole, emptiness 3 = **emptiness**, space, vacuum, oblivion, blankness, nullity, vacuity

▷ VERB 4 = **invalidate**, nullify, cancel, withdraw, reverse, undo, repeal, quash

volatile 1 = **changeable**, shifting, variable, unsettled, unstable, explosive, unreliable, unsteady OPPOSITE: stable 2 = **temperamental**, erratic, mercurial, up and down (*informal*), fickle, over-emotional OPPOSITE: calm

volley = **barrage**, blast, burst, shower, hail, bombardment, salvo, fusillade

volume 1 = **amount**, quantity, level, body, total, measure, degree, mass 2 = **capacity**, size, mass, extent, proportions, dimensions, bulk, measurements 3 = **book**, work, title, opus, publication, manual, tome, treatise 4 = **loudness**, sound, amplification

voluntarily = **willingly**, freely, by choice, off your own bat, of

your own accord, of your own volition

voluntary 1 = **intentional**, deliberate, planned, calculated, wilful OPPOSITE: unintentional 2 = **optional**, discretionary, up to the individual, open, unforced, at your discretion, open to choice OPPOSITE: obligatory 3 = **unpaid**, free, willing, pro bono (*law*)

volunteer = **offer**, step forward OPPOSITE: refuse

vomit 1 = **be sick**, throw up (*informal*), spew, chuck (*Austral & NZ informal*), heave (*slang*), retch 2 *often with* **up** = **bring up**, throw up, regurgitate, emit (*informal*), disgorge, spew out *or* up

vote NOUN 1 = **poll**, election, ballot, referendum, popular vote, plebiscite, straw poll, show of hands

▷ VERB 2 = **cast your vote**

voucher = **ticket**, token, coupon, pass, slip, chit, chitty (*Brit informal*), docket

vow NOUN 1 = **promise**, commitment, pledge, oath, profession, avowal

▷ VERB 2 = **promise**, pledge, swear, commit, engage, affirm, avow, bind yourself

voyage NOUN 1 = **journey**, trip, passage, expedition, crossing, sail, cruise, excursion

▷ VERB 2 = **travel**, journey, tour, cruise, steam, take a trip, go on an expedition

v

vulgar 1 = tasteless, common
OPPOSITE: tasteful **2 = crude**,
rude, coarse, indecent,
tasteless, risqué, ribald
3 = uncouth, unrefined,
impolite, ill-bred **OPPOSITE:**
refined
vulnerable 1 = susceptible,
helpless, unprotected,
defenceless, exposed, weak,
sensitive, tender **OPPOSITE:**
immune **2** (*Military*) **= exposed**,
open, unprotected, defenceless,
accessible, wide open, assailable
OPPOSITE: well-protected

waddle = shuffle, totter, toddle,
sway, wobble
wade 1 = paddle, splash, splash
about, slop **2 = walk through**,
cross, ford, travel across
wag VERB 1 = wave, shake,
waggle, stir, quiver, vibrate,
wiggle **2 = waggle**, wave,
shake, flourish, brandish,
wobble, wiggle **3 = shake**,
bob, nod
▷ **NOUN 4 = wave**, shake, quiver,
vibration, wiggle, waggle
5 = nod, bob, shake
wage NOUN 1 *often plural*
= payment, pay, remuneration,
fee, reward, income, allowance,
recompense
▷ **VERB 2 = engage in**, conduct,
pursue, carry on, undertake,
practise, prosecute, proceed
with
wail VERB 1 = cry, weep, grieve,
lament, howl, bawl, yowl
▷ **NOUN 2 = cry**, moan, howl,
lament, yowl
wait VERB 1 = stay, remain,
stop, pause, rest, linger, loiter,
tarry **OPPOSITE:** go **2 = stand**

by, hold back, hang fire **3 = be postponed**, be suspended, be delayed, be put off, be put back, be deferred, be put on hold (*informal*), be shelved
▷ NOUN **4 = delay**, gap, pause, interval, stay, rest, halt, hold-up
waiter = attendant, server, flunkey, steward, servant
waitress = attendant, server, stewardess, servant
waive 1 = give up, relinquish, renounce, forsake, drop, abandon, set aside, dispense with OPPOSITE: claim
2 = disregard, ignore, discount, overlook, set aside, pass over, dispense with, brush aside
wake¹ VERB **1 = awake**, stir, awaken, come to, arise, get up, rouse, get out of bed OPPOSITE: fall asleep **2 = awaken**, arouse, rouse, waken **3 = evoke**, recall, renew, stimulate, revive, induce, arouse, call up
▷ NOUN **4 = vigil**, watch, funeral, deathwatch, tangi (*NZ*)

USAGE NOTE
Both *wake* and its synonym *waken* can be used either with or without an object: *I woke/wakened my sister*, and also *I woke/wakened (up) at noon*. *Wake*, *wake up*, and occasionally *waken*, can also be used in a figurative sense, for example *Seeing him again woke painful memories*; and *It's time he woke up to*

his responsibilities. The verbs *awake* and *awaken* are more commonly used in the figurative than the literal sense, for example *He awoke to the danger he was in*.
wake² = slipstream, wash, trail, backwash, train, track, waves, path
▷ PHRASES: **in the wake of = in the aftermath of**, following, because of, as a result of, on account of, as a consequence of
walk VERB **1 = stride**, stroll, go, move, step, march, pace, hike **2 = travel on foot 3 = escort**, take, see, show, partner, guide, conduct, accompany
▷ NOUN **4 = stroll**, hike, ramble, march, trek, trudge, promenade, saunter **5 = gait**, step, bearing, carriage, tread **6 = path**, footpath, track, way, road, lane, trail, avenue, berm (*NZ*)
▷ PHRASES: **walk of life = area**, calling, business, line, trade, class, field, career
walker = hiker, rambler, wayfarer, pedestrian
wall 1 = partition, screen, barrier, enclosure **2 = barrier**, obstacle, barricade, obstruction, check, bar, fence, impediment
wallet = purse, pocketbook, pouch, case, holder, moneybag, e-wallet or eWallet
wander VERB **1 = roam**, walk, drift, stroll, range, stray, ramble,

prowl
▷ **NOUN** 2 = **excursion**, walk,
stroll, cruise, ramble, meander,
promenade, mosey (*informal*)
wanderer = **traveller**, rover,
nomad, drifter, gypsy, explorer,
rambler, voyager
wane 1 = **decline**, weaken,
diminish, fail, fade, decrease,
dwindle, lessen **OPPOSITE:** grow
2 = **diminish**, decrease, dwindle
OPPOSITE: wax
want **VERB** 1 = **wish for**, desire,
long for, crave, covet, hope for,
yearn for, thirst for **OPPOSITE:**
have 2 = **need**, demand, require,
call for 3 = **should**, need, must,
ought 4 = **desire**, long for, crave,
wish for, yearn for, thirst for,
hanker after, burn for 5 = **lack**,
need, require, miss
▷ **NOUN** 6 = **lack**, need, absence,
shortage, deficiency, famine,
scarcity, dearth **OPPOSITE:**
abundance 7 = **poverty**,
hardship, privation, penury,
destitution, neediness,
pennilessness **OPPOSITE:** wealth
8 = **wish**, will, need, desire,
requirement, longing, appetite,
craving
wanting 1 = **deficient**, poor,
inadequate, insufficient,
faulty, defective, imperfect,
unsound, bodger *or* bodgie
(*Austral slang*) **OPPOSITE:**
adequate 2 = **lacking**, missing,
absent, incomplete, short, shy
OPPOSITE: complete

war **NOUN** 1 = **conflict**,
drive, attack, fighting, fight,
operation, battle, movement
OPPOSITE: peace 2 = **campaign**,
drive, attack, operation,
movement, push, mission,
offensive, cyberwar
▷ **VERB** 3 = **fight**, battle,
clash, wage war, campaign,
combat, do battle, take up arms
OPPOSITE: make peace
ward 1 = **room**, department,
unit, quarter, division,
section, apartment, cubicle
2 = **district**, constituency, area,
division, zone, parish, precinct
3 = **dependant**, charge, pupil,
minor, protégé
▷ **PHRASES:** ward someone
off = **drive off**, resist, fight
off, hold off, repel, fend
off ▶ ward something off
1 = **avert**, fend off, stave off,
avoid, frustrate, deflect, repel
2 = **parry**, avert, deflect, avoid,
repel, turn aside
warden 1 = **steward**, guardian,
administrator, superintendent,
caretaker, curator, custodian
2 (*chiefly US & Canad*) = **jailer**,
prison officer, guard, screw
(*slang*) 3 (*Brit*) = **governor**, head,
leader, director, manager, chief,
executive, commander, baas
(*S African*) 4 = **ranger**, keeper,
guardian, protector, custodian,
official
wardrobe 1 = **clothes**
cupboard, cupboard, closet (*US*),

w

cabinet **2** = **clothes**, apparel, attire

warehouse = **store**, depot, storehouse, repository, depository, stockroom

wares = **goods**, produce, stock, products, stuff, commodities, merchandise

warfare = **war**, fighting, battle, conflict, combat, hostilities, enmity **OPPOSITE:** peace

warm ADJECTIVE **1** = **balmy**, mild, temperate, pleasant, fine, bright, sunny, agreeable **OPPOSITE:** cool **2** = **cosy**, snug, toasty (*informal*), comfortable, homely, comfy (*informal*) **3** = **moderately hot**, heated **OPPOSITE:** cool **4** = **thermal**, winter, thick, chunky, woolly **OPPOSITE:** cool **5** = **mellow**, relaxing, pleasant, agreeable, restful **6** = **affable**, kindly, friendly, affectionate, loving, tender, amicable, cordial **OPPOSITE:** unfriendly **7** = **near**, close, hot, near to the truth ▷ VERB **8** = **warm up**, heat, thaw (out), heat up **OPPOSITE:** cool down

▷ PHRASES: **warm something** *or* **someone up** = **heat**, thaw, heat up

warmth 1 = **heat**, snugness, warmness, comfort, homeliness, hotness **OPPOSITE:** coolness **2** = **affection**, feeling, love, goodwill, kindness, tenderness, cordiality, kindliness **OPPOSITE:** hostility

warn 1 = **notify**, tell, remind, inform, alert, tip off, give notice, make someone aware **2** = **advise**, urge, recommend, counsel, caution, commend, exhort, admonish

warning 1 = **caution**, information, advice, injunction, notification **2** = **notice**, notification, sign, alarm, announcement, alert, tip-off (*informal*), heads up (*US & Canad*) **3** = **omen**, sign, forecast, indication, prediction, prophecy, foreboding, portent, rahui (*NZ*) **4** = **reprimand**, admonition

warp VERB **1** = **distort**, bend, twist, buckle, deform, disfigure, contort, malform **2** = **become distorted**, bend, twist, contort, become deformed, become misshapen **3** = **pervert**, twist, corrupt, degrade, deprave, debase, debauch, lead astray ▷ NOUN **4** = **twist**, bend, defect, flaw, distortion, imperfection, kink, contortion

warrant VERB **1** = **call for**, demand, require, merit, rate, earn, deserve, permit ▷ NOUN **2** = **authorization**, permit, licence, permission, authority, sanction

warranty = **guarantee**, promise, contract, bond, pledge, certificate, assurance, covenant

warrior = **soldier**, combatant, fighter, gladiator, trooper, man-at-arms

wary 1 = **suspicious**, sceptical, guarded, distrustful, chary 2 = **watchful**, careful, alert, cautious, vigilant, circumspect, heedful **OPPOSITE:** careless

wash VERB 1 = **clean**, scrub, sponge, rinse, scour, cleanse 2 = **launder**, clean, rinse, dry-clean 3 = **rinse**, clean, scrub, lather 4 = **bathe**, bath, clean yourself, soak, douse, scrub yourself down 5 = **move**, overcome, touch, upset, stir, disturb, perturb, surge through 6 (*informal, used in negative constructions*) = **be plausible**, stand up, hold up, pass muster, hold water, stick, carry weight, be convincing
▷ NOUN 7 = **laundering**, cleaning, clean, cleansing 8 = **bathe**, dip, soak, scrub, rinse 9 = **backwash**, slipstream, path, trail, train, track, waves, aftermath 10 = **splash**, surge, swell, rise and fall, undulation 11 = **coat**, film, covering, layer, coating, overlay
▷ PHRASES: **wash something away** = **erode**, wear something away ▶ **wash something or someone away** = **sweep away**, carry off, bear away

waste VERB 1 = **squander**, throw away, blow (*slang*), lavish, misuse, dissipate, fritter away **OPPOSITE:** save 2 *followed by* **away** = **wear out**, wither
▷ NOUN 3 = **squandering**, misuse, extravagance, frittering away, dissipation, wastefulness, prodigality **OPPOSITE:** saving 4 = **rubbish**, refuse, debris, scrap, litter, garbage, trash, leftovers 5 *usually plural* = **desert**, wilderness, wasteland
▷ ADJECTIVE 6 = **unwanted**, useless, worthless, unused, leftover, superfluous, unusable, supernumerary **OPPOSITE:** necessary 7 = **uncultivated**, wild, bare, barren, empty, desolate, unproductive, uninhabited **OPPOSITE:** cultivated
▷ PHRASES: **waste away** = **decline**, dwindle, wither, fade, crumble, decay, wane, wear out

> **USAGE NOTE**
> *Waste* and *wastage* are to some extent interchangeable, but many people think that *wastage* should not be used to refer to loss resulting from human carelessness, inefficiency, etc: *a waste* (not *a wastage*) *of time, money, effort*, etc.

watch VERB 1 = **look at**, observe, regard, eye, see, view, contemplate, eyeball (*slang*) 2 = **spy on**, follow, track, monitor, keep an eye on, stake out, keep tabs on (*informal*), keep watch on 3 = **guard**, keep, mind, protect, tend, look after, shelter, take care of
▷ NOUN 4 = **wristwatch**,

timepiece, chronometer
5 = guard, surveillance, observation, vigil, lookout
watchdog 1 = guardian, monitor, protector, custodian, scrutineer **2 = guard dog**
water NOUN **1 = liquid**, H_2O, wai (*NZ*) **2** *often plural* **= sea**, main, waves, ocean, depths, briny
▷ VERB **3 = sprinkle**, spray, soak, irrigate, hose, dampen, drench, douse, fertigate (*Austral*) **4 = get wet**, cry, weep, become wet, exude water
▷ PHRASES: **water something down = dilute**, weaken, water, doctor, thin
waterfall = cascade, fall, cataract
wave VERB **1 = signal**, sign, gesture, gesticulate **2 = guide**, point, direct, indicate, signal, motion, gesture, nod **3 = brandish**, swing, flourish, wag, shake **4 = flutter**, flap, stir, shake, swing, wag, oscillate
▷ NOUN **5 = gesture**, sign, signal, indication, gesticulation **6 = ripple**, breaker, swell, ridge, roller, billow **7 = outbreak**, rash, upsurge, flood, surge, groundswell **8 = stream**, flood, surge, spate, current, flow, rush, tide
waver 1 = hesitate, dither (*chiefly Brit*), vacillate, falter, fluctuate, seesaw, hum and haw **OPPOSITE:** be decisive

2 = flicker, shake, tremble, wobble, quiver, totter
wax 1 = increase, grow, develop, expand, swell, enlarge, magnify **OPPOSITE:** wane **2 = become fuller**, enlarge
way 1 = method, means, system, process, technique, manner, procedure, mode **2 = manner**, style, fashion, mode **3** *often plural* **= custom**, manner, habit, style, practice, nature, personality, wont, tikanga (*NZ*) **4 = route**, direction, course, road, path **5 = access**, road, track, channel, route, path, trail, pathway **6 = journey**, approach, passage **7 = distance**, length, stretch
wayward = erratic, unruly, unmanageable, unpredictable, capricious, ungovernable, inconstant **OPPOSITE:** obedient
weak 1 = feeble, frail, debilitated, fragile, sickly, puny, unsteady, infirm **OPPOSITE:** strong **2 = slight**, faint, feeble, pathetic, hollow **3 = fragile**, brittle, flimsy, fine, delicate, frail, dainty, breakable **4 = unsafe**, exposed, vulnerable, helpless, unprotected, defenceless, unguarded **OPPOSITE:** secure **5 = unconvincing**, unsatisfactory, lame, flimsy, pathetic **OPPOSITE:** convincing **6 = tasteless**, thin, diluted, watery, runny, insipid **OPPOSITE:** strong

weaken 1 = **reduce**, undermine, moderate, diminish, lessen, sap **OPPOSITE:** boost 2 = **wane**, diminish, dwindle, lower, flag, fade, lessen **OPPOSITE:** grow 3 = **sap the strength of OPPOSITE:** strengthen

weakness 1 = **frailty**, fatigue, exhaustion, fragility, infirmity, feebleness, decrepitude **OPPOSITE:** strength 2 = **liking**, appetite, penchant, soft spot, passion, inclination, fondness, partiality **OPPOSITE:** aversion 3 = **powerlessness**, vulnerability, meekness, spinelessness, timorousness, cravenness, cowardliness 4 = **inadequacy**, deficiency, transparency, lameness, hollowness, implausibility, flimsiness, unsoundness 5 = **failing**, fault, defect, deficiency, flaw, shortcoming, blemish, imperfection **OPPOSITE:** strong point

wealth 1 = **riches**, fortune, prosperity, affluence, money, opulence **OPPOSITE:** poverty 2 = **property**, capital, fortune 3 = **abundance**, plenty, richness, profusion, fullness, cornucopia, copiousness **OPPOSITE:** lack

wealthy = **rich**, prosperous, affluent, well-off, flush (*informal*), opulent, well-heeled (*informal*), well-to-do, minted (*Brit slang*) **OPPOSITE:** poor

wear VERB 1 = **be dressed in**, have on, sport (*informal*), put on 2 = **show**, present, bear, display, assume, put on, exhibit 3 = **deteriorate**, fray, wear thin ▷ NOUN 4 = **clothes**, things, dress, gear (*informal*), attire, costume, garments, apparel 5 = **damage**, wear and tear, erosion, deterioration, attrition, corrosion, abrasion **OPPOSITE:** repair ▷ PHRASES: **wear off** = **subside**, disappear, fade, diminish, decrease, dwindle, wane, peter out

wearing = **tiresome**, trying, fatiguing, oppressive, exasperating, irksome, wearisome **OPPOSITE:** refreshing

weary ADJECTIVE 1 = **tired**, exhausted, drained, worn out, done in (*informal*), flagging, fatigued, sleepy, clapped out (*Austral & NZ informal*) **OPPOSITE:** energetic 2 = **tiring**, arduous, tiresome, laborious, wearisome **OPPOSITE:** refreshing ▷ VERB 3 = **grow tired**, tire, become bored

weather NOUN 1 = **climate**, conditions, temperature, forecast, outlook, meteorological conditions, elements ▷ VERB 2 = **withstand**, stand, survive, overcome, resist,

W

brave, endure, come through **OPPOSITE:** surrender to
weave 1 = **knit**, intertwine, plait, braid, entwine, interlace 2 = **zigzag**, wind, crisscross 3 = **create**, tell, recount, narrate, build, relate, make up, spin
web 1 = **cobweb**, spider's web 2 = **mesh**, lattice 3 = **tangle**, network
wed 1 = **get married to**, be united to **OPPOSITE:** divorce 2 = **get married**, marry, be united, tie the knot (*informal*), take the plunge (*informal*) **OPPOSITE:** divorce 3 = **unite**, combine, join, link, ally, blend, merge, interweave **OPPOSITE:** divide
wedding = **marriage**, nuptials, wedding ceremony, marriage service, wedding service
wedge VERB 1 = **squeeze**, force, lodge, jam, crowd, stuff, pack, thrust
▷ NOUN 2 = **block**, lump, chunk
weep = **cry**, shed tears, sob, whimper, mourn, lament, blubber, snivel **OPPOSITE:** rejoice
weigh 1 = **have a weight of**, tip the scales at (*informal*) 2 = **consider**, examine, contemplate, evaluate, ponder, think over, reflect upon, meditate upon 3 = **compare**, balance, contrast, juxtapose, place side by side 4 = **matter**, carry weight, count

weight NOUN 1 = **heaviness**, mass, poundage, load, tonnage 2 = **importance**, force, power, value, authority, influence, impact, import, mana (*NZ*)
▷ VERB 3 *often with* **down** = **load** 4 = **bias**, load, slant, unbalance
weird 1 = **strange**, odd, unusual, bizarre, mysterious, queer, eerie, unnatural **OPPOSITE:** normal 2 = **bizarre**, odd, strange, unusual, queer, unnatural, creepy (*informal*), freakish **OPPOSITE:** ordinary
welcome VERB 1 = **greet**, meet, receive, embrace, hail, karanga (*NZ*), mihi (*NZ*), haeremai (*NZ*) **OPPOSITE:** reject 2 = **accept gladly**, appreciate, embrace, approve of, be pleased by, give the thumbs up to (*informal*), be glad about, express pleasure *or* satisfaction at
▷ NOUN 3 = **greeting**, welcoming, reception, acceptance, hail, hospitality, salutation, haeremai (*NZ*) **OPPOSITE:** rejection
▷ ADJECTIVE 4 = **pleasing**, appreciated, acceptable, pleasant, desirable, refreshing, delightful, gratifying **OPPOSITE:** unpleasant 5 = **wanted** **OPPOSITE:** unwanted 6 = **free**
weld 1 = **join**, link, bond, bind, connect, fuse, solder 2 = **unite**, combine, blend, unify, fuse
welfare 1 = **wellbeing**, good, interest, health, security,

benefit, safety, protection
2 = **state benefit**, support, benefits, pensions, dole (slang), social security, unemployment benefit, state benefits, pogey (Canad)

well¹ ADVERB **1** = **skilfully**, expertly, adeptly, professionally, correctly, properly, efficiently, adequately **OPPOSITE**: badly
2 = **satisfactorily**, nicely, smoothly, successfully, pleasantly, splendidly, agreeably **OPPOSITE**: badly
3 = **thoroughly**, completely, fully, carefully, effectively, efficiently, rigorously
4 = **intimately**, deeply, fully, profoundly **OPPOSITE**: slightly
5 = **favourably**, highly, kindly, warmly, enthusiastically, approvingly, admiringly, with admiration **OPPOSITE**: unfavourably **6** = **considerably**, easily, very much, significantly, substantially, markedly
7 = **fully**, highly, greatly, amply, very much, thoroughly, considerably, substantially
8 = **possibly**, probably, certainly, reasonably, conceivably, justifiably **9** = **decently**, right, kindly, fittingly, fairly, properly, politely, suitably **OPPOSITE**: unfairly **10** = **prosperously**, comfortably, splendidly, in comfort, in (the lap of) luxury, without hardship
▷ ADJECTIVE **11** = **healthy**, sound, fit, blooming, in fine fettle, in good condition **OPPOSITE**: ill **12** = **satisfactory**, right, fine, pleasing, proper, thriving **OPPOSITE**: unsatisfactory **13** = **advisable**, proper, agreeable **OPPOSITE**: inadvisable

well² NOUN **1** = **hole**, bore, pit, shaft
▷ VERB **2** = **flow**, spring, pour, jet, surge, gush, spurt, spout
3 = **rise**, increase, grow, mount, surge, intensify

wet ADJECTIVE **1** = **damp**, soaking, saturated, moist, watery, soggy, sodden, waterlogged **OPPOSITE**: dry **2** = **rainy**, damp, drizzly, showery, raining, pouring, drizzling, teeming **OPPOSITE**: sunny **3** (informal) = **feeble**, soft, weak, ineffectual, weedy (informal), spineless, effete, timorous
▷ VERB **4** = **moisten**, spray, dampen, water, soak, saturate, douse, irrigate, fertigate (Austral) **OPPOSITE**: dry
▷ NOUN **5** = **rain**, drizzle **OPPOSITE**: fine weather
6 = **moisture**, water, liquid, damp, humidity, condensation, dampness, wetness **OPPOSITE**: dryness

whack (informal) VERB **1** = **strike**, hit, belt (informal), bang, smack, thrash, thump, swipe
▷ NOUN **2** = **blow**, hit, stroke,

W

belt (*informal*), bang, smack, thump, swipe **3** (*informal*) = **share**, part, cut (*informal*), bit, portion, quota **4** (*informal*) = **attempt**, go (*informal*), try, turn, shot (*informal*), crack (*informal*), stab (*informal*), bash (*informal*)

whale
• See panel **WHALES AND DOLPHINS**

wharf = **dock**, pier, berth, quay, jetty, landing stage

wheel NOUN **1** = **disc**, ring, hoop ▷ VERB **2** = **push**, trundle, roll **3** = **turn**, swing, spin, revolve, rotate, whirl, swivel **4** = **circle**, go round, twirl, gyrate

whereabouts = **position**, situation, site, location

whiff = **smell**, hint, scent, sniff, aroma, odour

whim = **impulse**, caprice, fancy, urge, notion

whine VERB **1** = **cry**, sob, wail, whimper, sniffle, snivel, moan **2** = **complain**, grumble, gripe (*informal*), whinge (*informal*), moan, grouse, grizzle (*informal*, *chiefly Brit*), grouch (*informal*) ▷ NOUN **3** = **cry**, moan, sob, wail, whimper **4** = **drone**, note, hum **5** = **complaint**, moan, grumble, grouse, gripe (*informal*), whinge (*informal*), grouch (*informal*)

whip NOUN **1** = **lash**, cane, birch, crop, scourge, cat-o'-nine-tails ▷ VERB **2** = **lash**, cane, flog, beat, strap, thrash, birch, scourge **3** (*informal*) = **dash**, shoot, fly, tear, rush, dive, dart, whisk **4** = **whisk**, beat, mix vigorously, stir vigorously **5** = **incite**, drive, stir, spur, work up, get going, agitate, inflame

whirl VERB **1** = **spin**, turn, twist, rotate, twirl **2** = **rotate**, roll, twist, revolve, swirl, twirl,

---

WHALES AND DOLPHINS

baleen whale	narwhal
beluga	pilot whale, black whale, *or* blackfish
blue whale *or* sulphur-bottom	
bottlenose dolphin	porpoise
bowhead	right whale *or* (*Austral*) bay whale
dorado	rorqual
Greenland whale	sei whale
greyback *or* grey whale	sperm whale *or* cachalot
humpback whale	toothed whale
killer whale, grampus, *or* orca	whalebone whale
minke whale	white whale

w

pirouette 3 = **feel dizzy**, swim, spin, reel, go round
▷ NOUN 4 = **revolution**, turn, roll, spin, twist, swirl, rotation, twirl 5 = **bustle**, round, series, succession, flurry, merry-go-round 6 = **confusion**, daze, dither (*chiefly Brit*), giddiness 7 = **tumult**, spin

whisk VERB 1 = **flick**, whip, sweep, brush 2 = **beat**, mix vigorously, stir vigorously, whip, fluff up
▷ NOUN 3 = **flick**, sweep, brush, whip 4 = **beater**, mixer, blender

whisper VERB 1 = **murmur**, breathe OPPOSITE: shout 2 = **rustle**, sigh, hiss, swish
▷ NOUN 3 = **murmur**, mutter, mumble, undertone 4 (*informal*) = **rumour**, report, gossip, goss (*informal*), innuendo, insinuation 5 = **rustle**, sigh, hiss, swish

white = **pale**, wan, pasty, pallid, ashen
• *See panel* SHADES FROM BLACK TO WHITE

white-collar = **clerical**, professional, salaried, nonmanual

whittle = **carve**, cut, hew, shape, trim, shave, pare
▷ PHRASES: whittle something away = **undermine**, reduce, consume, erode, eat away, wear away, cut down, cut, decrease, prune, scale down

whole NOUN 1 = **unit**, ensemble, entirety, totality OPPOSITE: part

▷ ADJECTIVE 2 = **complete**, full, total, entire, uncut, undivided, unabridged OPPOSITE: partial 3 = **undamaged**, intact, unscathed, unbroken, untouched, unharmed, in one piece OPPOSITE: damaged
▷ PHRASES: on the whole 1 = **all in all**, altogether, all things considered, by and large 2 = **generally**, in general, as a rule, chiefly, mainly, mostly, principally, on average

wholesale ADJECTIVE 1 = **extensive**, total, mass, sweeping, broad, comprehensive, wide-ranging, blanket OPPOSITE: limited
▷ ADVERB 2 = **extensively**, comprehensively, across the board, indiscriminately

wholly = **completely**, totally, perfectly, fully, entirely, altogether, thoroughly, utterly OPPOSITE: partly

whore = **prostitute**, tart (*informal*), streetwalker, call girl

wide ADJECTIVE 1 = **spacious**, broad, extensive, roomy, commodious OPPOSITE: confined 2 = **baggy**, full, loose, ample, billowing, roomy, voluminous, capacious 3 = **expanded**, dilated, distended OPPOSITE: shut 4 = **broad**, extensive, wide-ranging, large, sweeping, vast, immense, expansive OPPOSITE: restricted 5 = **extensive**,

w

general, far-reaching,
overarching 6 = **large**, broad,
vast, immense 7 = **distant**,
remote, off course, off target
▷ ADVERB 8 = **fully**, completely
OPPOSITE: partly 9 = **off target**,
astray, off course, off the mark

widen 1 = **broaden**, expand,
enlarge, dilate, spread, extend,
stretch **OPPOSITE:** narrow
2 = **get wider**, spread, extend,
expand, broaden **OPPOSITE:**
narrow

widespread = **common**,
general, popular, broad,
extensive, universal, far-
reaching, pervasive **OPPOSITE:**
limited

width = **breadth**, extent, span,
scope, diameter, compass,
thickness, girth

wield 1 = **brandish**, flourish,
manipulate, swing, use,
manage, handle, employ
2 = **exert**, maintain, exercise,
have, possess

wife = **spouse**, partner, mate,
bride, better half (*humorous*),
vrou (*S African*), wahine (*NZ*),
wifey (*informal*)

wild 1 = **untamed**, fierce, savage,
ferocious, unbroken, feral,
undomesticated, free, warrigal
(*Austral literary*) **OPPOSITE:**
tame 2 = **uncultivated**,
natural **OPPOSITE:** cultivated
3 = **stormy**, violent,
rough, raging, choppy,
tempestuous, blustery

4 = **excited**, crazy (*informal*),
enthusiastic, raving, hysterical
OPPOSITE: unenthusiastic
5 = **uncontrolled**, disorderly,
turbulent, wayward, unruly,
rowdy, unfettered, riotous
OPPOSITE: calm 6 = **mad**
(*informal*), furious, fuming,
infuriated, incensed, enraged,
very angry, irate, tooshie (*Austral
slang*), off the air (*Austral slang*)
7 = **uncivilized**, fierce, savage,
primitive, ferocious, barbaric,
brutish, barbarous **OPPOSITE:**
civilized
▷ PHRASES: the wilds
= **wilderness**, desert,
wasteland, middle of nowhere
(*informal*), backwoods, back of
beyond (*informal*)

wilderness = **wilds**, desert,
wasteland, uncultivated region

will NOUN 1 = **determination**,
drive, purpose, commitment,
resolution, resolve, spine,
backbone 2 = **wish**, mind,
desire, intention, fancy,
preference, inclination
3 = **choice**, prerogative, volition
4 = **decree**, wish, desire,
command, dictate, ordinance
5 = **testament**, bequest(s), last
wishes, last will and testament
▷ VERB 6 = **wish**, want, prefer,
desire, see fit 7 = **bequeath**,
give, leave, transfer, gift, hand
on, pass on, confer

willing 1 = **inclined**, prepared,
consenting, agreeable,

compliant, amenable **OPPOSITE:** unwilling 2 = **ready**, game (*informal*) **OPPOSITE:** reluctant

willingly = **readily**, freely, gladly, happily, eagerly, voluntarily, cheerfully, by choice **OPPOSITE:** unwillingly

willingness = **inclination**, will, agreement, wish, consent, volition **OPPOSITE:** reluctance

wilt 1 = **droop**, wither, sag, shrivel 2 = **weaken**, languish, droop 3 = **wane**, flag, fade

win VERB 1 = **be victorious in**, succeed in, prevail in, come first in, be the victor in **OPPOSITE:** lose 2 = **be victorious**, succeed, triumph, overcome, prevail, conquer, come first, sweep the board **OPPOSITE:** lose 3 = **gain**, get, land, achieve, earn, secure, obtain, acquire **OPPOSITE:** forfeit
▷ **NOUN** 4 = **victory**, success, triumph, conquest **OPPOSITE:** defeat
▷ **PHRASES: win someone over** *or* **round** = **convince**, influence, persuade, convert, sway, prevail upon, bring *or* talk round

wince VERB 1 = **flinch**, start, shrink, cringe, quail, recoil, cower, draw back
▷ **NOUN** 2 = **flinch**, start, cringe

wind[1] 1 = **air**, blast, hurricane, breeze, draught, gust, zephyr 2 = **flatulence**, gas 3 = **breath**, puff, respiration 4 = **nonsense**, talk, boasting, hot air, babble,

bluster, humbug, twaddle (*informal*), bizzo (*Austral slang*), bull's wool (*Austral & NZ slang*)
▷ **PHRASES: get wind of something** = **hear about**, learn of, find out about, become aware of, be told about, be informed of, be made aware of, hear tell of

wind[2] **VERB** 1 = **meander**, turn, bend, twist, curve, snake, ramble, twist and turn 2 = **wrap**, twist, reel, curl, loop, coil 3 = **coil**, curl, spiral, encircle
▷ **PHRASES: wind someone up** (*informal*) 1 = **irritate**, excite, anger, annoy, exasperate, nettle, work someone up, pique 2 = **tease**, kid (*informal*), have someone on (*informal*), annoy, rag (*informal*), rib (*informal*), josh (*informal*), vex ▶ **wind something up** 1 = **end**, finish, settle, conclude, tie up, wrap up, finalize 2 = **close down**, close, dissolve, terminate, put something into liquidation
▶ **wind up** = **end up**, be left, finish up, fetch up (*informal*), land up

windfall = **godsend**, find, jackpot, bonanza, manna from heaven **OPPOSITE:** misfortune

windy = **breezy**, wild, stormy, windswept, blustery, gusty, squally, blowy **OPPOSITE:** calm

wing NOUN 1 = **faction**, group, arm, section, branch

W

▷ **VERB** 2 = **fly**, soar, glide, take wing 3 = **wound**, hit, clip
wink VERB 1 = **blink**, bat, flutter 2 = **twinkle**, flash, shine, sparkle, gleam, shimmer, glimmer
▷ **NOUN** 3 = **blink**, flutter
winner = **victor**, champion, master, champ (*informal*), conqueror, prizewinner **OPPOSITE:** loser
winning ADJECTIVE
1 = **victorious**, first, top, successful, unbeaten, conquering, triumphant, undefeated 2 = **charming**, pleasing, attractive, engaging, cute, disarming, enchanting, endearing **OPPOSITE:** unpleasant
▷ **PLURAL NOUN** 3 = **spoils**, profits, gains, prize, proceeds, takings
wipe VERB 1 = **clean**, polish, brush, rub, sponge, mop, swab 2 = **erase**, remove
▷ **NOUN** 3 = **rub**, brush
▷ **PHRASES:** wipe something *or* someone out = **destroy**, massacre, erase, eradicate, obliterate, annihilate, exterminate, expunge
wisdom = **understanding**, learning, knowledge, intelligence, judgment, insight, enlightenment, erudition **OPPOSITE:** foolishness
wise 1 = **sage**, clever, intelligent, sensible, enlightened,

discerning, perceptive, erudite, grounded **OPPOSITE:** foolish 2 = **sensible**, clever, intelligent, prudent, judicious **OPPOSITE:** unwise
wish NOUN 1 = **desire**, want, hope, urge, intention, fancy (*informal*), ambition, yen (*informal*) **OPPOSITE:** aversion
▷ **VERB** 2 = **want**, feel, choose, please, desire, think fit
▷ **PHRASES:** wish for = **desire**, want, hope for, long for, crave, aspire to, yearn for, hanker for
wit 1 = **humour**, quips, banter, puns, repartee, wordplay, witticisms, badinage **OPPOSITE:** seriousness 2 = **humorist**, card (*informal*), comedian, wag, joker, dag (*NZ informal*) 3 = **cleverness**, sense, brains, wisdom, common sense, intellect, ingenuity, acumen **OPPOSITE:** stupidity
witch = **enchantress**, magician, hag, crone, sorceress, Wiccan
witchcraft = **magic**, voodoo, wizardry, black magic, enchantment, occultism, sorcery, Wicca, makutu (*NZ*)
withdraw 1 = **remove**, take off, pull out, extract, take away, pull back, draw out, draw back 2 = **take out**, extract, draw out
withdrawal = **removal**, ending, stopping, taking away, abolition, elimination, cancellation, termination
withdrawn
= **uncommunicative**, reserved,

retiring, distant, shy, taciturn, introverted, unforthcoming **OPPOSITE:** outgoing

wither 1 = **wilt**, decline, decay, disintegrate, perish, shrivel **OPPOSITE:** flourish 2 = **waste**, decline, shrivel 3 = **fade**, decline, perish **OPPOSITE:** increase

withering = **scornful**, devastating, humiliating, snubbing, hurtful, mortifying

withhold 1 = **keep secret**, refuse, hide, reserve, retain, conceal, suppress, hold back **OPPOSITE:** reveal 2 = **hold back**, suppress, keep back **OPPOSITE:** release

withstand = **resist**, suffer, bear, oppose, cope with, endure, tolerate, stand up to **OPPOSITE:** give in to

witness NOUN 1 = **observer**, viewer, spectator, looker-on, watcher, onlooker, eyewitness, bystander 2 = **testifier** ▷ VERB 3 = **see**, view, watch, note, notice, observe, perceive 4 = **countersign**, sign, endorse, validate

witty = **humorous**, funny, clever, amusing, sparkling, whimsical, droll, piquant **OPPOSITE:** dull

wizard = **magician**, witch, shaman, sorcerer, occultist, magus, conjuror, warlock, tohunga (NZ)

wobble VERB 1 = **shake**, rock, sway, tremble, teeter, totter 2 = **tremble**, shake

▷ NOUN 3 = **unsteadiness**, shake, tremble 4 = **unsteadiness**, shake, tremor

woe 1 = **misery**, distress, grief, agony, gloom, sadness, sorrow, anguish **OPPOSITE:** happiness 2 = **problem**, grief, misery, sorrow

woman = **lady**, girl, female, sheila (Austral & NZ informal), vrou (S African), adult female, charlie (Austral slang), chook (Austral slang), femme, wahine (NZ) **OPPOSITE:** man

womanly 1 = **feminine**, motherly, female, warm, tender, matronly, ladylike 2 = **curvaceous**, ample, voluptuous, shapely, curvy (informal), busty (informal), buxom, full-figured

wonder VERB 1 = **think**, question, puzzle, speculate, query, ponder, meditate, conjecture 2 = **be amazed**, stare, marvel, be astonished, gape

▷ NOUN 3 = **amazement**, surprise, admiration, awe, fascination, astonishment, bewilderment, wonderment 4 = **phenomenon**, sight, miracle, spectacle, curiosity, marvel, prodigy, rarity

wonderful 1 = **excellent**, great (informal), brilliant, outstanding, superb, fantastic (informal), tremendous,

w

magnificent, booshit (*Austral slang*), exo (*Austral slang*), sik (*Austral slang*), rad (*informal*), phat (*slang*), schmick (*Austral informal*) **OPPOSITE:** terrible
2 = **remarkable**, amazing, extraordinary, incredible, astonishing, staggering, startling, phenomenal **OPPOSITE:** ordinary

woo 1 = **seek**, cultivate
2 = **court**, pursue

wood NOUN **1** = **timber**, planks, planking, lumber (*US*) **2** = **firewood**, fuel, logs, kindling
▷ PLURAL NOUN **3** = **woodland**, forest, grove, thicket, copse, coppice, bushland

wooded = **tree-covered**, forested, timbered, sylvan (*poetic*), tree-clad

wooden 1 = **made of wood**, timber, woody, ligneous
2 = **expressionless**, lifeless, deadpan, unresponsive

wool 1 = **fleece**, hair, coat
2 = **yarn**

word NOUN **1** = **term**, name, expression **2** = **chat**, tête-à-tête, talk, discussion, consultation, confab (*informal*), heart-to-heart, powwow (*informal*)
3 = **comment**, remark, utterance **4** = **message**, news, report, information, notice, intelligence, dispatch, communiqué, heads up (*US & Canad*) **5** = **promise**, guarantee,

pledge, vow, assurance, oath
6 = **command**, order, decree, bidding, mandate
▷ VERB **7** = **express**, say, state, put, phrase, utter, couch, formulate

RELATED WORDS
adjectives: lexical, verbal

wording = **phraseology**, words, language, phrasing, terminology

work VERB **1** = **be employed**, be in work **2** = **labour**, sweat, slave, toil, slog (away), drudge, peg away, exert yourself **OPPOSITE:** relax **3** = **function**, go, run, operate, be in working order **OPPOSITE:** be out of order
4 = **succeed**, work out, pay off (*informal*), be successful, be effective, do the trick (*informal*), do the business (*informal*), get results **5** = **cultivate**, farm, dig, till, plough **6** = **operate**, use, move, control, drive, manage, handle, manipulate
7 = **manipulate**, form, fashion, shape, mould, knead
▷ NOUN **8** = **employment**, business, job, trade, duty, profession, occupation, livelihood **OPPOSITE:** play
9 = **effort**, industry, labour, sweat, toil, exertion, drudgery, elbow grease (*facetious*)
OPPOSITE: leisure **10** = **task**, jobs, projects, commissions, duties, assignments, chores, yakka (*Austral & NZ informal*)

11 = **handiwork**, doing, act, feat, deed 12 = **creation**, piece, production, opus, achievement, composition, handiwork
▷ **PHRASES**: work out = **solve**, find out, calculate, figure out

worker = **employee**, hand, labourer, workman, craftsman, artisan, tradesman

workman = **labourer**, hand, worker, employee, mechanic, operative, craftsman, artisan

works 1 = **factory**, plant, mill, workshop 2 = **writings**, output, canon, oeuvre (*French*) 3 = **mechanism**, workings, parts, action, movement, machinery

workshop 1 = **factory**, plant, mill 2 = **workroom**, studio

world 1 = **earth**, planet, globe 2 = **mankind**, man, everyone, the public, everybody, humanity, humankind 3 = **sphere**, area, field, environment, realm, domain
▷ **PHRASES**: a world of = **a huge amount of**, a mountain of, a wealth of, a great deal of, a good deal of, an abundance of, an enormous amount of, a vast amount of

worldly 1 = **earthly**, physical, secular, terrestrial, temporal, profane **OPPOSITE**: spiritual 2 = **materialistic**, grasping, selfish, greedy **OPPOSITE**: nonmaterialistic 3 = **worldly-wise**, knowing, experienced, sophisticated, cosmopolitan, urbane, blasé **OPPOSITE**: naive

worn = **ragged**, frayed, shabby, tattered, tatty, threadbare, the worse for wear

worried = **anxious**, concerned, troubled, afraid, frightened, nervous, tense, uneasy **OPPOSITE**: unworried

worry VERB 1 = **be anxious**, be concerned, be worried, obsess, brood, fret, agonize, get in a lather (*informal*) **OPPOSITE**: be unconcerned 2 = **trouble**, upset, bother, disturb, annoy, unsettle, pester, vex **OPPOSITE**: soothe
▷ **NOUN** 3 = **anxiety**, concern, fear, trouble, unease, apprehension, misgiving, trepidation **OPPOSITE**: peace of mind 4 = **problem**, care, trouble, bother, hassle (*informal*)

worsen 1 = **deteriorate**, decline, sink, decay, get worse, degenerate, go downhill (*informal*) **OPPOSITE**: improve 2 = **aggravate**, damage, exacerbate, make worse **OPPOSITE**: improve

worship VERB 1 = **revere**, praise, honour, adore, glorify, exalt, pray to, venerate **OPPOSITE**: dishonour 2 = **love**, adore, idolize, put on a pedestal **OPPOSITE**: despise
▷ **NOUN** 3 = **reverence**, praise, regard, respect, honour, glory, devotion, adulation

w

worth 1 = **value**, price, rate, cost, estimate, valuation **OPPOSITE:** worthlessness 2 = **merit**, value, quality, importance, excellence, goodness, worthiness **OPPOSITE:** unworthiness 3 = **usefulness**, value, quality, importance, excellence, goodness **OPPOSITE:** uselessness

worthless 1 = **valueless**, rubbishy, negligible **OPPOSITE:** valuable 2 = **useless**, unimportant, ineffectual, negligible **OPPOSITE:** useful 3 = **good-for-nothing**, vile, despicable, contemptible **OPPOSITE:** honourable

worthwhile = **useful**, valuable, helpful, profitable, productive, beneficial, meaningful, constructive **OPPOSITE:** useless

worthy = **praiseworthy**, deserving, valuable, worthwhile, admirable, virtuous, creditable, laudable **OPPOSITE:** disreputable

would-be = **budding**, self-styled, wannabe (*informal*), unfulfilled, self-appointed

wound NOUN 1 = **injury**, cut, hurt, trauma (*pathology*), gash, lesion, laceration 2 *often plural* = **trauma**, offence, slight, insult ▷ VERB 3 = **injure**, cut, wing, hurt, pierce, gash, lacerate 4 = **offend**, hurt, annoy, sting, mortify, cut to the quick

wrangle VERB 1 = **argue**, fight, row, dispute, disagree, contend, quarrel, squabble ▷ NOUN 2 = **argument**, row, dispute, quarrel, squabble, bickering, tiff, altercation

wrap VERB 1 = **cover**, enclose, shroud, swathe, encase, enfold, bundle up **OPPOSITE:** uncover 2 = **pack**, package, parcel (up), tie up, gift-wrap **OPPOSITE:** unpack 3 = **bind**, swathe **OPPOSITE:** unwind ▷ NOUN 4 = **cloak**, cape, stole, mantle, shawl ▷ PHRASES: wrap something up 1 = **giftwrap**, pack, package, bundle up 2 = **end**, conclude, wind up, terminate, finish off, round off, polish off (*informal slang*)

wrath = **anger**, rage, temper, fury, resentment, indignation, ire, displeasure **OPPOSITE:** satisfaction

wreck VERB 1 = **destroy**, break, smash, ruin, devastate, shatter, spoil, demolish, kennet (*Austral slang*), jeff (*Austral slang*) **OPPOSITE:** build 2 = **spoil**, ruin, devastate, shatter, crool *or* cruel (*Austral slang*) **OPPOSITE:** save ▷ NOUN 3 = **shipwreck**, hulk

wreckage = **remains**, pieces, ruin, fragments, debris, rubble

wrench VERB 1 = **twist**, force, pull, tear, rip, tug, jerk, yank 2 = **sprain**, strain, rick ▷ NOUN 3 = **twist**, pull, rip, tug,

jerk, yank **4 = sprain**, strain,
twist **5 = blow**, shock, upheaval,
pang **6 = spanner**, adjustable
spanner

wrestle = **fight**, battle, struggle,
combat, grapple, tussle, scuffle

wrinkle NOUN **1 = line**, fold,
crease, furrow, crow's-foot,
corrugation **2 = crease**, fold,
crumple, furrow, crinkle,
corrugation
▷ VERB **3 = crease**, gather,
fold, crumple, furrow, rumple,
pucker, corrugate **OPPOSITE:**
smooth

writ = **summons**, document,
decree, indictment, court order,
subpoena, arraignment

write 1 = record, scribble,
inscribe, set down, jot down
2 = compose, draft, pen, draw
up **3 = correspond**, get in touch,
keep in touch, write a letter,
drop a line, drop a note, e-mail

writer = **author**, novelist, hack,
scribbler, scribe, wordsmith,
penpusher

writing = **script**, hand,
printing, fist (*informal*), scribble,
handwriting, scrawl, calligraphy

wrong ADJECTIVE **1 = amiss**,
faulty, unsatisfactory,
not right, defective, awry
2 = incorrect, mistaken, false,
inaccurate, untrue, erroneous,
wide of the mark, fallacious
3 = inappropriate, incorrect,
unsuitable, unacceptable,
undesirable, incongruous,

unseemly, unbecoming
OPPOSITE: correct **4 = bad**,
criminal, illegal, evil, unlawful,
immoral, unjust, dishonest
OPPOSITE: moral **5 = defective**,
faulty, awry, askew
▷ ADVERB **6 = incorrectly**,
badly, wrongly, mistakenly,
erroneously, inaccurately
OPPOSITE: correctly **7 = amiss**,
astray, awry, askew
▷ NOUN **8 = offence**, injury,
crime, error, sin, injustice,
misdeed, transgression
OPPOSITE: good deed
▷ VERB **9 = mistreat**, abuse,
hurt, harm, cheat, take
advantage of, oppress, malign
OPPOSITE: treat well

Xx   Yy

X-ray = **radiograph**, x-ray image

yank VERB 1 = **pull**, tug, jerk, seize, snatch, pluck, hitch, wrench
▷ NOUN 2 = **pull**, tug, jerk, snatch, hitch, wrench, tweak

yarn 1 = **thread**, fibre, cotton, wool 2 (*informal*) = **story**, tale, anecdote, account, narrative, fable, reminiscence, urban myth

yawning = **gaping**, wide, huge, vast, cavernous

yearly ADJECTIVE 1 = **annual**, each year, every year, once a year
▷ ADVERB 2 = **annually**, every year, by the year, once a year, per annum

yearn *often with* **for** = **long**, desire, hunger, ache, crave, covet, itch, hanker after

yell VERB 1 = **scream**, shout, cry out, howl, call out, wail, shriek, screech OPPOSITE: whisper
▷ NOUN 2 = **scream**, cry, shout, roar, howl, shriek, whoop, screech OPPOSITE: whisper

yellow NOUN = **lemon**, gold, amber
▷ ADJECTIVE (*informal*)
• *See panel* **SHADES OF YELLOW**

SHADES OF YELLOW

almond	gold *or* golden
amber	jasmine
beige	lemon
bisque	magnolia
bistre	maize
buff	mustard
butternut	nankeen
canary yellow	oatmeal
champagne	ochre
cinnamon	old gold
citron	primrose
daffodil	saffron
eau de nil	straw
ecru	tea rose
eggshell	topaz
gamboge	tortoiseshell

yen = **longing**, desire, craving, yearning, passion, hunger, ache, itch

yet ADVERB 1 = **so far**, until now, up to now, still, as yet, even now, thus far, up till now 2 = **now**, right now, just now, so soon 3 = **still**, in addition, besides, to boot, into the bargain
▷ CONJUNCTION
4 = **nevertheless**, still, however, for all that, notwithstanding, just the same, be that as it may

yield VERB 1 = **bow**, submit, give in, surrender, succumb, cave in (*informal*), capitulate 2 = **relinquish**, resign, hand over, surrender, turn over, make over, give over, bequeath OPPOSITE: retain 3 = **produce**, give, provide, return, supply, bear, net, earn OPPOSITE: use up
▷ NOUN 4 = **produce**, crop, harvest, output 5 = **profit**, return, income, revenue, earnings, takings OPPOSITE: loss

yielding 1 = **soft**, pliable, springy, elastic, supple, spongy, unresisting 2 = **submissive**, obedient, compliant, docile, flexible, accommodating, pliant, acquiescent OPPOSITE: obstinate

yob *or* **yobbo** = **thug**, hooligan, lout, hoon (*Austral & NZ slang*), ruffian, roughneck (*slang*), tsotsi (*S African*), cougan (*Austral slang*),

y

scozza (*Austral slang*), bogan
(*Austral slang*)

young ADJECTIVE 1 = **immature**,
juvenile, youthful, little, green,
junior, infant, adolescent
OPPOSITE: old 2 = **early**,
new, undeveloped, fledgling
OPPOSITE: advanced
▷ NOUN 3 = **offspring**, baby,
litter, family, issue, brood,
progeny **OPPOSITE:** parent

youngster = **youth**, girl, boy,
kid (*informal*), lad, teenager,
juvenile, lass

youth 1 = **immaturity**,
adolescence, boyhood *or*
girlhood, salad days **OPPOSITE:**
old age 2 = **boy**, lad, youngster,
kid (*informal*), teenager, young
man, adolescent, teen (*informal*)
OPPOSITE: adult

youthful = **young**, juvenile,
childish, immature, boyish,
girlish **OPPOSITE:** elderly

Zz

zeal = **enthusiasm**, passion, zest,
spirit, verve, fervour, eagerness,
gusto **OPPOSITE:** apathy

zero 1 = **nought**, nothing, nil
2 = **rock bottom**, the bottom,
an all-time low, a nadir, as low as
you can get

zip VERB 1 = **speed**, shoot,
fly, flash, zoom, whizz
(*informal*) 2 (*~data*) = **compress**
(*computing*), archive (*computing*)
OPPOSITE: unzip
▷ NOUN 3 (*informal*) = **energy**,
drive, vigour, verve, zest, gusto,
liveliness **OPPOSITE:** lethargy

zone = **area**, region, section,
sector, district, territory, belt,
sphere

zoom = **speed**, shoot, fly, rush,
flash, dash, whizz (*informal*),
hurtle

LANGUAGE
FOR LIFE

CONTENTS

INTRODUCTION

A dictionary can tell you what a word means and when it can be used accurately. It cannot, though, give you guidance on how to write clearly and appropriately in a variety of situations. The *Collins Language for Life* has been written to help you express yourself effectively at work and at home. It includes advice on how to structure your writing, and how to adapt tone, style and content to different forms of communication – from formal letters and emails to social communication.

BEFORE YOU START WRITING

It is amazing how much more effective your writing will be with a bit of thinking time beforehand. There are three questions which you should be able to answer about any piece of writing, whether it's an email, text, letter or post:

- **Who am I writing to?** This will determine the style and tone that you use. If you are writing an email to a friend, for instance, then you are likely to use less formal language than if you are writing to apply for a job.

- **What do I want to say?** Make sure that all the information you want to communicate is included, and that it is set out as clearly as possible.

- **Why do I want to say it?** In other words, what do you want to happen as a result of your communication? Whether it's for a job application, to ask someone out on a date, or to offer your condolences for a bereavement, what you want to achieve should be clearly stated.

Once you've answered these questions, writing becomes much easier.

Tone

The tone of your writing expresses your attitude towards the reader. To achieve the tone you want, consider the following questions:

- If you were talking to your reader, what tone would your voice have?

- Is the language you are using too simple (patronising) or too difficult (pompous)?

- What is your relationship to the reader, are they your employer (formal, professional tone) or friend (informal, chatty tone)?

Then read through your writing to make sure it conveys the tone you intended.

Here are some tips for making your writing successful and some common traps to avoid.

👍 Tips:

- **Use plain English.** Aim for concise, simple expression which will make your writing easy to read.

- **Plan.** Think about what you want to say, and how you want to say it. Planning will save you time and make your writing more effective. It needn't take a lot of time but, even if you're only writing a text or a tweet, it will pay dividends.

- **Vary the length of your sentences.** Short sentences are powerful. Longer sentences can express more complicated thoughts, but try to keep them to a manageable length or else they become tiring to read! Try to stick to the principle of including one main idea in a sentence, and maybe one related point.

- **Use active rather than passive verbs.** It is usually better to use active verbs because it makes your writing simpler and less stuffy to read:
  The programme was watched by an audience of 13 million people (passive)
  13 million people watched the programme (active).
  The verb 'watched' is 'active' in the second example because it is linked to the subject – '13 million people'. The sentence is shorter and clearer as a result.

5

- **Read your work aloud.** If the sentences work well, it will be easy to read. Check that you have commas where there are natural pauses.

- **Think about register and tone.** Are you using the right level of formality ('register')? Does your writing accurately express your attitude to the subject and the reader ('tone')? How you address a best friend will be different from how you write to a potential employer.

- **Always check your writing before sending it – and then check it again!** You'll be surprised how easy it is to overlook mistakes. Computers have introduced new errors – for instance, did you delete the original passage that you copied and pasted later in the document? If you correct one word in a sentence, make sure the rest of it still makes sense.

> *I wish people would read through what they have written before pressing 'send'. It would save me a lot of time and make their applications more successful.*
>
> (HR manager)

Traps:

- **Jargon.** Specialist words which are understood by a particular group of people, or overly technical language. Don't talk about 'interfacing' with someone, if you simply mean 'talking' to them.

- **Clichés.** Words or phrases that are used too often, and have little meaning. They will annoy your reader and distract from what you are trying to say. Examples include sayings like, '*A different kettle of fish*,' and '*At the end of the day*'.

- **Long sentences.** Avoid sentences longer than 15–20 words – they can be difficult to read, and can usually be divided into clearer statements. If your sentences work well, they will be easy to read.

- **Repeating words.** Using the same word more than once in a sentence can be clumsy, and there is usually an alternative. For instance, '*The date of the English exam is the same date as the French exam*,' sounds better as, '*The English and the French exams are on the same date*.'

- **Long words.** Avoid using long or complex words for the sake of it, they can be replaced by shorter, clearer ones. For example using 'proffer' when you mean 'give' or 'articulate' when you mean 'say'.

- **Redundancy.** Avoid using ten words where two will do: '*I am meeting Sophie later,*' is clearer than, '*Sophie and I are due to hook up together at some point in the day.*' Also avoid **tautology** – saying the same thing twice: '*10 a.m. in the morning*' is either '*10 a.m.*' or '*10 in the morning.*'

- **Ambiguity.** Many words can be understood in more than one way. So, '*Clarice was really cold*' could mean that Clarice was unfriendly or that she was shivering. Put yourself in the reader's place to make sure that the meaning of your statement is clear.

- **Causing offence.** A simple rule to follow is: *treat everyone equally in your writing, regardless of sex, age, race, sexual orientation, or physical difference.* Be aware of current customs and values, and also consider different cultures. This is especially relevant if you are communicating with people around the world.

These are only a few points to consider before you start writing, but if you refer to them regularly, they will help you express yourself clearly and consistently in all your communications.

EMAIL

Emails are an important form of written communication in many people's lives. Whether at home or at work, we spend a lot of our time sending and receiving them. Email correspondence can feel more like a conversation than an exchange of letters. The tone is generally less formal, and the time between sending your message and getting a reply can be minutes or even seconds. The fact that it is instant can be good and bad. Good because it can be a very efficient way of corresponding; bad if you write quickly and carelessly.

Addressing emails

When addressing emails, the general rule of thumb is that the fewer people you email, the better. There are three address fields to consider, and each serves a different purpose:

- **'To':** this is for the address of the main recipient, or recipients, of the information or request to do something.

- **'Cc':** if you are simply informing someone of your actions or requests, put those people in the 'Cc' ('Carbon or Courtesy Copy') field.

- **'Bcc':** if you are copying someone in but you don't want the other addressees to know you should use the 'Bcc' ('Blind Carbon or Courtesy Copy'). This is frequently used for mailing large groups, where you don't want individuals to know who else is receiving the email.

> *Bear in mind that if you send an email to one person you are 95 per cent likely to get a reply; if you send it to 10 people the response rate drops to 5 per cent.*
>
> (Linguistics professor)

Greeting and ending

Emails on work-related issues or personal business require a formal style. You can never go wrong with 'Dear Mr Blake' or 'Dear Peter'. If the contact is long-standing and you are on a familiar footing then 'Hi Peter' is acceptable. In initial exchanges of formal email you might sign off in the same way that you would in a formal letter with 'Yours sincerely' or 'Yours faithfully'. As your correspondence gets onto a slightly less formal footing then 'Kind regards' or 'Best wishes' is fine.

Subject line

You can really help your correspondents by being precise in the subject line. For example if you send out a regular set of minutes by email, don't just write 'Launch Meeting Minutes', but add the date so people can quickly find what they are looking for. If your email contains a specific question it is good practice to add 'Q:' followed by the question in the subject line.

Layout

Use a paragraph per point you wish to make, and put headings above each paragraph if there are more than three. If your email is long and will require the reader to scroll down the screen, consider writing it as a Word document and attaching it to an email – long emails are not easy to read and respond to.

Content

Always remember that with email, your writing can be forwarded to anyone with a single mouse click. Be careful that what you write is not defamatory, offensive, or detrimental to you or your business.

> *Never forward without reading the whole email: you never know what indiscretions or traps are in there. Never put anything in an email you don't want the world to know.*
>
> (Local authority manager)

- Restrict the email to a single subject. If you want to email the same person or people about other issues, use separate emails. It makes filing and action points much easier to follow.

- Don't reply straight away to an email that irks you. You will not be able to hide your anger and will not make the situation better. Wait until you have calmed down enough to think through your response and compose a measured reply dealing with the points raised.

- Don't assume that the person you are writing to has the same cultural reference points, sense of humour, or values.

> *I know of people who communicate regularly with colleagues in Italy, where capitalization is used to show something is urgent whereas we read it as shouting.*
>
> (Marketing executive)

Attachments

Email is great for spreading information held in spreadsheets, pdfs and Word documents. But sending large attachments can cause headaches. Most email providers (and certainly most companies) allocate a storage limit to each email address; if an Inbox becomes too full, you cannot receive or send emails. So be considerate when you send anything as an attachment.

Replying

Sometimes you get an email which contains a series of questions. It is perfectly acceptable to reply to each of these questions by adding your comments (sometimes in a different colour or with your initials in square brackets before your answer) in the body of the original email. This saves you typing out the questions or writing replies that incorporate the original question. For example:

From: Asif Iqbal
To: Fiona McManus
SUBJECT: My paintings

Dear Fiona
Thank you very much for your email about the posters I sell. I've put my answers below your questions with [AI] after.

With thanks and all best wishes

Asif
Mobile: 011111 789456
www.asifiqbal.art.gallery.net

Do you have a website?
[AI] Yes. You can see all my work at www.asifiqbal.art.gallery.net
What sizes do the posters come in?
[AI] Anything from A5 to A1. I can also frame them to order – there's a selection of frames on the website.
What range of prices are there?
[AI] Prices start at $AUS 11.95 and can go up to $AUS 75.00
If you don't have a poster I want in stock, can you source it for me?
[AI] Of course, I'd be happy to help in any way. Have a look through the website and If you can't find what you want, just drop me a line and I'll do my best!

Formal email

The rules for writing formal emails are similar to those for formal letters.

- If you are communicating with someone for the first time you should adopt the structure of a formal letter.

- It is usual and proper to use a greeting of some sort when you begin your email. 'Dear' can never be misunderstood and rarely strikes the wrong note. If you are more familiar with the person you are writing to 'Hi' or 'Hello' is fine. If you're writing to close friends then use whichever greeting you are accustomed to in your social circle.

- If you are emailing someone for the first time without being invited to it is always proper to explain at the very start of the email who you are and why you are writing to them.

- Never leave the subject line blank. In most formal or professional correspondence you should aim to keep the email to one subject. Think clearly what the email is about and be as precise as you can. Keep the subject as short as possible as the recipient's inbox will often only display a limited amount of the line.

- If the email is going to be long it is polite to indicate this in the opening few sentences of the email.

- Structure your email so that each point is addressed in a separate paragraph. If you wish, it is entirely acceptable to add a heading to each paragraph. Your reader can then see at a glance the points you are covering.

- In formal emails, texting abbreviations and emoticons should be avoided.

- When you end your email use the same rules as with formal letters, using 'Yours faithfully' or 'Yours sincerely' as appropriate.

> *I avoid using multiple sub-clauses and long sentences and use lists or bullet points rather than block text.*
>
> (Marketing manager)

Informal emails

For emails to friends and family you can be more relaxed in your style and tone.

- 'Hi' or 'Hey' or other informal greetings are appropriate and you can sign off the email with 'See you' or 'lots of love' or other phrases.

- Even when you're writing to a friend remember that email can seem terse and abrupt if there is no greeting or sign-off.

- It is fine to use texting abbreviations and emoticons in informal emails – just make sure the person you're writing to understands them all!

> *I read the email back to myself as though I were reading someone else's email prior to sending.*
>
> (Course co-ordinator)

JOB APPLICATIONS

A covering letter and CV are usually the first things any prospective employer will see of you. If you want to get an interview for a job, it is important that these documents present you in the best possible light. The following sections deal with how to construct and write your covering letter and CV, and provide tips on how to apply for a job online.

Covering letter

The covering letter should convey confidence, enthusiasm, technical knowledge and demonstrate an understanding of what the job entails. It need not be long and it should not be a rehash of the accompanying CV. A short, clear, well-written covering letter can make all the difference between two candidates.

> *Some people think the covering letter is another CV. It's not. A covering letter is a way of introducing yourself to the employer and of providing a persuasive case for reading the CV and then getting an interview.*
>
> (HR Director)

The covering letter should alert the employer to the key points of a CV and show the match between the candidate and the job being advertised. In general it will consist of three paragraphs or so:

- **First paragraph.** Introduce yourself, say which job you are applying for and where you saw it. You can also include a general statement of why you want to apply for the job and how you feel about the company.

- **Second paragraph.** Provide information about your skills, strengths, qualifications and experience. Give specific examples of why you are the ideal candidate and don't simply restate your CV.

- **Final paragraph.** Conclude the letter expressing your desire to get the job and requesting an interview. You should also say what the best way to contact you is, and if there are any inconvenient dates. Always thank the employer for their time in considering your application.

FAQ

Q. *Should my letter be typed or handwritten?*

A. It should be typed on A4 paper. Only the signature should be handwritten.

Q. *To whom should I address my letter?*

A. If you do not know the name of the person who would deal with your application, call the company to find out their name.

Q. *Is it OK to send out the same letter to all those companies I'm interested in?*

A. No. Try to avoid general letters. Find out as much as you can about the company, and tailor your letter accordingly.

Q. *Should I mention salary in my accompanying letter?*

A. It is usually best not to touch on the subject of salary at this stage, unless requested in the advertisement.

Useful phrases

First of all, identify the job you are applying for:

- I would like to inquire as to whether there are any openings for junior telesales operators in your company.

- I am writing to apply for the post of senior marketing manager.

- I would like to apply for the position of online learning coordinator, as advertised on your website.

- I am writing to apply for the above post, as advertised in the Guardian of 8 August 2015.

Next, give some examples of personal achievements:

- I have gained experience in several major aspects of publishing.

- I co-ordinated the change-over from one accounting system to another.

- I developed designs for a new range of knitwear.

- I have supervised a team of telesales operators on several projects.

- I contributed to the development of our new database software.

Then outline your personal qualities:

- I see myself as systematic and meticulous in my approach to work.

- I am a fair and broad-minded person, with an ability to get on well with people from all walks of life.

- I am hardworking and business minded, and I tend to thrive under pressure.

Explain why you want this job:

- I am now keen to find a post with more responsibility.

- I now wish to find a more permanent full-time position.

- I would like to further my career in the field of production.

- I feel that your company's activities most closely match my own values and interests.

Express your willingness to attend an interview.

Here is an example covering letter:

15 Sandybank Drive
Derby
DX27 9LC
joelmanners@email.com
01245 645201

27 July 2015

Mr H Carson
Personnel Manager
Allied Derby Building Society
HR House
Illingworth Way
DERBY
DX3 9DF

Dear Mr Carson

Customer Services Manager

I am responding to the job advertised in the *Derby Express* and on your website on the 22nd July. I feel the job is just what I have been looking for, and reading the job description, I am sure that I have the right level of experience, aptitude and training. Your company's support and promotion of ethical investment has always impressed and inspired me and I would very much like to contribute to your success. My CV is attached.

For the past three years I have been Senior Customer Services Adviser at Cathedral County Bank, leading a team of seven people. Since I took on the role our positive response rate has risen by 10 per cent and customer satisfaction in the area I look after by 15 per cent. I was voted Employee of the Month three times by my colleagues in the period. While I am very happy in my job, the opportunities for promotion are limited and I do want to take on a more responsible role in my area of expertise.

I would welcome the opportunity to discuss my application further. Email is the best way to contact me and I am available for interview at your convenience. Thank you for taking the time to read my application.

Yours sincerely

Mr Joel Manners

Mr Joel Manners

- Avoid just sending a letter or email with 'Please find my CV attached'. Remember that this application is a two-stage process to try to get an interview. Each step in the process (covering letter and CV) has to make the employer want to take the next step.

- Remember the basics:
  - check all spelling and grammar two or three times
  - make sure you have spelled all names correctly
  - include all contact details
  - include any information that the job advertisement has specifically asked you to provide.

A speculative job application

- When applying for a job on a speculative basis, try to speak to the person responsible for recruitment in the appropriate department beforehand. This way, you will have a specific person to write to, as well as having established a relationship with them.

---

34 St Dunstan's Way
Vancouver
V6G 7D7

19 July 2015

Ms D Wallis
Youngs Accountancy and Finance
19 Lockwood Road
Vancouver
V9P 8K1

Dear Ms Wallis

post of software development co-ordinator

Thank you very much for taking the time to speak to me yesterday about the possibility of a position as software development co-ordinator with your company.

Please find attached a CV which highlights my prior professional experience, and the qualities which I feel make me suited to this position. You will see that I have a strong interest in, and knowledge of, staff management, and have gained extensive experience in handling large development projects and meeting deadlines.

I see myself as being well-organized and self-motivated, and have excellent communication skills. I am keen to develop my career with Youngs Accountancy and Finance, and so would very much appreciate the opportunity to discuss further my suitability for the post.

Please feel free to contact me, either by email: dgormanl@netserve.com, or by leaving a message on (604) 473 5522. I look forward to speaking to you soon.

Yours sincerely

D Gorman

Deborah Gorman

CV

Your CV exists to give a brief description of who you are, what you have done and what you can do.

> *What a lot of candidates forget is that the purpose of the CV is to get the interview – not the job. So they give way too much detail and don't tailor it to the role they are trying to get.*
>
> (HR Director)

- The language should always be 'active'. Avoid passive statements like 'Turnover growth of 25 per cent was achieved in the period,' say instead, 'I increased turnover for the period by 25 per cent.' Active language simplifies your statements and makes them easier to read.

- Use positive adverbs ('efficiently', 'successfully' 'effectively') so that your CV will convey a positive impression to your prospective employer.

CV structure

The most common CV format is called 'reverse chronological', meaning you start with your current job and work backwards. If your earliest jobs have little relevance to your current application, you can simply list the job title, company and the dates you worked there. Summarize your education after the employment section, and then add any additional skills and interests that may be of use to support your application.

You can see a sample CV on the next page:

Helena Shapur

12 Green Lane, Brighton, Sussex BT1 3EY
Email: h.sharpur@email.com
Mobile: 07123 456789

Personal profile

An enthusiastic, self-motivated professional, highly qualified in the field of online team management. My motivation is to use the web to help make the most of all businesses I work for. I have an in-depth understanding of a wide range of web technologies from Java to Ruby.

Career summary

2009 – present Development Team Leader, GoGetting.com

I joined the online travel company GoGetting.com as a development officer before being promoted in August 2012 to my current position. Since becoming team leader the site has had a threefold increase in unique visitors thanks to an extensive linking program I developed. As a result of the increased traffic, the company has given me extra responsibility to drive the marketing of the site with selected web partners. I manage a team of seven development officers and am in charge of a budget of £250,000.

2004 – 2009 Web Developer, Toprank Recruitment

Having learned a lot at my first company and really enjoyed the experience of working in web development, I joined this small recruitment start-up specializing in the catering trade. During the time I helped program the site's search engine and learned ASP, Java and SQL.
I was very proud to have seen one key module of the search engine's development through from design to implementation. The module generated five per cent extra revenue for the company while I was there. I learned a lot about effective teamwork in the process.

2002–2004 Junior programmer, Oakhampton Systems

This was a perfect job after graduation. I was part of a small graduate intake whose job was to develop and code account and customer databases. I went on site visits to understand what a client needed and understand the way the business works. I taught myself HTML in this period and designed the company's first website.

Education and qualifications

1998–2001 University of Windsor, BSC Computer Science (2:1)
1991–1998 Greenglades School, Windsor
3 A-levels: Mathematics (A), Physics (A), Chemistry (B)
10 GCSEs

Hobbies and interests

Between leaving school and starting university I worked for six months so that I could spend three months doing charity runs for Famine Relief, whom I continue to work for as a volunteer. I run long-distance competitively, enjoy cinema, computer games and chess.

References available on request

> *One of the worst mistakes a candidate can make is to send employers a 6-page 'novel' about their work experience, school qualifications and hobbies and pastimes – especially if it is written in size-9 font. Many managers skim read CVs so using short paragraphs and an almost report-like style will mean they are less likely to miss a candidate with relevant skills or experience. This is where editing down and making the CV relate to the job description/advert works to the candidate's advantage.*
>
> (HR Director)

BASIC GRADUATE CV

CV

Name	Kate Maxwell
Date of birth	29.02.92
Address	19, The Poplars, Bristol B10 2JU
Telephone	0117 123 4567
Email	katemaxwell@atlantic.net
Nationality	British

Education

20011–2015	**BA Hons in Modern Languages, University of Exeter** (final grade 2.1)
2009–2011	**Clifton Road Secondary School:** 3 'A' levels – French (A) German (A) History (B)
2004–2009	**Clifton Road Secondary School:** 8 GCSEs including Maths and English

Employment history

2011–2012	**Sales Assistant, Langs Bookshop, Bristol** I was responsible for training and supervising weekend and holiday staff.
2012–2013	**English Assistant, Lycée Benoit, Lyons** I taught conversational English to pupils aged 12–18, preparing the older students for both technical and more academic qualifications. I organized an educational trip to the UK for fourth year pupils.

Positions of responsibility held

2012–2013	**Entertainments Officer for University Student Social Society** I organized and budgeted for entertainment for a student society with over 1000 members.
2011–2014	**Captain of the university women's netball team** I was in charge of training, organizing and motivating the woman's team.

Other skills

Fluent French and German
Extensive knowledge of Microsoft Word, Excel and Access
I hold a clean driving licence

References

on request

Top ten CV tips

1. Adapt your CV to the job or prospective employer.

2. You have 30–60 seconds to attract your reader's attention so lay out your CV clearly – use a plain font like Arial, Trebuchet or Times New Roman – and keep it to the point. It should not be longer than 3 sides.

3. Remember the CV is a means of getting an interview, not getting the job.

4. Avoid gimmicks like thumbnail images or pictures – they distract from the words you are writing about yourself.

5. Focus your description of your current and previous experience on achievements and the contribution you have made to organizations. If possible quantify your achievements – 'my actions led to a saving of £xx' or, 'as a result profits were up by x per cent'.

6. Give examples of your skills and qualities – don't just say 'I am a natural leader', write a brief description of when you showed this attribute.

7. Avoid bullet points when describing your current and previous jobs. It's much better to write short paragraphs because you can give examples.

8. Format the document to make sure that the printed version reflects what you see on screen. Try not to waste paper by leaving just two or three sentences at the top of the last page.

9. Use 'active' verbs such as 'achieve', 'lead', 'manage'.

10. Finally carefully proofread your CV and, if you can, ask someone else to look at it as well.

How to send your CV

You can still post your CV if you wish but most HR professionals prefer to receive the document as an attachment to an email. This means that they can share the CV with the relevant staff or store it on their computer for future reference.

Online applications

Sometimes you will be asked to complete an application form online. Here are some tips to do this effectively:

- As for written job applications, you should write in a formal style.

- The online system will probably dictate the particular text format (the font and size of type) – you should take this into account when you draft your answers.

- It is useful to prepare a draft of the application and then transfer the information to the online form.

- Copy and save your answers regularly into a normal document in case the system crashes or you have to break off your application and start again.

- Just because the application is automatically filed online, it does not mean you should be any less rigorous in the editing and proofreading you do. If you can print the document out before you submit it, get someone you trust to read it over to look for errors and omissions.

WRITING FORMAL LETTERS

Emails and other digital media are the prevalent forms of communication for most of us today, at work and at home, but there are still occasions when a handwritten or typed letter is more appropriate.

This section lays out the basic structure and the rules which underpin most formal letter writing. Subsequent sections on Domestic Correspondence, Letters of Complaint and Social Communication look more closely at situations where formal letter writing is used, and give examples of good practice.

As with any written communication, your letter should be in three discernible parts:

- **An introduction.** This is where you introduce yourself, acknowledge any previous correspondence, and briefly state the reason why you are writing. Ideally it should be no longer than a paragraph of three or four sentences.

- **The middle.** This is the section where you expand your argument, provide further details, and raise any questions you have. The middle of the letter should be a series of paragraphs set out in a logical order. Each paragraph should make a clear, separate point. If the letter is long and covers a range of subjects, it may be appropriate to divide the contents by subheadings.

- **The ending, or conclusion.** The final paragraph should set out what you would like to happen as a result of the communication, whether that be a written response, a meeting to discuss the contents of the letter, or a demand for a refund.

Here is an example of a formal letter:

55 Torrance Close
Gorton
NSW 2234

25 August 2015

Mr L Dylan
Terrigan Building Ltd
340 Shorter Street
Terrigan
NSW 2234
Dear Mr Dylan

Estimate for extension to living room, 55 Torrance Close

I am writing to thank you for the written estimate which I received this morning. I have queries about a couple of details in your letter which I would like to be resolved before we proceed any further.

First, can you say exactly when you would propose to begin work on the extension? I realize this depends, to some extent, on how quickly you can finish your current project. I need to know which week work would commence in, however, so that I can make arrangements to store the living room furniture.

Second, can you tell me when you propose to fit the additional plumbing, so that I can arrange to stay with friends while there is no running water? Also, are there any other times when you anticipate that I shall be without water or electricity?

Finally, there is no mention of additional costs for materials. Can I assume, therefore, that these are included in the estimate you have provided for the overall cost of the extension?

Assuming I receive satisfactory answers in writing to these queries, I shall be happy to accept your proposal and go ahead with the project as discussed.

Yours sincerely

Tom Peterson

Tom Peterson

Points to remember:

- **Your address.** This should be written in the top right corner of the letter. Do not write your name here, and don't put commas after each line.

- **The date.** The date should come under your address, also on the right. It is common practice to write the date as 25 August 2015, instead of 25th August 2015.

- **The recipient's address.** Write this under the date, but on the left side of the page. Again, no punctuation is required.

- **The greeting.** If you are writing to a friend then you will use, 'Dear Luke,' for instance. Otherwise it should be 'Dear Mr Dylan.' Note that if you are writing to a woman and do not know whether she prefers to be addressed as 'Dear Mrs Dylan', or 'Dear Miss Dylan', then you should use 'Dear Ms Dylan.' If you do not know the person's name then use, 'Dear Sir or Madam'.

- **Headings.** If you are using a heading, then it should summarize the subject matter of the letter, and appear between the greeting and the first paragraph. Headings should be written in bold but not capital letters.

- **The ending.** If you have used the name of the person in the greeting, then you should end with 'Yours sincerely'. Otherwise end the letter with 'Yours faithfully'. 'Yours...' should always begin with a capital letter.

- **Punctuation.** It is not necessary to include a comma after the greeting or after the ending. Don't put full stops in initials – write 'Mr L H Dylan' instead of 'Mr L.H. Dylan'.

- **Signature.** Write your signature but include your typewritten name underneath.

- **Further contact details.** If you are including your email address or telephone number as contact details, then these should be included underneath your postal address:

55 Torrance Close
Gorton
NSW 2234
tpeterson@email.com
(02) 4254 6398

Once you have written your letter check that:

- You have explained why you are writing in the first paragraph.

- You have made all the points that you wanted to.

- Each sentence is clear, concise and unambiguous.

- You have not included too much information, or any irrelevant details.

- Your language has been courteous and polite, even if you are writing a letter of complaint.

- Check once more for spelling mistakes – it is surprisingly easy to miss them!

DOMESTIC CORRESPONDENCE

This section tackles the range of letters and correspondence that relates to you, your home, your finances and your family. The following points about content, style and tone apply equally whether you're writing a letter, an email, filling in an online form, or if you are speaking to someone on the phone:

- Use formal language.

- Include every detail that will make the letter easier to deal with.

- Lay the letter out clearly – breaking it down so that each paragraph contains a single point.

- Be explicit about what you want to happen next and introduce a timescale where appropriate.

- What you are writing may have legal implications, so take care with the details you include and the language you use.

- Provide as many contact details as you can.

- Write 'Yours sincerely' to end the letter if you know the surname of the person you are writing to. Write 'Yours faithfully' if you do not.

> *When I'm writing to a company, I always try and find out a specific person to address the letter to – or else it can just end up getting lost in the system.*
> (Teacher)

In the following section there is a selection of letters that many of us will have to write at some point:

- Housing problems

- Money-related correspondence

- Insurance claims

- Local authority correspondence

- School correspondence

Housing problems

To a landlord concerning outstanding repairs

In the first instance, simply list the repairs required, and ask the landlord to contact you so that a time may be arranged for them to be carried out.

> 56 Kayside Close
> Redditch
> Worcs.
> RD14 7NX
>
> 4 April 2015
>
> Dear Mr Fairchild
>
> I am writing to notify you that the following repairs to 56 Kayside Close require attention:
>
> There are several loose tiles on the roof.
> The kitchen tap is leaking.
> The sealant round the bath needs replacing.
>
> I would appreciate it if you would contact me as soon as possible to arrange a time to have these problems taken care of.
> Thank you very much.
>
> Yours sincerely
>
> *Matthew Chalmers*
>
> Matthew Chalmers

If you do not get a reply in a reasonable amount of time, write again, once more itemizing the repairs, and reminding the recipient how long you have been waiting. This time you might want to give the landlord a deadline, and show that you are aware of your rights in law.

Useful phrases

- Further to my previous correspondence, the following repairs to the above address remain outstanding: …

- I have been waiting for a considerable amount of time to have these repairs completed.

- By law, a landlord is responsible for providing and maintaining residence in a good state of repair.

- Please contact me immediately so that we may resolve this problem.

- I would be glad if you could see that the matter is resolved as soon as possible.

56 Kayside Close
Hawkes Bay
4230

1 May 2015

Dear Mr Fairchild

I refer to my letter of 4th April 2015 requesting repairs to be completed to 56 Kayside Close. The following items remain outstanding:

There are several loose tiles on the roof.
The kitchen tap is leaking.
The sealant round the bath needs replacing.

I have been waiting for a considerable amount of time to have these repairs completed. I would ask you to take care of this matter within one week of receipt of this letter.

I remind you that by law, a landlord is responsible for providing and maintaining residence in a good state of repair, and for complying with housing and maintenance standards.

Please contact me immediately so that we may resolve this problem.

Yours sincerely

Matthew Chalmers

Matthew Chalmers

Letter to a housing advice centre regarding unfair rent

If your landlord/landlady is trying to put the rent up and you don't agree to the increase, it may be worth negotiating with them. They may agree to a lower rent increase in return rather than having to relet the property. Alternatively, they may agree to increase the rent in stages over a period of time.

---

45 Victoria
Street
Headley
Northants.
NO3 7FS

16 April 2015

The Rents Adviser
Headley Housing Advice
4 The Row
Headley
Northants.
NO2 4TY

Dear Sir/Madam

Unfair rent query

I am writing to request your advice on an issue regarding what I consider to be an unfair increase in rent.

My landlord has recently increased my rent from £300 a month to £360 a month. Not only do I find this amount unreasonable, but I am also having difficulty sustaining the payments. Furthermore, there are several outstanding repairs to be attended to in the house.

I would be grateful if you could inform me of my rights, and let me know what, if anything, I can do to challenge this increase.

I look forward to hearing from you.

Yours faithfully

Katherine Gulliver

Katherine Gulliver

Letter to a housing advice centre regarding eviction

Most private tenants can only be evicted if their landlord gets a possession order from the court. If your landlord has evicted you without following the correct procedure this may be illegal.

34 Tadworth
Court
Ducksbury
Berkshire
RD7 4GN

3 June 2015

Dear Sir/Madam

eviction query

I am writing to request advice from you regarding a matter of urgency.

My landlord has just issued me with an eviction notice, due to come into force on 4 July 2015. His justification for this action is that I have not paid my rent for the last two months.

I am a single mother with two young children, and I have been unable to pay the rent due to the fact that my ex-husband has not kept up regular maintenance payments over the last four months.

Could you please inform me of my rights, and advise me on how I should proceed?

I look forward to hearing from you. If you wish to speak to me directly, please call me on 01456 783219.

Thank you in advance.

Yours faithfully

Sally Nettles

Sally Nettles

Money-related correspondence

Letter to a lender advising of difficulty in mortgage payment

If you are having problems with your mortgage repayments, or think you will have problems in the near future, it is always wise to contact the lender and alert them as soon as possible. In your correspondence explain the problem clearly and state that you are keen to keep paying as much as you can. Also show that you can be flexible and are willing to negotiate.

Useful phrases

- I am writing to inform you that I am anticipating having some difficulty in continuing to meet my mortgage payments.

- I am currently finding it hard to meet all my financial commitments.

- My employers went into liquidation two months ago.

- I have recently been made redundant.

- I am suffering from a long-term illness, and am no longer entitled to sickness pay.

- I was wondering if it would be possible to reduce my monthly payments.

- I would like to request that my mortgage payments be reduced from July.

- I am keen to continue paying as much as possible.

- I would be pleased to come into your office and discuss this matter further with you.

- Would it be possible to arrange an interview with you, so that we may come to some sort of arrangement?

- I do hope that you will give sympathetic consideration to my situation, and look forward to hearing from you.

12 Darwin Road
Canberra
2605

15 May 2015

Mr J McVee
Senior Credit Controller
Castle Building Society
17 Martyn Place
Canberra
2602

Dear Mr McVee

request for reduction in mortgage payments

I am writing to inform you that, due to my recent redundancy, I am anticipating having some difficulty in continuing to meet my mortgage payments.

I am making every attempt to find work elsewhere, but if I am unsuccessful, I would like to request that my mortgage payments be temporarily reduced from July, and the terms of my mortgage extended accordingly.

I am keen to continue paying as much as possible, and am currently in consultation with my financial adviser to calculate how much money I can reasonably afford each month.

Would it be possible to arrange an interview with you, so that we may come to some sort of arrangement?

I do hope that you will give sympathetic consideration to my situation, and look forward to hearing from you.

Yours sincerely

Jack Everett

Jack Everett

Insurance claims

Most of us find ourselves having to make a claim to an insurance company at some stage in our lives – whether it be as the result of a car accident, burglary, incident on holiday or some other regrettable occurrence.

The claim can be made verbally, online or in a written statement but whichever form it takes, it is important to consider the kind of language you use and the information that you include.

Ms C Hall
32, Lime Road
Saddleworth
Devon
SD2 8LN
christinehall@email.com
17 June 2015

Ms Ying
Claims Assessor
Admirable Insurance Company
Claims Avenue
Spottington
Hants
SP31 4AQ

My policy number: AIC008997/CH56.

Dear Ms Ying,

I am writing to make an insurance claim, resulting from an accident I was involved in on 16 June 2015. My car is covered by a comprehensive insurance policy which I took out with you some time ago. The policy number is included above.

The incident occurred at approximately 3pm at the junction of New Street and London Road in Saddleworth. The other driver, a Mr Steve Wall, turned right out of New Street and drove into the front passenger side of my vehicle, causing extensive damage to the bodywork and the headlights. I have enclosed a picture of the damage, together with a diagram showing the relative positions of the vehicles, and the direction they were travelling in at the time of the accident.

Mr Wall has admitted liability for the accident. His insurance company's details, together with his policy number, are also enclosed.

As a result of the incident, my car is not roadworthy. I need therefore, to arrange to collect a replacement car from one of your suppliers, which I am entitled to according to the terms of my policy. Can you advise me on the nearest garage and confirm my entitlement? Please let me know if there are any other details you require to process my claim, and also give me an indication of how long it will take to arrange the repair of my vehicle.

Yours sincerely

Ms C Hall

Ms C Hall

- The letter contains all the relevant information – such as dates, policy number, details of the incident – that the company is likely to require.

- In spite of the nature of the incident, the language is restrained – emotional language will not make your claim any more likely to succeed.

- The letter politely requests information from the insurance company which will move the claim on.

Local authority correspondence

Letter to planning authority inquiring whether planning permission is needed

Some minor developments (such as certain extensions to domestic property, or changes in the way a building is used) may not need express planning permission. With buildings that are listed for preservation, it is generally best to consult with the local planning authority before any changes are made.

If you are unsure whether your development requires planning permission, you should contact your local planning authority.

19 Limes Avenue
Cambridge
CB12 4LA
tel: 01356 721673

17 June 2015

The Planning Department
Cambridge District Council
University Road
Cambridge
CB2 7KS

Dear Sir/Madam

Inquiry re. necessity of planning permission

I am writing to inquire as to whether I will need to apply for planning permission for a proposed development I wish to undertake at the above address.

The specifications of the development are as follows:

description:
garage
location:
side of property
use:
car storage
dimensions:
floor surface area: 6m x 3.5m
height: 2.5m

If you require any further information, please do not hesitate to contact me at the telephone number above. I look forward to hearing from you.

Yours faithfully

Harriet Yates

Harriet Yates (Mrs)

Opposing a planning application

If you are making an objection to a planning proposal, check which aspects of the proposal you can object to and what deadlines the local authority have imposed. Comply with these and lay out your letter clearly, keeping the objections succinct and relevant.

Mr Anderson
Director of Planning
Lime Borough Council
Acacia Road
Lessington
County Durham
D5 1AA

Dear Mr Anderson,

Planning application number LBC123456/7A
Address of proposed extension: 77 Birchtree Row, Lessington, County Durham, D2 8LN

I am writing to object to the proposal to build an extension on the above property. There are several reasons for this.

Design
The very modern design of the proposed extension is in unsympathetic contrast to the Victorian style of all the houses in the area.

Privacy
The two-storey extension will affect the privacy of my property. The plans show a window that will look directly into my garden.

Natural light
The extension will block out the natural light I get in my conservatory all-year round.

Appropriateness of use
It is clear from the plans that the owner intends to make and sell drum kits from the property. This will have a significant impact on the local noise levels – the neighbourhood at the moment is very quiet.

I am sure that other local residents will be objecting as well, and I trust you will refuse this application on the basis that it most definitely contravenes your planning regulations.

I would be grateful if you could acknowledge this letter, confirm that it has been logged as an objection to the application within the deadline set by the council, and keep me informed as to the outcome. I can be contacted at the above address or via the email address at the top of this letter.

Yours Sincerely,

Mr C Hopkins

Mr C Hopkins

- The writer has found out the deadline for his objection and complied with it.

- He has found out and addressed the criteria on which the application will be judged.

- The headings highlight the grounds on which he is basing his objection.

Writing to your MP

When writing to your MP keep the letter to a single subject and make it as concise as possible. Remember to say what you want the MP to do as a result of your letter. At all times be courteous – just because you may disagree with his views, does not mean that you should be anything other than respectful in your writing.

Mr R Boscombe
27 Juniper Road
Flickcroft
West Midlands
reg.boscombe@email.com

15 April 2015

Derek Firbanks MP
House of Commons
Westminster
LONDON
SW1A 1AA

Dear Derek Firbanks

I am writing to draw your attention to the imminent closure of the Priory Centre on Sandhurst Road in Flickcroft. I am a parent whose child uses the premises for a theatre group on Saturday mornings. She finds the opportunity to learn about acting and to perform stimulating and great fun. The group also provides invaluable contact with other children from the area and with the community in general.

There are 120 children aged from six to 16 who attend the theatre classes every week – divided into three age bands. Last term my daughter's group staged a production dramatizing the history of the Priory Centre and its place in the local community.

The theatre group is by no means the only one affected. There are some 30 other activities put on for a huge range of people, including for elderly and disabled groups, at weekends and during the week.

The council plans to pass the plans at a meeting in three weeks' time. I, and many others, would be grateful if you could take this matter up with the leader of the council as a matter of urgency. The loss of the centre will create a huge gap in the cultural life of our community.

Please acknowledge this letter as soon as you can and let me know of your progress.

Yours sincerely,

Mr R Boscombe

Mr R Boscombe

- The letter starts with a very specific description of the problem.

- The writer includes his full address so that the MP knows the letter is from a constituent.

- The letter is about one issue which makes it much easier to deal with.

- Including anecdotes or some personal detail will help the MP remember the letter.

- The writer refers to others who are opposed to the closure. Including supporting evidence – be it a petition or the MPs involvement with or voting record on similar issues – will help the cause.

> *When contacting your MP, a short, handwritten or printed letter is*
> *most effective. Take the time to edit your letter for brevity and clarity.*
> *Try to make a single coherent point.*
>
> (Campaigning website)

Deferring jury service

A letter requesting you to serve on a jury is a serious matter – in the UK if you ignore it you could be prosecuted. If the dates you have been called for are very disruptive to your plans, or circumstances are such that you can't attend, then you should write asking for a deferment. The grounds for deferment will be laid out in the letter you receive.

Mr J Brown
The Moorings
Chettleworth
LINCOLNSHIRE
AG7 0BC
james.brown@email.com
01285 78945613

3 February 2015

Mr R Ball
Jury Central Summoning Bureau
Derby
DA1 9IO

Dear Mr Ball

Thank you for the letter dated January 30th inviting me to serve on a jury from March 27th. I would like to ask if it would be possible to defer this until sometime next year? My wife has recently had a car accident and suffered a serious injury. I have now had to become a full-time carer for her and as a consequence cannot leave the house for an extended period.

I would be very grateful if you could agree to this request, and if you require me to provide you with any further information, please do not hesitate to contact me.

I look forward to receiving your response.

Yours sincerely,

Mr James Brown

Mr James Brown

- It is more effective to provide specific details for your request: it decreases the likelihood of having to give more information and speeds up the process.

- Do not demand that your attendance is deferred.

School correspondence

There are a few occasions when it will be necessary to write, or email, your child's school about health matters, behaviour or other issues. Below are an email, two letters and a hand-written note giving examples of this kind of correspondence.

Explaining a child's absence due to ill health

> To: J Chalfont <jchalfont@derwentwaterschool.ed.uk
> From: kevin.bond@email.net
>
> Subject: Charlie Bond's absence 1st – 5th March
>
> Dear Mr Chalfont
>
> I am writing to explain why Charlie was absent from school last week (1st to 5th March). He woke up with a very sore throat on Sunday morning. We went to the doctor on Monday and Charlie was diagnosed with laryngitis. He started to feel better on Friday morning and is able to return to school today.
>
> Charlie is worried, as the exams approach, about keeping on top of his work, so I would be very grateful if you could let him know what he has missed and help him catch up.
>
> If you have any concerns, please do email or phone me on the number below.
>
> Yours sincerely
>
> Mr K Bond
> kevin.bond@email.net
> Tel: 01234 456789

- The letter quickly and clearly summarizes the course of events and includes evidence of the illness by referring to the doctor's diagnosis.

- The parent, having been very clear about the reason for absence, then presents his own concerns and is explicit about what he wants the teacher to do. The letter is useful and effective for the teacher, the parent and the pupil.

Recording concerns about bullying

Mrs J Trewin
'The Glade'
Farm Road
Kettering
XA7 2WR
janetrewin@email.com
01234 5678913

29 January 2015

Ms L Edge
Long Oak Primary School
West End Lane
Kettering
XA5 9LD

Dear Ms Edge

I am writing to follow up on our conversation on the phone two days ago. I'm afraid that Julia is still very upset when she gets home from school. The name-calling and exclusion from playground games seems to have carried on, in spite of the warning you said you gave the other children concerned. In fact, I fear that it may have made the problem worse.

As you can imagine this is causing Julia great distress and it is certainly affecting her desire to come to school and learn. I am very anxious to get this matter resolved with all possible speed, and request a meeting with you and the head of year at your earliest convenience.

Please telephone or email me as soon as you can to arrange this.

Yours sincerely

Mrs J Trewin

Mrs J Trewin

- The letter quickly summarizes the current situation to remind the teacher of the problem.

- The parent suggests a specific course of action and a timetable.

Excusing a child from religious instruction

67 Langley Avenue
Crawley
W. Sussex
RH8 3FX

12 July 2015

Mrs J Wilson
Langley Green Secondary School
Langley Drive
Crawley
RH8 4WA

Dear Mrs Wilson

religious instruction

My son, Aashir, will be attending your school from the beginning of next term, and I am writing to ask that he be excused from religious education classes.

He is being raised in the Muslim faith, and receives his religious instruction outside school.

Thank you very much for your understanding.

Yours sincerely

Mahira Pandit

Mahira Pandit (Mrs)

Non-completion of homework

Dear Mr Mitchell

John was unable to finish his essay that was due to be handed in today, as he was suffering from a severe migraine for most of yesterday evening.

He will make every effort to complete it tonight and hand it in tomorrow.

Thank you for your understanding.

Yours sincerely
Helen Maxwell

LETTERS OF COMPLAINT

Complaining about faulty goods or services is an unpleasant but common experience. Whatever your complaint, there are several points which you should bear in mind when composing a letter or email to increase your chances of receiving a satisfactory response:

- Make sure you are complaining to the right person. It may seem obvious, but if you have paid for something in cash or by credit card, then it is the seller of the goods or services who you should address your complaint to – not the manufacturer.

- Be aware of your rights under the Sales and Supply of Goods Act, the Trades Descriptions Act and related or equivalent legislation – these decree that goods or services must be found to be 'as described' when sold.

- There are consumer watchdogs and other bodies who can help you if you are given unsatisfactory responses to your complaints. You can also write to your MP or consult a solicitor, but these should be last measures which hopefully won't be necessary.

Useful phrases

- I am writing to express my dissatisfaction with the service I received from your ...

- At the time of booking it was agreed that ...

- However, on our arrival, we discovered that ...

- I recently bought ...(include colour, model and price) in your shop in ...

- When I tried to use this item, I discovered that ...

- I have contacted you by telephone three times and each time you have promised to visit and put the faults right.

- To date these problems have not been resolved.

- Under the terms of your guarantee, I would like to request a full reimbursement of the amount paid.

- I am withholding payment of the above invoice until I have heard your response to the points outlined above.

- Under the Goods and Services Act 1982, I am entitled to expect work to be carried out using due care and skill.

- If I do not hear from you within 14 days, I will have no choice but to take the matter further.

- Because of these faults I now consider you to be in breach of contract.

Letter or email of complaint concerning faulty goods

15 High Street
Corton
LANCS
LA12 3SH
fheadley@email.com

17 August 2015

Mr D Bryant
High Fi
3 The Parade
Soulton
LANCS
LA23 8GG

Dear Mr Bryant,

I am writing to complain about the Soundalive 411 headphones which I bought from your company, High Fi in Soulton, on 14 August.

When I plugged the headphones into my iPhone and listened to music through them, the sound in the left headphone was distorted at even low levels of volume – it was clear to me that they were faulty.

I returned them to your shop, a thirty mile round trip, but the salesperson who I originally dealt with disputed my claim – stating that the item had been sold in a satisfactory state. He suggested that I take up the complaint with you, as the owner of the shop.

The Sale of Goods Act 1979 makes it clear that goods be as described, fit for purpose and of satisfactory quality. I am therefore rejecting the headphones and request that you refund the £89 I paid, as the condition of the goods I received constitutes a breach of contract. I have enclosed a copy of my receipt.

I also require you to confirm whether you will arrange for the headphones to be collected from me at the above address, or will reimburse me for the cost of returning them by post?

I expect to receive a response detailing your proposals to satisfactorily settle my claim within seven days of this date.

Yours sincerely,

F Headley

Mr F Headley

- Although the writer has being treated badly by a member of staff, the tone of the letter is formal. Emotive language is likely to produce a defensive response, whereas a detailed and factual description of the problem is more likely to succeed.

- It is quite reasonable to seek compensation for the cost of returning a faulty item.

- Don't send originals of receipts and other documentary evidence with your complaint – especially if you have paid in cash. They may be the only way you have to prove purchase should you need to take the complaint further.

Letter to a travel agency complaining about a holiday

Customer Services department
Sunkissed Holidays
14 The Waterglades
Hintenbury
GLOS
FL34 7HH

Dear sir or madam

I am writing to complain about the holiday I booked through your company on 5 May this year (REF: BA12303/Maga003).

The booking stated that I would have a room with a balcony with ocean views, and that I would enjoy '5 star luxury' at the Mirabelle Resort, with 'top class international cuisine', and 'a choice of four swimming pools – two of which are reserved for adult use only.' Furthermore, the booking was on an 'all-inclusive basis, guaranteeing bar snacks, soft drinks and local brands of beers, wines and spirits', as and when I requested them.

The reality of my experience was very different. On arrival at the resort, I was allocated a room at the back of the hotel, with a view over a busy street. The noise from the traffic kept me awake at night.

The 'international cuisine' turned out to be a buffet featuring the same options practically every night – mostly fried food, chips and salad.

One of the swimming pools was closed for maintenance for the duration of my stay, and there was no attempt to keep any of the three remaining pools segregated for adult use.

Finally, the availability of drinks and bar snacks was very limited – peanuts were the only snack at the poolside bar, which also only had wine stocked on two days of the fourteen I was at the hotel.

I complained about each of these issues to your firm's representative at the resort – a Mr Stephens – during my first week's holiday. He said he would 'see what he could do'. I didn't hear back from him, and he failed to turn up for the 'rep meeting' in the second week. The hotel staff were unhelpful and told me they could do nothing to rectify any of the problems.

As a result of these issues, my holiday was ruined. I am therefore writing to you seeking compensation from your firm, which has clearly failed to deliver what was contractually agreed. I request that you reply within seven days, stating your proposal to compensate me.

Yours faithfully

Mrs B Pritchard

Mrs B Pritchard

- Use the company's own description of services to compare your experience with.

- Describe each aspect of your complaint concisely; state what you have done about it, and the response that you received from the relevant authority – in this case the holiday rep and the hotel staff.

48

Letter of complaint to a noisy neighbour

Mr G Barton
7 Chestnut Mansions
Pibble
Cumbria
PW12 3RR
gbarton@email.com

14 October 2015

Ms R Devlin
8 Chestnut Mansions
Pibble
Cumbria
PW12 3RR

Dear Ms Devlin

I am writing to you to formally register my complaint about the excessive noise that has been generated from your flat since you moved in two months ago.

As you know, I have complained in person to you five times in the past month about extremely loud music being played after 11 pm. You have assured me that you will 'not let it happen again,' only for me and my partner to have our sleep ruined the next weekend.

We have no objection to the occasional party or celebration, but your behaviour is inconsiderate and unreasonable. The interruption to our sleep patterns is affecting our concentration at work, and therefore I am giving you notice that if this happens again, without prior notice and agreement from us, I shall instruct my solicitor to begin legal proceedings to restrain you from excessive noise pollution.

Yours sincerely

Mr G Barton

Mr G Barton

- Legal action should only be threatened after attempts to complain less formally have failed. This letter is written after five such attempts.

- Be clear about what you expect to happen as a result of your complaint – how you expect the other party to modify their behaviour in this instance.

- Also spell out what course of action you intend to take should your demands not be met. You must follow through on this course of action, if you don't get a satisfactory response, or you will not be taken seriously in the future.

Letter complaining about shoddy workmanship

If you are dissatisfied with a piece of work which has been carried out for you discuss the problem with the tradesperson first, and give them a chance to put it right. If this doesn't work, put your complaint in writing giving a clear deadline. If you chose a contractor that belongs to a trade association, they may offer a conciliation or arbitration service to settle your dispute.

Keep copies of all letters sent and received and make a note of conversations.

77 Bishop Road
Newport
Gwent
NP3 5NQ

31 October 2015

The Customer Services Manager
L. Smart & Co. Contractors
17 Trevellyan Road
Cardiff
CA4 5GT

Dear Sir/Madam

Re: estimate 700003412

I am writing to express my dissatisfaction with the service I received from one of your builders recently.

Before accepting your estimate for the job, I was assured that the work would be completed by 10 October. Three weeks later, the work is still incomplete. Moreover, the work that has been done is defective. The new door that was fitted is not flush with the frame, and the lock is consequently very stiff.

If the work is not completed and the defect rectified within 14 days, I shall consider our contract to be at an end. I shall then instruct another firm to complete the work, and deduct the cost from your original price.

Yours faithfully

Douglas Fairburn

Douglas Fairburn

Complaining to a health authority

If you wish to make a complaint regarding healthcare treatment you have received you should address your letter to the Complaints Manager of the Local Health Authority. Start by giving the name of the doctor, GP or practitioner concerned and then provide a brief background to the case. Explain the problem clearly and if your complaint consists of a catalogue of errors, itemize them clearly and succinctly.

It is one of the NHS's officially stated core principles that it is committed to shaping its services around the needs and preferences of individual patients, their families and carers. You should not be afraid to voice your opinion.

---

7 Oaklands
Horley
RH6 2QT

17 November 2015

The Complaints Manager
East Surrey Local Health Authority
5 Market Street
Redhill
RH1 4GA

Dear Sir

I am writing to express my concern about the treatment that my elderly mother, Mrs Grace Harding, is currently undergoing. Her GP is Dr Middleton at the Longwood Surgery, Horley.

In 2010, my mother was diagnosed as suffering from shingles. Since that time she has experienced continual pain down the sides of her body.

However, she recently received a letter informing her that she would no longer be able to attend the pain clinic. She has been given no explanation as to the reasons for this decision from the health authority or from her doctor.

Since it is one of the NHS's officially stated core principles that it is committed to shaping its services around the needs and preferences of individual patients, I feel that you have a duty to ensure that she enjoys this later period of her life.

I would be glad to hear your comments on this case.

Yours faithfully

G. Glover

Gillian Glover

Complaining about financial services

If you are having problems with a bank you must complain to the firm in question before you can take your complaint to the financial ombudsman. When writing your letter remember to include your customer number of your policy or your account number. Enclose copies of any relevant documents that you believe support your case and always keep a copy of any letters between you and the firm. You may need to refer to them later.

4 Crow Lane
Wagga Wagga
2650

24 October 2015

The Customer Relations Manager
Castle Building Society
Short Street
Wagga Wagga
2650

Dear Sir/Madam

Complaint: savings acc. no. 9450001992

I wish to register my dissatisfaction with the service that I have received from the staff at your Brighton branch.

I opened a savings account, and arranged for a monthly standing order of $200 a month to be made from my current account, held at another bank. However, the last time I asked for a mini-statement, I noticed that there had not been a credit to my savings account for the previous two months, despite the fact that the money had been debited from my current account. Enclosed are copies of both the relevant statements.

I am therefore appealing to you for a thorough investigation into this matter, and look forward to hearing from you.

Yours faithfully

Patrick Horton

Patrick Horton

SOCIAL COMMUNICATION

> *And none will hear the postman's knock*
> *Without a quickening of the heart.*
> *For who can bear to feel himself forgotten?*

(W.H. Auden)

Although seemingly belonging to a different world – predating mobile phones, texts and tablet devices, all of which convey informal messages instantly and very well – there is still a time and a place for a carefully handwritten note or card, or printed invitation.

Types of correspondence in this category include:

- Thank-you notes
- Letters of apology
- Letters wishing a speedy recovery
- Letters of condolence
- Invitations

Here are some general points to consider when writing social communications:

Tone

Apart from invitations, the tone of most social communications is informal and friendly:

- Salutations can range from 'Dear' to 'Hi'.
- Language is usually quite conversational, with shortened sentences and contractions ('I'm', 'won't'); more emotive and less factual than in business correspondence.
- Endings are similarly warm – 'Lots of love'; 'Love'; 'Speak/write soon'; or slightly more formal such as 'Best wishes', 'Kind regards' or 'All the best' if you don't know your correspondent quite so well.

Format

Just because it is handwritten doesn't mean that a note shouldn't have a structure. It is still usual to have:

- An introductory line or paragraph, stating the purpose of the letter ('I was sorry to hear about your loss'; 'thank you for the birthday card...').

- A middle section expounding on the subject ('She was a wonderful woman...'; 'The party went really well, all things considered').

- An ending ('I shall hope to speak to you at the memorial service'; 'Let's meet up before another year goes by...').

> *One thing I can't stand? The computer-generated Christmas card – it's so impersonal – "Look, I can do a mail merge on my pc!" If you can't be bothered to handwrite a greetings card, don't bother!*
>
> (Publishing assistant)

Here are some examples of different kinds of social correspondence:

Thank-you note for a dinner party

A thank-you letter can be as varied as a formal letter: the writer's relationship with the recipient will determine the tone and language used.

Tuesday

Hi Moz,

I'm just popping this note through your letterbox to thank you so much for dinner on Saturday. Nigel and I had a wonderful evening. It was lovely to meet Sharon and Graham at last – you've talked about them so much over the years – and they were delightful company. I hope Ben has found the champagne cork (sorry about that!)

By the way, please, please send me your recipe for the chocolate mousse – it was exquisite, and Nigel talked of nothing else on Sunday.

You must come to ours for dinner soon.

Love to you both and thanks again,

Lizzie.

- Dating and address can be very informal – this is a note between friends, and knowledge of addresses and contact details can be assumed. Note that the writer uses her friend's nickname 'Moz', rather than full name. You wouldn't use this form of address if writing to a colleague, for example.

- The language is casual – contractions like 'you've' and 'I'm' are absolutely fine. "Please, please send me your recipe…' would be out of place in a formal letter, but it works here.
- In social communication you can refer to events without having to be explicit – here there was clearly an 'incident' with a champagne cork which was a shared source of humour.

Writing a letter of apology

If you feel compelled to apologize for your actions and wish to send the person concerned a letter of apology you should start by making it clear that you are saying sorry. State plainly what you are apologizing for and explain your actions or the mistake (as the case may be) as far as you can. Accept responsibility if you are at fault and try to suggest a means by which you can right the wrong. At the end of the letter, reiterate your apology.

Useful phrases
- I am writing to apologize for …
- I've just realized that …
- I can't tell you how sorry I am.
- I am sorry that …
- Due to …, I was unable to …
- I know it's no excuse, but …
- Unfortunately …
- I hope you will accept …
- Can I suggest …?
- Would you agree to …?
- Again, please accept my apologies (for …).
- In the meantime, many apologies again.

Letters wishing a speedy recovery

Informal wishes (card)

- Hoping you get well very soon.

- Wishing you a speedy recovery.

- Sorry to hear you're not well. We're thinking of you.

Formal wishes (letter)

- I was very sorry to hear of ...

- Please accept my sympathies ...

- ... and best wishes for a speedy recovery.

- It must be an anxious time for you.

- You have our deepest sympathy.

- Is there any way in which we can help?

- If there's anything I can do, please don't hesitate to let me know.

- We hope and trust you will soon be better.

- We are feeling for you.

Formal letter wishing someone a speedy recovery

Upper Steading 17 June, 2015

Dear Mr Grierson

We were very sorry to hear of your wife's sudden illness. Please accept our sympathies and give her our best wishes for a speedy recovery.

It must be a very anxious time for you. If there's anything we can do, please don't hesitate to let us know. In the meantime, we are thinking of you both.

Yours sincerely
Mary Fawkes

If the recipient is unlikely to make a full recovery, it is unwise to suggest that this might be the case.

Letter of condolence

46 Cork Lane
Lamington
Herts

12 May

Dear Stephen

I am writing to say how sorry I was to hear of your loss, and that I am thinking of you at this difficult time. Although I was aware that Helen was ill, I was nevertheless shocked to hear of her passing.

I know she was never happier than when she had met you, and the two of you made a lovely couple. She seemed to light up the life of everyone who met her.

I shall certainly attend the memorial service next Thursday, but if there is anything I can do in the meantime Stephen, please don't hesitate to call me. I'm sure Jo and Max are a great comfort to you at the moment.

Thinking of you all with love and affection.

Fiona

- The main point of difference with a thank-you letter, is that the writer should be acutely sensitive to the addressee's feelings, rather than trying to express their own emotions. The references made to the deceased in this letter are mainly in the context of her relationship with the bereaved partner, rather than the writer.

- A handwritten note can be more appropriate than a phone call in situations of grief and loss like this. Writing a letter also gives you more time to think about what you want to say, and how you want to say it.

- Note that the letter, although it is informal in address and tone, still has a discernible structure: the introductory sentence explains the purpose of the letter; the middle paragraph expands on the theme with the writer's memories of the deceased; and the final paragraph acknowledges the future by accepting an invitation and offering support.

> *It really helped to receive letters of support from friends. Even though I didn't feel like talking to anyone at the time, it was good to know that others appreciated Jim, and that people were thinking of me and the kids.*
>
> (Widow)

Invitations

Invitations are frequently made by email or by text these days, but there are occasions when a written or printed invitation is still the prevalent form of communication.

Occasions that might require an invitation include:

- Weddings
- Birthday parties

A wedding invitation

Boris and Isabel Andrews
request the pleasure of the company of
Phillip and Sally Bairstow
at the wedding of their daughter Florence
to James Chater
on Saturday July 18 2015
at St Bart's Church, Eggleton at 2pm.

R.S.V.P.
Isabel Andrews, The Gildings, Foxton Lane, Biblington, BB13 5TR
Tel: 01286 5543077.

- The most important feature of an invitation is that it must possess all the necessary information to allow the recipient to respond with an acceptance or a refusal. There is no point sending out wedding invitations to 400 guests without the date on them!

- Social invitations can be informal or formal. Formal invitations – to a wedding or a christening, for example – will usually be printed.

A birthday invitation

> YIKES!
> I'm (nearly) thirty!
> Help me get over it on Saturday 21 May
> at the Stag, Riddlesway, Broxton.
> There'll be drinking, dancing and a very special quiz
> – how can you refuse?
> Please RSVP as soon as possible,
> so I can sort out some eats for the night.
> See you there,
> Charlie Bright
> cbright@email.com
> 06785 4459881

- This invitation could be sent in the form of an email, handwritten note or printed card.

- The tone is humorous and the language (and punctuation) informal, which suits the occasion.

- The font is also deliberately informal.

- Note the promise of a 'very special quiz' to intrigue the reader and hopefully persuade them to attend.

- Even with this casual approach, the host has taken care to include all the information which the recipient will need to decide whether they can attend or not.

Replying to invitations

- When replying to invitations, match the style and formality of the invite.

- If you have to decline an invitation, it is good practice to sound apologetic, regretful and explain the reason why you cannot attend.

WRITING SPEECHES

At some point in your life you're going to have to stand up in front of a group of people and make a speech. It could be at a wedding, at work or at a friend's significant birthday party or your own. Whatever the occasion, there are some basic language rules you should follow to make your speech successful and memorable.

Preparation

As with all written work, preparation is the key to writing a good speech. There are some basics you should cover before you start to write:

- **Make sure you know who you're speaking to.** Always keep in mind all of your audience when you start preparing your speech. If the occasion is going to have a mix of people who you know well and some you know less well, then the tone and content will be less intimate than if you are speaking to good friends and family.

- **Decide or establish with the hosts how long your speech should be.** This could depend on the number of other speakers, the length of time the venue has been hired for, or what other entertainment or activities are planned.

- **Start your research early.** For example, if you are making a speech for a colleague's retirement, try and speak to old as well as current workmates so that you have a range of stories and views to draw from.

- **Think about the venue.** Is it likely to be noisy? Are the audience going to be sitting down and comfortable or standing and eager to move? A long, detailed speech in uncomfortable surroundings will quickly lose the audience's attention.

- **Decide on your main theme.** All good speeches have a central idea that the speaker wants to make – it doesn't matter whether the occasion is a eulogy, wedding or a speech to the student union.

Structure and content

When you have covered this ground, you can start to write the speech. There are three main parts to it:

The opening

This is perhaps the most important part of the speech. Work hard to make it effective:

- **Try to grab your audience's attention from the start.** Make a joke, a controversial statement, or do something unexpected and entertaining. The opening sets the tone for the rest of the speech.

- **Give a brief outline of what you are going to say.** This will help the audience anticipate which parts might be of particular interest to them, and give them a rough idea of how far into the speech you are at any one time.

The body

Having got your audience's attention, you now need to develop your themes:

- **The main theme.** Use the main theme as a thread working through the body of the speech. If you are going to spend a little time talking about related but not central themes, tell your audience what you are doing and why.

- **Use anecdotes.** If possible illustrate your themes with anecdotes. If you're saying what a kind person the bride or a colleague is, tell a story that shows this.

- **Use stories from other people.** Include quotes from friends, famous people or colleagues to vary the tone of the speech.

Above all remember that regardless of the precise aim of the speech, your duty is to entertain: you've asked for people's attention, it is your job to reward them.

The finish

Just as with the opening, you need to finish in a way that will make the speech memorable.

- **Recapping.** Before you end your speech, you should signal to the audience that you are winding up by recapping the points you have made and saying what you hope to have achieved.

- **Thanking your audience.** You should always thank them for their time and attention and leave them with a memorable phrase, statistic or story.

> *Remember, the golden rule of public speaking is to be yourself. An audience can tell when you're being natural and when you're not.*
>   (Professional public speaker)

Useful phrases for specific occasions

Weddings

At a traditional wedding, there are three main speeches: the bride's father's; the bridegroom's and the best man's. Nowadays the bride often speaks too. The speeches act as a way of saying thank you to different people and as a prelude to a toast by each speaker.

The bride's father

The bride's father proposes the main toast to the bride and groom and gives a general welcome and thank you to everyone for coming along. He should say a few indulgent words about his daughter and new son-in-law before proposing the toast. Useful phrases for the father of the bride include:

- 'On behalf of [name of wife] and myself, I would like to start by saying what a pleasure it is to welcome [groom's parents], [names of close relatives] and you all to this happiest of occasions...'
- 'As father of the bride, it is my great privilege....'
- 'I am honoured on the proudest day of my life to welcome you all to the wedding of...'
- 'It is now my pleasure to propose a toast to the happy couple. Please be upstanding and raise your glasses to the bride and groom [names]'
- 'Ladies and gentlemen, the bride and groom'.

The bridegroom

The bridegroom has the responsibility of responding to the bride's father, thanking people for coming, mentioning people who could not make it, and saying a few words about his bride. His toast should be to the bridesmaids. Some useful phrases include:

- 'I would like to thank you both [bride's father and mother's names] for welcoming me into the family'
- 'I'd like to thank [bride's father's name] for those very kind words...'.
- 'Thank you to our lovely bridesmaids for taking such good care of [bride's name] and getting her here on time...'

The best man

The best man's speech is traditionally a response on behalf of the bridesmaids – a point often overlooked as guests at a wedding wait for the speech billed as the main event! The best man will also toast the bride and groom's parents before proposing the final toast to the happy couple. Some useful phrases include:

- 'Firstly on behalf of the bridesmaid(s) [names], I'd like to thank [groom's name] for his kind words....'

- 'To the bride and groom's parents and those friends and relatives who couldn't make it today....'

- 'it gives me great pleasure to invite you to stand and raise your glasses in a toast to the bride and groom. We wish them every happiness in their life together...'

A eulogy

The eulogy is the moment at which the deceased is brought close, and a time when he or she steps away. It is at once a greeting and a letting go.

(Andrew Motion, former Poet Laureate)

A eulogy is a speech given at a memorial or funeral service that celebrates a person's life. If you are giving a eulogy the same rules apply as with any speech: know who your audience is and pitch the speech appropriately.

- Try to entertain as much as the circumstances allow: the audience will be on your side and a funny or appropriate anecdote will help release some of the emotions in the room.

- Be careful not to speak for too long – most eulogies are between three and five minutes; ten at the very most.

- Sometimes more than one person speaks in which case you should talk to the other speakers before the service to make sure you are not saying the same things.

- If you are the only person giving a eulogy, take time to gather the thoughts and anecdotes of other people.

Here are some useful questions to ask yourself (and others) when you are preparing to write your speech:

- How did I first meet the deceased?

- Is there a picture in your mind (of an event or occasion) that you associate with them in particular?

- What have others said to you about the deceased?

- What will you miss most about them?